Microsoft® XNA™ Game Studio Creator's Guide

Second Edition

About the Authors...

Stephen Cawood is a former Microsoft employee and recovering *Halo* fan. Stephen has written a number of books including *Augmented Reality: A Practical Guide*, *Microsoft Content Management Server 2002: A Complete Guide*, *The Unauthorized Halo 2 Battle Guide: Advanced Combat Techniques*, *The Black Art of Halo Mods*, and *Halo 2 Hacks*. Stephen currently works for Metalogix Software and lives in Halifax, Nova Scotia, with his wife Christa and two well-behaved kittens.

Pat McGee is a former games programmer and has worked on the *Clifford the Big Red Dog* video game series. In addition to writing the first edition of the *Microsoft XNA Game Studio Creator's Guide*, Pat has also written a book called *Games Programming in C++ and DirectX*. Since 2001, Pat has developed and taught several courses in games programming at the British Columbia Institute of Technology. Pat is an Instructor in the Software Systems Developer program at the British Columbia Institute of Technology. Pat lives in North Vancouver, British Columbia, with his wife Yumi and their son Owen.

About the Technical Editor

Nick Gravelyn is a two-time Microsoft MVP in the DirectX/XNA category. He has written countless articles and blog posts relating to XNA, and has recorded many hours of video tutorials. He is currently the owner and lead programmer of Metacreature, an indie software company.

Microsoft® XNA™ Game Studio Creator's Guide

Second Edition

Stephen Cawood
Pat McGee

New York Chicago San Francisco Lisbon London Madrid Mexico City
Milan New Delhi San Juan Seoul Singapore Sydney Toronto

The McGraw-Hill Companies

Sponsoring Editor
Roger Stewart

Editorial Supervisor
Patty Mon

Project Editor
Rachel Gunn

Acquisitions Coordinator
Carly Stapleton

Technical Editor
Nick Gravelyn

Copy Editor
Margaret Berson

Proofreader
Kristy Eldredge, Word One New York

Indexer
Ted Laux

Production Supervisor
Jim Kussow

Composition
Apollo Publishing Services

Art Director, Cover
Jeff Weeks

Cover Designer
Jeff Weeks

Library of Congress Cataloging-in-Publication Data

Cawood, Stephen.
Microsoft XNA Game Studio Creator's Guide / Stephen Cawood, Pat McGee.
-- 2nd ed.
p. cm.
ISBN 978-0-07-161406-1 (alk. paper)
1. Microsoft XNA (Computer file) 2. Computer games--Programming. 3. Computer games--Design. 4. Computer games. I. McGee, Pat. II. Title.
QA76.76.C672C395 2009
794.8'1526--dc22
2009009941

McGraw-Hill books are available at special quantity discounts to use as premiums and sales promotions, or for use in corporate training programs. To contact a special sales representative, please visit the Contact Us page at www.mhprofessional.com.

Microsoft® XNA™ Game Studio Creator's Guide, Second Edition

1234567890 FGR FGR 019

ISBN 978-0-07-161406-1
MHID 0-07-161406-0

I dedicate this book to my father, John Cawood. To protect his children from a future that would have included military service under an oppressive regime, my dad left our home in 1978 and moved to Canada. That decision provided me with the sort of opportunities that led to this book project. In 1994, when South Africa became a truly democratic country, my father once again did the right thing and returned. His goal was lofty—to help South Africa reach its potential—but that's what he worked for every day. I miss him and so does the rest of our family, but it is his homeland that misses him most of all.

—Stephen Cawood

To my wife Yumi for supporting me on this project and to my parents Jack and Donna McGee for assistance along the way.

—Pat McGee

Contents At A Glance

1	Set Up an XNA Development Environment	1
2	Developer Basics	7
3	Behind the Game Window	21
4	2D Games	31
5	Introduction to 3D Graphics Programming	55
6	Shaders	69
7	Animation Introduction	91
8	Character Movement	103
9	Texturing Your Game World	119
10	Adding Skies and Horizons to Your Levels	143
11	Index Buffers	155
12	Combining Images for Better Visual Effects	165
13	Score Tracking and Game Stats	191
14	3D Models	201
15	Vectors	233
16	Matrices	247
17	Building a Graphics Engine Camera	267

18	**Collision Detection**	285
19	**Ballistics**	305
20	**Particle Effects**	323
21	**Keyframe Animations**	343
22	**Lighting**	353
23	**Input Devices**	377
24	**Content Pipeline Processors**	401
25	**Terrain with Height Detection**	419
26	**Animated Models**	437
27	**Adding Audio to Your Game**	459
28	**Multiplayer Gaming**	491
29	**Networking**	505
	Index	527

Contents

ACKNOWLEDGMENTS, xix

INTRODUCTION, xxi

1 Set Up an XNA Development Environment 1

Set Up an XNA Development Environment, 2

Install the Software, 3

Join the Xbox 360 Creators Club, 3

Using XNA Game Studio Connect, 3

Connect Your PC to Your Xbox 360, 3

Deploying a Game to Your Zune, 4

Selling Your Games with LIVE Community Games, 5

Download the Examples for This Book, 5

XNA and Your PC Video Card, 6

2 Developer Basics 7

Managing the Code Project, 8

Opening Microsoft XNA Game Studio, 8

Creating a Game Studio Project, 8

Opening an Existing Game Studio Project, 8

Coding Differences Between Windows, the XBox 360, and the Zune, 9

Creating a Windows Game Project, 9

Creating an Xbox 360 Game Project, 10

Creating a Zune Game Project, 11

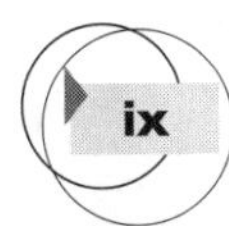

Editing Your Code, 12
Adding and Removing Code Files to and from the Project, 12
Compiling and Running Game Studio Projects, 12
Saving the Game Studio Project, 13
Deploying an Xbox 360 Game Project, 14
Debugging, 15
Error List, 15
Errors, 15
Warnings, 16
Pausing the Program to View Logic and Variable Values at Run Time, 16
Watch Lists, 18
Chapter 2 Review Exercises, 19

3 Behind the Game Window **21**

Creating the XNA Game Foundation, 22
Initializing the Game Application, 23
GraphicsDeviceManager, 24
SpriteBatch, 24
ContentManager, 24
Initialize(), 25
LoadContent(), 25
Drawing and Updating the Game Application, 25
Draw(), 26
Update(), 26
Closing the Game Application, 26
Basic XNA Game Window Example, 26
Chapter 3 Review Exercise, 28

4 2D Games **31**

The Two-Dimensional Coordinate System, 32
Using Image Files in 2D Games, 33
Content Pipeline Overview, 33
Loading and Storing Images, 33
Textures, 33
Animated Sprites, 34
Enabling Transparency, 35
Drawing and Animating Your Sprites, 35
Title Safe Region, 37

Adding Collision Detection, 37
Rectangle Collision Checking, 37
Transformation Matrices, 37
Per Pixel Collision Checking, 39
Handling User Input Devices, 40
Keyboard Input, 40
GamePad Input, 41
Porting your 2D Games to the Zune, 41
A Starter 2D Game Example, 42
Adding the Images, 42
Animating the Asteroid, 43
Controlling the Ship, 45
Adding in Collision Detection, 48
Completing the 2D Game, 52
Chapter Exercises, 53

5 Introduction to 3D Graphics Programming 55

Primitive Objects, 56
Drawing Syntax, 57
Primitive Object Types, 57
Vertex Types, 58
VertexDeclaration, 59
DrawUserPrimitives, 59
Drawing Primitive Objects Example, 59
Triangle Strip, 61
Triangle List, 63
Drawing a Line Strip, 65
Adding a Line List, 66
Adding a Point List, 67
Chapter 5 Review Exercises, 68

6 Shaders 69

Graphics Pipeline, 70
Shaders, 70
Shader Structure, 71
High Level Shader Language, 72
XNA's BasicEffect Class, 86
Setting Properties Within the BasicEffect Class, 87
Chapter 6 Review Exercises, 89

7 Animation Introduction **91**

Right Hand Rule, 92

Matrix Logic, 93

Transformation Order, 94

XNA Matrix Syntax, 94

Identity Matrix, 94

Scaling Matrix, 95

Rotation Matrices, 95

Translation Matrices, 95

Steps for Drawing a Primitive Object or a 3D Model, 96

Declaring and Initializing Individual Matrices, 96

Building the Cumulative World Matrix, 96

Setting the Shader Values, 96

Drawing the Object, 97

Applying Transformations: Earth and Moon Example, 97

Chapter 7 Review Exercises, 101

8 Character Movement **103**

Direction, 104

Calculating Direction Using Trigonometry, 104

Calculating Direction Using Speed, 105

Calculating Direction Using Vectors, 107

Scaling Animations with Time Lapse Between Frames, 108

Character Movement Example, 109

Chapter 8 Review Exercises, 118

9 Texturing Your Game World **119**

Texture Introduction, 120

UV Coordinates, 120

C# Syntax for Textures, 120

Shader Implementation for Textures, 122

Transparent Textures, 127

Alpha Channel, 127

Texture Tiling, 127

Texture Coloring, 128

Texture Example, 129

Billboarding Example, 140

Texture Coloring Example, 140

Chapter 9 Review Exercises, 141

10 Adding Skies and Horizons to Your Levels **143**

The Skybox, 144

Terragen Photorealistic Scenery Rendering Software, 145

Using Terragen to Create a Skybox, 146

Chapter 10 Review Exercises, 153

11 Index Buffers **155**

Index Buffers, 156

Managing Vertex Data with Index Buffers and Vertex Buffers, 158

Chapter 11 Review Exercises, 163

12 Combining Images for Better Visual Effects **165**

Sprites, 166

Image Frame Swapping for 2D Animations, 166

SpriteBatch, 166

Restoring 3D Drawing Settings After Drawing with a SpriteBatch, 167

Image Frame Animations, 169

Sprite on the Heads-Up-Display Example, 169

Animated Texture Example, 174

Multitexturing, 178

Multipass Rendering from the Shader's Technique, 178

Calling a Pass in the Shader, 179

Water Using Multitexturing Example, 179

Water Using Multitexturing Example, Continued: Adding Waves, 187

Chapter 12 Review Exercises, 190

13 Score Tracking and Game Stats **191**

Font Example: Displaying Text in the Game Window, 193

Loading the Font Type Data, 193

Ensuring Your Fonts Are Drawn in the Visible Portion of the Window, 196

Drawing the Font, 197

Font Example: Displaying a Frames-per-Second Count, 198

Chapter 13 Review Exercises, 200

14 3D Models **201**

3D Modeling Tools, 202

MilkShape 3D Intro Example: Creating a Windmill, 203

Loading the Model in XNA, 214

Loading the Models, 214

Drawing the Model In XNA, 215

Loading and Animating the Windmill in Code, 216

Adding a Car as a Third-Person Object, 219

Chapter 14 Review Exercises, 232

15 Vectors **233**

Vector Types, 234

Vector Addition, 234

Vector Subtraction, 236

Vector Scaling, 236

Vector Scaling, Example 1, 236

Vector Scaling, Example 2, 237

Normal Vectors, 238

Cross Product, 238

Cross Product Example, 239

Normalization, 240

Pythagorean Theorem, 241

Using the Pythagorean Theorem to Calculate the Vector Length, 241

Using Normalization to Compute the Unit Vector, 242

Using the Normalize( ) Method to Compute the Unit Vector, 243

Dot Product, 243

Dot Product Method, 244

Dot Product Example, 244

Chapter 15 Review Exercises, 246

16 Matrices **247**

Matrix Multiplication, 248

Matrix Types, 248

Transformation Matrices, 253

Translation Matrix, 254

Scaling Matrix, 256

Rotation Matrix X Axis, 258

Rotation Matrix Y Axis, 260

Rotation Matrix Z Axis, 262

Identity Matrix, 263

Chapter 16 Review Exercises, 265

17 Building a Graphics Engine Camera **267**

Camera Vectors, 268

Camera Matrices, 268

World Matrix, 269

View Matrix, 269

Projection Matrix, 269

Camera Example, 271

Creating the Camera Class Shell, 271

Initializing the Camera from Your Game Class, 272

Moving and Strafing, 274
Rotating the View, 277
Triggering Changes to the View from the Game Class, 282
Building the Base Code from Scratch Example, 284
Chapter 17 Review Exercises, 284

18 Collision Detection **285**
Fine-Tuning Your Collision Detection Systems, 286
Early Warning Systems, 287
ContainmentType, 287
BoundingSphere, 288
Initializing the Bounding Sphere, 288
Intersects(), 288
Contains, 288
BoundingBox, 288
Intersects(), 289
Contains(), 289
Collision Detection Example: Initializing and Drawing Bounding Spheres, 290
Collision Detection Example: Implementing BoundingSphere Collision Checking, 299
Collision Detection Example: Implementing BoundingBox Collision Checking, 302
Chapter 18 Review Exercises, 304

19 Ballistics **305**
Linear Projectiles, 306
Arcing Projectile, 306
Linear Projectiles Example, 309
Arcing Projectiles Example, 319
Chapter 19 Review Exercises, 321

20 Particle Effects **323**
Point Sprites, 324
Custom Vertex Declarations, 330
Fire Example Using Point Sprites, 331
Chapter 20 Review Exercises, 341

21 Keyframe Animations **343**
Interpolation, 344
Curves, 344

Keyframe Animation Example, 345
Chapter 21 Review Exercises, 351

22 Lighting 353

Lighting Methods, 354
Source Lights, 354
Reflective Lighting Properties of Materials, 355
Implementing Directional Lighting Using XNA's BasicEffect Class, 356
BasicEffect Default Lighting, 356
Directional Lighting Example, 357
Implementing Point Light Using the Phong Reflection Model, 362
Calculating Point Light, 364
Point Light in the Pixel Shader Example, 365
Point Light in the Vertex Shader Example, 373
Chapter 22 Review Exercises, 375

23 Input Devices 377

Handling Keyboard Input, 378
Handling Mouse Input, 379
Handling Controller Input, 379
Game Pad States, 380
Handling Pressed and Released States, 381
Thumbsticks, 381
Triggers, 382
Adjusting the Input Device Responsiveness, 382
Adding a Rumble, 382
Input Example, 383
Zune Input Handling, 396
Zune Input Device Example, 397
Chapter 23 Review Exercises, 399

24 Content Pipeline Processors 401

Content Processors, 402
ContentImporter, 403
ContentTypeWriter, 403
ContentTypeReader, 404
Custom Content Processor Example, 404
Building a Custom Content Processor in Windows, 405
Chapter 24 Review Exercises, 417

25 Terrain with Height Detection 419

Height Maps, 420
Creating a Height Map Using Terragen, 421

Height Map Code Example, 425

Chapter 25 Review Exercises, 436

26 Animated Models **437**

The Quake II Format, 438

A Closer Look at the .md2 Data, 439

Textures with .md2 Format, 440

Animating Models in Milkshape, 440

Creating the Quake II Model, 441

Loading Your Quake II Model in Code, 446

Loading and Controlling Quake II Models in Code, 451

Loading the Quake II Weapon, 454

Chapter 26 Review Exercises, 457

27 Adding Audio to Your Game **459**

About XACT, 460

The Song and SoundEffect Alternative, 460

Programming XACT Audio, 460

XACT Audio Project File, 461

Audio Engine, 461

Global Settings, 462

Wave Banks, 462

Sound Banks, 462

Space Audio Example: Part A, 464

Launching the XACT Authoring Tool, 465

Creating a Wave Bank, 465

Adding a Sound Bank, 465

Referencing the Spaceship Engines, Firing Sound, and Beeping Sounds, 466

Setting the Category Property for Beep0, 466

Creating an Infinite Loop, 467

Adding a Finite Loop, 467

Testing Your Audio, 468

Cue Instance Variables, 468

Creating a New RPC Preset, 469

Enabling Volume Attenuation, 471

Saving Your Audio Project, 473

Space Audio Example: Part B, 473

Loading, Drawing, and Animating the Spacecraft, 473

Space Audio Example: Part C, 477

Adding Audio, 477

Space Audio Example: Part D, 482

Adding 3D Audio, 482

Zune Audio Example, 487

Chapter 27 Review Exercises, 489

28 Multiplayer Gaming **491**

Viewport, 492

Creating Separate Cameras for Each Player, 493

Adjusting the View, 493

Adjusting the Projection, 493

Handling the User Input, 494

Split-Screen Code Example, 494

Chapter 28 Review Exercises, 503

29 Networking **505**

Peer-to-Peer Networks, 506

Client/Server Networks, 506

Efficient Bandwidth Use, 506

XNA's Code Framework, 507

GamerServicesComponent, 507

NetworkSession, 507

Session Events, 508

Local Network Gamer, 509

Updating the Session, 509

PacketWriter, 510

PacketReader, 510

Updating the Network, 511

Network Example: Peer to Peer, 511

Setting Up the Network Class, 511

Adding Network Capability to the Game Class, 514

Network Example: Client/Server, 521

Chapter 29 Review Exercises, 526

Index **527**

Acknowledgments

Thank you to people at Microsoft for a great game platform and for advocacy of our project. Thank you Andy Dunn (the ZMan) and Shawn Hargreaves for excellent community contributions. Nick Gravelyn has been an incredible resource for this project—Nick, we are very grateful for your help and input.

For guidance and assistance from the British Columbia Institute of Technology, thank you to Kevin Cudihee, Medhat Elmasry, Jason Harrison, and Dr. Benjamin Yu.

Thank you to a publishing team who are an excellent group to work with: Roger Stewart, Joya Anthony, Rachel Gunn, Carly Stapleton.

—Pat McGee

Big thanks go to Nick Gravelyn for his technical expertise. I'd also like to thank my agent Neil J. Salkind, Roger Stewart (our Editorial Director) from McGraw-Hill, and the rest of the MGH team: Joya Anthony, Rachel Gunn, and Carly Stapleton. It has been great working with MGH again and I look forward to our next project together. In the last, but not least, category, thanks go to my wife Christa for her support.

—Stephen Cawood

Credits:

CF-18 model, Eric Bancroft
Hotrod model, Sheila Nash
Zarlag model, Phillip T. Wheeler
For use of Terragen images, John McLusky:
  http://www.planetside.co.uk/terragen/
For support on MilkShape, Mete Cirigan:
  http://www.milkshape3d.com/
Permission to use *Quake II* model format granted under the GPL from id Software:
  http://www.idsoftware.com

Acknowledgments

Introduction

Source code for all examples in this book can be downloaded from http://www.mhprofessional.com/ and http://www.xnachinchilla.com

This book shows how to build complete 2D and 3D games with all essential components from scratch; shapes, image effects, animation, 3D model creation and use, graphics math, collision detection, 3D audio, split-screen, and networked games. All code examples are presented in an easy-to-follow, step-by-step format. This book targets development for the PC and Xbox 360 and introduces development for the Zune.

With the exception of the *Quake II* model loader code, all source code for all examples and solutions is presented on the pages of this book. All examples either begin with the minimal Microsoft XNA game template or they begin with a single base code project that is used throughout this entire book. Chapter 17 shows how to build this base code project from start to finish so you have a full understanding of the structures behind it.

This book is suited for readers with basic to advanced knowledge in a C-style programming language but who have not necessarily programmed 3D games. This book is also suited for readers who just want to cover a lot of ground in games programming fast with an easy-to-understand tutorial-style guide.

CHAPTER 1

Set Up an XNA Development Environment

THE release of the XNA platform—and specifically the ability for anyone to write Xbox 360 console games—was truly a major progression in the game-programming world. Before XNA, it was simply too complicated and costly for a student, software hobbyist, or independent game developer to gain access to a decent development kit for a major console platform. With the release of XNA Game Studio, the ground rules changed. Suddenly, anyone with a PC that has a decent graphics card can use the XNA platform to develop games not only for Windows, but also for the Xbox 360.

The XNA platform has continued to evolve, and with the release of XNA 3.0, XNA developers have provided the ability to write games for the Microsoft Zune MP3 Player. Also, XNA game developers may submit their games for distribution in the Xbox LIVE Community Games marketplace. We are pleased to offer this second edition to update our book for the latest developments in the XNA development platform. We have also taken the experience from writing our first edition to add improvements, making this our strongest XNA guide to date. We hope you enjoy reading it and that you find it helpful for learning XNA.

It will be fun to watch as a new strain of games springs forth from the labs of students, hobbyist game developers, small game shops—and you. Of course, commercial developers have larger budgets, teams of paid artists, and abundant resources on their side—however, commercial game developers are going to be taking notes and learning from the independent XNA developers who find new and interesting ways to warp the virtual world. There is a niche for you to fill and an opportunity for you to sell your games at the LIVE Community Games marketplace.

XNA Game Studio (GS) is the integrated development environment (IDE) for XNA. It is an add-on for Visual C# Express Edition or Visual Studio. Although some people prefer to use the full version of Visual Studio, Visual C# Express is free. Based on this, it is possible to develop Windows XNA games without any cost—aside from the price of your PC, and possibly your Zune.

However, if you want to write games for the Xbox 360, this is obviously not the case. There is an additional subscription charge for the Xbox 360 Creators Club (http://creators.xna.com). A Creators Club subscription allows you to deploy games from your Windows PC to the Xbox 360.

SET UP AN XNA DEVELOPMENT ENVIRONMENT

Follow these instructions to prepare your system for XNA development on the PC, Xbox 360, and Zune.

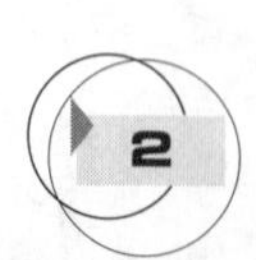

Install the Software

Before you can develop any games with XNA, you will need to download some free software from Microsoft.com. You will need to install Visual C# Express or Visual Studio with C# and then XNA Game Studio.

After you have installed the required software, you will be able to develop XNA games for Windows or the Zune. However, if you want to develop for the Xbox 360, you will need to complete the rest of the instructions in this section.

Join the Xbox 360 Creators Club

Before you are able to do any Xbox 360 game development, you will have to pay for a subscription to the Xbox 360 Creators Club. Fortunately, this is the only fee you will have to pay; everything else is free. To join the club, go to the XNA Creators Club website and sign up for a premium membership (http://creators.xna.com/en-us/membership).

Using XNA Game Studio Connect

After you have purchased a Creators Club premium membership, you will be able to sign in to Xbox LIVE and download the free XNA Game Studio Connect application.

To use the XNA Game Studio Connect utility, navigate to the Games blade on your Xbox 360, and then to the Demos and More section. Once there, select XNA Game Studio Connect and press A to launch the application. Next, press A to start the XNA Game Studio Connect.

When you have the launcher running, you will see three options: My XNA Games, Connect to Computer, and Settings. The My XNA Games option shows a list of games. Selecting a game gives you the options Play Game and Delete Game. Connect to Computer (which requires an active Xbox LIVE connection to verify your subscription) puts the Xbox 360 in the correct mode for deploying or debugging Xbox 360 Game projects in GS. The last option, Settings, allows you to generate a connection key. Select this option and you will receive instructions for how to add the connection key inside GS (under Tools | Options | XNA Game Studio and Xbox 360 Console).

Connect Your PC to Your Xbox 360

Before you can develop Xbox 360 games, you must set up a connection between your GS development PC and your Xbox 360. Follow these steps to establish the connection:

1. Make sure that your Xbox 360 is connected to Xbox LIVE, that you have a membership to the Xbox 360 Creators Club, and that you have downloaded the XNA Game Studio Connect application.

2. Ensure that you have Visual C# Express Edition (or Visual Studio) and GS installed on your development PC.
3. The Connect to Computer option is disabled the first time you run XNA Game Studio Connect. To enable it, you must go to Settings and select Generate Connection Key. At this point, you will see a connection key displayed. After you have added the connection key to GS (under Tools | Options | XNA Game Studio and Xbox 360 Console), your PC can deploy XNA projects to your Xbox 360.
4. From the XNA Game Studio Connect options, choose Connect to Computer. You must have the Xbox waiting in this mode before you try to debug or deploy from GS.

That's it! Now you will be able to develop XNA games for the Windows platform or the Xbox 360.

Deploying a Game to Your Zune

With the recent XNA 3.0 release, you can now deploy your XNA games to a Microsoft Zune device. Although the Zune does not support 3D graphics, you can still write your own games and play them on the small screen. The process of deploying games to the Zune is remarkably straightforward.

Once you have installed XNA GS, you simply need to plug in your Zune, add it as a recognized device, and then create an XNA game with the Zune game template. To test your ability to deploy games to the Zune, try downloading a Zune game project from the Creators Club website, deploying it to your Zune, and then playing the game.

Here is the process to deploy your own Zune games:

1. Open GS and create a game by choosing File | New Project | Zune Game (3.0).
2. Build the game as usual.
3. Physically connect your Zune to your PC. (Note that you should have already connected your device at least once and thereby updated to the latest version of the Zune firmware.)
4. Add your Zune to GS using Tools | XNA Game Studio Device Center. Set your Zune as the default.
5. Use the Deploy to Zune option to send your game to the device.
6. Play your Zune game!

Here are some points to remember when creating a Zune game:

- The Zune currently only plays 2D games.
- Screen resolution on all Zunes is 240×320 pixels.
- Game size should be restricted to a maximum of 2GB.
- Be wary of memory limitations when developing games for the Zune; keep your texture and audio content lean.
- The Zune does not implement 3D audio content created in the Cross Platform Audio Creation Tool (XACT). Instead it implements mp3 and WAV file playback using the SoundEffect, SoundEffectInstance, and Song classes.
- The Zune input device handling uses a subset of the input device library used for the game controller.

Selling Your Games with LIVE Community Games

Starting with the full release of GS 3.0, XNA game developers have the option of making their games public on the Xbox LIVE marketplace. When you submit your game, you have the option of choosing between a few different price levels. Microsoft has announced that XNA developers will retain up to 70 percent of the profit from the sale of community games on the Xbox 360.

To publish your game, you simply have to:

1. Develop a game. Note that there is a size limitation for games published on LIVE Community Games, so check how big your game can be before you start development.
2. Submit your game for peer review. Other Creators Club members will make sure your game follows the rules for publishing (for example, no copyright infringement, no unacceptable content, and the game actually works), and then they will either approve or reject your game.
3. Sell your game. You will need to refer to Microsoft's XNA Creators Club site for current detailed instructions.

Download the Examples for This Book

You can find all of the resources and solutions for the examples in this book available for download from the book's catalog page at www.mhprofessional.com and at XNAChinchilla.com (see the Introduction for more details).

XNA AND YOUR PC VIDEO CARD

Before you start installing the software required for XNA development, you should ensure that your PC meets the basic requirements for GS. One consideration is your video card; if your card does not meet the requirements, you will not be able to run GS projects on your PC.

If you have encountered the following GS error, you may have already discovered that your card has an issue:

"Could not find a Direct3D device that has a Direct3D9-level driver and supports pixel shader 1.1 or greater."

GS requires your PC's video card to support Shader Model 2.0 or greater. This should not be an issue, though, as most current computers ship with suitable graphics cards.

Now that you have your development environment ready to go, the next chapter will walk you through some of the most important features of the GS IDE.

CHAPTER 2

Developer Basics

IF you're itching to get coding, but are not familiar with Microsoft's integrated development environment (IDE), this chapter will help you use Microsoft XNA Game Studio (GS) to program, debug, and deploy your game projects. Once your PC, Zune, and Xbox 360 have been prepared as outlined in Chapter 1, "Set Up an XNA Development Environment," you are ready to code with GS.

MANAGING THE CODE PROJECT

GS is a first-class integrated development environment (IDE) that leverages the C# language. Although Microsoft Visual Studio and Microsoft Visual C# Express are both supported. Microsoft Visual C# Express is a free coding studio and it is very similar to Microsoft Visual C# .NET, enabling you to program, edit, debug, and deploy your C# applications. Compared to other freeware developer tools, GS is a Rolls Royce. Using this software, you can code in comfort and allow the IDE to improve your efficiency.

Opening Microsoft XNA Game Studio

To launch GS, from the Start menu select Programs and choose Microsoft XNA Game Studio or Microsft Visual C# 2008. GS will open the Start Page, which presents your recent projects, links to tutorials, and links to online articles, discussions, and events related to C# development.

Creating a Game Studio Project

A GS project will store references to all of your code files and resources that are used by your game application. There are currently three types of stand-alone XNA game projects: the Windows Game project, the Zune Game project, and the Xbox 360 Game project.

Each type of project references a slightly different instruction set. For example, the Windows Game project can be run on a PC, but the Xbox 360 Game project cannot because it uses a reduced instruction set that is required by the Xbox 360 console.

Opening an Existing Game Studio Project

A GS project can be opened by double-clicking the solution file. Solution files have an .sln extension. The project will launch GS and show the code editor, Solution Ex-

plorer, and Error List. If any of these items do not appear when the game studio is open, they can be opened individually from the View menu.

Coding Differences Between Windows, the Xbox 360, and the Zune

The base code that is automatically generated by GS for the Xbox 360 Game project is identical to the code generated for a Windows Game project. Some slight differences exist between the two instruction sets available, such as mouse support, which is only available in Windows. However, in the majority of cases, you can write your code in one project type and then copy your source files and resources to the other project type and you will still be able to run your project. The Xbox 360 is slightly stricter in enforcing variable default declarations, but even if you forget the differences, GS provides excellent debug information to inform you of any issues and how to resolve them when testing your code in one environment or the other.

You can have confidence that almost all the code you write for a Windows Game project is going to work in an Xbox 360 Game project, and vice versa. In most cases, platform compatibility will not be an issue because XNA is designed to work in both environments. Of course, you still need to test in both environments, but plan for an excellent level of compatibility between platforms.

The most important distinction for Zune programming is that the Zune does not currently support 3D graphics. When creating games for the Zune, you'll have to work with simpler 2D graphics. Also, the Zune does not implement 3D audio for projects created using the Cross Platform Audio Creation Tool. Instead the Zune uses a much lighter audio library for playing WAV and mp3 files which loads your audio content directly in code. Finally, the input device handling on the Zune is implemented using a subset of instructions used for device handling with the Xbox 360 game controller. Aside from including one extra instruction to regulate the frequency of updates between frames, the Zune Game project template code is identical to the Xbox 360 Game and Windows Game project templates.

Creating a Windows Game Project

You can create a project by selecting File and then New Project. At this point, several options are available to you. If you want your project to run on Windows, then choose the Windows Game icon that appears in the New Project dialog (see Figure 2-1). To proceed, you need to fill in each of the text boxes at the bottom of the New Project dialog. These values include the name of the project and the file path for the directory where you would like your project to be created.

FIGURE 2-1

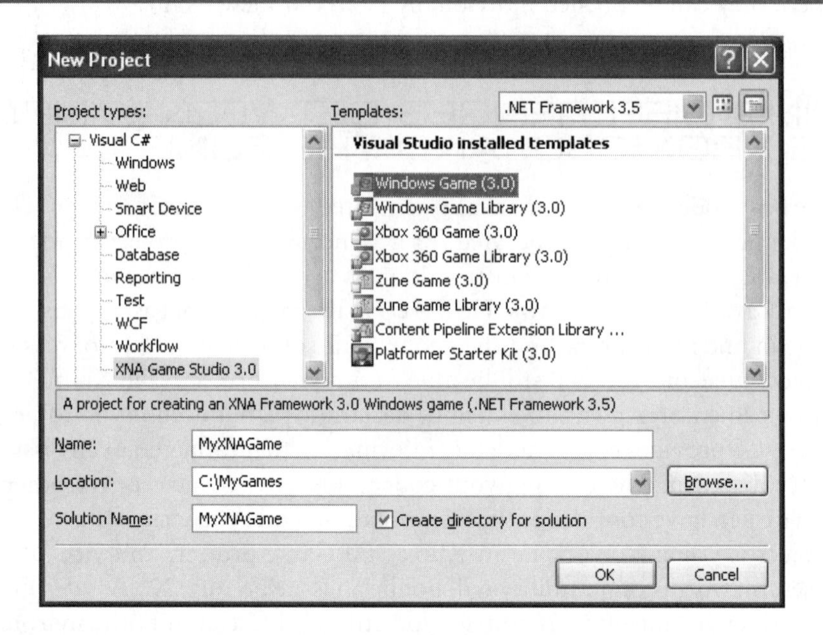

Selecting a project type and entering the file path and project name

When you first create a project, a code-editing window will open on the left (see Figure 2-2). The Solution Explorer in the right panel shows a listing of code files and may display resources such as a project icon and other items you have selected. The Error List at the bottom of the page displays error messages for lines of code that will not compile, warning messages such as information about variables that are not used, and instructions that are deprecated but have been allowed to compile.

If the code editor, Solution Explorer, or Error List do not appear, these options can be enabled from the View menu.

Creating an Xbox 360 Game Project

The creation of an Xbox 360 Game project is similar to creating a Windows Game project. But before you can actually run an Xbox 360 Game project, you will need to sign in to Xbox Live and download the XNA Game Studio Connect, as outlined in Chapter 1, "Set Up an XNA Development Environment." Once you have this installed, you will have to connect your PC to your Xbox 360. Connecting your PC to your Xbox 360 will be explained later in this chapter.

FIGURE 2-2

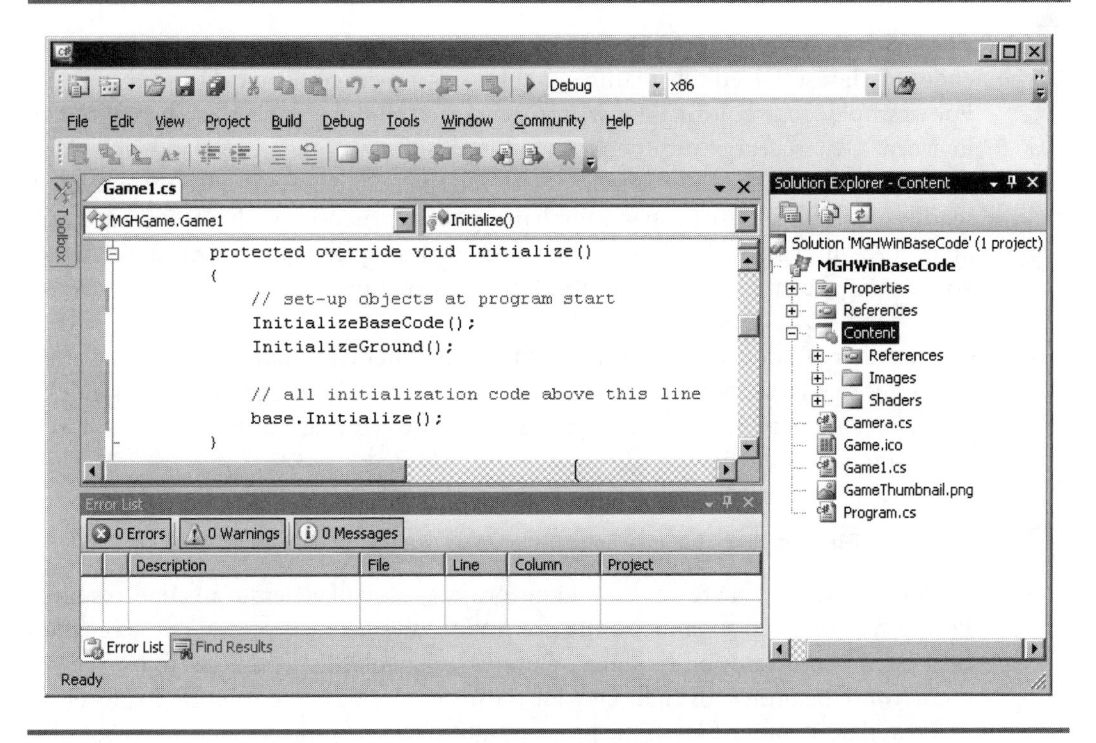

GS project with code window, Error List, and Solution Explorer

Once you have a connection from your PC to your Xbox 360, you will be able to compile an Xbox 360 Game project. Creating an Xbox 360 Game project is similar to creating a Windows Game project. The only difference is that you select the Xbox 360 Game icon in the New Project dialog. When you create the project, GS will generate the base code needed to build a game that runs on the Xbox 360. The development environment will look like the Windows Game project shown in Figure 2-2.

Creating a Zune Game Project

Creating a new project for the Zune is exactly the same as for the other project types: File | New project | Zune Game.

EDITING YOUR CODE

The GS code window offers a friendly environment for writing and editing your code. The latest IDE editing features enable you to write code quickly and accurately. For example, code coloring allows for easy readability by distinguishing comments in green, C# structures and functions in blue, and user-defined code in black. Also, incomplete lines of code are marked with red lines. Furthermore, AutoComplete is readily available to assist you in completing your instructions with methods and variables for your classes. ToolTips, which display descriptive summaries, appear when you hover the mouse over variables and instructions that are referenced from Microsoft's code libraries.

The other windows also provide features that will make your programming experience more enjoyable. For example, the Solution Explorer enables you to quickly navigate from page to page. In short, GS is rich with editing features that are waiting for you to discover them.

Adding and Removing Code Files to and from the Project

By default, when you create a new game project, GS will generate a Game1.cs file, a Program.cs file, and a Game.ico file (for a Windows Game project). You'll see these files listed in the Solution Explorer. Options are available to add files to (or remove them from) the project by right-clicking the project name in the Solution Explorer.

To add new source files to the project, right-click the project name in the Solution Explorer, choose Add, and then select New Item. In the New Item dialog that appears, a C# file can be created by selecting Code File. You must specify a name for the C# file in the Name box before the file can be added. Once you have provided a filename, click the Add button to have the file added to the project.

To add existing source files to the project, right-click the project name in the Solution Explorer, choose Add, and then select Existing Item; an Add Existing Item dialog will appear. By default, the Add Existing Item dialog displays all files listed in the source folder of the current project. When you left-click the source files to be added and click Add, GS will load the files into the project; after they have been added, they will be listed in the Solution Explorer.

Compiling and Running Game Studio Projects

You can use the Start Debugging action to compile your code, generate debugging information, and run the project in one step. In the case of an Xbox 360 Game project, this will also deploy the project to your Xbox 360. You can access the Start Debugging action from the Debug menu or by pressing the F5 key.

By default, both newly created Windows Game projects and Xbox 360 Game projects are generated with the source code needed to build a basic window. The output from compiling and debugging a brand new project will be a game window as shown in Figure 2-3.

Saving the Game Studio Project

When compiling, GS will automatically save all edits to the game project. Between builds, you can manually save changes to the *.cs file that is currently showing in the code editor, or you can save changes to the entire project. Under the File menu, three different options are available for saving the project: Save *.cs, Save *.cs As, and Save All.

FIGURE 2-3

The newly built game window

DEPLOYING AN XBOX 360 GAME PROJECT

When you have a project that is ready to run on your Xbox 360, you can use GS to deploy it to your Xbox. The first step of deployment requires that you go to your Xbox 360 and configure it to connect it to your PC. On the Games blade of the Xbox 360 Dashboard (under Demos and More), launching XNA Game Studio Connect will display the XNA Game Studio Connect main page (see Figure 2-4).

The Connect to Computer option is disabled the first time you run XNA Game Studio Connect. To enable it, you must go to Settings and select Generate Connection Key. After you generate the key, but before you accept it, you must enter the key number into GS on your PC. From GS, under Options | Tools, select XNA Game Studio Xbox 360 and click Add to launch the Add Xbox 360 Name and Connection Key dialog. In this dialog, you must enter a computer name so you can identify your PC connection and the connection key that was just generated. Once you complete this task, select Accept New Key from the Connection Key dialog on your Xbox 360 to finalize the process. After you have accepted the key, you will be brought back to the Settings dialog, which will now report [key set] to notify you that you were successful in applying the key on your Xbox 360. You can now select the Back button to return to the XNA Game Studio Connect page.

On the XNA Game Studio Connect page, select the Connect to Computer option and press the A controller button to make the connection.

FIGURE 2-4

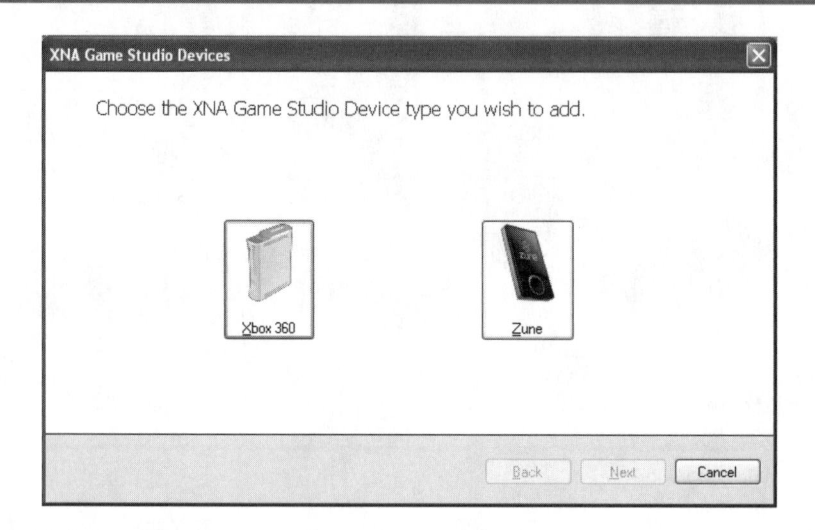

XNA Game Studio Connect main page

If you want to test your Xbox 360 Game project, select Start Debugging under the Debug menu (or press F5) to deploy and run your game on the Xbox 360.

Alternatively, if you just want to deploy your game to the Xbox 360, from GS, right-click the project name in the Solution Explorer and choose Deploy. This will enable you to play the game on your Xbox 360. The progress of your deployment will be displayed in the Output window of GS. The Connect to Computer screen will also show the deployment progress and a listing. When the deployment is complete, select the B button to back out of the Connect to Computer page. When the project has been loaded onto the Xbox 360, select My XNA Games and press the A controller button from the XNA Game Studio Connect page to display your XNA projects. You can select and run any that are listed.

DEBUGGING

There is no silver bullet when it comes to debugging techniques. However, having many techniques in your arsenal will aid your ability to examine (or trace) code, and it will help you write robust code quickly and efficiently.

Microsoft's development suites have earned a reputation for delivering exceptional debugging tools. In short, the debugging tools rock. It is no wonder that big game companies such as Electronic Arts use Microsoft's Visual Studio .NET for their coding environment. Most of the common debug features available in Visual Studio .NET can be also found in GS.

Error List

The Error List at the bottom of the project page is probably the first debugging tool you will encounter, and it will quickly become your best friend. If your code fails to compile, the Error List will show error messages alerting you to reasons why. Also, if the compiler finds an issue that isn't serious enough to cause a build error, the Error List will show a warning message.

Errors

When your project does not compile, the Error List will show all lines of code that failed—with an explanation of why each did not compile. Figure 2-5 shows the Error List reporting a missing semicolon. You can double-click the error message in the Error List to automatically move your cursor to the line that failed to compile; this feature is a huge timesaver.

FIGURE 2-5

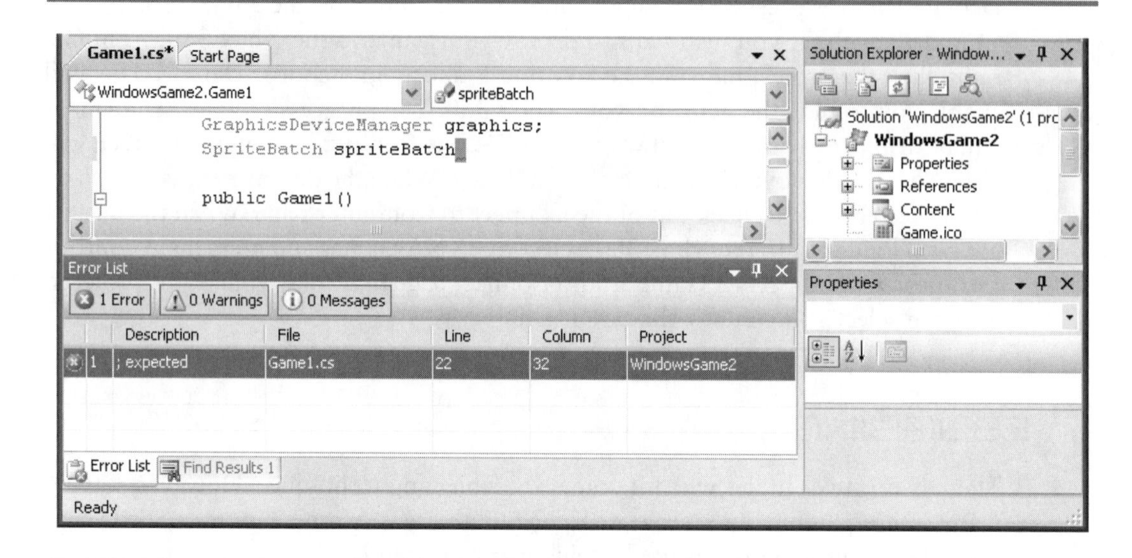

Error message in the Error List

Warnings

Warnings highlight code that compiles but should either be modified or removed. The warning in Figure 2-6 shows a variable that has been declared but is unused.

Keep in mind that expert developers pay attention to the warnings and aim to ship their code with zero warnings. Paying heed to warnings can also improve the readability and scalability of your code projects. Warnings will also help you identify deprecated methods and blocks of code that are unused. Finding replacements for deprecated methods will ensure your code is current with the latest code libraries, and it will also ensure that you're using the most secure code available. Removing unused variables will reduce the clutter in your project.

Pausing the Program to View Logic and Variable Values at Run Time

Microsoft's development environments, including GS, offer excellent tools for stopping your program in midstream so that you can check variable values and logic. If you are not already aware of these features, you should add them to your debugging procedures.

FIGURE 2-6

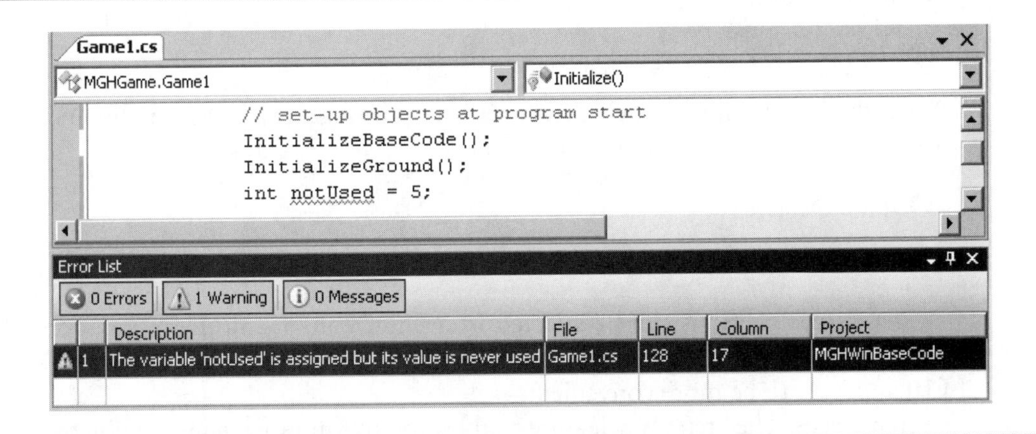

The Error List showing a warning about a variable that is declared but not used

Breakpoints

Breakpoints allow you to pause on a specific line of code while your program is running. The program will run until it encounters the instruction where your breakpoint is set. Once the breakpoint is hit, you will be able to examine variable values and program logic at that point in your application.

A breakpoint can be quickly set by left-clicking on the gray margin beside the instruction where the break should occur. When the breakpoint is added, a red dot will appear in the margin to flag the location of the break. Figure 2-7 shows a breakpoint in action—the program has been paused at the breakpoint. At this point, you can

FIGURE 2-7

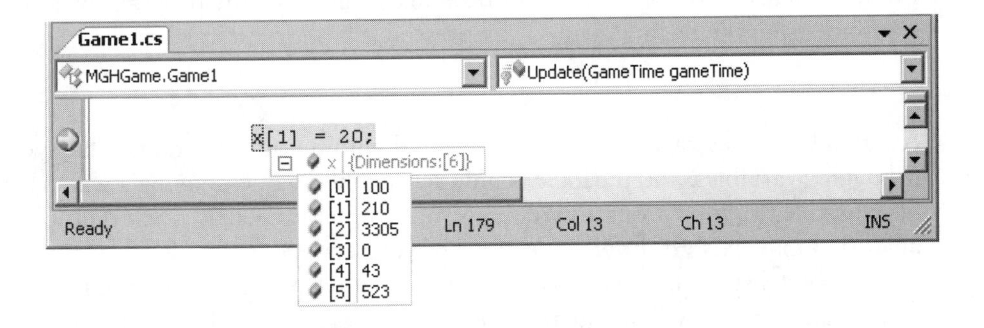

Pausing at a breakpoint to examine logic and variable values

hover your mouse over variable values to examine their them. ToolTips will appear as you hover over each variable.

Stepping

When the breakpoint is reached, you can step through the code, line by line, and watch your code execute in run time. There are two ways to step:

- Step Over (F10)
- Step Into (F11)

These step functions can be selected from the Debug menu. However, you will need to step through code frequently, so you will probably find the shortcut keys, F10 and F11, to be more convenient.

Step Over—The Step Over feature enables you to follow each instruction sequentially, line by line; this way, you can move through your code from one method to the next. Step Over will not enter a new method from a call statement. Being able to skip by a call statement to a method is useful when the method is known to work and there is no need for it to be examined.

Step Into—The Step Into feature also allows you to follow each instruction sequentially. However, unlike Step Over, Step Into will follow call statements into the methods that are being called. Step Into is helpful when you want to follow the code into every method and examine every branch of code.

Here is a simple way to remember the shortcut keys for Step Into and Step Over: F10ver and F11nto.

Resuming the Program

If the program has been paused by a breakpoint, and your examination of logic and variable values is complete, you can resume execution of the program by selecting Continue from the Debug menu or by pressing the shortcut key F5.

Watch Lists

A watch list tracks variables that are declared within your program. When you are debugging variables, and the logic behind setting their values, having a watch list for key variables in your program will help you to simultaneously track multiple variables that may exist in different sections of your code.

The watch list can be customized to your choice of specific variable values. Also, a watch can be added when you are running the program to a breakpoint. When the program pauses at the breakpoint, right-clicking the variable that needs to be tracked and selecting Add Watch will add it to the list. Figure 2-8 displays a watch list.

FIGURE 2-8

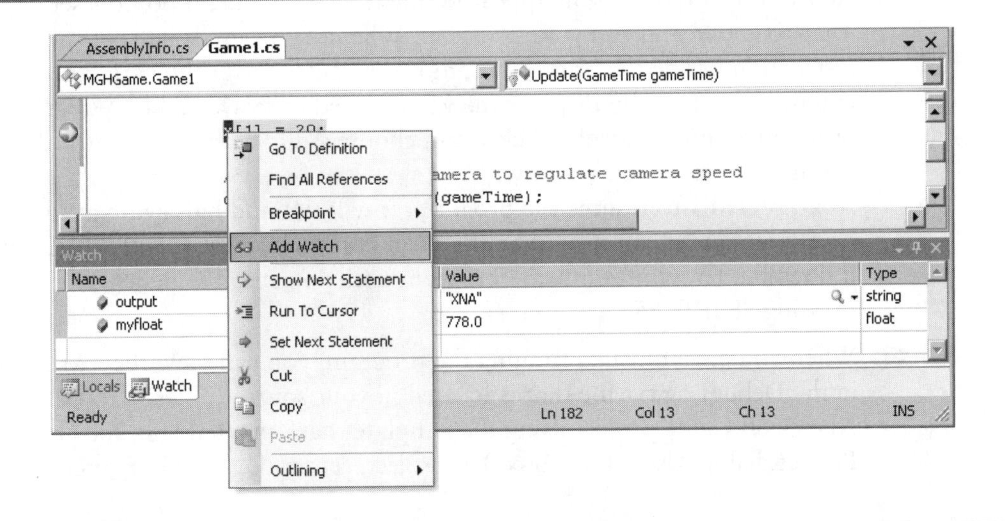

Adding a variable to a watch list

XNA Game Studio is a first-class integrated development environment for programming, editing, and deploying your applications. It is designed for ease of deployment on your Windows PC, Zune, and Xbox 360. XNA GS also offers an excellent suite of debugging tools to help you write solid code faster. In addition to using the built-in debugging features, you may also consider using an instance of the System.IO.StreamWriter to write and append debug text to your own log files.

It's amazing that GS is freeware. In our last book, we suggested that XNA would change the game world as we know it. Now with LIVE Community Games, the outlook for the future is even more optimistic. Have fun out there!

CHAPTER 2 REVIEW EXERCISES

To get the most from this chapter, try out these chapter review exercises.

1. Create a Windows Game project using the template that is available in the New Project dialog. Inside the Update() method, add this code:

```
int x = 5;
System.IO.StreamWriter sw
= new System.IO.StreamWriter(@"..\..\..\DebugLog.txt", true);
sw.Write("X = ");
sw.WriteLine(x);
sw.Close();
```

2. Create a breakpoint by clicking the left margin next to the instruction sw.Close(). A red dot will appear beside it when the breakpoint is set. Then, compile and run your program. When the program halts at the instruction beside the breakpoint, move the cursor over the variable x and note the ToolTip displays the value stored in this variable. While the program is running, right-click x and choose Add Watch to monitor the variable in the Watch window.
   Next, press F5 to resume the program. It will run and halt again at the breakpoint. You can then click the breakpoint in the left margin to remove it. Pressing F5 will resume the program until you stop the debugger by pressing SHIFT+F5.
3. When you have finished running the program, you can view the text output in the DebugLog.txt file that is located in your source folder. Create an Xbox 360 Game project using the template that is available in the New Project dialog. Using the Xbox 360 project, repeat the steps in Exercise 1.

CHAPTER 3

Behind the Game Window

THIS chapter explains the methods and objects behind 2D and 3D XNA game windows. Right off the bat, the XNA Game Studio (GS) project templates will automatically generate the code needed for building, updating, and displaying your game window. This means that the XNA platform offers a simple process for creating, drawing, and updating the foundation of your games. The flowchart shown in Figure 3-1 summarizes the steps required to build, update, and draw graphics within a game window.

CREATING THE XNA GAME FOUNDATION

Hardly any C# code is needed to generate and display a basic XNA game window—like the one shown in Figure 2-3. Chapter 2 explained how to create a game studio project for a Windows PC, a Zune device, or the Xbox 360 platform. These projects can be created using the Xbox 360, Zune, or Windows Game project tem-

FIGURE 3-1

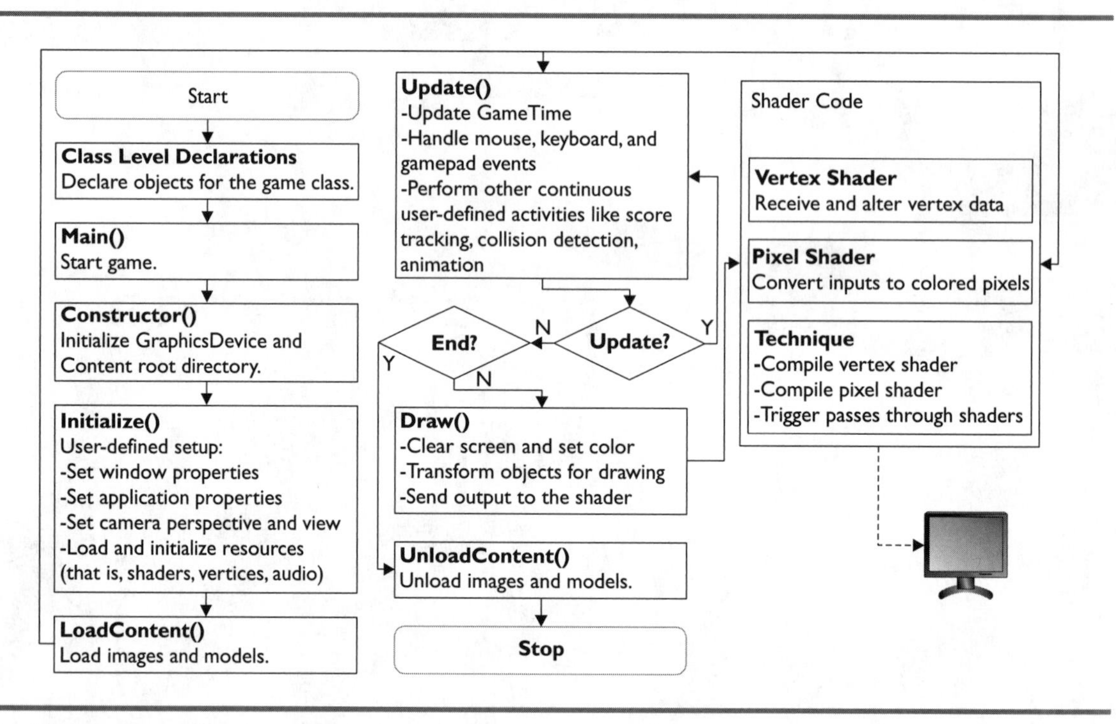

XNA application flow

plates—they generate practically identical code. For example, the only difference between the Windows and Xbox 360 templates is the namespace for the game class. The Windows template assigns the name WindowsGame1 by default and the Xbox 360 assigns the namespace Xbox360Game1—that's it. These templates provide the basic foundation you need to create an XNA game window.

Although the XNA code in these templates is basically the same, the XNA framework references for Windows, Zune, and Xbox 360 projects are different. If you want, you can write all of your code in one environment and then reference it in an Xbox 360, Zune, or Windows project to run it. Microsoft has intentionally made window creation and portability between projects simple. Obviously, Microsoft wants you to take the platform beyond the outer limits.

Initializing the Game Application

When you want to create a new XNA game project, the easiest method is to use the project templates that come with GS because the template adds the necessary project references for you. After you have installed the XNA framework, you can begin a new project, by following these steps:

1. From the Start menu, select Programs and choose Microsoft XNA Game Studio. Depending on your environment, you could also choose to open Microsoft Visual Studio, Microsoft Visual C#, or Microsoft Visual C# Express Edition.
2. From the main Visual Studio or Visual C# window, choose File | New Project.
3. Choose either the Windows Game, Zune, or Xbox 360 Game template.

Like any other C# application, an XNA application begins by referencing the assemblies and the namespaces required by the program. To plug into the XNA platform, you will need references to the XNA framework along with namespaces for Audio, Content, GamerServices, Graphics, Input, .Media, .Net and .Storage components. When you use a game project template, these namespaces are automatically added for you in the default Game1.cs file that is generated. To avoid potential naming conflicts for this class (with any identically named classes), a namespace is needed for the game class. For example, the Xbox 360 Game project template generates the namespace `Xbox360Game1` and the Windows Game project template generates the namespace `WindowsGame1`. The namespace is followed by a class declaration for the game application class, which both project templates declare as `Game1`. The templates also add the required assembly references for you.

GraphicsDeviceManager

Every XNA application requires a `GraphicsDeviceManager` object to handle the configuration and management of the graphics device. The `GraphicsDevice` class is used for drawing. The `GraphicsDeviceManager` object is declared at the module level:

```
GraphicsDeviceManager graphics;
```

The `GraphicsDeviceManager` object is initialized in the game class constructor, `Game1()`:

```
graphics = new GraphicsDeviceManager(this);
```

SpriteBatch

The `SpriteBatch` object provides access to methods for drawing images, referred to as *sprites*, in the game window. Only one `SpriteBatch` object is needed in your game, and you can use it to draw as many sprites as you choose. Microsoft's game project template declares a `SpriteBatch` object at the top of the game class for you:

```
SpriteBatch            spriteBatch;
```

The `SpriteBatch` object is then initialized in the `LoadContent()` method:

```
spriteBatch = new SpriteBatch(GraphicsDevice);
```

ContentManager

The `ContentManager` is used to load, manage, and dispose of binary media content through the content pipeline. When it is referenced in the game project, this object can load graphics and media content. If you generate your game projects with an XNA template, the root directory for your content will be defined in the constructor of the game class, `Game1()`:

```
Content.RootDirectory = "Content";
```

With this declaration in place, you will need to reference your image, audio, and models from this Content node in the Solution Explorer.

Initialize()

After the `GraphicsDeviceManager` object has been created, you can override the `Initialize()` method to trap the one-time game startup event.

`Initialize()` is a natural place to trigger basic setup activities such as the following:

- Setting window properties such as the title or full-screen options
- Setting up your camera to view a 3D game world
- Initializing vertices for storing position, color, and image coordinates that you will use throughout the program
- Initializing shaders to convert your primitive objects to pixel output
- Setting up other game objects

LoadContent()

The `LoadContent()` override method is generated by the game project templates. The method is used to load binary image and model content through the content pipeline. `LoadContent()` is called after `Initialize()`, and for our examples, this is sufficient to handle our needs. However, if you want to experiment with `DeviceReset` events on your own, you can use `LoadContent()` to reload your media resources when the `DeviceReset` event occurs.

DRAWING AND UPDATING THE GAME APPLICATION

Once an XNA application is initialized, it enters a continuous loop that alternates between drawing and updating the application. Generally, `Update()` is called more frequently than the `Draw()` method. The XNA framework calls these methods for you. So you don't have to worry about triggering them in your own code. All code for drawing graphics objects in the window is triggered from the `Draw()` method. The `Update()` method contains code for updating objects, handling events within the application, and triggering your own defined events—such as checking for game object collisions, handling keyboard or game pad events, tracking the score, and tending to other game features that require maintenance every frame. Both of these functions are performed for every frame that is shown to the player.

Draw()

The Draw() method handles the drawing (also known as *rendering*) for the game program. Throughout the 3D examples in this book, the Draw() routine is basically the same. Draw() starts by clearing the screen background, setting the screen color, and then drawing graphics to the screen.

Update()

The Update() method is used to check and handle game-time events. The Xbox 360, Zune and Windows Game project templates automatically add this method. Events typically handled here include mouse clicks, keyboard presses, game-pad control events, and timers. Update() is also a place for many other activities that require continuous checks or updates. Update() activities might include advancing animations, detecting collisions, or tracking and modifying game scores.

CLOSING THE GAME APPLICATION

The XNA game project templates automatically add an override for the UnloadContent() method. This method will dispose of your managed graphics media when the game program shuts down. The UnloadContent() method also conveniently frees your memory resources even when the game application is closed unintentionally.

BASIC XNA GAME WINDOW EXAMPLE

This example shows all of the C# code that is generated by the Xbox 360, Zune, and Windows Game project templates. When the New Project dialog box is used to create a game project, two source files are generated for your project. One of these is the Program1.cs file, which begins and launches the game application:

```
using System;

namespace WindowsGame1{
    static class Program{
        // main entry point for the application.
        static void Main(string[] args){
```

```
            using (Game1 game = new Game1()){
                game.Run();
            }
        }
    }
}
```

The second default file is the Game1.cs file. This file is generated to house the game class that initializes, updates, and closes the game application:

```
using System;
using System.Collections.Generic;
using Microsoft.Xna.Framework;
using Microsoft.Xna.Framework.Audio;
using Microsoft.Xna.Framework.Content;
using Microsoft.Xna.Framework.GamerServices;
using Microsoft.Xna.Framework.Graphics;
using Microsoft.Xna.Framework.Input;
using Microsoft.Xna.Framework.Net;
using Microsoft.Xna.Framework.Storage;

namespace WindowsGame1{
    public class Game1 : Microsoft.Xna.Framework.Game{
        GraphicsDeviceManager   graphics;
        SpriteBatch             spriteBatch;

        public Game1()
        {   // initialize graphics device and content directory
            graphics                = new GraphicsDeviceManager(this);
            Content.RootDirectory   = "Content";
        }

        protected override void Initialize()
        {   // set up non-graphics related content at program start
            base.Initialize();
        }
```

```
        protected override void LoadContent()
        {   // set up graphics content
            spriteBatch = new SpriteBatch(GraphicsDevice);
        }

        protected override void UnloadContent()
        {   // dispose of graphics content
        }

        protected override void Update(GameTime gameTime)
        {   // animations, collision checking, event handling

            // exit on Xbox 360 when Back button pressed
            if (GamePad.GetState(PlayerIndex.One).Buttons.Back
            == ButtonState.Pressed)
                this.Exit();

            // all update code placed here before base.Update()
            base.Update(gameTime);
        }

        protected override void Draw(GameTime gameTime)
        {   // clear window and color background
            graphics.GraphicsDevice.Clear(Color.CornflowerBlue);

            // all drawing triggered here above base.Draw()
            base.Draw(gameTime);
        }
    }
}
```

That's all of the C# code needed to draw an XNA game window. As you can see, creating and displaying a window is fairly simple. The code is generated by the GS project template and will run on your Xbox 360, Zune, or Windows PC.

CHAPTER 3 REVIEW EXERCISE

To get the most from this chapter, try out this chapter review exercise.

1. Create an XNA Windows Game project. Then make the following changes.

a. Set breakpoints in the `Game1()`, `Initialize()`, `LoadContent()`, `Update()`, `Draw()`, and `UnloadContent()` methods by left-clicking in the grey margin beside each method in the code window. A red dot will appear in the grey margin to indicate that your breakpoint has been set.

b. Next, run your project. Notice that your program will halt at the breakpoint in `Game1()`. Press F5 to advance to `Initialize()` and then press F5 again to advance to `LoadContent()`. Note that these first three methods are always called in this sequence and only one time.

c. Then press F5 repeatedly to alternate between the `Update()` and `Draw()` methods. Note that `Update()` and `Draw()` are called continuously—with `Update()` being called more frequently. To stop your application, press SHIFT+F5.

d. Once you have done this, notice how `UnloadContent()` is entered. At this point you can press F10 to end your application. Finally, if you want to clear your breakpoints, left-click beside each breakpoint in the code window and then press F9.

CHAPTER 4

2D Games

ALTHOUGH there was a time when it seemed as though 2D Games were going to be lost forever within the casing of 1980s video game cartridges, that is certainly not the case today. The rerelease of 2D arcade classics, and the resounding success of Xbox LIVE Arcade, have shown that 2D games can still be fun, relevant, and even profitable.

While you may not be looking to build the next Space Invaders, there is another benefit of 2D Games that makes them worth studying—they can be much easier to create than 3D games. Covering 2D games is also a nice way to start learning about XNA because you can very quickly cover many techniques and get exciting results. For this chapter, you will notice we create a solid 2D game foundation from scratch with hardly any code.

In this chapter, we'll introduce 2D games with an "Asteroid Starter" example that you can use as a starting point for your own 2D game. This simple version should be rich enough to demonstrate the most important 2D-specific coding structures. Specifically, this code sample demonstrates the most essential routines to create interactive 2D animation and 2D collision detection. In some of the later chapters we show all of the steps for adding other structures to your 2D code—such as other types of animation, advanced input handling, fonts, and audio. These specific examples from later chapters are referenced at the end of the chapter.

THE TWO-DIMENSIONAL COORDINATE SYSTEM

Exciting interactive 2D game graphics are possible largely through the animation of images in the game window. A 2D coordinate system is used to position these images and to determine which sections of the image are drawn. The horizontal width and vertical height dimensions of the window and of all images drawn in it are measured in pixels. Note that X pixel column values start at 0 on the left and increase towards the right. Y pixel row values begin at 0 at the top and increase downwards (see Figure 4-1).

FIGURE 4-1

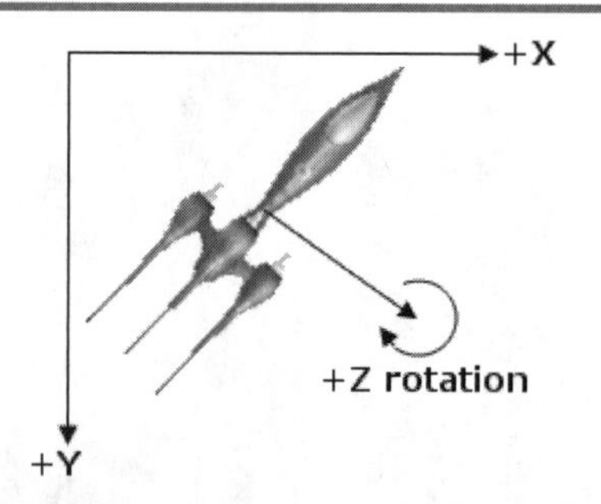

Window and Image X pixel values increase to the right and Y pixel values increase downward

USING IMAGE FILES IN 2D GAMES

XNA supports automatic loading and drawing of bmp, dds, dib, hdr, jpg, pfm, png, ppm, and tga image files. This range of image file formats is most likely all you need. If your images are in another format, you may be able to convert them to a supported format or you can build your own custom loader.

You may choose one format over another due to image quality, but be aware that large image file sizes will eat into your memory, so you need to balance quality with efficiency when selecting an image format.

Note: If you have images that use transparency, you can expect high quality and stable results with png and tga formats.

Content Pipeline Overview

XNA's *Content Pipeline* is the framework that enables automatic loading of supported media formats. As far as image formats are concerned, already having the content pipeline in place saves you from having to write your own image file loader and it provides you with a trusted series of methods to efficiently load your game assets. The Content Pipeline is extensible in case you need to use media file formats that XNA does not support. Chapter 24, "Content Pipeline Processors," provides an example of how to create a custom image loader for a *raw* image file.

Note: Technically, the content pipeline has nothing to do with rendering. For instance, on Windows, you can use Texture2D.FromFile and bypass the entire content pipeline process and still render. The content pipeline's sole purpose is to perform build-time processing of assets to put them into a more appropriate format for quicker loading at runtime.

LOADING AND STORING IMAGES

When using XNA's Content Pipeline, image files are loaded and stored using a Texture2D object. A SpriteBatch object is then used to draw it and you can add code to create an animation.

Textures

Texture objects load and store your image file data. They are referenced when drawing your images in the window. These objects are declared with the Texture2D class:

```
Texture2D   texture2D;
```

To use the Content Pipeline to load your images (with a simple relative file path), they need to be added to your game project under the Content node in the Solution

FIGURE 4-2

Images referenced in the Solution Explorer

Explorer. You may want to create a sub-folder under the Content node for your image files. Either way, when you are ready to load your image files, right-click the Content node or sub-folder and select Add | Existing Item. From the Add Existing Item | Content dialog, you can navigate to the image files. After selecting the file and choosing Add you will see the image file referenced in your project under the Content node (see Figure 4-2).

Using a relative path from the Content node is possible because the Content directory property is set in the game class constructor with the RootDirectory attribute. This instruction is actually generated by the XNA game template wizard:

```
Content.RootDirectory = "Content";
```

When using the Content Pipeline to load your images, the image file extension must not be referenced in your code. If you include the extension, your project won't compile. The file extension is referenced in your project data when the image file is added in the Solution Explorer. Texture2D objects are initialized from the LoadContent() method when the program begins:

```
Texture2D  texture2D = Content.Load<Texture2D>(String filePath);
```

ANIMATED SPRITES

You will often hear the term *sprite* in game programming discussions. A 2D sprite is an animated texture. Sprites are used in all kinds of exciting 2D effects such as character animation, explosions, and more.

Sprite objects are created from the SpriteBatch class. You only need one SpriteBatch object to draw all of your 2D textures and this is already declared and initialized for you in the code generated by the game template wizard. When you use XNA's wizard to create a Windows, Zune, or Xbox 360 game project, you will see a SpriteBatch declaration at the top of the game class:

```
SpriteBatch             spriteBatch;
```

After you use the wizard to generate your code, you will also find that the SpriteBatch object is initialized in the LoadContent() method:

```
spriteBatch            = new SpriteBatch(GraphicsDevice);
```

Enabling Transparency

When drawing sprites, the SpriteBatch Draw() method triggers the actual rendering. All drawing occurs between the Begin() and End() methods.

The Begin() method has three overloads to specify how sprites are drawn. However, when starting basic 2D games programming, you can use the defaults. AlphaBlend mode ensures that pixels which are set to be transparent in an image editor (such as Adobe Photoshop or Gimp) are not drawn at run-time:

```
spriteBatch.Begin(spriteBlendMode.AlphaBlend);      // Additive|AlphaBlend|None
```

Drawing and Animating Your Sprites

The SpriteBatch Draw() method has several overloads. The Draw() method chosen for this chapter is used because it offers a simple but powerful way to animate your sprites. Here is the Draw() method that we will use:

```
spriteBatch.Draw(
    Texture2D      texture2D,     // 2D image object
    Vector2        position,      // window XY position in pixels
    Rectangle      null,          // sourceRectangle
    Color          color,         // use white for original image color
    float          rotation,      // rotation angle in radians
    Vector2        origin,        // origin (use middle pixel in image)
    float          scale,         // scale size (1 is the original size)
    SpriteEffects spriteEffect, // FlipHorizontally|FlipVertically|None
    float          layerDepth);   // layer depth
```

There are several parameters, so we'll discuss the ones you need to modify.

Setting the Texture

The first parameter of this method is for specifying the Texture2D object that you draw. This texture stores the image data.

Updating the Sprite Position

The second parameter in the Draw() method sets the sprite's pixel position in the game window. You can use this value to create lateral and diagonal movement by updating the sprite position each frame—this resets the X and Y coordinates:

```
Vector2 position = new Vector2(float X, float Y);
```

If you multiply your increments to the X and Y values by the time lapse between frames, you can ensure your sprites move at the same rate on all computer systems regardless of their processing power.

Updating the Sprite Rotation

The fifth parameter in our Draw() method overload is the angle used to rotate your sprite. In XNA, the angle of rotation is usually measured in radians—not degrees. As you know, the angle of a circle equals 360 degrees (which equals 2π radians). This rotation is about the Z axis as shown in Figure 4-1. If you multiply your increment to the rotation by the time lapse between frames (for every frame) this will ensure your sprite rotates at the same rate on all machines regardless of processing power.

Setting the Sprite Origin at the Sprite Center

When you draw your sprite at an XY position in the window, you must specify the XY position of the sprite that is mapped to that window location. The single pixel that corresponds to the window position where the sprite is drawn is known as the *origin*. To be consistent with the material in this book, and to ensure your rotations and collision detection code work properly, you need to set the origin at the middle pixel of the image. Also, to ensure your pixel is truly at the middle of your image, we recommend you trim out unused pixels in the margins that surround your image.

Resizing the Sprite

The 7th parameter of the Draw() method below is for setting the size of your sprite. Most of the time, you are going to want to set this value to 1.0f, so that you draw the sprite at its original size. You could double the size of your sprite with a value of 2.0f, or you could shrink the sprite to half the size with a value of 0.5f. However, the collision code implemented later in this chapter requires that the sprite is drawn at its original size. Until you are more familiar with this code, we recommend you leave the scale value at 1.0f.

Setting the Layer Depth

The last parameter in the Draw() method sets the order in which the sprites are drawn. A sprite that is assigned a large depth value will be placed further back in the drawing order. In other words, it will be covered by sprites that have lower-layer depth values if they are positioned at the same location. But you don't have to set the layer depth value, you could just set all depth values to 0.0f and manually implement the drawing order in the Draw() method. If you take the manual route, the images that are drawn on top are the ones drawn last.

All SpriteBatch drawing routines are terminated with the End() method:

```
spriteBatch.End();
```

Title Safe Region

When running XNA projects on a PC, you see the entire window. However, when running your games on the Xbox 360, up to 20% of the view may be truncated by the television display. The visible region in this scenario is referred to as the *title safe region*. If you want to run games on the Xbox 360, you must ensure that your most important graphics (such as heads-up displays, scores, etc.) are visible in the title safe region. The code sample included with this chapter shows how to do this. The routine generates the X and Y pixel positions for each corner of the margin around the title safe area and returns this data in a Rectangle object.

ADDING COLLISION DETECTION

Collision detection allows you to determine if your game objects overlap. You'll use collision detection when you need to know if a puck hits the boards or heaven forbid, an asteroid hits your rocket ship. 2D collision detection routines are quite different than 3D collision detection algorithms, but some of the principals are the same. Wherever you implement collision detection, you should use an efficient check to determine if your objects are in close proximity. If the objects are close, you can apply a more exhaustive but precise check to determine if your sprites actually overlap. By using these two methods instead of just the precise one, you can save valuable processing time.

Rectangle Collision Checking

For 2D games, the *Rectangle* class is used for an efficient but broad check for collisions between your sprites. To create a Rectangle object, you need to pass in the top-left pixel XY position of your sprite and the pixel width and height of your sprite.

Transforming Your Rectangle

As your bounding rectangles are repositioned and rotated, you will need to calculate the updated position of each corner. You use *transformations* to generate these values. These transformations are calculated using a series of matrices. Each matrix stores one transformation and all matrices in this series are multiplied together to generate one cumulative transformation. You don't really need to understand the matrix math to use the transformation matrices effectively. There are more important topics to cover first, but if you really want more detail on matrix math you can find it in Chapter 16, "Matrices."

Transformation Matrices

Matrices are applied slightly differently in a 2D environment compared to a 3D environment. We actually use three-dimensional matrices to manipulate our 2D sprites.

This might sound strange, however, it does make sense if you consider that changing the sprite's direction on X and Y requires a rotation about the Z axis.

To get the versatility we need for implementing collision detection, this chapter introduces the *Z rotation matrix* and the *translation* matrix.

Z Rotation Matrix

The Z rotation matrix is generated using the CreateRotationZ() method. CreateRotationZ() receives an angle in radians as a parameter and uses it to generate a matrix that will rotate sets of vertices around the Z axis:

```
Matrix rotationZ =  Matrix.CreateRotationZ(float radians);
```

Translation Matrix

2D translations are lateral movements on X and Y. The translation matrix is created using the CreateTranslation() method. The CreateTranslation() method receives three floating point values to set the lateral movement on X and Y. The last parameter, Z, is set to 0.0f for 2D since the drawing is done in two dimensions:

```
Matrix.CreateTranslation(float x, float y, float Z);
```

Building the Cumulative Transformation

Cumulative transformation matrices for transforming a set of vertices are calculated by multiplying each individual transformation matrix with the others in this series. Here is an example of a cumulative matrix being generated by multiplying the translation matrix and rotation matrix together:

```
Matrix cumulativeTransform
= Matrix.CreateTranslation(X,Y,Z) * Matrix.CreateRotationZ(radians);
```

The Intersects() Method

After your rectangle corners are transformed, the Intersects() method determines if one rectangle overlaps another.

```
bool Rectangle rectangle0.Intersects(Rectangle rectangle1);
```

FIGURE 4-3

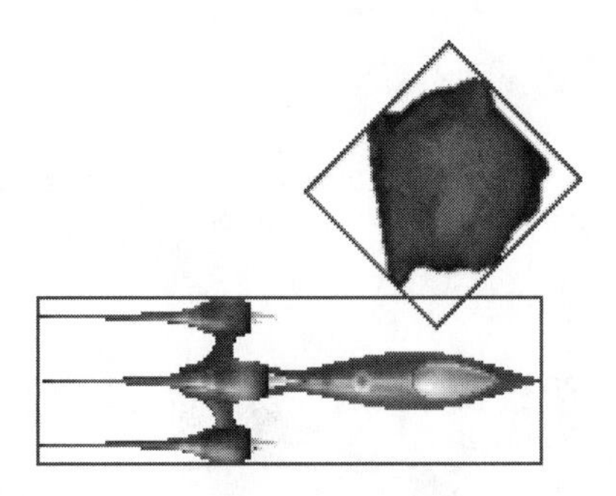

False bounding rectangle collision

There are problems with this method. Figure 4-3 shows a situation where a collision is detected, but there actually is no collision. Another—more accurate—routine is required to check for collisions, but you should still use rectangle collision checking to determine if it is even worth executing a more accurate routine. Rectangle collision checking requires little processing so it will save a lot of heavy lifting.

Per Pixel Collision Checking

Say your bounding rectangle collision check returns a true result which indicates that two sprites have collided. As shown in Figure 4-3, it is possible for the solid portions of the image to not be touching. You don't want to react to this false collision. In a 2D game, you can use a pixel collision checking algorithm to be more accurate. Here is a high-level view of how pixel collision checking works.

The left section of Figure 4-4 shows two sprites drawn at their origin (their centers) at the top left of the window where X=0, Y=0 before each sprite is rotated and translated. The middle section of Figure 4-4 shows each transformed sprite when a bounding rectangle collision is detected. On the right of Figure 4-4, to make pixel collision checking calculations easier, the rocket sprite is treated as if it were drawn at the original starting position (at X=0, Y=0). The asteroid sprite is translated and rotated as before. Then, the asteroid sprite is transformed by the inverse transformation of the rocket sprite.

FIGURE 4-4

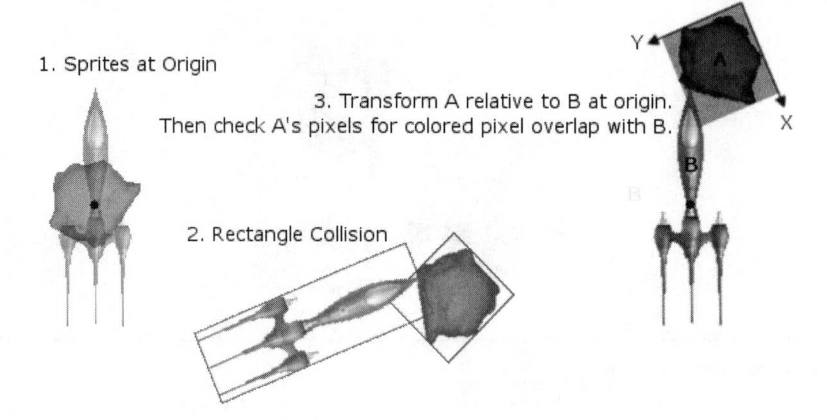
1. Sprites at Origin
2. Rectangle Collision
3. Transform A relative to B at origin.
Then check A's pixels for colored pixel overlap with B.
Y
X
A
B

Steps for checking colored pixel overlap for accurate collision detections

HANDLING USER INPUT DEVICES

The last topic introduced in this chapter is user input device handling. User input devices are easy to implement and you may find this example is enough to not only get you started, it may be all you need to take full advantage of the options available for keyboard and game controller input. If you want more detail though, you can go to Chapter 23, "Input Devices."

Keyboard Input

The KeyboardState class allows you to poll for keyboard IsKeyDown and IsKeyUp states for all keys on the keyboard. The KeyboardState object retrieves the current key states with the GetState() method:

```
KeyboardState keyboardState = Keyboard.GetState();
```

You can use a Keys object to determine if a key is being pressed or released. The example below shows a check to determine if the A key is pressed:

```
bool keyboardState.IsKeyDown(Keys.A);
```

GamePad Input

You can also plug a game controller into your PC or Xbox. In case a game controller is being used, you can add the GamePadState object to listen for button press, *DPad*, *bumper*, *trigger*, and *thumbstick* events using the GetState() method. On the Xbox 360, up to four game controllers are supported. You can specify the player with an integer in the GetState() method with an index.

```
GamePadState  gamePad  = GamePad.GetState(int PlayerIndex);
```

The IsConnected property is used to check if the game pad is actually active on your PC or Xbox 360:

```
bool gamePad.IsConnected
```

The game pad thumbstick controls return floating point values ranging between -1.0f and 1.0f when they are shifted horizontally and vertically. X=-1.0f for all the way left, X=0.0f for the middle, and X=1.0f for the all the way right. Similarily, the Y values are -1.0f when these controls are pulled down, Y=0.0f when the control is at rest in the middle, and Y=1.0f when these controls are pushed all the way forward:

```
float rightSideways, rightForwards, leftSideways, leftForwards;
rightSideways = gamePad.ThumbSticks.Right.X; rightForwards = gamePad.ThumbSticks.Right.Y;
 leftSideways = gamePad.ThumbSticks.Left.X;   leftForwards = gamePad.ThumbSticks.Left.Y;
```

PORTING YOUR 2D GAMES TO THE ZUNE

The screen resolution for the Zune is either 240x320 or 320x240 pixels depending on how you rotate your Zune. You can set these dimension with code similar to the following:

```
this.graphics.PreferredBackBufferWidth  = 240;
this.graphics.PreferredBackBufferHeight = 320;
this.graphics.ApplyChanges();
```

If you are developing a game for the Zune you are better off to build the game with this specified resolution during the design and build phase. Shrinking your sprites and other resources into a smaller area may work but you will be wasting valuable Zune space. For more information on Zune development please see Chapter 1.

A STARTER 2D GAME EXAMPLE

The starter 2D game you'll be creating for this chapter features a rocket that the user can navigate around the screen. The object of the game is to fly the rocket around without heading off into space or making contact with the spinning asteroid rock that bounces back and forth across the screen.

This example shows all of the steps needed to draw and control animated sprites and how to implement proper collision detection.

Unlike almost all other examples in this book (which use the book's base code for a 3D framework), this example begins with the XNA game template. If you want, you can find the solution for this example in the book's download, but we recommend you follow these steps instead. Working through the example will help you learn how to implement this game.

You can build the project template by launching Visual Studio. From the menu, first select File | New Project. Then, under Project Types in the New Project dialog select XNA Game Studio 3.0. From there you can select the Windows Game, Xbox 360 Game, or Zune template depending on where you want to run your game—the code is the same. After you assign your project a name, and specify a location for it, click OK and you are ready to go.

Adding the Images

The first part of this demonstration shows how easy it is to draw a sprite.

Variable Setup

When setting up the project, some variables are needed at the top of the game class to store the texture, position, dimension, and direction information for the rocket and the asteroid:

```
Texture2D  shipTexture, rockTexture;                      // image files

Vector2    shipPosition = new Vector2(100.0f, 100.0f);// position data
Vector2    rockPosition = new Vector2(100.0f, 29.0f);

float      shipRotation, rockRotation;                    // rotation radians

Vector2    shipCenter;    int shipWidth, shipHeight;  // ship dimensions
Vector2    rockCenter;    int rockWidth, rockHeight;  // rock dimensions
```

You can use the ship and asteroid images from the Images folder in the book's download. They have been designed with transparent backgrounds. Of course, you may want to try using your own images for this example. These images need to be referenced in the Solution Explorer as shown in Figure 4-2 (near the start of this chapter). The texture objects are initialized in the LoadContent() method. Also, after the textures are loaded, the texture's Height and Width properties are used to store the texture dimensions and pixel centers. This will help you reference the properties later:

```
shipTexture = Content.Load<Texture2D>("Images\\ship");
rockTexture = Content.Load<Texture2D>("Images\\asteroid");

rockWidth   = rockTexture.Width;      rockHeight = rockTexture.Height;
shipWidth   = shipTexture.Width;      shipHeight = shipTexture.Height;
rockCenter  = new Vector2(rockWidth/2, rockWidth/2);
shipCenter  = new Vector2(shipWidth/2, shipHeight/2);
```

You can now draw your images by placing the following code block inside the Draw() method:

```
spriteBatch.Begin(SpriteBlendMode.AlphaBlend); // start drawing 2D images
    spriteBatch.Draw(rockTexture, rockPosition, null, Color.White,
               rockRotation, rockCenter, 1.0f, SpriteEffects.None, 0.0f);
    spriteBatch.Draw(shipTexture, shipPosition, null, Color.White,
               shipRotation, shipCenter, 1.0f, SpriteEffects.None, 0.0f);
spriteBatch.End();                             // stop drawing 2D images
```

If you run your code now, you will see the asteroid and spaceship.

Animating the Asteroid

In XNA, animations are created by updating position and rotation values every frame. These updates are scaled by the time lapse between frames to ensure the animations run at a uniform speed on all systems. You may have seen some older games that didn't have this feature (such as Microsoft Hearts). If these games were run on a system much faster than the typical processor when the game was developed, the games would run so fast that they could be unplayable. Variables are needed at the top of the game class to assist in tracking the asteroid's lateral speed, rotation speed, and direction:

```
float rockSpeed, rockRotationSpeed;
bool  move         = true;
```

When the program begins, inside Initialize() you need to assign some speed values to set rates for the sprite's continuous lateral and rotational movement:

```
rockSpeed            = 0.16f;
rockRotationSpeed    = 0.3f;
```

To ensure your most important graphics stay within the title safe area of your window, you need to specify the area. The TitleSafeRegion() method is used in your game class to return the margins of a rectangle that surrounds the visible area on your game display. This method returns a Rectangle object which contains the Top, Bottom, Left, and Right margin values of this title safe area:

```
Rectangle TitleSafeRegion(int spriteWidth, int spriteHeight){
#if Xbox
    // some televisions only show 80% of the window
    Vector2     start         = new Vector2();    // starting pixel X & Y
    const float MARGIN        = 0.2f;             // only 80% visible on
                                                  // Xbox 360
    start.X =  graphics.GraphicsDevice.Viewport.Width * MARGIN/2.0f;
    start.Y =  graphics.GraphicsDevice.Viewport.Height
          * (1 - MARGIN/2.0f);
    // ensure image drawn in safe region on all sides
    return new Rectangle(
          (int)start.X,                           // surrounding safe area
          (int)start.Y,                           // top,left,width,height
          (int)(1.0f-MARGIN)*Window.ClientBounds.Width  - spriteWidth,
          (int)(1.0f-MARGIN)*Window.ClientBounds.Height - spriteHeight);
#endif
    // show entire region on the PC or Zune
    return new Rectangle(0,0,Window.ClientBounds.Width  - spriteWidth,
                             Window.ClientBounds.Height - spriteHeight);
}
```

Next is the code to update the position and orientation of the rock; this happens for each frame. A rotation is added in to make them look more interesting. In the asteroid code, unlike the rocket, there are checks for the screen bounds (e.g., Window.ClientBounds.Width). These checks ensure that the rock doesn't leave the viewable area of the screen. If the rock hits the side, it reverses direction and heads straight back the other way.

```
private void UpdateAsteroid(GameTime gameTime){
    // time between frames
    float timeLapse = (float)gameTime.ElapsedGameTime.Milliseconds;

    if (move == true)
    {   // asteroid centered at the middle of the image
        Rectangle safeArea = TitleSafeRegion(rockWidth/2, rockHeight/2);
```

```
        // asteroid right edge exceeds right window edge
        if (rockPosition.X > safeArea.Right){
            rockPosition.X = safeArea.Right;     // move it back
            rockSpeed     *= -1.0f;              // reverse direction
        }
        // asteroid left edge precedes the left window edge
        else if (rockPosition.X - rockCenter.X < 0){
            rockPosition.X = rockCenter.X;       // move it back
            rockSpeed     *= -1.0f;              // reverse direction
        }
        // asteroid within window bounds so update rockPosition
        else
            rockPosition.X += rockSpeed * timeLapse;

        // Scale radians by time between frames so rotation is uniform
        // rate on all systems. Cap between 0 & 2PI for full rotation.
        const float  SCALE = 50.0f;
        rockRotation += rockRotationSpeed * timeLapse/SCALE;
        rockRotation  = rockRotation % (MathHelper.Pi * 2.0f);
    }
}
```

Updates to the asteroids' position and rotation values should be done from the Update() method:

```
UpdateAsteroid(gameTime);
```

If you run your code now, the asteroid will move back and forth continuously.

Controlling the Ship

In this example, the ship angle is determined using input from either the LEFT and RIGHT arrow keys, or from the left thumbstick's X value on the game controller. The change to the rotation is scaled by the time lapse between frames to ensure a uniform rotation. Since the angle of a circle is 360 degrees (2π radians), the cumulative ship rotation, stored in the "shipRotation" variable, is modded by 2π to keep the rotation angle between 0 and 2π at all times.

```
private float RotateShip(GameTime gameTime){
    float rotation = 0.0f;
    float speed    = gameTime.ElapsedGameTime.Milliseconds/300.0f;
```

```
    if (!move) // collision has occurred so don't rotate ship any more
        return rotation;

    // handle user input
    KeyboardState keyboard = Keyboard.GetState();
    GamePadState  gamePad  = GamePad.GetState(PlayerIndex.One);

    if(!gamePad.IsConnected){                              // keyboard input
        if(keyboard.IsKeyDown(Keys.Right)
        && keyboard.IsKeyDown(Keys.Left)){
            // don't rotate if Right or Left not pressed
        }
        else if(keyboard.IsKeyDown(Keys.Right))           // right
            rotation = speed;
        else if (keyboard.IsKeyDown(Keys.Left))           // left
            rotation =-speed;
    }
    else                                                   // controller input
        rotation = gamePad.ThumbSticks.Left.X * speed;

    // update rotation based on time scale and only store between 0 & 2pi
    shipRotation += rotation;
    shipRotation  = shipRotation % (MathHelper.Pi * 2.0f);
    return shipRotation;
}
```

Trigonometry is used to implement the forward and backward movement of the rocket ship. The ship moves when the user presses the UP or DOWN arrow keys or when they shift the left thumbstick.

Now for a quick trigonometry primer. We use these formulas to calculate the distance moved in the X and Y planes. Where:

```
Sinϕ  = Opposite/Hypotenuse     and     Cosϕ = Adjacent/Hypotenuse
```

We can say:

```
X = Opposite = Hypotenuse*Sinϕ and     Y = Adjacent  = Hypotenuse*Cosϕ
```

In the case of our rocket ship, shown in Figure 4-5, we have already stored the ship's rotation angle and if we treat the speed as the hypotenuse we can calculate the change on X and Y.

FIGURE 4-5

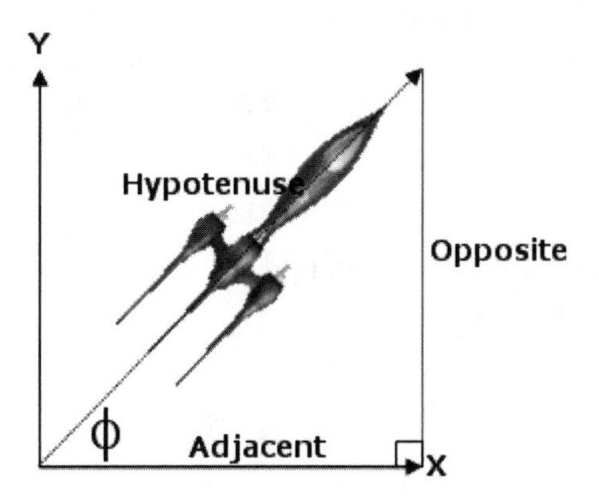

The angle of the rocket ship

MoveShip() implements this algorithm from the game class to allow the user to control the direction and movement of the rocket ship:

```
private void MoveShip(GameTime gameTime){
    const float SCALE = 20.0f;                          // speed
    float       speed = gameTime.ElapsedGameTime.Milliseconds/100.0f;

    KeyboardState keyboard = Keyboard.GetState();       // user input
    GamePadState  gamePad  = GamePad.GetState(PlayerIndex.One);

    if (move && !gamePad.IsConnected){  // KEYBOARD
        if (keyboard.IsKeyDown(Keys.Down) && keyboard.IsKeyDown(Keys.Up)){
            // Up and Down pressed at same time so do not move
        }
        if (keyboard.IsKeyDown(Keys.Up)){                // forwards
            shipPosition.X += (float)Math.Sin(shipRotation)*speed*SCALE;
            shipPosition.Y -= (float)Math.Cos(shipRotation)*speed*SCALE;
        }
        else if (keyboard.IsKeyDown(Keys.Down)){         // reverse
            shipPosition.X -= (float)Math.Sin(shipRotation)*speed*SCALE;
            shipPosition.Y += (float)Math.Cos(shipRotation)*speed*SCALE;
        }
    }
```

```
    else if(move){                              // GAMEPAD
        shipPosition.X += (float)Math.Sin(shipRotation) *
                          gamePad.ThumbSticks.Left.Y*speed*SCALE;
        shipPosition.Y -= (float)Math.Cos(shipRotation) *
                          gamePad.ThumbSticks.Left.Y*speed*SCALE;
    }
}
```

The ship rotation and movement updates are triggered from the Update() method to ensure consistency each frame:

```
RotateShip(gameTime);
MoveShip(gameTime);
```

Adding in Collision Detection

In the high-level view of the collision detection algorithms discussed earlier, we explained that a bounding rectangle algorithm can be used as a quick check to determine if texture borders intersect. If a bounding rectangle occurs, pixel comparisons are made between the two textures to determine if two colored pixels overlap. Now let's look at the code.

First, identifiers are used to distinguish the rock and rocket ship objects:

```
const int   ROCK     = 0;     const int   SHIP     = 1;
Color[]     rockColor;        Color[]     shipColor;
```

These color values are initialized at the end of LoadContent() after the textures are loaded:

```
rockColor = new Color[rockTexture.Width * rockTexture.Height];
rockTexture.GetData(rockColor);
shipColor = new Color[shipTexture.Width * shipTexture.Height];
shipTexture.GetData(shipColor);
```

To keep things simple, we store the color data for each texture in an array. The following routine is added to the game class to return the specific color for each pixel in each sprite:

```
public Color PixelColor(int objectNum, int pixelNum){
    switch (objectNum){
        case ROCK:
            return rockColor[pixelNum];
```

```
        case SHIP:
            return shipColor[pixelNum];
    }
    return Color.White;
}
```

The PixelCollision() and TransformRectangle() methods implemented here are based on code samples provided from the XNA Creator's Club website (http://creators.xna.com). This site is a fantastic resource for anyone working with the XNA framework. Basically, the PixelCollision() method transforms sprite A by A's original transformation and then transforms it again by the inverse of sprite B's transformation. These calculations express sprite A with the same relative positioning to sprite B during the bounding rectangle collision. However, B is treated as if it hasn't moved from the original starting pixel position at X=0, Y=0.

When traversing across and downward through A's rows of pixels, a unit change in X and a unit change in Y must be calculated to determine the increment for X and Y values of each neighboring pixel. Unit normal vectors are used to calculate these rates of change. Normal vectors and unit vectors are discussed in more detail in Chapter 15, "Vectors,", but we recommend you stay focused on this chapter and the others leading up to it.

For each pixel in sprite A: if it is colored, the position is used to retrieve the pixel color from sprite B if it exists. If both pixels are colored a collision has occurred (refer to Figure 4-4):

```
public bool PixelCollision(
            Matrix transformA, int pixelWidthA, int pixelHeightA, int A,
            Matrix transformB, int pixelWidthB, int pixelHeightB, int B){
    // set A transformation relative to B. B remains at x=0, y=0.
    Matrix AtoB = transformA * Matrix.Invert(transformB);

    // generate a perpendicular vectors to each rectangle side
    Vector2 columnStep, rowStep, rowStartPosition;
    columnStep  = Vector2.TransformNormal(Vector2.UnitX, AtoB);
    rowStep     = Vector2.TransformNormal(Vector2.UnitY, AtoB);

    // calculate the top left corner of A
    rowStartPosition = Vector2.Transform(Vector2.Zero, AtoB);

    // search each row of pixels in A. start at top and move down.
    for (int rowA = 0; rowA < pixelHeightA; rowA++){
        // begin at the left
        Vector2 pixelPositionA = rowStartPosition;
```

```
        // for each column in the row (move left to right)
        for (int colA = 0; colA < pixelWidthA; colA++){
            // get the pixel position
            int X = (int)Math.Round(pixelPositionA.X);
            int Y = (int)Math.Round(pixelPositionA.Y);

            // if the pixel is within the bounds of B
            if (X >= 0 && X < pixelWidthB && Y >= 0 && Y < pixelHeightB){
                // get colors of overlapping pixels
                Color colorA = PixelColor(A, colA + rowA * pixelWidthA);
                Color colorB = PixelColor(B, X    + Y    * pixelWidthB);

                // if both pixels are not completely transparent,
                if (colorA.A != 0 && colorB.A != 0)
                    return true;                    // collision
            }
            // move to the next pixel in the row of A
            pixelPositionA += columnStep;
        }
        // move to the next row of A
        rowStartPosition += rowStep;
    }
    return false;                                   // no collision
}
```

When checking for bounding rectangles, the Transform() method generates a cumulative transformation matrix according to the sprites' current rotation and position. But first, this method shifts the sprite to the origin. It then performs the Z rotation and translation on X and Y and returns the cumulative result:

```
public Matrix Transform(Vector2 center, float rotation, Vector2 position)
{   // move to origin, scale (if desired), rotate, translate
    return  Matrix.CreateTranslation(new Vector3(-center, 0.0f)) *
            // add scaling here if you want
            Matrix.CreateRotationZ(rotation) *
            Matrix.CreateTranslation(new Vector3(position, 0.0f));
}
```

When checking for collisions between the bounding rectangles of each sprite, each corner of each rectangle must be transformed. Then a new rectangle is generated using the top left vertex from the newly transformed corners and the X and Y distance to the opposite corner. TransformRectangle() does this from the game class:

```
public static Rectangle TransformRectangle(Matrix transform, int width,
                                                          int height){

    // Get each corner of texture
    Vector2 leftTop     = new Vector2(0.0f,  0.0f);
    Vector2 rightTop    = new Vector2(width, 0.0f);
    Vector2 leftBottom  = new Vector2(0.0f,  height);
    Vector2 rightBottom = new Vector2(width, height);

    // Transform each corner
    Vector2.Transform(ref leftTop,     ref transform, out leftTop);
    Vector2.Transform(ref rightTop,    ref transform, out rightTop);
    Vector2.Transform(ref leftBottom,  ref transform, out leftBottom);
    Vector2.Transform(ref rightBottom, ref transform, out rightBottom);

    // Find the minimum and maximum corners
    Vector2 min = Vector2.Min(Vector2.Min(leftTop, rightTop),
                  Vector2.Min(leftBottom, rightBottom));
    Vector2 max = Vector2.Max(Vector2.Max(leftTop, rightTop),
                  Vector2.Max(leftBottom, rightBottom));

    // Return transformed rectangle
    return new Rectangle((int)min.X, (int)min.Y,
                         (int)(max.X - min.X), (int)(max.Y - min.Y));
}
```

The driving routine which should be added to check for collisions is added to the game class. The pixel collision routine is expensive, so it is not entered until a bounding rectangle collision has been established. First, the asteroid and ship sprites are transformed and rectangle collision is used to determine if both sprites are close. If the two objects are close, then pixel collision detection is triggered to search for overlapping colored pixels:

```
private void CheckCollisions(){
    Matrix      shipTransform, rockTransform;
    Rectangle   shipRectangle, rockRectangle;

    // transform the rectangles which surround each sprite
    rockTransform = Transform(rockCenter, rockRotation, rockPosition);
    rockRectangle = TransformRectangle(rockTransform, rockWidth,
                                       rockHeight);
    shipTransform = Transform(shipCenter, shipRotation, shipPosition);
```

```
    shipRectangle = TransformRectangle(shipTransform, shipWidth,
                                             shipHeight);
    // collision checking
    if (rockRectangle.Intersects(shipRectangle)) // rough collision check
        if (PixelCollision(                      // exact collision check
            rockTransform, rockWidth, rockHeight, ROCK,
            shipTransform, shipWidth, shipHeight, SHIP))
                move = false;
}
```

The collision checking routine is called from Update() after the ship and asteroids are updated:

```
CheckCollisions();
```

If you run the program now, you will see a moving rock and a ship that you can control with the arrow keys. If your rocket ship gets hit by an asteroid, you will no longer be able to move your ship and the asteroid will stop moving. That's it! You have built your own 2D starter game.

COMPLETING THE 2D GAME

After reading the code discussion in this chapter, you will see that you can create a very powerful 2D game foundation in minutes. The sample discussed shows all steps needed to implement animated sprites, handle user input devices, and perform 2D collision detection. However, we are sure you want to build a complete 2D game and this book does explains how to do so from start to finish. After reading this chapter, you can also follow the steps in the following chapters to complete your 2D framework:

Chapter	Title
12	*"Combining Images for Better Visual Effects," SpriteBatch on the Heads-Up-Display Example*
13	*"Score Tracking and Game Statistics," Font Example: Displaying a Frames-per-Second Count*
23	*"Zune Input Device Example"*

We also think you will find adapting the following chapters to suit a 2D game is a simple process:

Chapter	*Title*
23	*"Zune Input Device Example"*
29	*"Networking"*

Lastly, if you are deploying your 2D games to the Zune please read Chapter 1, "Set Up an XNA Development Environment," for steps and best practices on porting code to the Zune.

CHAPTER EXERCISES

1. Add another sprite to your game.
2. Change the behavior of the rock so that it doesn't move in a straight line.
3. Add collision code that prevents the rocket from leaving the screen.
4. Add more code to launch a missile from the rocket when you press the space bar. For an additional hint on how to do this, see the section on "Adjusting the Input Device Responsiveness" for toggling states in Chapter 23, "Input Devices."

CHAPTER 5

Introduction to 3D Graphics Programming

THIS chapter discusses the basic elements and methods for drawing primitive 3D game graphics with points, lines, and triangles. By the end of this chapter, you will be able to use these structures to build something like a simple village in a 3D world. Learning how to draw basic shapes in a game window might not grab you at first, but all great graphic effects, and even 3D models, begin with the structures presented here.

3D graphics start with shapes that are created from points, lines, or triangles. These basic elements are referred to as *primitive objects*. Primitive objects are drawn in 3D space using a Cartesian coordinate system where position is mapped in the X, Y, and Z planes (see Figure 5-1).

Even complex shapes are built with a series of points, lines, or triangles. A static 3D model is basically made from a file containing vertex information that includes X, Y, Z position, color, image coordinates, and possibly other data. The vertices can be rendered by outputting points for each vertex, with a grid of lines that connects the vertices, or as a solid object that is built with a series of triangles—which are linked by the vertices.

PRIMITIVE OBJECTS

Complex shapes are created with primitive objects that regulate how the vertices are displayed. The vertex data could be rendered as points, linear grids, or solid triangles (see Figure 5-2).

FIGURE 5-1

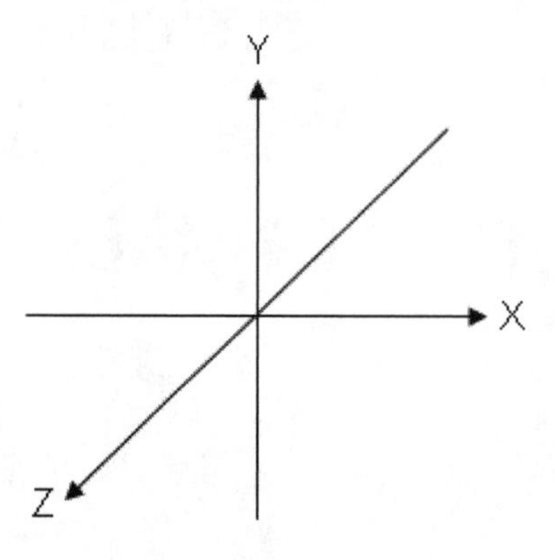

Cartesian coordinate system for drawing in 3D

FIGURE 5-2

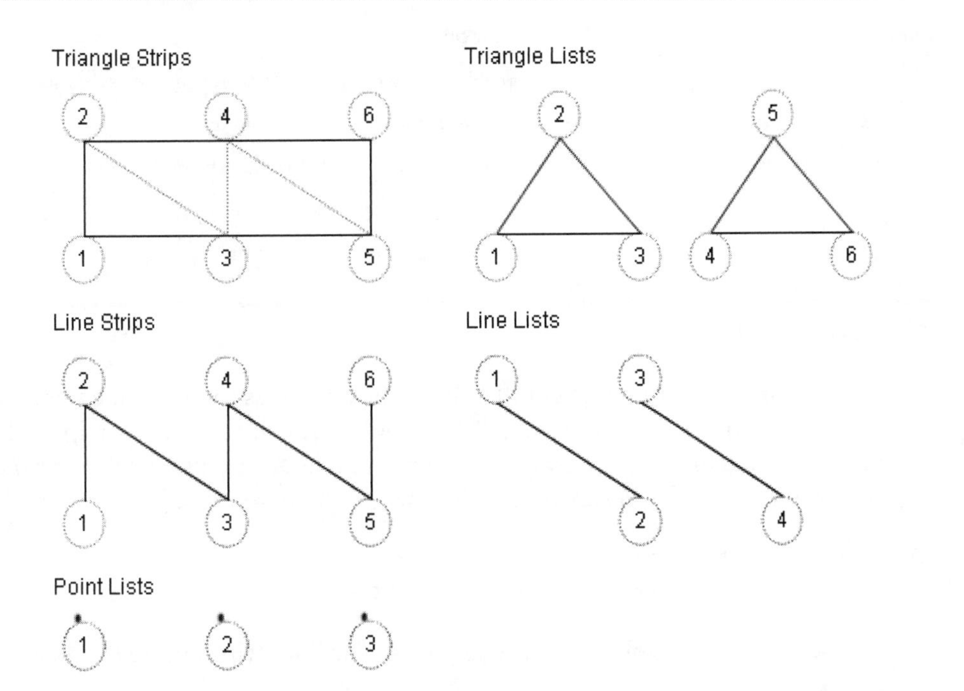

Primitive strips and lists

DRAWING SYNTAX

XNA delivers simple syntax for drawing shapes from primitive objects.

Primitive Object Types

Table 3-1 details the five common primitive object types. You will notice that triangles and lines can be drawn in *strips* or in *lists*. Lists are required for drawing separate points, lines, or triangles. Strips, on the other hand, are more efficient where the lines or triangles are combined to create a complex shape—such as a 3D model.

TABLE 5-1

Primitive Type	Function
TriangleStrip	Enables linking of triangles to create complex solid shapes
TriangleList	Enables groups of separate triangles
LineStrip	Enables linking of lines to create wire grids
LineList	Enables groups of separate lines
PointList	Enables groups of separate points

Common Primitive Types

Strips are also more efficient than lists when it comes to saving memory and, as a result, they enable faster drawing. When you're drawing a triangle strip, adding one more vertex to the strip generates one more triangle. A strip practically cuts the memory requirements for vertex data in half when compared to a list:

```
Total triangle list vertices  = Ntriangles * 3 vertices
Total triangle strip vertices = Ntriangles + 2 vertices
```

The same logic applies for drawing lines. The line strip is more efficient for complex grids:

```
Total line list vertices  = Nlines * 2 vertices
Total line strip vertices = Nlines + 1 vertex
```

Vertex Types

A *vertex object* stores vertex information, which can include X, Y, and Z positions, image coordinates, a normal vector, and color. The XNA platform offers four predefined vertex formats that are fairly self-explanatory (see Table 5-2).

TABLE 5-2

Vertex Storage Format	Function
VertexPositionColor	Stores X, Y, Z and color coordinates
VertexPositionTexture	Stores X, Y, Z and image coordinates
VertexPositionColorTexture	Stores X, Y, Z, color, and image coordinates
VertexPositionNormalTexture	Stores X, Y, Z positions, a normal vector, and image coordinates

Storage Formats for Vertex Buffers

VertexDeclaration

A `VertexDeclaration` object stores the vertex format for the data contained in each vertex of the shape or model. Before drawing the object, the graphics device must be set to use the correct format to allow for proper retrieval of vertex data from each vertex array. Here is the syntax required to declare and initialize the `VertexDeclaration` object:

```
VertexDeclaration vertexDeclaration
= new VertexDeclaration(graphics.GraphicsDevice,
      VertexPositionColor.VertexElements);
```

Before an object is drawn, the graphics device's `VertexDeclaration` property is assigned so that it can retrieve the vertex data and render it properly:

```
graphics.GraphicsDevice.VertexDeclaration = vertexDeclaration;
```

DrawUserPrimitives

When an object is drawn using primitive types, five items are set just before it is rendered:

1. The vertex type is declared.
2. The primitive type is set so that drawings can be rendered using points, lines, or triangles.
3. The vertex array that stores the X, Y, Z, color, texture, and normal data used for drawing is assigned.
4. The starting element in the vertex array is set.
5. The total count for the primitives to be drawn is assigned.

This information is passed to the `DrawUserPrimitives()` method:

```
graphics.GraphicsDevice.DrawUserPrimitives<Vertex Storage Format>(
     PrimitiveType                 primitiveType,
     VertexPositionColorTexture[]  vertexData,
     int                           startingVertex,
     int                           primitiveCount);
```

DRAWING PRIMITIVE OBJECTS EXAMPLE

This demonstration shows how to draw using the five common primitive objects with vertex data. These objects are arranged to draw a Martian's face (see Figure 5-3). The Martian's eyes are made using six vertices that draw two separate white

FIGURE 5-3

Final output for the drawing primitive objects example

triangles in a triangle list. Two vertices are used in a point list to make two tiny black pupils for these eyes. A green triangle is drawn using a third triangle in the triangle list to create the skin of the Martian's face. The Martian's mouth is made using five vertices to draw three triangles in one red triangle strip. The nose is drawn using three vertices in one line strip that makes two separate lines. Two yellow eyebrows are drawn using four vertices in a line list. At first glance, the output from this demonstration might seem limited, but keep in mind that primitive objects are the foundation of any 3D world, so understanding them is worth your time.

This example begins with either the MGHWinBaseCode project or the MGH360BaseCode project in the BaseCode folder in the download from this book's web site. The basic code for each of these projects is identical. The framework differences between the two allow the MGHWinBaseCode project to run on your PC and the MGH360BaseCode project to run on the Xbox 360.

With this base code, you can move through the 3D world either by moving the left thumbstick on the game controller up or down or by pressing the UP or DOWN ARROW on the keyboard. Moving the left thumbstick to the left or right allows you to *strafe*—as do the LEFT and RIGHT ARROW keys on the keyboard. If you prefer, you can also use the W, A, S, and D keys to move and strafe while viewing your 3D world. Moving the right thumbstick, or the mouse, allows you to adjust the view. Before you start this example, you may want to run the project and experiment in the basic 3D world.

When drawing in 3D with XNA, you have to use a shader. To draw primitives from vertices that store position and color, you must have a shader that can process vertices with position and color. Shaders will be discussed in the next chapter, Chapter 6. In a nutshell, shaders receive vertex data from the C# application, apply filters, and then perform other user-defined operations such as texturing, coloring, and lighting. The output from the shader is pixel output in your game window.

For this example to work properly, you need to reference the shader file named PositionColor.fx in your project. It is already referenced in the base code. Chapter 6 shows how to add and reference this shader in addition to explaining how all of this code works.

Triangle Strip

When you work through the next portion of this example, and you run your project, three triangles will appear together to create the Martian's mouth.

You must declare a vertex array in your game class to store five vertices containing position and color information for the three triangles that will be drawn in the strip. To do so, add this code:

```
private VertexPositionColor[] triangleStrip = new VertexPositionColor[5];
```

Next, a method containing code to initialize the positions and colors for each vertex in the triangle strip can be added to the game class:

```
private void InitializeTriangleStrip(){
    Color color = Color.Red;        // mouth

    triangleStrip[0]
    = new VertexPositionColor(new Vector3(-0.15f, 1.40f, -3.0f), color);
    triangleStrip[1]
    = new VertexPositionColor(new Vector3(-0.10f, 1.37f, -3.0f), color);
    triangleStrip[2]
    = new VertexPositionColor(new Vector3(-0.00f, 1.40f, -3.0f), color);
    triangleStrip[3]
    = new VertexPositionColor(new Vector3( 0.10f, 1.37f, -3.0f), color);
    triangleStrip[4]
    = new VertexPositionColor(new Vector3( 0.15f, 1.40f, -3.0f), color); }
```

The method `InitializeTriangleStrip()` should be called at the end of `Initialize()` to set up the array of vertices for the triangle strip when the program begins:

```
InitializeTriangleStrip();
```

Next, you need a method in the game class for drawing the primitive object from the vertex array. For most examples throughout this book, the drawing of primitive shapes is done in five simple steps:

1. Declare transformation matrices for scaling, moving, and rotating your graphics.

2. Initialize the transformation matrices.
3. Build the cumulative transformation by multiplying the matrices.
4. Set the shader parameters.
5. Select the vertex type, primitive type, and number of vertices, and then draw the object.

The first three steps involve setting up a cumulative matrix to transform the object through scaling, translations, and rotations. Transformations are covered in Chapter 7. More detail is presented in Chapter 6 to explain step 4 (where the shader variables are set). For the purpose of introducing vertices and primitive shapes in this chapter, we'll focus on step 5.

For our demonstration, the drawing in step 5 is implemented with a method called `PositionColorShader()`. `PositionColorShader()` has already been added to the base code. The drawing instructions contained in this method are nested between the `Begin()` and `End()` methods for the pass to the PositionColor.fx shader. The graphics device `VertexDeclaration` property is assigned the `VertexPositionColor` storage type. This property allows the graphics device to retrieve the data in the correct format, which in this case contains color and position data. The `DrawUserPrimitives()` method is assigned the `<VertexPositionColor>` format, the primitive type is set for surface type output, and the vertex array `vertexData` is specified as the source of vertices with color and position data. The last two parameters of the `DrawUserPrimitives()` method select the offset of the vertex array and the total primitives to be drawn:

```
private void PositionColorShader(PrimitiveType primitiveType,
            VertexPositionColor[] vertexData, int numPrimitives){
    positionColorEffect.Begin();       // begin using PositionColor.fx
    positionColorEffect.Techniques[0].Passes[0].Begin();

    // set drawing format and vertex data
    graphics.GraphicsDevice.VertexDeclaration = positionColor;
    graphics.GraphicsDevice.DrawUserPrimitives<VertexPositionColor>(
                            primitiveType, vertexData, 0, numPrimitives);

    positionColorEffect.Techniques[0].Passes[0].End();
    positionColorEffect.End();          // stop using PositionColor.fx
}
```

For all primitives drawn in this example, you are going to draw each object at the position where their vertices were defined earlier. To do this, you add the

DrawObjects() method to the game class. DrawObjects() uses the vertex data you declare at the program start to call PositionColorShader() to perform the drawing:

```
void DrawObjects(){
    // 1: declare matrices
    Matrix world, identity;

    // 2: initialize matrices
    identity    = Matrix.Identity;

    // 3: build cumulative world matrix using I.S.R.O.T. sequence
    // identity, scale, rotate, orbit(translate & rotate), translate
    world       = identity;

    // 4: set the shader parameters
    positionColorEffectWVP.SetValue(world *
                              cam.viewMatrix * cam.projectionMatrix);

    // 5: draw object - set primitive type, vertex data, # of primitives
    PositionColorShader(PrimitiveType.TriangleStrip, triangleStrip, 3);
}
```

All drawing is triggered from inside the Draw() method before the base.Draw() instruction:

```
DrawObjects();
```

Try running this version of the program, and you'll find that the graphics output is displayed in the game window. More specifically, three red triangles in a strip will appear in front of your view.

Triangle List

When you need to draw separate triangles, the triangle list is handy. To continue with this example, you will create white eyes and a green face for the Martian by displaying two triangles in a list. A vertex array with room for nine vertices (for three triangles) is needed to store the position and color data that will be used to draw the triangles. To set up this array, add the following declaration to the top of the game class:

```
private VertexPositionColor[] triangleList  = new VertexPositionColor[9];
```

A method for initializing each vertex in the triangle list, `InitializeTriangleList()`, is needed in the game class:

```
private void InitializeTriangleList(){
    Color color = Color.White;  // left eye
    triangleList[0]
    = new VertexPositionColor(new Vector3(-0.20f, 1.5f, -3.0f), color);
    triangleList[1]
    = new VertexPositionColor(new Vector3(-0.15f, 1.6f, -3.0f), color);
    triangleList[2]
    = new VertexPositionColor(new Vector3(-0.10f, 1.5f, -3.0f), color);

    color = Color.White;        // right eye
    triangleList[3]
    = new VertexPositionColor(new Vector3( 0.20f, 1.5f, -3.0f), color);
    triangleList[4]
    = new VertexPositionColor(new Vector3( 0.15f, 1.6f, -3.0f), color);
    triangleList[5]
    = new VertexPositionColor(new Vector3( 0.10f, 1.5f, -3.0f), color);

    color = Color.Green;        // face
    triangleList[6]
    = new VertexPositionColor(new Vector3( 0.5f, 1.7f, -3.05f), color);
    triangleList[7]
    = new VertexPositionColor(new Vector3( 0.0f, 1.2f, -3.05f), color);
    triangleList[8]
    = new VertexPositionColor(new Vector3(-0.5f, 1.7f, -3.05f), color);
}
```

Call `InitializeTriangleList()` from `Initialize()` to fill the vertex array with data that can be used to draw the three triangles in the list:

```
InitializeTriangleList();
```

At the end of `DrawObjects()`, after the triangle strip is drawn, the triangle list can be rendered. The drawing of the three new and separate triangles in a list is triggered by calling `PositionColorShader()` with new parameters for primitive type, vertices, and total primitive objects. Drawing more than one primitive object from the same `PositionColorShader()` method is possible because both primitive objects use the same vertex format, `VertexPositionColor`. Notice that the `PrimitiveType` specified for this new addition is `TriangleList` and the total number of primitives rendered in the list is three. The data in our vertex array for the triangle list, `triangleList`, is being referenced when drawing the triangle list:

```
PositionColorShader(PrimitiveType.TriangleList, triangleList, 3);
```

When you run the new version of the program, it will show the three triangles in the strip to create the Martian's mouth, two triangles in a triangle list to create the white eyes, and one triangle in the triangle list to create the green face.

Drawing a Line Strip

You have seen how triangles can be created and drawn using strips and lists. The same logic applies for drawing lines. For this next portion of the example, a line strip will be used to draw the Martian's nose. The line strip might be useful for you if you ever want to show a wire grid between the vertices that make the 3D object. You undoubtedly have seen this effect used when rendering 3D models or terrain with line strips instead of triangle strips.

A vertex array must be declared with the position and color data that build the line strip. For this example, enough room will be given to store two lines in the strip. In other words, three vertices are required. To declare the vertex array, add this code to the module declarations section:

```
private VertexPositionColor[] lineStrip = new VertexPositionColor[3];
```

Next, add a method to store the vertex information for each of the vertices in the line strip. For each vertex, the X, Y, and Z position is specified and the color is assigned.

```
private void InitializeLineStrip(){
    Color color  = Color.Red;         // nose
    lineStrip[0]
    = new VertexPositionColor(new Vector3(-0.05f, 1.46f,-3.0f), color);
    lineStrip[1]
    = new VertexPositionColor(new Vector3( 0.00f, 1.55f,-3.0f), color);
    lineStrip[2]
    = new VertexPositionColor(new Vector3( 0.05f, 1.46f,-3.0f), color);
}
```

To initialize the line strip when the program begins, add the call statement for InitializeLineStrip() to the end of the `Initialize()` method:

```
InitializeLineStrip();
```

Finally, code for drawing our line strip is added as the last line in the DrawObjects() method after the setup for the rendering has been completed. This instruction uses the PositionColorShader() method to draw two lines in a strip using position and color data from the lineStrip array:

```
PositionColorShader(PrimitiveType.LineStrip, lineStrip, 2);
```

When you run the game application, the output will use the line strip to draw the Martian's nose.

Adding a Line List

Now that drawing lines using strips has been demonstrated, this next section of code will show how to add two lines that are drawn using a list. Each line in the list requires two separate vertices. The vertex array needed to store each vertex in the line list is declared in the module declarations section of the game class.

```
private VertexPositionColor[] lineList = new VertexPositionColor[4];
```

A method, InitializeLineList(), for initializing each vertex in the line list with X, Y, Z, and color data, is added to the methods section:

```
private void InitializeLineList(){
    Color color = Color.Yellow;      // eyebrows
    lineList[0]
    = new VertexPositionColor(new Vector3(-0.18f, 1.60f,-3.0f), color);
    lineList[1]
    = new VertexPositionColor(new Vector3(-0.12f, 1.63f,-3.0f), color);
    lineList[2]
    = new VertexPositionColor(new Vector3( 0.12f, 1.63f,-3.0f), color);
    lineList[3]
    = new VertexPositionColor(new Vector3( 0.18f, 1.60f,-3.0f), color);
}
```

InitializeLineList() is called from Initialize() to set up the line list when the program begins:

```
InitializeLineList();
```

Finally, a new instruction should be added to the very end of the DrawObjects() method to render the line list. The first parameter of the PositionColorShader() method sets the LineList type, the second parameter selects the `lineList` array as the source of vertex data for the primitive object being drawn, and the third parameter sets the total number of lines that are rendered.

```
PositionColorShader(PrimitiveType.LineList, lineList, 2);
```

When you run the program, two separate lines will be drawn in as the Martian's eyebrows.

Adding a Point List

Now for our final primitive object—the point list. In this portion of the demonstration, two points from a list will be added to the window.

First, a class declaration for a vertex array is used to store each point in the list using the position and color format:

```
private VertexPositionColor[] pointList = new VertexPositionColor[2];
```

Next, a method is required to initialize each vertex in the point list with X, Y, Z position data and color information. To do this, add the following method to the game class:

```
private void InitializePointList(){
    Color color = Color.Black;        // pupils
    pointList[0]
    = new VertexPositionColor(new Vector3(-0.15f, 1.53f,-3.0f), color);
    pointList[1]
    = new VertexPositionColor(new Vector3( 0.15f, 1.53f,-3.0f), color);
}
```

The point list should be initialized when the program starts. A call to `InitializePointList()` from the `Initialize()` method will do this:

```
InitializePointList();
```

Now the point list can be drawn. Add the following call to `PositionColorShader()` at the end of the `DrawObjects()` method. The parameters indicate that a `PointList` is being rendered, the vertex data should be read from the `pointList` vertex array, and two points are being drawn:

```
PositionColorShader(PrimitiveType.PointList, pointList, 2);
```

When you run the program, two points will appear in the middle of the Martian's eyes.

This chapter has shown how to draw 3D graphics. The vertices and primitive surfaces drawn with these simple shapes are the foundation for all 3D game graphics. Even fiery effects and 3D models begin with vertices and primitive surfaces.

CHAPTER 5 REVIEW EXERCISES

To get the most from this chapter, try out these chapter review exercises:

1. Implement the step-by-step examples presented in this chapter, if you have not already done so.
2. Using primitive objects, create the face of a cat with ears and whiskers.
3. Use line and triangle primitives to create a small house with a roof and fence around it. You can use triangle strips, triangle lists, line strips, and line lists.

CHAPTER 6

Shaders

XNA uses shader-based rendering to convert vertex data into pixel output. This method achieves high performance because shaders perform graphics processing at breakneck speed on your graphics card. Whether you use your own shader or XNA's `BasicEffect` shader, you must use some type of shader to draw 3D graphics from your XNA code. The shader also gives you the power to customize the way your vertices are displayed. Shaders can be used to manipulate all vertex properties (for example, color, position, and texture). The ability to provide additional vertex processing through the shader makes it possible to use them for implementing lighting, blending effects such as transparency, and multitexturing. For some effects—such as point sprites for fire, multitexturing, and custom lighting—you will need to write your own shader to implement the effect.

GRAPHICS PIPELINE

In discussions about shaders, you will often hear references to the graphics pipeline. The *graphics pipeline* refers to the process of converting vertex and primitive input into pixel output. Vertex and pixel shaders, of course, play a key role in this processing. The vertex shader applies transformations to the vertex inputs. When the transformed vertices are passed to the shader, the output that is not visible to the player is clipped and the back faces are removed (this is called *culling*). Rasterization is performed to convert the vector data to an output image. And interpolation is performed between vertices to uniformly distribute vertex data between coordinates. In the pixel shader, coloration and texturing are applied before outputting pixels to the screen. Figure 6-1 provides a high-level summary of the graphics pipeline operations.

Shaders

Shaders offer you some control over how processing is done in the graphics pipeline. In most cases, you will want to write your own shader code. This section explains why and shows you how to do it.

FIGURE 6-1

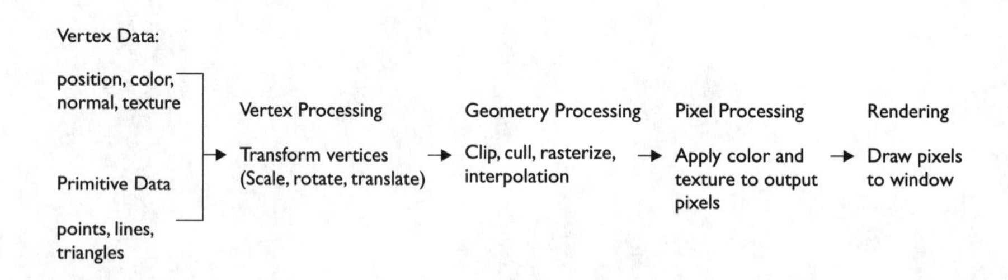

Graphics pipeline summary

Shader Structure

The shader shown here does nothing more than receive vertices that contain color and position data. The vertex shader receives this data, and then outputs the position data to the graphics pipeline. The vertex shader output (that can be modified by the pixel shader) is interpolated before it reaches the pixel shader. The pixel shader receives the color data and outputs it as pixels in your screen. The shader code shown here is actually the same code that is contained in the PositionColor.fx file in your game project:

```
float4x4 wvpMatrix  : WORLDVIEWPROJ;

struct VSinput{
    float4 position : POSITION0;
    float4 color    : COLOR0;
};
struct VStoPS{
    float4 position : POSITION0;
    float4 color           : COLOR0;
};
struct PSoutput{
    float4 color    : COLOR0;
};

// alter vertex inputs
void VertexShader(in VSinput IN, out VStoPS OUT){
     // transform vertex
    OUT.position    = mul(IN.position, wvpMatrix);
    OUT.color       = IN.color;
}

// alter vs color output
void PixelShader(in VStoPS IN, out PSoutput OUT){
    float4 color    = IN.color;
    OUT.color       = clamp(color, 0, 1); // range between 0 and 1
}

// the shader starts here
technique BasicShader{
    pass p0{                                // declare & initialize ps & vs
        vertexshader    = compile vs_1_1 VertexShader();
        pixelshader     = compile ps_1_1 PixelShader();
    }
}
```

Vertex Shaders

A *vertex shader* is the portion of the shader that performs operations on each vertex received from your XNA code. You can use the vertex shader to alter and draw any vertex property. It can be used for per-vertex lighting, modifying position, changing color, or adjusting image coordinates. For example, the vertex shader may alter this information using other inputs such as transformations or filtering. When alterations to each vertex are complete, the color and texture output is sent to a pixel shader for further processing (if desired). Position and normal data may also be passed to the pixel shader if any calculations require this information. However, the position and normal data cannot be altered once it leaves the vertex shader.

At the very least, the vertex shader must output position data. Elements that are passed to the pixel shader are interpolated across the polygon before they are sent to the pixel shader.

Pixel Shaders

Pixel shaders convert vertex data from the vertex shader into colored pixel data. The pixel shader cannot manipulate the position or normal vector information, but it can perform per-pixel operations to implement lighting, coloration, texture sampling, and blending. In terms of volume, per-pixel operations are more expensive than per-vertex operations. However, effects such as lighting are noticeably richer when you do them in the pixel shader, so there are times when the performance hit is worth it. When processing in the pixel shader is complete, the pixel shader outputs colored pixels for display in the window.

Technique and Passes

A *technique* defines the vertex shaders and pixel shaders used during each pass through the pixel-rendering process. In most cases, drawing is done in one pass. However, you might want to specify more than one pass if you have to implement blended textures (through multitexturing). Chapter 12 shows an example of a multipass technique used to create running water.

High Level Shader Language

For XNA games, most shaders are written in Microsoft's High Level Shader Language (HLSL). HLSL syntax resembles C syntax, and because C# is also a member of the C family, the data types, conditional structures, loops, functions, and other syntax used in HLSL code are easy transitions for an XNA coder.

You could write your shaders in assembly language, but assembly syntax is more difficult to read and is more prone to incompatibilities between graphics cards. Also, because HLSL and XNA were designed for implementation on the Xbox 360, and they were both created by Microsoft, you are certainly going to want to write most (if not all) of your shader code in HLSL.

Initially, game programmers only wrote shaders in assembly language, but assembly code is specific to video card hardware and this caused issues. Graphics card manufacturers such as NVIDIA, AMD (formerly ATI), and others have similar assembly code instruction sets, but differences between video cards sometimes cause shader incompatibilities. Because of this, games that use cutting-edge shader code, or shader code that is unique to a graphics card vendor, may not port well to machines that use other types of graphics cards. If you are only developing for the Xbox 360, you could use the latest HLSL features as long as they run on your Xbox 360. If you are writing code to run on PCs, you should consider potential differences in graphics cards when writing your shaders.

For the XNA platform, Microsoft recommends that your PC graphics card support at least Shader Model 2.0. However, shaders written using Shader Model 1.1 will run on the Xbox 360.

Shader Inputs and Outputs

Parameters that are received and returned from the vertex and pixel shaders can be passed either through parameter lists in the shader headers or through *structs*. Either way, the data fields are denoted with semantics to bind the inputs and outputs passed between shaders and to bind the data from the shader to the graphics pipeline.

Shader Semantics

A shader semantic binds shader input to vertex data that is output from your XNA code. Shader semantics are also used to bind inputs and outputs together for passing data between shaders. In other words, a *semantic* is a syntactical element that denotes a piece of data that is passed between your XNA code, shaders, and the graphics pipeline. You can specify shader semantics for color, texture coordinates, normal vectors, position data, and more. Because it is possible to input more than one instance of a specific data type, you must use a numeric suffix to define the data type instance when referencing it more than once.

Common Vertex Shader Input Semantics Here are some common vertex shader inputs that allow you to pass vertex properties from your XNA code to the vertex shader:

```
COLOR[n]      // color
NORMAL[n]     // normal vector
```

```
POSITION[n] // vertex position
PSIZE[n]    // point size for point sprites
TEXCOORD[n] // texture coordinates
```

The number, denoted by `[n]`, specifies the instance of the data type since you can have more than one field storing data of the same type.

Common Vertex Shader Output Semantics Vertex shader output semantics denote the data that is passed from a vertex shader to the pixel shader, where more processing can be performed on the vertex inputs, or to the graphics pipeline, where the vertex data is channeled for display in the window. You use semantics to bind the data that is passed between the vertex shader and the pixel shader. The outputs from the vertex shader use these semantics:

```
COLOR[n]    // color
POSITION[n] // position
PSIZE       // size for point sprites
TEXCOORD[n] // texture coordinates
```

Common Pixel Shader Input Semantics The pixel shader can modify the color and texture data; it receives this information through the semantics shown here. You will notice that the position semantic is absent. The pixel shader can receive position information to implement calculations for effects such as lighting. However, the pixel shader cannot alter the position information because it is sent to the graphics pipeline from the vertex shader.

```
COLOR[n]     // color
TEXCOORD[n]  // texture coordinates
```

Common Pixel Shader Output Semantics In most cases—and throughout this book—the only output returned from the pixel shader is the color of a pixel. Fittingly, the main output semantic for the pixel shader is the `COLOR` semantic:

```
COLOR[n]     // output color
```

Shader Data Types

When looking at HLSL code, you will notice that the shader data types are very similar in syntax to XNA data types. Table 6-1 compares the XNA data types with the HLSL data types used in this book.

TABLE 6-1

XNA Data Type	HLSL Data Type
Matrix	*float4x4*
Texture2D	*Texture*
struct	*struct*
int	*int*
float	*float*
Vector2	*float2 // array with two elements*
Vector3	*float3 // array with three elements*
Vector4	*float4 // array with four elements*
Color	*float3 (with no alpha blending) or float4 (with alpha blending)*

Comparison of XNA Data Types with Shader Data Types

HLSL Intrinsic Functions

HLSL provides several functions, and they are fully documented on Microsoft's MSDN website (www.msdn.com). Table 6-2 is a reference for the intrinsic functions used in this book. They are explained in more detail as they are used in each chapter.

Flow Control Syntax

Shaders implement C-like syntax for loops and conditional structures. Loop structures include for-loops, do-while loops, and while-loops. HLSL if-else syntax is the same syntax used for any C-style language.

Referencing the Shader in Your XNA Project

To use shaders, your XNA application needs to load and reference them. The XNA platform makes this task easy by providing an `Effect` class with methods for loading and compiling the shader. Your XNA code can modify global shader variables through the `EffectParameter` class.

TABLE 6-2

HLSL Intrinsic Functions	Inputs	Component Type	Outputs
`abs(a)`	*a is a scalar, vector, or matrix.*	`float, int`	*Absolute value of a*
`clamp(a, min, max)`	`clamp(a, min, max)`	`float, int`	*Clamped value for a*
`cos(a)`	*a is a scalar, vector, or matrix.*	`float`	*Same dimension as a*
`dot(a, b)`	*a and b are vectors.*	`float`	*A scalar vector (dot product)*
`mul(a, b)`	*a and b can be vectors or matrices, but the a columns must match the b rows.*	`float`	*Matrix or vector, depending on the inputs*
`normalize(a)`	*a is a vector.*	`float`	*Unit vector*
`pow(a, b)`	*a is a scalar, vector, or matrix. b is the specified power.*	*a is a float. b is an integer.*	a^b
`saturate(a)`	*a is a scalar, vector, or matrix.*	*a is a float.*	*a clamped between 0 and 1*
`sin(a)`	*a is a scalar, vector, or matrix.*	`float`	*Same dimension as a*
`tan(a)`	*a is a scalar, vector, or matrix.*	`float`	*Same dimension as a*
`tex2D(a,b)`	*a is a sampler2D. b is a vector.*	*a is a sampler2D. b is a two-dimensional float.*	*Vector*

HLSL Intrinsic Functions

Referencing the Shader File in Your XNA Project

Shaders are loaded by the content pipeline, so you need to reference the *.fx file, which contains the shader code, under the Content node in the Solution Explorer. The base code in this book groups all .fx files in a subfolder called Shaders (under the Content node). To create a new shader in your project, right-click the Content node, in the Solution Explorer (or any subfolder where you keep your shaders). Then, select Add | New Item. In the Add New Item dialog, select the Effect File template. You can overwrite the shader name, which defaults to Effect1.fx. Note that the *.fx extension is the required extension for your shader file. Once the name is entered, click Add to add this file to your project. Game Studio will add code to generate a shader code shell, so you will need to manually delete this code to start fresh.

Alternatively, you can add a prewritten shader to your project from the Solution Explorer by right-clicking your project's Content node or any subdirectory under this node and selecting Add | Existing Item. From there, you can select the *.fx file from the Add Existing Item dialog that appears.

Effect

An `Effect` object allows you to load and compile the shader code, to finalize any variable changes that you made to the shader, and, of course, to send vertex data from your XNA code to the shader. The `Effect` class is used for declaring the `Effect` object:

```
private Effect                          effect;
```

When the shader is referenced in your project from the Solution Explorer, it can be read using the `Load()` method. HLSL shader files traditionally are named with an .fx extension. However, when the shader is referenced in the Solution Explorer, the .fx extension is dropped from the filename in the load statement:

```
effect = content.Load<Effect>("DirectoryPath\\ShaderName");
```

EffectParameter

`EffectParameter` objects allow you to set global variables in the shader from your XNA code. The `EffectParameter` class is used when declaring this object:

```
private EffectParameter             effectParameter;
```

When you have defined the `EffectParameter` object in your XNA code, you can then use it to reference global shader variables. An `Effect` object's `Parameters` collection stores references to all the global shader variables. The collection is indexed by the global variable name. Thus, the following line stores a reference to a global shader variable:

```
effectParameter = effect.Parameters[string shaderVariableName];
```

Once the `EffectParameter` objects have been declared and initialized, you assign the value using the `SetValue()` method:

```
effectParameter.SetValue(DataValue);
```

The parameter used in SetValue() must match the data type of the variable being set.

Drawing with the Shader

When you draw with the shader, you must select the shader (and the shader's technique) to execute your vertex and pixel processing code. There are several syntax variations for this. Here is a common approach that we use throughout the book:

```
Effect    effect.Begin();
Effect    effect.Techniques[0].Passes[0].Begin();
```

As soon as the shader is finished drawing, deselect it with the End() method:

```
Effect    effect.End();
Effect    effect.Techniques[0].Passes[0].End();
```

Committing Changes to the Shader

For performance reasons, the preferred way to set variable values within the shader (using the EffectParameter's SetValue() method) is to assign the values before calling the Begin() method for the Effect object. Calling Begin() finalizes the changes to the values.

CommitChanges()

You may encounter situations where you want to assign values to your shader variables after you have called Effect.Begin(). As soon as you finish setting any shader values, though, you must use the CommitChanges() method to finalize these changes in your shader:

```
effect.CommitChanges();
```

Position Color Shader Example: Referencing the Shader

This example demonstrates one of the most basic shaders. This shader does nothing more than output a primitive surface that uses a set of vertices for storing color and position. You will make adjustments to the shader so you can use your XNA code to change the color and position of the vertices that are drawn from the shader. In this case, the blue component of the rectangular surface will be set to automatically increment and decrement between 0 (for no blue) and 1 (for full blue)—this will create a flashing effect. The rectangular surface's position on the X axis will also be automatically incremented and decremented from the shader using a timescale, which will make it slide back and forth.

In Chapter 5, we covered graphics basics for drawing primitive surfaces that use vertices for storing position and color. The example in this chapter takes the material discussed in Chapter 5 a little further by showing how to control the vertex data output from the shader. On the surface, this example may not appear to offer anything remotely useful for a video game implementation, but remember that this example has been kept simple to introduce the topic. Shaders will be discussed again in this book, and you will definitely benefit from your efforts to understand this example. Chapter 9 shows how to use the shader to texture your primitive surface with images; Chapter 12 shows how to create multitexturing effects using shaders; Chapter 20 explains how shaders can be implemented for fiery effects; and Chapter 22 demonstrates how to create advanced lighting using shaders.

All code discussed in the "Referencing the Shader" portion of the "Position Color Shader Example" is already added to your base code.

If you are trying this example for the first time, this demonstration begins with either the MGHWinBaseCode project or the MGH360BaseCode project—both can be found in the BaseCode folder in the download from the book's website. However, if you are following the steps in Chapter 17, continue with the project that you started in Chapter 17 to build the base code from scratch.

Adding Your Shader Code

The PositionColor.fx file must be referenced in your project from the Solution Explorer. This shader receives color and position data from your XNA code and renders points, lines, and surfaces with it.

All of the code in this shader is from the shader sample at the start of this chapter. This is the same PositionColor.fx file that is in the base code project. However, if you are following the "Building the Base Code From Scratch Example," you will need to add it to your Shaders folder under your project's Content node.

Referencing Your Shader from Your XNA Code

To reference a shader in your XNA code, you need an `Effect` object. Also, when drawing your object with this shader, you need an `EffectParameter` object to set the world-view-projection (WVP) matrix. This positions your object, so it can be viewed properly in your window. The WVP matrix is explained in Chapter 17. The `Effect` and `EffectParameter` objects should be added at the top of the game class so they can be used in your project. These declarations must be added to your "Building the Base Code From Scratch Example" project from Chapter 17:

```
private Effect              positionColorEffect;    // shader object
private EffectParameter     positionColorEffectWVP; // set window view
```

After your shader has been referenced in the Solution Explorer, you need to load it from the `InitializeBaseCode()` method. This allows you to compile and reference your shader when the program begins. Also, the `EffectParameter` object, `positionColorEffectWVP` (declared earlier), is initialized to reference the `wvpMatrix` global variable in the shader. Note that the file path is hard-coded to the PositionColor.fx file in the Shaders folder:

```
positionColorEffect     = Content.Load<Effect>("Shaders\\PositionColor");
positionColorEffectWVP  = positionColorEffect.Parameters["wvpMatrix"];
```

Preparing your XNA Code for Drawing with the PositionColor.fx Shader

A `VertexDeclaration` object prepares the `GraphicsDevice` to retrieve and draw your data with a specific format. In this case, we need one to set the device for retrieving and drawing position and color vertices. This declaration is made at the top of the game class:

```
private VertexDeclaration                positionColor;
```

Next, the `VertexDeclaration` instance, `positionColor`, is referenced in the `InitializeBaseCode()` method:

```
positionColor            = new VertexDeclaration(graphics.GraphicsDevice,
                                 VertexPositionColor.VertexElements);
```

All drawing that uses this new shader must be triggered between the `Begin()` and `End()` statements for the `Effect` object `positionColorEffect`. The vertex shaders and pixel shaders that you will use are set inside each pass. But, in this case, only one pass is used in the shader. All drawing is done from within the `Begin()` and `End()` methods for the pass. The following method is added to the base code for drawing with the PositionColor.fx shader:

```
private void PositionColorShader(PrimitiveType primitiveType,
             VertexPositionColor[] vertexData, int numPrimitives){
    positionColorEffect.Begin();        // begin using PositionColor.fx
    positionColorEffect.Techniques[0].Passes[0].Begin();
```

```
    // set drawing format and vertex data then draw primitive surface
    graphics.GraphicsDevice.VertexDeclaration = positionColor;
    graphics.GraphicsDevice.DrawUserPrimitives<VertexPositionColor>(
                            primitiveType, vertexData, 0, numPrimitives);

    positionColorEffect.Techniques[0].Passes[0].End();
    positionColorEffect.End();        // stop using PositionColor.fx
}
```

The PositionColor.fx shader is now defined and is initialized in your code, and the `PositionColorEffect()` method is in place to draw with it. If you are following the "Building the Base Code From Scratch Example" from Chapter 17, your base code project is now complete and it is identical to the one we have been using throughout the book.

Position Color Shader Example: Drawing with Your Shader

This section shows how to draw a surface with the PositionColor.fx shader. You need to declare a set of vertices that can use our newly referenced shader. Because the shader is designed to modify only position and color, it makes sense that the vertex definition is also set to store only color and position. This declaration in the game class at the module level will enable its use throughout the class:

```
private VertexPositionColor[] vertices = new VertexPositionColor[4];
```

A method is required to initialize the vertices that you will use to build the rectangular surface. Therefore, you'll add the `InitializeVertices()` method to the game class to define each corner vertex of this rectangle:

```
private void InitializeVertices(){
    Vector3 position    = Vector3.Zero;
    Color   color       = Color.White;

    // initialize coordinates used to draw white surface
    position    = new Vector3(-3.0f, 3.0f, -15.0f);        // top left
    vertices[0] = new VertexPositionColor(position, color);
    position    = new Vector3(-3.0f,-3.0f, -15.0f);        // bottom left
    vertices[1] = new VertexPositionColor(position, color);
    position    = new Vector3(3.0f, 3.0f, -15.0f);         // top right
    vertices[2] = new VertexPositionColor(position, color);
    position    = new Vector3(3.0f,-3.0f, -15.0f);         // bottom right
    vertices[3] = new VertexPositionColor(position, color);
}
```

To initialize the vertices that will be used to build the rectangle when the program starts, `InitializeVertices()` is called from the `Initialize()` method:

```
InitializeVertices();
```

The code used to draw the rectangle from the vertices that have been declared follows the same five steps described in the preceding chapter. Step 4 of this method makes use of the new `EffectParameter` by setting the matrix in the new shader for positioning the rectangle relative to the camera.

```
private void DrawRectangle(){
    // 1: declare matrices
    Matrix world, translation;

    // 2: initialize matrices
    translation = Matrix.CreateTranslation(0.0f, -0.9f, 0.0f);

    // 3: build cumulative world matrix using I.S.R.O.T. sequence
    // identity, scale, rotate, orbit(translate & rotate), translate
    world = translation;

    // 4: set the shader variables
positionColorEffectWVP.SetValue( world * cam.viewMatrix
                                       * cam.projectionMatrix);

    // 5: draw object - select primitive type, vertices, # of primitives
    PositionColorShader(PrimitiveType.TriangleStrip, vertices, 2);
}
```

To make our output a little more dramatic, replace the existing `Draw()` method with this revision. This new version of the `Draw()` method makes the background of our world black, so all we'll see is the rectangle that is drawn with the new shader:

```
protected override void Draw(GameTime gameTime){
    graphics.GraphicsDevice.Clear(Color.Black); // clear screen
    DrawRectangle();                            // build graphics
    base.Draw(gameTime);                        // display buffer
}
```

If you ran the project with the current modifications, it would show a white stationary rectangle with a black background.

One of the first modifications you will make is to modify the blue component of the RGB colors that are rendered. In the shader, you can do this by creating a global variable at the top of the PositionColor.fx file:

```
float   blueIntensity;
```

Next, you need a function inside the PositionColor.fx file to change the blue component of the RGB color that is drawn from the shader. Note that you use the color vector's `b` component to adjust the blue intensity by assigning to it the global variable `blueIntensity`:

```
float4 AdjustBlueLevel(){
    float4 color;
    color.r = 0.0f;              color.g = 0.0f;
    color.b = blueIntensity;     color.a = 1.0f;
    return color;
}
```

NOTE Shader functions must be declared before they are used in the shader; otherwise, the shader file will not compile. This requirement, of course, applies when placing `AdjustBlueLevel()` in the shader, and the same logic applies for the `ChangePosition()` function that follows.

The code that outputs the color from the vertex shader to the pixel shader must now change to handle the modifications to the blue component. Note that when you are multiplying vectors in HLSL, the product becomes $(a_1*b_1,a_2*b_2,a_3*b_3,a_4*b_4)$. Replace the existing color assignment in the vertex shader with this version to alter the blue component:

```
OUT.color = IN.color * AdjustBlueLevel();
```

To reference the `blueIntensity` shader variable used to adjust the blue component from your XNA code, you declare the `EffectParameter` `positionColorEffectBlue`. In the Game1.cs file, add a module declaration for it:

```
private EffectParameter positionColorEffectBlue;
```

Next, to initialize this object, add the following line to the `InitializeBaseCode()` method of your game class (after the code where the `Effect` object, `positionColorEffect`, has been loaded and initialized):

```
positionColorEffectBlue          =
positionColorEffect.Parameters["blueIntensity"];
```

Class-level variables are used to adjust the blue component of the color that is output every frame. Also, a Boolean value is used to track whether the floating point is increasing or decreasing, and a float is used to track the actual value:

```
private float   blue            = 0.0f;
private bool    increaseBlue    = true;
```

A method is used to increase or decrease the value of the blue component each frame. The blue portion of the RGB color ranges between 0 and 1, where 0 is no color and 1 is full blue. Each frame, this value is incremented or decremented by a scaled amount based on the time difference between frames. This time scalar ensures the color change is at the same rate regardless of the system that shows the animation. Add the `UpdateBlueLevel()` method to your game class to implement this routine:

```
void UpdateBlueLevel(GameTime gameTime){
    // use elapsed time between frames to increment color for
    // a smooth animation at same speed on all systems
    if(increaseBlue)
        blue += (float)gameTime.ElapsedGameTime.Milliseconds/1000.0f;
    else
        blue -= (float)gameTime.ElapsedGameTime.Milliseconds/1000.0f;

    if (blue <= 0.0f)          // decrease blue till blue < 0
        increaseBlue = true;
    else if (blue >= 1.0f)     // increase blue till blue > 1
        increaseBlue = false;

    positionColorEffectBlue.SetValue(blue); // set blue in shader
}
```

To update the blue color each frame, you call `UpdateBlueLevel()` from the `Update()` method:

```
UpdateBlueLevel(gameTime);
```

If you run the code now, you will notice that the blue color component changes; it will range from between 0 and 1. Because the red and green colors are set at 0, the color range for the rectangle is between black and dark blue.

Next, you will make another change to automatically adjust the position of the rectangle—to move it side to side on the X axis. To enable this, in the global variable section of the shader, you declare a variable to store the value of the position on the X plane:

```
float  positionX;
```

This function, added to the shader, changes the value of the X position:

```
float4 ChangePosition(float4 position){
    position.x      += positionX;
    return             position;
}
```

To implement the change in the vertex shader, replace the assignment for `position` with the instruction that follows. This takes the current position and shifts it on the X axis by the amount stored in the *positionX* global variable:

```
OUT.position = mul(ChangePosition(IN.position), wvpMatrix);
```

Back in your XNA code, an `EffectParameter` is required to reference the *positionX* global variable in the shader:

```
private EffectParameter positionColorEffectX;
```

To initialize this effect parameter inside `InitializeBaseCode()`, after the `Effect` object is set up, add the following instruction to reference the *positionX* shader variable from the Effect's collection:

```
positionColorEffectX = positionColorEffect.Parameters["positionX"];
```

With a reference to a shader variable that is used to modify the position of the rectangle, some XNA code can be added to actually track the X value and reset it. Add the float X declaration to store the current X increment for the rectangle. Also, add the *increasingX* Boolean variable to track whether the variable is to be incremented or decremented:

```
private float   X              = 0.0f;
private bool    increasingX    = true;
```

The code for updating the X increment is added to the game class:

```
void UpdatePosition(GameTime gameTime){
    // use elapsed time between frames to increment X to create animation
    // at same speed on all systems that run this code
```

```
    if (increasingX)
        X += (float)gameTime.ElapsedGameTime.Milliseconds/1000.0f;
    else
        X -= (float)gameTime.ElapsedGameTime.Milliseconds/1000.0f;

    if (X <= -1.0f)          // decrease X till less than -1
        increasingX = true;
    else if (X >= 1.0f)      // increase X till greater than 1
        increasingX = false;

    positionColorEffectX.SetValue(X);     // set new X value in shader
}
```

Updates to the X increment for the rectangle are triggered from the `Update()` method every frame:

```
UpdatePosition(gameTime);
```

When you run this version of the code, you will see a flashing blue rectangle that moves from side to side.

XNA's BasicEffect Class

XNA offers the `BasicEffect` class, which actually is a built-in shader that you can use to render your 3D graphics. On one hand, compared to writing your own HLSL, the `BasicEffect` class does not offer you as much flexibility to customize the way your vertex data is filtered, blended, and displayed as pixel output. However, on the other hand, you can rely on the `BasicEffect` class to quickly and simply implement lighting, and it is especially useful for rendering 3D models. Chapter 14 demonstrates the use of the `BasicEffect` shader to render and light 3D models. The BasicEffect class lighting properties are explained and implemented in Chapter 22.

The code for the `BaseEffect` shader has been shared by Microsoft so that XNA coders can learn from how it was developed (see http://creators.xna.com/en-us/utilities/basiceffectshader).

A `BasicEffect` object is instantiated with the `BasicEffect` class:

```
BasicEffect   basicEffect
= new BasicEffect(GraphicsDevice device, EffectPool effectPool);
```

Setting Properties Within the BasicEffect Class

When drawing objects using the `BasicEffect` class, you will need to set the World, View, and Projection matrices to implement object movement, scaling, and rotations and to position your objects in the window so they can be seen properly as your players view the 3D world. These matrices are explained in more detail in Chapter 17. When you are implementing a custom shader (as demonstrated earlier in the chapter), an `EffectParameter` is used to set these matrix values. With the `BasicEffect` class, you don't have to create an `EffectParameter` object for each variable you want to set. Instead, you can assign these values to the `BasicEffect`'s `World`, `View`, and `Projection` properties:

```
Matrix basicEffect.World      = Matrix worldMatrix;
Matrix basicEffect.View       = Matrix viewMatrix;
Matrix basicEffect.Projection = Matrix projectionMatrix;
```

Similar to the custom shader, whenever you change the state of the `BasicEffect` shader—by assigning a value to one of the `BasicEffect`'s attributes—you have to finalize the change by calling the `CommitChanges()` method (although only if you have changed attributes between a `Begin()` and `End()` pair):

```
basicEffect.CommitChanges();
```

Techniques and Passes within the BasicEffect Class

Similar to a custom shader that you would write on your own, the `BasicEffect` class uses a technique to define the vertex and pixel shaders, and to set the total number of passes used to render an object each frame. To use the `BasicEffect` shader when drawing your objects, you use the following construct to select the technique and pass(es) within it. All drawing is performed between the `Begin()` and `End()` methods for the `BasicEffect` object:

```
basicEffect.Begin();
foreach (EffectPass pass in basicEffect.CurrentTechnique.Passes){
    pass.Begin();
        // rendering is done here
    pass.End();
}
basicEffect.End();
```

BasicEffect Class Example

This demonstration shows how to convert the existing base code to use the `BasicEffect` class to draw the ground with a grass texture. Currently, the base code uses the shader Texture.fx. Note that this demonstration uses texturing to apply images to the surfaces you draw before a proper explanation is given. Chapter 9 provides a more detailed explanation of how the texturing works.

This example begins with either the MGHWinBaseCode or the MGH360BaseCode base code from the BaseCode folder in the download from this book's website. Converting it to use the BasicEffect class to draw the textured ground can be done in two steps.

First, you will need to declare an instance of the `BasicEffect` at the top of the game class so that you can use it throughout the class:

```
BasicEffect basicEffect;
```

The `BasicEffect` instance should be initialized when the program begins in `Initialize()`. Regenerating this `BasicEffect` instance anywhere else on a continuous basis will slow down your program considerably, so you should only do it when the program starts:

```
basicEffect     = new BasicEffect(graphics.GraphicsDevice, null);
```

Next, replace the existing `DrawGround()` method in the game class with this new version, which uses a `BasicEffect` object to do the rendering. Most of the routine remains the same. However, in step 4, the `World`, `View`, and `Projection` properties for the `BasicEffect` class are set to provide it with information about the camera. This way, it can render the ground and be seen properly by the camera. Also in step 4, the texture is set to the grass texture. These changes are then committed to the shader. In step 5, the `BasicEffect` technique is selected and the rendering is done in the passes that have been automatically selected by the technique.

Replace the existing version of `DrawGround()` with this routine to draw the ground with the `BasicEffect` shader:

```
private void DrawGround(){
    // 1: declare matrices
    Matrix  world, translation;

    // 2: initialize matrices
    translation = Matrix.CreateTranslation(0.0f, 0.0f, 0.0f);
```

```
    // 3: build cumulative world matrix using I.S.R.O.T. sequence
    // identity, scale, rotate, orbit(translate & rotate), translate
    world        = translation;

    // 4: set the shader variables
    basicEffect.World               = world;
    basicEffect.View                = cam.viewMatrix;
    basicEffect.Projection          = cam.projectionMatrix;
    basicEffect.TextureEnabled      = true;
    basicEffect.Texture             = grassTexture;

    // 5: draw object - select shader, vertex type, then draw surface
    basicEffect.Begin();
    foreach (EffectPass pass in basicEffect.CurrentTechnique.Passes){
        pass.Begin();
        graphics.GraphicsDevice.VertexDeclaration = positionColorTexture;
        graphics.GraphicsDevice.DrawUserPrimitives
                  <VertexPositionColorTexture>(
                  PrimitiveType.TriangleStrip, groundVertices, 0, 2);
        pass.End();
    }
    basicEffect.End();
}
```

When you run this code, the textured ground will appear as before, but this time it will be rendered using the `BasicEffect` class.

If you have ever seen the NVIDIA or AMD shader demos, you would agree that shaders can be used for some incredibly slick graphics effects. The shader examples in this chapter have intentionally been kept simple by comparison, but will gradually become more complex as the chapters progress.

CHAPTER 6 REVIEW EXERCISES

To get the most from this chapter, try out these chapter review exercises:

Implement the step-by-step examples in this chapter, but make the following changes:

1. In the first example, try adding a field with a `POSITION` semantic to the pixel shader output struct and notice that it can't be done. Why is this?

2. In the first example, replace the instruction in the vertex shader that defines the color output with the following:

```
OUT.color = IN.color
```

3. In the pixel shader, replace the instruction that defines the color output with this:

```
OUT.color = IN.color * ChangeBlueValue();
```

When you run the code after this change, the output will be the same as before, but the color transformation will be performed on a per-pixel basis rather than a per-vertex basis.

CHAPTER 7

Animation Introduction

AFTER working through Chapter 5, you should now be comfortable building structures with lines and triangles. If you create a butterfly, a bird, a car, an airplane, or even a monster out of lines and triangles, you will surely want to animate your 3D object. Animation is the key ingredient that will bring life to your creations.

Animating an object requires that you have the ability to rotate, move, or even resize the object. The process of scaling and moving objects is referred to as a *transformation*. Transformations include:

- Setting the *identity* as a default for the World matrix if no transformations are specified.
- *Scaling* to resize the object.
- Using *translations* for horizontal, vertical, up, down, and diagonal movements on the X, Y, and Z planes.
- *Rotating* an object about its own axis. This is referred to as a *revolution*.
- *Rotating* an object about an external fixed point. This is referred to as the object's *orbit*.

XNA offers several methods for performing transformations. Familiarity with these methods is crucial since they greatly reduce the amount of code you have to write to bring movement to your 3D environment.

While this chapter may seem to be somewhat trivial, the topic of transformations is extremely important. For new graphics programmers, understanding this chapter and Chapter 8 is essential to harnessing XNA and taking control of your 3D animations.

RIGHT HAND RULE

Like all 3D graphics libraries, XNA allows you to create 3D worlds on a Cartesian graph with X, Y, and Z axes. The orientation of each axis on the graph, with respect to the other axes, defines the direction for positive and negative translations and rotations. With an upright Y axis, it is possible to have an X axis that runs either outward to the left or to the right, and a Z axis that increases either in a forward or backward direction. The XNA developer team has implemented the Cartesian coordinate system from a Right Hand Rule perspective. Figure 7-1 shows the Right Hand Rule implementation used in this book, where positive movement in the X, Y, and Z planes is:

- Toward the right on the X axis
- Upward on the Y axis
- Toward the viewer on the Z axis

FIGURE 7-1

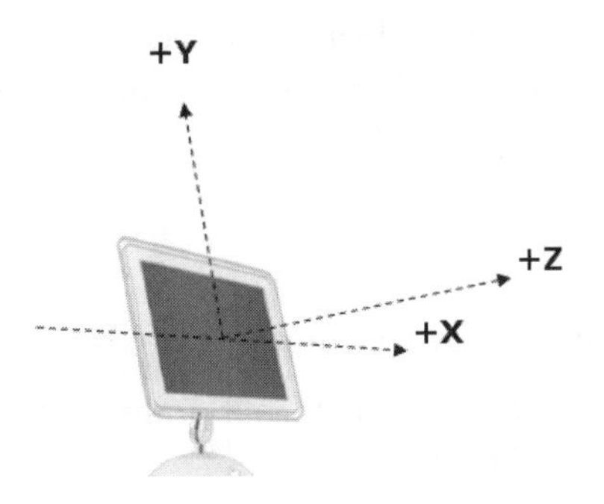

Applying the Right Hand Rule

In this case, there is a common mnemonic device to remember the positive direction for a rotation about X, Y, and Z. Imagine standing with your back to the monitor so you are facing the viewer. Next, imagine gripping the X, Y, or Z axis with your right hand and your right thumb extended in the direction of the arrow shown in Figure 7-1. When you curl your fingers about the axis in a counterclockwise direction, this is the positive rotation.

MATRIX LOGIC

3D transformations are performed using matrix algebra. With this in mind, XNA provides several methods to automate the process of building and applying matrices to resize, rotate, and translate objects in 3D space. More detail about the underlying linear algebra is provided in Chapter 16. However, even after the math behind the matrices is explained, the XNA methods for applying matrix transformations will remain crucial as a fast and efficient way to perform transformations.

Each type of transformation is implemented with a separate matrix. Scaling an object, rotating an object about X, Y, and Z, and translating an object all require separate transformation matrices. Once each individual transformation matrix has been defined, they are combined using multiplication to build one cumulative transformation matrix. This cumulative matrix is referred to as the *World matrix*.

Transformation Order

The order in which the matrices for scaling, rotating, and translating are combined is significant. For successful transformations, we strongly recommend that you combine individual transformations in the following order:

1. Set the *identity*.
2. *Scale* the object.
3. *Revolve* or rotate the object about its axis.
4. *Orbit* the object about an external point. (This involves a translation followed by a rotation.)
5. *Translate* the object.

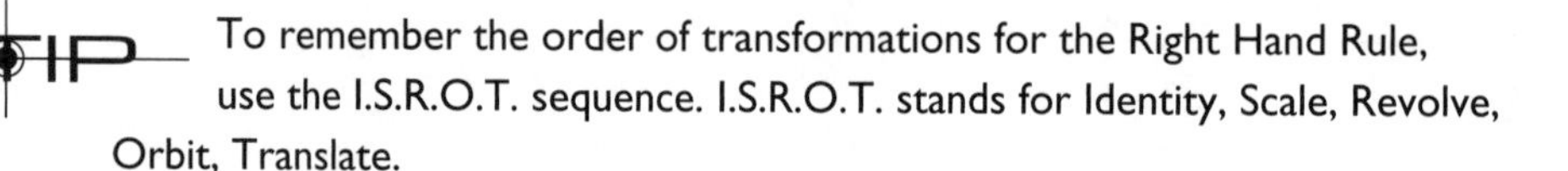

TIP To remember the order of transformations for the Right Hand Rule, use the I.S.R.O.T. sequence. I.S.R.O.T. stands for Identity, Scale, Revolve, Orbit, Translate.

XNA MATRIX SYNTAX

XNA stores matrices in the `Matrix` type. The `Matrix` type stores data used to calculate transformations. Most of the time, XNA will automate your use of matrices, so you do not have to fuss about the data or structure of your matrices. Occasionally, you will want to work with matrices more closely to perform complex transformations. Chapter 16 explains their structure in more detail.

Identity Matrix

You cannot actually transform an object with the identity matrix. The identity matrix is only used as a default matrix to initialize the cumulative transformation matrix, known as the World matrix, in the shader when no other transformations are assigned. If the identity matrix is the only matrix used in the World transformation, the primitive surface or 3D model will be drawn wherever the X, Y, and Z coordinates for this object are defined.

Multiplying a data matrix by the identity matrix gives the data matrix as a product. Whenever there are transformations, you can omit the identity matrix from your calculation and still end up with the same transformation. XNA provides an instance for you that can be obtained with the reference `Matrix.Identity`:

```
Matrix matrix = Matrix.Identity;
```

Scaling Matrix

The scaling matrix is used to resize objects drawn using primitives or 3D models. The `Matrix.Scale()` method can be used to generate a scaling matrix based on the amount of resizing needed on X, Y, and Z. The `Matrix.Scale()` method accepts three float parameters to set the amount of sizing on the X, Y, and Z planes.

```
Matrix matrix = Matrix.Scale(float X, float Y, float Z);
```

Here are some examples of scaling:

```
// half size on X, Y, and Z
Matrix matrix = Matrix.CreateScale(0.5f, 0.5f, 0.5f);
// double size on X, Y, and Z
Matrix matrix = Matrix.CreateScale(2.0f, 2.0f, 2.0f);
// double Y, but X and Z stay the same
Matrix matrix = Matrix.CreateScale(1.0f, 2.0f, 1.0f);
```

Rotation Matrices

Rotations about each of the X, Y, and Z axes are implemented with another matrix. XNA provides a separate method for generating each of these rotation matrices. The input parameter for each method requires an angle in radians. Remember that 2π radians = 360 degrees.

```
Matrix matrix = Matrix.CreateRotationX(float radians);
Matrix matrix = Matrix.CreateRotationY(float radians);
Matrix matrix = Matrix.CreateRotationZ(float radians);
```

Translation Matrices

XNA provides a one-step, user-friendly method to build a simultaneous translation along the X, Y, and Z planes. Here is the syntax:

```
Matrix matrix = Matrix.CreateTranslation(float X, float Y, float Z);
```

STEPS FOR DRAWING A PRIMITIVE OBJECT OR A 3D MODEL

The routine used to draw an object using primitives or a 3D model can be implemented in many ways. For consistency and clarity, most examples in this book follow this routine for drawing objects that use primitives:

1. Declare the transformation matrices.
2. Initialize the transformation matrices.
3. Build the total cumulative transformation matrix, known as the World matrix, using the I.S.R.O.T. sequence.
4. Set the shader variables.
5. Draw the object.

For effective transformations, center the vertices that define your objects at the origin. Failing to do this can create unwanted translations that are difficult to handle and debug.

Declaring and Initializing Individual Matrices

Steps 1 and 2 of this recommended drawing routine require the declaration and initialization of each individual transformation matrix. As a minimum, the identity matrix is created to initialize the World matrix in the shader if no transformations are set.

Building the Cumulative World Matrix

In step 3 of this drawing routine, the cumulative World matrix is built by multiplying the individual matrices together. The I.S.R.O.T. sequence must be used to build this matrix. However, if a scale, rotation, orbit, or translation is performed, you can omit the identity matrix.

Setting the Shader Values

In step 4 of the drawing routine, the product of the transformation matrices, also known as the World matrix, is set in the shader. You may also set other variables in the shader, such as textures or colors, if you need to modify these values when rendering.

Drawing the Object

Step 5 of this recommended routine involves drawing the output. In the preceding chapter, steps for selecting the vertex type and drawing surfaces using primitive objects were explained in detail. However, this last step could be modified to draw 3D models. Either way, the steps taken to apply the transformations remain the same.

Applying Transformations: Earth and Moon Example

This example demonstrates transformations by drawing simple `Earth` and `Moon` objects. Both the `Earth` and `Moon` objects are actually just triangles. The earth is shown revolving about its own axis. The moon is shown with its own revolution as it also orbits around the earth (see Figure 7-2).

This example begins with either the MGHWinBaseCode project or the MGH360BaseCode project found in the BaseCode folder on this book's website.

A vertex array to store the position and color elements for each of the three vertices in the triangle is required. To create an array that can store this vertex information (which can be used throughout the game class) in your Game1.cs file, add the following class-level declaration:

```
private VertexPositionColor[] triangleVertex = new  VertexPositionColor[3];
```

To implement a continuous rotation for both the earth and moon, module-level variables are used in the game class. These variables store the current rotation about the Y axis.

```
float earthRotation, moonRotation;
```

Adding the `InitializeTriangle()` method to your game class initializes the vertices used by both the earth and moon. To ensure a smooth animation, the vertices are centered about the origin when they are initialized:

```
private void InitializeTriangle(){
    Vector3 position   = new Vector3( 0.5f, 0.0f, 0.0f);        // right
    triangleVertex[0] = new VertexPositionColor(position, Color.Orange);
    position           = new Vector3( 0.0f, 0.5f, 0.0f);        // top
    triangleVertex[1] = new VertexPositionColor(position, Color.Green);
    position           = new Vector3(-0.5f, 0.0f, 0.0f);        // left
    triangleVertex[2] = new VertexPositionColor(position, Color.Orange);
}
```

FIGURE 7-2

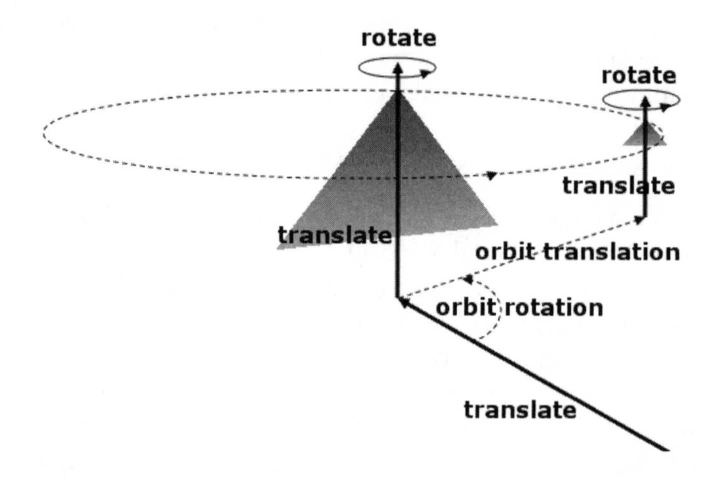

Earth and moon example

The vertices for the earth and moon are set when the program begins, so `InitializeTriangle()` is called from the `Initialize()` method:

```
InitializeTriangle();
```

When animating the triangle, a time-scaled increment is made to the triangle's rotation during each `Update()`. This rotation value is modded by 2π to clamp the value between 0 and 2π.

```
earthRotation += gameTime.ElapsedGameTime.Milliseconds/1000.0f;
earthRotation  = earthRotation%(2.0f * MathHelper.Pi);
moonRotation  += (float)TargetElapsedTime.Milliseconds/750.0f;
moonRotation   = moonRotation %(2.0f * MathHelper.Pi);
```

Here are the five recommended steps for drawing the revolving Earth object:

1. Declare the matrices.
2. Initialize the matrices. The identity matrix is initialized as a default matrix in the event of no transformations. (Try leaving it out of the transformation,

and notice you still get the same result.) A matrix that generates the earth's revolution on the Y axis is computed based on a constantly changing angle (in radians). Every frame, the angle is incremented with a value based on the time lapse between frames. This time-scaled increment to the rotation angle ensures that the animation appears smoothly while maintaining a constant rate of change. Scaling the increment based on time is necessary because durations between frames can vary depending on other tasks being performed by the operating system. Finally, a translation is created to move the earth 0.5 units upward on the Y axis and 8.0 units inward on the Z axis.

3. The World matrix is built by multiplying each of the matrices in the transformation using the I.S.R.O.T. sequence.
4. The World matrix used to transform the earth is passed to the shader as part of the World*View*Projection matrix.
5. The triangle is rendered by drawing vertices with a triangle strip.

Adding `DrawEarth()` to the game class provides the code needed for transforming and drawing the `Earth`:

```
private void DrawEarth(){
    // 1: declare matrices
    Matrix world, translation, rotationY;

    // 2: initialize matrices
    rotationY   = Matrix.CreateRotationY(earthRotation);
    translation = Matrix.CreateTranslation(0.0f, 0.5f, -8.0f);

    // 3: build cumulative World matrix using I.S.R.O.T. sequence
    // identity, scale, rotate, orbit(translate & rotate), translate
    world = rotationY * translation;

    // 4: set shader parameters
    positionColorEffectWVP.SetValue(world * cam.viewMatrix
                                     * cam.projectionMatrix);


    // 5: draw object - select primitive type, vertices, # primitives
    PositionColorShader(PrimitiveType.TriangleStrip, triangleVertex, 1);
}
```

Next, the DrawMoon() method implements the same five-step drawing routine to transform and render the same vertices as a Moon object. The moon has its own revolution about the Y axis, and it also orbits around the earth. In addition, the moon is scaled to one-fifth the size of the earth.

The DrawMoon() method performs all of the same transformations as the DrawEarth() method. Plus, DrawMoon() implements scaling and an orbit. All of the matrices declared in the DrawEarth() method are declared in DrawMoon() to perform the same transformations. Also, additional matrices are declared and set in this method to handle the scaling and orbit. The scale is set to draw the object at one-fifth the size of the earth by assigning the scale matrix the following value:

```
Matrix.CreateScale(0.2f, 0.2f, 0.2f);
```

Remember that the orbit is a two-step process that involves a translation followed by a rotation. When the World matrix is built, the crucial I.S.R.O.T. sequence is used to ensure that the matrices are multiplied in the proper order:

```
    world      = scale * rotationY * orbitTranslation * orbitRotationY
               * translation;
```

Since the same vertices are used for drawing the Moon and the Earth, steps 4 and 5 of DrawMoon() are identical to those in DrawEarth().

```
private void DrawMoon(){
    // 1: declare matrices
    Matrix world, scale, rotationY, translation,
           orbitTranslation, orbitRotationY;

    // 2: initialize matrices
    scale            = Matrix.CreateScale(0.2f, 0.2f, 0.2f);
    rotationY        = Matrix.CreateRotationY(moonRotation);
    translation      = Matrix.CreateTranslation(0.0f, 0.8f,-8.0f);
    orbitTranslation = Matrix.CreateTranslation(0.0f, 0.0f,-1.0f);
    orbitRotationY   = Matrix.CreateRotationY(moonRotation);

    // 3: build cumulative World matrix using I.S.R.O.T. sequence
    // identity, scale, rotate, orbit(translate & rotate), translate
    world            = scale * rotationY * orbitTranslation
                     * orbitRotationY * translation;
```

```
    // 4: set the shader parameters
    positionColorEffectWVP.SetValue(world * cam.viewMatrix
                                    * cam.projectionMatrix);

    // 5: draw object - select primitive type, vertices, # of primitives
    PositionColorShader(PrimitiveType.TriangleStrip, triangleVertex, 1);
}
```

Both the `DrawEarth()` and `DrawMoon()` methods are called from the `Draw()` method in the game class:

```
DrawEarth();
DrawMoon();
```

When you compile and run this code, it will show the earth as a revolving triangle being orbited by a revolving moon (refer to Figure 7-2).

Spend the time you need to ensure that you understand transformations. It is not an overly complex topic, but it can be challenging for beginner graphics programmers who do not give transformations the learning time the topic deserves. You will enjoy the rest of the book more when you have mastered this introduction to animation.

Be fearless when experimenting with your transformations. When you test and run your projects, you will probably know right away if your transformations are working properly. Of course, use the documentation presented in this section as a guide to understanding the topic. The real learning will happen when you try to create your own transformations.

CHAPTER 7 REVIEW EXERCISES

To get the most from this chapter, try out these chapter review exercises.

1. Implement the step-by-step example presented in this chapter, if you have not already done so.
2. Using primitives, create a stationary airplane with a rotating propeller that is made from triangles, as in the following illustration. When initializing the vertices that store the propeller, be sure to center the X, Y, and Z coordinates around the origin. Failure to center the X, Y, and Z coordinates of your surface about the origin will offset your rotations and will lead to strange results when unbalanced objects are transformed (see Figure 7-3).

FIGURE 7-3

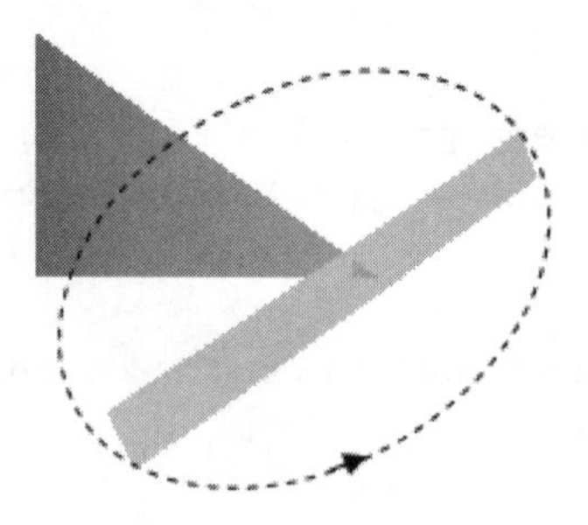

Primitive airplane with rotating propeller

3. When you finish Exercise 2, transform your propeller so it serves as a rotor for a helicopter. Using the same set of vertices, write another procedure to transform and render the same rectangle used for the main rotor as a back rotor, as shown here in Figure 7-4.

FIGURE 7-4

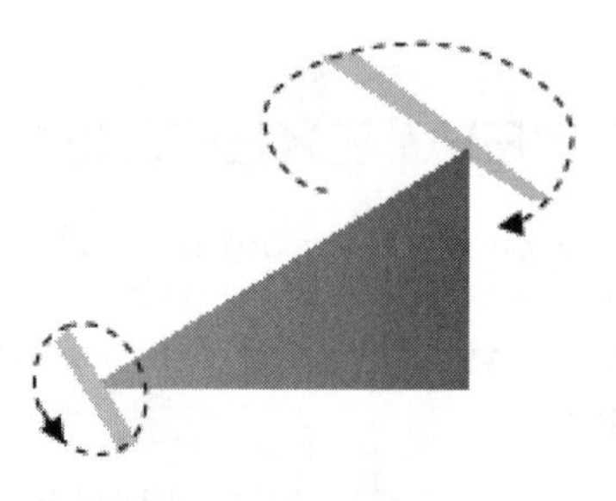

Helicopter with top and back rotors using the same vertices

CHAPTER 8

Character Movement

AFTER reading and applying the material covered in Chapter 7, you should be comfortable performing simple animations with translations and rotations. For most gamers, it is not enough just to make a bird flap its wings or make the propeller of an airplane spin; anybody with half an ounce of curiosity wants to see these objects actually fly. This chapter introduces a simple animation method that allows moving objects to travel independently within your 3D world.

Additional methods for enabling the movement of objects are covered in Chapter 21.

Regardless of the method used to move objects and characters, basic movement is generated by updating the X, Y, and Z position coordinates, as well as the rotation angles of the moving object rendered at every frame.

DIRECTION

When you animate vehicles that fly, drive, sail, or glide, you most likely expect them to point in the direction they are traveling. Calculating the angle of direction can be done using several methods. Without this calculation, your vehicles could look as if they are flying backward or even sideways. Trigonometry offers a simple intuitive approach to calculate the angle of direction—this method will be used often throughout this book. However, computing direction can also be done with vectors. Using vectors to calculate direction is actually a more powerful method for implementing rotations of direction because they offer a simpler means to implement complex transformations for directions in all planes.

Calculating Direction Using Trigonometry

The trigonometry applied in this chapter is actually quite simple and only involves using the arctangent function. The arctangent function enables calculations of direction about the Y axis when the X and Z coordinates of the object are known.

When the Right Hand Rule is used, all positive rotations are counterclockwise. To calculate an object's angle about the Y axis, draw a line from the object's position to the preceding axis in the rotation to create a right-angle triangle. The tangent of the angle between the hypotenuse and the axis can be calculated with the following equation:

```
tan ϕ side length / adjacent side length (where ϕ is the angle)
```

This equation can be rearranged to isolate the angle:

```
ϕ = tan-1 (opposite / adjacent)
ϕ = atan (opposite / adjacent)
```

Figure 8-1 shows the angle about the Y axis in relation to the hypotenuse, opposite, and adjacent sides of the right-angle triangle.

Calculating Direction Using Speed

When Y is constant, the change in X and Z, during each frame, measures speed. On a three-dimensional graph, the X and Z speed combination will always fall in one of four quadrants, depending on whether each of the X and Z speeds is positive or negative.

Calculating Direction Using the Math.Atan() Function

To calculate the angle of direction about the Y axis, create an imaginary right-angle triangle by drawing a line from the X, Z coordinate to the preceding X or Z axis. This line must be perpendicular to the X or Z axis. You can use XNA's `Math.Atan()` function to compute the angle of rotation about the Y axis using the corresponding X and Z values as opposite and adjacent parameters:

```
double radians = Math.Atan( (double)opposite/(double)adjacent );
```

FIGURE 8-1

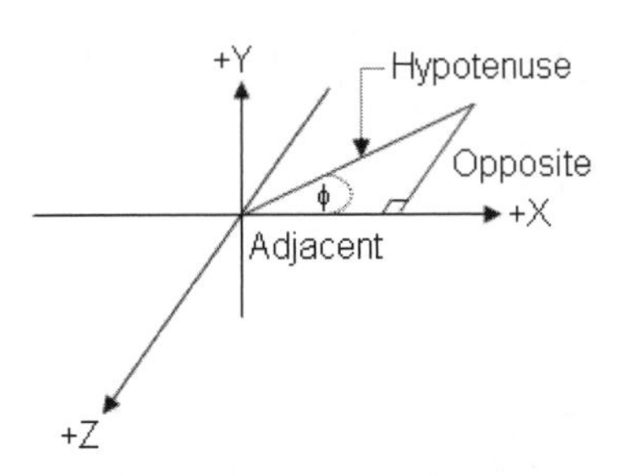

Hypotenuse, opposite, and adjacent sides of a right-angle triangle

FIGURE 8-2

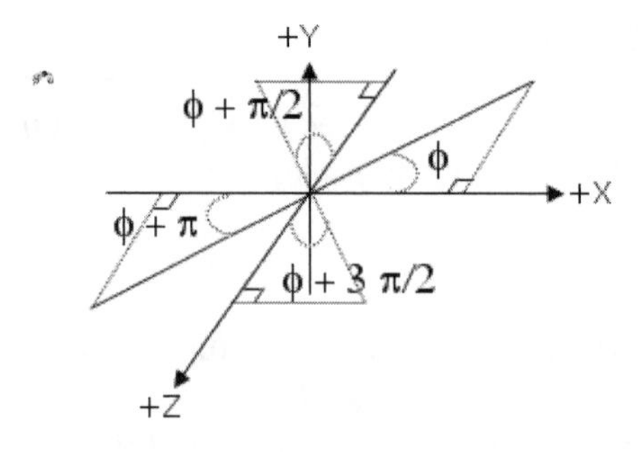

Calculating angle of direction about the Y axis using speed quadrants

The `Math.Atan()` function then returns the angle of rotation about Y for the immediate quadrant. An offset that equals the total rotation for the preceding quadrants is added to this angle to give the total rotation in radians. Figure 8-2 illustrates the relationship between the X and Z speeds for each quadrant and their offsets.

When the `Math.Atan()` function is used, each quadrant uses a slightly different equation to generate the rotation about the Y axis. These individual quadrant equations are summarized in Table 8-1.

Understanding this basic trigonometry can help you develop algorithms to generate your own direction angles.

TABLE 8-1

Quadrant	*Offset*	*Equation*
1	0	`Math.Atan (-z/x)`
2	$\pi/2$	`Math.Atan (-x/-z) + π/2`
3	π	`Math.Atan (z/-x) + π`
4	$3\pi/2$	`Math.Atan (x/z) + 3π/2`

Quadrant Equations to Calculate the Angle of Direction About the Y Axis

Calculating Direction Using the Math.Atan2() Function

Thankfully, there is an easier way to employ trigonometry to calculate the angle of direction about the Y axis. The `Math.Atan2()` function eliminates the need to factor quadrant differences into the calculations. To compute the angle of rotation about the Y axis with the `Math.Atan2()` function, the calculation becomes this:

```
double radians = Math.Atan2((double) X / (double) Z)
```

This equation can be used to calculate the angle of direction about the Y axis for all quadrants.

Both the `Math.Atan()` and `Math.Atan2()` functions will be demonstrated in the example presented in this chapter.

Calculating Direction Using Vectors

Calculating direction using vectors is the more powerful method. The math behind implementing vectors of direction is explained in more detail later, in Chapters 15, 16, and 17, so you may choose to read these chapters first for a better understanding of how the vectors work. The vector logic for calculating direction is being presented ahead of these chapters to ensure you have a better way to move your vehicles, vessels, and aircraft through your 3D world.

The vectors that describe the orientation of a moving object can be summarized using the `Look`, `Up`, and `Right` vectors. These vectors describe the moving object's direction and uprightness (see Figure 8-3).

The `Look` vector, also known as the `Forward` vector, is calculated from the difference in the view position and the position of the object. When you are animating objects, the `Look` vector could also be the same as the object's speed vector. The `Up` vector describes the upright direction. For most objects that are animated in this book, the starting upright direction is 0, 1, 0. When we stand on our own two feet, we have an `Up` vector of 0, 1, 0. The `Right` vector describes the perpendicular from the surface created by the `Up` and `Look` vectors. The `Right` vector can be used for a strafe in addition to assisting with the computation of angles of direction.

If the `Up` vector is known, the `Right` vector can be calculated using the cross product of the `Look` and `Up` vectors. The `Right` vector equals the cross product of the `Up` and `Look` vectors.

FIGURE 8-3

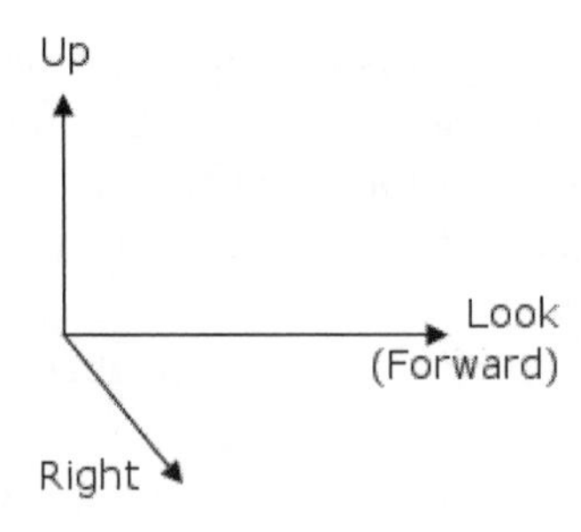

Direction vectors

When these vectors are normalized, or scaled so their lengths range between -1 and 1, they can be used in a matrix that calculates the direction. The cells of the matrix are defined with the data from the three direction vectors:

```
M.M11 = R.X;  M.M12 = R.Y;  M.M13 = R.Z;  M.M14 = 0.0f; //Right
M.M21 = U.X;  M.M22 = U.Y;  M.M23 = U.Z;  M.M24 = 0.0f; //Up
M.M31 = L.X;  M.M32 = L.Y;  M.M33 = L.Z;  M.M34 = 0.0f; //Look
M.M41 = 0.0f; M.M42 = 0.0f; M.M43 = 0.0f; M.M44 = 1.0f;
```

XNA's `Matrix` struct actually exposes each of these three direction vectors by name. If we create a transformation matrix called `direction`, we can reference these vectors with the `Matrix` struct's `Right`, `Up`, and `Forward` properties:

```
Vector3 right   = direction.Right;
Vector3 up      = direction.Up;
Vector3 look    = direction.Forward;
```

An example showing how to implement this structure is presented later in the chapter.

Scaling Animations with Time Lapse Between Frames

When animating objects, it is essential to ensure that your animations run at the same speed regardless of the processing power of the system that runs them. If you are a starving student, you might only be able to afford a slow PC—maybe with an older graphics card—but the computers in the labs at your college or university might be faster, or vice versa. If you develop your games on a slow PC, and you don't regulate the timing of your animations, they will look as if they are playing in fast forward when you run them on a faster PC. The reverse is true if you develop your games on a super-charged PC and then run them on a slower machine. Also, when you port your games over to the Xbox 360, you are almost certain to experience a difference in processing power compared to your development PC. To compound this issue, every frame of your game will exert different demands on the processor, and you might be running other programs in the background that are stealing valuable processor cycles. With all of these varying system and performance factors to consider, a mechanism to control the speed of your animations is a must-have item.

The trick to controlling animation speed is simple. The equation used to control the translation speed looks like this:

```
Vector3 Position += Increment.XYZ * TimeBetweenFrames / ConstantScale;
```

Controlling rotation speed is similar:

```
float radians    += Increment * TimeBetweenFrames / ConstantScale;
```

These equations offer a self-adjusting mechanism to account for varying frame rates. For example, a faster machine will produce more frames, but the animation won't run faster, because the time scale will reduce the increment for each frame. In the end, you will have more frames and a smoother animation, but the animation speed will be the same as an animation that runs on a slower machine. If you do not factor in the time difference between frames, your animations will run at uncontrollable speeds.

Character Movement Example

In this example, you will animate a single-prop aircraft so that it flies within the boundaries of your virtual world. Of course, you will also ensure that the plane is pointing in the direction it's supposed to fly; first with methods that use trigonometry and then with methods that use direction vectors. This example demonstrates how to use animations that involve translations and rotations, how to animate an object at a constant speed, and how to calculate the angle of direction using a constant speed.

To keep this example simple, the airplane is built with nothing more than a triangle for the body and a spinning rectangle for the propeller (see Figure 8-4).

FIGURE 8-4

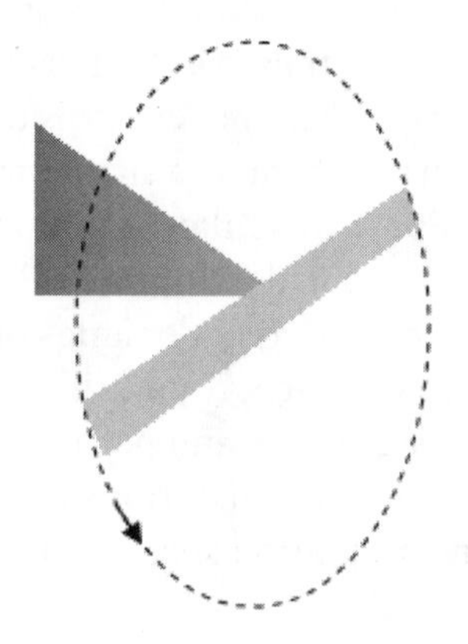

Airplane animation

If you want, you can easily swap these primitive objects with 3D models; the sequence of instructions to create the transformation for the animation would remain identical.

This example begins with either the files in the MGHWinBaseCode project or the MGH360BaseCode project from the BaseCode folder on this book's website.

A Stationary Airplane with a Spinning Propeller

This first part of the demonstration explains how to create an airplane using a stationary triangle and a rotating rectangle that is perpendicular to the front tip of the triangle. Two separate objects for storing vertices are needed: the body of the airplane and the propeller. Their declarations are required in the module-level area of the game class:

```
VertexPositionColor[] airplaneVertices  = new VertexPositionColor[3];
VertexPositionColor[] propellerVertices = new VertexPositionColor[4];
```

Code to initialize each vertex—in both the airplane and the propeller—sets the position and color values for each coordinate. Note that the vertices for each object are centered around the origin. As explained previously, any space from the origin to the center of an object is actually a translation that will literally send your object into an orbit when you rotate it. If you have already felt the mental pain from trying to debug this problem before realizing your vertices are not centered—welcome to the club! The methods `InitializeAirplaneBody()` and `InitializePropeller()` are added to the game class to initialize each array of vertices:

```
private void InitializeAirplaneBody(){
    Vector3 position;
    Color   color         = Color.Orange;

    position              = new Vector3(0.0f,-0.25f, 0.5f); // lower front
    airplaneVertices[0] = new VertexPositionColor(position, color);
    position              = new Vector3(0.0f, 0.25f,-0.5f); // top back
    airplaneVertices[1] = new VertexPositionColor(position, color);
    position              = new Vector3(0.0f,-0.25f,-0.5f); // lower back
    airplaneVertices[2] = new VertexPositionColor(position, color);
}
private void InitializePropeller(){
    Vector3 position;
    Color   color          = Color.LightBlue;

    position               = new Vector3(-0.5f, 0.05f, 0.0f);// top left
    propellerVertices[0] = new VertexPositionColor(position, color);
    position               = new Vector3(-0.5f,-0.05f, 0.0f);// lower left
    propellerVertices[1] = new VertexPositionColor(position, color);
    position               = new Vector3(0.5f,  0.05f, 0.0f);// top right
    propellerVertices[2] = new VertexPositionColor(position, color);
    position               = new Vector3(0.5f, -0.05f, 0.0f);// lower right
    propellerVertices[3] = new VertexPositionColor(position, color);
}
```

To initialize the propeller and the airplane body, when the program begins, call `InitializeAirplaneBody()` and `InitializePropeller()` from `Initialize()`:

```
InitializeAirplaneBody();
InitializePropeller();
```

In the beginning of this demonstration, the airplane is drawn as a stationary object. A translation matrix generated by the instruction:

```
translation  = Matrix.CreateTranslation(0.0f, 0.75f, -8.0f);
```

moves the plane in a one-time translation 0.75 units up the Y axis and -8.0 units inward along the Z axis. A slight rotation is generated with this instruction:

```
rotationY      = Matrix.CreateRotationY(MathHelper.Pi/8.0f);
```

This makes it easier to view the airplane from the camera's starting position. When the rotation and translation are combined, the I.S.R.O.T. (Identity, Scale, Revolve, Orbit, Translate) sequence is used to build the cumulative transformation:

```
world          = rotationY * translation;
```

`DrawAirplaneBody()` declares and initializes the transformation matrices in the first two steps. Then, the cumulative World matrix is built in the third step. In the fourth step, the cumulative transformation stored in the World matrix is sent to the shader. Finally, in the fifth step, the triangle is drawn from the transformed vertices. `DrawAirplaneBody()` is added to the game class to transform and render the vertices for the triangle.

```
private void DrawAirplaneBody(){
    // 1: declare matrices
    Matrix world, translation, rotationY;

    // 2: initialize matrices
    translation  = Matrix.CreateTranslation(0.0f, 0.75f, -8.0f);
    rotationY    = Matrix.CreateRotationY(MathHelper.Pi/8.0f);

    // 3: build cumulative world matrix using I.S.R.O.T. sequence
    // identity, scale, rotate, orbit(translate & rotate), translate
    world        = rotationY * translation;

    // 4: set shader parameters
    positionColorEffectWVP.SetValue(world * cam.viewMatrix
                                          * cam.projectionMatrix);
    // 5: draw object - primitive type, vertices, total primitives
    PositionColorShader(PrimitiveType.TriangleStrip,airplaneVertices,1);
}
```

Instructions for rendering the propeller are similar to steps taken to position and draw the airplane. The main difference in `DrawPropeller()` is the inclusion of a continuous rotation about the Z axis. Adding a variable to the game class to store rotation on the Z axis will permit updates to this variable with each frame. This data can be used to generate the continuous rotation.

```
float propellerSpin;
```

In this example, the propeller is assumed to be rotating counterclockwise, so the calculation that generates the value for *propellerSpin* is always greater than or equal to 0. If you need to reverse the rotation so it is negative, negating *propellerSpin* will generate clockwise rotation. The DrawPropeller() method is added to the game class to transform and draw the vertices; this creates a spinning rectangle. A time lapse between frames is obtained with the TargetElapsedTime.Milliseconds attribute. Note that an orbit is required. Non-orbit transformations are performed to move the propeller to the center of the airplane body. Then, a translation across the body of the aircraft and a rotation in the airplane body's direction are required to move the propeller from the aircraft's center to the aircraft's nose. This translation and rotation away from the center of the aircraft is the orbit.

```
private void DrawPropeller(GameTime gameTime){
    // 1: declare matrices
    Matrix world, translation, orbitTranslate, orbitRotateY, rotationZ;

    // 2: initialize matrices
    // continous rotation - restrict it between 0 and 2pi
    propellerSpin  += gameTime.ElapsedGameTime.Milliseconds/50.0f;
    propellerSpin   = propellerSpin % (MathHelper.Pi * 2.0f);
    rotationZ       = Matrix.CreateRotationZ(propellerSpin);

    orbitTranslate  = Matrix.CreateTranslation(0.0f,-0.25f, 0.5f);
    orbitRotateY    = Matrix.CreateRotationY(MathHelper.Pi/8.0f);
    translation     = Matrix.CreateTranslation(0.0f, 0.75f, -8.0f);
    // 3: build cumulative world matrix using I.S.R.O.T. sequence
    // identity, scale, rotate, orbit(translate & rotate), translate
    world = rotationZ * orbitTranslate * orbitRotateY * translation;

    // 4: set shader parameters
    positionColorEffectWVP.SetValue(world * cam.viewMatrix
                                          * cam.projectionMatrix);
    // 5: draw object - primitive type, vertices, # of primitives
    PositionColorShader(PrimitiveType.TriangleStrip, propellerVertices, 2);
}
```

Both `DrawAirplaneBody()` and `DrawPropeller()` are called from the `Draw()` method where all drawing for your game application is triggered:

```
DrawAirplaneBody();
DrawPropeller(gameTime);
```

When you run this code, a stationary airplane body and a propeller that rotates on the Z axis will appear (refer to Figure 8-4).

A Flying Airplane with a Spinning Propeller

For your airplane to move, it needs speed. And to calculate the speed, the current position must be tracked at every frame. Add the `Vector3` variables, *`speed`* and *`airplanePosition`*, to the game class to enable speed and position tracking for the airplane:

```
Vector3 speed;
Vector3 airplanePosition = new Vector3(0.0f, 0.75f, -8.0f);
```

When the speeds are initialized, they can be randomized. Using the `InitializeSpeed()` method in your game class randomizes the airplane's speed when the program starts. This helps to ensure that the airplane's route varies each time the game is run:

```
void InitializeSpeed(){
    Random randomNumber =  new Random();
    speed.X      = -1.0f - randomNumber.Next(3);
    speed.Z      = -1.0f - randomNumber.Next(3);
}
```

The speed can be randomized at the beginning of the game by calling `InitializeSpeed()` from the `Initialize()` method:

```
InitializeSpeed();
```

If updates to the airplane's position are not monitored and adjusted, the airplane is going to fly off into outer space. A check is needed to determine whether the X and Z world boundaries are exceeded—in which case the corresponding speed on X or Z is reversed. To allow the airplane to travel, the `UpdateAirplanePosition()` method is added to the game class. This method updates the airplane's position for every frame. A time scale is obtained by dividing the total milliseconds between frames by 1,000. Multiplying this scaled time value by the speed ensures that the animation will run at the same rate regardless of the system. For this example, the outcome ensures that the airplane will take the same time to travel from point A to point B regardless of the computer's processing power, the varying demands of your game each frame, and the background processing on your system outside your game.

```
void UpdateAirplanePosition(GameTime gameTime){
    // change corresponding speed if beyond world's X and Z boundaries
    if (airplanePosition.X > BOUNDARY || airplanePosition.X < -BOUNDARY)
        speed.X *= -1.0f;
    if (airplanePosition.Z > BOUNDARY || airplanePosition.Z < -BOUNDARY)
        speed.Z *= -1.0f;
    // increment position by speed * time scale between frames
    float timeScale      = gameTime.ElapsedGameTime.Milliseconds/1000.0f;
    airplanePosition.X  += speed.X * timeScale;
    airplanePosition.Z  += speed.Z * timeScale;
}
```

The `UpdateAirplanePosition()` method is called from the `Update()` method to ensure that the airplane's position variable is adjusted for each frame:

```
UpdateAirplanePosition(gameTime);
```

When this updated vector variable is applied—in a translation matrix against the airplane's body—it moves the airplane to the current position. Replacing the existing `CreateTranslation()` instruction inside `DrawAirplaneBody()` and `DrawPropeller()` will include the updated translation in the transformation:

```
translation = Matrix.CreateTranslation(airplanePosition);
```

When you run this program, the airplane will fly around the world and remain within the boundaries. However, there is still a problem with this version of the example. The airplane has no sense of direction and therefore appears to fly sideways.

Setting the Angle of Direction with Math.Atan()

This portion of the example adds the ability to point the airplane in the direction it is traveling. The rotation implemented in this `RotationAngle()` method uses quadrants to calculate the angle of rotation about the Y axis:

```
float RotationAngle(){
    float PI        = MathHelper.Pi;
    float rotationY = 0.0f;

    // 1st quadrant
```

```
    if (speech.X >= 0.0f && speed.Z <= 0.0f)
        rotationY =             (float)Math.Atan(-speed.Z/+speed.X);
    // 2nd quadrant
    else if (speed.X <= 0.0f && speed.Z <= 0.0f)
        rotationY = PI/2.0f   + (float)Math.Atan(-speed.X/-speed.Z);
    // 3rd quadrant
    else if (speed.X <= 0.0f && speed.Z >= 0.0f)
        rotationY = PI        + (float)Math.Atan(+speed.Z/-speed.X);
    // 4th quadrant
    else if (speed.X >= 0.0f && speed.Z >= 0.0f)
        rotationY = 3*PI/2.0f + (float)Math.Atan(+speed.X/+speed.Z);
    return rotationY + PI / 2.0f;
}
```

Replacing the instruction for the creation of the Y rotation matrix—inside `DrawAirplaneBody()`—creates a rotation about Y that matches the direction of the aircraft:

```
rotationY     = Matrix.CreateRotationY(RotationAngle());
```

This same replacement must be applied in the `DrawPropeller()` method to rotate the propeller properly about the Y axis:

```
orbitRotateY     = Matrix.CreateRotationY(RotationAngle());
```

When you compile and run this code, the airplane will fly through the world and will point in the direction it is traveling.

Setting the Angle of Direction with Math.Atan2()

You could actually replace the existing `RotationAngle()` method with this simpler version to get the same result. The longer version was shown first to demonstrate how this simpler version actually works:

```
float RotationAngle(){
    return (float)Math.Atan2((double)speed.X,(double)speed.Z);
}
```

This finished example shows an airplane that flies within the boundaries of the 3D world and points in the direction it is traveling. The only difference with this last change is the simplified instruction.

Setting the Angle of Direction Using Vectors

As explained earlier, the direction vectors can be used to generate a rotation matrix. To use the Look (speed), Up, and Right vectors to calculate the angle of direction, add this method to your game class:

```
Matrix DirectionMatrix(){
    // LOOK (FORWARD) vector stores forward direction
    Vector3 L = speed;
            L.Normalize();
    // Default UP in this case is (0, 1, 0)
    Vector3 U = new Vector3(0.0f, 1.0f, 0.0f);
            U.Normalize();
    // RIGHT is cross product (perpendicular) of UP and LOOK
    Vector3 R = Vector3.Cross(U, L);
            R.Normalize();

    Matrix M=new Matrix();// compute direction rotation matrix M
    M.M11= R.X;    M.M12=R.Y;    M.M13=R.Z;    M.M14=0.0f; //RIGHT
    M.M21= U.X;    M.M22=U.Y;    M.M23=U.Z;    M.M24=0.0f; //UP
    M.M31= L.X;    M.M32=L.Y;    M.M33=L.Z;    M.M34=0.0f; //LOOK
    M.M41= 0.0f;   M.M42=0.0f;   M.M43=0.0f;   M.M44=1.0f;
    return M;
}
```

Then, to replace the trigonometry reference in calculating the Y rotation angle, in DrawAirplaneBody(), replace the instruction that creates the Y rotation matrix with the following instruction:

```
rotationY       = DirectionMatrix();
```

Inside DrawPropeller() you can change the rotation. As discussed, you perform the non-orbit tranformations to move the propeller to the center of the aircraft. Then you perform the orbit to move the propeller out to the nose of the aircraft.

```
orbitRotateY     = DirectionMatrix();
```

When you run your code, the airplane exhibits the same behavior by flying through the world pointing in the direction it is traveling.

Once you become comfortable with the code in this chapter, and the previous one for animation, you will have more control over the look and feel of your game. Being able to control the movement of your vehicles, objects, and other beings will lead to many interesting avenues for creating great graphics effects and game play.

CHAPTER 8 REVIEW EXERCISES

To get the most from this chapter, try out these chapter review exercises.

1. Implement the step-by-step exercises presented in this chapter, if you have not already done so.
2. Create a helicopter with a spinning top and side rotor, like the one shown in the following illustration. Make the helicopter fly continuously within the boundaries of your world and ensure that it points in the direction it is traveling. Use the `Look`, `Up`, and `Right` vectors to calculate the helicopter's angle of direction (refer to Figure 8-5).

FIGURE 8-5

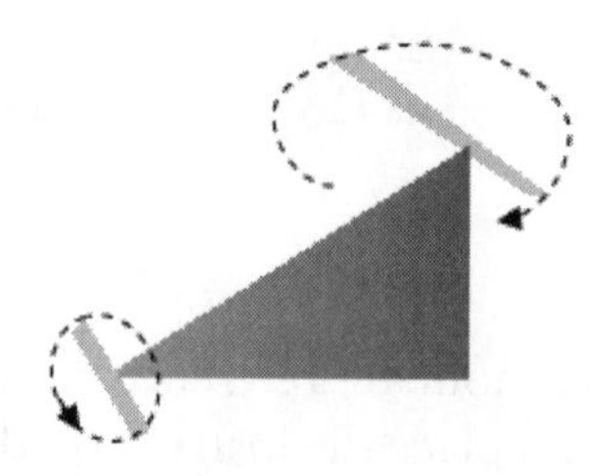

Helicopter with spinning side rotor and top rotor

CHAPTER 9

Texturing Your Game World

ANYTHING that appears in a video game needs to be textured; this includes everything from plants to people. If things aren't textured well, your game just won't look right. But don't worry, because we've got you covered. After completing this chapter, you will be able to cover your virtual surfaces with images, create tiling patterns, shade images with color, add transparency to images, and make 2D images appear as 3D objects.

TEXTURE INTRODUCTION

Textures are images applied to surfaces that are created using primitive objects. The wide variety of texture attributes within the XNA platform gives developers the power to blend and manipulate textures to create an infinite number of exciting visual effects. For example, textures can be colored, filtered, blended, and transformed at run time. Considering the importance of quality texturing, it's no surprise that XNA offers impressive support for presenting and manipulating texture data. XNA supports .bmp, dds, .dib, .hdr, .jpg, .pfm, .png, .ppm, and .tga image formats for textures.

UV Coordinates

UV coordinates specify a point in the texture; they are commonly referred to as *texture coordinates*. Texture coordinates are different from X, Y, and Z position coordinates because a texture is a two-dimensional object that is mapped onto a three-dimensional polygon. The texture's two-dimensional coordinate data is stored inside the vertex along with each X, Y, and Z position coordinate. When a texture is mapped on a one-to-one basis to a rectangular object, both U and V coordinates take a minimum value of 0 and a maximum value of 1. Figure 9-1 shows the UV coordinate settings of textures that are mapped on a one-to-one basis in three different planes.

C# Syntax for Textures

Textures are loaded and manipulated in C# using a `Texture2D` object. The object is declared with the following syntax:

```
Texture2D textureObject;
```

FIGURE 9-1

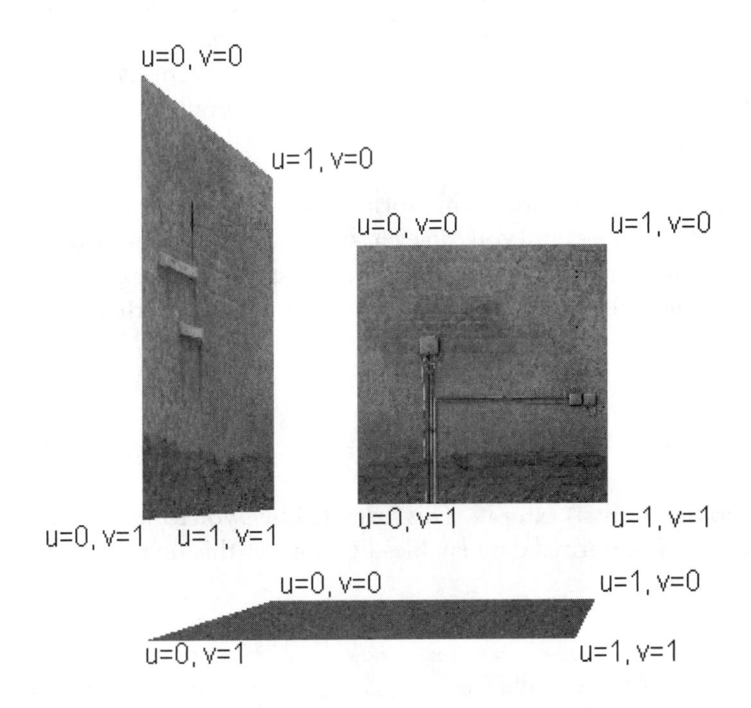

UV coordinates when mapping textures on the X, Y, and Z axes

Using the ContentManager Class to Load Textures

The `ContentManager` class is an XNA component used for loading binary content such as images. To use the `ContentManager`, you are required to reference your media content from the Content node of your project. Once images have been added to your project, the `ContentManager`'s `Load()` method can load the image files into `Texture2D` objects. The `Load()` method only requires the directory path and image name. The image file extension (*.bmp for example) is not required. In this example, the Images folder is located in the Content folder, which can be found in the same directory as the C# source files. The syntax shown here is used to load an image from the game project's Images folder within the project's Content node:

```
Texture2D texture = Content.Load<Texture2D>("Images\\imageName");
```

Vertex Types for Textures

Previous examples used a *VertexPositionColor* variable for storing vertex data. This variable type lacked the ability to store image information, so until now, the 3D graphics have been limited to basic shapes and colors. Three vertex formats allow for storage of image coordinates; they will literally add another dimension to your graphics:

VertexPositionColorTexture This format allows you to apply image textures to your primitive shapes, and you can even shade your images with color. For example, with this vertex type you could draw a rectangle with an image texture and then you could show it again with a different shade of color. The vertex variable declaration syntax is:

```
VertexPositionColorTexture  vertex = new
VertexPositionColorTexture(Vector3 position, Color color, Vector2 uv);
```

VertexPositionNormalTexture This format allows you to add textures to your primitive objects. The normal data enables lighting for this textured format. The vertex declaration syntax is:

```
VertexPositionNormalTexture  vertex = new
VertexPositionNormalTexture(Vector3 position, Vector3 normal, Vector2 uv);
```

VertexPositionTexture This format only permits storage of position and texture data. It may be useful if you don't need lighting and were concerned about saving space or improving performance for large amounts of vertices. The vertex declaration syntax is:

```
VertexPositionTexture  vertex = new
VertexPositionTexture(Vector3 position, Vector2 uv);
```

Shader Implementation for Textures

Texturing is applied in the shader. The shader code needed to texture objects is similar to the shader explained in Chapter 6. However, some changes to the code are required to enable textures. The additions required are:

- A global *Texture* variable
- A `Sampler` object for filtering the texture

- Vertex shader input and output vertex data types that include UV coordinates
- Pixel shader code that applies the texture data to the pixels that are output

HLSL Texture Variable

The `Texture` data type is used to store and apply the image within the shader. The declaration for a texture is usually made in the global section of the shader:

```
uniform    extern    Texture    textureImage;
```

HLSL Sampler Object

A `Sampler` object defines properties or filters in the shader for drawing. The `Sampler` is like a brush type that can be used to apply the texture to the primitive surface. Here is the `Sampler` used in the texture shaders throughout this book:

```
sampler textureSampler = sampler_state{
    Texture      = <textureImage>;
    magfilter    = LINEAR;          // magfilter - bigger than actual
    minfilter    = LINEAR;          // minfilter - smaller than actual
    mipfilter    = LINEAR;
};
```

In this code, you can see that the filter properties are declared. A `minfilter` tells the shader how to draw the texture on the object if the object is smaller than the actual texture. A `magfilter` tells the program how to draw the texture if the object is larger than the texture. A `mipfilter` assists in resizing the image up close and far away, so your surfaces will not be as jagged around the edges. This method of sampling is actually very common and applies the image clearly against a primitive surface, as you would expect to see in a standard photo that can be printed in both small and large sizes. In this case, the filter properties for the shader are `LINEAR`. A linear `Sampler` state tells the shader to take the portion of the texture defined by the UV coordinates and spread it evenly over the area defined by the corresponding X, Y, and Z values for each vertex. This process of projecting image data between vertices is known as *linear interpolation*.

UV Coordinates Within the Shader Until now, the input and output data declarations in the vertex shader only enabled vertices for color and position. For textures, the vertex shader input and output must be declared to handle not only position and color but also UV coordinate data. The following struct defines the structure of each vertex that is passed to the vertex shader:

```
struct VSinput{                                // input to vertex shader
    float4 position      : POSITION0; // position semantic x,y,z,w
    float4 color         : COLOR0;    // color semantic    r,g,b,a
    float2 uv            : TEXCOORD0; // texture semantic  u,v
};
```

The following struct defines the output from the vertex shader. The output data type will also serve as the pixel shader's input data type.

```
struct VStoPS{                                 // vertex shader output
    float4 position      : POSITION0; // position semantic x,y,z,w
    float4 color         : COLOR;     // color semantic    r,g,b,a
    float2 uv            : TEXCOORD0; // texture semantic  u,v
};
```

The texture output for the vertex shader is defined in the vertex shader with the following instruction:

```
OUT.uv = IN.uv;
```

tex2D If a pixel shader is used when texturing is applied, the `tex2D()` function is often used to return output that combines the texture information with the filter. The syntax for the conversion would appear as:

```
OUT.color        = tex2D(textureSampler, IN.uv);
```

Shader Code for Applying Textures

This complete listing of shader code applies textures to vertices and renders objects built from vertices that store X, Y, and Z positions, as well as UV texture coordinates and color. This shader is similar to the initial shader used in the preceding examples. However, the shader used previously could only render objects constructed from position and color data. The new shader also applies image textures to your objects, making them more visually appealing. You can find this shader code in the Texture.fx file in the Shaders folder on this book's website.

```
float4x4                wvpMatrix :WORLDVIEWPROJ;//world view proj matrix
uniform extern texture textureImage;              // store texture

// filter (like a brush) for showing texture
```

```
sampler textureSampler = sampler_state{
    Texture     = <textureImage>;
    magfilter   = LINEAR;           // magfilter - bigger than actual
    minfilter   = LINEAR;           // minfilter - smaller than actual
    mipfilter   = LINEAR;
};
// input to vertex shader
struct VSinput{                         // input to vertex shader
    float4 position     : POSITION0; // position semantic x,y,z,w
    float4 color        : COLOR0;    // color semantic    r,g,b,a
    float2 uv           : TEXCOORD0; // texture semantic  u,v
};
// vertex shader output
struct VStoPS{                          // vertex shader output
    float4 position     : POSITION0; // position semantic x,y,z,w
    float4 color        : COLOR;     // color semantic    r,g,b,a
    float2 uv           : TEXCOORD0; // texture semantic  u,v
};
// pixel shader output
struct PSoutput{                        // pixel shader output
    float4 color        : COLOR0;    // colored pixel is output
};

// alter vertex inputs
void VertexShader(in VSinput IN, out VStoPS OUT){
    OUT.position    = mul(IN.position, wvpMatrix); // transform object
                                                    // orient it in camera
    OUT.color       = IN.color;                     // send color to p.s.
    OUT.uv          = IN.uv;                        // send uv's to p.s.
}

// convert color and texture data from vertex shader to pixels
void PixelShader(in VStoPS IN, out PSoutput OUT){
    // use texture for coloring object
    OUT.color       = tex2D(textureSampler, IN.uv);

    // this next line is optional - you can shade the texturized pixel
    // with color to give your textures a tint. Do this by multiplying
    // output by the input color vector.
    OUT.color      *= IN.color;
}
```

```
// the shader starts here
technique TextureShader{
    pass p0{
        // texture sampler initialized
        sampler[0]  = (textureSampler);

        // declare and initialize vs and ps
        vertexshader= compile vs_1_1 VertexShader();
        pixelshader = compile ps_1_1 PixelShader();
    }
}
```

That's all of the shader code needed to receive vertices with position, color, and texture coordinates to transform this data into textured objects.

C# EffectParameter for Setting the Shader's Texture Value

An `EffectParameter` object for the texture is required in the C# code to tell the shader what image to use when rendering a textured polygon. As discussed in Chapter 6, the `EffectParameter` object is declared in the application with the following syntax:

```
Effect              textureEffect;
EffectParameter     textureEffectImage;
```

When the program begins, the `EffectParameter` object is assigned the name of the `texture` variable in the shader:

```
textureEffectImage
= textureEffect.Parameters["textureVariableName"];
```

Later, when an image needs to be selected for rendering, the `EffectParameter` object is assigned a texture using the `SetValue()` method. If you set the value before entering the shader, the assignment takes place when the shader pass begins. However, if the shader's `Effect.Begin()` method has already been called to start drawing, you should always call `CommitChanges()` immediately after assigning a shader variable, or it will not be set in the shader:

```
textureEffectImage.SetValue(Texture2D   texture2D);
```

An image texture is not applied to a surface until the surface is drawn from the shader. You might consider keeping your texture assignments organized by executing them where your other shader parameters are set.

TRANSPARENT TEXTURES

At some point, you may want to create a transparency effect. For example, you could make the background pixels of an image invisible while all other pixels in the texture are rendered in their original color. You likely have seen this transparency effect applied with tree images, a heads-up display, or a stylish custom dashboard that always faces the viewer. It is possible to create this effect when using a mask that is stored in the *.dds format. It is also possible to create *.png or *.tga images with transparent pixels in your favorite photo editor, such as Adobe Photoshop or the freeware program, GIMP, and then draw them using XNA code so that the transparent pixels do not appear.

Alpha Channel

An alpha channel can be used to "mask" all pixels of a specific color in an image. Alpha data is stored in the last color byte of a pixel—after the red, green, and blue bytes. When alpha blending is enabled in your XNA code and the alpha channel is active, transparency is achieved for the pixels where the alpha setting is set to 0.

TEXTURE TILING

Tiling is a very simple effect that creates a repeating pattern of an image on the surface of a primitive object. Tiling is also a performance-friendly effect that looks great on brick or stone surfaces, such as walls and streets. However, tiling can even be implemented for grass and soil as long as the image is created so that the edges match the neighboring edges of the same image. In fact, the grass texture in the MGHWinBaseCode and MGH360BaseCode projects is tiled ten times horizontally and vertically to make the grass look more dense and lush. If you look at the UV coordinates inside `InitializeGround()`, you will notice that they range between 0 and 10 instead of between 0 and 1. Figure 9-2 shows another example of tiling where the image is repeated ten times along both the rows and columns. The original texture is on the left, and the tiled surface is on the right.

Using a small image to cover a large surface makes tiling a useful way to increase the performance of your textures and decrease the size of your image files.

FIGURE 9-2

Tiling effect

TEXTURE COLORING

It is possible to color your image textures at run time. This technique might be handy for a number of instances—maybe you need your texture to be darker and you can't wait for the artist to fix it, so you decide to shade it in your code. Maybe you want to create a stone pattern; you could use the same image to draw all stones but alternate the shade to create more contrast on the surface.

The Texture.fx shader is already able to apply colors, which are stored in the vertices, to any textured item. If a non-white color is stored in the vertices, the image in the texture will be shaded by this color.

To demonstrate how this works, it helps to examine the vertex shader and pixel shader. The vertex shader input receives the color stored in the vertices. The user-defined struct that stores the vertex shader output stores this color information. The vertex shader output, by design, serves as the input for the pixel shader. This vertex shader code receives the color from the vertices that are set in your C# code and passes it to the pixel shader:

```
void VertexShader(in VSinput IN, out VStoPS OUT){
    OUT.position    = mul(IN.position, wvpMatrix); // transform object
                                                   // orient it in viewer
    OUT.color       = IN.color;                    // send color to p.s.
    OUT.uv          = IN.uv;                       // send uv's to p.s.
}
```

The pixel shader can only return colored pixels as output. On the first line of the shader, the texture is applied to each vertex using the `tex2D()` function, which uses the `textureSampler` filter and UV coordinates as input parameters. The pixel shader uses linear interpolation to shade and texture the area between the vertices. On the second line, this optional instruction is added, which multiplies the colored pixel by the color that is stored in the vertices. This modification, in effect, applies a color to the image texture:

```
void PixelShader(in vsOutput IN, out psOutput OUT)
{   // apply texture to vertices using textureSampler filter
    OUT.color    = tex2D(textureSampler, IN.uv);
    // apply color from v.s. - p.s. interpolates between verts
    OUT.color   *= IN.color;
}
```

Texture Example

This example begins with either the MGHWinBaseCode project or the MGH360BaseCode project, which can be found at the BaseCode folder on this book's website. This project already has textured ground and uses the Texture.fx file described earlier in this chapter. Aside from the shader already being present, this demonstration shows how to add in new textured objects from scratch. This demonstrates the texturing process from start to finish. Each surface will be transformed into place, and the accompanying textures will be applied to each of them. Part A of this example demonstrates how to add in the ground that is used in the base code. By the time Part B of this example is complete, a textured side wall and a textured back will also be visible.

In Part C of this example, a tree texture with transparency will be added. This tree will use a "billboarding" technique, which allows it to always face the viewer—regardless of the camera's angle. Figure 9-3 shows the billboard tree from different camera angles.

FIGURE 9-3

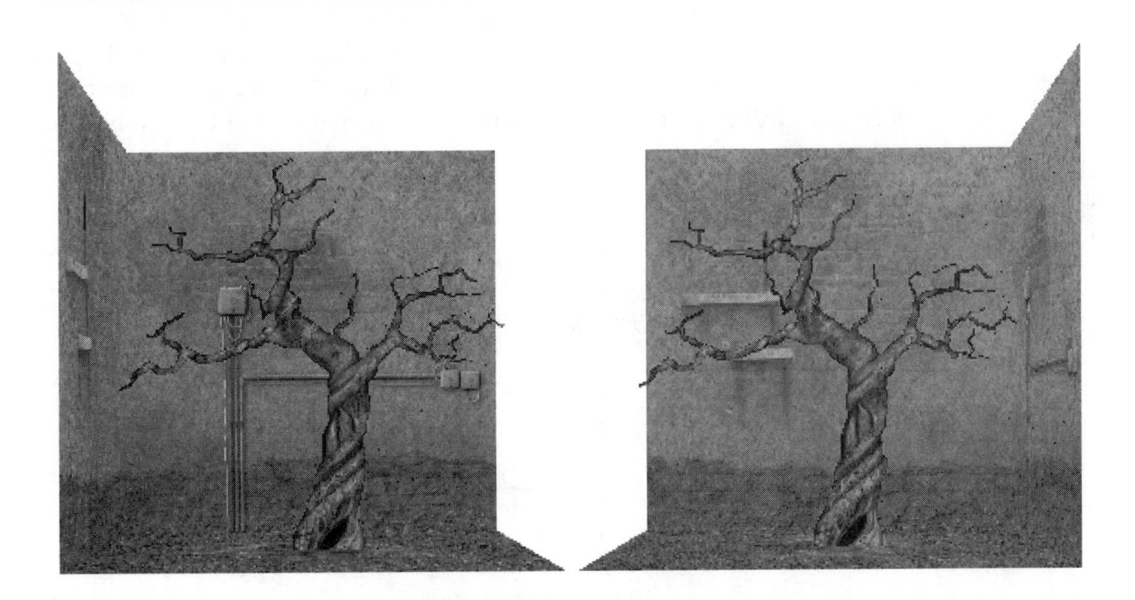

Billboarding applied to tree so it always faces viewer

Texture Example, Part A: Adding the Grass Texture

To demonstrate how to load an opaque texture into any 3D game project, and to draw it, Part A of this example will include adding the grass texture that is used in the base code. If you are following the "Building the Base Code from Scratch" example from Chapter 17, you will need to follow the steps in this section. If you are working through this chapter and have already started with the MGHWinBaseCode project or the MGH360BaseCode project, you can skip this section and go to Part B. However, if you are reading Chapter 9 for the first time, you should probably still read this section so that you can understand how the texture is set up from the very beginning.

When you are applying textures in a 3D game, you require a shader that can handle the texture-mapping data. The Texture.fx code presented earlier in this chapter can do the job. This shader must be referenced from the Content node of your game project. You can find the Texture.fx file in the Shaders folder on this book's website. To keep your different project files organized, create a Shaders folder under the Content node and add your Texture.fx shader file there. In Figure 9-4, you can see your Texture.fx file referenced from the Solution Explorer.

At the top of the game class, you require an `Effect` object to load and access your shader. `EffectParameter` objects are also required to allow you to set values in your shader from your C# game code. In this case, you will need two `EffectParameter` objects. The first `EffectParameter`, `textureEffectWVP`, allows you to define how your world will be seen by your

FIGURE 9-4

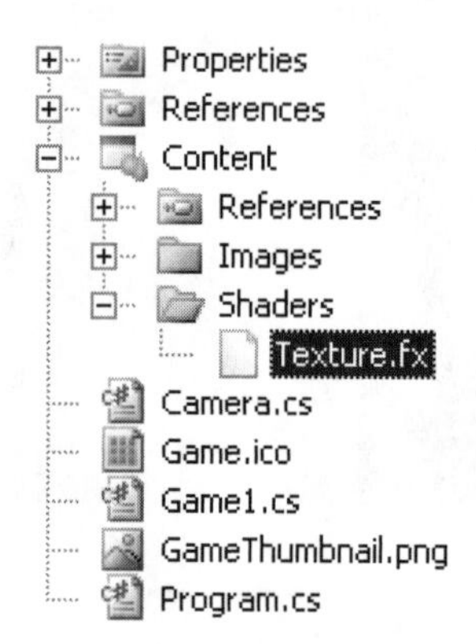

Shader reference in the Solution Explorer

camera. The second EffectParameter, textureEffectImage, allows you to set the texture that is applied against surfaces that are drawn from the shader:

```
Effect              textureEffect;      // shader object
EffectParameter     textureEffectWVP;   // cumulative matrix w*v*p
EffectParameter     textureEffectImage; // texture parameter
```

The Microsoft XNA game project template automatically generates a folder named "Content" for loading your shaders and media. Also, the project template automatically adds a line of code to set the Content.RootDirectory property to this directory. To load your texture shader when the program begins, and to set your game project references to the shader's camera settings and texture variables, add these instructions to the InitializeBaseCode() method:

```
textureEffect           = Content.Load<Effect>("Shaders\\Texture");
textureEffectWVP        = textureEffect.Parameters["wvpMatrix"];
textureEffectImage      = textureEffect.Parameters["textureImage"];
```

When drawing objects that have textures, the GraphicsDevice needs to retrieve data from the vertex variable in the proper format. A new VertexDeclaration object is declared in the module declarations section so that the graphics device can later retrieve the correct position, color, and UV data.

```
private VertexDeclaration  positionColorTexture;
```

Later, in the InitializeBaseCode() method, you need more code to set the VertexDeclaration object to store the VertexPositionColorTexture type:

```
positionColorTexture    = new VertexDeclaration(graphics.GraphicsDevice,
                          VertexPositionColorTexture.VertexElements);
```

As you have seen when you run the base code, the ground is created using a square surface that is covered with a grass texture. The sides of the square are set to have the length equivalent to the constant BOUNDARY. If you are building the base code, a declaration for BOUNDARY is required at the top of the game class:

```
private const float BOUNDARY = 16.0f;
```

A Texture2D object is required to load and access the image file at run time, so a declaration for the texture object is also needed at the top of the game project:

```
private Texture2D        grassTexture;
```

The grass.jpg image will be used to texture the ground. This file can be found in the Images folder in the download for this book. It is loaded in your project using the `Load()` method when the program begins. The code here works under the assumption that you have created an Images folder under the Content node in the Solution Explorer and you have copied the grass.jpg file to the Images folder, so it is referenced from there. To create an Images folder, right-click the Content node in the Solution Explorer and then click Add New Folder. To reference the image file from there, right-click the Images folder, select Add, and then navigate to the grass.jpg file and select it. Add this instruction to load the grass texture inside the `LoadContent()` method:

```
grassTexture = Content.Load<Texture2D>("Images\\grass");
```

You will need an array of vertices to store the position, color, and UV texture-mapping data. The declaration is made at the top of the game class so it can be initialized and then used for drawing the ground.

```
VertexPositionColorTexture[] groundVertices = new
VertexPositionColorTexture[4];
```

Next, add `InitializeGround()` to the game class to store the vertices with position, color, and UV coordinates. For the ground vertices, the UV coordinates are set to tile the image ten times along the horizontal and vertical. The image has been designed specifically to create a repeating pattern that is not easily detected by the naked eye. Tiling the image allows it to be drawn with a higher resolution of detail.

```
private void InitializeGround(){
    const float BORDER = BOUNDARY;
    Vector2     uv     = new Vector2(0.0f, 0.0f);
    Vector3     pos    = new Vector3(0.0f, 0.0f, 0.0f);
    Color       color  = Color.White;

    // top left
    uv.X= 0.0f; uv.Y= 0.0f;    pos.X=-BORDER; pos.Y=0.0f; pos.Z=-BORDER;
    groundVertices[0] = new VertexPositionColorTexture(pos, color, uv);
    // bottom left
    uv.X= 0.0f; uv.Y=10.0f;    pos.X=-BORDER; pos.Y=0.0f; pos.Z=BORDER;
    groundVertices[1] = new VertexPositionColorTexture(pos, color, uv);
    // top right
    uv.X=10.0f; uv.Y= 0.0f;    pos.X= BORDER; pos.Y=0.0f; pos.Z=-BORDER;
    groundVertices[2] = new VertexPositionColorTexture(pos, color, uv);
    // bottom right
```

```
    uv.X=10.0f; uv.Y=10.0f;    pos.X= BORDER; pos.Y=0.0f; pos.Z=BORDER;
    groundVertices[3] = new VertexPositionColorTexture(pos, color, uv);
}
```

To set up the ground vertices when the program begins, add the call to InitializeGround() inside Initialize():

```
InitializeGround();
```

When rendering the new textured surfaces, you need to select the correct shader, but it is possible to use more than one shader for drawing. Just be certain of two things:

- When an effect is selected, all code for rendering should be triggered between the texture shader effect's `Begin()` and `End()` methods.
- The shader effect's `End()` method must be executed before another shader effect begins.

When you are setting parameters in the shader, the more performance-friendly and common approach is to set these parameters before `Begin()` is called for the `Effect` object. `Effect.Begin()` sets all of the render states. However, if you need to set an effect parameter after `Begin()`, you would need to finalize this state by calling `Effect.CommitChanges()` or it will not be set.

While the shader is active, you can then specify the vertex type and call `DrawUserPrimitives()` to draw your textured surface. `DrawUserPrimitives()` in this case must specify a textured vertex type. Then the primitive type, vertices, vertex offset, and number of primitive objects are supplied as parameters to this method. Add `TextureShader()` to your game class to trigger use of the Texture.fx shader and to draw your textured objects with it. If you are using a prebuilt version of the base code, this project already contains this method:

```
private void TextureShader(PrimitiveType  primitiveType,
            VertexPositionColorTexture[] vertexData, int numPrimitives){
    textureEffect.Begin();       // begin using Texture.fx
    textureEffect.Techniques[0].Passes[0].Begin();

    // set drawing format and vertex data then draw surface
    graphics.GraphicsDevice.VertexDeclaration = positionColorTexture;
    graphics.GraphicsDevice.DrawUserPrimitives
                            <VertexPositionColorTexture>(
                            primitiveType, vertexData, 0, numPrimitives);
    textureEffect.Techniques[0].Passes[0].End();
    textureEffect.End();         // stop using Textured.fx
}
```

The code needed to draw textured surfaces, like your grass-covered ground, follows the same steps that are taken when drawing surfaces with only color and position coordinates. The main differences are in step 4 and step 5. In step 4, an `EffectParameter` object is used to assign a texture in the shader. In step 5, the `TextureShader()` routine is called to select the appropriate shader and to draw with it. Add `DrawGround()` to your game class to implement this routine:

```
private void DrawGround(){
    // 1: declare matrices
    Matrix world, translation;

    // 2: initialize matrices
    translation = Matrix.CreateTranslation(0.0f, 0.0f, 0.0f);

    // 3: build cumulative world matrix using I.S.R.O.T. sequence
    // identity, scale, rotate, orbit(translate & rotate), translate
    world = translation;

    // 4: set shader parameters
    textureEffectWVP.SetValue(world*cam.viewMatrix*cam.projectionMatrix);
    textureEffectImage.SetValue(grassTexture);

    // 5: draw object - primitive type, vertex data, # primitives
    TextureShader(PrimitiveType.TriangleStrip, groundVertices, 2);
}
```

To trigger the drawing, DrawGround() must be called from inside `Draw()`:

```
DrawGround();
```

If you are working through the Chapter 17 exercise, "Building the Base Code from Scratch," and have completed these steps, you are now done adding all of the code required for texturing your surfaces. You can view your textured ground when you run the project now.

Texture Example, Part B: Adding Two More Opaque Textures

In this next portion of the example, two wall textures will be applied to the surfaces to create a side wall and back wall. To store the new wall images, you will require `Texture2D` objects, so declarations are needed for the wall textures in the game class declarations area:

```
private Texture2D backWallTexture, sideWallTexture;
```

The backwall.jpg and sidewall.jpg images will be used to texture both walls. They can be found in the Images folder on this book's website. They are loaded in your project using the Load() method when the program begins. Add these two image files to the Content\Images directory of your project and add them to your project using the Solution Explorer. If the Images folder does not exist, right-click the Content node in your game project and select Add | New Folder to launch the dialog that allows you to add an Images folder. Then, once you have an Images folder under the Content node, right-click it, select Add, and then navigate and select each of the image files. Add these instructions to load each texture inside the LoadContent() method:

```
backWallTexture = Content.Load<Texture2D>("Images\\backwall");
sideWallTexture = Content.Load<Texture2D>("Images\\sidewall");
```

The vertices used to draw the walls store position, color, and UV coordinates to map the images onto this surface. An array of VertexPositionColorTexture coordinates is needed:

```
private VertexPositionColorTexture[] surfaceVertex = new
VertexPositionColorTexture[4];
```

The method InitializeSurface() initializes the vertices with the position, color, and UV coordinates that you will use to create a rectangular surface for each wall. The UV coordinates will be mapped with U along the X axis and with V along the Z axis.

Add InitializeSurface() to the game class to create these vertices with position, color, and UV coordinates:

```
private void InitializeSurface(){
    Vector2 uv      = new Vector2(0.0f, 0.0f);
    Vector3 pos     = new Vector3(0.0f, 0.0f, 0.0f);
    Color   color   = Color.White;

    // A. top left, B. bottom left, C. top right, D. bottom right
    uv.X=0.0f; uv.Y=0.0f;   pos.X=-BOUNDARY; pos.Y=0.0f; pos.Z=-BOUNDARY;
    surfaceVertex[0] = new VertexPositionColorTexture(pos, color, uv);//A
    uv.X=0.0f; uv.Y=1.0f;   pos.X=-BOUNDARY; pos.Y=0.0f; pos.Z=BOUNDARY;
    surfaceVertex[1] = new VertexPositionColorTexture(pos, color, uv);//B
    uv.X=1.0f; uv.Y=0.0f;   pos.X=BOUNDARY; pos.Y=0.0f; pos.Z=-BOUNDARY;
    surfaceVertex[2] = new VertexPositionColorTexture(pos, color, uv);//C
    uv.X=1.0f; uv.Y=1.0f;   pos.X=BOUNDARY; pos.Y=0.0f; pos.Z=BOUNDARY;
    surfaceVertex[3] = new VertexPositionColorTexture(pos, color, uv);//D
}
```

The data for the surface is assigned at the beginning of the program. To do this, call `InitializeSurface()` from the `Initialize()` method:

```
InitializeSurface();
```

You will reuse the `DrawSurfaces()` method to draw the side wall, back wall, and tree. An identifier for the surface to be drawn is passed as an argument to `DrawSurfaces()`. These surface-identifier declarations have to be added to the top of the game class so they can be recognized in the methods that use them:

```
const int SIDE = 0; const int BACK = 1;
```

Next, you must add `DrawSurfaces()` to the game class to transform each wall into position, to apply a texture, and to render each textured surface using the same set of vertices. Each time a surface is drawn, a switch selects the specific transformations and texture for the surface. When the texture is selected, it is set in the shader using the `EffectParameter` object's `SetValue()` method. Once the cumulative transformation has been set, the `WorldViewProjection` matrix value is set in the texture shader using another `EffectParameter` object, `textureEffectWVP`. The world-view projection-matrix is used in the shader to position each surface so that it can be seen properly by the camera.

```
private void DrawSurfaces(int surfaceNum)
{   // shrink walls and tree then position them relative to world size
    const float SCALAR          =  0.08f;
    float       edge            =  SCALAR * BOUNDARY;
    float       Z               = -0.5f   * BOUNDARY;

    // 1: declare matrices
    Matrix world, scale, translation, rotationY, rotationX;

    // 2: initialize matrices
    scale       = Matrix.CreateScale(SCALAR, SCALAR, SCALAR);
    rotationX   = Matrix.CreateRotationX(MathHelper.Pi/2.0f);
    rotationY   = Matrix.CreateRotationY(0.0f);
    translation = Matrix.CreateTranslation(0.0f, 0.0f, 0.0f);

    switch (surfaceNum){
    // set transformations and texture for each surface instance
    case BACK:
```

```
        translation = Matrix.CreateTranslation(0.0f, edge, Z);
        textureEffectImage.SetValue(backWallTexture); break;
    case SIDE:
        rotationY   = Matrix.CreateRotationY(MathHelper.Pi/2.0f);
        translation = Matrix.CreateTranslation(-edge, edge, Z + edge);
        textureEffectImage.SetValue(sideWallTexture); break;
    }
    // 3: build cumulative world matrix using I.S.R.O.T. sequence
    // identity, scale, rotate, orbit(translate & rotate), translate
    world = scale * rotationX * rotationY * translation;

    // 4: set shader parameters
    textureEffectWVP.SetValue(world*cam.viewMatrix*cam.projectionMatrix);

    // 5: draw object - primitive type, vertices, # primitives
    TextureShader(PrimitiveType.TriangleStrip, surfaceVertex, 2);
}
```

With your `DrawSurfaces()` method in the game class, you can now call it twice to draw each textured wall. These call statements, of course, belong in the `Draw()` method:

```
DrawSurfaces(SIDE);
DrawSurfaces(BACK);
```

When you compile and run the program, the output will show the two textured walls and textured ground.

Texture Example, Part C: Transparent Textures

This example shows how to draw a tree without the background pixels. The example continues with the code created for Part B, but some extra setup is required to load the tree texture. You will need a `Texture2D` object declaration at the top of the game class to store the tree image so that it can be referenced throughout the class:

```
private Texture2D treeTexture;
```

The tree.png file used to create the tree texture must be loaded when the program begins. Once your tree.png file has been added to the Content\Images directory of your project and is referenced in the Solution Explorer, this file can be loaded in your XNA code using the `LoadContent()` method:

```
treeTexture  =  Content.Load<Texture2D>("Images\\tree");
```

An identifier definition is added (at the top of the game class) so it can be used in the `DrawSurfaces()` method to select the tree texture and to apply the appropriate transformations when drawing it:

```
const int TREE = 2;
```

With the identifiers for the tree and total surfaces in place, the `DrawSurfaces()` method can be used to draw the tree using the same vertices that are used to map the wall and ground textures. In `DrawSurfaces()`, an additional case is required inside the switch to handle the texture selection and transformations that move the tree into place:

```
    case TREE:
        float treeScale  = SCALAR / 1.5f;
        scale       = Matrix.CreateScale(treeScale,treeScale,treeScale);
        translation = Matrix.CreateTranslation( 0.0f, treeScale
                                        * BOUNDARY, 0.88f * Z);
        textureEffectImage.SetValue(treeTexture);     break;
```

To draw the tree, alpha blending is applied so that the transparent pixels will not be rendered. The `SourceBlend` property selects the image pixel and masks it with the `DestinationBlend` layer. Pixels with an active alpha channel will be made transparent after the masking operation. Once the tree is drawn, the alpha blending property, `AlphaBlendEnable`, is turned off. In the `Draw()` method, you must add this code inside the `Begin()` and `End()` methods for the texture effect since `DrawSurfaces()` references this effect. Also, you must place the code to draw the tree after the code that draws the opaque surfaces; this allows the transparent object to overlay the opaque objects.

```
graphics.GraphicsDevice.RenderState.AlphaBlendEnable = true;
graphics.GraphicsDevice.RenderState.SourceBlend      = Blend.SourceAlpha;
graphics.GraphicsDevice.RenderState.DestinationBlend =
Blend.InverseSourceAlpha;
DrawSurfaces(TREE);
graphics.GraphicsDevice.RenderState.AlphaBlendEnable = false;
```

With the right adjustments to your game application, you will now be able to look through the branches of the tree and see what's on the other side. However, if you ran the code now, you would notice that while the tree appears with a transparent background, it only looks real when the camera is facing the texture directly. When the camera faces another direction, the illusion is spoiled because the viewer can easily see that a two-dimensional image is being used. At some angles, the surface will appear to be paper thin to the viewer. In *Halo 2*, you can see an example of how this can happen. On the Delta Halo level, it is possible to climb onto a cliff that overlooks the level; the cliff was not intended to be accessible, but once you climb up, you can clearly see that the bushes on the cliff are 2D. In fact, you can walk right through them and see that they are only a pixel deep.

Billboarding can help solve the two-dimensional problem. *Billboarding* is a common technique that makes two-dimensional images appear as though they are three-dimensional objects; this works regardless of the camera position or angle. The algorithm for billboarding involves rotating the texture about the Y axis by the angle of the camera's look direction. (Refer to Chapter 17 for an explanation of how the `Look` (Forward) vector is obtained.) For the billboarding effect to work, the vertices that create the textured face must be centered at the origin. Also, the object must be centered in the image (see Figure 9-5).

FIGURE 9-5

Objects within billboarded images must be centered on the X axis.

Billboarding Example

This example begins with the solution from the transparency code in Part C of the previous example. In Chapter 8, logic is used to rotate the object drawn about the Y axis so that it points in the direction it travels. This same logic can be used to rotate the tree about the Y axis so it always faces the viewer and will consequently always look like a bushy tree at any camera angle. In Figure 9-3 you can see the tree face the viewer regardless of the angle.

As in Chapter 8, the `Atan2()` function uses the changes in direction on X and Z as parameters to calculate the angle of direction about the Y axis. However, for this case, the camera's `Look` vector is used to obtain the direction parameters. The `Look` direction equals the `View` position minus the camera position. (Refer to Chapter 17 for more detail on the `Look` vector that stores the direction of the camera.)

Adding `GetViewerAngle()` to the game class provides a method that returns the rotation angle about the Y axis. This angle matches the camera's angle about the Y axis. When the tree is rotated about the Y axis (by the amount returned from this function), the tree will always face the viewer:

```
float GetViewerAngle()
{   // use camera look direction to get
    // rotation angle about Y
    float x = cam.view.X - cam.position.X;
    float z = cam.view.Z - cam.position.Z;

    return (float)Math.Atan2(x, z) + MathHelper.Pi;}
```

Inside `DrawSurfaces()`, in the case that handles the `TREE` identifier, you need to add code to reset the Y rotation matrix based on the camera's rotation about the Y axis. This creates the billboard effect that makes the tree look real from a distance.

```
rotationY = Matrix.CreateRotationY(GetViewerAngle());
```

After you have made these changes, try running the program. The tree will appear like a nice, full, bushy tree, regardless of the angle of the camera.

Texture Coloring Example

This example shows how to colorize your image textures. This example begins with the solution from the previous example. You can also find this solution in the Solutions folder in this book's download. The discussion in this section shows how to change the color of the texture for the back wall.

In the InitializeSurface() method, replace the line that sets the color for the vertices from white to red:

```
Color color = Color.Red;
```

When you run your code after this change you will see that the textures drawn with these modified vertices are rendered with a red tint.

By now, you should see that applying images makes the 3D world a lot more interesting. Simple effects such as tiling, color, transparency, and billboarding can be applied with little effort.

CHAPTER 9 REVIEW EXERCISES

Here are some exercises that focus on some of the key points for applying texture effects:

1. Try the step-by-step examples presented in this chapter, if you have not already done so.
2. State four differences between a shader that enables texturing and a shader that only handles position and color.
3. List the objects that need to be added to the C# code to add in a second shader that allows textures.
4. List the states that must be set to enable transparency.
5. Create a building and apply textures to the sides. Add a billboarded tree, cactus, or flower that you create with transparency.

CHAPTER 10

Adding Skies and Horizons to Your Levels

THIS chapter explains how to create a realistic sky effect with an infinite horizon. By the time you finish working through this chapter, the sunny blue atmosphere you create will look so tranquil and inviting that you may want to crawl inside your 3D world and never leave.

THE SKYBOX

The structure that houses the images that create the sky and horizon is often referred to as a *skybox*. When the skybox is built properly, it is seamless—you can't tell where it begins or ends. Figure 10-1 shows three different camera views of a 3D world from within a skybox.

A skybox is built using six images to create the sides, sky, and ground for the horizon. Each individual image is shown in Figure 10-2.

To create the effect of an infinite horizon, each of the four wall images and the sky image translate with the camera, but the ground image remains stationary. The result allows you to see the ground move underneath you as you travel, but you will never reach the horizon.

The walls of your virtual world are draped so that they fall slightly below the ground. This means that the bottom edges of the walls are hidden. Figure 10-3 illustrates the stationary ground and its position relative to the moving ceiling and draped walls.

FIGURE 10-1

Viewing a skybox from different camera angles

FIGURE 10-2

Six images used to make the skybox

Terragen Photorealistic Scenery Rendering Software

Excellent tools are available to create your skybox. Terragen (http://www.planetside.co.uk/) from Planetside is a popular utility for generating photorealistic scenery that you can use for spectacular landscapes, seascapes, and skyscapes. The beauty of Terragen is also evident in its ease of use.

Thanks to Planetside, a link to the download for the noncommercial edition of Terragen is included on the website for this book. The noncommercial version is free for personal use. However, the registered commercial version offers access to support, the ability to render larger and higher-quality images, enhanced anti-aliasing modes, and, of course, permission to deploy works created using Terragen for commercial purposes. Refer to the Planetside website for licensing and update details.

FIGURE 10-3

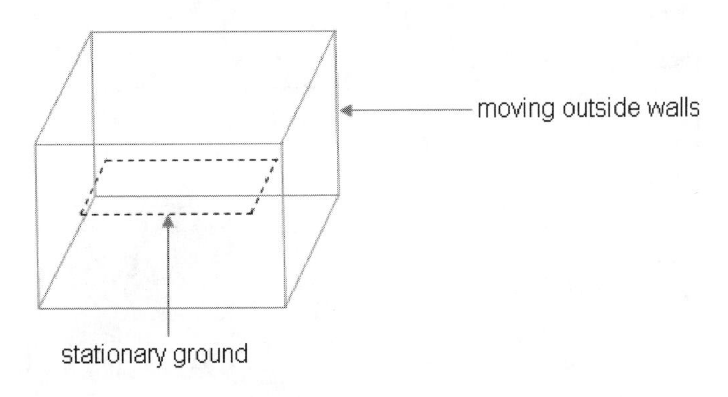

Moving ceiling and draped walls with a stationary ground of skybox

Using Terragen to Create a Skybox

This demonstration explains the steps needed to create the six images used to make a skybox.

When you open Terragen, the application launches the main window, presented in Figure 10-4.

Setting Up the Terragen Project

When you are setting up a Terragen project, you should assign several properties before you create your images. This ensures consistency among the images you generate. The properties you need to set govern image size, magnification, quality, camera position, and target position for generating land and sky scenery.

Sizing the Image To ensure consistent sizing for all images, you should give each image in the skybox the same pixel width and height dimensions. To set the dimensions, click the Image Size button to open the Render Settings dialog. On the Image tab of the Render Settings dialog, you can enter numeric values for Width and Height (both values are in pixels). For this demonstration, a size of 512 pixels by 512 pixels is recommended.

FIGURE 10-4

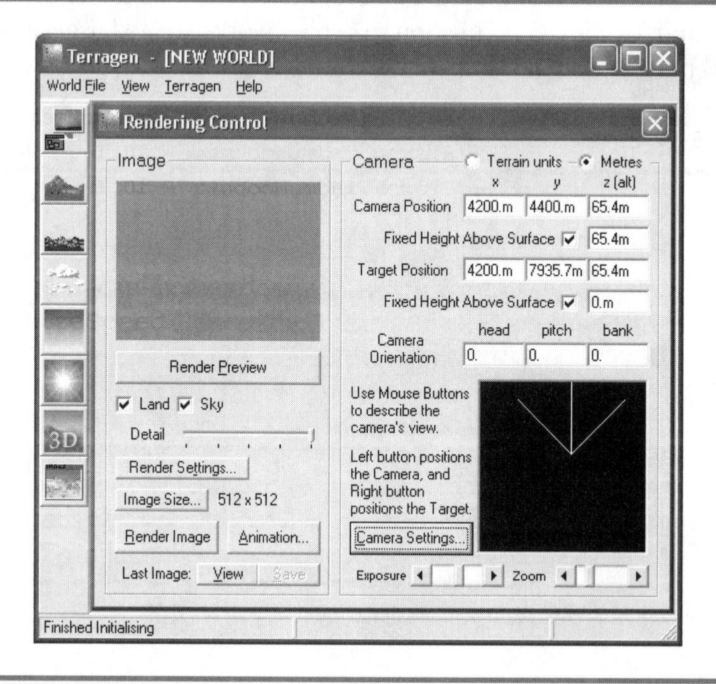

Terragen main window

A higher pixel count enables better-quality images, but higher pixel counts also reduce the memory available. This may lower the frame rate in your game because it takes more processing power for the game engine to render the sky.

Setting the Zoom Magnification The camera's zoom magnification must be set to 1 to ensure that the images are scaled properly when creating each snapshot for the sides of the skybox. This setting can be adjusted using the Zoom Magnification slider in the Camera Settings dialog, which you can access by clicking the Camera Settings button in Terragen's main window.

Setting the Image Quality You can specify additional filter settings to improve image quality. For example, you can adjust values for atmosphere and cloud effects. To do this from Terragen's main window, click the Render Settings button. This opens the Render Settings dialog. In this dialog, you can increase the Accuracy settings for Atmosphere and Cloud Shading from the Quality tab. If you want to avoid pixelation, it is strongly recommended that you select high levels of accuracy for Atmosphere and Cloud Shading.

Setting the Detail Level If you want to ensure that your images are rendered with minimal pixelation, you must set the Detail slider on Terragen's main window to full strength. Leaving the slider at a lower setting reduces the image-generation time, but the pixelation is noticeably worse; this problem will be magnified when the image is used for the skybox. Figure 10-4 shows Terragen's main window with the Detail setting at full strength.

Setting the Camera and Target Positions While working in the main window of your Terragen project, it is possible to specify the position of the camera and the target position viewed by the camera. You can experiment with these settings if you choose. The settings used while creating the skybox images for this chapter are summarized in Table 10-1. If you are new to Terragen, we recommend that you try these settings; they will allow you to create a skybox similar to the one shown in Figure 10-1. These settings are also visible in Terragen's Rendering Control dialog (see Figure 10-4).

TABLE 10-1

Setting	*X*	*Y*	*Z*
Camera Position	*4200.m*	*4400.m*	*65.4m*
Fixed Height Above Surface		*Yes*	*65.4m*
Target Position	*4200.m*	*7935.7m*	*65.4m*
Fixed Height Above Surface	*Yes*		*0.0m*

Camera Position and Target Position Settings

Checking the Land and Sky Options Select the Land and Sky options in Terragen's main window to generate ground and cloudscapes for your scenery.

Creating Each Image: Assigning Head, Pitch, and Bank Properties

If you followed the instructions in the previous section, your global settings for the Terragen project will be set. Each individual image, in the skybox, will have specific settings that generate a unique picture that fits with the other images that make the skybox.

Setting Up Each Snapshot When all of your images are assembled in the box, the edges of each picture must match up with the edges of the neighboring picture. To achieve a perfect set of matching images, you must give the camera a carefully planned and unique angle for each snapshot. Terragen refers to these camera direction settings as `Head`, `Pitch`, and `Bank` attributes. These attributes set direction on the X, Y, and Z planes. Later in this chapter, a code example shows you how to load and display Terragen images in your game project. For the code example to work properly, you must generate the named image files and their corresponding `Head`, `Pitch`, and `Bank` properties with the settings summarized in Table 10-2.

Rendering and Saving Each Image To create each image from Terragen's main window, enter the Head, Pitch, and Bank settings and then click Render Image. A bitmap appears in the resulting Image dialog. You can then save the image by clicking the Save button in the top-left corner of the Image dialog.

After completing the steps for creating each image, you should have a directory that contains your brand new front.bmp, back.bmp, left.bmp, right.bmp, sky.bmp,

TABLE 10-2

Image Name	**Camera Orientation**		
	`Head`	`Pitch`	`Bank`
front.bmp	*0*	*0*	*0*
left.bmp	*90*	*0*	*0*
back.bmp	*180*	*0*	*0*
right.bmp	*–90*	*0*	*0*
sky.bmp	*–90*	*90*	*0*
ground2.bmp	*–90*	*–90*	*0*

Camera Direction Settings for Each Image of the Skybox

and ground2.bmp images. You can now load these into your game project and create the skybox.

Skybox Code Example This example takes your new images and renders them to create a seamless sky with an endless horizon. For this example, you can use either the MGHWinBaseCode project or the MGH360BaseCode project from the book's download.

Once the base project is ready, you will need to load the images you created with Terragen. To add the images to your project, copy them into the Images directory under the Content node that already exists in your project. Next, click the Show All Files button in the Solution Explorer, select the new images that appear under the Images folder, and then right-click and choose Include in Project. When you are done, you will see all of your skybox images referenced under the Images folder in the Solution Explorer.

Now that your images are referenced in your game project; the next step is to declare variables for storing them. These must be declared at the top of your game class.

```
Texture2D    frontTexture, backTexture,  groundTexture,
             leftTexture,  rightTexture, skyTexture;
```

To assign these images at startup, place the image-loading code inside the `LoadContent()` method:

```
frontTexture    = Content.Load<Texture2D>("Images\\front");
backTexture     = Content.Load<Texture2D>("Images\\back");
leftTexture     = Content.Load<Texture2D>("Images\\left");
rightTexture    = Content.Load<Texture2D>("Images\\right");
groundTexture   = Content.Load<Texture2D>("Images\\ground2");
skyTexture      = Content.Load<Texture2D>("Images\\sky");
```

Textured ground already exists in the base project. It is currently tiled ten times, but the skybox ground texture is not designed for tiling. Inside `InitializeGround()`, all uv.X or uv.Y values set to 10.0f must be replaced with code that sets them to 1.0f to ensure that the texture is mapped to the ground surface on a one-to-one basis. Also, to replace the existing image with the ground2.bmp image from Terragen, in step 4 of `DrawGround()` (marked by the comments in the code), replace the instruction that sets the texture using *`grassTexture`* with an instruction to use the *`groundTexture`* image:

```
textureEffectImage.SetValue(groundTexture);
```

If you try the program now, you will see the same 3D world, but this time the ground will be covered with the texture you created in Terragen.

Once the ground is properly rendered with the texture, the surrounding walls and ceiling of the skybox can be added. By design, the edges of the skybox surround the outer perimeter of the world, so the skybox walls must be bigger than the world walls. A class-level definition for the skybox panel size must be proportionately larger than the world boundary size:

```
private const float          EDGE = BOUNDARY * 2.0f;
```

A set of vertices is required to store the vertex position, texture, and color information for a rectangle that can be used to make each surface of the skybox. This same surface can be redrawn using a different set of rotations and translations to create each panel of the skybox as long as the appropriate texture is used each time it is drawn. Because only one rectangular surface is required to draw all sides of the skybox, the vertex array only needs to be declared with room for four sets of coordinates:

```
private VertexPositionColorTexture[] skyVertices = new
VertexPositionColorTexture[4];
```

The `InitializeSkybox()` method contains the necessary code to set up the vertices that can be used to render a skybox panel. As mentioned earlier, the same four vertices are used to draw each panel. Remember that the length of the panels must be greater than the length of the world size. The module-level definition, EDGE, is used to set the X and Z values of each vertex to ensure that the panels are large enough to surround the perimeter of the 3D world.

Each time these coordinates are used to draw a panel, they must be rotated and translated into position. Notice how the rectangle's X, Y, and Z coordinates are centered about the origin where X=0, Y=0, and Z=0. This enables easier rendering.

Note that the UV coordinates that enable texture mapping are between 0.003f and 0.997f. This shortened range from the usual 0.0f to 1.0f setting removes the white seam that outlines each bitmap. The UV offset of 0.003f preserves the illusion of the skybox.

```
private void InitializeSkybox(){
    Vector3 pos    = Vector3.Zero;
    Vector2 uv     = Vector2.Zero;
    Color   color  = Color.White;

    const float MAX=0.997f; // offset to remove white seam at image edge
    const float MIN=0.003f; // offset to remove white seam at image edge
```

```
    // set position, image, and color data for each vertex in rectangle
    pos.X=+EDGE; pos.Y=-EDGE;        uv.X=MIN; uv.Y=MAX; //Bottom R
    skyVertices[0]=new VertexPositionColorTexture(pos, color, uv);

    pos.X=+EDGE; pos.Y=+EDGE;        uv.X=MIN; uv.Y=MIN; //Top R
    skyVertices[1]=new VertexPositionColorTexture(pos, color, uv);

    pos.X=-EDGE; pos.Y=-EDGE;        uv.X=MAX; uv.Y=MAX; //Bottom L
    skyVertices[2]=new VertexPositionColorTexture(pos, color, uv);

    pos.X=-EDGE; pos.Y=+EDGE;        uv.X=MAX; uv.Y=MIN; //Top L
    skyVertices[3]=new VertexPositionColorTexture(pos, color, uv);
}
```

To be sure the skybox is initialized only once, add the call statement to the `Initialize()` method:

```
InitializeSkybox();
```

To draw each panel of the skybox, you must add the `DrawSkybox()` method to the game class. This method is designed to iterate through all five moving panels of the skybox, transform each panel into place, and render it with the correct texture. Step 1 declares a set of matrices and initializes each matrix with a default value. In step 2, the transformations are assigned so that the sides and the ceiling of the skybox are drawn where they belong. Also in step 2, the corresponding texture for each panel is set. In step 3, the I.S.R.O.T. sequence is used to calculate the cumulative transformation. Of course, this order of transformations is crucial and cannot change. The last extra translation, `camTranslation`, translates the skybox panels so that they move with the camera and give the illusion of an unreachable horizon.

```
private void DrawSkybox(){
    const float DROP = -1.2f;

    // 1: declare matrices and set defaults
    Matrix world;
    Matrix rotationY     = Matrix.CreateRotationY(0.0f);
    Matrix rotationX     = Matrix.CreateRotationX(0.0f);
    Matrix translation   = Matrix.CreateTranslation(0.0f, 0.0f, 0.0f);
    Matrix camTranslation    // move skybox with camera
    = Matrix.CreateTranslation(cam.position.X, 0.0f, cam.position.Z);

    // 2: set transformations and also texture for each wall
```

```
    for (int i = 0; i < 5; i++){
        switch (i){
        case 0: // BACK
            translation = Matrix.CreateTranslation(0.0f, DROP, EDGE);
            textureEffectImage.SetValue(backTexture); break;
        case 1: // RIGHT
            translation = Matrix.CreateTranslation(-EDGE, DROP, 0.0f);
            rotationY   = Matrix.CreateRotationY(-(float)Math.PI/2.0f);
            textureEffectImage.SetValue(rightTexture); break;
        case 2: // FRONT
            translation = Matrix.CreateTranslation(0.0f, DROP, -EDGE);
            rotationY   = Matrix.CreateRotationY((float)Math.PI);
            textureEffectImage.SetValue(frontTexture); break;
        case 3: // LEFT
            translation = Matrix.CreateTranslation(EDGE, DROP, 0.0f);
            rotationY   = Matrix.CreateRotationY((float)Math.PI/2.0f);
            textureEffectImage.SetValue(leftTexture); break;
        case 4: // SKY
            translation = Matrix.CreateTranslation(0.0f,EDGE+DROP, 0.0f);
            rotationX   = Matrix.CreateRotationX(-(float)Math.PI/2.0f);
            rotationY   =
                       Matrix.CreateRotationY(3.0f*MathHelper.Pi/2.0f);
            textureEffectImage.SetValue(skyTexture); break;
        }
        // 3: build cumulative world matrix using I.S.R.O.T. sequence
        world = rotationX * rotationY * translation * camTranslation;

        // 4: set shader variables
        textureEffectWVP.SetValue(world * cam.viewMatrix
                                        * cam.projectionMatrix);

        // 5: draw object - primitive type, vertices, # primitives
        TextureShader(PrimitiveType.TriangleStrip, skyVertices, 2);
    }
}
```

To trigger the code to draw the skybox from the `Draw()` method, add this instruction:

```
DrawSkybox();
```

When you run this project, your majestic skybox will surround your world. As you move, you discover that you can never reach the horizon.

However, this example is not yet complete. You may have discovered that you can travel over the edge of the ground and see the bottom of the skybox—this spoils the illusion. To fix this problem, Chapter 18 shows how to add collision detection just inside the outer edges of your world to prevent players from reaching the world's edge where they can see the bottom of your skybox.

Note that there is another common method for building a skybox, which involves creating a model of the top half of a sphere and mapping a sky texture to it. However, there are some advantages to using Terragen. Terragen generates the images for you and also has the ability to create terrain to match your sky and horizon. The creation of terrain with height detection will be explained in Chapter 27.

Whether you use Terragen or a 3D model, coding a skybox is easy, and it will go a long way towards fully immersing your players in the game.

CHAPTER 10 REVIEW EXERCISES

To get the most from this chapter, try out these chapter review exercises.

1. Create your own skybox by following the steps outlined in this chapter.
2. In your code solution from Exercise 1, change the `min` and `max` declarations so that the range falls between 0.0f and 1.0f. Then run the project and look at the seams around the bitmaps. Notice how the original offset prevents the white seam from appearing.

CHAPTER 11

Index Buffers

ON the surface, a chapter dedicated to building an indexed grid of vertices might not seem very exciting, but once you see this code used in future chapters, you'll change your mind. The index buffer is a powerful and efficient structure for referencing large amounts of vertex data. The index buffers in conjunction with vertex buffers also enable dynamic updates to position, texture, color, and surface normal data. Together, these two functions enable great effects such as water and hilly terrain. Remember what water looked like in *Frogger*? Now, think of what water looks like in *Halo 3*. Which do you prefer? If water ripples do not interest you, how about terrain that isn't flat, or beautifully lit surfaces that use per-vertex lighting? These are the sort of effects you can create with index buffers.

INDEX BUFFERS

If you rendered a surface or polygon with a large set of data to construct a series of line or triangle strips, you would run into a problem. Using the methods you have applied until now, you would find that much of the vertex data needs to be stored twice. The diagram on the left in Figure 11-1 shows how non-indexed vertices are duplicated when drawing a line strip. In this case, multiple rows of data are used to create a rectangular surface. The diagram on the right in Figure 11-1 shows how indexing reduces storage requirements because each vertex only needs to be stored once. This memory saving amounts to a substantial performance improvement and allows you to use far more interesting effects in your games.

FIGURE 11-1

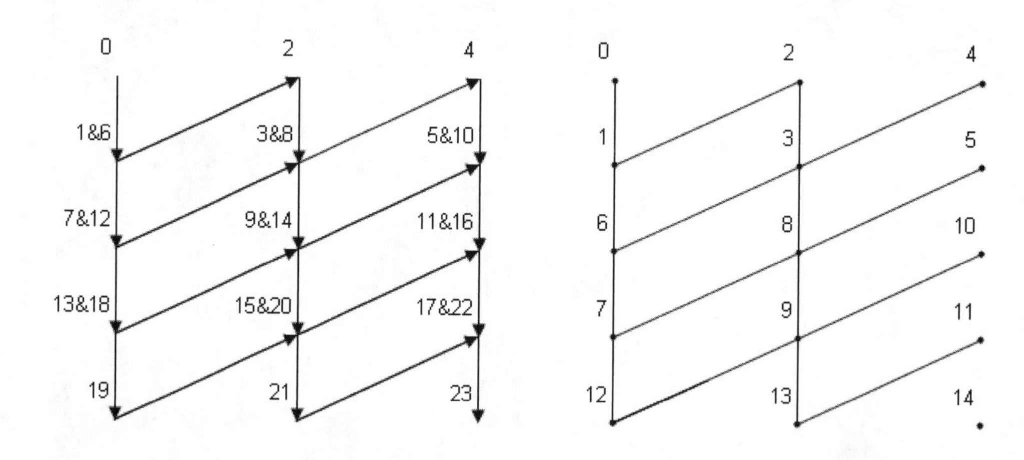

Total vertices stored for non-indexed data (left) versus indexed data (right)

All indexed vertices in the vertex buffer must be stored in a sequence that enables proper rendering of the 3D object being drawn. The sequence must be arranged so that several subsets of vertices can be used for drawing in succession to render the complete surface. When the index buffer is declared, it is sized to store one subset of vertices. The vertices are referenced using a short array:

```
short[] indexArray = new short[int subsetVertexCount];
```

In Figure 11-2, indices for a subset of six vertices are stored in a short array. Later, while the surface is being rendered, the index reference will be applied four times to reference four subsets of six vertices to build the rectangle.

The index buffer is declared using the `IndexBuffer` class. Here is the syntax:

```
IndexBuffer indexBuffer = new IndexBuffer(
                              GraphicsDevice  graphicsDevice,
                              Type            indexType,
                              int             elementCount,
                              BufferUsage     usage);
```

The `graphicsDevice` and `elementCount` parameters are self-explanatory. `indexType` is the data type used for values that are stored. `BufferUsage` specifies how the buffer memory is to be allocated. The available `BufferUsage` options are `None` as the default, `WriteOnly` for efficient writing and rendering, and `Points` for point sprites. The `Points` option will be covered in Chapter 20.

FIGURE 11-2

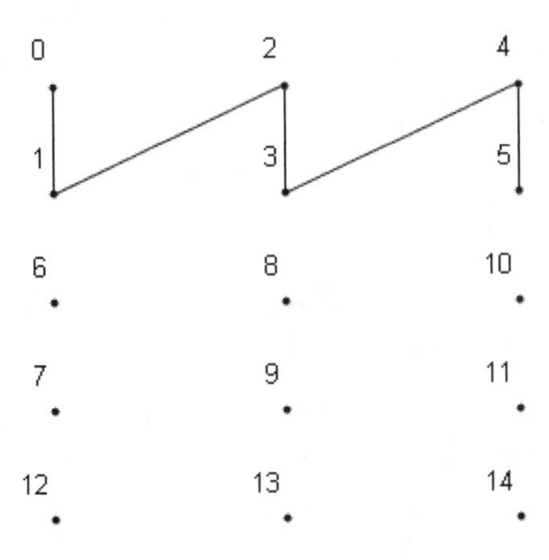

The index buffer is designed to reference two rows of data in the grid at a time while drawing.

Once the indices have been defined, the `SetData()` method stores the index references in the index buffer. There are several overrides for this method, but for our needs, all you have to do is pass in the array of indices:

```
SetData<T>(T[] data);
```

Managing Vertex Data with Index Buffers and Vertex Buffers

By themselves, the `VertexPositionColor`, `VertexPositionColorTexture`, `VertexPositionTexture`, and `VertexPositionNormalTexture` objects that you have used will not permit live updates to the position, color, texture, and normal data. `DynamicVertexBuffer` objects in combination with index buffers, on the other hand, will permit updates to large amounts of vertex data. You are going to want a structure like this when creating an effect such as water.

When initialized, the constructor for the vertex buffer takes parameters for the current graphics device, vertex type, element count, and buffer usage for memory allocation:

```
VertexBuffer(   GraphicsDevice        graphicsDevice,
                Type                  vertexType,
                int                   elementCount,
                BufferUsage           usage);
```

As explained above, `BufferUsage` options are `None` as the default, `WriteOnly` for efficient writes to memory and for efficient drawing, and `Points` for point sprites.

After the vertex data is loaded into an array, the vertex data is moved into the vertex buffer with the `VertexBuffer` object's `SetData()` method. There are several variations of this method. The method used here only passes the array of vertices:

```
SetData(VertexBuffer[] vertexBuffer)
```

Rendering Vertex Buffers with an Index Buffer Reference

The draw method you use for dynamic vertex buffers—using index buffers—differs in three ways from the draw methods you have used until now:

1. The `SetSource()` method is used to set the vertex buffer that stores the grid, the starting element, and the size of the vertex type in bytes:

```
graphics.GraphicsDevice.Vertices[0].SetSource(
    VertexBuffer     vertexBuffer,
    int              startingElement,
    int              sizeOfVertex
);
```

2. The GraphicsDevice's Indices object is set with the corresponding IndexBuffer object you defined during the program setup:

```
graphics.GraphicsDevice.Indices = indexBuffer;
```

3. The DrawIndexedPrimitives() method is used to reference a series of vertex subsets that are rendered in succession to draw the entire polygon or surface. DrawIndexedPrimitives() is called for each vertex subset.

```
graphics.GraphicsDevice.DrawIndexedPrimitives(
        PrimitiveType   primitiveType,
        int             startingPointInVertexBuffer,
        int             minimumVerticesInBuffer,
        int             totalVerticesInBuffer,
        int             indexBufferStartingPoint,
        int             indexBufferEndPoint);
```

Grid Using Index Buffer Example

This code will implement an index buffer and dynamic vertex buffer to draw a rectangle from a set of vertices that is three vertices wide and five vertices long (see Figure 11-3). Drawing a rectangle with a set of vertices that uses index buffers might seem like a lackluster chore, but don't be fooled. Index buffers have grit. This little example serves as the foundation for creating water waves in Chapter 12, creating terrain with height detection in Chapter 25, and enabling better lighting across primitive surfaces in Chapter 22.

This example begins with either the MGHWinBaseCode or MGH360BaseCode project in the BaseCode folder on this book's website.

FIGURE 11-3

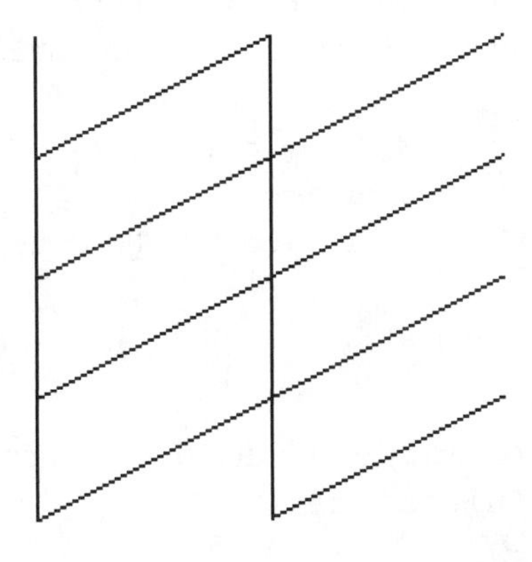

Grid rendered from an index buffer

To make this vertex reference system work, an index buffer to reference a grid of vertices is required. Also, a vertex buffer object is needed to store the vertices. A vertex declaration type is used to set up the buffer when it is being initialized. Add these object declarations to the top of your game class:

```
private IndexBuffer  indexBuffer;   // reference vertices
private VertexBuffer vertexBuffer;  // vertex storage
```

The rows and columns used to draw the rectangle will be referenced with identifiers to help explain how the vertices are arranged. Add these identifiers to the top of the game class.

```
const   int     NUM_COLS = 3;
const   int     NUM_ROWS = 5;
```

Indices for referencing the vertex buffer are initialized when the program begins. The index buffer array is sized to store the total number of vertices contained in one subset of the vertex buffer. The code that you need to set up the index reference is contained in the `InitializeIndices()` method. Add this method to set up your index reference:

```
private void InitializeIndices(){
    short[]     indices;                        // indices for 1 subset
    indices     = new short[2 * NUM_COLS];      // sized for 1 subset
    indexBuffer = new IndexBuffer(
                        graphics.GraphicsDevice,// graphics device
                        typeof(short),          // data type is short
                        indices.Length,         // array size in bytes
                        BufferUsage.WriteOnly); // memory allocation

    // store indices for one subset of vertices
    // see Figure 11-2 for the first subset of indices
    int counter = 0;
    for (int col = 0; col < NUM_COLS; col++){
        indices[counter++] = (short)col;
        indices[counter++] = (short)(col + NUM_COLS);
    }
    indexBuffer.SetData(indices);               // store in index buffer
}
```

To initialize the short array and index buffer when the program begins, add the call statement to the `Initialize()` method:

```
InitializeIndices();
```

A `VertexBuffer` object is initialized to store the vertices used to build the primitive surface. The `VertexBuffer` object in this example is static and only stores the vertices that are used to draw the grid or surface. Still, the vertex buffer works in conjunction with the index buffer as a reference to reduce the total number of vertices that build the grid or surface. This type of static vertex buffer is especially useful for drawing lit objects or even terrain where many vertices are needed for detail. When setting up a vertex buffer, the vertex data is generated and is stored in a temporary array. Once all of the vertex values have been assembled, the vertex data is then stored in the vertex buffer using the `SetData()` method. To set up your vertices in this efficient buffer, add `InitializeVertexBuffer()` to your game class:

```
private void InitializeVertexBuffer(){
    vertexBuffer = new VertexBuffer(
                   graphics.GraphicsDevice,          // graphics device
                   typeof(VertexPositionColorTexture), // vertex type
                   NUM_COLS * NUM_ROWS,              // element count
                   BufferUsage.WriteOnly);           // memory use

    // store vertices temporarily while initializing them
    VertexPositionColorTexture[] vertex
                    = new VertexPositionColorTexture[NUM_ROWS*NUM_COLS];

    // set grid width and height
    float colWidth  = (float)2 * BOUNDARY/(NUM_COLS - 1);
    float rowHeight = (float)2 * BOUNDARY/(NUM_ROWS - 1);

    // set position, color, and texture coordinates
    for (int row=0; row < NUM_ROWS; row++){
        for (int col=0; col < NUM_COLS; col++){
            // set X, Y, Z
            float X      = -BOUNDARY + col * colWidth;
            float Y      = 0.0f;
            float Z      = -BOUNDARY + row * rowHeight;
            vertex[col + row * NUM_COLS].Position = new Vector3(X, Y, Z);

            // set color
            vertex[col + row * NUM_COLS].Color = Color.White;

            // set UV coordinates to map texture 1:1
            float U      = (float)col/(float)(NUM_COLS - 1);
            float V      = (float)row/(float)(NUM_ROWS - 1);
            vertex[col + row * NUM_COLS].TextureCoordinate
```

```
                = new Vector2(U, V);
            }
        }
        // commit data to vertex buffer
        vertexBuffer.SetData(vertex);
    }
```

The vertices must be set when the program begins, so add a call to initialize the grid vertices in the `Initialize()` method:

```
InitializeVertexBuffer();
```

When a dynamic vertex buffer is being rendered, the `SetSource()` method reads data from the vertex buffer that was initialized earlier. The vertex format is passed into the `SetSource()` method, so the `GraphicsDevice` knows how to extract the data, and the `GraphicsDevice`'s `Indices` property is assigned the index buffer. Finally, `DrawIndexedPrimitives()` is executed once for each subset of strips in the grid. Add `DrawIndexedGrid()` to the games class:

```
private void DrawIndexedGrid(){
    // 1: declare matrices
    Matrix world, translation;

    // 2: initialize matrices
    translation = Matrix.CreateTranslation(0.0f, -0.5f, 0.0f);

    // 3: build cumulative world matrix using I.S.R.O.T. sequence
    world       = translation;

    // 4: set shader parameters
    textureEffectWVP.SetValue(world*cam.viewMatrix*cam.projectionMatrix);
    textureEffectImage.SetValue(grassTexture);

    // 5: draw object - select vertex type, vertex source, and indices
    graphics.GraphicsDevice.VertexDeclaration = positionColorTexture;
    graphics.GraphicsDevice.Vertices[0].SetSource(vertexBuffer, 0,
                            VertexPositionColorTexture.SizeInBytes);
    graphics.GraphicsDevice.Indices           = indexBuffer;

    // start using Texture.fx
    textureEffect.Begin();
    textureEffect.Techniques[0].Passes[0].Begin();
```

```
    // draw grid one row at a time
    for (int Z = 0; Z < NUM_ROWS - 1; Z++){
        graphics.GraphicsDevice.DrawIndexedPrimitives(
            PrimitiveType.LineStrip, // primitive
            Z * NUM_COLS,            // start point in buffer for drawing
            0,                       // minimum vertices in vertex buffer
            NUM_COLS * NUM_ROWS,     // total vertices in buffer
            0,                       // start point in index buffer
            2 * (NUM_COLS - 1));     // end point in index buffer
    }
    // stop using Texture.fx
    textureEffect.Techniques[0].Passes[0].End();
    textureEffect.End();
}
```

To draw the grid, call `DrawIndexedGrid()` from the `Draw()` method:

```
DrawIndexedGrid();
```

Also, to see the grid when it renders, you will need to comment out the instruction to `DrawGround()`.

When you run the program, the grid appears as shown earlier in Figure 11-3. However, if the grid is drawn with triangle strips, the output will fill in the area between the vertices and display a rectangle. This will happen if you change `LineStrip` to `TriangleStrip` in `DrawIndexedGrid()`.

Bystanders might not be impressed that you just created a rectangular surface, but don't let that bother you. Let's put this demo on the backburner for now. We'll return to it in later chapters to let it rip.

CHAPTER 11 REVIEW EXERCISES

To get the most from this chapter, try out these chapter review exercises.

1. Try the step-by-step example in this chapter, but this time change the number of rows to 125 and the number of columns to 55. View the project using line strips and triangle strips.
2. Compared to methods that are used in previous chapters for storing vertices without an index reference, how many vertices are saved when using an index buffer to draw a grid that is 60 rows high and 35 rows wide?

3. The example presented in this chapter shows how to use a static `VertexBuffer` object with index buffers. What is the advantage of doing this? What type of vertex buffer permits updates to vertices at run time?
4. List three ways that the `DrawIndexedPrimitives()` method is different from the `DrawUserPrimitives()` method.

CHAPTER 12

Combining Images for Better Visual Effects

THIS chapter demonstrates various ways of combining images to generate compelling visual effects; more specifically, sprites and multitexturing will be discussed. By the end of the chapter, you will be able to use image files that store more than one image frame to create cool heads-up display (HUD) animations in your 2D or 3D games. You will also be able to blend two textures together to generate intricate detail for effects such as terrain or a water simulation. Although games are not defined solely by their aesthetics, no one has ever complained that a game's graphics looked too good. Your players will appreciate any effort you put into maximizing your visual effects.

SPRITES

As discussed in Chapter 4, a *sprite* is an animated 2D image. You can animate sprites by moving them in the window. Also, if your sprite has more than one frame, you can swap frames to animate them.

Image Frame Swapping for 2D Animations

Image frame swapping creates an animation similar to old-style page-flipping animations used to create simple cartoons. The sprite is animated at run time by adjusting the texture's UV coordinates at fixed time intervals. Sprites store multiple image frames because adjusting UV coordinates at run time—to switch image frames—is faster than switching to a different image file.

For 3D games, a 2D sprite offers a very simple way to customize and animate the heads-up display, or a game dashboard. This type of sprite could be used to create an animated radar scope on the console of a flight simulation game.

SpriteBatch

For the 2D effect, a sprite object is created with the `SpriteBatch` class:

```
SpriteBatch spriteBatch = new SpriteBatch(GraphicsDevice);
```

A `SpriteBatch` object is actually already included in the XNA template project code that is generated using the New Project dialog box. For our purposes this is the only one you will need.

Primitive objects are not needed to display the image when using `SpriteBatch` methods. As a result, setting up the sprite is easier than setting up textured primitive surfaces; the `SpriteBatch` object draws the image on its own. For the 2D object, all drawing is done between the `SpriteBatch` object's `Begin()` and `End()` methods.

The syntax for the `Draw()` method is designed for drawing on a 2D window. The first parameter references the `Texture2D` object that stores the image file; the second parameter references the position, height, and width of a rectangle in the 2D window; and the third parameter references the starting pixel's X and Y position in the image and the height and width—in pixels—to be drawn. The fourth parameter sets the color of the sprite in case you want to shade it differently from the colors already in the image.

Be aware that there are several other overrides for `SpriteBatch.Draw()`; however, this is the one that we'll be using for our examples:

```
SpriteBatch.Draw(
    // Texture2D object
    Texture2D texture,
    // window
    new Rectangle(
        int topLeftXWindowCoord,
        int tpLeftYWindowCoord,
        int displayWidthInPixels,
        int displayHeightInPixels),
    // image source
    new Rectangle(
        int startingXPixel,
        int startingYPixel,
        int pixelWidthDrawn,
        int pixelHeightDrawn),
    // color
    Color   Color.ColorType);
```

The rendering for a `SpriteBatch` object is still triggered from the `Draw()` method.

Restoring 3D Drawing Settings After Drawing with a SpriteBatch

If your 3D game uses 2D sprites, you need to be aware of how this will impact your drawing routines. The 2D `SpriteBatch` automatically resets the `GraphicsDevice`'s render states to draw 2D graphics in the window. While this is helpful, if the settings are not restored to enable 3D rendering, you may not see your 3D graphics—and if you do, they may not display properly. Ideally, when rendering your `SpriteBatch` objects, you should draw them last in the `Draw()` method so that they layer on top of the 3D graphics.

Your graphics device states should be reset to turn off transparency and to re-enable 3D graphics after drawing with the SpriteBatch. You must also reset the culling option back to the default used by your game. Culling designates the face of an object that is not drawn, so it should be the face that is not visible to the user. Culling options include CullClockwiseFace, CullCounterClockwiseFace, and None. The base code uses CullMode.None to prevent your surfaces from disappearing just in case you mistakenly arrange your vertices in the same order as your culling option. However, for performance gains, you definitely will want to cull nonvisible sides of your surfaces when you are rendering large groups of vertices, so be aware that you have this option.

The following code for resetting the state belongs in the Draw() method right after you draw with SpriteBatch:

```
graphics.GraphicsDevice.RenderState.CullMode = CullMode.None; // no cull
graphics.RenderState.DepthBufferEnable = true;          // enable 3D on Z
graphics.RenderState.AlphaBlendEnable  = false;         // end transparent
graphics.RenderState.AlphaTestEnable   = false;         // per pixel test
                                                        // enable tiling
graphics.SamplerStates[0].AddressU     = TextureAddressMode.Wrap;
graphics.SamplerStates[0].AddressV     = TextureAddressMode.Wrap;
```

Instead of manually resetting the render states, you can add SaveStateMode.SaveState as a parameter for the SpriteBatch object's Begin() instruction when drawing it. This will restore the render states back to their original settings before the sprite is drawn. It's important to note that this saves and restores all the render states, so it's more costly than restoring the render states by hand:

```
spriteBatch.Begin(SpriteBlendMode.AlphaBlend,
                  SpriteSortMode.Immediate,SaveStateMode.SaveState);
```

Rendering Sprites Within the Title Safe Region of the Window

When running games on the Xbox 360, some televisions will only show 80 percent of the game window. The PC shows 100 percent of the window, so some adjustments may be needed to account for this platform difference. Here is a routine that returns the bottom-left pixel in the window for drawing a SpriteBatch object so that it is positioned properly in the visible region of the window regardless of where the project runs:

```
Rectangle TitleSafeRegion(Texture2D texture, int numFrames){
    int windowWidth          = Window.ClientBounds.Width;
    int windowHeight         = Window.ClientBounds.Height;

    // some televisions only show 80% of the window
    const float UNSAFEAREA   = 0.2f;
    const float MARGIN       = UNSAFEAREA / 2.0f;

    // return bounding margins
    int top, left, height, width;
    left    = (int)(windowWidth * MARGIN);
    top     = (int)(windowHeight * MARGIN);
    width   = (int)((1.0f - UNSAFEAREA) * windowWidth - texture.Width);
    height  = (int)((1.0f - UNSAFEAREA) * windowHeight
            - texture.Height/numFrames);
    return new Rectangle(left, top, width, height);}
```

IMAGE FRAME ANIMATIONS

The `SpriteBatch` class is limited to drawing images that are flat. To perform image frame swapping inside the 3D world, you must use textured primitives without the `SpriteBatch` class to animate your textures. Animating textures through image frame swapping is useful for effects such as flashing signs and blinking lights inside your world. When a sprite is drawn in a 3D environment, the image frames are swapped at regular intervals by adjusting the UV coordinates.

Sprite on the Heads-Up-Display Example

This example animates a two-frame sprite. In this example, the `SpriteBatch` class is used to swap frames within the image so that it appears in the 2D game window as a blinking light. Figure 12-1 shows the sprite image on the right and the warning light animation on the left. The two images on the left will be swapped at each interval. To the gamer, the light appears to blink on and off every 0.5 seconds.

This example begins with either the MGHWinBaseCode project or the MGH360BaseCode project found in the BaseCode folder on this book's website. A `Texture2D` object is used to load and reference the image. To try this example, first add this declaration to the top of the game class:

```
private Texture2D                         spriteTexture;
```

FIGURE 12-1

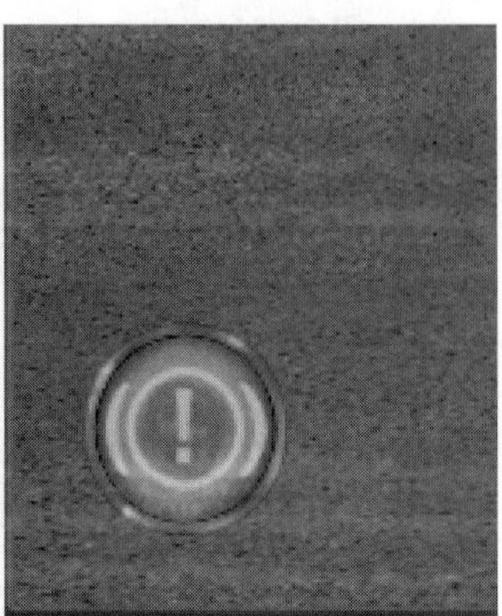

An animated sprite in the game window

A timer is used to trigger the frame change for the sprite, which creates the blinking light animation. To implement the timer, class-level declarations are required to store the frame number (frameNum), the time spent in the current timer interval (intervalTime), and the time lapse since the last interval (previousIntervalTime):

```
int            frameNum             = 1;
private double intervalTime         = 0; // time in current interval
private double previousIntervalTime = 0; // interval time at last frame
```

Next, the Timer() method is added to the methods section to check for the completion of each 0.5-second interval. The Timer() method calculates the remainder of the amount of time since the interval started, divided by 500 milliseconds. When the remainder has increased compared to the remainder calculated for the previous frame, the interval is incomplete. When the remainder has decreased since the previous frame, a new interval has been entered, and the Timer() method returns a positive result. The positive result triggers a frame swap for the sprite. Checking the remainders in this manner prevents the variable from growing beyond the variable's storage capacity, because it is reset every interval. Even though the remainder is usually positive when a new interval is detected, the overshot from the interval start is miniscule, and tracking the remainder makes this algorithm self-correcting. In this manner, the Timer() implements animations that appear to be synchronized with real time:

```
bool Timer(GameTime gameTime){
    bool resetInterval = false;

    // add time lapse between frames and keep value between 0 & 500 ms
    intervalTime += (double)gameTime.ElapsedGameTime.Milliseconds;
    intervalTime  = intervalTime % 500;

    // intervalTime has been reset so a new interval has started
    if (intervalTime < previousIntervalTime)
        resetInterval = true;

    previousIntervalTime = intervalTime;
    return resetInterval;
}
```

The warninglight.png file is also loaded by code into the `Texture2D` object in the `LoadContent()` method. The warninglight.png file can be obtained from the Images folder on this book's website. The image needs to be added to the Images folder in your project so it can be loaded by the content pipeline. To reference this in your project, right-click the Images folder in the Solution Explorer, choose Add, and then select Existing Item. A dialog will appear that allows you to navigate to the image and select it. Once the warninglight.png file is selected, it will appear in your project within the Solution Explorer, and you can then load it with the following instruction:

```
spriteTexture = Content.Load<Texture2D>("Images\\warninglight");
```

To ensure that the sprite is positioned properly in the game window, add the routine that was discussed earlier to retrieve the starting pixel for drawing in the window:

```
Rectangle TitleSafeRegion(Texture2D texture, int numFrames){
    int windowWidth         = Window.ClientBounds.Width;
    int windowHeight        = Window.ClientBounds.Height;

    // some televisions only show 80% of the window
    const float UNSAFEAREA  = 0.2f;
    const float MARGIN      = UNSAFEAREA / 2.0f;

    // return bounding margins
    int top, left, height, width;
    left    = (int)(windowWidth * MARGIN);
    top     = (int)(windowHeight * MARGIN);
```

```
    width   = (int)((1.0f - UNSAFEAREA) * windowWidth - texture.Width);
    height  = (int)((1.0f - UNSAFEAREA) * windowHeight
            - texture.Height/numFrames);
    return new Rectangle(left, top, width, height);
}
```

The next method to add is `DrawAnimatedHud()`. `DrawAnimatedHud()` checks the timer to see if the set interval has completed. If the timer returns a `true` value—indicating that it just ticked into a new interval—the frame in the image is incremented or reset. The `SpriteBatch` object calls the `Begin()` method to start the drawing. `Begin()` allows the developer to set the `SpriteBlendMode` option to specify the type of blending. This could include:

- `AlphaBlend` For removing masked pixels
- `Additive` For summing source and destination colors
- `None` For standard rendering

If you want to remove the transparent pixels, you can use `SpriteBlendMode.AlphaBlend` as a parameter in the `SpriteBatch`'s `Begin()` method. The picture in the warninglight.png file was created with a transparent background, so the pixels will not appear when the image is drawn with alpha blending.

The `SpriteBatch`'s `Draw()` method applies four parameters. The first parameter is the `gameTime` object, which is applied to ensure that the animation runs at a consistent speed. The second parameter is the X and Y position for the starting pixel where the sprite is to be drawn. A `Texture2D` object is passed as a third parameter to allow you to set the width and height of the area to be drawn. The fourth parameter is the total number of frames, which allows you to split up the image so it is drawn one section at a time. To draw the sprite so it is positioned properly in the window, add `DrawAnimatedHud()` to your project:

```
void DrawAnimatedHUD(GameTime  gameTime, Vector2 startPixel,
                     Texture2D texture,  int     numFrames){
    // get width and height of the section of the image to be drawn
    int width  = texture.Width;                 // measured in pixels
    int height = texture.Height / numFrames; // measured in pixels

    if (Timer(gameTime)){
        frameNum += 1;                          // swap image frame
        frameNum  = frameNum%numFrames;         // set to 0 after last frame
    }
    spriteBatch.Begin(SpriteBlendMode.AlphaBlend);
    spriteBatch.Draw(
```

```
        // texture drawn
        texture,

        // area of window used for drawing
        new Rectangle((int)startPixel.X, // starting X window position
                      (int)startPixel.Y, // starting Y window position
                      width, height),    // area of window used
        // area of image that is drawn
        new Rectangle(0,                 // starting X pixel in texture
                      frameNum*height,   // starting Y pixel in texture
                      width, height),    // area of image used
        // color
        Color.White);
    spriteBatch.End();
}
```

`DrawAnimatedHud()` needs to be called in the `Draw()` method, but only after instructions for the drawing of 3D objects are called. This allows the 2D sprite to overlay the 3D graphics:

```
const int NUM_FRAMES = 2;
Rectangle safeArea = TitleSafeRegion(spriteTexture, NUM_FRAMES);
Vector2 startPixel = new Vector2(safeArea.Left, safeArea.Bottom);
DrawAnimatedHUD(gameTime, startPixel, spriteTexture, NUM_FRAMES);
```

As mentioned earlier, the `SpriteBatch` object automatically adjusts the render state of the `GraphicsDevice` object to draw in 2D but does not change it back. To draw in 3D, the original settings must be reset in the `Draw()` method after the `SpriteBatch` object is drawn:

```
// A: Culling off   B: Enable 3D   C: transparency off   D: pixel testing
graphics.GraphicsDevice.RenderState.CullMode           = CullMode.None;//A
graphics.GraphicsDevice.RenderState.DepthBufferEnable = true;          //B
graphics.GraphicsDevice.RenderState.AlphaBlendEnable  = false;         //C
graphics.GraphicsDevice.RenderState.AlphaTestEnable   = false;         //D

// re-enable tiling
graphics.GraphicsDevice.SamplerStates[0].AddressU
    = TextureAddressMode.Wrap;
graphics.GraphicsDevice.SamplerStates[0].AddressV
    = TextureAddressMode.Wrap;
```

When you run the program, the light will appear as shown back in Figure 12-1.

Animated Texture Example

The previous example is useful for implementing 2D sprites in the game window. This example shows how to create a similar effect for textures used inside your 3D world. When the example is complete, a flashing "danger" sign will appear in your game. Maybe you don't need a flashing danger sign, but you need a flashing billboard on your speedway, or maybe you want to display scrolling text on one of the objects in your 3D world. An animated texture can do this. You could even use a similar effect to create a cartoon in your game.

To get these effects off the window and inside your game world, you will need to use textured primitive objects. The frames in the image are swapped by modifying the UV coordinates at the start of each interval. The fraction of the image displayed in each frame is based on the total frames stored in the image. The image used for this example has just two frames. Figure 12-2 shows the two frames of the image on the left and the animation on the right at different intervals.

This example begins with either the MGHWinBaseCode project or the MGH360BaseCode project in the BaseCode folder on this book's website. Also, the dangersign.png file must be downloaded from this book's website and referenced in your project from the Solution Explorer.

An array of four vertices will be used to render a triangle strip with a danger-sign texture. This vertex object declaration is needed at the top of the game class so the vertices can be stored, updated, and used for drawing while the game runs:

```
private VertexPositionColorTexture[] vertices
        = new VertexPositionColorTexture[4];
```

FIGURE 12-2

Two frames of an image (left) and animation (right)

The position, texture, and color data are set when the program begins. Add `InitializeAnimatedSurface()` to the game class to set up these vertices for the rectangle used to display the danger sign:

```
private void InitializeAnimatedSurface(){
    Vector2 uv  =   new Vector2(0.0f, 0.0f);
    Vector3 pos =   new Vector3(-0.5f, 1.0f, 0.0f);
    Color   col =   Color.White;

    vertices[0]=new VertexPositionColorTexture(pos,col,uv);// top left
    pos.X=-0.5f; pos.Y=0.0f; pos.Z=0.0f;      uv.X=0.0f; uv.Y=1.0f;
    vertices[1]=new VertexPositionColorTexture(pos,col,uv);// lower left
    pos.X= 0.5f; pos.Y=1.0f; pos.Z=0.0f;      uv.X=1.0f; uv.Y=0.0f;
    vertices[2]=new VertexPositionColorTexture(pos,col,uv);// top right
    pos.X= 0.5f; pos.Y=0.0f; pos.Z=0.0f;      uv.X=1.0f; uv.Y=1.0f;
    vertices[3]=new VertexPositionColorTexture(pos,col,uv);// lower right
}
```

The four vertices that are used to draw the rectangle with the danger-sign texture must be initialized when the program launches. To do this, inside `Initialize()`, add the following call to `InitializeAnimatedSurface()`:

```
InitializeAnimatedSurface();
```

Also, a `Texture2D` object is required to store the texture, so a declaration for `signTexture` needs to be in the module declarations area of the game class:

```
private Texture2D signTexture;
```

The dangersign.png file (shown in Figure 12-2) must be read into memory when the program begins. To do this, add a statement to load the image in the `LoadContent()` method:

```
signTexture = Content.Load<Texture2D>("Images\\dangersign");
```

The texture's frame must alternate every 500 milliseconds, so a timer is used to track when these intervals are completed. To assist with setting up the timer and swapping texture frames, module-level declarations are used to store the current frame number as well as the times of the current and previous frame:

```
private double  intervalTime          = 0;
private double  previousIntervalTime  = 0;
```

The timer code used for this example follows the same algorithm used in the previous example. This time, it will set the interval used to display each section of the image. Add `Timer()` to enable frame swapping every 500 milliseconds:

```
bool Timer(GameTime gameTime){
    bool resetInterval = false;

    // add time lapse between frames and keep value between 0 & 500 ms
    intervalTime += (double)gameTime.ElapsedGameTime.Milliseconds;
    intervalTime  = intervalTime % 500;

    // intervalTime has been reset so a new interval has started
    if (intervalTime < previousIntervalTime)
        resetInterval = true;

    previousIntervalTime = intervalTime;
    return resetInterval;
}
```

When animating textures, you must update the UV coordinates to switch frames. The current frame is tracked with the variable *frameNum*, which is declared at the top of the game class:

```
int frameNum = 0;
```

Since the texture frames are arranged vertically in this example, when the timer signals the completion of an interval, the V coordinate for each vertex is adjusted to switch frames. `UpdateTextureUV()` requires three parameters to implement this routine. A `GameTime` argument controls the speed of the animation. A `Texture2D` parameter provides height and width properties for the image file that is referenced. Lastly, the number of frames is passed so the image can be properly sectioned into separate frames. Adding `UpdateTextureUV()` to your game class provides the routine needed to swap the frames of your image at regular intervals. This swapping creates the animation effect:

```
void UpdateTextureUV(GameTime gameTime,Texture2D texture,int numFrames){
    int width       = texture.Width;     // image width in pixels
    int height      = texture.Height;    // image height in pixels
    int frameHeight = height/numFrames;  // height of image section drawn

    if (Timer(gameTime)){
        frameNum += 1;                     // swap image frame
        frameNum  = frameNum % numFrames; // set to zero after last frame
    }
```

```
    float U, V; // update UV coordinats
    // top left
    U = 0.0f;   V = (float)frameNum * frameHeight/height;
    vertices[0].TextureCoordinate = new Vector2(U,V);
    // bottom left
    U = 0.0f;   V = (float)((frameNum + 1.0f) * frameHeight)/height;
    vertices[1].TextureCoordinate = new Vector2(U, V);
    // top right
    U = 1.0f;   V = (float)frameNum * frameHeight/height;
    vertices[2].TextureCoordinate = new Vector2(U,V);
    // bottom right
    U = 1.0f;   V = (float)((frameNum + 1.0f) * frameHeight)/height;
    vertices[3].TextureCoordinate = new Vector2(U,V);
}
```

`UpdateTextureUV()` is called from the `Update()` method to map a different portion of the image to the surface each interval:

```
const int NUM_FRAMES = 2;
UpdateTextureUV(gameTime, signTexture, NUM_FRAMES);
```

The `DrawAnimatedTexture()` routine is identical to the routines used for drawing any textured object that you have used until now. Check the comments in this code for details:

```
private void DrawAnimatedTexture(){
    // 1: declare matrices
    Matrix world, translation;

    // 2: initialize matrices
    translation = Matrix.CreateTranslation(0.0f, 0.0f, -BOUNDARY / 2.0f);

    // 3: build cumulative world matrix using I.S.R.O.T. sequence
    world = translation;

    // 4: set shader parameters
    textureEffectWVP.SetValue(world*cam.viewMatrix*cam.projectionMatrix);
    textureEffectImage.SetValue(signTexture);

    // 5: draw object - primitive type, vertices, #primitives
    TextureShader(PrimitiveType.TriangleStrip, vertices, 2);
}
```

Inside the Draw() method, just before the End() method is called for the texture shader, the animated texture needs to be drawn. When transparency is involved, the transparent objects must be rendered last. In other words, they are drawn after the opaque 3D objects. To enable transparency, several RenderStates for the GraphicsDevice must be adjusted. Alpha blending must be enabled by setting AlphaBlendEnable = true. The opaque pixels are drawn by setting SourceBlend = Blend.SourceAlpha, and the masked portion of the image is filtered out by setting DestinationBlend = Blend.InverseSourceAlpha. Alpha blending is disabled when the drawing is complete.

Add the following code to set up transparency for your textured surface and to render it as the last item in your list of 3D objects that are drawn:

```
graphics.GraphicsDevice.RenderState.AlphaBlendEnable = true;
graphics.GraphicsDevice.RenderState.SourceBlend      = Blend.SourceAlpha;
graphics.GraphicsDevice.RenderState.DestinationBlend
                                                   = Blend.InverseSourceAlpha;
DrawAnimatedTexture();
graphics.GraphicsDevice.RenderState.AlphaBlendEnable = false;
```

When you run the program, it will show a flashing danger sign in the 3D world, as shown earlier in Figure 12-2. Unlike the sprite example, this sign can be viewed from different angles as a player travels through the world.

MULTITEXTURING

Multitexturing is a technique that blends two or more images into one texture. Multitexturing offers interesting possibilities for creating graphics effects, such as adding detail texturing to terrain, simulating currents of water, and changing the appearance of existing textures at run time.

Multitexturing uses multipass rendering to blend more than one textured surface each frame. Each render of the object is triggered during one *pass* in the shader. (There are several references to shaders in this example, so you may find a review of Chapter 6 to be helpful.) The developer can set each pass to specify how the objects are filtered, textured, and drawn.

Multipass Rendering from the Shader's Technique

A shader that implements multitexturing is almost identical to the shader used for applying textures in Chapter 9. The only difference with a multipass shader is that the technique implements more than one pass. In each pass, different blending and filtering can be triggered and different functions within the shader can be executed. This technique demonstrates typical syntax for a multitexturing shader:

```
technique MultiTexture{
    pass p0 // first pass
    {       // declare and initialize vs and ps
        Vertexshader = compile vs_1_1 VertexShader();
        pixelshader  = compile ps_1_1 PixelShader();
    }
    pass p1 // second pass
    {       // declare and initialize vs and ps
        Vertexshader = compile vs_1_1 VertexShader();
        Pixelshader  = compile ps_1_1 PixelShader();
    }
}
```

Calling a Pass in the Shader

Each pass is called between the effect's `Begin()` and `End()` methods. The code syntax presented here is similar to code that would be used to select and execute two passes within the shader. Note that in each pass a separate textured surface is rendered:

```
effect.Begin();                           // start shader
effect.Techniques[0].Passes[0].Begin();   // *START 1ST PASS
drawObject(SURFACE0);                     // draw 1st surface
effect.Techniques[0].Passes[0].End();     // *END 1ST PASS

effect.Techniques[0].Passes[1].Begin();   // *START 2ND PASS
drawObject(SURFACE1);                     // draw 2nd surface
effect.Techniques[0].Passes[1].End();     // *END 2ND PASS

effect.End();                             // end shader
```

Water Using Multitexturing Example

In this example, a multitexturing technique simulates a flowing river. To create the water, this example uses two images of rocks that resemble what you might find near a riverbed (see Figure 12-3). The first image (on the left) serves as the blurred river bottom. The second image (on the right) is used for the water surface. The second image is a picture of similar stones that uses a lighter shade for easier blending. In every frame, the second image's texture coordinates are adjusted so that it appears to slide over the first texture.

The image on the right is actually created from three identical images. The middle image is inverted to ensure a seamless wraparound when the maximum V texture coordinate is reached and reset back to the start. Only one-third of the second texture is shown at a time. In each frame, the visible portion of the texture is shifted by a scaled increment, based on the time lapse between frames.

The images are combined using a shiny blend to give the illusion of light bouncing off the water.

This example shows how to create a clear dynamic water effect by blending the two images. This code begins with the solution from the "Grid Using Index Buffer Example" section in Chapter 11.

FIGURE 12-3

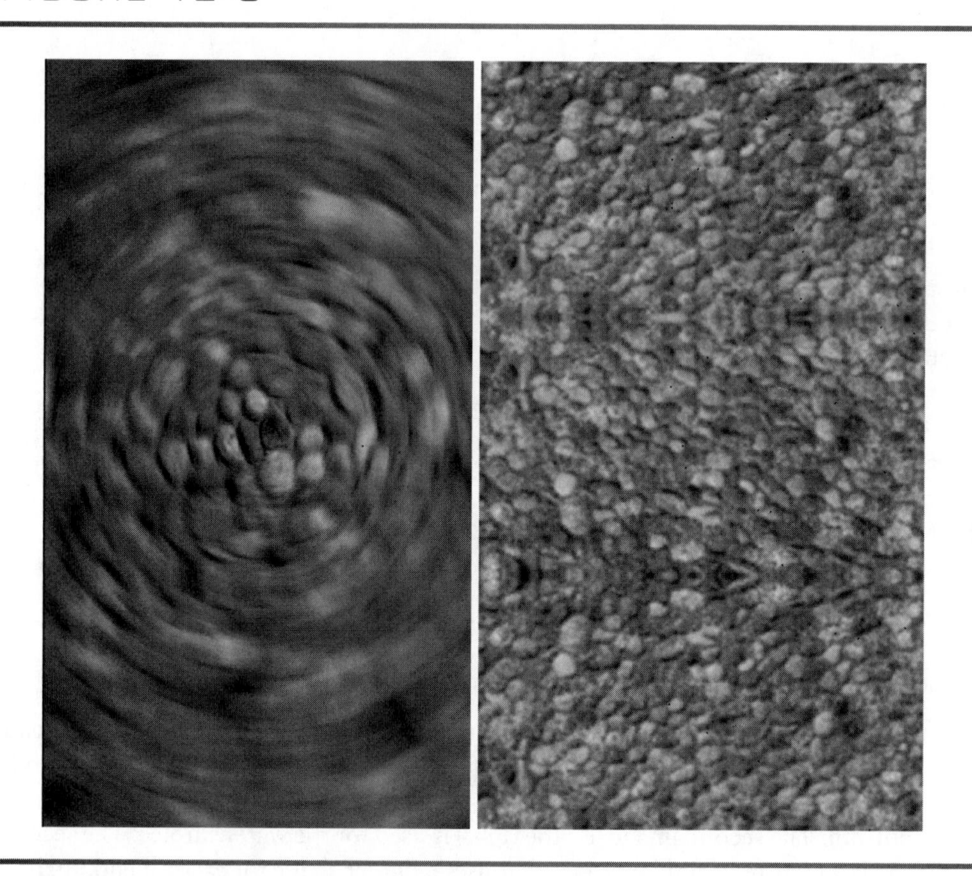

Stationary texture (left) and moving texture (right)

One of the first items that must be modified is the shader. Replace the technique in the Texture.fx file with this version to enable multipass rendering. This revision calls the same vertex shader and pixel shader twice. Before each pass is called, the application sets the texture so that a different textured surface is rendered during each pass:

```
technique multiTexture{
    pass p0 // first pass
    {   // declare and initialize vs and ps
        vertexshader= compile vs_1_1 VertexShader();
        pixelshader = compile ps_1_1 PixelShader();
    }
    pass p1 // second pass
    {   // declare and initialize vs and ps
        vertexshader= compile vs_1_1 VertexShader();
        pixelshader = compile ps_1_1 PixelShader();
    }
}
```

At the class level within the game class, constants are declared to identify each surface in the multitexture:

```
const int SURFACE0 = 0; const int SURFACE1 = 1; const int NUM_LAYERS = 2;
```

To generate the effect of more naturally rounded waves, more vertices are required. At the top of the game class, replace the existing definitions for the total number of columns and rows, in the vertex grid, with these revised declarations:

```
private const int NUM_COLS = 30;
private const int NUM_ROWS = 30;
```

Two `Texture2D` objects are required to store each layer used to create the running water. During each pass in the shader, only one of the textures is applied—depending on whether the riverbed or moving watery surface is being rendered. To make both textures available throughout the game class, a `Texture2D` array is declared at the top of the class:

```
private Texture2D[] waterTexture = new Texture2D[NUM_LAYERS];
```

The two images of rocks—water0.bmp and water1.bmp—will need to be in the Images folder under the Content node in your game project so they can be loaded with `Load()` in the `LoadContent()` method. You can download the image files from this book's website. They can be found in the Images folder. Place this code in the `LoadContent()` method so that the images will be loaded when the program begins:

```
waterTexture[SURFACE0] = Content.Load<Texture2D>("Images\\water0");
waterTexture[SURFACE1] = Content.Load<Texture2D>("Images\\water1");
```

The UV coordinates for each surface in the multitextured water will be used differently. The riverbed will remain stationary but the UV coordinates for the running water will be updated dynamically. Later, in the example, the Y coordinates for all vertices in each surface will be adjusted every frame to create a wave pattern. Since the position is going to be updated, a `DynamicVertexBuffer` object is needed to store each set of vertices. Replacing the existing class-level `VertexBuffer` declaration from the Chapter 11 "Index Buffer" example with this `DynamicVertexBuffer` array declaration will permit efficient dynamic updates to large numbers of vertices every frame:

```
// offscreen storage and updates
VertexPositionColorTexture[] surface0
   = new VertexPositionColorTexture[NUM_ROWS * NUM_COLS];
VertexPositionColorTexture[] surface1
    = new VertexPositionColorTexture[NUM_ROWS * NUM_COLS];

// buffer for drawing
DynamicVertexBuffer[] vertexBuffer = new DynamicVertexBuffer[2];
```

A different set of vertices is used for each surface in this multitexture effect so they can be updated independently of each other. This structure is different than the previous index buffer from Chapter 11, which does not permit dynamic updates to the vertices at run time. To set up the dynamic vertex structure, replace the existing `InitializeVertexBuffer()` method with this one:

```
private void InitializeVertexBuffer(){
    for(int i=0; i<NUM_LAYERS; i++)      // vertex buffer for drawing
        vertexBuffer[i] = new DynamicVertexBuffer(
          graphics.GraphicsDevice,
          NUM_COLS*NUM_ROWS*VertexPositionColorTexture.SizeInBytes,
          BufferUsage.WriteOnly | BufferUsage.Points);

    // set grid width and height
    float colWidth  = (float)2*BOUNDARY/(NUM_COLS - 1);
    float rowHeight = (float)2*BOUNDARY/(NUM_ROWS - 1);
```

```
    for (int i = 0; i < NUM_LAYERS; i++){
        for (int row = 0; row < NUM_ROWS; row++){
            for (int col = 0; col < NUM_COLS; col++)
            {   // set X, Y, Z
                float X = -BOUNDARY + col*(colWidth);
                float Y =  0.0f;
                float Z = -BOUNDARY + row*(rowHeight);
                surface0[col+row*NUM_COLS].Position = new Vector3(X,Y,Z);
                surface1[col+row*NUM_COLS].Position = new Vector3(X,Y,Z);

                // set color
                surface0[col + row*NUM_COLS].Color  = Color.White;
                surface1[col + row*NUM_COLS].Color  = Color.White;

                // set UV coordinates to map texture 1:1
                Vector2
                UV = new Vector2((float)col/((float)NUM_COLS - 1.0f),
                                 (float)row/((float)NUM_ROWS - 1.0f));
                surface0[col + row*NUM_COLS].TextureCoordinate = UV;
                surface1[col + row*NUM_COLS].TextureCoordinate = UV;
            }
        }
        if (i == SURFACE0)
            vertexBuffer[SURFACE0].SetData(surface0);
        else if(i == SURFACE1)
            vertexBuffer[SURFACE1].SetData(surface1);
    }
}
```

The top layer of water appears to move because of adjustments to the vertical texture coordinate. This requires that you add a class-level declaration to store adjustments for the V coordinate:

```
private float                          verticalAdjustment = 0.0f;
```

The method `UpdateMovingSurface()` is added to shift the vertical texture coordinate, V, each frame. This procedure updates the V coordinate for all vertices in the grid.

```
void UpdateMovingSurface(GameTime gameTime){
    const float VISIBLE_SECTION = 1.0f/3.0f;     // show only 1/3 of image
```

```
    const float TIME_SCALE      = 20000.0f;     // adjust V by time scale

    verticalAdjustment                          // time scale V increment
        -= (float)gameTime.ElapsedGameTime.Milliseconds/TIME_SCALE;

    // if V reaches 0 reset it to 2/3 to wrap the texture
    if (verticalAdjustment < 0.0f)
        verticalAdjustment      = VISIBLE_SECTION*2.0f;

    for (int row = 0; row < NUM_ROWS; row++){
        for (int col = 0; col < NUM_COLS; col++){
            // U doesn't change but V does
            // only 1/3 of moving water image shows at a time
            // this calculation allows for vertical wrap around
            // SURFACE1 V starts at 2/3 and ends at 0
            // SURFACE0 V starts at 1 and ends with 1/3
            float U = surface1[col + row*NUM_COLS].TextureCoordinate.X;
            float V = verticalAdjustment
                + VISIBLE_SECTION*(float)row/((float)NUM_ROWS - 1.0f);
                surface1[col + row*NUM_COLS].TextureCoordinate
                = new Vector2(U, V);
        }
    }
    // need to release the buffer before resetting it
    graphics.GraphicsDevice.Vertices[0].SetSource(null, 0, 0);
        vertexBuffer[SURFACE0].SetData(surface0);
        vertexBuffer[SURFACE1].SetData(surface1);
}
```

Since the texture coordinates must be updated between each frame, the call to update the water surfaces is placed in the `Update()` method:

```
UpdateMovingSurface(gameTime);
```

A new version of `DrawIndexedGrid()` is needed to replace the version you used at the beginning of this example. This revision is a pared-down version that selects the indices and vertices for each specific layer before drawing it. Only the top face is rendered for the performance gain, so `CullMode` is set to omit the clockwise face. To enable this change so that `DrawIndexedGrid()` can serve for drawing both surfaces, replace the existing version of `DrawIndexedGrid()` with this one:

```
private void DrawIndexedGrid(int layer){
    graphics.GraphicsDevice.VertexDeclaration = positionColorTexture;
    graphics.GraphicsDevice.Vertices[0].SetSource(vertexBuffer[layer], 0,
                                VertexPositionColorTexture.SizeInBytes);
    graphics.GraphicsDevice.Indices = indexBuffer;
    graphics.GraphicsDevice.RenderState.CullMode  // don't draw back face
                                                  // for efficiency
                                       = CullMode.CullClockwiseFace;
    // draw grid one row at a time
    for (int Z = 0; Z < NUM_ROWS - 1; Z++){
        graphics.GraphicsDevice.DrawIndexedPrimitives(
            PrimitiveType.TriangleStrip,// primitive
            Z * NUM_COLS,              // start point in buffer for drawing
            0,                         // minimum vertices in vertex buffer
            NUM_COLS * NUM_ROWS,       // total vertices in buffer
            0,                         // start point in index buffer
            2 * (NUM_COLS - 1));       // end point in index buffer
    }
    // reset to no culling
    graphics.GraphicsDevice.RenderState.CullMode = CullMode.None;
}
```

DrawWater() is needed in the game class to apply the texture for each surface and to set the appropriate blending filters before drawing the surface from DrawIndexedGrid(). This code selects two passes in the shader. The first pass implements standard texturing for the riverbed. During the second pass, alpha blending is enabled to create a semitransparent watery surface. A SourceBlend and DestinationBlend setting of Blend.One creates a shiny brightness on the second surface:

```
private void DrawWater(int layer){
    // 1: declare matrices
    Matrix world, translation;

    // 2: initialize matrices
    translation = Matrix.CreateTranslation(0.0f, -0.5f, 0.0f);

    // 3: build cumulative world matrix using I.S.R.O.T. sequence
    world = translation;
```

```
    // 4: set shader variables
    textureEffectWVP.SetValue(world*cam.viewMatrix*cam.projectionMatrix);
    textureEffectImage.SetValue(waterTexture[layer]);

    // 5: draw object
    // begin multiTexture using modified Texture.fx shader
    textureEffect.Begin();                                  // start shader

    switch (layer){
    case SURFACE0:
        textureEffect.Techniques[0].Passes[0].Begin(); // *START 1ST PASS
        DrawIndexedGrid(SURFACE0);                     // draw 1st layer
        textureEffect.Techniques[0].Passes[0].End();   // *END 1ST PASS
        break;
    case SURFACE1:
        // enable shiny blending (dest and source are both one)
        graphics.GraphicsDevice.RenderState.AlphaBlendEnable = true;
        graphics.GraphicsDevice.RenderState.SourceBlend      = Blend.One;
        graphics.GraphicsDevice.RenderState.DestinationBlend = Blend.One;

        textureEffect.Techniques[0].Passes[1].Begin(); // *START 2ND PASS
        DrawIndexedGrid(SURFACE1);                     // draw 2nd layer
        textureEffect.Techniques[0].Passes[1].End();   // *END 2ND PASS

        // restore graphics device for standard 3D rendering
        graphics.GraphicsDevice.RenderState.AlphaBlendEnable = false;
        break;
    }
    textureEffect.End();                                    // end shader
}
```

Replacing the call statement to `DrawIndexedGrid()` with these call statements will implement multitexturing through two passes using the modified Texture.fx file:

```
DrawWater(SURFACE0);
DrawWater(SURFACE1);
```

At this point, you can compile and run your program. The output will show a clear, bright moving surface that simulates water (see Figure 12-4).

FIGURE 12-4

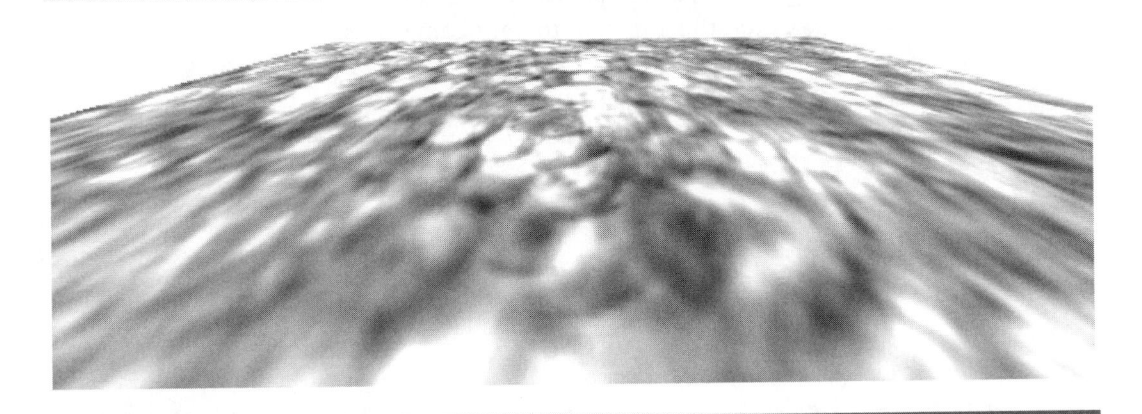

Clear water, no waves

Water Using Multitexturing Example, Continued: Adding Waves

This next portion of the example adds waves to the water. The algorithm uses a sine function, shown here, to update the Y value of each vertex in the grid at every frame.

The sine wave equation offers properties to control the wave frequency, number of waves, and height (amplitude).

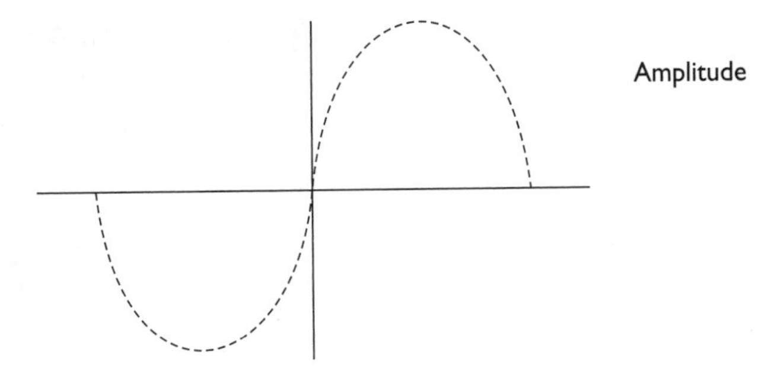

Start with the code from the last solution, "Water Using Multitexturing Example."

To begin with this next section of our demonstration, a float variable declaration at the top of the game class is required to store the sine wave cycle increment:

```
private float           cycleIncrement;
```

`SineCycle()` traces a floating-point value through a sine wave's cycle over time. The function is only executed once per frame but is used to update each Y value for all vertices in the grid. Add this function to your game class:

```
float SineCycle(GameTime gameTime){
    // less than full cycle of sine wave retrieves between 0 and 1.
    // full cycle for sine wave is 2*PI.
    if (cycleIncrement < 1)
        cycleIncrement
        += 0.0000005f * (float)gameTime.ElapsedGameTime.Milliseconds;
    // adjust when sine wave cycle complete
    else
        cycleIncrement = cycleIncrement - 1;
    return cycleIncrement;
}
```

As discussed, `SineCycle()` is called only once per frame to trace a value on the sine wave over time. The point on the sine wave that is returned is added to the V coordinate for each point in the grid. This sum is used for setting the Y value of each point in the grid. The result is a set of oscillating Y values that follow the sine wave as it rises and falls over time.

`SetWaterHeight()` receives the sum of the texture's V coordinate plus the point in the sine wave over time. This sine wave equation returns a Y value for the coordinate that corresponds with the V coordinate:

$$Height = Amplitude = \sin(WaveCountPerCycle * PointInCycle * 2\pi)$$

Add the `SetWaterHeight()` method to the game class:

```
float SetWaterHeight(float cycleTime){
    const float FREQUENCY = 6.0f;          // wave count per cycle
    const float AMPLITUDE = 1.0f/15.0f;    // wave height

    // generates height based on V coord and sine equation
    return (AMPLITUDE * (float)Math.Sin(FREQUENCY * cycleTime
                  * 2.0f * (float)Math.PI) - 0.4f);
}
```

The X, Y, Z information is the same for both the stationary image layer and the moving image layer. Since the stationary layer is drawn first, the Y value that changes with the sine wave over time can be set for this layer and the changes will apply to both image layers. Adding this code to reset the X, Y, and Z coordinates inside the nested for-loop for `UpdateMovingSurface()` will create a dynamically changing Y value that simulates the wave for both layers over time:

```
float X = surface1[col + row * NUM_COLS].Position.X;
float Y = SetWaterHeight(V + SineCycle(gameTime));
float Z = surface1[col + row * NUM_COLS].Position.Z;
surface0[col + row * NUM_COLS].Position = new Vector3(X, Y, Z);
surface1[col + row * NUM_COLS].Position = new Vector3(X, Y, Z);
```

When you run this program, it shows the moving dynamic texture and the waves rippling through the object. The effect is actually quite beautiful (see Figure 12-5). You can try building this example, or you can download the completed example from the Solutions folder on this book's website.

There are various ways to combine images for creating exciting graphics effects. Sprites are used to animate a series of image frames that are stored in an image file. Multitexturing can be used to blend two images together and provide more detail or dynamic movement for the texture.

FIGURE 12-5

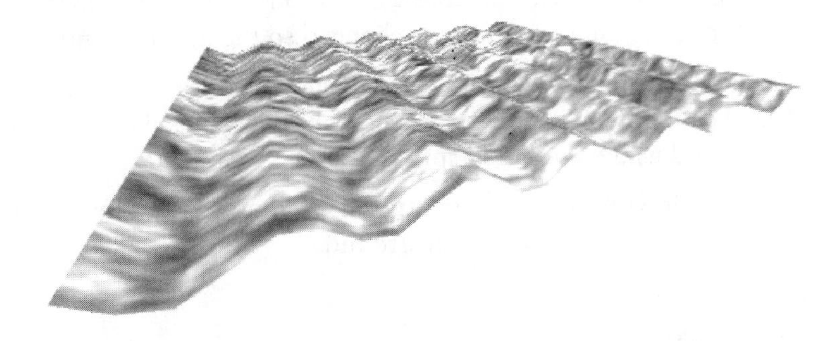

Surf's up!

CHAPTER 12 REVIEW EXERCISES

To get the most from this chapter, try out these chapter review exercises.

1. Try the step-by-step examples presented in this chapter, if you have not already done so.
2. For your solution to the SpriteBatch example, remove the code that manually resets the `RenderState` properties for the `GraphicsDevice` in the `Draw()` method. Then, add code to automatically restore the render states after the `SpriteBatch` object is drawn. Automatically restoring the render states can be done in `DrawAnimatedHud()` by replacing the `SpriteBatch` object's `Begin()` instruction with code similar to this:

   ```
   spriteBatch.Begin(SpriteBlendMode.AlphaBlend,
                     SpriteSortMode.Immediate,SaveStateMode.SaveState);
   ```

   Try running your code and notice that the output appears to be the same as before.
3. Replace your `Begin()` statement in Exercise 2 with an instruction similar to the following statement and then run your project:

   ```
   spriteBatch.Begin();
   ```

   Notice how the ground and all other 3D objects disappear when the render states are not restored.
4. With the solution for the 2D sprite and the original 2D sprite settings, call `DrawAnimatedHud()` before `DrawGround()`. Notice that you cannot see the sprite unless the view is changed so the ground is not covering it.
5. Create your own sprite with three or more frames. In the same project, show the sprite as a 2D `SpriteBatch` object. Display your sprite in the 3D world using a textured sprite.
6. Use multitexturing to make it appear as if moving shadows cast from the clouds are traveling across the ground.

CHAPTER 13

Score Tracking and Game Stats

BEING able to display status information about players, and their scores, is fundamental to any game dashboard. For example, you might need to show statistics such as health, fuel level, the current map name, or maybe even the opponents' names. In the end, your ability to present this information boils down to having access to a font library that can overlay 2D text on your game's 2D or 3D environment. As you would expect, XNA offers an excellent font library for this purpose.

The two examples in this chapter demonstrate how to write text and numeric output to the game window. When you are finished (depending on which project you start with), your output will be similar to the window display shown in Figure 13-1.

FIGURE 13-1

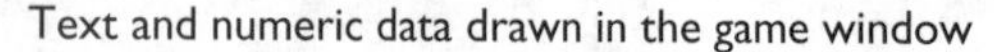

Text and numeric data drawn in the game window

FONT EXAMPLE: DISPLAYING TEXT IN THE GAME WINDOW

This example explains the steps to display the string "Score Tracking and Game Stats" in the top-left corner of the game window. You could use the same technique to show your name, display your scores, or to show other important statistics—like your shield strength or health level.

This example can begin with either the Windows or Xbox 360 starter projects from the BaseCode folder on the book's website. Alternatively, you could add this font example code to a new project generated by Visual Studio's project template.

Loading the Font Type Data

Once you have chosen a starter project, you will use the XNA font class, so you will need to add a reference to the font type description data, in the Solution Explorer. The font can be added by right-clicking the Content node, choosing Add and selecting New Item. Once you have the Add New Item – Content dialog open, you can add a font by choosing the Sprite Font template icon. For this exercise, call your file "MyFont."

Once you click Add, this will generate an XML file called MyFont.spritefont, which is then automatically placed in your project. At this point you will see the spritefont file referenced in the Solution Explorer (refer to Figure 13-2).

FIGURE 13-2

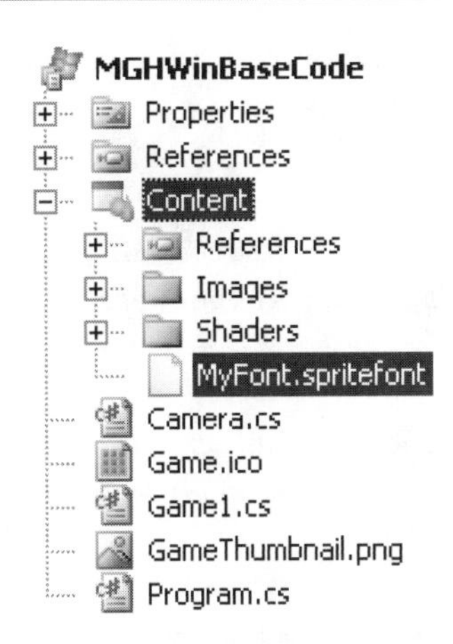

Font is properly referenced under the Content node.

If you view the contents of the spritefont file, you will see XML code that stores the font properties. You can adjust these elements to change the size of the font and the spacing between characters, and you can also set the font to be Regular, Bold, Italic, or Bold Italic in the `<Style>` element.

To reference a TrueType font on your PC or Xbox 360, you will need to adjust the `<FontName>` element value in the spritefont file. In this example we will load a Courier New font, so to do this, you must replace the FontName element with:

```
<FontName>Courier New</FontName>
```

Once you have made this adjustment, your XML code will appear in the MyFont.spritefont file as follows:

```
<?xml version="1.0" encoding="utf-8"?>
<!--
This file contains an xml description of a font, and will be read by the
XNA Framework Content Pipeline. Follow the comments to customize the
appearance of the font in your game, and to change the characters which
are available to draw with.-->
<XnaContent
 xmlns:Graphics="Microsoft.Xna.Framework.Content.Pipeline.Graphics">
  <Asset Type="Graphics:FontDescription">

    <!--Modify this string to change the font that will be imported.-->
    <FontName>Courier New</FontName>

    <!--Size is a float value, measured in points. Modify this value to
    change the size of the font.-->
    <Size>14</Size>

    <!--Spacing is a float value, measured in pixels. Modify this value
    to change the amount of spacing in between characters.-->
    <Spacing>0</Spacing>

    <!--UseKerning controls the layout of the font. If this value is
    true, kerning information will be used when placing characters.-->
    <UseKerning>true</UseKerning>

    <!--Style controls the style of the font. Valid entries are
    "Regular", "Bold", "Italic", and "Bold, Italic", and are case
    sensitive.-->
    <Style>Regular</Style>
```

```
    <!--If you uncomment this line, the default character will be
    substituted if you draw or measure text that contains characters
    which were not included in the font.-->
    <!-- <DefaultCharacter>*</DefaultCharacter>-->

    <!--CharacterRegions control what letters are available in the font.
    Every character from Start to End will be built and made available
    for drawing. The default range is from 32, (ASCII space), to 126,
    ('~'), covering the basic Latin character set. The characters are
    ordered according to the Unicode standard. See the documentation for
    more information.-->
    <CharacterRegions>
      <CharacterRegion>
        <Start>&#32;</Start>
        <End>&#126;</End>
      </CharacterRegion>
    </CharacterRegions>
  </Asset>
</XnaContent>
```

For now, aside from changing the FontName, you can leave the default spritefont file settings as they were originally generated. However, you can edit the elements in this file further to change the size, weight (boldness), italics, and other properties if desired.

Loading the Font

Fonts are drawn using a SpriteFont object, which you must declare at the top of the game class:

```
private SpriteFont spriteFont;
```

The SpriteFont object actually is a sprite, so the corresponding data behind it should be read in the LoadContent() method. This object is loaded by first retrieving the font description data from the spritefont file. Since the spritefont file is referenced in the Content folder, you do not need to specify a directory when loading it. To load this file with the Load() method, you must pass the name of the spritefont filename without the file extension:

```
spriteFont = Content.Load<SpriteFont>("MyFont");
```

Ensuring Your Fonts Are Drawn in the Visible Portion of the Window

We have already discussed the need to designate a title safe region in Chapter 4. This avoids truncating your graphics when running your games on the Xbox 360. Since fonts are 2D, and you do not want your fonts to be truncated, you will need to display your text in a title-safe region. A `TitleSafeRegion()` method was used in Chapter 4 to generate a rectangle that stores the top, bottom, left, and right margins around the safe area. An alternate, but similar, version of the `TitleSafeRegion()` method will be used in this chapter to calculate the starting pixel position on the window for each string that is written to it.

This new `TitleSafeRegion()` method receives a string and a `SpriteFont` object as parameters. It then uses the `SpriteFont`'s `MeasureString()` method to retrieve the width and height of the string. The `MeasureString()` method uses the string to determine the output width and it uses the `SpriteFont` object to calculate the height of the font. Here is the revised version of the `TitleSafeRegion()` method to conveniently generate margins for the visible display area from game class:

```
Rectangle TitleSafeRegion(string outputString, SpriteFont font){
    Vector2 stringDimensions = font.MeasureString(outputString);
    int    stringWidth  = (int)stringDimensions.X; // string pixel width
    int    stringHeight = (int)stringDimensions.Y; // font pixel height

    // some televisions only show 80% of the window
    const float UNSAFEAREA    = 0.2f;
    const float MARGIN        = UNSAFEAREA/2.0f;

    // calculate title safe bounds for string
    int          top, left, safeWidth, safeHeight;
    top          = (int)(Window.ClientBounds.Height*MARGIN);
    left         = (int)(Window.ClientBounds.Width *MARGIN);
    safeWidth    = (int)((1.0f-UNSAFEAREA)*Window.ClientBounds.Width)
                 - stringWidth;
    safeHeight   = (int)((1.0f-UNSAFEAREA)*Window.ClientBounds.Height)
                 - stringHeight;

    return new Rectangle(left, top, safeWidth, safeHeight);
}
```

Drawing the Font

The font render is triggered from the Draw() method. It is drawn using an overridden DrawString() method from the SpriteBatch class. The DrawString() parameters for this override include the FontBatch object, an output string, the starting top-left pixel position on the window where the string is drawn, and color.

Whenever you draw a 2D SpriteBatch object, the process must start with the Begin() method and finish with the End() method. If you are adding your font code to a 3D game project, call your font drawing code after all your other objects are rendered. This ensures that your text displays at the forefront of the window. Otherwise your text will be covered by other objects that are rendered later by the Draw() method.

Saving Your Render States

When drawing 2D objects with a SpriteBatch object, XNA automatically adjusts the GraphicsDevice object to render in 2D. This makes drawing with SpriteBatch objects easy, but you have to be careful because the original GraphicsDevice settings are not restored. If the GraphicsDevice settings are not restored, your 3D objects may disappear and your tiled images may be thrown out of whack. You can get some hair-raising results if you forget and think your game code is broken. To automatically restore the settings (after drawing 2D fonts in your 3D games), use the SaveStateMode.SaveState property as the third parameter in an overridden version of the Begin() method. Be aware, though, that SaveStateMode.SaveState can cause performance issues if you use it a lot in your game, so you may want to manually reset your graphics device to avoid this performance hit. Restoring the graphics device manually is described in Chapter 12. Here is the code to draw your output:

```
private void DrawFonts(GameTime gameTime){
    string      outputString;
    Rectangle   safeArea;

    // start drawing font sprites
    spriteBatch.Begin(SpriteBlendMode.AlphaBlend,  // enable transparency
                      SpriteSortMode.Immediate,    // use manual order
                      SaveStateMode.SaveState);    // store 3D settings
        outputString    = "Score Tracking and Game Stats";
        safeArea        = TitleSafeRegion(outputString, spriteFont);
        spriteBatch.DrawString(spriteFont, outputString, new Vector2(
                        safeArea.Left, safeArea.Top), Color.Yellow);
```

```
    // stop drawing - and 3D settings are restored if SaveState used
    spriteBatch.End();
}
```

This font output will display after you trigger it from the `Draw()` method:

```
DrawFonts(gameTime);
```

When you compile and run this code, the words "Score Tracking and Game Stats" will appear at the top-left corner of the title safe region in the game window.

FONT EXAMPLE: DISPLAYING A FRAMES-PER-SECOND COUNT

This next example takes the solution from the previous example a little further with some extra code to display numeric data in the window. In this example, a frame count will be shown at the bottom-right of the window.

To create the frames-per-second count, you will use a timer like the one presented in Chapter 12. In this example, the total frames rendered during 1-second intervals are counted. When each 1-second interval is complete, the total frame count generated is displayed on the screen for the second that follows—until a new count is tallied and displayed.

Some setup is required to store the count and interval times, so you will need to add the following variable declarations (for storing the counter and time values) at the top of your game class:

```
private double fps, fpsCounter;
private double intervalTime         = 0;    // time in current interval
private double previousIntervalTime = 0;    // interval time at last frame
```

The timer method discussed in Chapter 12 must also be added to measure the frame count in 1-second intervals. A value of 1000 milliseconds is assigned for the interval to ensure that the timer returns a `true` value for every second.

```
bool Timer(GameTime gameTime){
    bool resetInterval = false;

    // add time lapse between frames and keep value between 0 & 1000 ms
    intervalTime += (double)gameTime.ElapsedGameTime.Milliseconds;
    intervalTime  = intervalTime % 1000;
```

```
    // intervalTime has been reset so a new interval has started
    if (intervalTime  < previousIntervalTime)
        resetInterval = true;

    previousIntervalTime = intervalTime;
    return resetInterval;
}
```

The code that counts and stores the number of frames per second is also added to the game class. The count you see in the window is actually the total generated in the previous 1-second interval:

```
public String FramesPerSecond(GameTime gameTime){
    if (Timer(gameTime)){   // check if 1 second is up
        fps = fpsCounter;   // 1 second complete so assign new FPS value
        fpsCounter  = 0;    // reset counter to 0 to start new interval
    }
    else
        fpsCounter += 1;    // increment counter when interval incomplete

    return "Frames Per Second: " + fps.ToString();
}
```

Before drawing the text, the starting top-left pixel position is needed to right-justify the string at the bottom-right, title-safe corner of the window. The `Update()` method is not necessarily called the same number of times as the `Draw()` method. This code belongs in the `DrawFonts()` routine immediately before `spriteBatch.End()` is called:

```
outputString     = FramesPerSecond(gameTime);
safeArea         = TitleSafeRegion(outputString, spriteFont);
spriteBatch.DrawString(spriteFont, outputString, new Vector2(
                   safeArea.Right,safeArea.Bottom), Color.Yellow);
```

When you run this code, the frame count appears at the bottom right of the window. Drawing information to the screen is not only useful for your gamers, but you may also find the frames-per-second routine useful when testing your code's performance.

CHAPTER 13 REVIEW EXERCISES

To get the most from this chapter, try out these chapter review exercises.

Try the step-by-step examples presented in this chapter, but make the following changes.

1. Use a Times New Roman font to display the "Score Tracking and Game Stats" title and use a Courier New font to display the frames-per-second count.
2. Create a custom score board. Increment the score every time the spacebar is pressed.
3. Change the size of your font to 24 points.

CHAPTER 14

3D Models

BY now, you may be thinking that you'd like to add some more realistic models to your game world—maybe an airplane, a rocket, or a castle. You could add them by hand-coding a bunch of textured primitive objects, but that would be way too much work. The obvious way to efficiently develop a complex 3D object is with a 3D modeling application. Learning to work with 3D models is a giant step in understanding game development. It allows you to add realistic and exciting-looking objects to your game world. By the end of this chapter—after you have created your own models and animated them in code—you will certainly choose the use of 3D models over hand-coded primitive objects when possible.

Once you have developed a 3D model, you can import it into your game and control it with your code. The two supported model formats currently for XNA are .x and .fbx. Microsoft has provided a library of code to load these models into XNA for you. If you really wanted, you could use other model file formats in your game, but you'd have to write a model loader.

3D MODELING TOOLS

Autodesk Maya, Autodesk 3D Studio Max, and Softimage XSI are three of the most popular modeling tools for professional game artists, but these packages are expensive. That's not to say they aren't worth their cost; these packages are definitely worth it if you can afford them. If you are a student, you may be able to purchase an educational license for a fraction of the cost of a commercial license.

Most high-end modeling tools, such as Maya or 3ds Max, have the ability to export to Microsoft's .x format or Alias's .fbx format if you install the right combination of plug-ins. However, converting other model formats to .x or .fbx can be a finicky process. If you plan to use a modeling tool, then experiment with it first so that you are sure about the tool's requirements for successful conversions.

An inexpensive, but popular, lightweight 3D modeling program is MilkShape, by chUmbaLum sOft. MilkShape is used for the examples in this book because it is one of the easiest modeling tools to learn. In addition, MilkShape's support for the .fbx format is excellent. MilkShape also imports from and exports to over 70 relevant model file types for games. Even if you decide later that you prefer a different modeling tool, MilkShape is a great application to use when you are learning how to create 3D models. chUmbaLum sOft offers a free 30-day trial version. The purchase price is surprisingly inexpensive—$35 (U.S.) at the time this book was written. A link to their 30-day trial version is available on this book's website.

If you have used MilkShape up until XNA 3.0 and shortly after this version was released, you may find these models are not textured when loading them in an XNA 3.0 project. The XNA team upgraded their model loader in XNA 3.0 to stay current with the .FBX format but MilkShape had not yet made this change. chUmbaLum sOft is aware of this issue and this problem should be resolved before the book is released.

If you still find old MilkShape models that do not load properly in XNA 3.0 or later, there is another work-around. You can import these models into MilkShape and export them to .OBJ format. Then you can import the .OBJ files into the free model design tool, Blender. You can then export these models from Blender back to .FBX and they will retain their texture data for XNA 3.0. You likely will not need to take these extra steps but be aware of it in case you are confronted with any compatibility issues.

MilkShape 3D Intro Example: Creating a Windmill

This first example shows you how to create a windmill using MilkShape. Later, a code demo will show you how to load and animate the windmill in your game application.

When you finish creating the model and program the animation in code, it will look similar to the one in Figure 14-1.

The process of creating a 3D model helps to demonstrate how models can be loaded and manipulated in your code. But, if you decide that you are not interested in 3D modeling, or if you use other modeling tools, you can skip this section. All of the models presented in this chapter can be found in the Models folder on this book's website. On the other hand, you might find you actually enjoy the break from programming. MilkShape is such a great utility, even if you use other modeling tools, that you might discover a feature that can assist you in your model creation, such as converting one model format to another or performing quick edits to your model.

FIGURE 14-1

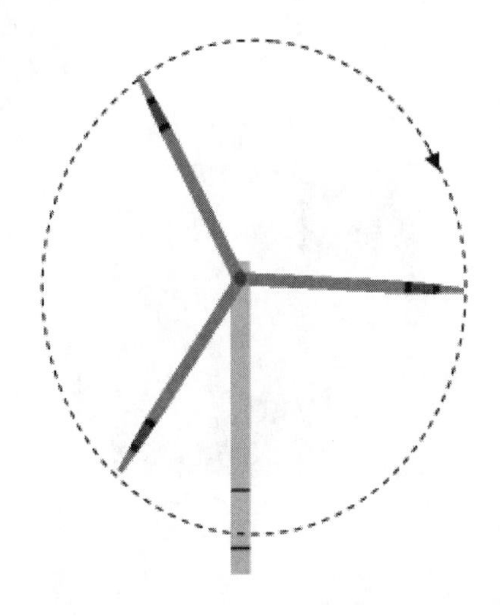

A windmill model animated in code

Creating a New Project

Starting MilkShape automatically opens the designer studio environment. Most of the controls can be found in the gray panel on the right. Four different viewports are located on the left, as shown in Figure 14-2.

Each viewport offers a view of the model from a different angle. As with similar applications, the viewport serves to guide you when you're working with your model. Different views can also offer easier access to specific sets of vertices when you're adding, modifying, or deleting parts of the model. You can change the view in each of the four ports by right-clicking the port and choosing from Front, Back, Left, Right, Top, Bottom, and 3D (from the Projection submenu). The first six views are self-explanatory. The 3D view offers you the ability to see a solid model as it would appear in a game. When you're in 3D view, right-clicking the viewport and choosing Textured will show the model with the texture applied.

FIGURE 14-2

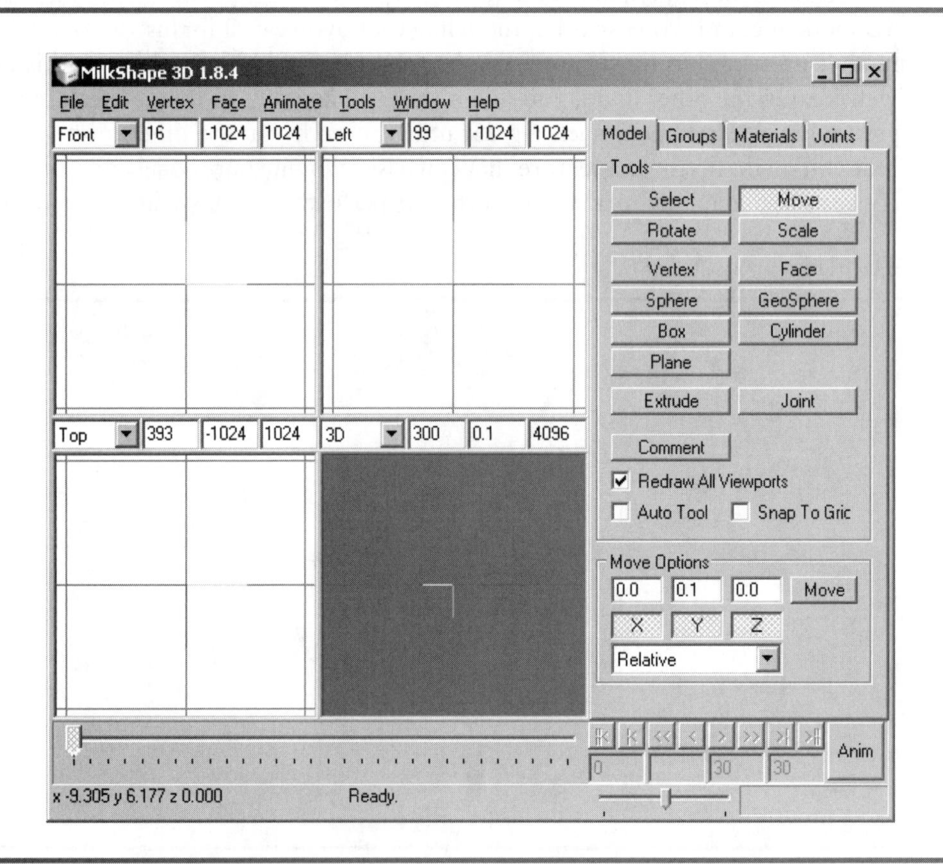

MilkShape 3D designer studio

In the Window menu is the Show Viewport Caption option, which is useful because it labels each view as Front, Left, Right, and so on. You can easily lose your bearings after switching between views, so this option can help you keep track of your model from different angles.

Adding a Box

Now it's time to start designing. First, you need to create a base for the windmill. To do this, find the Model tab, click the Box button, and click and drag in one of the viewports. A box will emerge as you drag your mouse with the left mouse button pressed down. After you have added the box and resized it, the box shape will resemble the large one on the left shown in Figure 14-3.

If the box is incorrectly sized, you can always scale it into shape. In order to scale it, the box must be selected. To select the box, on the Model tab, click the Select button and choose Group in the Select Options area. Then click inside one of the viewports and drag the mouse over the box. When the box is selected, it will be highlighted in red.

You can scale the box using either the Scale button or the mouse. The Scale button is used for intricate scaling and it is located on the right gray panel of the Model tab. When the Scale button in the Tools group is clicked, a Scale Options group will appear further down on the right panel. You can enter scale amounts here for the X, Y, and Z planes. Repeatedly clicking the Scale button in the Scale Options group will resize the selected group(s) according to the values that are set for the X, Y, and Z planes. You may find it easier to manually scale the box using the mouse. To use the mouse for scaling, choose Scale on the Model tab and then resize the object by dragging the cursor in the viewport to compress or stretch the box as needed.

FIGURE 14-3

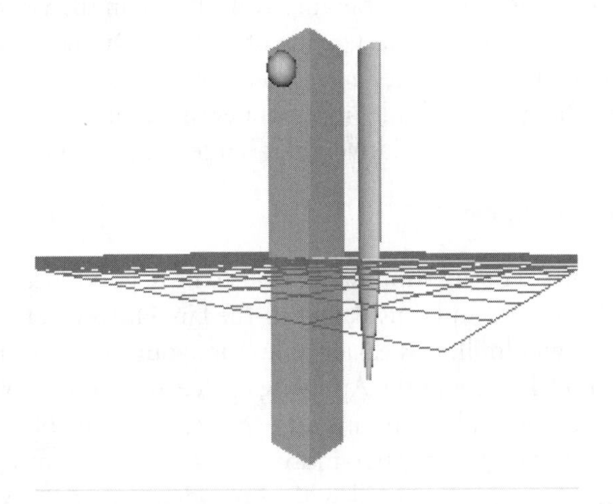

Box base, rounded fan blade, and sphere

Adding a Sphere

The next step is to add a pin to your windmill. The windmill needs a pin to fasten the windmill fan to the base. Once the pin has been added, scaled, and moved into place, it will appear similar to the one in Figure 14-3

Your pin will be a sphere added to the top face of the windmill base. To add your pin, select the Model tab and click the Sphere button—it's in the Tools group in the right panel. Then, click into one of the viewports and drag with your left mouse button down. The sphere will grow as the cursor is dragged outward from the center. You may need to resize the sphere. If you do, when you finish scaling, the pin size should be proportionate to the windmill base. The next step is to move the sphere into the correct position. On the Groups tab in the right panel, select the sphere group. Click the Move button. Then, click in a viewport and use the mouse to drag the sphere to the place where it belongs.

Adding a Cylinder

Next, you will add a cylinder to serve as one of the blades for the windmill's fan. You will use scaling to flatten and shape the blade in a proportion similar to what is shown in Figure 14-3.

On the Model tab in the right panel, click the Cylinder button. Then click in one of the viewports and drag the mouse. In one continuous movement, with the left mouse button pressed, size the cylinder so it is proportionate to the windmill base created by the box and pin.

You'll notice that the cylinder looks too round to be a windmill blade. You definitely need to flatten it. It is also possible that your cylinder is too short or too long, so you may need to scale it up or down accordingly. You could scale it using Scale Options or manually adjust it by dragging your mouse in the viewport. You may scale the entire cylinder or only a select group of vertices. On the Model tab, after clicking Select, you may choose Vertex, Face, Group, or Joint to isolate your vertices for scaling or transforming your cylinder in a manner that is most efficient. When the scaling is done, you should have a relatively flat blade with a point at the end.

Applying a Texture

Now that the pieces of the windmill appear to be in good form, you may be tempted to duplicate the blades and finish creating the fan. However, first you should apply a texture to your windmill. It is easier to texture your model at this point because the pieces of the model are separate. Applying the texture piece by piece is easier than trying to get the texture right with one large piece. After one blade is textured the way you want, it can be duplicated two more times and rotated into place to complete the windmill fan. Having a windmill with three identical well-textured fans will look very impressive. To texture the fan, you will apply a windmill.bmp file. A copy can be found in the Images folder on the book's website.

It is common for one image to contain the textures for an entire 3D model. Having all of the textures in one file greatly simplifies the code required to load and apply the textures to a model. With this in mind, 3D modelers often combine a cross-section of different textures in one image file. The windmill.bmp file contains a cross-section of images to map the texture on different parts of the model.

In MilkShape, textures can be set up on the Materials tab in the right panel. On the Materials tab, click New. A gray ball will appear when the material has been generated.

Two-thirds of the way down the right panel on the Materials tab, you will find two buttons labeled <none>. Click on the top one to launch the Open dialog, which will prompt you to select an image. In this case, a bitmap (.bmp file) is being used, but any image format that is supported by XNA will work. These image formats include .bmp, .dds, .dib, .jpg, .png, and .tga. Navigate to the windmill.bmp file. Select the image and click Open in the Open dialog. The name of the loaded image will appear on the Materials tab.

To reduce any difficulties during model format conversions and exporting to *.fbx, it is recommended that you use only one texture for your model. After you export to .fbx from MilkShape, XNA will demand that you use images that have height and width pixel dimensions that are a power of 2. Before creating the model, it is further recommended that you first test your texture by exporting a simple model that uses this image to *.fbx and then load and display it from your XNA code. When the program loads your model and tries to draw it, Game Studio will inform you if there are any issues with the image. Test your model by loading it in your game on a regular basis to ensure that it continues to load and display properly from your code. You may experience issues with compressed image formats such as .jpg, so consider sticking with the .bmp, .tga, or .png format where possible.

Assigning the Material to the Blade

Now that an image has been loaded, you can start texturing your model with it. You could start by giving the cylinder a texture to make it appear as if it has been painted with a decal. To do this, on the Groups tab, click on the cylinder group in the group listing and then click Select. The cylinder should be the only object that is selected; this is indicated by a red highlight in the viewports.

Now that the cylinder is the only object selected, return to the Materials tab and click Assign. Then, from the Window menu, select Texture Coordinate Editor. The Texture Coordinate Editor dialog will open.

Choose Front in the lower drop-down menu. Make sure that the cylinder is selected in the top drop-down menu. If the model and image do not appear, select the cylinder from the drop-down menu and click Remap. After you select the cylinder group and do the remapping, if the image and cylinder group do not appear in the Texture Coordinate Editor, the group wasn't assigned properly. To correct this, exit from the Texture Coordinate Editor and reselect the cylinder group only. Then on the Materials tab, click Assign and return to the Texture Coordinate Editor.

Once the cylinder appears in the Texture Coordinate Editor, the cylinder wireframe can be moved, scaled, and rotated into place over the section of the image that contains the decal for the windmill blade. (This section of the image is the rectangular strip that runs along the left side of the image.) The section of image underneath the cylinder's vertex group automatically wraps around the entire group of vertices. Figuring out how to wrap textures around your models may require some trial and error. But with a little practice, you will be able to plan your model components so that they're easier to texture. You may find that your model groups need to be split apart or revised so that you can map textures on them as you had originally intended. The buttons in the right panel of the Texture Coordinate Editor allow you to select your group or individual vertices to move, rotate, and scale them to find the best possible fit over the image section that is needed for the texture. In this case, the windmill fan blade fits nicely on top of the image section. Figure 14-4 shows the windmill blade before and after it is positioned over the corresponding section of image used to texture it.

Once the best fit has been achieved for the selected group, close the Texture Coordinate Editor. When you close the Texture Coordinate Editor, texture coordinates are assigned to the model where the model was last placed. The 3D viewport on the bottom right will show how the texture wrapped on the model component. Right-click the 3D viewport and choose Textured. The windmill fan blade will appear with the texture on it as in Figure 14-5.

FIGURE 14-4

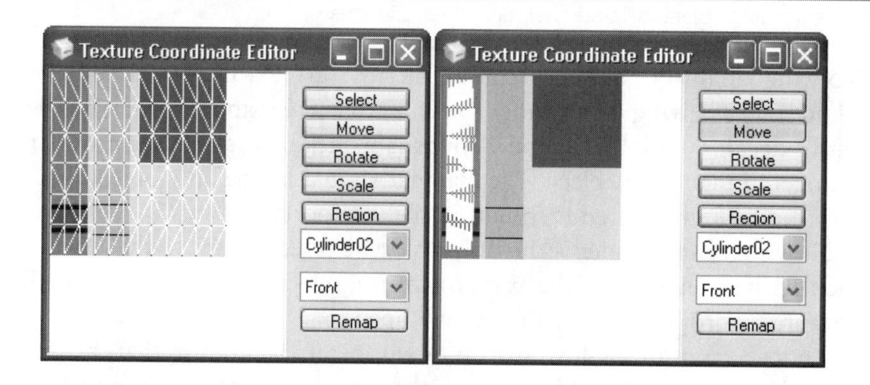

Texture Coordinate Editor while texturing the fan blade

FIGURE 14-5

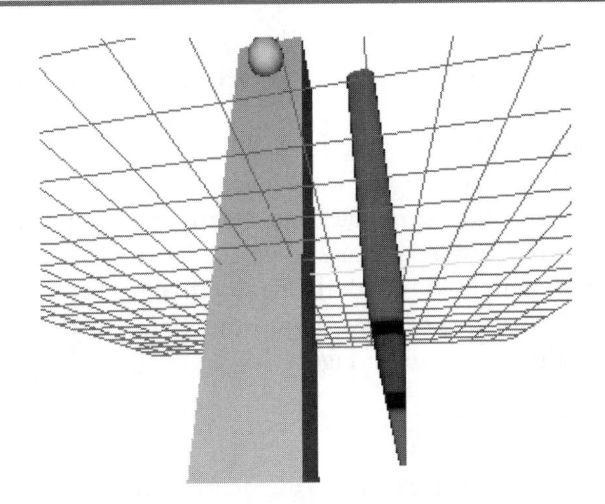

Properly textured windmill fan blade viewed in 3D viewport

Assigning the Material to the Box and Sphere

Repeat the process described previously to map the box and sphere groups individually to other sections in the texture.

Duplicating the Blade

Now that everything has been textured properly, you can complete the fan. The first blade is already textured. When this blade is duplicated, the copy will also be textured in an identical manner. Because of this, the matching blades will look sharp in the final product. To do this, on the Model tab, click the Select button. Then, in the Select Options area, choose Group. Once there, click into the viewport and drag over the group of vertices in the blade. The entire blade is now highlighted. Finally, from the Edit menu, choose Duplicate Selection. A new blade will appear on top of the original one.

Rotating the Duplicate Blade about the Z Axis

At this point, the duplicate blade is selected. Before doing anything else, choose the Rotate button on the Model tab. In the Rotate Options area that appears midway down the right panel, enter **120** in the Z plane, set X and Y to **0**, and then click the Rotate button. This will rotate the new blade by 120 degrees on the Z axis. The result will be two duplicate blades that appear at different angles around the Z axis.

Next, you will create the third blade. While the new blade is still selected, from the Edit menu choose Duplicate Selection again. A new blade will appear on top of the original one. Next, choose the Rotate button on the right panel. In the Rotate Options area, enter **120** in the Z plane and then click Rotate. This will rotate the new blade.

The three blades have now been forged. It is time to move them into position. Select one of the blades, and choose the Move button on the Model tab. Click into the top-right viewport. Make sure you have a front view by right-clicking the viewport and selecting Front. While holding down the left mouse button, drag the selected blade so the base matches up with the base of one of the other blades. Repeat these steps to join the remaining blade with the other two. The three blades should now be positioned together as shown in Figure 14-6.

Merging the Groups

Now that the blades are all textured with identical markings and are placed together, you should merge them into one group. Having the blades in one group will help later when you write code to animate the fan. It will be a lot easier to transform one fan rather than three separate blades. On the Groups tab, select each of the cylinders in the groups list. Click the Regroup button on the Groups tab. When you do this, the three blades will be merged into one. Select the new merged group and enter the name, **fan**, beside the Rename button and then click Rename.

FIGURE 14-6

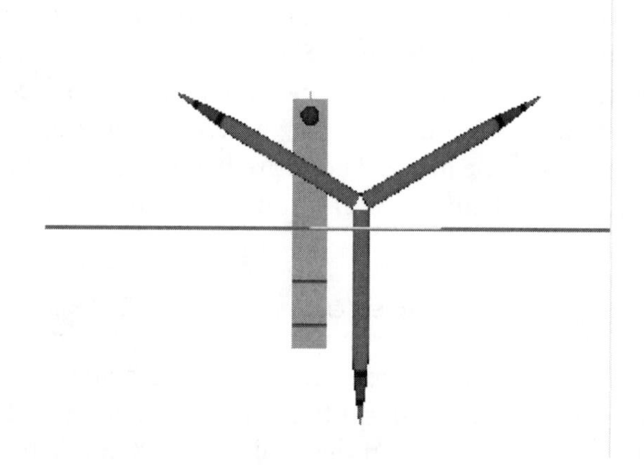

Original blade with two duplicate blades

Deselect the fan and select the box and sphere. Repeat the regroup process for the box and sphere to weld them together. When the merged box and sphere are selected on the Groups tab, enter the name, **base**, beside the Rename button. Click the Rename button to assign the name to the newly merged group, as shown in Figure 14-7.

Positioning the Model at the Point of Origin

Before exporting your model pieces, make sure they are centered at the origin (X = 0, Y = 0, Z = 0). If you do not center your models at the origin, complex animations will be very difficult to implement. Any extra distance away from the origin will create a translation that may cause trouble if you rotate the object in code. As explained in Chapter 8, a translation followed by a rotation creates an orbit. When you create objects that are animated programmatically, the unwanted orbit will be very hard to fix in code. If you don't move the model to the origin in the designer, you might waste a lot of time trying to debug this issue when the problem isn't actually in your code. To avoid these pitfalls, professional game developers will usually ask the modeler to position the model so it rests at the point of origin. Both the fan and windmill base should be centered at the origin.

Adding a Joint

A *joint* is the root of the model hierarchy. It is used to identify the center of the mesh.

FIGURE 14-7

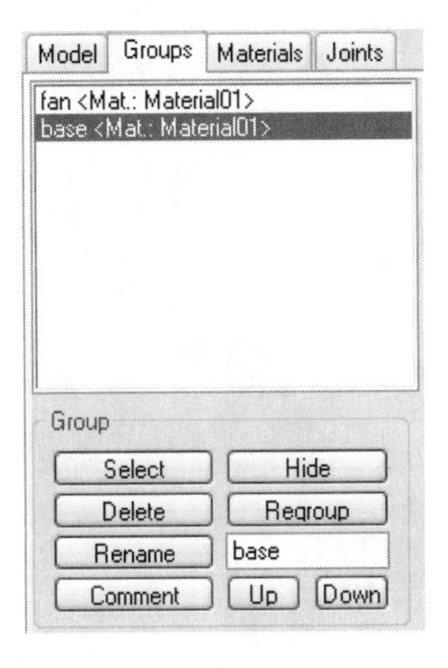

Group listing after merging and renaming

The XNA model loader currently does not require that a joint exist when exporting to *.fbx. However, adding a joint to your MilkShape model in your project is still strongly recommended in case it is required for a future export or by a different format. When MilkShape was used for creating models for XNA's predecessor, DirectX, most DirectX Software Developers Kit releases required a joint for the .x format, but a few releases did not. This made it confusing for MilkShape designers who discovered their models would not load in certain releases of DirectX. To ensure that your model exports can load in your XNA code for future releases, take the extra 30 seconds to add the joint.

The joint can be added from the Model tab. To do this, click on the Joint button and then left-click once over the origin in one of the viewports. If you don't quite get your joint in the exact center of origin, click the Select button. In the Select Options area that appears, choose Joint. Left-click into a viewport and drag around the joint to select it so the joint is highlighted in red. Next, click the Move button on the Model tab. Once in Move mode, you can left-click on the selected joint with your mouse and drag it into place. The joint should appear where the two model pieces are centered at the point of origin, as shown in Figure 14-8.

Saving the Project

Your MilkShape project is now complete. You should save the project and keep it archived in case you decide that you want to modify it. MilkShape projects save as *.ms3d files. Using the ms3d project file type is strongly recommended in case you want to reopen your project later for editing. It is possible to import other file formats into MilkShape, but you may discover unwanted alterations, such as lost group in-

FIGURE 14-8

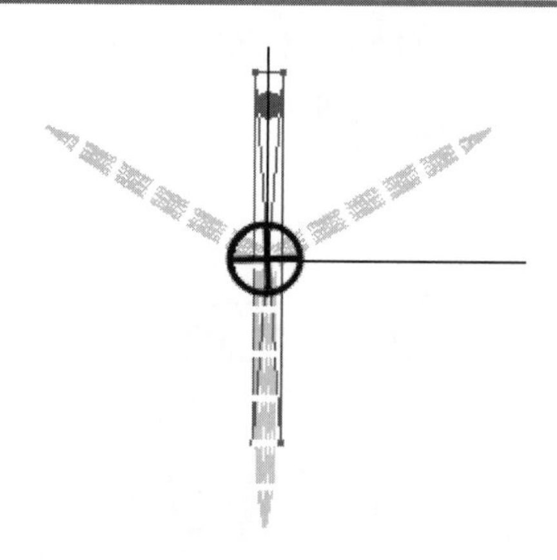

Joint, base, and fan all centered at the origin

formation. Save the project with the name Windmill.ms3d to the same directory where the windmill.bmp file is located. Make sure you store the Windmill.ms3d and windmill.bmp files in a safe place.

Exporting the Model from the Project to the .fbx Format

Next, you are going to export your model to the .fbx format. To keep things simple, you are going to export the fan and windmill base separately. Exporting each piece separately to its own .fbx file allows you to load the pieces separately and animate them individually in your code. After you export the model, you will be able to load and display the windmill base as a stationary object. To create a rotation animation, you will load the fan separately and give it a constant rotation around the Z axis. When the windmill base and the rotating fan are positioned properly, the model will look like an animated windmill in your 3D game.

Exporting the Windmill Base

To prevent the loss of any valuable models, create a copy of your archived project. Open the copy and delete the fan. Next, click on File, then Export. Choose Alias FBX File format in the lengthy list of available model formats that appears. Enter **base.fbx** in the Filename text box of the Export dialog. Export the base.fbx file to the same directory where the windmill.bmp file is located, using the default options. Close the project and do not save it. You have now exported the base of the windmill. The next step is to export the fan.

Exporting the Fan

Reopen your copy of the MilkShape project. This time, delete the windmill base from your project. Next, click on File, then Export. Choose the Alias FBX format from the list of formats that appears. Enter **fan.fbx** in the Filename text box of the Export dialog. Export the fan.fbx file to the same directory where the windmill.bmp file is located. Close the project, but do not save it.

Concluding the MilkShape Demonstration

After working through this chapter, you will have created four files: fan.fbx, base.fbx, windmill.bmp, and windmill.ms3d. The *.fbx and *.bmp files will be loaded in the game project in the next example.

Naturally, you encounter a learning curve when you first create models with MilkShape, but at this point, you probably agree that the job of creating a simple model was not too challenging. If your first few models turn out lousy, do not be alarmed. Most model design newbies do not produce stellar models on their first few tries. But with a little bit of practice, it will not take long for you to ramp up on MilkShape. You can create incredible models in MilkShape once you experiment, learn its limitations, and then learn to push its limits. The simplicity of MilkShape, and its flexibility, make this a product well worth the low price requested after the free 30-day trial ends.

Creating the windmill by using the modeling tool is certainly more interesting and easier than coding it with a series of textures and primitive objects. With only a little bit of practice, you could probably build the same windmill presented in this demo in 5 minutes or less.

LOADING THE MODEL IN XNA

Now that your windmill is built and exported, you can load and animate your masterpiece in code.

The `Model` class provides a simple and effective way to quickly load models, transform them, and of course draw them. Currently the .x and .fbx formats are supported.

The `Model` class uses a skeletal hierarchy to store and draw the vertices of a model. The skeleton is made of bones, and each bone has a transformation associated with it. Mesh data containing vertices with position, normals, and texturing information is attached to each bone in the model and moves with the bone when it is transformed.

Loading the Models

Models are loaded through the content pipeline with the `Load()` method:

```
Model model = Content.Load<Model>("model directory\\modelName");
```

To successfully load each model, you must reference each one in the Solution Explorer.

Skeletal Hierarchy

A *matrix array* stores the transformation matrices for positioning each bone in the model skeleton. For nonanimated models, usually the bone count is 1, so only one transformation is applied to the entire model.

```
Matrix   BoneTransformations = new Matrix[int    model.Bones.Count];
```

The skeletal hierarchy is designed for bone animation. But, as mentioned, currently there is no official animated model loader code for the XNA release. Even so, when drawing static models, it is possible to have more than one bone in your model that has a separate mesh attached to each bone. Each bone has a transformation, and the transformations are cumulative as you travel down the hierarchy from the skeleton's root. As an example, you could think of the spine as the root. The upper leg takes on the transformation of the spine and adds a transformation of its own. The lower leg takes on the cumulative transformation of the spine and upper leg in addition to adding its own transformation. The foot takes on the cumulative transformations of all these bones, plus it adds its own transformation to the series. The foot is a child of the lower leg, and the lower leg is a child of the upper leg, and so on. Conversely, the spine is the parent of the upper leg, which in turn is the parent of the lower leg. This hierarchy of bones is ideal for transforming and animating multiple meshes.

When the model is created, the bone transformation matrices associated with the model are stored in the `Model` class using the `CopyAbsoluteBoneTransformsTo()` method exposed by the `Model` object:

```
Model   model.CopyAbsoluteBoneTransformsTo(Matrix  boneTransformations);
```

DRAWING THE MODEL IN XNA

It is possible to have more than one mesh in a model where each mesh is considered a separate unit of vertex position, texture, and normal data. While rendering the model, the routine searches the `Model` object for each `ModelMesh` object, transforms it according to the World matrix, sets lighting (if desired), and draws it. To iterate through each mesh of the `Model` object, a foreach-loop searches through each `ModelMesh` object:

```
foreach (ModelMesh mesh in model.Meshes);
```

Another loop nested inside the `ModelMesh` loop is required to properly show your model in the game world and to add lighting (if desired):

```
    foreach (BasicEffect effect in mesh.Effects);
```

Before drawing the model, you can apply lighting to the model using XNA's `BasicEffect` class, which was introduced in Chapter 6. Once inside the effect loop, to show all objects in your game properly relative to the camera, you must store the game class's View and Projection matrices in the `BasicEffect` shader through the effect parameters:

```
BasicEffect  effect.View       = Matrix world;
BasicEffect  effect.Projection = Matrix world;
```

To apply transformations to all meshes within the model, you must multiply each mesh's bone transformation matrix by the cumulative transformation matrix, or *World matrix*. The product is stored in the `BasicEffect shader, which applies the final transformation to the mesh drawn.`

```
effect.World = carMatrix[mesh.ParentBone.Index] * WorldMatrix;
```

You can use XNA's `BasicEffect` class to also add lighting to the model. More information will be provided in Chapter 22 to explain how to customize your lighting. For this chapter, the default lighting is applied to the model:

```
effect.EnableDefaultLighting();
```

To draw each mesh in the model, `ModelMesh`'s `Draw()` method is called to render it:

```
ModelMesh   mesh.Draw();
```

Loading and Animating the Windmill in Code

This example takes the windmill you made in MilkShape and animates it in code. When you are finished working through this example, your windmill will look like the one presented earlier in Figure 14-1.

This code example begins with either the MGHWinBaseCode or MGH360BaseCode project found in the BaseCode folder on this book's website. Also, your fan.fbx and base.fbx files, along with the windmill texture (windmill.bmp) models, must be added to your project so they can be loaded in the content pipeline. Or, if you don't want to build these models, you can find the fan.fbx, base.fbx, and windmill.bmp files in the Models folder. These three files need to be placed in a Models folder in your project so they can be loaded properly.

To store the fan and base models separately, two separate `Model` objects are declared at the module level of the game class. Matrices for transforming the meshes in each model are also included with this declaration so they can be set later when the models are loaded.

```
Model       baseModel;      Model       fanModel;
Matrix[]    fanMatrix;      Matrix[]    baseMatrix;
```

The same code will be reused to draw each model, so identifiers are needed to distinguish between the windmill base and fan model. These definitions are used throughout the game class, so they need to be added at the top of the game class.

```
const int WINDMILL_BASE = 0; const int WINDMILL_FAN = 1;
```

The two models are loaded separately with the ContentManager's Load() method using a <Model> template. When each model is loaded, the bone matrices are stored in a Matrix object for that model. These examples have only one bone, so any transformations applied to them will apply to the entire model. The CopyAbsoluteBoneTransformsTo() method copies the transformations for all bones in the model into an array that the model object can use. To set these models up when the program begins, add these instructions to the LoadContent() method:

```
baseModel   = Content.Load<Model>("Models\\base");
baseMatrix  = new Matrix[baseModel.Bones.Count];
baseModel.CopyAbsoluteBoneTransformsTo(baseMatrix);

fanModel    = Content.Load<Model>("Models\\fan");
fanMatrix   = new Matrix[fanModel.Bones.Count];
fanModel.CopyAbsoluteBoneTransformsTo(fanMatrix);
```

To create a continuous rotation for the windmill fan, a module-level variable, *fanRotation*, is used. The module-level variable stores the total rotation in radians and is incremented each frame. Adding it at the module level allows you to store the variable and read its updated value each frame:

```
private float fanRotation = 0.0f; // stores rotation of windmill fan
```

Drawing the windmill base is actually very simple. The first three steps for rendering a model are identical to the steps used to draw a primitive object using vertex types. The transformation matrices are declared and initialized just as you have done before when you rendered primitive objects from vertex types. As described in Chapter 7, the same I.S.R.O.T. sequence of transformations applies here to transform each Model object. In this case, scaling and a translation will be performed for both models. Every time you load a model, you have to resize it so that it is proportionate to your game world. The fan is rotated about the Z axis too, so an additional transformation on the Z axis is required. A time-scaled value is used to perform the rotation to keep the rotation speed constant regardless of the system used. The scaled time lapse is added to *fanRotation*, which stores total radians for the rotation. *fanRotation* is reset to equal the remainder of *fanRotation* divided by 2π. This extra step to store the remainder rather than the actual cumulative value maintains the same rotation about the Z axis while preventing variable overflow.

In step 4 of DrawWindmill(), once the cumulative transformation matrix has been built, it is multiplied against the transformation matrix for each mesh in the model. If you are working with a model that is centered at the origin and only has one mesh, the mesh's matrix would be equivalent to the identity matrix. If your model is not centered at the origin, your transformations are going to take on an additional translation, so you may need to check this if your models are not animating properly. The product of the bone matrix and the World matrix is passed to the World matrix variable in XNA's `BasicEffect shader`. At the same time, you also need to store the View and Projection matrices from your game class in the `BasicEffect's` variables. The shader needs this information to position your models so they can be seen properly by the camera.

Lighting is also enabled in step 4 using the `EnableDefaultLighting()` method. Refer to Chapter 22 for more information on how to use the different lighting options that come with the `BasicEffect` class.

Finally, the model can be drawn using the `ModelMesh` object's `Draw()` method. Add `DrawWindmill()` to your game class to transform and render your fan and windmill:

```
void DrawWindmill(Model model, int modelNum, GameTime gameTime){
    graphics.GraphicsDevice.RenderState.CullMode    // don't draw backface
                  = CullMode.CullClockwiseFace;  // when many vertices

    foreach (ModelMesh mesh in model.Meshes){
        // 1: declare matrices
        Matrix world, scale, rotationZ, translation;

        // 2: initialize matrices
        scale       = Matrix.CreateScale(0.1f, 0.1f, 0.1f);
        translation = Matrix.CreateTranslation(0.0f, 0.9f, -4.0f);
        rotationZ   = Matrix.CreateRotationZ(0.0f);

        if (modelNum == WINDMILL_FAN){
            // calculate time between frames for system independent speed
            fanRotation += gameTime.ElapsedRealTime.Ticks / 6000000.0f;
            // prevent var overflow - store remainder
            fanRotation  = fanRotation % (2.0f * (float)Math.PI);
            rotationZ    = Matrix.CreateRotationZ(fanRotation);
        }
        // 3: build cumulative world matrix using I.S.R.O.T. sequence
        // identity, scale, rotate, orbit(translate&rotate), translate
        world           = scale * rotationZ * translation;

        // 4: set shader parameters
        foreach (BasicEffect effect in mesh.Effects){
            if (modelNum == WINDMILL_BASE)
                effect.World  = baseMatrix[mesh.ParentBone.Index]* world;
```

```
            if (modelNum == WINDMILL_FAN)
                effect.World  = fanMatrix[mesh.ParentBone.Index] * world;
            effect.View       = cam.viewMatrix;
            effect.Projection = cam.projectionMatrix;
            effect.EnableDefaultLighting();
        }
        // 5: draw object
        mesh.Draw();
    }
    // stop culling
    graphics.GraphicsDevice.RenderState.CullMode = CullMode.None;
}
```

To draw both models, call them from the `Draw()` method:

```
DrawWindmill(baseModel, WINDMILL_BASE, gameTime);
DrawWindmill(fanModel,  WINDMILL_FAN,  gameTime);
```

When you run this program, you will see how great the windmill looks in your game. The output shows your windmill with the fan rotating about the Z axis (refer to Figure 14-1). You may find that additional scaling, rotations, or translations are needed to move your own models into place depending on how your windmill was built. In the end, you will find you can create, load, and render 3D models with very little effort.

Adding a Car as a Third-Person Object

This example shows how to draw a model car as a third-person object. When you use the third-person view, your camera is behind the object wherever you travel in the 3D world. When this example is complete, not only will the car drive in front of you as you move the camera through the 3D world, but the wheels of the car will spin when you move and the front wheels will pivot about the Y axis as you turn.

One car model and one tire model will be used for this example. They can be found in the Models folder on this book's website. Note that these models are intentionally positioned at the origin with the joint, as shown in Figure 14-9. Having everything centered at the origin ensures that the transformations done in code generate the expected behavior.

Figure 14-10 shows the car after the wheel has been transformed and drawn once in each wheel well.

When this demonstration is complete, the model car and wheel will be drawn as the third person, so your camera will always be positioned behind it.

The code example begins with the MGHWinBaseCode project or the MGH360BaseCode project found in the BaseCode folder.

FIGURE 14-9

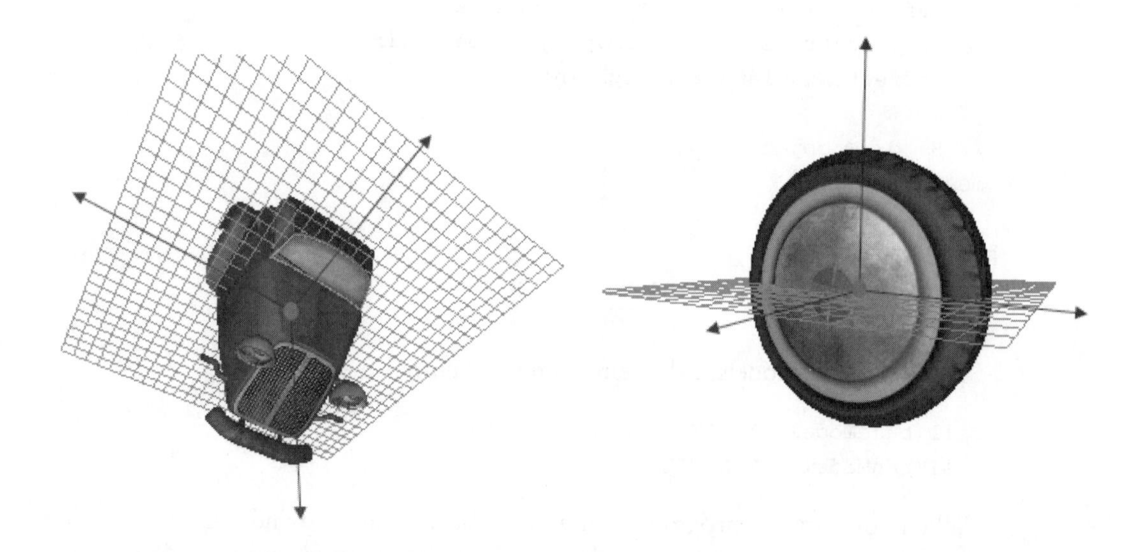

Models centered at the origin with a joint in the middle

FIGURE 14-10

One model car and one model wheel redrawn four times

You can find the hotrod.fbx, wheel.fbx, and car.tga files in the Models folder on this book's website. To reference them in your project, add a Models folder under the Content node and place these files there. You will need to add a reference to the two *.fbx files from the Models folder inside the Solution Explorer. To do this, right-click the project name in the Solution Explorer. Then choose Add and then New Folder. This will create a Models folder. Next, right-click the Models folder and choose Add an Existing Item. Finally, navigate to the hotrod.fbx and wheel.fbx files and select them. When you do this, they will be added to the Models folder. You will also need to add the car.tga file to the Models directory in your project.

In code, two separate model objects are used to draw the model car. One object stores the car, and the other stores a wheel. Also, a matrix array for each model is needed to store the bone transformations for their meshes when the two models are loaded. These bone transformations will be implemented later when the models are drawn to position them so they can be seen properly by the camera. Add these declarations for the model objects, and their matrix arrays at the top of the game class so the two models can later be loaded, transformed, and drawn:

```
Model       carModel;   Model       wheelModel;
Matrix[]    carMatrix;  Matrix[]    wheelMatrix;
```

Adding the next six lines of code to the `LoadContent()` method will load the models using the `ContentManager` object. The transformation matrices for each mesh in both models will be stored in a mesh array with the `CopyAbsoluteBoneTransformsTo()` method. The code loads your models from the Models folder referenced from the Content node of your project. The wheel.fbx, hotrod.fbx, and car.tga files need to be there for a successful load.

```
carModel     = Content.Load<Model>("Models\\hotrod");
carMatrix    = new Matrix[carModel.Bones.Count];
carModel.CopyAbsoluteBoneTransformsTo(carMatrix);

wheelModel   = Content.Load<Model>("Models\\wheel");
wheelMatrix  = new Matrix[wheelModel.Bones.Count];
wheelModel.CopyAbsoluteBoneTransformsTo(wheelMatrix);
```

To obtain a better look at the car from behind so you can see the front wheels pivot, an adjustment to the camera is made so it looks slightly downward toward the ground. In the constructor for the camera class, replace the view direction with this instruction to angle the camera downward. The X and Z values remain the same, but the Y value is down 0.07 units from 0.9f:

```
view         = new Vector3(0.0f, 0.83f,-0.5f);
```

To adapt the camera's look and feel for a car, obviously you cannot strafe with a car, so in the Update() method comment out the instruction that triggers strafing:

```
// cam.Strafe(Strafe());
```

To position the car and wheels ahead of the camera, a translation on the Z axis is needed. A variable declared at the class level to store this translation is required so that the methods that draw the tires and wheels can use the same variable. Using the same translation amount variable in both methods makes it easy to adjust the car's distance from the camera.

```
const float Z_OFFSET = 2.10f;
```

To understand the logic behind turning the wheels and the response of the controls, consider the process behind parallel parking a car. You have to consider the car's direction when turning the steering wheel while moving backward and forward as you position the car beside the roadside curb. You have to look where you're going too, so you don't hit the cars around you. The logic is similar when programming a third-person car.

For this routine, if the game pad is in use, the left thumbstick's Y property is obtained to determine whether the car is moving forward or backward. The left thumbstick's Y value ranges from –1 for reverse to +1 for forward. If the left thumbstick is resting at the center, where Y = 0.0f, the car is not moving so the view is not changed. If the game pad is not connected, the UP and DOWN ARROW keys, or the W and S keys, are used to move the car and the RIGHT and LEFT ARROW keys, or the A and D keys, are used to turn it. To coordinate the changes in view with the game controls, the following version of the ChangeView() method replaces the existing one. This revised version only permits changes to the view that occur when the car turns. You can read more about the viewer code in Chapter 17.

```
Vector2 ChangeView(GameTime gameTime){
    const float SENSITIVITY          = 200.0f;
    const float VERTICAL_INVERSION   =  -1.0f;    // vertical view control

    // handle change in view using right and left keys
    KeyboardState kb      = Keyboard.GetState();
    GamePadState  gp      = GamePad.GetState(PlayerIndex.One);
    int        middleX    = Window.ClientBounds.Width/2;
    int        middleY    = Window.ClientBounds.Height/2;
    Vector2 change        = new Vector2(0.0f, 0.0f);

    if (gp.IsConnected == true) // give gamepad precedence
        change.X          = gp.ThumbSticks.Right.X
```

```
                        * SENSITIVITY;
    else{
#if !XBOX
        float scaleY    = VERTICAL_INVERSION * (float)
                          gameTime.ElapsedGameTime.Milliseconds/100.0f;
        float scaleX    = (float)
                          gameTime.ElapsedGameTime.Milliseconds/400.0f;
        // get cursor position
        mouse           = Mouse.GetState();

        // cursor not at center on X
        if (mouse.X != middleX)
            change.X    =(mouse.X - middleX)/scaleX;

        // reset cursor back to center
        Mouse.SetPosition(middleX, middleY);
#endif
    }
    // use game pad
    if (gp.IsConnected == true){
        // no forward or backward movement so don't change view
        if (gp.ThumbSticks.Left.Y == 0.0f)
            change.X    = 0.0f;
        // driving in reverse - the view must match the wheel pivot
        else if (gp.ThumbSticks.Left.Y < 0.0f)
            change.X   *= -1.0f;
    }
    // use keyboard
    else{
        if (kb.IsKeyDown(Keys.Right) || kb.IsKeyDown(Keys.D))
            change.X    = SENSITIVITY; // right
        else if (kb.IsKeyDown(Keys.Left) || kb.IsKeyDown(Keys.A))
            change.X    =-SENSITIVITY; // left
        if (!kb.IsKeyDown(Keys.Down) && !kb.IsKeyDown(Keys.Up) &&
            !kb.IsKeyDown(Keys.S) && !kb.IsKeyDown(Keys.W))
            change.X    = 0.0f;           // not moving
        else if (kb.IsKeyDown(Keys.Down) || kb.IsKeyDown(Keys.S))
            change.X   *=-1.0f;           // driving in reverse so adjust
    }                                     // view and wheel pivot
    return change;
}
```

Then, to ensure the camera viewer follows the car, replace the existing call to `cam.SetView()` from `Update()` with these four instructions:

```
Vector2 view = ChangeView(gameTime);
view.Y       = 0.0f; // disable vertical view changes
view.X      /= 2.7f; // restrict view to match car's turning radius
cam.SetView(view);
```

The code used to draw the car is similar to the code used to draw the windmill base and fan. The transformations are a little more complex, but they still follow the I.S.R.O.T. sequence. The references used to create the car in the modeling tool were different from the XNA environment. The car needs to be scaled down from its original size so it is proportionate to the 3D world generated in the base code. Also, to make the car bottom horizontal with the ground, it must be rotated on the X axis. Once these initial transformations have been performed, some additional translations and a rotation are needed to move the car out ahead of the camera so you can see it at all times from a third person perspective wherever you go. We are also going to reuse some of this code later when drawing the wheels and also in Chapter 18 when implementing collision detection. To enable code reuse we have broken the transformation series into the ScaleModel(), OffsetFromCamera(), CarYDirection(), and TransformCar() methods. These are needed in the game class at this point to animate the car:

```
Matrix ScaleModel(){
    const float SCALAR = 0.002f;
    return Matrix.CreateScale(SCALAR, SCALAR, SCALAR);
}
Vector3 OffsetFromCamera(){
    const float CARHEIGHTOFFGROUND = 0.195f;
    Vector3 offsetFromCamera
                  = new Vector3(0.0f, CARHEIGHTOFFGROUND, Z_OFFSET);
    return offsetFromCamera;
}
float CarYDirection(Camera tempCam){
    return (float)Math.Atan2(tempCam.view.X - tempCam.position.X,
                             tempCam.view.Z - tempCam.position.Z);
}
Matrix TransformCar(Camera camera){
    // 1: declare matrices and other variables
    Vector3 offsetFromCamera = OffsetFromCamera();
    Matrix rotationX, translation, orbitTranslate, orbitRotate;
```

```
    // 2: initialize matrices
    rotationX        = Matrix.CreateRotationX(-(float)Math.PI / 2.0f);
    orbitTranslate   = Matrix.CreateTranslation(offsetFromCamera);
    orbitRotate      = Matrix.CreateRotationY(CarYDirection(camera));
    translation      = Matrix.CreateTranslation(camera.position.X, 0.0f,
                                                camera.position.Z);
    // 3: build cumulative world matrix using I.S.R.O.T. sequence
    // identity, scale, rotate, orbit(translate & rotate), translate
    return rotationX * orbitTranslate * orbitRotate * translation;
}
```

Figure 14-11 explains the transformations to make viewing the car as a third person possible.

FIGURE 14-11

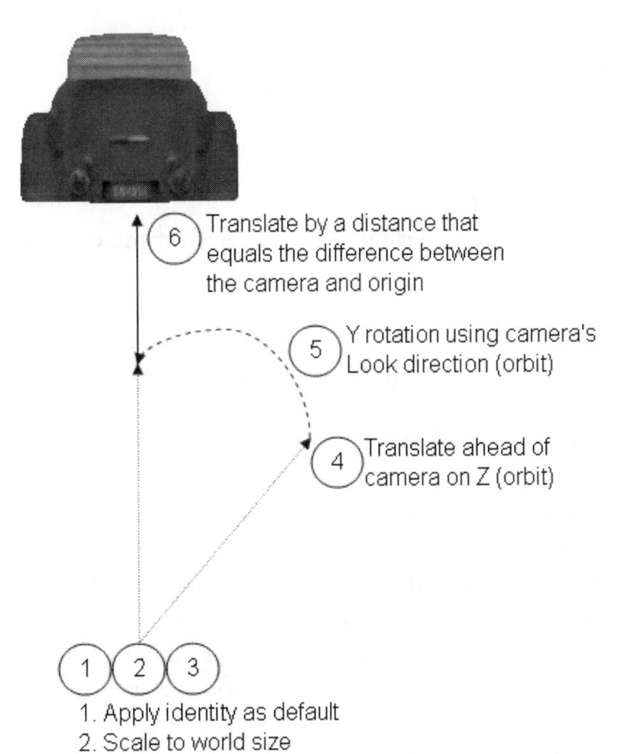
6
Translate by a distance that equals the difference between the camera and origin
5
Y rotation using camera's Look direction (orbit)
4
Translate ahead of camera on Z (orbit)
1
2
3
1. Apply identity as default
2. Scale to world size
3. Rotate on X so car is horizontal

Transformations for positioning the car in front of the camera

As explained in the windmill model example, when the model is drawn, the BasicEffect shader is used, so the World, View, and Projection matrices must be set to transform it. Also, when the car is drawn, default lighting is enabled since the BasicEffect shader makes this easy to do. Add DrawCar() to transform, light, and draw your car so it appears from third person you can always see in front of your camera:

```
void DrawModel(Model model, Matrix[] modelMatrix, Matrix world){
    foreach (ModelMesh mesh in model.Meshes){
        foreach (BasicEffect effect in mesh.Effects){
            // 4: set shader variables
            effect.World      = modelMatrix[mesh.ParentBone.Index]*world;
            effect.View       = cam.viewMatrix;
            effect.Projection = cam.projectionMatrix;
            effect.EnableDefaultLighting();
            effect.CommitChanges();
        }
        // 5: draw object
        mesh.Draw();
    }
}
```

The car is ready for rendering. To draw it, add the call statement to the end of Draw():

```
Matrix transform = TransformCar(cam);
DrawModel(carModel, carMatrix, ScaleModel() * transform);
```

When you run the program now, you will see the car but without the wheels. The code for adding the wheels is not much different from the code used to load and draw the car model. However, the wheels must also spin when the car moves and they must pivot when the car turns.

The distance travelled each frame is used to increment the tire's spin. A variable, *tireSpin*, is declared at the top of the game class to store and update the tire rotation in radians. Since the difference between the camera's current and previous position is needed, a variable to store the camera's previous position is also required:

```
private float    tireSpin;
private Vector3  previousPosition;
```

The camera's previous position needs to be stored at the top of the `Update()` method in the game class before the camera's position is modified:

```
previousPosition = cam.position;
```

The wheels are spun forward as long as you shift the left thumbstick up or press the UP ARROW key. The wheels spin backward if you shift the left thumbstick down or press the DOWN ARROW key. Change in distance divided by the tire radius is used to calculate the increment to the tire's rotation angle each frame. Add `Spin()` to spin your wheels as your car moves forward or backward:

```
private float Spin(GameTime gameTime){
    KeyboardState kb = Keyboard.GetState();
    GamePadState  gp;
    gp                = GamePad.GetState(PlayerIndex.One);

    // generate time scaled increment for tire rotation
    float timeScale = gameTime.ElapsedGameTime.Milliseconds/170.0f;

    // game pad connected - car not moving forward or reverse
    if (gp.ThumbSticks.Left.Y == 0.0f && gp.IsConnected)
        return 0.0f; // don't Spin wheels

    // game pad not connected - car not moving forward or reverse
    else if (!kb.IsKeyDown(Keys.Up) && !kb.IsKeyDown(Keys.W) &&
    !kb.IsKeyDown(Keys.Down) && !kb.IsKeyDown(Keys.S) && !gp.IsConnected)
        return 0.0f; // don't Spin wheels

    // down key or left stick down so reverse tires
    if (kb.IsKeyDown(Keys.Down) || kb.IsKeyDown(Keys.S)
        || gp.ThumbSticks.Left.Y < 0.0f)
        timeScale *= -1.0f;

    // increment tire and prevent variable overflow with modulus
    tireSpin += timeScale;
    tireSpin  = tireSpin % (2.0f * (float)Math.PI);

    // return increment to X rotation for tire
    return tireSpin;
}
```

Next, some extra code is needed to pivot the front wheels when you turn the car. While the car is moving forward or backward, an adjustment to the view either from shifting the right thumbstick left or right or from pressing the LEFT or RIGHT ARROW key will cause the wheels to pivot. You can also pivot the wheels when the car is stationary and there is no change to the view.

If the game pad is in use, the right thumbstick's X property is obtained to adjust the rotation angle about the Y axis for both wheels. The right thumbstick's X property ranges from -1 to 1. This X value is scaled to provide a suitable pivot angle in radians for the front wheels.

If you are using the keyboard only, the change in view from pressing the RIGHT or LEFT ARROW key or the A and D keys is used to set the rotation angle. When you're using the keyboard, the change in view is used to obtain the rotation angle. Since the change in view is determined before the pivot angle is calculated, matching the wheel pivot to the change in view avoids conflicts in direction if you are pressing the UP and DOWN ARROW keys or the W and S keys at the same time. The pivot angle in radians is negated if the car is driving in reverse, so the front wheels pivot properly while you back up.

Add `PivotWheel()` to the game class to rotate your front tires about the Y axis when you want to turn your wheels:

```
private float PivotWheel(GameTime gameTime){
    float          pivot = 0.0f;
    KeyboardState kb     = Keyboard.GetState();
    GamePadState  gp     = GamePad.GetState(PlayerIndex.One);

    // turn wheel about Y axis if right stick shifted on X
    if (gp.IsConnected == true)
        pivot              = gp.ThumbSticks.Right.X/2.7f;
    // turn wheel about Y axis if LEFT, RIGHT, A, or D keys pressed
    else{
        Vector2 view     = ChangeView(gameTime);
        pivot              = view.X/470.0f;
        if (Move() < 0.0f)            // driving in reverse
            pivot *= -1.0f;
        else if (Move() == 0.0f)      // car stopped but pivot tires
            if (kb.IsKeyDown(Keys.Right) || kb.IsKeyDown(Keys.D))
                pivot   = 0.41f;
            else if (kb.IsKeyDown(Keys.Left) || kb.IsKeyDown(Keys.A))
                pivot   =-0.41f;
    }
```

```
    return pivot;
}
```

To identify each wheel throughout the game class, these constant declarations are required at the top of this class:

```
const int FRONTLEFT = 0;    const int FRONTRIGHT = 1;
const int BACKLEFT  = 2;    const int BACKRIGHT  = 3;
```

The code for drawing the wheel is structurally identical to the other draw routines presented in this chapter. Only one wheel model is actually being used, but it is being drawn four times. The transformations to rotate, spin, and position each wheel into place may look hefty, but they are actually simple when you realize that they, too, follow the I.S.R.O.T. sequence. Figure 14-12 summarizes the transformations applied to each wheel.

FIGURE 14-12

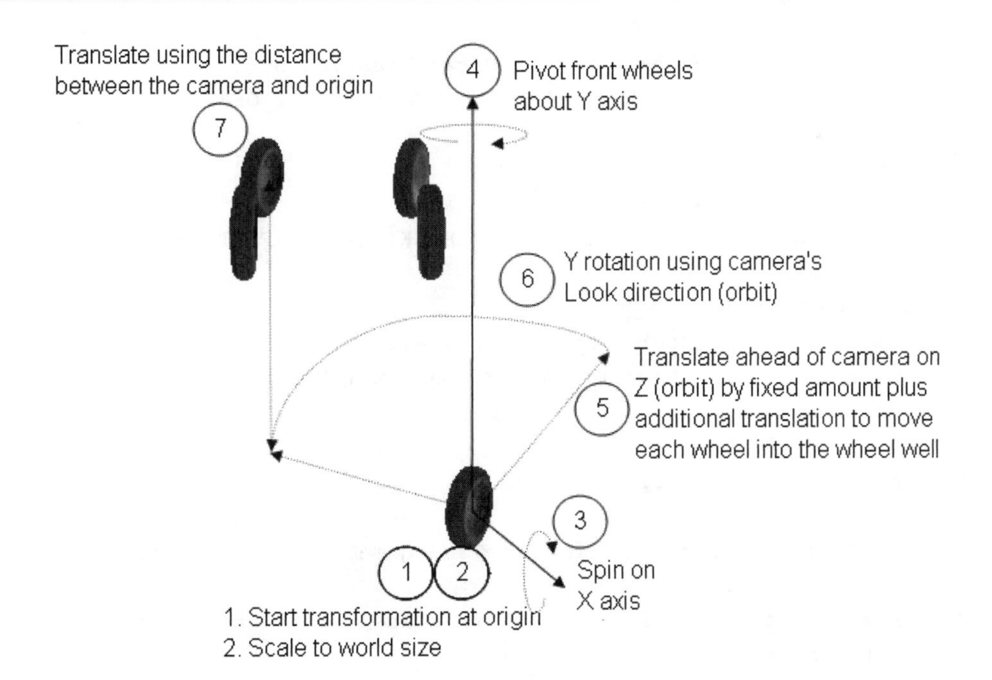

Transformations for each wheel

The transformations described are implemented in the following WheelOffset() and TransformWheel() methods:

```
Matrix WheelOffset(int wheelNum){
    Matrix offsetFromCenter = Matrix.Identity;
    const float WHEELRADIUS = 0.126f;
    const float FRONT_MAX_X = 0.23f;
    const float FRONT_MAX_Z = 0.251f;
    const float BACK_MAX_X  =  0.24f;
    const float BACK_MAX_Z  = -0.29f;
    Vector3 FRONT
            = new Vector3(FRONT_MAX_X, WHEELRADIUS, FRONT_MAX_Z);
    Vector3 BACK
            = new Vector3(BACK_MAX_X, WHEELRADIUS, BACK_MAX_Z);
    switch (wheelNum){
        case FRONTLEFT:
            offsetFromCenter = Matrix.CreateTranslation(
            new Vector3( FRONT.X, FRONT.Y, FRONT.Z + Z_OFFSET));
            break;
        case FRONTRIGHT:
            offsetFromCenter = Matrix.CreateTranslation(
            new Vector3(-FRONT.X, FRONT.Y, FRONT.Z + Z_OFFSET));
            break;
        case BACKLEFT:
            offsetFromCenter = Matrix.CreateTranslation(
            new Vector3( BACK.X, BACK.Y, BACK.Z + Z_OFFSET));
            break;
        case BACKRIGHT:
            offsetFromCenter = Matrix.CreateTranslation(
            new Vector3(-BACK.X, BACK.Y, BACK.Z + Z_OFFSET));
            break;
    }
    return offsetFromCenter;
}
Matrix TransformWheel(int tireNum, GameTime gameTime, Camera camera){
    // 1: declare matrices
    Matrix rotationX, rotationY, orbitTranslate, orbitRotationY,
           translation;
    // 2: initialize matrices
    rotationX         = Matrix.CreateRotationX(0.0f);
    rotationY         = Matrix.CreateRotationY(0.0f);
    orbitTranslate    = WheelOffset(tireNum);
```

```
    orbitRotationY     = Matrix.CreateRotationY(CarYDirection(camera));
    translation        = Matrix.CreateTranslation(camera.position.X, 0.0f,
                                                  camera.position.Z);
    switch (tireNum){
        case FRONTLEFT:
            rotationX = Matrix.CreateRotationX(-Spin(gameTime));
            rotationY = Matrix.CreateRotationY(+(float)Math.PI
                                              - PivotWheel(gameTime));
            break;
        case FRONTRIGHT:
            rotationX = Matrix.CreateRotationX(+Spin(gameTime));
            rotationY = Matrix.CreateRotationY(-PivotWheel(gameTime));
            break;
        case BACKLEFT:
            rotationX = Matrix.CreateRotationX(-Spin(gameTime));
            rotationY = Matrix.CreateRotationY(+(float)Math.PI);
            break;
        case BACKRIGHT:
            rotationX = Matrix.CreateRotationX(+Spin(gameTime));
            break;
    }
    // 3: build cumulative world matrix using I.S.R.O.T. sequence
    // identity, scale, rotate, orbit(translate & rotate), translate
    return rotationX * rotationY * orbitTranslate * orbitRotationY
                                                  * translation;
}
```

Add the following code to `Draw()` to transform, light, and draw the wheel model four times so that each wheel is positioned properly around the car:

```
const int NUM_WHEELS = 4;
for(int i = 0; i <=NUM_WHEELS; i++){
    transform = TransformWheel(i, gameTime, cam);
    DrawModel(wheelModel, wheelMatrix, ScaleModel() * transform);
}
```

Now the wheels are ready to be drawn. Inside `Draw()`, add the call statement to draw the wheels to view them with your car:

After compiling and running your project, you will be able to drive through the 3D world in comfort. Driving around in this model hot rod is definitely a lot more interesting than driving around in a hand-coded primitive object. Point your wheels and go.

CHAPTER 14 REVIEW EXERCISES

To get the most from this chapter, try out these chapter review exercises.

1. Follow the step-by-step examples presented in this chapter, if you have not already done so.
2. Explain how models that are not saved at the origin cause unbalanced transformations.
3. Replace the primitive objects in the airplane example shown in Chapter 8 with an airplane model and propeller model that you create in MilkShape. When you create the airplane model, be sure to use only one image for the texture, as explained in the guidelines in this chapter.

CHAPTER 15

Vectors

A *vector* is a multidimensional object that stores data such as position, distance, and speed. Vectors are a key pillar in the structure of any 3D graphics engine because they are used to create animations, implement collision detection, set lighting, launch ballistics, and more. Understanding vector math is essential if you want to invent impressive special effects for your games. The good news is that vector math is simple.

VECTOR TYPES

A three-dimensional vector stores X, Y, and Z coordinates, which are often used for describing position and direction. However, a vector could be two-dimensional, in which case it would only store X and Y coordinates. A two-dimensional vector is often used for setting position coordinates for 2D sprites or UV coordinates for textures. A vector could even have four dimensions (that is, it would store X, Y, Z, and W coordinates). The W coordinate might be used to specify the alpha color for setting transparency along with red, green, and blue parameters in the X, Y, and Z values of the same vector. Alternatively, the W coordinate might be added on to the end of a three-dimensional vector to ensure that the total vector columns match the total rows of a 4×4 matrix so the objects are compatible for multiplication.

The Microsoft.Xna.Framework library provides three vector types: Vector2, Vector3, and Vector4. Each vector contains a similar set of methods to perform mathematical operations on the vectors, but each set of operators is tailored for the total dimensions in the corresponding vector type. You will see these vector operations in various graphics and game algorithms, so it is worth understanding them—and it's even better when you can use them to customize your own graphics algorithms. The logic behind vector math operations is the same for each of the three vector types, and each type makes it easy to perform addition, subtraction, and scaling. The vector types also provide methods for performing more complex operations. This includes calculating a vector's length, calculating a perpendicular vector from a surface, and finding the angle between two vectors.

VECTOR ADDITION

Vector addition is essential for many game algorithms. You have already been using vector addition to move an object by updating its coordinates. This technique was first covered in Chapter 8. Here is the formula for summing two 3D vectors (A and B):

```
A + B = {Ax + Bx, Ay + By, Az + Bz}
```

Here's an example of vector addition. If vector A stores a position of X=5, Y=3, Z=0, and vector B stores a change in position of X=4, Y=-2, Z=0, then the sum equals X=9, Y=1, Z=0. This is the manual calculation:

```
|5| + | 4| = |9|
|3|   |-2|   |1|
|0|   | 0|   |0|
```

To perform this calculation in code, start with the "Font Example: Displaying Text in the Game Window" solution in Chapter 13, and add the `VectorCalculation()` method to the game class. This new method adds vectors A and B and then displays their sum as text in the game window:

```
String VectorCalculation(){
    Vector3 A, B, C;
    A = new Vector3(5.0f, 3.0f, 0.0f);
    B = new Vector3(4.0f,-2.0f, 0.0f);
    C.X=A.X+B.X;     C.Y=A.Y+B.Y;     C.Z=A.Z+B.Z;

    return     "X = " + C.X.ToString() + "  Y = " + C.Y.ToString()
         + "   Z = " + C.Z.ToString();
}
```

To trigger the calculation and show the result in the top of the game window, inside the `DrawFonts()` method, replace the line

```
spriteBatch.DrawString(spriteFont, outputString, new Vector2(
                       safeArea.Left, safeArea.Top), Color.Yellow);
```

with this revised version that calls the `VectorCalculation()` method:

```
spriteBatch.DrawString(spriteFont, VectorCalculation(), new Vector2(
                       safeArea.Left, safeArea.Top), Color.Yellow);
```

When you run this code, the output will show the same sum for X, Y, and Z that was demonstrated earlier in the manual addition.

You could actually replace the three instructions that separately assign values to C.X, C.Y, and C.Z to perform the sum in `VectorCalculation()` with this revision:

```
C = A + B;
```

When you run this program, you will see the same output as before, but there is considerably less code behind the addition.

VECTOR SUBTRACTION

Vector subtraction is essential any time you want to calculate the distance between two vectors. If vector A (5, 3, 0) is decremented by B (4, –2, 0), the resulting vector would be defined by X=1, Y=5, Z=0:

```
|5| - | 4| = |1|
|3|   |-2|   |5|
|0|   | 0|   |0|
```

To implement vector subtraction in your code, start with the solution from the previous example and make the following changes. To calculate the difference between vector A and vector B, replace the instruction that performs the addition for C inside `VectorCalculation()` with the following:

```
C = A - B;
```

When you run this code, the vector that results from the subtraction is displayed in the game window as X = 1, Y=5, Z = 0. Notice that these totals for X, Y, and Z match the difference you calculated manually.

VECTOR SCALING

Scaling a vector's magnitude up or down involves multiplying a vector by a scalar value. When you're working with the `Vector2`, `Vector3`, and `Vector4` objects, the scalar must be a floating-point number. Of course, there are endless possibilities for using vector scaling in your game and graphics routines. In Chapter 7, vector scaling was used to maintain an animation at a constant rate. To regulate the animation speed so that it runs at the same rate on both fast and slow machines, the direction vector is multiplied by the time lapse between frames.

Vector Scaling, Example 1

To demonstrate vector scaling, consider a vector where X=9, Y=1, and Z=0. Then multiply the vector by 2. The product equals

```
X = 9*2        Y = 1*2        Z = 0*2
```

The new vector is X = 18, Y = 2, Z = 0.

To perform this scaling in code, replace the `VectorCalculation()` method from the previous example with this new version:

```
String VectorCalculation(){
    Vector3 vector  = new Vector3(9.0f, 1.0f, 0.0f);
    float   scale   = 2.0f;
            vector *= scale;

    return "X = " + vector.X.ToString() + "  Y = " + vector.Y.ToString()
       + "  Z = " + vector.Z.ToString();
}
```

When you compile and run this code, the text output will show the same product that you calculated manually: X = 18, Y = 2, Z = 0.

You may also use a divisor to scale a vector by a fraction. One common example of this operation is in the creation of unit vectors to scale the range so each vector component is between -1 and 1. Unit vectors are essential for ensuring consistency when working with direction vectors and even when using vectors for graphics effects such as lighting.

Vector Scaling, Example 2

To demonstrate vector scaling with a divisor, consider vector A (9, 1, 0) divided by 2; you would end up with the following calculation:

```
X = 9/2 Y = 1/2 Z = 0/2
```

The new vector is defined with the coordinates X = 4.500, Y = 0.500, and Z = 0.000. The direction information is the same, but the magnitude is reduced to half the original amount.

To implement this vector operation in code, begin with the solution for the preceding scaling example. Then, replace the instruction to multiply the vector with a float to apply the divisor:

```
vector /= scale;
```

The output of this code reads "X=4.5 Y = 0.5 Z = 0," which is equivalent to the quotient from your manual calculation.

NORMAL VECTORS

A *normal* is a special type of vector that is perpendicular to a flat surface. In other words, a normal is a vector that points outward from a face at an angle of 90 degrees. The normal represents direction, so the position is irrelevant. Figure 15-1 shows a normal vector pointing outward from a face. In game programming, normal vectors have uses that range from implementing lighting to building a camera.

When you're computing normal vectors from a flat surface, the simplest flat surface possible is built by two vectors joined at the tail end.

Cross Product

The cross product formula is used to calculate a normal vector for a surface that is created by two vectors. It uses the two surface vectors as inputs. The cross product between vectors A and B equals the following:

$$A \times B = (A_y*B_z - A_z*B_y, \quad A_z*B_x - A_x*B_z, \quad A_x*B_y - A_y*B_x)$$

The set of coordinates generated from the cross product represents the normal direction vector. The order of the surface vectors used in the cross product will affect the direction of the normal vector. When applying the cross product using the Right Hand Rule, you can use a mnemonic device to determine the direction of the normal vector. You can determine the direction of the normal by positioning your right thumb so it runs in the direction of vector A. Then position your hand so your right index finger points in the direction of vector B. The palm of your right hand will point

FIGURE 15-1

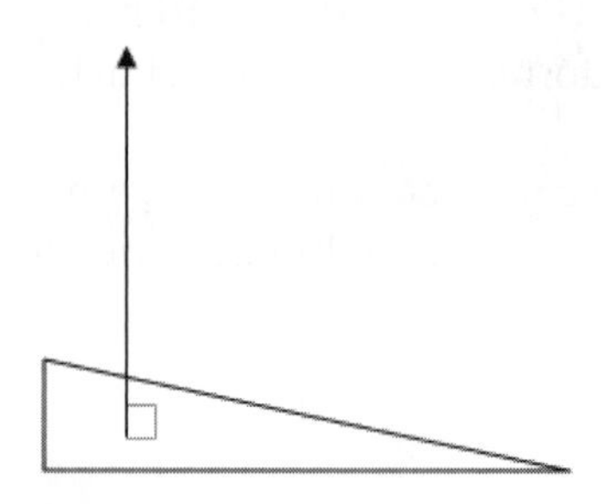

Normal vector

in the direction of the normal vector that results from the cross product between vector A and vector B.

XNA's `Cross()` method automates the process of calculating the cross product to generate the normal. The syntax is

```
Vector3 crossproduct = Vector3.Cross(Vector3 vectorA, Vector3 vectorB);
```

Cross Product Example

This example shows you how to calculate a normal in both directions. The surface is defined by vector A (9, 0, 0) and vector B (9, 1, 0). Here is the manual cross-product calculation to generate the normal direction vector:

$$
\begin{aligned}
& A \times B \\
&= (A_y*B_z - A_z*B_y, \quad A_z*B_x - A_x*B_z, \quad A_x*B_y - A_y*B_x) \\
&= (0*0 - 0*1, 0*9 - 9*0, 9*1 - 0*9) \\
&= (0, 0, 9)
\end{aligned}
$$

The manual calculation verifies the prediction that X and Y equal 0. Also, the normal vector is traveling in a positive direction (on the Z axis) from the surface created by vectors A and B. The image on the left in Figure 15-2 shows the two surface vectors together with the positive normal vector that was just calculated.

FIGURE 15-2

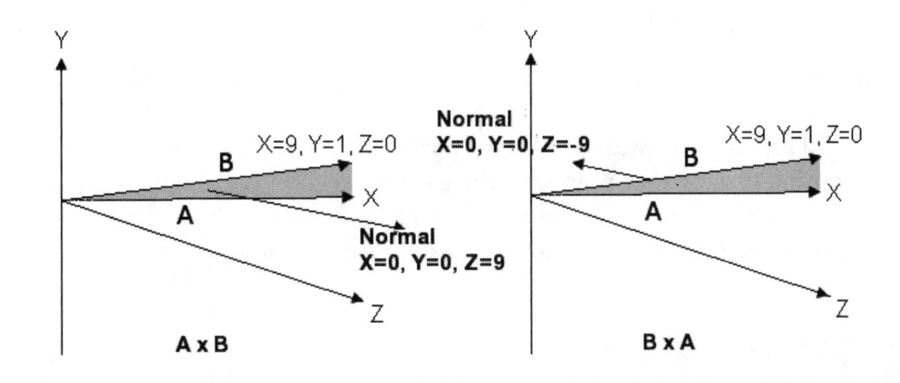

Cross product A × B (left) and cross product B × A (right)

To show this cross product calculation in code, use the solution from the previous code example and replace the `VectorCalculation()` method with this version:

```
String VectorCalculation(){
    Vector3 A = new Vector3(9.0f, 0.0f, 0.0f);          // A
    Vector3 B = new Vector3(9.0f, 1.0f, 0.0f);          // B
    Vector3 C = new Vector3(A.Y*B.Z - A.Z*B.Y,          // compute normal
                            A.Z*B.X - A.X*B.Z,   A.X*B.Y - A.Y*B.X);

    return "X = " + C.X.ToString() + "  Y = " + C.Y.ToString()
          + "  Z = " + C.Z.ToString();
}
```

The output of this code will show the values "X = 0 Y = 0 Z = 9."

This cross-product calculation code can be simplified further. The definition for vector C can be replaced with a definition that uses the `Cross()` method:

```
Vector3 C = Vector3.Cross(A, B);
```

Once again, after you insert and run this code, the resulting vector is computed as X = 0, Y = 0, Z = 9.

So far, in this example, you have generated a normal vector with a positive direction. You can reverse the normal vector's direction by swapping the vector parameters in the `Cross()` method. Swapping vector A and vector B parameters in the `Cross()` method reverses the order in which the surface vectors are used in the cross product. To try this, replace the existing definition for vector C with this revision in the `VectorCalculation()` method:

```
Vector3 C = Vector3.Cross(B, A);
```

The result of swapping vector parameters in the `Cross()` method will output a normal vector that points in a negative direction on Z with the coordinates X=0, Y=0, Z=-9. The image on the right in Figure 15–2 shows how the normal vector points inward from the face in a negative direction.

NORMALIZATION

The process of scaling vectors to unit vectors is known as *normalization*. A *unit vector* is a set of numbers that have been expressed in the same ratio as the original vector, but the vector components are scaled to a fraction that ranges between –1 and +1. The vector length is scaled to 1. Often, when you're comparing properties such as direction or speed, magnitude is not important, but relative change on the X, Y, and Z planes is important. A normalized vector allows such comparisons on a uniform scale while the individual vector components (X, Y, Z) retain the same relative size to each other as the original vector.

The normal vector is calculated by dividing the X, Y, and Z coordinates of a vector by the total vector length:

```
unitVector.X = Vector.X/VectorLength
unitVector.Y = Vector.Y/VectorLength
unitVector.Z = Vector.Z/VectorLength
```

The vector length is calculated using the Pythagorean Theorem.

Pythagorean Theorem

As you'll remember from math class, the Pythagorean Theorem states that for a right-angle triangle, $A^2+B^2=C^2$ (where C is the length of the hypotenuse, and A and B represent the lengths of the other two sides). In the context of three-dimensional vectors, the vector length can be calculated with the following equation:

$$\text{Vector length} = \sqrt{X^2+Y^2+Z^2}$$

To apply the Pythagorean Theorem for vectors, you create a right-angle triangle by dropping a line from the head of the vector so that it intersects the nearest axis at 90 degrees. Together, the original vector, the right-angle line, and the axis create a right-angle triangle.

Using the Pythagorean Theorem to Calculate the Vector Length

This example shows how you can use the Pythagorean Theorem to calculate the vector length. It starts with a vector having values of X=9, Y=1, and Z=0. Calculating the length of the hypotenuse, in effect, returns the vector length.

Implementing the Pythagorean Theorem gives you the following:

$$\text{Vector Length} = \sqrt{9^2+1^2+0^2} = 9.055$$

To compute and display vector length in code, replace the existing `VectorCalculation()` method (in the code solution from the last example) with this new version:

```
String VectorCalculation(){
    Vector3 vector  = new Vector3(9.0f, 1.0f, 0.0f);
```

```
    float   length  = (float)Math.Sqrt(vector.X * vector.X
                    + vector.Y * vector.Y  +  vector.Z * vector.Z);

    return "Vector length   = " + length.ToString("N3");
}
```

When you run this code, the vector length 9.055 is generated and displayed in the game window.

XNA provides the `Length()` method to automate the vector's length calculation. If you replace the declaration for length in `VectorCalculation()` with this instruction, the same result will be generated:

```
float   length  = vector.Length();
```

When you run the code now, the vector length that appears in the game window will remain the same. The length of 9.055 is still computed and shown in the window.

Using Normalization to Compute the Unit Vector

After the length has been calculated, you can scale the original vector to a unit vector by dividing the X, Y, and Z values in the original vector by the vector length. Here is the manual calculation:

```
unitVector.X = Vector.X/VectorLength = 9/9.055 = 0.99
unitVector.Y = Vector.Y/VectorLength = 1/9.055 = 0.11
unitVector.Z = Vector.Z/VectorLength = 0/9.055 = 0.00
```

In this case, the calculated unit vector is much smaller than the original vector, but the unit vector contains the same proportion of direction or speed information. The angle of the vector remains the same as the original vector (9, 1, 0), but the vector is shorter.

To calculate the unit vector in code, and show it in the window, replace the current `VectorCalculation()` method from the previous example's solution with this version:

```
String VectorCalculation(){
    Vector3 vector      = new Vector3(9.0f, 1.0f, 0.0f);
    float   length      = (float)vector.Length();
    Vector3 unitVector  = vector/length;

    return "X = " + unitVector.X.ToString("N3")
```

```
    + "    Y = " + unitVector.Y.ToString("N3")
    + "    Z = " + unitVector.Z.ToString("N3");
}
```

When you run this version of the code, the text in the window reads "X = 0.994 Y=0.110 Z = 0.000."

Using the Normalize() Method to Compute the Unit Vector

XNA provides the `Normalize()` method to automate the generation of the unit vector so that you no longer need to divide the original vector by the length. The syntax for the `Normalize()` method is

```
Vector3 unitVector = Vector3.Normalize(Vector3 vector);
```

A `Normalize()` method also exists for objects derived from the Vector2 and Vector4 types. The syntax is identical to that for the Vector3 type:

```
Vector2 unitVector = Vector2.Normalize(Vector2 vector);
Vector4 unitVector = Vector4.Normalize(Vector4 vector);
```

The solution from the previous example can be reimplemented using the `Normalize()` method. To use this method, replace the declaration for `unitVector` in `VectorCalculation()` with this version:

```
Vector3 unitVector = Vector3.Normalize(vector);
```

Also, in `VectorCalculation()`, delete the vector-length calculation because it is no longer required. The output from this revised method generates the same unit vector as before, but with less code.

DOT PRODUCT

The dot product is used to find the angle between vectors and is essential for many 3D graphics routines. The dot product can be used for calculating trajectory angles, angles of reflection, or even light intensity. If you have two vectors, as in Figure 15-3, the dot product can be computed with the following equation:

```
cosθ
= unitVectorA . unitVectorB
= unitVectorA.x * unitVectorB.x + unitVectorA.y * unitVectorB.y +
  unitVectorA.z * unitVectorB.z
```

The dot product formula can be rearranged to give the angle:

```
θ = cos-1(unitVectorA . unitVectorB)
```

For the material in this book, the dot product is used in Chapter 22.

Dot Product Method

XNA provides the `Dot()` method to help automate the calculation of the dot product:

```
float dotproduct = Vector3.Dot(Vector3 unitVectorA, Vector3 unitVectorB);
```

Dot Product Example

This example shows how to use the dot product to calculate the angle between vector A where X=0, Y=5, Z=0 and vector B where X=5, Y=5, and Z=0, as shown in Figure 15-3.

To perform this calculation manually, first calculate the unit vector for A:

```
unitVectorA = A/lengthA
```

Length A= $\sqrt{0^2+5^2+0^2}$ =5

```
Ax/lengthA = 0.000, Ay/lengthA = 1.000, Az/lengthA = 0.000
```

Then, calculate the unit vector for B:

```
unitVectorB = B/lengthB
```

Length A= $\sqrt{0^2+5^2+0^2}$ =7.072

```
Bx/lengthB = 0.707, By/lengthB = 0.707, Bz/lengthB = 0.000
```

FIGURE 15-3

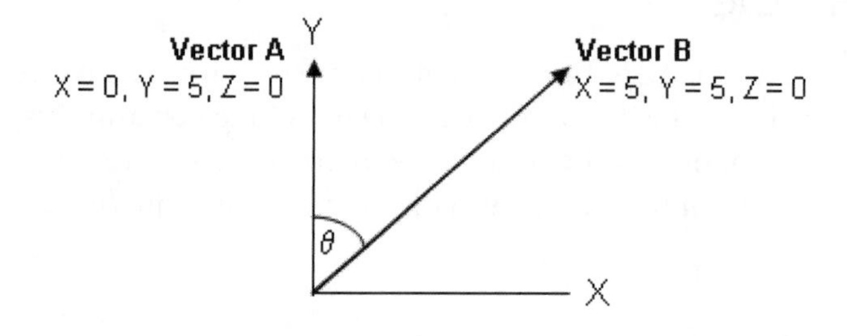

Calculating the angle between vectors using the dot product

Next, using the dot product definition, you can calculate the value for cos θ:

```
cosθ
= unitVectorA . unitVectorB
= unitVectorA.x * unitVectorB.x + unitVectorA.y * unitVectorB.y +
  unitVectorA.z * unitVectorB.z
= 0.000 * 0.707 + 1.000 * 0.707 + 0.0000 * 0.000
= 0.707
```

The result can be rearranged to isolate the value for θ which is the angle being sought:

```
θ = cos⁻¹(0.707) = 0.785 radians
2π radians = 360 degrees
θ = 0.785 radians * (360 degrees/2π radians) = 45 degrees
```

To perform this calculation for the angle between the two vectors in code, replace the old `VectorCalculation()` method with this revision:

```
String VectorCalculation(){
    Vector3 A            = new Vector3(0.0f, 5.0f, 0.0f);
    Vector3 B            = new Vector3(5.0f, 5.0f, 0.0f);
    Vector3 unitVectorA = Vector3.Normalize(A);
    Vector3 unitVectorB = Vector3.Normalize(B);
    float   dotProduct  = Vector3.Dot(unitVectorA, unitVectorB);
    float   radians     = (float)Math.Acos((double)dotProduct);
    float   degrees     = radians * 360.0f/MathHelper.Pi/2.0f;

    return "Angle in Degrees = " + degrees.ToString("N3");
}
```

When you run the code, the text in the window will read "Angle in Degrees = 45.000."

Vector lingo is daunting if you haven't used it before or studied it for many years. If you studied vectors in high school, chances are you never associated them with cool graphics and game code, so they may not have stuck with you. As far as game code goes, you can get a lot of mileage from the formulas presented in this chapter. The formulas covered here appear in all types of game algorithms and effects in the wide world of games programming.

CHAPTER 15 REVIEW EXERCISES

To get the most from this chapter, try out these chapter review exercises.

1. Implement the step-by-step examples shown in this chapter, if you have not already done so.
2. Create a pyramid, composed of line lists, that is centered at the origin. Generate normals for each of the five faces and render them as line lists. Draw each of the five normal vectors as line lists as well.
3. Normalize the normal vectors in Exercise 2. Run and view your project after the normals have been converted to unit vectors.
4. If you are feeling ambitious, use the dot product to calculate the angle between the normal vector and the ground for each of the pyramid sides. Print this data in the game window.

CHAPTER 16

Matrices

MATRIX math is a branch of linear algebra, and all 3D graphics programmers can benefit from understanding it. In video game development, matrices are used to store data such as vertices and information about how to transform an object. Matrices are simply grids of rows and columns, but they are essential for scaling, rotating, and translating objects in 3D space. You will have noticed by now that matrix calculations are used throughout your XNA and shader code for performing transformations, controlling your camera, and even drawing 3D models. Understanding how these matrix methods work will provide you with a better understanding of 3D game engines. Most of the time, you can get away with just using XNA matrix methods to automatically create matrices and to implement your transformations. However, for complex vector transformations, you may need to be able to build your own matrices for the calculations.

In Chapter 8, a matrix is manually created to compute the flight path of an airplane. In Chapter 19, a matrix is manually built to implement a vector transformation that determines the starting position and direction of a rocket. In cases like these, understanding the matrix math can definitely help to simplify your transformations.

MATRIX MULTIPLICATION

This section introduces matrix multiplication and prepares you for performing manual transformations later in the chapter. The product of two matrices is obtained by multiplying the rows of matrix A by the columns of matrix B (where matrix A is on the left side of the operator). For the multiplication to be possible, the total number of columns in matrix A must equal the total number of rows in matrix B.

Matrix Types

XNA's Matrix type enables storage of 3×3 matrices (3 rows by 3 columns) and 4×4 matrices (4 rows by 4 columns). Each cell in the matrix grid can be accessed by referencing the matrix and suffixing it with the cell's row and column, where the top-left cell begins at row 1, column 1. Each cell stores a float:

```
float cellvalue = Matrix matrix.MRC
```

For example, `matrix.M11` represents the value in row 1, column 1. `Matrix.M13` represents the value in row 1, column 3.

Matrix Multiplication Example: 1×4 Matrix * 4×4 Matrix

This example shows how to multiply a 1×4 matrix by a 4×4 matrix. We'll first show the multiplication done by hand so that you can see each step of the calculation.

Later, the same operation will be shown in code. For this example, a vector with X=2, Y=1, Z=0, and W=0 will be multiplied by a 4×4 matrix.

Manual Calculation To set up the equation, the vector is placed on the left side of the multiplication operator, and the 4×4 matrix is placed on the right, as shown here:

```
| 2   1   0   0   |   X   |  2   1   3   1   |
                          |  1   2   4   1   |
                          |  0   3   5   1   |
                          |  2   1   2   1   |
```

The row on the left is multiplied by each column on the right. The following formula is used for each of the four columns of vector C, where A represents the matrix on the left and B represents the matrix on the right:

```
for(int c=1; c<=4; c++)
     C1c = A11*B1c + A12*B2c + A13*B3c + A14*B4c
```

Implementing the formula gives you the following:

```
|( 2*2 + 1*1     ( 2*1 + 1*2     ( 2*3 + 1*4     ( 2*1 + 1*1
|+ 0*0 + 0*2)    + 0*3 + 0*1)    + 0*5 + 0*2)    + 0*1 + 0*1)
=
| 5   4   10   3   |
```

The product of A * B, therefore, is a new vector with X=5, Y=4, Z=10, and W=3.

Calculation in Code The previous computation will now be performed in code. This allows you to print the calculation results in the game window. To begin, start with the solution for the "Font Example: Displaying Text in the Game Window" section of Chapter 13. This solution can be found in the Solutions folder on this book's website.

Since we will be displaying rows and columns of numeric data, we need to have a suitable font type to align the text in each cell. To keep things simple, this example uses the Courier New font, which is a *monospace*, or nonproportional, font, which means that all characters are the same width. A monospace font ensures that each character is the same pixel width. This is useful because having alphabetical and numeric characters of the same width simplifies the data formatting calculations.

Once you have the project open, to improve readability, add the `Cell()` method so you can create an evenly spaced string for each cell. This method will right-align the columns when they are displayed in a matrix grid. `Cell()` first formats the data in each cell so it appears as a floating-point number with two decimal places. Then `Cell()` compares the length of the data string with the number of spaces allotted for each cell. `Cell()` does this by adding extra spaces until the total character count for the string matches the number of spaces allotted for each cell. When the string has been created, it is returned to the calling function:

```
public string Cell(float cell){
    string      cellDisplay     = cell.ToString("N2"); // 2 decimals
    const int   CELL_WIDTH      = 8;                   // 8 chars wide
    int         numDigits       = cellDisplay.Length;

    // right align text and add padding on left
    for (int i = 0; i < CELL_WIDTH - numDigits; i++)
        cellDisplay = " " + cellDisplay;
    return cellDisplay;
}
```

To display the cell data (for the product matrix) as text in the game window, you will require the `DrawMatrix()` method. Add it to your game class so that you can convert each cell of the product matrix to a string, combine cells to form each row of the matrix, and then draw each row of the matrix in the window.

```
public void DrawMatrix(Matrix C){
    String[] row = new String[4];                       // output strings
    row[0] = Cell(C.M11) + Cell(C.M12) + Cell(C.M13) + Cell(C.M14);
    row[1] = Cell(C.M21) + Cell(C.M22) + Cell(C.M23) + Cell(C.M24);
    row[2] = Cell(C.M31) + Cell(C.M32) + Cell(C.M33) + Cell(C.M34);
    row[3] = Cell(C.M41) + Cell(C.M42) + Cell(C.M43) + Cell(C.M44);

    spriteBatch.Begin(SpriteBlendMode.AlphaBlend,   // enable transparency
                      SpriteSortMode.Immediate,     // use manual order
                      SaveStateMode.SaveState);     // preserve 3D settings

    for (int i = 0; i < 4; i++){                        // draw 4 matrix rows
        Rectangle safeArea = TitleSafeRegion(row[i], spriteFont);
        float      height = spriteFont.MeasureString(row[i]).Y;

            spriteBatch.DrawString(
                      spriteFont,                       // font
                      row[i],                           // row string
                      new Vector2(safeArea.Left,        // top left pixel
                            safeArea.Top+(float)i*height),
                      Color.Yellow);                    // color
```

```
    }
    spriteBatch.End();
}
```

When you open the solution, you must add the `MultiplyMatrix()` method to the game class so it can initialize two matrices and calculate their product. For this example, the code declares matrix A and initializes it to store the vector in the first row. Initially, when the constructor for the Matrix type is referenced, all cells in matrix A are initialized to 0. The vector's X, Y, Z, and W components are assigned to the four cells of the first row of matrix A. The cell data for the matrix on the right side of the operator is assigned to matrix B; then A and B are multiplied together to generate the product matrix.

```
public Matrix MultiplyMatrix(){
    Matrix A = new Matrix();
    Matrix B = new Matrix();

    // store vector in first row - all other cells equal 0
    A.M11 = 2.0f; A.M12 = 1.0f; A.M13 = 0.0f; A.M14 = 0.0f;

    // initialize matrix B
    B.M11 = 2.0f; B.M12 = 1.0f; B.M13 = 3.0f; B.M14 = 1.0f;
    B.M21 = 1.0f; B.M22 = 2.0f; B.M23 = 4.0f; B.M24 = 1.0f;
    B.M31 = 0.0f; B.M32 = 3.0f; B.M33 = 5.0f; B.M34 = 1.0f;
    B.M41 = 2.0f; B.M42 = 1.0f; B.M43 = 2.0f; B.M44 = 1.0f;

    return A * B;
}
```

To trigger the methods that calculate the matrix product and display the output, replace the line

```
DrawFonts(gameTime);
```

inside `Draw()` with the following:

```
DrawMatrix(MultiplyMatrix());
```

When you run this code, the product matrix will appear in the window:

```
5.00    4.00    10.00    3.00
0.00    0.00     0.00    0.00
```

```
0.00    0.00    0.00    0.00
0.00    0.00    0.00    0.00
```

This result verifies that the code, C = A * B (where A, B, and C are `Matrix` objects), generates the same product as shown in the lengthy manual calculation.

Matrix Multiplication Example: 4×4 Matrix * 4×4 Matrix

This next example demonstrates how to multiply a 4×4 matrix by a 4×4 matrix. Knowing how to do this by hand is very useful because all of the transformations you have been implementing in your XNA code involve multiplying 4×4 matrices by 4×4 matrices. You will first see how the multiplication can be performed manually, and then how you can do it in code.

Manual Calculation For this case, the following two matrices, A and B, are to be multiplied:

```
A   X   B   =
| 2    1   0   0   |   X   |   2   1   3   1   |
|-1   -2   0   0   |       |   1   2   4   1   |
| 3    1   0   0   |       |   0   3   5   1   |
|-3    2   2   0   |       |   2   1   2   1   |
```

When you're calculating the product of a 4×4 matrix by a 4×4 matrix, the formula to multiply the rows of matrix A by the columns of matrix B is

```
for(r=1; r<=4; r++)
    for(c=1; c<=4;c++)
        Crc =A1*B1c + A2*B2c + A3*B3c + A4*B4c
```

When the formula is implemented by hand, the calculation looks like this:

```
|( 2*2 + 1*1     ( 2*1 + 1*2     ( 2*3 + 1*4     ( 2*1 + 1*1
|+ 0*0 + 0*2)    + 0*3 + 0*1)    + 0*5 + 0*2)    + 0*1 + 0*1)
|(-1*2 - 2*1     (-1*1 - 2*2     (-1*3 - 2*4     (-1*1 - 2*1
|+ 0*0 + 0*2)    + 0*3 + 0*1)    + 0*5 + 0*2)    + 0*1 + 0*1)
|( 3*2 + 1*1     ( 3*1 + 1*2     ( 3*3 + 1*4     ( 3*1 + 1*1
|+ 0*0 + 0*2)    + 0*3 + 0*1)    + 0*5 + 0*2)    + 0*1 + 0*1)
|(-3*2 + 2*1     (-3*1 + 2*2     (-3*3 + 2*4     (-3*1 + 2*1
|+ 2*0 + 0*2)    + 2*3 + 0*1)    + 2*5 + 0*2)    + 2*1 + 0*1)
=
```

```
| 5    4    10    3    |
|-4   -5   -11   -3    |
| 7    5    13    4    |
|-4    7     9    1    |
```

Calculation in Code After performing the long-winded manual calculation, you can appreciate the simplicity of being able to compute the same result with the instruction C = A * B.

Using the code solution from the previous example, in `MultiplyMatrix()`, replace the instructions that set the individual cell values for matrix A with the following version (matrix B remains the same as the previous example, so no changes are required to it):

```
A.M11 = 2.0f;   A.M12 = 1.0f;   A.M13 = 0.0f;   A.M14 = 0.0f;
A.M21 =-1.0f;   A.M22 =-2.0f;   A.M23 = 0.0f;   A.M24 = 0.0f;
A.M31 = 3.0f;   A.M32 = 1.0f;   A.M33 = 0.0f;   A.M34 = 0.0f;
A.M41 =-3.0f;   A.M42 = 2.0f;   A.M43 = 2.0f;   A.M44 = 0.0f;
```

When you run the code, you will see the result does indeed match the manual calculation:

```
| 5.00    4.00    10.00    3.00    |
|-4.00   -5.00   -11.00   -3.00    |
| 7.00    5.00    13.00    4.00    |
|-4.00    7.00     9.00    1.00    |
```

At this point, we can say when multiplying a 4×4 matrix by a 4×4 matrix that the manual calculation can be executed in one line with the following instruction:

```
Matrix C = A * B
```

TRANSFORMATION MATRICES

As mentioned earlier in this chapter, when drawing primitive shapes and 3D models, you use matrices to transform sets of vertices. Through the study of linear algebra, specific matrices have been defined to scale, rotate, and translate sets of vertices. In Chapter 7, the I.S.R.O.T. (Identity, Scale, Revolve, Orbit [translation and rotation], Translate) sequence of matrices is used to ensure balanced transformations. The same logic applies when you are using transformation matrices that have been created manually. If the matrices are multiplied in an incorrect order, the transformations will also be incorrect.

When matrix calculations are performed in XNA, they are applied using the Right Hand Rule perspective, which was explained in Chapter 7. This chapter applies the transformation matrices from a Right Hand Rule perspective to suit the XNA framework.

When you perform transformations on an object, the data matrix containing the X, Y, Z, and W coordinates is located on the left of the multiplication operator. The transformation matrix is located on the right.

Translation Matrix

Translation matrices store lateral transformations along the X, Y, and Z planes. Here is the format for the translation matrix:

```
| 1  0  0  0  |
| 0  1  0  0  |
| 0  0  1  0  |
| X  Y  Z  1  |
```

When you are presented with a 4×4 matrix with 1s along the diagonal, values for X, Y, Z at the bottom, and 0s elsewhere, you can conclude the matrix will perform a translation of X units along the X plane, Y units along the Y plane, and Z units along the Z plane.

Handling the W Component

When a vector representing the X, Y, and Z coordinates of an object is transformed using a translation matrix, the W component in the fourth column of the data matrix must be set to 1.

Failing to set all values in the fourth column of the data matrix to 1 will lead to inaccurate translations.

Translation Matrix Example

Imagine that the vertex (X=2, Y=1, Z=0) is transformed by the matrix on the right. The vector data matrix is located on the left. Note that the fourth column representing the W component is set to 1. The translation matrix for the format described here must be located on the right side of the operator for the calculation to work properly.

```
| 2  1  0  1  |  X  | 1  0  0  0  |
                    | 0  1  0  0  |
                    | 0  0  1  0  |
                    | 3  5  0  1  |
```

Viewing this vertex and translation matrix gives you enough information to determine that the vertex with the coordinates X=2, Y=1, and Z=0 will be transformed by three units in the positive X direction, and five units in the positive Y direction. If this is correct, the product of the vertex and translation matrix should move the vertex to X=5, Y=6, and Z=0. Figure 16-1 shows the coordinate in its original position before the predicted translation (on the left) and after the predicted translation (on the right).

To verify the prediction, you can try this calculation in code. To set up the data matrix, replace the code that initializes the cells in matrix A with this revision to initialize the vector data. The remaining rows will take on the default of 0 in each cell.

```
// store vector in first row - all other cells equal 0 by default
A.M11 = 2.0f; A.M12 = 1.0f; A.M13 = 0.0f; A.M14 = 1.0f;
```

Next, to set up the translation matrix, replace the code that assigns matrix B with this revision:

```
B.M11 = 1.0f;    B.M12 = 0.0f;    B.M13 = 0.0f;    B.M14 = 0.0f;
B.M21 = 0.0f;    B.M22 = 1.0f;    B.M23 = 0.0f;    B.M24 = 0.0f;
B.M31 = 0.0f;    B.M32 = 0.0f;    B.M33 = 1.0f;    B.M34 = 0.0f;
B.M41 = 3.0f;    B.M42 = 5.0f;    B.M43 = 0.0f;    B.M44 = 1.0f;
```

If you run this code, the output that appears in the window matches the prediction that the new coordinates are X=5, Y=6, and Z=0:

```
5.00   6.00   0.00   1.00
0.00   0.00   0.00   0.00
0.00   0.00   0.00   0.00
0.00   0.00   0.00   0.00
```

FIGURE 16-1

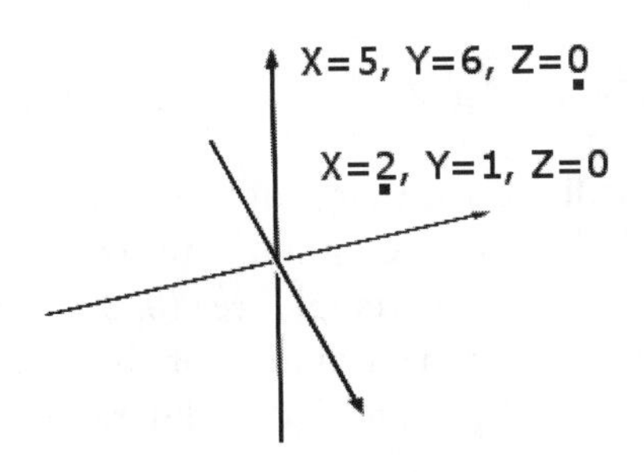

Translating an object with the translation matrix

The translation moved the original vertex three units in the positive X direction, and five units in the positive Y direction.

Translation Matrix Example Using the CreateTranslation() Method

Since Chapter 7, we have used the method `CreateTranslation(float x, float y, float z)` to automatically generate the translation matrix. This method actually generates a translation matrix that is identical to the translation matrix we just created manually. If you replace the code inside `MultiplyMatrix()` that assigns cell values to matrix B with the following instruction, you will generate an identical matrix:

```
B = Matrix.CreateTranslation(3.0f, 5.0f, 0.0f);
```

Therefore, when you compile and run the code, the product matrix will also be identical.

Scaling Matrix

Scaling matrices are used any time an object needs to be resized. You will often need to scale your 3D models because modeling tools usually generate them in a size that is different from the size needed for your game project. The following matrix represents a standard matrix for performing scaling operations. At a glance, this scaling matrix contains information to expand or shrink an object in the X, Y, and Z planes. The X, Y, and Z scaling factors are set on the diagonal down from the top left to the bottom right. The digit, one, is needed in the bottom-right corner, and zeros are placed elsewhere to make this matrix a scaling matrix.

```
X   0   0   0
0   Y   0   0
0   0   Z   0
0   0   0   1
```

Scaling Matrix Example

In this example, you will use a scaling matrix to double the size of a triangle. A triangle is represented with the matrix containing the triangle vertices on the left. The vertex coordinates used to build the triangle are ((0, 0, 0), (1, 4, 0), (4, 2, 0)). The scaling matrix that doubles the size of the triangle is on the right. In the first three rows of the data matrix on the left, the X, Y, and Z coordinates for the three triangle vertices are stored. One triangle vertex is stored in each of the first three rows. When multiplying the triangle vertices by the scaling matrix (to double the size), you can use the following matrix equation:

```
| 0  0  0  0 |   X   | 2  0  0  0 |
| 1  4  0  0 |       | 0  2  0  0 |
| 4  2  0  0 |       | 0  0  2  0 |
| 0  0  0  0 |       | 0  0  0  1 |
```

By looking at the scaling matrix—and without performing any calculations—it is apparent that the size of the existing triangle is going to be doubled. In Figure 16-2, you can see that the size of the triangle has doubled when a vector set was transformed with the scaling matrix.

Inside `MultiplyMatrix()`, replace the code that assigns values to the cells of matrix A with the following revision to initialize the data matrix for the triangle:

```
A.M11 = 0.0f;    A.M12 = 0.0f;    A.M13 = 0.0f;    A.M14 = 0.0f;
A.M21 = 1.0f;    A.M22 = 4.0f;    A.M23 = 0.0f;    A.M24 = 0.0f;
A.M31 = 4.0f;    A.M32 = 2.0f;    A.M33 = 0.0f;    A.M34 = 0.0f;
A.M41 = 0.0f;    A.M42 = 0.0f;    A.M43 = 0.0f;    A.M44 = 0.0f;
```

FIGURE 16-2

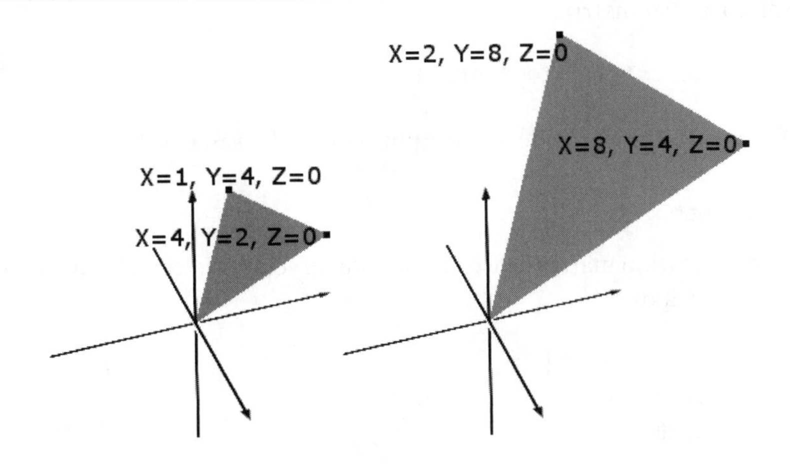

Before scaling and after scaling

Next, replace the code that initializes matrix B with this version to initialize a scaling matrix:

```
B.M11 = 2.0f;   B.M12 = 0.0f;   B.M13 = 0.0f;   B.M14 = 0.0f;
B.M21 = 0.0f;   B.M22 = 2.0f;   B.M23 = 0.0f;   B.M24 = 0.0f;
B.M31 = 0.0f;   B.M32 = 0.0f;   B.M33 = 2.0f;   B.M34 = 0.0f;
B.M41 = 0.0f;   B.M42 = 0.0f;   B.M43 = 0.0f;   B.M44 = 1.0f;
```

When the program is run, the output displays coordinates for the triangle that has been doubled:

```
0.00   0.00   0.00   0.00
2.00   8.00   0.00   0.00
8.00   4.00   0.00   0.00
0.00   0.00   0.00   0.00
```

The triangle coordinates in the output matrix are graphed on the right side of Figure 16-2.

Scaling Matrix Example Using the CreateScale() Method

In Chapter 7, the `CreateScale(float x, float y, float z)` method was introduced as a way to automatically generate the scaling matrix. Replace the instructions that manually assign the scaling matrix with this simpler revision to generate an identical matrix:

```
B = Matrix.CreateScale(2.0f, 2.0f, 2.0f);
```

When you run the code, the output will be the same as before.

Rotation Matrix X Axis

The X rotation matrix is used to transform sets of vertices by an angle of θradians about the X axis:

```
|  1   0      0      0   |
|  0   cosθ   sinθ   0   |
|  0  -sinθ   cosθ   0   |
|  0   0      0      1   |
```

Rotation Matrix X Axis Example

This example applies the X rotation matrix to rotate a triangle by 45 degrees (π/4). The original set of coordinates (before the rotation) is in the left matrix, and the X rotation matrix is located on the right:

```
| 0  0  0  0 |  X  | 1   0          0          0 |
| 1  4  0  0 |     | 0   cos(π/4)   sin(π/4)   0 |
| 4  2  0  0 |     | 0  -sin(π/4)   cos(π/4)   0 |
| 0  0  0  0 |     | 0   0          0          1 |
```

If you were to multiply this by hand, the result would be

```
0.00   0.00   0.00   0.00
1.00   2.83   2.83   0.00
4.00   1.41   1.41   0.00
0.00   0.00   0.00   0.00
```

Figure 16-3 shows how the triangle would be positioned before and after the rotation.

Now we will show this implementation of the rotation matrix in code by using the solution from the previous example. To create a rotation matrix of π/4 radians about

FIGURE 16-3

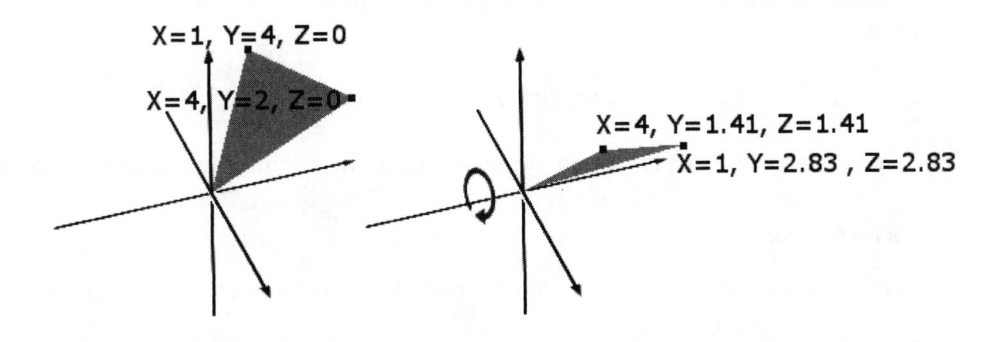

Rotation of a triangle using the X rotation matrix

the X axis, replace the instructions that initialize matrix B with the following version inside `MultiplyMatrix()`:

```
float sin = (float)Math.Sin(Math.PI / 4.0);
float cos = (float)Math.Cos(Math.PI / 4.0);
B.M11 = 1.0f;    B.M12 = 0.0f;    B.M13 = 0.0f;    B.M14 = 0.0f;
B.M21 = 0.0f;    B.M22 =  cos;    B.M23 = sin;     B.M24 = 0.0f;
B.M31 = 0.0f;    B.M32 = -sin;    B.M33 = cos;     B.M34 = 0.0f;
B.M41 = 0.0f;    B.M42 = 0.0f;    B.M43 = 0.0f;    B.M44 = 1.0f;
```

When you compile and run this code, the product matrix equals the result that you computed by hand:

```
0.00   0.00   0.00   0.00
1.00   2.83   2.83   0.00
4.00   1.41   1.41   0.00
0.00   0.00   0.00   0.00
```

This matrix stores the coordinates of the triangle after it has been rotated about the X axis, as shown in Figure 16-3.

X Axis Rotation Example Using the CreateRotationX() Method

Prior to this chapter, the `CreateRotationX(float radians)` method has been used to generate the same X rotation matrix as the manually created matrix. To calculate the same transformation for the triangle, replace the initial declaration for the X rotation matrix with a matrix that is generated using the `CreateRotationX()` method:

```
B = Matrix.CreateRotationX((float)(Math.PI / 4.0));
```

The resulting product is obviously the same, but the calculation requires less code.

Rotation Matrix Y Axis

The matrix shown here is a predefined matrix that rotates a set of vertices around the Y axis by θ radians:

```
|  cosθ   0   -sinθ   0  |
|  0      1    0      0  |
|  sinθ   0    cosθ   0  |
|  0      0    0      1  |
```

Rotation Matrix Y Axis Example

This example demonstrates the use of the Y rotation matrix to rotate a set of triangle coordinates by π/4 radians about the Y axis. The data matrix is on the left, and the Y rotation matrix is on the right:

```
|  0   0   0   0  |   X   |  cos(π/4)   0   -sin(π/4)   0  |
|  1   4   0   0  |       |  0          1    0          0  |
|  4   2   0   0  |       |  sin(π/4)   0    cos(π/4)   0  |
|  0   0   0   0  |       |  0          0    0          1  |
```

If you multiplied this out by hand, the result would be

```
|  0      0    0      0  |
|  0.71   4   -0.71   0  |
|  2.83   2   -2.83   0  |
|  0      0    0      0  |
```

Figure 16-4 shows the triangle coordinates before and after the multiplication that performs the rotation.

To implement the Y rotation in code, replace the code that initializes matrix B with a rotation matrix to rotate the vertices by π/4 radians:

```
float sin = (float)Math.Sin(Math.PI / 4.0);
float cos = (float)Math.Cos(Math.PI / 4.0);
B.M11 =  cos;   B.M12 = 0.0f;   B.M13 = -sin;   B.M14 = 0.0f;
B.M21 = 0.0f;   B.M22 = 1.0f;   B.M23 = 0.0f;   B.M24 = 0.0f;
B.M31 =  sin;   B.M32 = 0.0f;   B.M33 =  cos;   B.M34 = 0.0f;
B.M41 = 0.0f;   B.M42 = 0.0f;   B.M43 = 0.0f;   B.M44 = 0.0f;
```

FIGURE 16-4

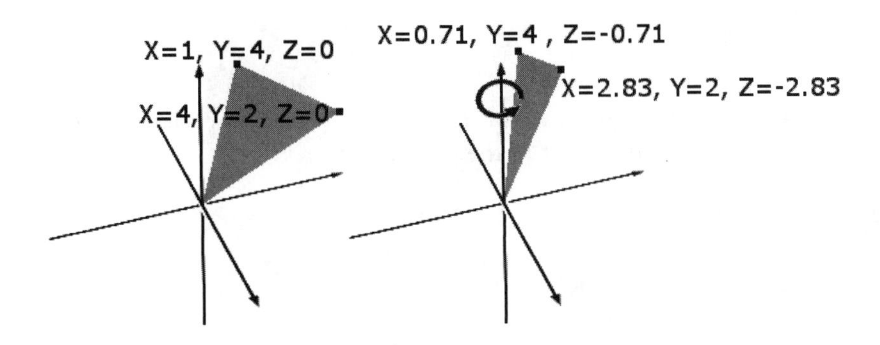

Y axis rotation before and after the transformation matrix is applied

When you run this program, the product matrix stores the triangle's new coordinates after they are rotated by π/4 units around the Y axis (see Figure 16-4).

Y Axis Rotation Example Using the CreateRotationY() Method

In Chapter 7, the `CreateRotationY(float radians)` method was used to generate an identical Y rotation matrix as the one presented in this chapter. You can replace the code that initializes matrix B with the following instruction and it will produce the same result:

```
B = Matrix.CreateRotationY(MathHelper.Pi/4.0f);
```

When you run this code, the product matrix will be the same as before, but this version requires less code.

Rotation Matrix Z Axis

The following matrix is the classic matrix for rotations of θ radians on the Z axis:

```
|   cosθ    sinθ    0   0   |
|  -sinθ    cosθ    0   0   |
|   0       0       1   0   |
|   0       0       0   1   |
```

Rotation Matrix Z Axis Example

In this example, the triangle coordinates on the left are transformed with the Z rotation matrix by π/4 radians (45 degrees) about the Z axis:

```
|  0   0   0   0  |  X  |   cos(π/4)    sin(π/4)    0   0   |
|  1   4   0   0  |     |  -sin(π/4)    cos(π/4)    0   0   |
|  4   2   0   0  |     |   0           0           1   0   |
|  0   0   0   0  |     |   0           0           0   1   |
```

When you calculate the multiplication by hand, the new triangle coordinates—after the rotation—will appear in the product matrix:

```
 0.00   0.00   0.00   0.00
-2.12   3.54   0.00   0.00
 1.41   4.24   0.00   0.00
 0.00   0.00   0.00   0.00
```

FIGURE 16-5

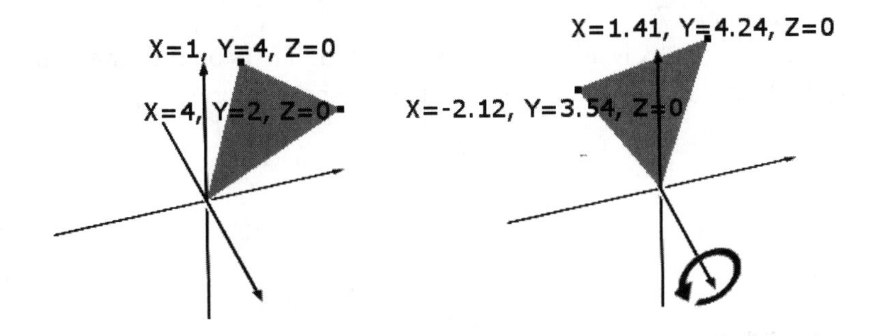

Z axis rotation before and after the transformation matrix is applied

Figure 16-5 shows the triangle before and after the rotation.

To try this in code, replace the assignment of matrix B with the following code to create a rotation about the Z axis of π/4 radians:

```
float sin = (float)Math.Sin(Math.PI / 4.0);
float cos = (float)Math.Cos(Math.PI / 4.0);
B.M11 =  cos;    B.M12 =  sin;    B.M13 = 0.0f;    B.M14 = 0.0f;
B.M21 = -sin;    B.M22 =  cos;    B.M23 = 0.0f;    B.M24 = 0.0f;
B.M31 = 0.0f;    B.M32 = 0.0f;    B.M33 = 1.0f;    B.M34 = 0.0f;
B.M41 = 0.0f;    B.M42 = 0.0f;    B.M43 = 0.0f;    B.M44 = 1.0f;
```

Z Axis Rotation Example Using the CreateRotationZ() Method

The `CreateRotationZ(float radians)` matrix will generate a matrix identical to the one just declared for matrix B. Replacing the existing matrix assignment with this instruction will generate the same result:

```
B = Matrix.CreateRotationZ(MathHelper.Pi/4.0f);
```

Identity Matrix

When a set of vertices is multiplied by the identity matrix, the product equals the original vertex matrix. In other words, nothing changes in the original data matrix. It may seem pointless to use the identity matrix since it does not actually perform a transformation. However, the identity matrix is included in the recommended I.S.R.O.T. sequence of transformations to ensure that the World matrix is initialized properly when no other transformation matrix is applied. By default, an identity matrix is used in the World matrix to initialize it. The World matrix is explained in more detail in Chapter 17.

The identity matrix is defined for a matrix that has 1s on the diagonal from the top left to the bottom right, and 0s elsewhere, as shown here:

```
| 1  0  0  0  |
| 0  1  0  0  |
| 0  0  1  0  |
| 0  0  0  1  |
```

Identity Matrix Example

This example shows that when a data matrix is multiplied by an identity matrix, the result equals the data matrix. In other words, A*B=A (where B is an identity matrix). In this case, the vertices for a triangle are multiplied by the identity matrix. The product equals the original set of vertices for the triangle:

```
| 0  0  0  0  |X|  1  0  0  0  |=|  0  0  0  0  |
| 1  4  0  0  | |  0  1  0  0  |=|  1  4  0  0  |
| 4  2  0  0  | |  0  0  1  0  |=|  4  2  0  0  |
| 0  0  0  0  | |  0  0  0  1  |=|  0  0  0  0  |
```

To perform this calculation in code, replace the assignment for matrix B with this revision:

```
B.M11 = 1.0f;   B.M12 = 0.0f;   B.M13 = 0.0f;   B.M14 = 0.0f;
B.M21 = 0.0f;   B.M22 = 1.0f;   B.M23 = 0.0f;   B.M24 = 0.0f;
B.M31 = 0.0f;   B.M32 = 0.0f;   B.M33 = 1.0f;   B.M34 = 0.0f;
B.M41 = 0.0f;   B.M42 = 0.0f;   B.M43 = 0.0f;   B.M44 = 1.0f;
```

When you run this code, the product matrix displayed in the game window equals matrix A (which defines the triangle).

Identity Matrix Example Using Matrix.Identity

Until now, the predefined matrix (`Matrix.Identity`) has been used for the identity matrix. This matrix is equivalent to the one you just created manually. If you replace the assignment for matrix B with

```
B = Matrix.Identity;
```

the outcome will be the same.

Matrices enable transformations in 3D space. Understanding linear algebra and the defined transformation matrices will allow you to develop better graphics algorithms and have deeper control of your graphics engine. This will be especially helpful when you need to build your own matrices to perform transformations for vectors. See Chapter 8 and Chapter 19 for examples of when this technique is necessary.

CHAPTER 16 REVIEW EXERCISES

1. Try the step-by-step examples discussed in this chapter.
2. Starting with a triangle with the coordinates

```
A{-0.23f, -0.2f, -0.1f)
B{ 0.23f, -0.2f, -0.1f)
C{ 0.0f,   0.2ff, 0.1f)
```

manually compute the unit normal. Then manually translate the triangle, together with its unit normal, 2 units on Z, and –0.35 units on X. Scale the triangle and normal by 3.5 on X, Y, and Z. Rotate the triangle and normal by π/3 radians on X and π/4 radians on Z. When performing this transformation, do not use any variations of the following methods:

```
CreateScale(float X, float Y, float Z);
CreateRotationX(float radians);
CreateRotationY(float radians);
CreateRotationZ(float radians);
CreateTranslation(float X, float Y, float Z);
Cross();
Normalize();
```

When the program is run, the final result shows both the triangle and the triangle's unit normal pointing out from it. Both the triangle and normal vector are

- Translated 2 units on Z and –0.35 units on X
- Scaled by 3.5 on X, Y, and Z
- Rotated π/3 radians on X
- Rotated π/4 radians on Z

CHAPTER 17

Building a Graphics Engine Camera

A great number of elements contribute to the "feel" of a video game. The physics, sounds, music, graphics, 3D models, and many other factors all influence the gamer's experience. These things are important, but possibly none is as important as the camera you create for your game. The camera is the heart of the graphics engine. This book shows how to add and customize the components you need for game graphics, but it's the camera that allows your players to see your world.

A camera lets your viewer travel through a virtual world; it can be thought of as the player's lens. The camera includes logic for responding to the game's controls so the user can adjust their view and position within the 3D world.

The 3D camera code is so fundamental that it is included in the base code for almost all of this book's examples. This chapter explains how the base code was created and shows you how to build it from scratch. You can also use the step-by-step explanation from this chapter to add a camera to your own game projects.

CAMERA VECTORS

Most cameras are constructed with logic that applies a common set of vectors and matrices. The structure is often described and manipulated with a set of five vectors:

- `View` Stores the target position focused on by the camera.
- `Position` Stores the camera's position.
- `Up` Stores the upright direction.
- `Look` Stores the direction of the lens `(View - Position)`. (The `Look` vector is also known as the `Forward` vector.)
- `Right` Stores the normal vector from the `Look` and `Up` vectors.

Figure 17-1 shows the position and directional vectors that describe a camera's position and orientation.

CAMERA MATRICES

For a camera to function properly (so that all objects in the world are seen correctly), three matrices are used. Together, they transform the objects seen by the camera, the angle at which these objects appear, and the range of visibility. These three matrices are known as the World matrix, the View matrix, and the Projection (Perspective)

FIGURE 17-1

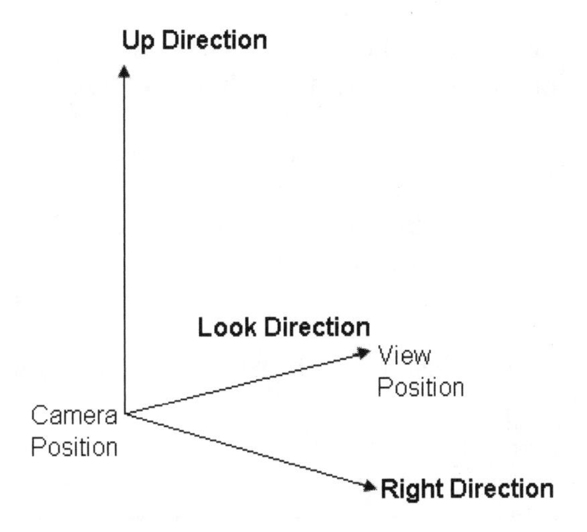

Position and directional vectors that make a camera

matrix, respectively. The WVP matrix you have been sending to your shader in this book's examples thus far is a product of these three matrices.

World Matrix

You have already been working with the World matrix to transform vertices and 3D models. The World matrix converts model and vertex coordinates to world coordinates so they map properly to the 3D world space. You have used both XNA transformation functions for creating the rotations, translations, and scaling, and you have also seen how to perform these calculations manually.

View Matrix

The View matrix defines what the camera sees by setting the camera's direction.

Projection Matrix

The Projection matrix sets the visibility for the camera. A large projection creates a wide-angle lens. Another way to say this is that the Projection matrix describes the *frustum*, which is the cone-shaped view seen by the camera. The frustum has front and back boundaries on the Z axis known as the *near clip plane* and the *far clip plane*, respectively.

The Projection matrix builds the frustum using the function `Matrix.CreatePerspectiveFieldOfView()`, which takes five parameters:

```
Matrix projectionMatrix = Matrix.CreatePerspectiveFieldOfView(
                          float  fieldOfView, // angle of visibility
                          float  aspectRatio, // width/height
                          float  nearClip,    // first visible point on Z
                          float  farClip);    // last visible point on Z
```

Figure 17-2 shows a diagram of the frustum created with the Projection matrix.

FIGURE 17-2

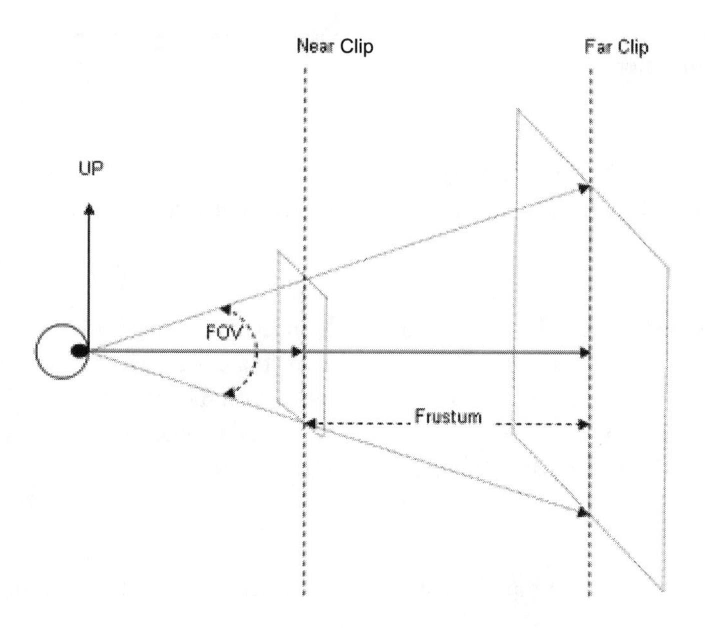

Projection described by field of view (FOV), aspect ratio, and clip space

CAMERA EXAMPLE

The camera code presented in this example shows everything you need to implement a camera that can be used for first-person shooter games, racing games, and many others. In fact, the code explained here is the same code used in the MGHWinBaseCode and MGH360BaseCode base code projects.

You can begin with either the Windows Game project or Xbox 360 Game project template to generate your game application shell. The camera you add will move and strafe with arrow keypress events; W, A, S, and D keypress events; or left stick-shift events. The camera's view will change with either mouse movements or right thumbstick shift events.

Creating the Camera Class Shell

You will first need to add an empty Camera.cs file to your project. It needs the following class structure:

```
using System;
using System.Collections.Generic;
using Microsoft.Xna.Framework;

namespace CameraViewer{
    public class Camera{}
}
```

When you have created your base `Camera` class, it will need some class-level variables for storing the camera vectors, projection and view matrices, and a time variable for moving the camera at a regulated speed:

```
public      Vector3     position, view, up;
public      Matrix      projectionMatrix, viewMatrix;
private     float       timeLapse = 0.0f;
```

Obviously, the `Camera()` constructor initializes the class. It starts by creating a camera that uses the vectors `View`, `Position`, and `Up`; these vectors store the direction, position, and orientation of the camera, respectively. When you are defining these vectors, the Y value for the camera's position and view is set to 0.9f to elevate the camera position and view above the ground:

```
public Camera(){
    position    = new Vector3(0.0f, 0.9f, 0.0f);
```

```
    view         = new Vector3(0.0f, 0.9f,-0.5f);
    up           = new Vector3(0.0f, 1.0f, 0.0f);
}
```

In the camera class, SetFrameInterval() provides an interface for setting a scaled measure based on the time difference between the current frame and the previous frame. This time measure is then used to create a scalar value for incrementing or decrementing the position and view of the camera when it is moved. The time scale enables smooth lateral and diagonal camera translations along the X axis and the Z axis. Because you're measuring the time between frames, the translations are performed at the same speed regardless of the system running the application.

```
public void SetFrameInterval(GameTime gameTime){
    timeLapse = (float)gameTime.ElapsedGameTime.Milliseconds;
}
```

To orient the camera properly, a view matrix is set using the CreateLookAt() method in the SetView() routine:

```
public void SetView(){
    viewMatrix    = Matrix.CreateLookAt(position, view, up);
}
```

After initializing your camera class, you must create a projection matrix to define the frustum. In other words, adding SetProjection() to the camera class defines what the camera lens sees:

```
public void SetProjection(int windowWidth, int windowHeight)
{   // parameters are field of view, width/height, near clip, far clip
    projectionMatrix
    =   Matrix.CreatePerspectiveFieldOfView(MathHelper.Pi/4.0f,
        (float)windowWidth/(float)windowHeight, 0.005f, 1000.0f);
}
```

Initializing the Camera from Your Game Class

To reference the camera in your game class, include the camera's namespace, CameraViewer, in your Game1.cs file:

```
using  CameraViewer;
```

The camera is instantiated from the game class with the following line:

```
private Camera    cam = new Camera();
```

Adding a camera to the game template helps to enable 3D graphics, but some extra setup is required to make 3D graphics possible. First, the CullMode should be specified at the application launch. In our case, CullMode is set to None so 3D objects are drawn in their entirety. Enabling culling leads to efficient rendering because it will clip the back face. However, this can lead to confusion when you are starting out with graphics programming as you may mistakenly arrange your vertices in the order that is culled. If your vertices are arranged in the same order as the culling sequence, they will not be drawn. You might not always remember to check culling if this happens, so we have purposely turned culling off. Even so, we strongly recommend that you implement culling when drawing large models or surfaces with high vertex counts. In this framework you could easily set culling immediately before drawing large objects and then set this property back to CullMode.None afterward if you wanted.

Next, when setting up the projection matrix, the window Width and Height parameters are used to help define the camera's cone of view. Both instructions are called from the InitializeBaseCode() method in the game class. This is necessary because the frustum for most 3D games only needs to be defined once. This might change, though, if you are using a split-screen game as discussed in Chapter 28:

```
private void InitializeBaseCode()
{   // see both sides of objects drawn
    graphics.GraphicsDevice.RenderState.CullMode = CullMode.None;
    // set camera matrix
    cam.SetProjection(Window.ClientBounds.Width,
                      Window.ClientBounds.Height);
}
```

InitializeBaseCode() is called from the Initialize() method that sets up the game:

```
InitializeBaseCode();
```

Every frame, a call to SetFrameInterval() (from the start of the Update() method) updates the time tracking between frames so the camera will move at uniform speed on any system:

```
cam.SetFrameInterval(gameTime);
```

We have defined our Projection matrix when the program begins. When drawing our 3D objects, we transform each one using a World matrix. The last camera matrix needed at this point is the View, which is set from each frame from the Update() method and controls the camera's current direction:

```
cam.SetView();
```

Moving and Strafing

Once you have defined the basic camera, you can add methods to enable the viewer to move forward, backward, or sideways (strafing) in the 3D world. Updating the camera's position while moving also requires updating the visible scenery.

Enabling Forward, Backward, and Sideways Movement in Camera.cs

`UpdatePositionAndView()` is added to the camera class to increment the camera position along X and Z. This increment is taken from the direction vector, which is scaled by the time between frames. The camera's view is also incremented by the same amount to ensure that updates to the scenery match the changes to the camera's position:

```
public void UpdatePositionAndView(Vector3 direction, float speed){
    speed       *= (float)timeLapse;
    direction   *= speed;
    position.X  += direction.X; position.Z  += direction.Z;
    view.X      += direction.X; view.Z      += direction.Z;
}
```

The camera's `Move()` method allows the viewer to move forward and backward whenever the user presses the UP or DOWN ARROW key, the W or S key, or when shifting the left thumbstick on the game controller. The actual "move" is implemented by incrementing the camera's `View` and `Position` vectors by the camera's `Look` direction. The `Look` direction is normalized to ensure a uniform comparison of elements in the direction vector:

```
public void Move(float speed){
    Vector3         look    = new Vector3(0.0f, 0.0f, 0.0f);
    Vector3         unitLook;
    const float     SCALE   = 0.005f;
    speed                  *= SCALE;

    look.Y                  = view.Y;
    look.X                  = view.X - position.X;
    look.Z                  = view.Z - position.Z;

    // get new camera direction vector
    unitLook = Vector3.Normalize(look);

    UpdatePositionAndView(unitLook, speed);
}
```

A similar feature to add to your camera is the ability to strafe. A *strafe* is a side-to-side camera movement. If you're a fan of first-person shooter games, you know how fundamental strafing can be to a game. Whether you're playing *Quake*, *Doom*, *Halo*, or *Call of Duty*, moving side to side is often your only defense against taking enemy fire.

The code needed to perform this action is almost identical to the code used for creating forward and backward movement. Only one extra instruction is needed to convert the forward direction vector into a strafe direction vector:

```
Vector3 right    = Vector3.Cross(unitLook, up);
```

The strafe vector is perpendicular to the surface created by the `Look` and `Up` vectors. This new vector is referred to as the `Right` vector. A time-scaled increment based on the `Right` vector is then used to update the camera's position and view from the `Strafe()` method. Adding the `Strafe()` method to the camera class provides the code needed to generate sideways camera movement:

```
public void Strafe(float speed){
    Vector3             look      = Vector3.Zero;
    Vector3             unitLook;
    const float         SCALE     = 0.005f;
    speed                        *= SCALE;

    look.Y              = view.Y;
    look.X              = view.X - position.X;
    look.Z              = view.Z - position.Z;
    unitLook            = Vector3.Normalize(look);

    // update camera position and view with right vector direction
    Vector3 right    = Vector3.Cross(unitLook, up);
    UpdatePositionAndView(right, speed);
}
```

Triggering Forward, Backward, and Sideways Movement from the Game Class

You should add some code to the `Update()` method to allow the game player to exit the game gracefully when pressing the B button on the controller or the ESC key on the keyboard. Some code already exists in the `Update()` method to allow players to exit the game when pressing the Back button on the controller. However, there is no keypress event for exiting on the PC if no controller is used. Since the PC mouse cursor is repositioned at the window center each frame, allowing the player to end the game with a keypress event is essential because she will not be able to click the close button in the top right of the window. To enable the gamer to close the game application with either a Back button press on the controller or an ESC keypress on the keyboard, replace the existing exit event code in the `Update()` method with this block of code:

```
KeyboardState kbState = Keyboard.GetState();

if (GamePad.GetState(PlayerIndex.One).Buttons.Back == ButtonState.Pressed
    || kbState.IsKeyDown(Keys.Escape))
{ this.Exit(); }
```

Forward and backward movement is triggered by shifting the game pad's left thumbstick up and down, or by pressing either the UP and DOWN ARROW keys on the keyboard, or pressing the W and S keys on the keyboard. This `Move()` method handles user input from the game class:

```
float Move(){
    KeyboardState kb     = Keyboard.GetState();
    GamePadState  gp     = GamePad.GetState(PlayerIndex.One);
    float         move   = 0.0f;
    const float   SCALE = 1.50f;

    if (gp.IsConnected){ // left stick shifted left/right
        if(gp.ThumbSticks.Left.Y != 0.0f)
            move = (SCALE * gp.ThumbSticks.Left.Y);
    }
    else                              // no gamepad - use UP&DOWN or W&S
        #if !XBOX
        if( kb.IsKeyDown(Keys.Up) || kb.IsKeyDown(Keys.W))
            move = 1.0f;              // Up or W - move ahead
        else if(kb.IsKeyDown(Keys.Down) || kb.IsKeyDown(Keys.S))
            move =-1.0f;              // Down or S - move back
        #endif
}
```

The code that retrieves the strafe value in the game class is executed when the user shifts the left thumbstick on the controller from side to side, when the user presses the A or D keys, or when the user presses the LEFT or RIGHT ARROW key. This code returns an amount between -1.0f and +1.0f when the user shifts the left thumbstick. If the game controller is not connected, either -1 is returned when the LEFT ARROW key is pressed or +1 is returned when the RIGHT ARROW key is pressed:

```
float Strafe(){
    KeyboardState kb = Keyboard.GetState();
    GamePadState  gp = GamePad.GetState(PlayerIndex.One);

    // using gamepad leftStick shifted left / right for strafe
    if (gp.IsConnected){
        if(gp.ThumbSticks.Left.X != 0.0f)
            return gp.ThumbSticks.Left.X;
    }
    // using keyboard - strafe with Left&Right or A&D
    else if (kb.IsKeyDown(Keys.Left) || kb.IsKeyDown(Keys.A))
        return -1.0f;   // strafe left
    else if (kb.IsKeyDown(Keys.Right) || kb.IsKeyDown(Keys.D))
        return 1.0f;    // strafe right
    return 0.0f;
}
```

The camera's `Move()` and `Strafe()` methods are triggered from `Update()`—just before setting the view—to enable continuous checks for these events:

```
cam.Move(Move());
cam.Strafe(Strafe());
```

If you have implemented all of the code shown so far in your project, you already have a camera that moves forward, backward, and sideways. To see your camera in action, you will have to draw an object to act as a visible reference to show that you are actually moving. If you run your code without drawing anything, all you will see is an empty CornflowerBlue world and you won't be able to tell which way is up.

Rotating the View

This next portion of this example demonstrates how to rotate the camera's `View` vector about the X and Y axes—based on the position of the mouse or right thumbstick. Be aware that the camera `Position` vector and camera `Up` vector are not changed by the mouse movements or shifts of the right thumbstick; only the `View` vector is modified by this section of code. This vector allows you to look in different directions without actually changing your position.

But before you dive into the code, here's a description of quaternion theory, which is the system you'll use to enable changes to the view.

Quaternion Theory

The following section of code, which updates the camera view for the mouse movement, is based on quaternion theory. By definition, a *quaternion* is a special type of vector that stores a rotation around an axis. Quaternion math is used to calculate an increment to update the camera's Look vector.

We can express the value of the Look vector like this:

```
Look      = View - Position
```

By rearranging this equation we can say the following:

```
View      = Look + Position
```

If the quaternion represents the updated Look vector, then

```
Updated View = Updated Look Vector + Position
```

Updated Look Vector

The formula for calculating the updated Look vector is:

```
qRotation * qLook * qRotation' (qRotation' is the conjugate of qRotation)
```

Each of the three operands will be discussed next.

Local Rotation Quaternion

The first quaternion that is used to calculate the updated Look vector, qRotation, is a local rotation. Quaternion theory provides a formula for computing the local rotation. In this case, the local rotation is generated using a direction vector for X, Y, and Z. Rotations about the X axis are applied using the Look vector. Rotations about the Y axis are applied using the Right direction vector. The rotation angle stored in the W component is obtained from the deviation of the mouse (or thumbstick) from the center of the window. With this information, we can generate the local rotation by writing the following:

```
qRotation.W = cos(MouseDeviationFromCenter/2)
qRotation.X = UnitDirection.X * sin(MouseDeviationFromCenter/2)
qRotation.Y = UnitDirection.Y * sin(MouseDeviationFromCenter/2)
qRotation.Z = UnitDirection.Z * sin(MouseDeviationFromCenter/2)
```

Using the Look Vector as a Quaternion

The next quaternion used in the formula for the updated Look vector is based on the Look direction:

```
qLook.X = Look.X   qLook.Y = Look.Y   qLook.Z = Look.Z qLook.W = 0
```

Conjugate Quaternion

A *conjugate quaternion* is used to calculate the updated `Look` vector. The conjugate is created by negating a quaternion vector's X, Y, and Z components:

```
Quaternion conjugate
= (-Quaternion.X, -Quaternion.Y, -Quaternion.Z, Quaternion.W)
```

Quaternion Product

The equation for multiplying two quaternion is as follows:

$$(Quaternion_1 * Quaternion_2).W = w_1x_2 - x_1w_2 + y_1y_2 - z_1z_2$$
$$(Quaternion_1 * Quaternion_2).X = w_1x_2 + x_1w_2 + y_1z_2 - z_1y_2$$
$$(Quaternion_1 * Quaternion_2).Y = w_1y_2 - x_1z_2 + y_1w_2 + z_1x_2$$
$$(Quaternion_1 * Quaternion_2).Z = w_1z_2 + x_1y_2 - y_1x_2 + z_1w_2$$

Updating the View

The updated `Look` vector is obtained using the product of local rotation, look, and conjugate quaternions.

```
Updated Look Vector = qRotation * qLook * qRotation'
```

With the result from this product, the `View` can be updated:

```
Updated View         = Updated Look Vector + Position
```

Now you will apply this logic to the graphics engine to update your view.

Updating the View in the Camera Class

`RotationQuaternion()` can be added to the camera class to generate the local rotation quaternion based on the direction vector. The first parameter of this method represents the shift of the mouse or thumbstick from the resting position. The second parameter is a direction vector that can be either the `Look` or `Right` vector:

```
private Vector4 RotationQuaternion(float degrees, Vector3 direction){
    Vector4 unitAxis = Vector4.Zero;
    Vector4 axis     = new Vector4(direction, 0.0f);

    // only normalize if necessary
    if ((axis.X != 0 && axis.X != 1) || (axis.Y != 0 && axis.Y != 1) ||
        (axis.Z != 0 && axis.Z != 1)){
```

```
        unitAxis = Vector4.Normalize(axis);
    }

    float angle = degrees * MathHelper.Pi/180.0f;
    float sin   = (float)Math.Sin(angle/2.0f);

    // create the quaternion.
    Vector4 quaternion = new Vector4(0.0f, 0.0f, 0.0f, 0.0f);
            quaternion.X = axis.X * sin;
            quaternion.Y = axis.Y * sin;
            quaternion.Z = axis.Z * sin;
            quaternion.W = (float)Math.Cos(angle/2.0f);

    return  Vector4.Normalize(quaternion);
}
```

Next, you'll add the UpdateView() method. UpdateView() computes the product of these three quaternions and uses it to update the player's view:

```
private void UpdateView(float rotationAmount, Vector3 direction)
{   // local rotation quaternion
    Vector4 Q    = RotationQuaternion(rotationAmount, direction);

    Vector4 look = Vector4.Zero;
    look.X       = view.X - position.X;
    look.Y       = view.Y - position.Y;
    look.Z       = view.Z - position.Z;

    // rotation quaternion * look
    Vector4 Qp;
    Qp.X    = Q.W*look.X + Q.X*look.W + Q.Y*look.Z - Q.Z*look.Y;
    Qp.Y    = Q.W*look.Y - Q.X*look.Z + Q.Y*look.W + Q.Z*look.X;
    Qp.Z    = Q.W*look.Z + Q.X*look.Y - Q.Y*look.X + Q.Z*look.W;
    Qp.W    = Q.W*look.W - Q.X*look.X - Q.Y*look.Y - Q.Z*look.Z;

    // conjugate is made by negating quaternion x, y, and z
    Vector4 conj = new Vector4(-Q.X, -Q.Y, -Q.Z, Q.W);

    // updated look vector
    Vector4 Qlook;
```

```
    Qlook.X = Qp.W*conj.X + Qp.X*conj.W + Qp.Y*conj.Z - Qp.Z*conj.Y;
    Qlook.Y = Qp.W*conj.Y - Qp.X*conj.Z + Qp.Y*conj.W + Qp.Z*conj.X;
    Qlook.Z = Qp.W*conj.Z + Qp.X*conj.Y - Qp.Y*conj.X + Qp.Z*conj.W;
    Qlook.W = Qp.W*conj.W - Qp.X*conj.X - Qp.Y*conj.Y - Qp.Z*conj.Z;

    // cap view at ground and sky
    if (Qlook.Y > -0.49f && Qlook.Y < 0.49f){
        // updated view equals position plus the quaternion
        view.X = position.X + Qlook.X;
        view.Y = position.Y + Qlook.Y;
        view.Z = position.Z + Qlook.Z;
    }
}
```

The camera class uses the `ChangeView()` method to receive changes in `View` direction from the game class and apply them to the camera orientation. `ChangeView()` checks whether the mouse or right stick has been shifted. If no movement is detected, the method exits and no changes to the view are performed. Otherwise, a relative measure for the X and Y rotations is generated based on the deviation of the mouse from the center of the window. Rotations about the X axis are applied using the `Right` vector. Rotations about the Y axis are applied using the `Up` vector:

```
public void ChangeView(float X, float Y)
{   // exit if no change to view
    if (X == 0 && Y == 0)
        return;

    float       rotationX,                      rotationY;
    const float SCALEX = 50.0f;  const float SCALEY = 2000.0f;
    Vector3     look   = view - position;

    // tilt camera up and down
    Vector3 right       = Vector3.Cross(look, up);
            rotationX   = Y / SCALEX;
    UpdateView(rotationX, Vector3.Normalize(right));

    // swivel camera left and right
    rotationY = X * timeLapse / SCALEY;
    UpdateView(-rotationY, up);
}
```

With ChangeView() in the game class, it will adjust the camera view according to shifts of the mouse or left thumbstick. A revised SetView() method in the camera class replaces the existing one to process changes to the camera's Look direction for each frame:

```
public void SetView(Vector2 viewChange){
    ChangeView(viewChange.X, viewChange.Y);
    viewMatrix    = Matrix.CreateLookAt(position, view, up);
}
```

Triggering Changes to the View from the Game Class

Back inside the game class, the camera needs to be enabled for manipulation by the game controller, keyboard, and mouse. The camera will function on the PC like a first-person shooter, where a typical configuration uses the mouse to change the view. XNA provides the Mouse and MouseState classes to handle the mouse on a PC.

When run on the PC, the mouse has to be enabled in the game class. The mouse will adjust the view by checking the distance from the center of the window to the mouse. At the top of the game class, a MouseState object is declared:

```
#if !XBOX
        MouseState mouse;
#endif
```

The game class's ChangeView() method receives changes in view on X and Y that are triggered from the game class by mouse movements, or by shifts to the right thumbstick. After the relative changes in view have been captured and processed on the PC, the Mouse class SetPosition() method moves the cursor back to the center of the window so the mouse's relative change from the center of the window can be calculated in the next frame. Otherwise, the camera will use the right stick's deviation from the center to calculate the change in view:

```
Vector2 ChangeView(GameTime gameTime){
    const float SENSITIVITY           = 250.0f;
    const float VERTICAL_INVERSION    =-1.0f;      // vertical view control

    // negate to reverse
    // handle change in view using right and left keys
    KeyboardState   kbState           = Keyboard.GetState();
    int          widthMiddle          = Window.ClientBounds.Width/2;
    int          heightMiddle         = Window.ClientBounds.Height/2;
    Vector2      change               = Vector2.Zero;
```

```
    GamePadState gp      = GamePad.GetState(PlayerIndex.One);
    if (gp.IsConnected == true)                  // gamepad on PC / Xbox
    {
        float   scaleY   = VERTICAL_INVERSION * (float)
                           gameTime.ElapsedGameTime.Milliseconds/50.0f;
        change.Y         = scaleY * gp.ThumbSticks.Right.Y * SENSITIVITY;
        change.X         = gp.ThumbSticks.Right.X * SENSITIVITY;
    }
    else{                                        // mouse only (on PC)
#if !XBOX
        float scaleY     = VERTICAL_INVERSION * (float)
                           gameTime.ElapsedGameTime.Milliseconds/100.0f;
        float scaleX     = (float)
                           gameTime.ElapsedGameTime.Milliseconds/400.0f;
        // get cursor position
        mouse = Mouse.GetState();

        // cursor not at center on X
        if (mouse.X != widthMiddle){
            change.X     = mouse.X - widthMiddle;
            change.X    /= scaleX;
        }
        // cursor not at center on Y
        if (mouse.Y != heightMiddle){
            change.Y     = mouse.Y - heightMiddle;
            change.Y    /= scaleY;
        }
        // reset cursor back to center
        Mouse.SetPosition(widthMiddle, heightMiddle);
#endif
    }
    return change;
}
```

To update your camera's view from the game class (for each frame), replace the existing call to `SetView()` from the `Update()` method with this revision that changes the view based on how the mouse or right thumbstick is shifted:

```
cam.SetView(ChangeView(gameTime));
```

If you run your code now, your project will have a fully functional camera enabled. To actually see it moving, you need to draw some kind of reference, such as ground, a triangle, or a 3D model. The camera moves and strafes with the left thumbstick or ARROW keys. It changes view with the right thumbstick or the mouse.

With this camera, your game players now have full access to journey into the world hosted by your graphics engine.

BUILDING THE BASE CODE FROM SCRATCH EXAMPLE

Not only is the camera viewer the heart of the base code, but this camera viewer discussion completes our explanation of how the base code works. You can actually build the base code starting with the solution from this last example. When you add the code from the "Texture Example, Part A: Adding the Grass Texture" demonstration in Chapter 9, you will see the grassy ground when you run the project. Then, you can follow the steps listed in Chapter 6 in "Position Color Shader Example: Referencing the Shader" to add the simple shader for drawing surfaces with colored vertices. Finally, inside `InitializeBaseCode()`, add the following instruction to write the title of this book on the status bar and complete the base code:

```
Window.Title = "Microsoft® XNA Game Studio Creator's Guide 2nd Edition";
```

You have just created the base code for this book. If you have followed the discussions behind this code, you should now be able to say you understand how the base code works and, using this book as your reference, you can create it from scratch.

CHAPTER 17 REVIEW EXERCISES

To get the most from this chapter, try out these chapter review exercises.

Follow the step-by-step examples presented in this chapter, but make the following changes.

1. Add an option to "invert" the camera. This is a common first-person shooter game feature that allows players to reverse the direction of the Up and Down view control.
2. Add an option to move the camera forward on the PC when the left mouse button is pressed.

CHAPTER 18

Collision Detection

COLLISION detection determines whether two objects overlap and therefore have collided in your virtual world. Accurate collision detection is fundamental to a solid game engine. Without collision detection, your cars would drive off the road, your people would walk through buildings, and your camera would travel through cement walls. Collision detection is also fundamental when dealing with any sort of missiles. For example, if you had faulty detection applied to a rocket, you might successfully hit your target and not receive credit—or possibly even worse, your enemies might miss a shot at you and be credited with a hit. These sorts of problems are occasionally evident in commercial games, but to avoid player frustration, you should strive to have excellent collision detection. This chapter shows you how to use collision detection to add boundaries around your game objects.

XNA has two main types for implementing collision detection. They are:

1. `BoundingBox`
2. `BoundingSphere`

Implementing collision detection with these types involves encasing your physical game objects either with invisible boxes or spheres. Obviously, a box will better suit a rectangular high-rise building, while a bounding sphere offers a better fit for rounded objects such as a domed arena. Together, these two collision types deliver a powerful range of options that allow you to implement efficient collision checking in any situation.

FINE-TUNING YOUR COLLISION DETECTION SYSTEMS

For irregular shapes—such as an alien ship—you can use a group of smaller boxes or spheres for each section. Compared to boxes, spheres are easier to transform and they use less storage space, so you'll want to use spheres when you can.

Also, XNA's model loader exposes mesh objects in the .X models and .FBX models. Each mesh within a model is assigned a bounding sphere with a properly sized radius. With this system already in place, you can load your model in a modeling tool such as Blender or MilkShape, and add spheres using the designer to cover the surface of your model. You then need to delete your original model group(s) from this model project. After exporting your cluster of spheres as a separate model, you can load them in your XNA project and extract bounding-sphere information at run time. This means you can rapidly and accurately build your collision detection systems using a model design tool and the XNA Framework. Figure 18-1 shows models with spheres added before the original meshes were deleted.

FIGURE 18-1

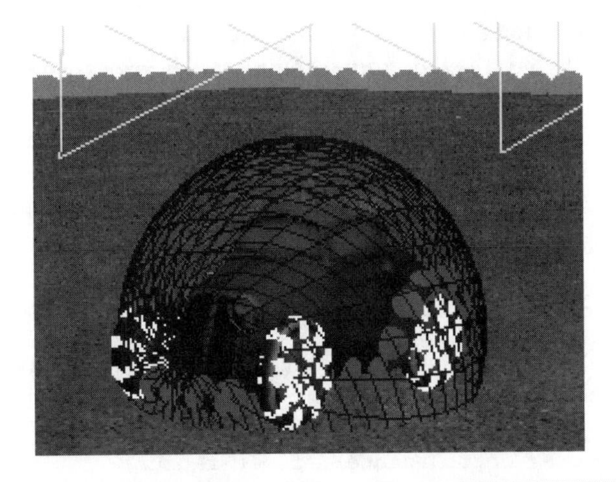

Additional spheres surrounding the original mesh are used for collision detection.

EARLY WARNING SYSTEMS

As you continue to add bounding spheres or bounding boxes to improve the accuracy of your collision detection, you may encounter a performance decrease if too much collision checking is required each frame. For this reason, you need broad collision-checking routines to first detect if two objects are within close proximity of each other before doing anything else. These early warning systems only need to compare a few large blunt bounding spheres or boxes to check for collisions. Whenever a close proximity between large bounding objects is established, more intensive and accurate collision-checking routines can be used. A decent early warning system avoids the need to run exhaustive sets of routines every frame.

CONTAINMENTTYPE

Both `BoundingSphere` and `BoundingBox` types use a `ContainmentType` to describe the extent of surface overlap. These containment types include `Contains`, `Disjoint`, and `Intersect`. This allows you to determine if your spheres or boxes contain or intersect each other. A `Disjoint` condition occurs when the collision objects are completely separate.

BoundingSphere

The use of bounding spheres is popular because spheres can easily be transformed and compared and they do not require much processing power. The bounding-sphere method involves creating an invisible sphere around each object that needs collision detection. If the distance between the centers of the two spheres is less than the sum of their radii, a collision is detected. You don't have to actually perform these calculations, though, because XNA's accompanying methods for the `BoundingSphere` type already do it for you.

Initializing the Bounding Sphere

When you initialize the bounding sphere, you will specify the location of the center of the sphere using a three-dimensional vector and the radius of the sphere.

```
public BoundingSphere(Vector3 center, float radius);
```

Intersects()

The `BoundingSphere Intersects()` method has several overloads. Two common overloads allow comparisons between the current bounding sphere and either a sphere or bounding box that can be passed in as parameters.

```
public bool Intersects(BoundingBox box);
public bool Intersects(BoundingSphere sphere);
```

Contains

The bounding-sphere object offers the `Contains()` method to compare the bounding sphere with another bounding sphere, a bounding box, or a three-dimensional position.

```
public void Contains(ref BoundingSphere  sphere,
                     out ContainmentType result);
public void Contains(ref BoundingBox box, out ContainmentType result);
public void Contains(ref Vector3 point, out ContainmentType result);
```

BoundingBox

The `BoundingBox` type offers collision checking for objects contained within rectangular 3D space. When you initialize this type, you pass in the minimum and maximum positions for the corners of your bounding box:

```
BoundingBox boundingBox = new BoundingBox(Vector3 min, Vector3 max);
```

The BoundingBox type in XNA is not axis aligned, so if you rotate or animate your bounding box you will have to reinitialize it each frame to reset the new minimum and maximum corners. This is not a practical solution because the bounding box shape will change significantly at different angles of a rotation.

In spite of limitations you might face with the bounding box, it really is a valuable structure—especially for rectangular objects that stay in one place. In the code demonstration later, you will see how over one hundred spheres that line the walls of the world are replaced with one large box for a giant leap in providing efficient collision detection.

Intersects()

Similar to the BoundingSphere Intersects() method, the BoundingBox Intersects() method has several overloads. Two common overloads allow comparisons between the current bounding sphere and either a sphere or bounding box that can be passed in as parameters.

```
public bool Intersects(BoundingBox box);
public bool Intersects(BoundingSphere sphere);
```

Contains()

The BoundingBox Contains() method has several variations. Here are three common ways to use the Contains() method:

1. Comparing one bounding box with another:

   ```
   public void Contains(ref BoundingBox box, out ContainmentType result);
   ```

2. Comparing a bounding box with a bounding sphere:

   ```
   public void Contains(ref BoundingSphere  sphere,
                        out ContainmentType result);
   ```

3. Comparing a bounding box with a single three-dimensional position:

   ```
   public void Contains(ref Vector3 point, out ContainmentType result);
   ```

The second Contains() overload mentioned is very exciting because it allows you to compare your boxes with spheres, giving you many possibilities to generate the best fit for your objects. We will show an example of this overload later in this chapter to generate a very efficient and well-fitted collision-detection routine between the car and the box that surrounds the world.

COLLISION DETECTION EXAMPLE: INITIALIZING AND DRAWING BOUNDING SPHERES

This example shows how to build a collision detection framework to implement XNA's `BoundingSphere` and `BoundingBox` objects. Usage of bounding spheres is emphasized because spheres are easier to update and transform than bounding boxes. The framework provided here also allows you to draw your bounding spheres while you debug your code so you can ensure that your spheres are sized and positioned properly.

This example begins with the solution from the "Adding a Car as a Third-Person Object" example from Chapter 14. You will first modify the code by manually adding bounding spheres around the edge of the world. Then, in a modeling tool, you will add a group of spheres for the car and wheel. Once you add your cluster of spheres, you will delete the original model and export it to .fbx format. Once you have exported your sphere group, you will load them in your project to obtain the bounding-sphere center and radius information.

When you are finished working with the `BoundingSphere` portion of this example, you will have a world that is divided into four quarters. Four large spheres each circle one quarter of the smaller spheres that line the wall of the world. A large sphere also surrounds the entire car, which moves with the camera. If a collision is detected between the large sphere around the car and one of the small spheres on the wall in the current quarter of the world, a more exhaustive routine checks for collisions between all car spheres and wall spheres within that world quadrant. See Figure 18-2.

At the end of this demonstration—since our world is a rectangle—you will replace the spheres that surround our world with just one bounding box for even larger per-

FIGURE 18-2

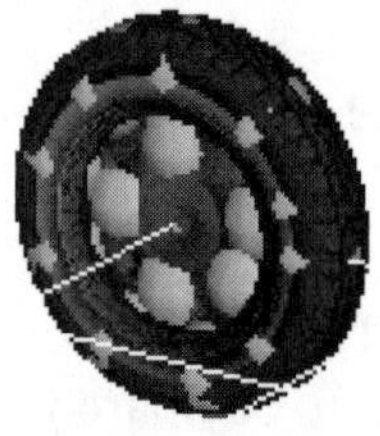

Different sphere groups for varying levels of efficiency and accuracy

formance gains. The final solution provides fast and accurate collision detection between the car and the world walls.

Once you have the solution from Chapter 14 open, add a code file named Vertices.cs to create a series of PositionColor vertices for drawing a sphere using line strips. The vertices are arranged in a grid of slices or columns and stacks, which are rows. You need to add this code to the Vertices.cs file to generate your sphere vertices:

```
using System;
using Microsoft.Xna.Framework;
using Microsoft.Xna.Framework.Graphics;

namespace MGHGame{
    public class SphereVertices{
        private Color   color;
        private int     numPrimitives;
        private Vector3 offset = Vector3.Zero;

        public SphereVertices(Color vertexColor, int totalPrimitives,
                              Vector3 position){
            offset          = position;
            color           = vertexColor;
            numPrimitives   = totalPrimitives;
        }
        public VertexPositionColor[] InitializeSphere(int numSlices,
                                     int numStacks, float radius){
            Vector3[] position = new Vector3[(numSlices + 1)
                               * (numStacks + 1)];
            float angleX, angleY;
            float rowHeight    = MathHelper.Pi / numStacks;
            float colWidth     = MathHelper.TwoPi / numSlices;
            float X, Y, Z, W;

             // generate horizontal rows (stacks in sphere)
            for (int stacks = 0; stacks <= numStacks; stacks++){
                angleX = MathHelper.PiOver2 - stacks * rowHeight;
                Y      =  radius * (float)Math.Sin(angleX);
                W      = -radius * (float)Math.Cos(angleX);

                // generate vertical columns (slices in sphere)
                for (int slices = 0; slices <= numSlices; slices++){
                    angleY = slices * colWidth;
```

```
                X       = W * (float)Math.Sin(angleY);
                Z       = W * (float)Math.Cos(angleY);

                // position sphere vertices at offest from origin
                position[stacks * numSlices + slices] =
                new Vector3(X+offset.X, Y+offset.Y, Z+offset.Z);
            }
        }
        int i = -1;
        VertexPositionColor[] vertices
              = new VertexPositionColor[2 * numSlices * numStacks];
        // index vertices to draw sphere
        for (int stacks = 0; stacks < numStacks; stacks++){
            for (int slices = 0; slices < numSlices; slices++){
                vertices[++i] = new VertexPositionColor(
                    position[stacks * numSlices + slices], color);
                vertices[++i] = new VertexPositionColor(
                    position[(stacks + 1) * numSlices + slices],

                             color);

            }
        }
        return vertices;
    }
  }
}
```

Now that the vertex building code is in place, you need to add another code file called Sphere.cs to generate a list of bounding spheres. When the `SHOW` constant is set to true in the game class, vertex data is generated for drawing the spheres. If `SHOW` is set to false, the vertex data is not generated. In either case, though, the `AddSphere()` routine generates a dynamic list of spheres for each group that is represented by an instance of the `Sphere` class:

```
using System;
using System.Collections.Generic;
using Microsoft.Xna.Framework;
using Microsoft.Xna.Framework.Graphics;

namespace MGHGame{
```

```
    public struct SphereData{
        public VertexPositionColor[] vertices;
        public BoundingSphere        boundingSphere;
    }
    class Sphere{
        const int               SLICES     = 10;
        const int               STACKS     = 10;
        public List<SphereData> sphere = new List<SphereData>();

        private int             numPrimitives = 0;
        public int PrimitiveCount { get { return numPrimitives; } }

        public PrimitiveType primitiveType = PrimitiveType.LineStrip;
        private Color        vertexColor   = Color.White;

        private bool         show;
        public bool          Show { get { return show;  } }

        public Sphere(bool showSphere){
            show          = showSphere;
        }
        public void AddSphere(float radius, Vector3 position,
                              Color color){
            SphereData sphereData              = new SphereData();
            sphereData.boundingSphere.Center = position;
            sphereData.boundingSphere.Radius = radius;

            if (show){
                numPrimitives = SLICES * STACKS * 2 - 1;
                SphereVertices sphereVertices
                = new SphereVertices(color, numPrimitives, position);
                sphereData.vertices
                = sphereVertices.InitializeSphere(SLICES,STACKS, radius);
            }
            sphere.Add(sphereData);
        }
    }
}
```

Our sphere group objects and corresponding lists are initialized from the game class. Each list of spheres is associated with one separate collision object. For example, we have a separate group of spheres for each wheel, the car, and sections of the wall within our world. For blunt but fast initial collision detection, we have one group named `bigCar` that stores only one sphere surrounding the entire car. This large sphere is checked with spheres along the wall. The smaller car spheres are only checked if the large sphere registers a collision. Also, to cut down on the number of wall spheres that are checked each frame, the world is divided into four sets of spheres. The quadrant that contains the car is also where the player is currently located. This means that only one of the four quadrants needs to be checked for collisions.

To help track the groups of spheres, named enumerations are used. A separate sphere list is created for each named group. Each group of spheres implements collision detection for one specific object.

```
public enum Group {
    wheelFL, wheelFR, wheelBL, wheelBR, // wheels
    // bigCar stores one large sphere for initial collision checks
    // car holds many small spheres for accuracy - but they are only checked
    // when bigCar registers a collision
    car, bigCar,
    // wall spheres divided into 4 groups
    wallBackRight, wallBackLeft, wallFrontLeft, wallFrontRight,
    // wall spheres grouped according to location within 4 world quadrants
    worldBackRight, worldBackLeft, worldFrontLeft, worldFrontRight
}
const int TOTAL_SPHERE_GROUPS = 14;
Sphere[]  sphereGroup = new Sphere[TOTAL_SPHERE_GROUPS];
const bool SHOW       = true; // set to false during release
```

The following helper method, `WallSphere()`, is added in the game class to add spheres to the list:

```
 void WallSphere(Group group, float X, float Z, float radius){
    Color color          = Color.Yellow;
    Vector3 position     = new Vector3(X, 0.0f, Z);
    sphereGroup[(int)group].AddSphere(radius, position, color);
}
```

When the program begins in the game class, `InitializeWallSpheres()` manually adds spheres around the edges of our world. This method also adds four larger spheres to determine the quadrant where the car is located:

```
void InitializeWallSpheres(){
    // initialize vertices around border of world
```

```
sphereGroup[(int)Group.wallBackRight]  = new Sphere(SHOW);
sphereGroup[(int)Group.wallBackLeft]   = new Sphere(SHOW);
sphereGroup[(int)Group.wallFrontRight] = new Sphere(SHOW);
sphereGroup[(int)Group.wallFrontLeft]  = new Sphere(SHOW);

Vector3 wall;
const float RADIUS = 0.3f;
const float SPHERE_INCREMENT = 2.0f;

// 1st qtr
wall = new Vector3(BOUNDARY, 0.0f, -BOUNDARY);

// small spheres right and left - back half of world
while (wall.Z < 0.0f){
    WallSphere(Group.wallBackRight, wall.X, wall.Z, RADIUS);
    WallSphere(Group.wallBackLeft, -wall.X, wall.Z, RADIUS);
    wall.Z += SPHERE_INCREMENT * RADIUS;
}
// small spheres right and left - front half of world
while (wall.Z < BOUNDARY){
    WallSphere(Group.wallFrontRight, wall.X, wall.Z, RADIUS);
    WallSphere(Group.wallFrontLeft, -wall.X, wall.Z, RADIUS);
    wall.Z += SPHERE_INCREMENT * RADIUS;
}
// small spheres right side of world - back and front
wall = new Vector3(BOUNDARY, 0.0f, -BOUNDARY);
while (wall.X > 0.0f){
    WallSphere(Group.wallBackRight,  wall.X,  wall.Z, RADIUS);
    WallSphere(Group.wallFrontRight, wall.X, -wall.Z, RADIUS);
    wall.X -= SPHERE_INCREMENT * RADIUS;
}
// small spheres left side of world - top and bottom
while (wall.X > -BOUNDARY){
    WallSphere(Group.wallBackLeft,  wall.X,  wall.Z, RADIUS);
    WallSphere(Group.wallFrontLeft, wall.X, -wall.Z, RADIUS);
    wall.X -= SPHERE_INCREMENT * RADIUS;
}
// separate world into 4 quadrants
sphereGroup[(int)Group.worldBackRight]  = new Sphere(SHOW);
sphereGroup[(int)Group.worldBackLeft]   = new Sphere(SHOW);
sphereGroup[(int)Group.worldFrontLeft]  = new Sphere(SHOW);
```

```
    sphereGroup[(int)Group.worldFrontRight] = new Sphere(SHOW);

    // large spheres - each one surrounds 1 quarter of world
    float radius = BOUNDARY;
    WallSphere(Group.worldBackRight, BOUNDARY, -BOUNDARY, radius);
    WallSphere(Group.worldBackLeft, -BOUNDARY, -BOUNDARY, radius);
    WallSphere(Group.worldFrontLeft, -BOUNDARY, BOUNDARY, radius);
    WallSphere(Group.worldFrontRight, BOUNDARY, BOUNDARY, radius);
}
```

You can now add `ExtractBoundingSphere()` to retrieve and store bounding-sphere radius and position data from your sphere models:

```
void ExtractBoundingSphere(Model tempModel, Color color, int groupNum){
    // set up model temporarily
    Matrix[] tempMatrix         = new Matrix[tempModel.Bones.Count];
    tempModel.CopyAbsoluteBoneTransformsTo(tempMatrix);

    // generate new sphere group
    BoundingSphere sphere       = new BoundingSphere();
    sphereGroup[groupNum]       = new Sphere(SHOW);

    // store radius, position, and color information for each sphere
    foreach (ModelMesh mesh in tempModel.Meshes){
        sphere                  = mesh.BoundingSphere;
        Vector3 newCenter       = sphere.Center;
        Matrix transformMatrix  = ScaleModel();
        sphereGroup[groupNum].AddSphere(sphere.Radius, sphere.Center,
                                        color);
    }
}
```

If you compare the process of manually adding bounding spheres on your own to adding spheres in a designer tool, you will find that it is a lot easier and more accurate to use a modeling tool. To generate the necessary groups of bounding spheres, you need to import the hotrod.fbx model and wheel.fbx models into either MilkShape or some other modeling tool such as Blender. Next, you have to add spheres around the edges of each model using the designer so they can be used for collision checking. When you are done, delete the original meshes so you are left only with the surrounding spheres. At this point, you can export these sphere groups as .fbx models. We have already created these sphere groups in MilkShape and they are contained in the hotrodSpheres.fbx, bigCarSpheres.fbx, and wheelSpheres.fbx files, which you can find in the Models folder on the book's website. These model files must be referenced under the content node so you can load their bounding-sphere information at run time.

The InitializeModelSpheres() routine loads these models and passes their references to the ExtractBoundingSphere() method to retrieve and store the radius and center data contained inside each file. Since this routine only stores the model data on the stack, the unused model data is released from memory when the method finishes. In other words, you do not have to worry about storing a bunch of unused models in memory during the course of your game. Add InitializeModelSpheres() to your game class to temporarily load these new models:

```
void InitializeModelSpheres(){
    // smaller fine spheres around car
    Model sphereModel = Content.Load<Model>("Models\\hotrodSpheres");
    ExtractBoundingSphere(sphereModel, Color.Red, (int)Group.car);

    // load big sphere surrounding the car for broad collision checking
    sphereModel = Content.Load<Model>("Models\\bigCarSphere");
    ExtractBoundingSphere(sphereModel, Color.Blue, (int)Group.bigCar);
    // same wheel drawn four times each with different transformation
    // for convenience same wheel is loaded four times to create a
    // separate collision object for each wheel
    sphereModel = Content.Load<Model>("Models\\wheelSpheres");
    ExtractBoundingSphere(sphereModel, Color.White, (int)Group.wheelFL);
    ExtractBoundingSphere(sphereModel, Color.White, (int)Group.wheelFR);
    ExtractBoundingSphere(sphereModel, Color.White, (int)Group.wheelBL);
    ExtractBoundingSphere(sphereModel, Color.White, (int)Group.wheelBR);
}
```

You can now call your sphere-loading routines from Initialize():

```
InitializeWallSpheres();
InitializeModelSpheres();
```

Since the sphere group models used in this example were created using a different modeling tool than the original model designer, they need to be scaled differently. The SphereScalar() and ScaleSpheres() methods are needed in the game class at this stage to apply scaling when you transform and draw your bounding spheres:

```
float SphereScalar(){
    return 0.2f;
}
```

```
Matrix ScaleSpheres(){
    // spheres created with different modeling tool so scaled differently
    return Matrix.CreateScale(SphereScalar(), SphereScalar(),
                              SphereScalar());
}
```

The bounding spheres are drawn with the `PositionColor` vertex format. If the spheres are derived from meshes in a model, they must be scaled and transformed according to the relative size and corresponding model transformation. If the spheres do not need any further transformation at run time, you can just draw them where they are originally set up. Adding `DrawSpheres()` to your game class will draw the bounding spheres as transformed objects in their respective groups when `DRAW` is set to true:

```
private void DrawSpheres(int group, Camera camera, GameTime gameTime){
    Matrix world;
    for (int j = 0; j < sphereGroup[group].sphere.Count; j++){
        if (sphereGroup[group].Show){
            world = Matrix.Identity;
            // draw car spheres
            if (group == (int)Group.car || group == (int)Group.bigCar)
                world = ScaleSpheres() * TransformCar(camera);
            // draw wheels
            if (group==(int)Group.wheelBL || group==(int)Group.wheelBR
            ||  group==(int)Group.wheelFL || group==(int)Group.wheelFR)
                 world = ScaleSpheres()
                       * TransformWheel(group, gameTime, camera);
            // 4: set variables in shader
            positionColorEffectWVP.SetValue(world
                       * cam.viewMatrix * cam.projectionMatrix);
            // 5: draw object - primitive type, vertex data, # primitives
            PositionColorShader(sphereGroup[group].primitiveType,
            sphereGroup[group].sphere[j].vertices,
                        sphereGroup[group].PrimitiveCount);
        }
    }
}
```

To see your spheres, call `DrawSpheres()` from the `Draw()` method inside your game class:

```
for (int i = 0; i <TOTAL_SPHERE_GROUPS; i++)
     DrawSpheres(i, cam, gameTime);
```

Try your code now to see the bounding spheres. If you do, you will see the spheres shown in Figure 18-2.

Collision Detection Example: Implementing BoundingSphere Collision Checking

Now that we can see that our spheres are accurately transformed, we can add collision detection. Add `Collision()` below to your game class to perform a simple check between the two spheres to determine if they intersect:

```
bool Collision(BoundingSphere A, BoundingSphere B){
    if (A.Intersects(B) )
        return true;
    return false;
}
```

`WallCollision()` iterates through each sphere in the car list and compares it with each sphere in the wall list to check for collisions. Since the car is moving and the car spheres were built in a different model designer than the original model, you will need to scale each bounding sphere differently than the original model:

```
public bool WallCollision(Camera camera, int wallGroup, int carGroup){
    // check selected car and selected wall spheres for collisions
    for (int i = 0; i < sphereGroup[carGroup].sphere.Count; i++){
        for (int j = 0; j < sphereGroup[wallGroup].sphere.Count; j++){
            Matrix transform           = ScaleSpheres()
                                       * TransformCar(camera);
            // generate temp bounding sphere with transformed sphere
            BoundingSphere tempSphere =
            sphereGroup[carGroup].sphere[i].boundingSphere.Transform(
                                        transform);
            tempSphere.Radius
                = SphereScalar()
                * sphereGroup[carGroup].sphere[i].boundingSphere.Radius;
            if (Collision(sphereGroup[wallGroup].sphere[j].boundingSphere,
                tempSphere))
                return true;
        }
    }
    return false;
}
```

When checking collisions for objects that move with the camera, you need to ensure that the camera doesn't move or change views before a collision is detected. For this reason, a copy of the camera is used to check for collisions before the actual game camera is updated. CameraCopy() is added to the game class to return a duplicate of the current camera settings:

```
public Camera CameraCopy(GameTime gameTime){
    Camera tempCamera          = new Camera();
    tempCamera.SetFrameInterval(gameTime);
    tempCamera.position        = cam.position;
    tempCamera.view            = cam.view;
    tempCamera.viewMatrix      = cam.viewMatrix;
    tempCamera.up              = cam.up;
    tempCamera.projectionMatrix = cam.projectionMatrix;
    return tempCamera;
}
```

Since the collision checking is applied to a car that moves with the camera, the bulk of the collision routines are driven from the following UpdateCamera() method. With a copy of an updated camera, we first determine the quarter of the world where the car is located. Then comparisons are made between the big sphere around the entire car and the small spheres within the current world quadrant. If a collision is registered at this point, the small spheres surrounding the car are checked with the small wall spheres in the current world quadrant. In the event of a car collision, the camera is not updated, so the car is prevented from driving through the wall. If a collision does not occur, the car and camera are updated. UpdateCamera() is needed in the game class to provide proper camera collision behavior:

```
public void UpdateCamera(GameTime gameTime) {
    // adjust tempCam time, position, and view
    cam.SetFrameInterval(gameTime);
    Camera tempCam         = CameraCopy(gameTime);

    // handle move
    float move             = Move();
    tempCam.Move(move);

    // handle view change
    Vector2 view    = ChangeView(gameTime);
            view.X/= 2.7f;
    tempCam.SetView(view);
```

```
    for (int qtr = (int)Group.worldBackRight; qtr <=
                   (int)Group.worldFrontRight; qtr++){
        // broad check to determine which quarter of the world we're in
        if (WallCollision(tempCam, qtr, (int)Group.bigCar)){
            int wallPart = 0;
            switch (qtr){
                case (int)Group.worldBackRight:
                    wallPart = (int)Group.wallBackRight;  break;
                case (int)Group.worldBackLeft:
                    wallPart = (int)Group.wallBackLeft;   break;
                case (int)Group.worldFrontLeft:
                    wallPart = (int)Group.wallFrontLeft;  break;
                case (int)Group.worldFrontRight:
                    wallPart = (int)Group.wallFrontRight; break;
            }
            // if collision with big sphere and wall check car parts
            if (WallCollision(tempCam, wallPart,  (int)Group.bigCar)){
                if (WallCollision(tempCam, wallPart,(int)Group.car)     ||
                    WallCollision(tempCam, wallPart,(int)Group.wheelBL)||
                    WallCollision(tempCam, wallPart,(int)Group.wheelBR)||
                    WallCollision(tempCam, wallPart,(int)Group.wheelFL)||
                    WallCollision(tempCam, wallPart,(int)Group.wheelFR))
                    return;
            }
        }
    }
    // if no collision move the tempCam and move boxes with it
    cam.Move(move);
    cam.SetView(view);
}
```

Replace the original code with the following lines of code in the `Update()` method:

```
cam.SetFrameInterval(gameTime);
cam.Move(Move());
Vector2 view     = ChangeView(gameTime);
view.Y           = 0.0f;
view.X          /= 2.7f;
cam.SetView(view);

previousPosition = cam.position;
```

with this call statement to also trigger collision checking for the camera:

```
UpdateCamera(gameTime);
```

If you run your game project now, it will show the collision checking. A system like this can be very effective for collision detection between complex shapes.

COLLISION DETECTION EXAMPLE: IMPLEMENTING BOUNDINGBOX COLLISION CHECKING

You may notice a performance decrease when the car is close to the wall because the most exhaustive collision detection methods run in this region. You can avoid this lag by dividing the wall into eighths or even sixteenths or by inventing some other creative scheme. If the wall were an irregular shape, you would need to implement a series of sphere subsets to alleviate the processing demands of collision checking each frame. However, since the 3D world in the base code is rectangular and stationary, this situation is ideal for implementing a bounding box. Because of this, you can replace all of our bounding spheres around the world with one single bounding box. This change offers an enormous performance increase. To make this change, add a declaration for a bounding box at the top of the game class:

```
BoundingBox worldBox;
```

Then, inside `Initialize()`, set up the bounding box to fit around the entire world. The minimum Y value is set well below the ground to avoid any false collisions between the wall and any objects that are slightly below ground level:

```
worldBox = new BoundingBox(new Vector3(-BOUNDARY, -5.0f, -BOUNDARY),
                           new Vector3( BOUNDARY,  7.0f,  BOUNDARY));
```

Next, add this `WallCollision()` overload to your game class to check for collisions between your world box and car spheres:

```
public bool WallCollision(Camera camera, int carGroup){
    // check selected car and selected wall spheres for collisions
    for (int i = 0; i < sphereGroup[carGroup].sphere.Count; i++){
            Matrix transform = ScaleSpheres()
                             * TransformCar(camera);
            // generate temp bounding sphere with transformed sphere
            BoundingSphere tempSphere =
```

```
            sphereGroup[carGroup].sphere[i].boundingSphere.Transform(
                                    transform);
            tempSphere.Radius
                = SphereScalar()
                * sphereGroup[carGroup].sphere[i].boundingSphere.Radius;
            // check to see if car sphere intersects bounding box edge
            if (worldBox.Contains(tempSphere) ==
                ContainmentType.Intersects)
                return true;
    }
    return false;
}
```

Finally, you can replace the current `UpdateCamera()` method with this new version. This revision initially passes in the large car sphere to perform broad checking between the car and world box. If a collision registers, then the small spheres are checked with the world box. As you can see, the processing requirements under this latest revision are miniscule:

```
public void UpdateCamera(GameTime gameTime){
    // adjust tempCam time, position, and view
    cam.SetFrameInterval(gameTime);
    Camera tempCam = CameraCopy(gameTime);

    // handle move
    float move = Move();
    tempCam.Move(move);

    // handle view change
    Vector2 view = ChangeView(gameTime);
    view.X /= 2.7f;
    tempCam.SetView(view);

    // if collision with big sphere and wall check car parts
    if (WallCollision(tempCam, (int)Group.bigCar)){
        if (WallCollision(tempCam, (int)Group.car) ||
         WallCollision(tempCam, (int)Group.wheelBL) ||
         WallCollision(tempCam, (int)Group.wheelBR) ||
         WallCollision(tempCam, (int)Group.wheelFL) ||
         WallCollision(tempCam, (int)Group.wheelFR))
            return;
    }
```

```
    // if no collision move the tempCam and move boxes with it
    cam.Move(move);
    cam.SetView(view);
}
```

When you run your code, you will notice that you have very accurate collision detection and no drain on performance. With bounding spheres, bounding boxes, and methods to generate spheres very quickly, XNA really does offer you a very flexible and robust platform for collision detection.

CHAPTER 18 REVIEW EXERCISES

To get the most from this chapter, try out these chapter review exercises.

1. If you have not done so already, follow the step-by-step examples shown in this chapter.
2. Change the bounding-sphere solution to divide your world up into eighths.
3. Create a 3D model spaceship that travels back and forth in the world along the Z axis. Add spheres to the model to generate collision detection data. Be sure to encase the entire model with one large sphere to perform broad collision checking. Delete your model and export your sphere groups. Load these sphere models into your project to implement the collision between your new model and the camera.

CHAPTER 19

Ballistics

BALLISTICS describes the flight of projectiles. When considering ballistics in the context of a game, you might think of obvious choices such as grenades, bullets, cannon balls, or rockets. Ballistics could even include throwing bananas, shooting squirt guns, or throwing baseballs. Regardless of the implementation, ballistics certainly will liven up your game.

This chapter explains two common ballistics algorithms. The first algorithm, referred to as the *Linear Projectile algorithm*, provides a routine for launching a fast-moving projectile where its speed on the X, Y, and Z planes remains constant. This first algorithm is suitable for projecting a laser beam, a bullet, or an extremely fast-moving missile that only needs to be shown over a short range. The second algorithm, referred to in this book as the *Arcing Projectile algorithm*, builds on the first algorithm. The difference is that the second algorithm considers the gravitational pull that acts on the projectile until it hits the ground.

LINEAR PROJECTILES

The Linear Projectile algorithm works under the assumption that the projectile will maintain a constant speed on the X, Y, and Z planes until the object is out of sight. For example, Figure 19-1 shows rockets flying in a linear path from the camera.

When the projectile is launched, the linear projectile travels in a path that follows the camera's `Look` direction. The `Look` vector gives us constant speeds for X, Y, and Z. Remember from Chapter 17 that the `Look` direction vector equals the difference between the `View` position vector and the camera `Position` vector.

The initial rate of change (in distance over time on the X, Y, and Z planes) when a projectile takes flight is known as the *launch speed*. Launch speed is based on the `Look` direction to ensure that the object projects outward from the camera toward the target. The total launch speed is scaled by each `Look` vector component in each of the corresponding X, Y, and Z planes. Figure 19-2 illustrates how the individual velocity components are derived.

At every frame during the projectile's flight, the position of the projectile is updated by adding the projectile's current position with the projectile velocity multiplied by time, as shown here:

$$\text{Projectile Position}_{xyz} = \text{Launch Position}_{xyz} + \text{Velocity}_{xyz} * \text{Time}$$

ARCING PROJECTILE

The Linear Projectile routine only works for bullets or other objects that appear to fly in a straight line. For events where the effects of gravity are apparent—such as a catapult launch or a grenade toss—the Arcing Projectile algorithm is needed to make the

FIGURE 19-1

Rockets following a linear path with a constant speed and direction

ballistic look real and to give the player control over the trajectory, height, and distance traveled. Higher launch speeds and trajectories help to overcome gravity, and ensure that the ballistic has a longer flight before hitting the ground.

FIGURE 19-2

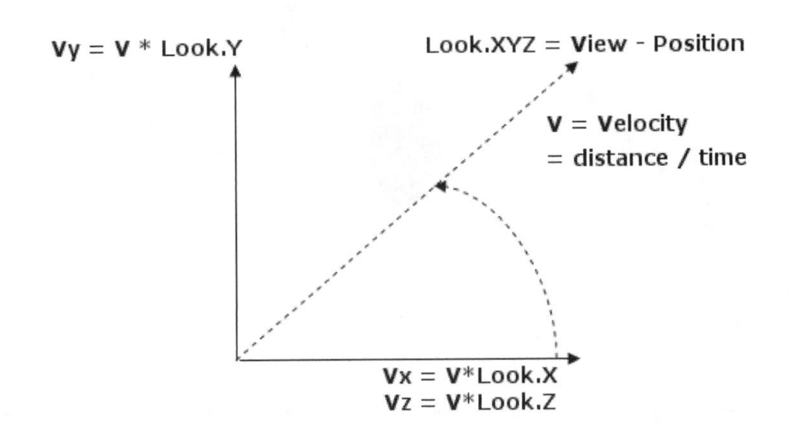

Deriving X, Y, and Z velocities using the Look direction

Figure 19-3 shows several rockets at various elevations (on the Y axis) and at different stages of flight. Over time, the projectiles lose momentum and gravity pulls them to the ground. The overall effect creates a nice arcing projectile path.

Game developers will often use real-world physics to create more realistic graphics effects. The physical properties that they consider may include gravity, friction, force, velocity, acceleration, viscosity, and much more. In case you're wondering, game development companies will often implement pseudo-physics in their algorithms. As long as the effect looks correct and is efficient, an approximation of the laws of physics is usually the faster and more effective alternative. After all, as a simulation approaches reality, it can become so complex that it loses its value. However, even when the code deviates from the laws of physics, realistic algorithms usually consider some portion of the real physical model.

Once the launch velocity and direction have been obtained, the effect of gravity can be computed and the X, Y, and Z positions of the projectile can be calculated over time. The X and Z positions are calculated using the same equations as the Linear Projectile algorithm to obtain the projectile's position over time:

$$X_t = X_{start} + V_x * t$$
$$Z_t = Z_{start} + V_z * t$$

The Arcing Projectile algorithm treats the calculation of the Y position over time as a special case that also considers gravity. Initially, the projectile's velocity is powerful enough to defy gravity—otherwise, there would be insufficient energy to launch

FIGURE 19-3

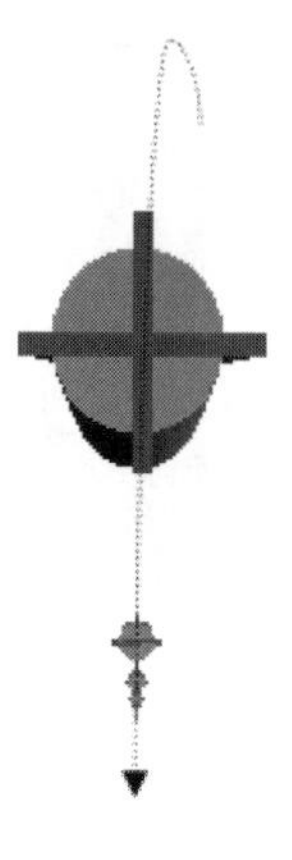

Considering the effect of gravity over time

the projectile into the air. However, over time, the projectile loses its momentum and gravity becomes the strongest force on the object. This gravitational pull is defined by a constant value of acceleration, *g*, which represents the Earth's gravity. The accepted value for *g* equals 9.8 meters / second^2 (32 ft/s^2). After the Earth's gravity is factored in, the equation used for calculating the Y position over time becomes:

$$Y_t = Y_{start} + V_y * t - 0.5 * g * t^2$$

Implementing these projectile algorithms in code is simple. The first example in this chapter implements the Linear Projectile algorithm. Then, in the example that follows, the Linear Projectile algorithm is converted into an Arcing Projectile algorithm.

LINEAR PROJECTILES EXAMPLE

This example demonstrates how to add projectiles that can be launched on a linear path from a rocket launcher, as shown back in Figure 19-1.

In this example, you will shoot ten rockets into the air at a time. When a trigger or spacebar event occurs, the first available rocket (that is not already in flight) is launched. At the time of launch, the rocket is given a position and direction to start it on an outward journey from the tip of the rocket launcher. The rocket launcher's position and direction are based on the camera's current position and `Look` direction. Also, during the launch, the activation state for the projectile is set to `true`, and remains set to `true` until the projectile reaches the end of the path. The activation state prevents the projectile from being reused while it is in flight. The projectile properties are reset every time the projectile is launched.

This example begins with either the MGHWinBaseCode or MGH360BaseCode project located in the BaseCode folder on this book's website.

You will create a `Projectile` class to assist with the implementation of your projectiles. You will use `Projectile` to keep track of each rocket and to update its position. The `Projectile` class can be created from scratch in the Solution Explorer. To generate it, right-click the project and choose Add New Item. Then, choose the Code File icon and enter **Projectile.cs** as the Name in the Add New Item dialog. When you click Add, GS will generate an empty Projectile.cs file.

First, add the following code shell to start your `Projectile class:`

```
using Microsoft.Xna.Framework;
namespace Projectiles{
    public class Projectile{
    }
}
```

Class-level declarations are also required for storing the position, direction, and activation state of each projectile. An additional variable, for storing the size of the world, enables a check to determine whether the projectile has flown out of sight. This tells you when to deactivate the projectile. To allow access to these variables throughout the class, we place their declarations at the top of the `Projectile` class (inside the class declaration):

```
public  Vector3  position, previousPosition; // rocket position
private Vector3  speed;                      // relative change in X,Y,Z
public  Matrix   directionMatrix;            // direction transformations
public  bool     active;                     // visibility
private float    boundary;                   // edge of world on X and Z
private float    seconds;                    // seconds since launch
private Vector3  startPosition;              // launch position
```

When the program begins, each projectile needs to be created only once. After they are created, the projectiles remain inactive until the user launches them. Later, you will add a method to deactivate a projectile when it flies past the boundaries of the world. To set the projectile flight range and activation state when the projectile is initialized, add this constructor to the `Projectile` class:

```
public Projectile(float border){
    boundary = border;
    active   = false;
}
```

The projectile's position, direction, and activation state are set according to the camera's position and `Look` direction at the time of the launch. The rocket speed is actually based on the direction, which is a relative change in X, Y, and Z. Including the `Launch()` method in the `Projectile` class will enable proper initialization of these attributes during the launch.

```
public void Launch(Vector3 look, Vector3 start){
    position = startPosition = start;     // start at camera
    speed    = Vector3.Normalize(look);   // unitize direction
    active   = true;                      // make visible
    seconds  = 0.0f;                      // used with gravity only
}
```

As discussed in Chapter 8, an object's direction can be calculated from the object's speed vector. Adding `SetDirectionMatrix()` to your `Projectile` class will provide the method you need to make your rocket point in the direction it is traveling. This routine applies to both the Linear Projectile algorithm and the Arcing Projectile algorithm. For the Linear Projectile algorithm, the rocket direction remains constant as the rocket travels outwards. For the Arcing Projectile algorithm, `SetDirectionMatrix()` will launch the rocket with the original launcher direction, and then it will gradually drop the rocket, nose downward, as the gravitational pull takes over:

```
private void SetDirectionMatrix(){
    Vector3 Look    = position - previousPosition;
    Look.Normalize();
    Vector3 Up      = new Vector3(0.0f, 1.0f, 0.0f); // fake Up to get

    Vector3 Right   = Vector3.Cross(Up, Look);
    Right.Normalize();
            Up      = Vector3.Cross(Look, Right);    // calculate Up with
    Up.Normalize();                                  // correct vectors

    Matrix matrix   = new Matrix(); // compute direction matrix
    matrix.Right    = Right;
    matrix.Up       = Up;
    matrix.Forward  = Look;
    matrix.M44      = 1.0f;         // W is set to 1 to enable transforms
    directionMatrix = matrix;
}
```

The projectile's position is updated before being drawn each frame. Also, in every frame, the projectile's position is incremented by a time-scaled direction vector, which ensures that the rocket flies in the path set by the camera when the rocket is launched. When the projectile location exceeds one of the outer boundaries, it is deactivated so that it can be deactivated and made available for the next launch. The `UpdateProjectile()` method implements this routine. Adding `UpdateProjectile()` to the projectile class ensures that your projectile positions are updated while they are active. The method also deactivates the projectiles after they reach the outer limits of your world.

```
public void UpdateProjectile(GameTime gameTime){
    previousPosition = position; // archive last position
    position        += speed     // update current position
                     *  (float)gameTime.ElapsedGameTime.Milliseconds/90.0f;
    SetDirectionMatrix();
```

```
    // deactivate if outer border exceeded on X or Z
    if (position.Z > 2.0f * boundary || position.X > 2.0f * boundary ||
        position.Z <-2.0f * boundary || position.X <-2.0f * boundary)
        active = false;
}
```

The `Projectile` class for a Linear Projectile algorithm is now complete, so you can reference it from Game1.cs. Adding the namespace reference at the top of the Game1.cs file enables your use of this new class:

```
using Projectiles;
```

To use the `Projectile` class, you need to declare instances of it inside the game class. An array of 10 is used here, but if you wanted, you could create a more dynamic structure with an `ArrayList`:

```
const   int          NUM_ROCKETS = 10;
private Projectile[] rocket      = new Projectile[NUM_ROCKETS];
```

With these declarations, you should set up each of these ten projectiles from the `Initialize()` method when the program begins. Passing the size of the world to the constructor will allow us to deactivate the rocket later when it flies beyond the outer boundaries of the world:

```
for (int i = 0; i < NUM_ROCKETS; i++)
    rocket[i] = new Projectile(BOUNDARY);
```

To make this example more interesting, a model of a rocket will be used for the projectiles. To reference this model in the game class, add a class-level declaration for the model and the matrix to the game class. Also, the starting Y value used in the rocket and launcher transformations is tracked with the variable declared here as *BASE_HEIGHT*:

```
Model       rocketModel;        Matrix[] rocketMatrix;
Model       launcherModel;      Matrix[] launcherMatrix;
const float BASE_HEIGHT         = 0.6f;  // start height for models
```

The rocket and rocket launcher models are loaded from the rocket.fbx and launcher.fbx files. Adding the `InitializeModels()` method to your game class provides the code to load these models using the `ContentManager` object. The directory path in this code assumes you have copied the rocket.fbx, rocket.bmp, launcher.fbx, and launcher.bmp files from the Models folder on this book's website.

Once the rocket.fbx and launcher.fbx models are referenced from the Solution Explorer, `InitializeModels()` can initialize the model objects and their transformation matrices:

```
void InitializeModels(){
    rocketModel     = Content.Load<Model>("Models\\rocket");
    rocketMatrix    = new Matrix[rocketModel.Bones.Count];
    rocketModel.CopyAbsoluteBoneTransformsTo(rocketMatrix);
    launcherModel   = Content.Load<Model>("Models\\launcher");
    launcherMatrix = new Matrix[launcherModel.Bones.Count];
    launcherModel.CopyAbsoluteBoneTransformsTo(launcherMatrix);
}
```

To initialize the rocket, when the program begins, call `InitializeModels()` from `LoadContent()`:

```
InitializeModels();
```

TIP Remember to only reference the models in your project. Both the models and textures should be placed in the Models folder. However, the content pipeline is unable to load more than one file with the same name from the same folder because no extension is required.

Now that the models have been loaded, projectile objects can be created to track each rocket's direction and whereabouts. Declaring ten projectile objects in the game class in the module declarations area will make them available for your use throughout the game class.

Next, we'll draw the rocket launcher. The rocket launcher travels with the camera and rotates about the X axis—with changes to the view position on Y whenever the user moves the mouse or right thumbstick up or down. The model rocket launcher was designed to simplify the transformations for this movement. The rocket launcher's base is positioned at the origin, and the barrel is centered around the Z axis and is positioned further out on Z. By design of the camera, the launcher's rotation range about the X axis is half a circle (or π radians). If the rocket launcher is pointed directly upward, the view position on Y would equal 0.5, and if the rocket launcher is pointed directly downward, the view position would be –0.5 (see Figure 19-4).

As discussed in Chapter 7, because XNA uses the Right Hand Rule, a negative rotation around the X axis will point the launcher upward. Using the same logic, a positive rotation about the X axis will point the launcher downward. The launcher must be rotated about the X axis to match the camera's `Look` direction about the Y axis.

FIGURE 19-4

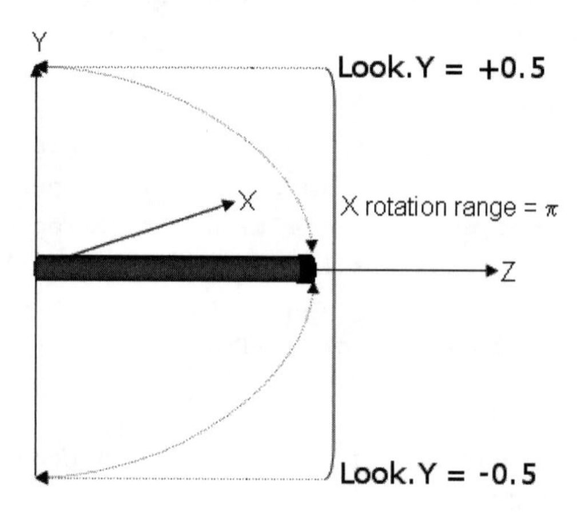

Rocket launcher rotation range around the X axis

With this information, you can calculate the rocket launcher's rotation angle about the X axis with the following equation:

```
rotationX     = Matrix.CreateRotationX(-MathHelper.Pi*look.Y );
```

The launcher must also be rotated about the Y axis to match the camera's `Look` direction about the Y axis. And finally, to finish the transformation using the I.S.R.O.T. sequence, the launcher must be translated by an amount that is equivalent to the distance from the origin to the camera. An extra shift downward on the Y axis is added to this translation to move the launcher downward slightly so it does not block your view.

Add `DrawLauncher()` to your game class to move and rotate the rocket launcher with your camera:

```
private void DrawLauncher(Model model){
    // 1: declare matrices
    Matrix world, translation, scale, rotationX, rotationY;

    // 2: initialize matrices
    scale        = Matrix.CreateScale(0.002f, 0.002f, 0.002f);
    translation  = Matrix.CreateTranslation(cam.position.X, BASE_HEIGHT,
                                            cam.position.Z);
```

```
    Vector3 look = cam.view - cam.position;
    rotationX    = Matrix.CreateRotationX(-MathHelper.Pi*look.Y );
    rotationY    = Matrix.CreateRotationY((float)Math.Atan2(look.X,
                                                          look.Z));

    // 3: build cumulative matrix using I.S.R.O.T. sequence
    // identity,scale,rotate,orbit(translate & rotate),translate
    world = scale * rotationX * rotationY * translation;

    // 4: set shader parameters
    foreach (ModelMesh mesh in model.Meshes){
    foreach (BasicEffect effect in mesh.Effects){
        effect.World      = launcherMatrix[mesh.ParentBone.Index]*world;
        effect.View       = cam.viewMatrix;
        effect.Projection = cam.projectionMatrix;
        effect.EnableDefaultLighting();
        effect.SpecularPower = 0.01f;
    }
    // 5: draw object
    mesh.Draw();
    }
}
```

To actually see the rocket launcher, you obviously need to call the method to draw it. Adding `DrawLauncher()` to the end of the `Draw()` method will draw the rocket when other objects are rendered:

```
DrawLauncher(launcherModel);
```

Because the rocket launcher's rotation angle about the X axis changes with the view position on Y, if the right thumbstick or mouse shifts the view all the way up or all the way down, you can actually see the base of the launcher, which spoils the effect. Inside the camera class in the `UpdateView()` method, you'll replace the code that caps the Y view position so that it can no longer exceed 0.30 or fall below –0.10, which prevents you from pointing the launcher into the ground. The end result is that whatever angle you point, it looks as though you are always holding the rocket launcher:

```
const float LOWER_LIMIT = -0.1f;    const float UPPER_LIMIT = 0.3f;
          if (Qlook.Y > LOWER_LIMIT && Qlook.Y < UPPER_LIMIT)
```

The code that you use to launch the rocket (from the game class) is contained in the `LaunchRocket()` method. This routine searches through the array of projectiles and finds the first inactive projectile available. When an inactive projectile is found, `LaunchRocket()` sets the starting position and direction to equal the camera position and `Look` direction.

The transformations use the I.S.R.O.T. sequence. Their implementation to angle and position the rocket at the tip of the launcher is summarized in the comments included with this code.

The starting position is needed to help track the location of each rocket. To create the required transformation, and record the initial starting position of the rocket, we can use the matrix math discussed in Chapter 8 and Chapter 16. Once the starting position is computed using matrices, the first row of the matrix that contains the position information is stored in a vector. This position vector can be used later to update the position of the rocket by incrementing the position by a time-scaled direction vector. As you can see, it really does pay to understand how to employ linear algebra beyond just using the `Matrix` objects and methods that are shipped with XNA.

Add `LaunchRocket()` to your game class to find the first available rocket when a launch is triggered and to calculate and store the starting position and direction of the rocket:

```
private void LaunchRocket(int i){
    Matrix  orbitTranslate, orbitX, orbitY, translate, position;
    Vector3 look, start;

    // create matrix and store origin in first row
    position       = new Matrix(); // zero matrix
    position.M14 = 1.0f;           // set W to 1 so you can transform it

    // move to tip of launcher
    orbitTranslate = Matrix.CreateTranslation(0.0f, 0.0f, -0.85f);

    // use same direction as launcher
    look = cam.view - cam.position;

    // offset needed to rotate rocket about X to see it with camera
    float offsetAngle = MathHelper.Pi;

    // adjust angle about X with changes in Look (Forward) direction
    orbitX     = Matrix.CreateRotationX(offsetAngle-MathHelper.Pi*look.Y);

    // rocket's Y direction is same as camera's at time of launch
    orbitY     = Matrix.CreateRotationY((float)Math.Atan2(look.X,look.Z));
```

```
    // move rocket to camera position where launcher base is also located
    translate = Matrix.CreateTranslation(cam.position.X,BASE_HEIGHT,
                                         cam.position.Z);
    // use the I.S.R.O.T. sequence to get rocket start position
    position  = position *  orbitTranslate * orbitX * orbitY * translate;

    // convert from matrix back to vector so it can be used for updates
    start     = new Vector3(position.M11, position.M12, position.M13);
    rocket[i].Launch(look, start);
}
```

At this point, the projectile objects are initialized and your launcher is in place. Your rockets are ready, but a mechanism is required to trigger their launch. In this case, you will add code to initiate their launch when the left mouse button is clicked, or when the right trigger on the controller is pressed. To ensure that all ten rockets are not launched during this press event—which lasts over several frames— the current and previous states of the game pad and mouse are compared. To enable this input device state checking, you must add a declaration for game pad and mouse states at the class level:

```
#if !XBOX
        MouseState mouseCurrent, mousePrevious;
#endif
        GamePadState    gamepad, gamepadPrevious;
```

The projectile trigger events can now be handled at the end of the `Update()` method. In this block of code, you will update the mouse and game-pad states. Then you can determine new mouse button click or trigger-pull events by comparing the button press states in the current frame with release states from the previous frame:

```
// refresh key and button states

#if !XBOX
    mouseCurrent = Mouse.GetState();
#endif
gamepad          = GamePad.GetState(PlayerIndex.One);

// launch rocket for right trigger and left click events
if (gamepad.Triggers.Right > 0 && gamepadPrevious.Triggers.Right == 0
#if !XBOX
||  mouseCurrent.LeftButton  == ButtonState.Pressed
 && mousePrevious.LeftButton == ButtonState.Released
#endif
```

```
){  // if launch event then launch next available rocket
    for (int i = 0; i < NUM_ROCKETS; i++)
        if (rocket[i].active == false){
            LaunchRocket(i);
            break;
        }
}
// archive current state for comparison next frame
gamepadPrevious     = gamepad;
#if !XBOX
    mousePrevious   = mouseCurrent;
#endif
```

In each frame, the locations of all projectiles must be updated so each can be animated properly along its trajectory path. The code used to trigger the update for each projectile position belongs at the end of the `Update()` method in the game class:

```
// update rockets that are in flight
for (int i = 0; i < NUM_ROCKETS; i++)
    if (rocket[i].active)
        rocket[i].UpdateProjectile(gameTime);
```

Only one method is used to draw each projectile. The details are explained in the comments:

```
private void DrawRockets(Model model, int i){
    // 1: declare matrices
    Matrix world, scale, rotateX, translate;

    // 2: initialize matrices
    scale     = Matrix.CreateScale(0.0033f, 0.0033f, 0.0033f);
    rotateX   = Matrix.CreateRotationX(-MathHelper.Pi/2.0f);
    translate = Matrix.CreateTranslation(rocket[i].position);

    // 3: build cumulative matrix using I.S.R.O.T. sequence
    world = scale * rotateX * rocket[i].directionMatrix * translate;

    // 4: set shader parameters
    foreach (ModelMesh mesh in model.Meshes){
        foreach (BasicEffect effect in mesh.Effects){
```

```
            effect.World           = rocketMatrix[mesh.ParentBone.Index]
                                   * world;
            effect.View            = cam.viewMatrix;
            effect.Projection      = cam.projectionMatrix;
            effect.EnableDefaultLighting();
            effect.SpecularPower = 16.5f;
        }
        // 5: draw object
        mesh.Draw();
    }
}
```

To ensure that projectiles are actually drawn, `DrawRockets()` needs to be called from the `Draw()` method. This code loops through all projectile objects and draws the active ones at their current position with their corresponding direction:

```
for (int i = 0; i < NUM_ROCKETS; i++)
    if (rocket[i].active)
        DrawRockets(rocketModel, i);
```

When you compile and run this program, it shows the Linear Projectile algorithm in action. Whenever the left mouse button is clicked, or a game controller trigger is pulled, a rocket is launched. Each projectile shoots outward until it reaches an arbitrary boundary located at the outer limits of the world.

ARCING PROJECTILES EXAMPLE

This Arcing Projectiles example picks up where the Linear Projectile algorithm ends. When this example is complete, and the effect of gravity is factored in, the flight of each projectile will rise to a peak and then follow a descending path to the ground. Most of the code in this revised routine remains the same. However, the method that updates the rocket position will be replaced so that the gravitational pull over time is taken into consideration. In this new routine, however, initially the linear projectile algorithm is implemented long enough for the projectile to safely leave the barrel of the launcher in case it is moving. Use of constant speed at the onset creates a mini turbo boost so your players don't risk blowing themselves up every time they pull the trigger. Once the rocket is far enough away from the launcher, gravity kicks in—then the count to the touchdown begins.

The `UpdateProjectile()` method updates the position by factoring speed over time. In Y's case, the height is also adjusted with the pull of gravity over time.

SetDirectionMatrix() makes this effect even more realistic by adjusting the rocket's direction. The transformation matrix set when calling this method ensures that the rocket flies in the proper direction about the Y axis, and it also gives the rocket a tilt on the X axis, so it points upward as it climbs and then lowers as the rocket descends to the ground.

Replace the existing UpdateProjectile() method with this one to implement the change:

```
public void UpdateProjectile(GameTime gameTime){
    previousPosition = position;      // store position from last frame

    // gravity takes over after rocket clears the launcher
    Vector3 distanceTravelled = position - startPosition;
    if (distanceTravelled.Length() > 1.8f)
    {                                 // gravity time starts ticking
        seconds    += gameTime.ElapsedGameTime.Milliseconds/1000.0f;
        const float GRAVITY = 9.8f;   // gravity constant and scaling
        const float SCALAR  = 0.0784f;

        position.X += speed.X*seconds;// X uses speed vs time
        position.Z += speed.Z*seconds;// Z uses speed vs time
        position.Y += speed.Y*seconds - 0.5f*GRAVITY*seconds*seconds
                   * SCALAR;          // Y uses speed and gravity vs time
    }
    // turbo boost needed for rocket to clearly leave the launcher
    else
        position += speed             // speed uses constant scalar
              *(float)gameTime.ElapsedGameTime.Milliseconds/90.0f;

    SetDirectionMatrix();             // rocket direction considers speed

    if (position.Y < -0.5f)           // de-activate if below ground
        active = false;
}
```

Running the program now shows the projectiles rising in an arc. When the peak is reached, they rotate gradually so they point downward and fall back to the ground. On reaching the ground, they are deactivated and made ready for the next launch.

Whether you are allowing your players to throw a ball or deploy weaponry, your ballistics are ready for launch.

CHAPTER 19 REVIEW EXERCISES

To get the most from this chapter, try out these chapter review exercises.

1. Follow the step-by-step examples shown in this chapter to implement the Linear Projectile algorithm and Arcing Projectile algorithm, if you have not already done so.
2. State how the projectile update routine for linear projectiles differs from that for arcing projectiles.
3. Replace the model rocket with your own 3D object and make it point in the direction that it travels. Add bounding-sphere collision detection to an object in your world so that something happens when you hit it.

CHAPTER 20

Particle Effects

PARTICLE algorithms enable effects such as rain, explosions, fire, smoke, sparkles, and much more. You could say that the effects created by the particle algorithm are only limited by your imagination. Compare the non-particle-based explosions in *Space Invaders* with an explosion that uses a particle algorithm—like a rocket explosion in id Software's *Quake*. *Quake*'s rocket effect is substantially more interesting.

A *particle* is a user-defined object that sets, stores, and updates properties for a group of related items. Each group or class of particles shares a similar but slightly randomized set of properties (for example, a group of rain particles, snow particles, fire particles, or smoke particles). Particles are usually assigned properties for life, size, color, position, and speed. As an example, a snowflake would have a starting position somewhere up in the sky, so the X and Z positions would be random but the starting position for Y would definitely be positive. The snow particle's life starts at the beginning of the particle's descent and ends when the snowflake reaches the ground. The snowflakes are small, but each one varies slightly in size. The snowflake's color property would be set to a shade of white. The snowflake's speed would definitely be negative on the Y axis, but the X and Z speeds are random. The Y speed of the snowflake particle is varied and slow enough to allow for the snow to drift to the ground.

There is no set syntax or rule for defining particles—they have different properties based on their implementation. Particles are usually regenerated on a continuous basis, but some randomization is normally present for creating a dynamic and ever-changing special effect.

When drawing particles, you often need transparency to remove background pixels. This generates the image you need for your effect—such as rain, fire, or an explosion. You could use billboarded triangle strips for this task, or you might consider using point sprites.

Because particle algorithms can be expensive in terms of system bandwidth, you should be careful not to create too many particles. Using point sprites will certainly help reduce the drag on performance to allow you to use hundreds and possibly thousands of particles in your game. Game developers use particle algorithms when they want to show off brilliant special effects, but when performance is an issue, they may choose a textured sprite instead of a particle algorithm.

POINT SPRITES

To improve performance, point sprites are often used for particle algorithms. A *point sprite* is a resizable textured vertex that always faces the camera. Here are three noteworthy characteristics of point sprites that make them suitable for rendering particles:

- A point sprite only uses one vertex, so it saves space and boosts performance.
- When point sprites are enabled, textures are automatically mapped to them, so there is no need to store or set or map UV coordinates in your XNA code.
- Point sprites always face the camera, so there is no need to implement code to adjust their angle to view them from various directions.

Point sprites can only be enabled through a shader. Much of the shader code is similar to code you have used in this book to draw a textured primitive surface. As discussed in Chapter 6, your shader usually begins with global variables that can be set from your XNA application. Here are declarations that you will need in your point sprite shader to set the texture and sizing from your XNA code:

```
texture     textureImage;                 // stores texture
float       fade;                         // fade as near end of life
float4x4    projection   : PROJECTION;    // viewport perspective matrix
float4x4    wvpMatrix    : WORLDVIEWPROJ;// world view projection matrix
float       viewportHeight;               // current viewport height
```

The same texture sampler used throughout this book, and explained in Chapter 9, will also work for this point sprite shader:

```
// filter (like a brush) for showing texture
sampler textureSampler = sampler_state{
    Texture = <textureImage>;
    magfilter = LINEAR; // magfilter when bigger than actual size
    minfilter = LINEAR; // minfilter when smaller than actual size
    mipfilter = LINEAR; // to resize images close and far away
};
```

Until now, your XNA code has been using XNA's preset `VertexDeclaration` to define the type of vertex data for drawing primitive-based surfaces using data such as texture coordinates, position, color, or normal information. These preset definitions are convenient, but sometimes you will want to customize your vertex definitions. To be able to access features such as setting the point sprite size, you need to create your own custom vertex definition in your XNA code. This ensures that the data sent from your XNA project is compatible with your vertex shader inputs. This will allow you to size your point sprite from your XNA code.

The vertex shader input for a point sprite still receives color and position information from your XNA application—as has been done in previous shader examples. However, the texture coordinate mapping is automatic, so you don't need to set UV coordinates in your XNA code or send them to the vertex shader. For you to pass the point sprite size to your vertex shader from your XNA code, the size variable defined for your vertex shader input must be tagged with the `PSIZE` semantic:

```
struct VSinput{
    float4 position : POSITION0;
    float4 color    : COLOR0;
    float1 size     : PSIZE0;
};
```

The output from the vertex shader is also different from the shader code that is used for texturing objects. When we're texturing primitive surfaces, the output from our vertex shader includes elements for color, position, and texture data. When implementing point sprites, the vertex shader also outputs the size element, and this must be denoted by the `PSIZE` semantic. You actually have to invent some data for the texture coordinate, which might seem weird, but some graphics cards require UV coordinates to exist when they leave the vertex shader.

```
struct VSoutput{
    float4 position : POSITION0;
    float1 size     : PSIZE;
    float4 color    : COLOR0;
    float4 UV       : TEXCOORD0;
};
```

Because of differences in point sprite handling on the Xbox 360 and the PC, we need to create a separate set of output specifically for the pixel shader. This allows you to use your shader on either platform. The Xbox 360 requires that UV coordinates be handled with a four-float vector denoted by a `SPRITETEXCOORD` semantic, and Windows requires the UV coordinates to be handled with a two-float vector denoted by a `TEXCOORD0` semantic. You may think having the extra output from the vertex shader is odd—and it is odd. However, being able to channel the `VSoutput` data to the graphics pipeline and the `PSinput` data to the pixel shader is necessary to run the same shader code on both your PC and Xbox 360.

```
struct PSinput{
    #ifdef XBOX
        float4 UV   : SPRITETEXCOORD;
    #else
        float2 UV   : TEXCOORD0;
    #endif
        float4 Color: COLOR0;
};
```

The vertex shader is similar to ones you've used before, but some extra values are added here to set up the point sprite for creating 3D fire in the next demonstration. The scale value, `fade`, reduces the size of each fire particle as it rises in the air and diminishes before being regenerated. `fade` is also used to darken the color of the particle as it rises away from the core of the fire.

Handling the texture data output for a point sprite from the vertex shader is notably different from a shader that just applies the usual texturing. The point sprite texture is automatically applied to the point sprite when it is sent to the pixel shader, so it doesn't matter what UV coordinates you set in the vertex shader. The data structure for the texture coordinate output from the vertex shader just needs to be in place. A vector with four floats is assigned to the texture output variable. This works both on the PC and on the Xbox. In the case of the PC, the vector will be truncated to a two-float vector.

The pixel shader actually performs the final processing on the color and texture data. However, to appease graphics card differences, and to allow this code to run on the PC and Xbox, two separate output streams have been created. Depending on your graphics card, if you leave this code out, your point sprites may not appear on your PC. The `VSoutput` data is sent into the graphics pipeline, and the `PSinput` data is sent to the pixel shader for further processing of color and UV data.

To ensure that the point sprite is sized properly, the following equation is used:

```
OUT.size        =(IN.size*
                 (projection._m11/OUT.position.w)*(viewportHeight/2))
                 *fade;
```

As you can see, this size routine veers away from the standard sizing methods that you might expect. The point sprite size is processed on the graphics card and it relies on the distance from the camera (`projectedPosition.w`), scaling for changes to the camera's field of view (`projection._m11`), and the viewport height. By viewport we mean the section of window that is set for each player in a full screen or split-screen environment. Also note that the vertex shader's output position value is used after the world-view-projection matrix has been applied to it.

```
void VertexShader(in VSinput IN, out VSoutput OUT){
    OUT.position    = mul(IN.position, wvpMatrix);

    // projection._m11     - Scaling information from camera's projection
    //                       to adjust to changing fields of view.
    // projectedPosition.w - Distance from the camera.
    // viewportHeight      - Height of the current projection in the
    //                       window.  See Chapter 28, "Multiplayer
    //                       Gaming," for more detail.
```

```
    OUT.size         =(IN.size*
                      (projection._m11/OUT.position.w)*(viewportHeight/2))
                      *fade;
    OUT.color        = (1.0f, 1.0f, 1.0f, 1.0f);
    OUT.UV           = (1.0f, 1.0f);

    // pass these values to the pixel shader
    PSinput          ps;
    ps.Color         = IN.color * fade;
    ps.UV            = (1.0f, 1.0f, 0.0f, 0.0f);
}
```

In the pixel shader, the texture coordinate values are extracted from the XY coordinates of the texture input. On the Xbox 360, these values are extracted from the ZW coordinates, and they may be negative. This tip and other tips on point sprite sizing are attributed to Shawn Hargreaves, an XNA platform developer at Microsoft and also a very outstanding XNA community contributor. (Great work, Shawn.) Shawn sums up the UV coordinate strangeness with a simple "Crazy, huh?":

```
float4 PixelShader(PSinput IN) : COLOR0{
    float2          UV;
    #ifdef XBOX
        UV          = abs(IN.UV.zw);
    #else
        UV          = IN.UV.xy;
    #endif
    return tex2D(textureSampler, UV)*IN.Color;
}
```

Finally, in the technique, some rendering states need to be set to create a shiny particle with a transparent background. Point sprites can be enabled in the shader by setting the `PointSpriteEnable` state to `true`. `AlphaBlendEnable` must be set to `true` to enable transparency. An `SrcBlend` setting of `SrcAlpha` and a `DestBlend` property of 1 will make the point sprite very shiny. If you just need a transparent point sprite texture but without the shiny filter, you could set the destination blend to `InvSrcAlpha`. When the `DestBlend` state is 1, the shiny particle will only appear against dark backgrounds because the brightness does not offer enough contrast to make it visible against lighter backgrounds. An additional `PointSize_Min` render state property has been added to enable scaling the point sprite to 0. You may not need this on your PC, but you will need it on the Xbox 360. Add this technique to set up your shader to run on both platforms:

```
technique PointSpriteTechnique{
    pass p0{
```

```
        // texture sampler initialized
        sampler[0]              = (textureSampler);
        PointSpriteEnable       = true;     // needed for point sprite
        PointSize_Min           = 0;        // enable scaling to 0 on xbox
        AlphaBlendEnable        = true;     // enable transparency
        SrcBlend                = SrcAlpha; // turn off transparent pixels
        DestBlend               = One;      // shiny blending
        ZWriteEnable            = false;    // disable 3D rendering

        // declare and initialize vs
        vertexshader = compile vs_1_1 VertexShader();
        // declare and initialize ps
        pixelshader = compile ps_1_1 PixelShader();
    }
}
```

For this case, the default state of `ZWriteEnable` is set to false; this disables the Z plane for 2D rendering and blends the sprites together. Without blending, the transparency effect for the point sprites may be spoiled for larger particles because the transparent edges will appear layered on top of each other when rendered with other sprites. Figure 20-1 shows how this layering appearance can backfire. Note how the top of the flame is distorted by poor layering.

If you set `ZWriteEnable` to `false` (to blend the point sprites), you will also need to ensure that you draw your point sprites after your other models and primitive surfaces are rendered. Otherwise, any 3D objects that you draw later will appear to be on top of the point sprites. This drawing order issue is demonstrated later in the chapter.

This shader can now be used to create great flashy effects.

FIGURE 20-1

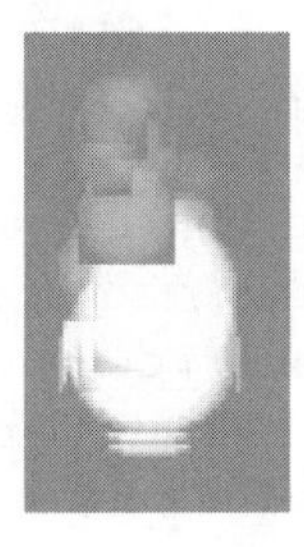

Unwanted layering of point sprites when ZWriteEnable is true

CUSTOM VERTEX DECLARATIONS

As mentioned earlier, XNA's preset VertexDeclarations are convenient but limited. For example, these preset vertex formats do not include an element for storing point sprite size. To set the point size from your XNA code, you will need to create a custom vertex to include this element. You may actually want to customize your vertex format to include other information—such as additional texture data, blend weights, fog, and much more. In other words, you create a vertex format to store the elements you need. Each data field in your vertex declaration is referred to as a VertexElement. An example of how to add VertexElement objects to your custom vertex definition appears later in this chapter. To set this up, you need to create a struct that stores data for each VertexElement. When declaring each VertexElement in your custom format definition, you use the following parameters:

```
VertexElement(
short stream,                          // stream source - 0 if only 1 stream
short offset,                          // offset in bytes for current element
VertexElementFormat elementFormat,// data type
VertexElementMethod elementMethod,// which data to calculate during render
VertexElementUsage  elementUsage, // Color, PointSize, TextureCoordinate,
                                   // Normal, Depth, Fog, BlendWeight, etc
byte usageIndex);                  // semantic instance of elementUsage
```

To initialize your data, you use your struct type to declare a vertex variable. Data is then stored in the fields of this vertex variable. Once your data is set, a VertexBuffer object is then initialized to store your custom vertex format. The contents of your vertex variable array are then assigned to this vertex buffer for use when rendering.

A VertexDeclaration object is also declared to store your custom definition:

```
VertexDeclaration vertexDeclaration = new VertexDeclaration(
                  GraphicsDevice      graphics,
                  VertexElement[]     customVertex.VertexElements);
```

This VertexDeclaration object is used later to set this property for the GraphicsDevice object, so it can read the data and render graphics using the newly defined vertex format. When you are drawing with the new vertex format, the vertex data is read from the VertexBuffer object and is rendered using the DrawPrimitives() method. The point sprite uses the PointList primitive type because only one vertex is needed for each point sprite.

```
GraphicsDeviceManager        graphics.GraphicsDevice.DrawPrimitives
(PrimitiveType. PointList, int  startVertex, int  primitiveCount);
```

FIRE EXAMPLE USING POINT SPRITES

This example takes the PointSprite.fx shader described earlier, creates a compatible custom vertex format in your XNA code, and shows you how to create a fire effect. It begins with either the MGHWinBaseCode or MGH360BaseCode project. This example is kept simple for easy learning, but the intent is to also inspire you with new ideas about how to create great effects. This example takes one image of a fire particle with a transparent background and turns it into fire. Figure 20-2 shows the fire from a torch at different frames.

In the Solution Explorer, reference the PointSprite.fx shader just described in this chapter. You can find this shader file in the Shaders folder on this book's website.

In your XNA code, this shader is referenced with the `Effect` object, `pointSpriteEffect`. This `Effect` object needs to be declared at the class level of your game class so it can be used throughout the class. Along with this declaration, some `EffectParameters` are also needed so you can set the WVP matrix, texture value, and scaling values in this shader from your XNA code:

```
Effect          pointSpriteEffect;              // shader object
EffectParameter pointSpriteEffectWVP;           // cumulative matrix w*v*p
EffectParameter pointSpriteEffectTexture;       // texture parameter
EffectParameter pointSpriteEffectFade;          // reduce size & color
EffectParameter pointSpriteEffectProjection; // camera projection
EffectParameter pointSpriteEffectViewport;      // viewport height
```

FIGURE 20-2

Fire from a torch during different frames

With these objects in place, your shader can be loaded and compiled, and your XNA code can be given access to its global variables. This setup needs to be done when the program begins. Therefore, in `Initialize()`, add the instructions to load your shader and to reference the shader's global variables:

```
pointSpriteEffect           = Content.Load<Effect>("Shaders\\PointSprite");
pointSpriteEffectWVP        = pointSpriteEffect.Parameters["wvpMatrix"];
pointSpriteEffectTexture    = pointSpriteEffect.Parameters["textureImage"];
pointSpriteEffectFade       = pointSpriteEffect.Parameters["fade"];
pointSpriteEffectProjection = pointSpriteEffect.Parameters["projection"];
pointSpriteEffectViewport   = pointSpriteEffect.Parameters["viewportHeight"];
```

The shader is now in place and ready for use, but a custom vertex format that is compatible with the shader inputs is required. Here is the class-level struct that stores the `VertexElements` (color, position, and point sprite size, as described earlier):

```
private struct CustomVertex{
    // struct fields
    private Vector3     position;
    private Vector4     color;
    private float       size;

    // create a new format with position, color, and size elements
    public static readonly VertexElement[] VertexElements =
    new VertexElement[]
    {                                                       // position
    new VertexElement(0, 0,                 VertexElementFormat.Vector3,
        VertexElementMethod.Default,        VertexElementUsage.Position, 0),
                                                            // color
    new VertexElement(0, sizeof(float)*3,VertexElementFormat.Vector4,
        VertexElementMethod.Default,        VertexElementUsage.Color, 0),
                                                            // size
    new VertexElement(0, sizeof(float)*7,VertexElementFormat.Single,
        VertexElementMethod.Default,        VertexElementUsage.PointSize,0),
    };

    // constructor for custom vertex element
    public CustomVertex(Vector3 position, Vector4 color, float size){
        this.position   = position;
        this.color      = color;
        this.size       = size;
    }
}
```

With the new vertex type in place, we can create an array that stores vertices using this new format. We'll also need to create a `VertexBuffer` object to serve as a data source while rendering our vertices. A `VertexDeclaration` object is also required to set the `GraphicsDevice` object, so it can read and draw using your new vertex format. Adding their declaration to the game class will make them available later:

```
CustomVertex[]       pointSpriteVertex       = new CustomVertex[1];
VertexBuffer         vertexBuffer;
VertexDeclaration    customVertexType;
```

Now you can initialize the particle vertex—you actually only need one vertex to do this. Once the data is set, it is then stored in a vertex buffer that serves as the data source during rendering. The vertex declaration is also initialized here, so the custom definition can be referenced by the `GraphicsDevice` when reading and drawing primitive surfaces with this new vertex format:

```
void InitializeParticleVertex(){
    Vector3 position = new Vector3(0.0f, 0.0f, 0.0f);       // origin
    Vector4 color    = new Vector4(0.7f, 0.8f, 0.0f, 1.0f); // yellow
    float   size     = 0.05f;                               // size
    pointSpriteVertex[0]
                = new CustomVertex(position, color, size); // set data
    vertexBuffer = new VertexBuffer(graphics.GraphicsDevice,// store data
                  pointSpriteVertex.Length * 32, BufferUsage.WriteOnly);
    vertexBuffer.SetData(pointSpriteVertex);
    customVertexType
                = new VertexDeclaration(                    // define format
                  graphics.GraphicsDevice, CustomVertex.VertexElements);
}
```

To initialize your custom vertex data, vertex buffer stream, and `VertexDeclaration` object when the program begins, call `InitializeParticleVertex()` from `Initialize()`:

```
InitializeParticleVertex();
```

Next, the texture used for the point sprite needs to be loaded. Only one image is needed to create a flashy fire effect, but you could add more to make the effect more varied and even more impressive. The image shown here is the one used for the particle texture.

To load your image using the `ContentManager`, you must reference the image file, particle.png, in your project's Images folder as well as in the Solution Explorer. The particle.png file can be obtained from the Images folder in the download from this book's website. The image is stored in a Texture2D object called `particleTexture`. Add this declaration to the modules area of your game class:

```
Texture2D   particleTexture;
```

To load your texture with other textures when the program starts, add the load statement to the `LoadContent()` method:

```
particleTexture = Content.Load<Texture2D>("Images\\particle");
```

To store and update the fire particles, you use a particle class. To store this class, add a Particle.cs source file to your project. Here is the class shell:

```
using System;
using System.Collections.Generic;
using System.Text;
namespace Particles{
    class Particle
    {    }
}
```

To access vital XNA functions from your new class, you need to include the XNA graphics framework declarations at the top of the Particle.cs file:

```
using Microsoft.Xna.Framework;
```

Declarations for the classic particle properties described at the beginning of the chapter belong in the module level of your particle class. Position, speed, life, and a fade rate in your particles are essential to build a fire.

```
public  Vector3 position;  // X, Y, Z position.
public  Vector3 speed;     // Rate of movement on X, Y, Z plane.
public  float   life;      // Die when life <= 0.0f. New life = 1.0f.
private float   fadeRate;  // Every particle dies at a different rate.
```

You are also going to need to add a constructor; otherwise, your class will not compile when you reference it from another class:

```
public Particle(){}
```

It would not make sense to continuously create a new particle each time an old particle has run its course. Instead, processing time is saved by forcing the particles to be effectively "reborn" after they die. In the case of a fire algorithm, the fire particles start at the base and rise upward. As each particle leaves the furnace core, it cools down and grows faint until it finally burns out and dies. The function `ResetParticle()` then rejuvenates the particle and it begins a new life. Every time the particle is regenerated, it is given a randomized position, fade rate, and speed. This randomization makes the fire more interesting.

Also note that these particle properties will often need a minimum or a maximum value to ensure that they fall within an acceptable range. For example, if the fade rate is not set to a minimum of 60, you'll discover very quickly that the longer-living particles will take over. These longer-living particles are like mutants that won't die off as nature intended. If your fire is overtaken by longer-living particles, eventually the core of your fire will become so dispersed that the flames will burn out and you will be left with a scattering of particles floating off into the atmosphere.

When you're customizing your own particle algorithms, these properties won't just jump into your head. Give yourself time for trial and error when setting up your particle properties and then see what looks best during your test phase. For this example, the properties have been provided for you. Here is the `ResetParticle()` procedure to add to your particle class:

```
public void ResetParticle(Random rand){
    life            = 1;                    // give a full life
    position        = Vector3.Zero;         // set to origin

    // set fade rate
    int fadeFactor = 60 + rand.Next(0, 70); // between 60 and 129
    fadeRate       = (1 + (float)fadeFactor)/50.0f;

    // set X speed
    int randomXSpeed = rand.Next(-40, 40);   // min -40 and max 39
    speed.X          = (float)(randomXSpeed + 1)/300.0f;
    // set Y speed
    int randomYSpeed = rand.Next(0, 15);     // min 0 and max 14
    speed.Y          = (float)(randomYSpeed + 1)/23.0f;
    // set Z speed
    speed.Z          = 0.0f;
}
```

A method is required to update the particles. The particle position property is incremented by the speed scaled by the time between frames. The scale regulates the speed so that the animation appears at the same rate regardless of the processing power of the machine that runs the algorithm.

Particle life is reduced by the fade rate at each frame. If the life value falls below zero, then the particle is reincarnated. In this case, the fire particle is born at the bottom by the fire source, and it then rises upward on a randomized path. Eventually, the particle gets too far away from the fire, grows smaller, and dims until it is invisible. At this point, the particle is regenerated again. To achieve this effect, add the `UpdateParticle()` procedure to your particle class. This code ensures that the particles live according to their destiny.

```
public void UpdateParticle(GameTime gameTime, Random rand){
    float time  = (float)gameTime.ElapsedGameTime.Milliseconds/1000.0f;
    position   += speed*time;        // update position
    life       -= fadeRate*time;     // update speed

    // regenerate particle if life falls below zero
    if (life < 0)
        ResetParticle(rand);
}
```

Back in Game1.cs, a reference to this new particle class is required. The particle class's namespace must be added at the top of Game1.cs so the game class can find it:

```
using Particles;
```

Several particles are needed to collectively build the fire. Through trial and error while experimenting with different numbers of particles when writing this algorithm, we found that 100 particles appeared to simulate a decent fire, both up close and from a distance. You may find as you customize your own particle algorithms that you don't need as many particles, especially if the effect is only viewed from a distance. Sometimes you may need more to create a more full-bodied particle effect. For this routine, 100 particles look good from different distances. Declaring 100 particle objects in your game class will allow you to track and update each particle's size, location, and color while drawing one point sprite in each particle's place.

```
private const int NUM_PARTICLES = 100;
private Particle[]                particle;
```

A `Random` object is declared and initialized at the top of your game class to seed the random generation of properties for each particle:

```
Random rand = new Random();
```

All particles are born when the game application begins. An array of particle objects makes it easy to generate fire particles when your program kicks into gear. By the time your window opens, you will likely catch the tail end of the particles springing to life in a full-fledged fire. The fire is started from the game application's `Initialize()` method:

```
particle = new Particle[NUM_PARTICLES];
for (int i = 0; i < NUM_PARTICLES; i++){
    particle[i] = new Particle();
    particle[i].ResetParticle(rand);
}
```

For every frame, the position for each fire particle must be adjusted so that the particle rises at the object's own random rate. Of course, after each frame, the particle is one step closer to its own death as its life is gradually reduced by its fade rate. The particle object's update method will check whether the life is reduced to zero—in which case a new life and an entirely different set of properties will be generated to start the particle on a new path from the core of the fire. This ensures that your particles don't stand still. Add this routine to update your particle objects inside the `Update()` method of your game class:

```
for (int i = 0; i < NUM_PARTICLES; i++)
    particle[i].UpdateParticle(gameTime, rand);
```

A `SaveStateMode.SaveState` parameter is needed in the `Begin()` method to restore the `GraphicsDevice` settings after the point sprites have been rendered. Performing this restore is necessary; otherwise, the `GraphicsDevice` object's depth setting is disabled. Your other non–point sprite objects will look strange if the original `GraphicsDevice` states are not restored. Try running the code with `SaveStateMode` enabled to see the code work correctly, then run your code without including this parameter to see how the background is off-color and 3D models have no depth when the `GraphicsDevice` settings have been thrown out after the point sprite is drawn.

Before the fire is drawn, the `GraphicsDevice` object is set to retrieve vertex buffer data from and render data using the new vertex format. The data is then read from the vertex buffer, and the vertex is drawn using a point list:

```
void ParticleShader(VertexBuffer vertexBuffer){
    pointSpriteEffect.Begin(SaveStateMode.SaveState);
    pointSpriteEffect.Techniques[0].Passes[0].Begin();

    graphics.GraphicsDevice.VertexDeclaration = customVertexType;
    int stride = vertexBuffer.SizeInBytes;
    graphics.GraphicsDevice.Vertices[0].SetSource(vertexBuffer, 0, stride);
    graphics.GraphicsDevice.DrawPrimitives(PrimitiveType.PointList, 0, 1);
```

```
    pointSpriteEffect.Techniques[0].Passes[0].End();
    pointSpriteEffect.End();
}
```

The code required to draw the particle using point sprites is very similar to code that draws any textured primitive surface. Scaling for the entire group of particles is triggered once—based on the distance between the camera and the group of particles. Each fire particle is rendered individually. The group of particles is moved into position and then each individual particle is translated from the fire base to its own position in the roaring fire. The particle's life level, which ranges between 0 for dead and 1 for full life, is passed to the shader so it can be used to fade the color of the flame and shrink the size as each particle rises away from the core of the fire:

```
private void DrawParticles(){
    // 1: declare matrices
    Matrix  world, translateParticle, translateGroup;
    // scale the point sprite by cam distance to the group of particles
    Vector3 particlesPosition = new Vector3(0.0f, 0.42f, -5.0f);

    // 2: initialize matrices
    translateGroup = Matrix.CreateTranslation(particlesPosition);

    for (int i = 0; i < NUM_PARTICLES; i++){
        // translate each individual particle
        translateParticle = Matrix.CreateTranslation(particle[i].position);

        // 3: build cumulative world matrix using I.S.R.O.T. sequence
        // identity, scale, rotate, orbit(translate & rotate), translate
        world = translateGroup * translateParticle;

        // 4: set shader variables
        pointSpriteEffectWVP.SetValue(
                   world*cam.viewMatrix*cam.projectionMatrix);
        pointSpriteEffectTexture.SetValue(particleTexture);
        pointSpriteEffectFade.SetValue(particle[i].life);
        pointSpriteEffectProjection.SetValue(cam.projectionMatrix);
        pointSpriteEffectViewport.SetValue(
                                     GraphicsDevice.Viewport.Height);
        // 5: draw object-select vertex type, primitive type, # primitives
        ParticleShader(vertexBuffer);
    }
}
```

Inside the `Draw()` method, a call can be made to draw the fire:

```
DrawParticles();
```

Finally, as one last touch to make the example a little more interesting, we'll add a model torch. For this to work, the torch.fbx file must be referenced from a Models folder under the Content node in the Solution Explorer. The torch.bmp texture will also need to be placed in the Models folder in your project but doesn't need to be referenced. If the torch.bmp texture is referenced from the Solution Explorer, it will be confused with the torch.fbx model because they both use the same name. The torch.fbx and torch.bmp files can be found in the Models folder on this book's website.

The logic and methods used to load and draw the models are the same as explained in Chapter 14, so the details behind these next steps will be minimal. First, declarations in the game class are required to store the torch model object and the array for the torch's bone transformations:

```
Model torchModel;   Matrix[] matTorch;
```

This `InitializeTorch()` method includes the code to load the torch and set the transformation matrix for the meshes in it. Placing this in the game class allows you to load the model:

```
void InitializeTorch(){
    torchModel = Content.Load<Model>("Models\\torchModel");
    matTorch   = new Matrix[torchModel.Bones.Count];
    torchModel.CopyAbsoluteBoneTransformsTo(matTorch);
}
```

`InitializeTorch()` can be called from the `Initialize()` method to read in the torch.fbx file when the program begins:

```
InitializeTorch();
```

You can add this next method to your game class to draw the torch:

```
private void DrawTorch(Model model){
    // 1: declare matrices
    Matrix world, translation, scale;

    // 2: initialize matrices
    scale       = Matrix.CreateScale(0.50f, 0.50f, 0.50f);
    translation = Matrix.CreateTranslation(0.0f, 0.35f, -5.0f);

    foreach (ModelMesh mesh in model.Meshes){
        // 3: build cumulative matrix using I.S.R.O.T. sequence
```

```
        // identity,scale,rotate,orbit(translate & rotate),translate
        world   = scale * translation;
        foreach (BasicEffect effect in mesh.Effects){ // 4a. pass wvp
            effect.World      = matTorch[mesh.ParentBone.Index] * world;
            effect.View       = cam.viewMatrix;
            effect.Projection = cam.projectionMatrix;
                                                      // 4b. set lighting
            effect.EnableDefaultLighting();
            effect.SpecularPower = 0.01f;
        }
        // 5: draw object
        mesh.Draw();
    }
}
```

The method to draw the torch model is triggered from `Draw()` along with the other draw routines that are called. `DrawTorch()` must be called before the point sprites are rendered to ensure that the point sprites are layered properly over the 3D model:

```
DrawTorch(torchModel);
```

To observe deviant layering when `ZWriteEnable` is false, try calling `DrawTorch()` after drawing the point sprites. You will notice that the flame no longer appears to come from the torch, as shown in Figure 20-3.

FIGURE 20-3

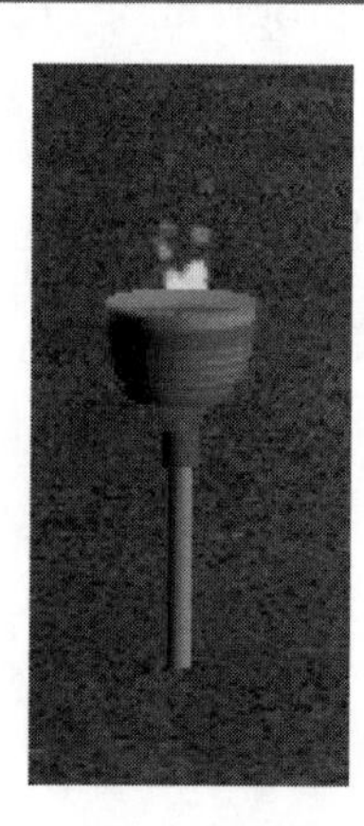

Draw order issues for point sprites when ZWriteEnable is false

Setting ZWriteEnable in the shader to false ensures that the point sprites will be blended together. However, sometimes setting ZWriteEnable to true looks good when the background is colored the same as the pixels that are supposed to be transparent, or when the particles are small or disperse. You can always experiment to see what looks good, but remember that a PC game may be played in several different environments—on different-sized windows. You should consider this in your decision as to whether or not to use ZWriteEnable.

With the DestBlend state set to 1 in the shader, shiny blending is applied. As a result, the point sprite can only be seen against darker backgrounds. To ensure that you can see the fire against the background, replace the instruction that clears the background and resets the color inside the Draw() method with this new instruction:

```
graphics.GraphicsDevice.Clear(Color.Black);
```

When you run your program, it will show a steady, ever-changing body of fire. As you back away from the fire, the size of the particles will scale properly to match the size of the primitive ground surface and model torch. At any angle the fire particles will face the camera, so you don't need to have any billboarding code.

This is a cool effect, but it's really only the beginning of what you can do with point sprites and particle effects. This particle effect would be ideal for creating explosions, exhaust trails from missiles, stardust, and more. You could even increase the number of textures used or the particle types to make the fire more interesting.

CHAPTER 20 REVIEW EXERCISES

To get the most from this chapter, try out these chapter review exercises.

1. Try the step-by-step examples provided in this chapter, if you have not already done so.
2. Starting with the existing algorithm, create an additional particle stream to simulate smoke from your fire.
3. Modify your fire algorithm to create an explosion.

CHAPTER 21

Keyframe Animations

KEYFRAME animations combine a timer and interpolation to determine the location of game objects. The term *keyframe* comes from the world of hand-drawn animation. The senior artists would draw the "key frames" and then other artists would create the "in-betweens." In computer games, the keyframes still define the most important stages of the animation, but interpolation is used to fill in the frames in between. This can mean interpolating the position or orientation of an object. For example, in a racing game, you might want to include a pace car when the cars are under a caution flag. Using keyframes, you can control the course that the pace car follows as it leads the pack and then eventually drives off into the pit. By the end of this chapter, you will be able to use keyframes to map out a route and regulate the speed of this sort of animation.

The proper technique is to use a timeline to control the speed of animations; this allows the animation to be rendered at the same speed regardless of the system that runs it. Until now, the examples in this book have generated translational animations by incrementing X, Y, and Z coordinates by a product of the increment unit and the difference in time between the current and previous frame. Interpolation is a similar process, but it offers other possibilities for moving objects on linear and curved paths. For translations or rotations, a path may be defined for the object and a specific duration of time may be assigned for completing the path.

INTERPOLATION

Interpolation can be used to project the location of a game object based on the expected time of arrival at the destination. For example, if the time between the starting frame and ending frame of an object is 10 seconds, and the object is expected to travel 5 units on the X plane and 10 units on the Z plane, then interpolation can be used to estimate the object's location at any time between 0 and 10 seconds. At 4 seconds, interpolation would project the object to be at X = 2 and Z = 4.

CURVES

When mapping out keyframes on your timeline, you probably won't always want your vehicles traveling in a straight line. You might want to use a curve to map out a path for a keyframe animation. This chapter uses Bézier curves to fulfill this role, but you could use other types of curves for the same task. Most splines are calculated by similar methods as the Bézier curve, so the Bézier curve provides a good example of how this family of curves can be implemented in your game algorithms.

The Bézier curves in this chapter use four points: a start point, an end point, and two control points (see Figure 21-1). The control points provide the user with a way to stretch or compress the curve. Stretching the control points will "push" or "pull" the curve into different shapes.

FIGURE 21-1

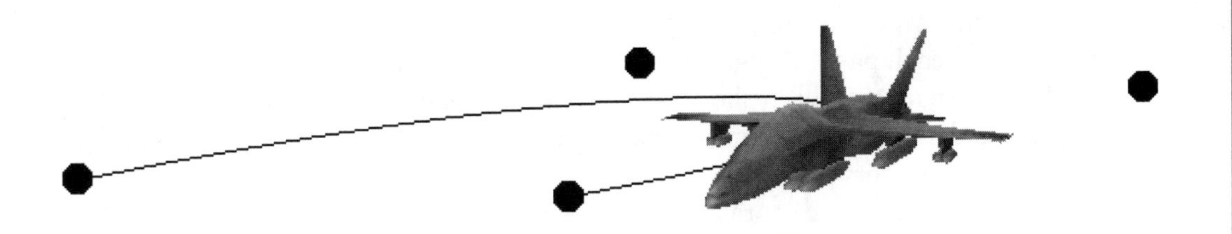

Jet travels along Bezier curve that has four control points

The formula for finding a point on a Bézier curve is based on the relative position between the start of the curve (0 percent) and the end of the curve (100 percent):

$$
\begin{aligned}
\text{Point on Bezier Curve} = \; & V_{start} * (1 - fraction)^3 \\
+ \; & V_{control\ 1} * 3 * fraction * (1 - fraction)^2 \\
+ \; & V_{control\ 2} * 3 * fraction^2 * (1 - fraction) \\
+ \; & V_{end} * fraction^3
\end{aligned}
$$

The following example puts this formula to use.

KEYFRAME ANIMATION EXAMPLE

This example demonstrates a timed animation that moves a model CF-18 Hornet fighter jet on a fixed route. Two parts of the route are defined by straight lines and two parts of the route are defined by Bézier curves. The CF-18 fighter jet and route are shown in Figure 21-2.

FIGURE 21-2

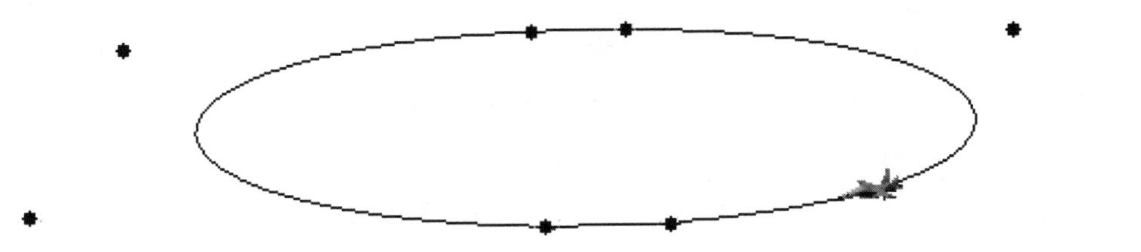

CF-18 fighter jet, animated using a series of straight lines and Bézier curves

The code for this example starts with either the MGHWinBaseCode or the MGH360BaseCode project available on this book's website.

A fixed period is specified for completing the combined sections. The total animation time needed to complete all combined routes is 11,200 milliseconds (11.2 seconds). At each pass through `Update()`, the algorithm checks to determine how far along the path the object should be at that specific time. The position of the CF-18 is projected using the keyframes, which store the fixed end points of the lines and points on the Bézier curves.

The first step is to store each route. Two Bézier curves are being used, and two lines are being used. The Bézier curve stores four control points:

```
private Vector3[] bezierA   = new Vector3[4]; // route 1
private Vector3[] lineA     = new Vector3[2]; // route 2
private Vector3[] bezierB   = new Vector3[4]; // route 3
private Vector3[] lineB     = new Vector3[2]; // route 4
```

This first routine will initialize the jet's route:

```
private void InitializeRoutes(){
    // length of world quadrant
    const float END = -BOUNDARY;
    // 1st Bezier curve control points (1st route)
    bezierA[0] = new Vector3( END+5.0f, 0.4f, 5.0f);          // start
    bezierA[1] = new Vector3( END+5.0f, 2.4f, 3.0f*END);      // ctrl 1
    bezierA[2] = new Vector3(-END-5.0f, 4.4f, 3.0f*END);      // ctrl 2
    bezierA[3] = new Vector3(-END-5.0f, 5.4f, 5.0f);          // end
    // 1st line between Bezier curves (2nd route)
    lineA[0]   = new Vector3(-END-5.0f, 5.4f, 5.0f);          // start
    lineA[1]   = new Vector3(-END-5.0f, 5.4f, -5.0f);         // end
    // 2nd Bezier curve control points (3rd route)
    bezierB[0] = new Vector3(-END-5.0f, 5.4f, -5.0f);         // start
    bezierB[1] = new Vector3(-END-5.0f, 4.4f, -3.0f*END);     // ctrl 1
    bezierB[2] = new Vector3( END+5.0f, 2.4f, -3.0f*END);     // ctrl 2
    bezierB[3] = new Vector3( END+5.0f, 0.4f, -5.0f);         // end
    // 2nd line between Bezier curves (4th route)
    lineB[0]   = new Vector3( END+5.0f, 0.4f, -5.0f);         // start
    lineB[1]   = new Vector3( END+5.0f, 0.4f, 5.0f);          // end
}
```

You call the jet initialization routine from `Initialize()`:

```
InitializeRoutes();
```

Next, you must add module declarations to initialize the time for the whole trip and each individual section of the trip:

```
private float[]      keyFrameTime     =   new float[4];
private float        tripTime         =   0.0f;
private const float TOTAL_TRIP_TIME =  11.2f;
private const int    NUM_KEYFRAMES    =   4;
```

To initialize the timeline, you will provide five values. Each of the total times between keyframes is stored. Also, the total trip time is stored.

```
private void InitializeTimeLine(){
    keyFrameTime[0] = 4.8f; // time to complete route 1
    keyFrameTime[1] = 0.8f; // time to complete route 2
    keyFrameTime[2] = 4.8f; // time to complete route 3
    keyFrameTime[3] = 0.8f; // time to complete route 4
}
```

Call the time-initialization routine from `Initialize()`:

```
InitializeTimeLine();
```

The next step is to add module declarations for storing the Y rotation of the jet model. This will correct the jet so that it is always pointing in the correct direction:

```
Vector3 currentPosition, previousPosition;
float   Yrotation;
```

After the jet is pointing in the proper direction, your next hurdle is keeping track of which route the jet is currently flying. Because we know how long each route will take, it's easy to check the time, and then figure out which route the jet is currently following. The `KeyFrameNumber()` function performs this check:

```
private int KeyFrameNumber(){
    float timeLapsed = 0.0f;
    // retrieve current leg of trip
    for (int i = 0; i < NUM_KEYFRAMES; i++)
    {
        if (timeLapsed > tripTime)
            return i - 1;
        else
            timeLapsed += keyFrameTime[i];
    }
    return 3; // special case for last route
}
```

The next function uses the Bézier curve to figure out what part of the curve your object is on. Unlike the last function, which checked the time, this one is checking the physical location of the jet. For this example, we need two different ways of determining position; the first one checks the position on the Bézier curve:

```
private Vector3 GetPositionOnCurve(Vector3[] bezier, float fraction){
            // returns absolute position on curve based on relative
    return  // position on curve (relative position ranges from 0% to 100%)
    bezier[0] * (1.0f - fraction) * (1.0f - fraction) * (1.0f - fraction) +
    bezier[1] * 3.0f * fraction * (1.0f - fraction) * (1.0f - fraction) +
    bezier[2] * 3.0f * fraction * fraction * (1.0f - fraction) +
    bezier[3] * fraction * fraction * fraction;
}
```

The second position-checking function uses linear interpolation to figure out which part of a line the model jet is on:

```
private Vector3 GetPositionOnLine(Vector3[] line, float fraction){
    // returns absolute position on line based on relative position
    // on curve (relative position ranges from 0% to 100%)
    Vector3 lineAtOrigin = line[1] - line[0];
    return line[0] + fraction*lineAtOrigin;
}
```

The next function to add, `UpdateKeyframeAnimation()`, is the workhorse of this example. It uses all of the logic that you have added to update the animation. The function determines which part of the route the fighter jet is on and then uses the appropriate check to find out where it should be on that route:

```
private void UpdateKeyframeAnimation(GameTime gameTime){
    // update total trip time, use modulus to prevent variable overflow
    tripTime    += (gameTime.ElapsedGameTime.Milliseconds/1000.0f);
    tripTime     = tripTime%TOTAL_TRIP_TIME;

    // get the current route number from a total of four routes
    int routeNum = KeyFrameNumber();

    // sum times for preceding keyframes
    float keyFrameStartTime = 0.0f;
    for (int i = 0; i < routeNum; i++)
        keyFrameStartTime += keyFrameTime[i];

    // calculate time spent during current route
```

```
    float timeBetweenKeys = tripTime - keyFrameStartTime;

    // calculate percentage of current route completed
    float fraction = timeBetweenKeys/keyFrameTime[routeNum];

    // get current X, Y, Z of object being animated
    // find point on line or curve by passing in % completed
    switch (routeNum){
    case 0: // first curve
        currentPosition = GetPositionOnCurve(bezierA, fraction); break;
    case 1: // first line
        currentPosition = GetPositionOnLine(lineA, fraction);    break;
    case 2: // 2nd curve
        currentPosition = GetPositionOnCurve(bezierB, fraction); break;
    case 3: // 2nd line
        currentPosition = GetPositionOnLine(lineB, fraction);    break;
    }
    // get rotation angle about Y based on change in X and Z speed
    Vector3 speed     = currentPosition - previousPosition;
    previousPosition = currentPosition;
    Yrotation         = (float)Math.Atan2((float)speed.X, (float)speed.Z);
}
```

This update function obviously needs to be called from `Update()`:

```
UpdateKeyframeAnimation(gameTime);
```

Next, you need to add the jet model to your program. To start the process of loading the fighter jet model, add these module declarations:

```
Model       jetModel;
Matrix[]    jetMatrix;
```

When you initialize the CF-18 model, make sure the cf18.x file is referenced in the Models folder under the Content node within your project (with the matching cf18Color.jpg file). If the Models folder is not present, you will need to add one. You can find these files in the Models folder on this book's website. Add this code to load and initialize the jet from inside the `LoadContent()` method (this code is explained in Chapter 14):

```
jetModel    = Content.Load<Model>("Models\\cf18");
jetMatrix   = new Matrix[jetModel.Bones.Count];
jetModel.CopyAbsoluteBoneTransformsTo(jetMatrix);
```

Now it's time to actually draw the jet model. Most of this code should be familiar to you—it has been used throughout this book. Lighting with the `BasicEffect` object is explained in Chapter 22.

```
private void DrawCF18(Model model){
    // 1: declare matrices
    Matrix scale, translate, rotateX, rotateY, world;

    // 2: initialize matrices
    translate    = Matrix.CreateTranslation(currentPosition);
    scale        = Matrix.CreateScale(0.1f, 0.1f, 0.1f);
    rotateX      = Matrix.CreateRotationX(0.0f);
    rotateY      = Matrix.CreateRotationY(Yrotation);

    // 3: build cumulative world matrix using I.S.R.O.T. sequence
    // identity, scale, rotate, orbit(translate & rotate), translate
    world        = scale * rotateX * rotateY * translate;

    // set shader parameters
    foreach (ModelMesh mesh in model.Meshes){
        foreach (BasicEffect effect in mesh.Effects){
            effect.World       = jetMatrix[mesh.ParentBone.Index] * world;
            effect.View        = cam.viewMatrix;
            effect.Projection = cam.projectionMatrix;
            effect.EnableDefaultLighting();
            effect.SpecularColor = new Vector3(0.0f, 0.0f, 0.0f);
            effect.CommitChanges();
        }
        mesh.Draw();
    }
}
```

The final step to set up this example is to call `DrawCF18()` from `Draw()`:

```
DrawCF18(jetModel);
```

When the program is run, it shows the jet model being interpolated over an 11.2-second interval. The first 0.8 seconds are spent on each straight line, and 4.8 seconds are spent on each Bézier curve. Interpolation is used to estimate where the jet should be at each frame. The CF-18 Hornet's path used is outlined back in Figure 21-2.

The keyframe animation created in this chapter is actually similar to a timeline animation you would create in Macromedia Flash or chUmbaLum sOft's MilkShape. As you can see, it's easy to implement a keyframe animation in code.

CHAPTER 21 REVIEW EXERCISES

To get the most from this chapter, try out these chapter review exercises.

1. Implement the step-by-step example demonstrated in this chapter, if you have not already done so.
2. Begin with the completed airplane example from Chapter 8, and convert this solution so that it uses three Bézier curves to move the airplane on a path in the X, Y, and Z planes.

CHAPTER 22

Lighting

A good lighting system is often a key differentiator between a high-quality game and an amateur game. If you're not sure about this, walk into any arcade and look at the games around you. Most likely, you will be more impressed with the games that use advanced lighting techniques. By adding interesting lighting—even in small amounts—you can excite your players' eyes with the details of your game.

This chapter shows you how to program the lighting inside your virtual worlds. Once you start using different lighting techniques and adding multiple light sources to your games, you might be surprised by how much detail becomes visible. Even with subtle lighting, bumps, cracks, and depth that formerly went unnoticed will materialize.

When setting up your lights, it is strongly recommended that you add only one light at a time. This ensures that you know exactly how each new light affects your environment. Even when professional game artists light a scene, they will usually start by working with one main light to establish the right mood and ambience before adding other lights.

LIGHTING METHODS

There are many different ways to implement lighting. On the XNA platform, lighting must be applied using a shader. You can use XNA's `BasicEffect` shader, or you can write your own shader to implement customized lighting.

Most light-simulation models break the light into different components so that you can describe the source of the light and the reflective properties of the materials that are being lit. Source lights can range from the sun, to a fire, or even a light bulb. Materials being lit might be bright, shiny, or reflective—like a golden ore. In comparison, dull materials, such as unfinished wood or dark cloth, will reflect very little light.

Source Lights

Source lights generate light. This chapter presents two types of source light:

- **Directional light** An example of directional light is the sun. This type of light source has no position, does not fade, is infinite, and has a direction.
- **Point light** An example of point light is a light bulb. Point light has a range and a position, and it shines in all directions.

Reflective Lighting Properties of Materials

Reflective lighting properties define how light radiates from and around the materials being lit. Reflective lighting properties are just as important as source lights because they define the shininess, color, and brightness of the materials being lit. The three common types of reflective light properties are ambient, diffuse, and specular.

Ambient Light

Ambient light is background light that has no source. The ambience is created by light bouncing off surrounding objects in all directions. The ambient property defines how background light colors and brightens materials in a scene. Here are some points to keep in mind:

- Ambient light is scattered background light and is everywhere in a scene.
- Ambient light has no direction.

Diffuse Light

Diffuse light defines how a source light colors and brightens materials in its path. Diffuse light increases as the angle between the light and the surface normal decreases.

Specular Light

The *specular* property defines a material's shininess, gloss, or highlights. Specular light reflected from a surface depends on the viewer's angle to the surface and the light's angle to the surface. Glass, water, metal, and some plastics have high specular levels. Earth, concrete, and dull-colored materials have lower specular levels. Here are some points to keep in mind:

- Specular light is like a highlight that makes an object shiny.
- Specular light is used for simulating shiny, plastic, glossy, or metallic objects.

Reflective Normals

As described in Chapter 15, a *normal* is a directional vector that is perpendicular to a surface. When lighting is implemented, a normal vector is used to calculate the intensity of the light reflected from the surface. Each normal is drawn at right angles to the surface being rendered.

When rendering complex shapes using primitive objects, you will need to calculate the normal and store it with each vertex. Refer to Chapter 15 for details on how to calculate normals. Most models already store the normal data with each vertex used to build the model. These normal vectors are used to reflect light when a light source shines on them. When you are implementing lighting with a vertex shader, more normals will offer higher-definition lighting. You will definitely want to use more vertices for your vertex shader–based lighting; otherwise, the effect will fall flat. To increase performance, when using large numbers of vertices, you should consider using an index buffer for rendering primitive objects with vertex shader–based lighting.

IMPLEMENTING DIRECTIONAL LIGHTING USING XNA'S BASICEFFECT CLASS

As mentioned in Chapter 6, XNA includes the `BasicEffect` class to access and implement built-in shader effects. This class exposes methods for setting shader properties to assist in implementing directional lighting. In Chapter 14, the `BasicEffect` class is used to implement default lighting for the models. It is a fuss-free way of getting decent lighting quickly.

BasicEffect Default Lighting

The easiest way to implement lighting with the `BasicEffect` class is to use the `EnableDefaultLighting()` method, which automatically sets directional lighting for you.

When implementing either default lighting or custom lighting with the `BasicEffect` class, you must set the `LightingEnabled` property to `true`:

```
public bool             LightingEnabled { get; set; }
```

Regardless of the type, light is simulated with adjustments to the brightness and coloration of an object. The color is usually stored in a vector. You can get and set global lighting color properties with the following methods:

```
public Vector3          AmbientLightColor { get; set; }
public Vector3          DiffuseColor { get; set; }
public Vector3          SpecularColor { get; set; }
public float            SpecularPower { get; set; }
```

Default lighting turns on three directional lights, which you can choose to disable or alter as needed. You don't actually need to use the default lighting. Instead, you can enable each directional light and customize it as you choose. Each directional light has an Enabled, Direction, DiffuseColor, and SpecularColor property that you can get or set:

```
bool    DirectionalLight0.Enabled
Vector3 DirectionalLight0.Direction
Vector3 DirectionalLight0.DiffuseColor
Vector3 DirectionalLight0.SpecularColor
bool    DirectionalLight1.Enabled
Vector3 DirectionalLight1.Direction
Vector3 DirectionalLight1.DiffuseColor
Vector3 DirectionalLight1.SpecularColor
bool    DirectionalLight2.Enabled
Vector3 DirectionalLight2.Direction
Vector3 DirectionalLight2.DiffuseColor
Vector3 DirectionalLight2.SpecularColor
```

XNA's default lighting option is a great way to quickly generate decent-looking directional light.

Directional lighting under the BasicEffect class is especially effective for lighting 3D models because it is easy to set up. For this case, the BasicEffect class implements lighting through the vertex shader. When the vertex data is sent to the pixel shader, it is interpolated between vertices. The definition of the light is enhanced with more vertices, so you may want to consider reducing the storage requirements by using an index buffer when drawing primitive objects.

Directional Lighting Example

This example implements directional lighting with XNA's BasicEffect class. Because the BasicEffect class implements vertex lighting, more vertices are needed for smoother application of light across the object surface or a higher definition of light. Higher-definition light is especially noticeable for specular lighting.

Because many vertices for storing surface normals are needed to enhance the lighting when the BasicEffect shader is used, this example uses our friend the index buffer. This demonstration starts with the solution from Chapter 11, section titled "Grid Using Index Buffer Example," which already has an index buffer set up. Surface normals are needed in the example. Figure 22-1 shows a before (left) and after (right) look at how directional lighting from this demonstration will change the look of the environment.

The subtle effect directional lighting has on detail makes it exciting to use. Most of the time, directional lighting is implemented in a daytime setting, so there will already be a high level of ambience and diffuse lighting around to brighten the area.

FIGURE 22-1

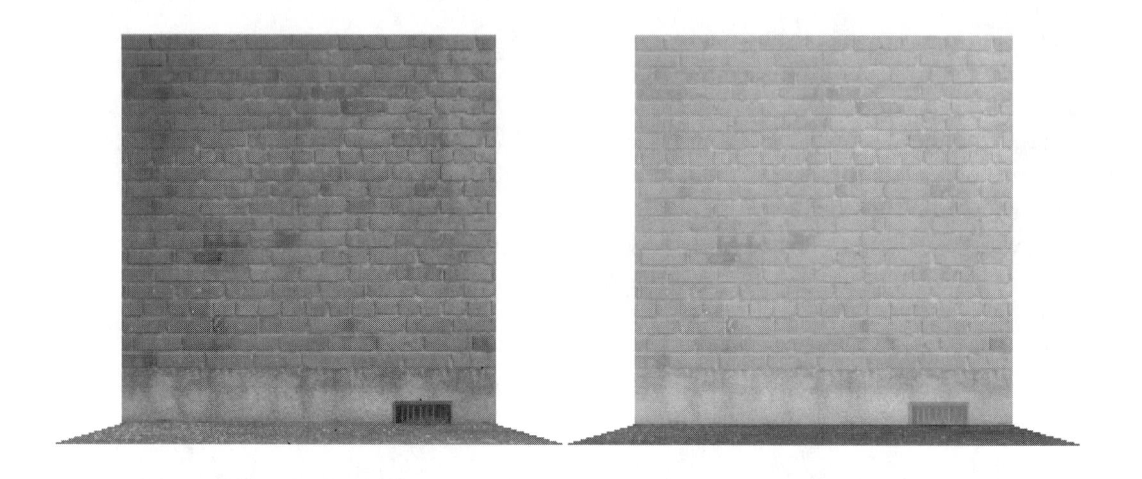

Before and after directional lighting

With the `BasicEffect` class, the specular light increases the brightness of the primitive surface face.

Once you have the original index buffer solution from Chapter 11 open, you may notice that the `PositionColorTexture` type was used to store the vertex data. This needs to change because normal data is also required to enable lighting. A few minor changes are needed. To implement lighting with a vertex that stores normal data, you must add a new `VertexDeclaration` to the top of the game class:

```
private VertexDeclaration positionNormalTexture;
```

The vertex declaration must be initialized when the program begins. This can be done by adding the statement to initialize it with a `VertexPositionNormalTexture` vertex type in `InitializeBaseCode()`:

```
positionNormalTexture = new VertexDeclaration(graphics.GraphicsDevice,
                        VertexPositionNormalTexture.VertexElements);
```

We almost have what we need. To change the vertex type, inside `InitializeVertexBuffer()` replace the instruction that sets the color property with an instruction to store the normal. The vertices stored in this method are used to draw a ground surface, so a suitable normal vector is X = 0.0f, Y = 1.0f, and Z = 0.0f:

```
vertex[col + row * NUM_COLS].Normal = new Vector3(0.0f, 1.0f, 0.0f);
```

To complete the change to enable normal data storage, inside `InitializeVertexBuffer()` replace each of the references to `VertexPositionColorTexture` with the following:

```
VertexPositionNormalTexture
```

A higher number of vertices will improve the definition of the lighting. You can easily increase the total vertices by adjusting the definitions for the row and column totals, which define the vertices used to build the indexed surface. To ensure that you have a suitable number of vertices to display the light for this demonstration, replace the current row and column definitions with these modified declarations:

```
const int NUM_COLS = 20;
const int NUM_ROWS = 20;
```

Now that a set of vertices is in place to enable high-definition lighting, changes can be made to implement the lighting using XNA's built-in `BasicEffect` shader. A reference to it is needed in the game class:

```
BasicEffect basicEffect;
```

To set up the `BasicEffect` object to apply lighting to a textured primitive, you must set the `TextureEnabled` and `LightingEnabled` properties to `true`. In this example, a fairly high level of ambient lighting is set, and the specular power is set to a noticeable level. Only one directional light is enabled, and the diffuse and specular color properties are set. The RGB color properties, for each type of light, range between 0 and 1. The direction is normalized to ensure consistent direction on the X, Y, and Z planes. Finally, the directional light is set to shine downward on the Y axis (-1) and inward on the Z axis (-1).

```
private void InitializeBasicEffect(){
    basicEffect = new BasicEffect(graphics.GraphicsDevice, null);
    basicEffect.TextureEnabled  = true; // needed if objects are textured
    basicEffect.LightingEnabled = true; // must be on for lighting effect
    basicEffect.SpecularPower   = 5.0f; // highlights
    basicEffect.AmbientLightColor
                    = new Vector3(0.6f, 0.6f, 0.5f);  // background light
    basicEffect.DirectionalLight0.Enabled = true;     // turn on light
    basicEffect.DirectionalLight0.DiffuseColor        // diffuse color
                    = new Vector3(0.2f, 0.2f, 0.2f);  // rgb range 0 to 1
    basicEffect.DirectionalLight0.SpecularColor       // highlight color
```

```
                 = new Vector3(0.5f, 0.5f, 0.37f); // rgb range 0 to 1
    basicEffect.DirectionalLight0.Direction          // set normalized
    = Vector3.Normalize(new Vector3(0.0f,-1.0f,-1.0f));// direction
}
```

To initialize the BasicEffect properties when the program begins, you call InitializeBasicEffect() from Initialize():

```
InitializeBasicEffect();
```

You need two Texture2D objects to store and apply the floor and wall images. To do this, add these object declarations at the top of your game class:

```
private Texture2D floorTexture;
private Texture2D wallTexture;
```

Of course, be sure to add the corresponding Stonefloor.jpg and Brickwall.jpg files (available from the Images folder on this book's website) to your project's Images folder under the Content node so they can be loaded when the program runs. When these images are referenced in your project, you will be able to load them when the following load instructions are placed inside the LoadContent() method:

```
wallTexture  = Content.Load<Texture2D>("Images\\Brickwall");
floorTexture = Content.Load<Texture2D>("Images\\Stonefloor");
```

Next is the code to draw the grid. Most of the code is used to set up the transformation to move each surface into place. The Texture property for the BasicEffect object is set to the appropriate Texture2D object if either the floor or wall is being drawn. The World, View, and Projection matrices are set to position the surfaces properly in the camera's view. The view also provides the BasicEffect class with information on the viewer's Look direction, which will help implement specular lighting. The GraphicsDevice's VertexDeclaration property is set with the *positionNormalTexture* variable to assign it the VertexPositionTextureNormal format for data retrieval and rendering. All drawing performed by the BasicEffect shader is done between the Begin() and End() for each pass. Replace the existing version of DrawIndexedGrid() with this revision to render the stone wall and ground texture surfaces:

```
private void DrawIndexedGrid(string surfaceName){
    // 1: declare matrices
    Matrix world, translate, rotationX, scale, rotationY;

    // 2: initialize matrices
```

```
scale     = Matrix.CreateScale(0.8f, 0.8f, 0.8f);
rotationY = Matrix.CreateRotationY(0.0f);
rotationX = Matrix.CreateRotationX(0.0f);
translate = Matrix.CreateTranslation(0.0f, -3.6f, 0.0f);

// create two walls with normals that face the user
if (surfaceName == "wall"){
    rotationX = Matrix.CreateRotationX(MathHelper.Pi/2.0f);
    translate = Matrix.CreateTranslation(0.0f, 9.20f,-12.8f);
    basicEffect.Texture = wallTexture;
}
else if(surfaceName == "ground")
    basicEffect.Texture = floorTexture;// set ground image

// 3: build cumulative world matrix using I.S.R.O.T. sequence
// identity, scale, rotate, orbit(translate & rotate), translate
world = scale * rotationX * rotationY * translate;

// 4: finish setting shader variables
basicEffect.World       = world;
basicEffect.Projection  = cam.projectionMatrix;
basicEffect.View        = cam.viewMatrix;

// 5: draw object
graphics.GraphicsDevice.VertexDeclaration = positionNormalTexture;
graphics.GraphicsDevice.Vertices[0].SetSource(vertexBuffer, 0,
                        VertexPositionNormalTexture.SizeInBytes);
graphics.GraphicsDevice.Indices           = indexBuffer;

// avoid drawing back face for large numbers of vertices
graphics.GraphicsDevice.RenderState.CullMode =
                        CullMode.CullClockwiseFace;
basicEffect.Begin();

foreach (EffectPass pass in basicEffect.CurrentTechnique.Passes){
    pass.Begin();
    graphics.GraphicsDevice.Vertices[0].SetSource(vertexBuffer, 0,
                            VertexPositionNormalTexture.SizeInBytes);
    // draw grid one row at a time
    for (int Z = 0; Z < NUM_ROWS - 1; Z++){
        graphics.GraphicsDevice.DrawIndexedPrimitives(
```

```
            PrimitiveType.TriangleStrip, // primitive type
            Z * NUM_COLS,                // start point in vertex buffer
            0,                           // vertex buffer offset
            NUM_COLS * NUM_ROWS,         // total verts in vertex buffer
            0,                           // index buffer offset
            2 * (NUM_COLS - 1));         // index buffer end
        }
        pass.End();
    }
    basicEffect.End();
   // disable culling
   graphics.GraphicsDevice.RenderState.CullMode = CullMode.None;
}
```

To draw the textured wall and floor surfaces using the same vertex and index buffer, replace the call to `DrawIndexedGrid()` with these two instructions:

```
DrawIndexedGrid("wall");
DrawIndexedGrid("ground");
```

When you run this program, you will notice how the walls are brightened by the light. Try experimenting with the normal and direction values and notice their effect on the brightness level. Also, try changing the ambient RGB color values to 1.0f. Notice that other lights no longer have an effect as long as ambience is at full strength. Increase the specular value to 50.0f and notice how the highlights on the ground and wall radiate.

IMPLEMENTING POINT LIGHT USING THE PHONG REFLECTION MODEL

Once you have directional lighting working, you may want more lighting effects to differentiate a constant source of sunlight from lighting that has a position and range. Scenes that take place outside, during the day, may be fine with directional light. Scenes that are located indoors, or that take place at night, are going to need a different type of light. Point light offers a dramatic way to reveal the details of your 3D world by creating a sphere of light that can brighten the surrounding area. Point light is used to radiate light from a light bulb, fire, torch, or lantern.

When building point light, we use the Phong reflection model to describe the relationship between ambient, diffuse, and reflective light. The model is actually very simple. It was authored by Bui Tuong Phong in 1973. The simplicity and effectiveness of the Phong reflection model has made it a popular method for computer-generated lighting simulations even today. Phong's reflection model states that the shade value for each surface point equals

```
Ambient Color * Ambient Intensity
  + Diffuse Color  * Diffuse Intensity * N.L
  + Specular Color * Specular Intensity * (R.V)^α
```

where

```
L = Light direction
V = Viewpoint vector
N = Surface normal
R = Reflection vector = 2 * (N.L) * N - L
α = An exponential factor for specular light that varies according
    to the user
```

Figure 22-2 illustrates how the Phong reflection model implements light, normal, view, and reflection vectors to predict values for ambient, diffuse, and reflective light.

The angle θ decreases as the view vector and reflection vector converge. As θ decreases, cos θ increases and the specular or shiny reflection increases. The specular light is brightest when the view direction is exactly opposite to the reflection vector.

As α decreases, the diffuse light increases. In other words, the directional reflection is brightest when the light shines in a direction directly opposite to the normal vector.

FIGURE 22-2

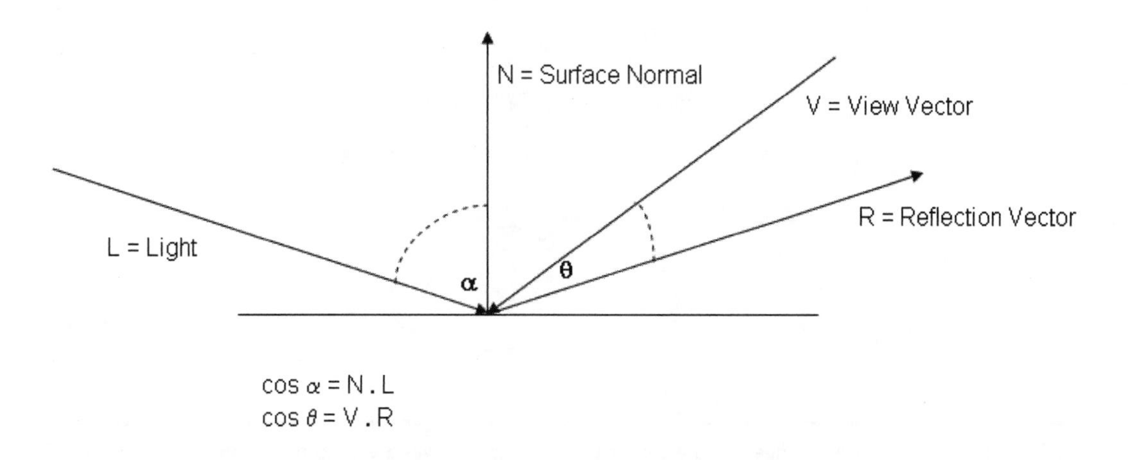

Lighting vectors used in the Phong reflection model

If you need to understand the math in more detail, or you need a refresher on dot products and vector math, consider reviewing Chapter 15.

Calculating Point Light

Because point light shines in all directions, when you are calculating the diffuse component for each pixel, or vertex, the light direction vector can be calculated by subtracting the surface position from the point light position. The dot product of the light direction and surface normal gives the cosine of the angle between them. As the angle becomes smaller, in more direct light, the cosine approaches 1—which yields a light with full intensity. Therefore, the brightest light appears on the portion of the surface that is closest to the light; from there the light fades outward. The result is a great-looking globe of light in the center, with the light fading away from the center. Figure 22-3 shows the relationship between the light position and normal vector. The portion of the surface that is closest to the point light is the brightest, and the light fades outward as the angle between the light vector and surface normal increases.

FIGURE 22-3

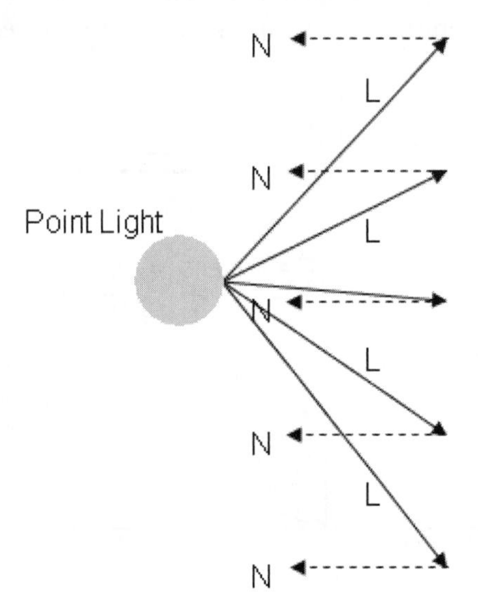

The dot product L.N is strongest at the center and fades as it moves away from the center.

Point Light in the Pixel Shader Example

The next example demonstrates a point light implementation in the pixel shader. It shows how to add a point light that moves with your camera as you travel through the world. If you wanted, you could easily set the position of this light to a constant value to simulate a stationary indoor light bulb. When you complete this example, a constant directionless light will illuminate your way. You can imagine using this sort of effect for a player's torch. If you wanted, this code could be modified to add a flicker to the light source to simulate a torch, a candle, a lantern, or a fire.

When the lighting calculations are performed in the pixel shader, the shading is automatically interpolated between pixels to show a gorgeously smooth, shiny light in the 3D world. Bear in mind that the processing demands of performing pixel-shading operations are expensive, so this effect needs to be used sparingly. However, it is attractive, and you can use it to liven up the parts of your game that you want noticed. After this demonstration of point light in the pixel shader, we'll view another example that shows how to perform the same calculations from the vertex shader when you feel the need for speed. Vertex shader–based lighting is not as attractive as lighting from the pixel shader, but it still delivers a punch.

The pixel shader–based point light does not actually need many vertices to produce high-definition light. This is because the pixel shader interpolates lighting between pixels. Even so, this example begins with the solution from the previous example, which uses an index buffer that offers potential for using large sets of vertices. You could actually skip the index buffer for pixel shader–based light. However, when this same example is converted to implement lighting from the vertex shader, you will want a larger number of vertices to produce high-definition lighting, so the index buffer is being used.

This example begins with the solution from the previous example. The shader code is contained in the PointLightPS.fx file, which can be found in the Shaders folder on this book's website. To try this illuminating example, add the PointLightPS.fx file to the Shaders folder in your project. All of the shader code in the PointLightPS.fx file will be presented here in sequential order so that you can see how the point light is generated.

Point Light Example: The Shader Code

The globals section of the shader declares values that are accessed by the effect parameters in the game application. The global values allow you to send in different values for the camera and transformation matrices, textures, point light color, and point light intensity:

```
float4x4    wvpMatrix;
float4x4    worldMatrix;
```

```
float4      lightPosition;
float4      color;
float       lightIntensity;
Texture     textureImage;
```

Because the lighting is going to be applied to an image, the texture effect parameter and sampler will also be included. A texture sampler, like the one used in Chapter 9, defines how to filter your images:

```
sampler textureSampler          = sampler_state{
    Texture                     = (textureImage);
    Minfilter                   = LINEAR;
    Magfilter                   = LINEAR;
    Mipfilter                   = LINEAR;
};
```

The input struct for the vertex shader allows you to retrieve and manipulate the position, normal, and texture data for each vertex:

```
struct VSinput{
    float4 position             : POSITION0;
    float3 normal               : NORMAL0;
    float2 UV                   : TEXCOORD0;
};
```

The output struct from the vertex shader gives you control over the data that you send to the pixel shader. The position is computed by multiplying the vertex by the WVP matrix so it can be viewed properly by the camera. However, the position is also expressed as *transformedPosition*, which is the normalized product of the vertex position multiplied by the cumulative transformation matrix. *transformedPosition* will be used in the pixel shader to compute the light direction vector for the point light. The normal, *normal*, is also transformed and normalized, so it too can be used in the pixel shader to compute the dot product between the light vector, L, and the normal vector, N. Additional texture semantics allow you to pass your calculated data to the pixel shader from the vertex shader.

```
struct VStoPS{
    float4 position             : POSITION;  // position for view & cam
    float3 transformedPosition  : TEXCOORD0; // transformed position
    float2 UV                   : TEXCOORD1; // uv data
    float3 normal               : TEXCOORD2; // unit normal
    float4 ambientColor         : COLOR0;
};
```

In most cases, the pixel shader output is just a color for each pixel. By the time the output has been generated for each pixel, the pixel shader will have blended a shade of color against the texture. The color is altered by the light—hence the light is just a shade of color. The struct used for the pixel shader output only returns an RGBA color vector:

```
struct PSoutput{
    float4 color                    : COLOR;
};
```

The effect of ambience can easily be simulated by multiplying an RGBA color vector by an intensity coefficient. In your shader code, you can decide how much ambience you want to add. For this example, the ambient light intensity has been turned down to 0.1f to allow you to see the effect of the specular and diffuse point light:

```
float4 AmbientLight(){
    // ambient is just a color vector*intensity
    float4 color                    = (1.0f, 1.0f, 1.0f, 1.0f);
    float intensity                 = 0.05f;
    return color*intensity;
}
```

A yellow specular light has been added to make the brick wall look as if it is covered with a bright finish. You will notice the yellow shine as you move closer to the wall.

If your object should have a glossy sheen—like a brand new Corvette—you will need a high level of specular light. Phong's reflection model calculates specular highlights using the reflection vector and the view direction. The equation to generate the specular light is

```
Specular Color * Specular Intensity * (R .V)^α
```

where R = 2 * N.L * N – L.

`SpecularLight()` implements this calculation to return an RGBA vector with color added to represent the specular light:

```
float4 SpecularLight(VStoPS IN){
    float4 specularColor;
    float4 intensity                = 0.2f;
    float4 color                    = { 1.0f, 1.0f, 0.0f, 1.0f };
    float3 unitNormal               = IN.normal; // N
    float3 lightDirection
          = normalize(lightPosition - IN.transformedPosition);
```

```
    float3 unitDirection        = normalize(lightDirection); // L
    // (N.L) - dot product of surface normal and light direction
    float cosine                = dot(unitNormal, unitDirection);
    // R = 2*(N.L)*N - L
    float3 reflection    = normalize(2*cosine*unitNormal - unitDirection);
    // (R.V)^n specular reflection.
    float specularLevel = pow(dot(reflection, unitDirection), 2);
    specularColor        = color*intensity*specularLevel;
    return specularColor;
}
```

The diffuse light is simply the dot product between the light direction vector and the object being lit. The dot product approaches 1 for full intensity with the directness of the light to the surface. When this calculation is done in the pixel shader, the result is interpolated between pixels to produce a nice, smooth-looking light. As you move the camera closer to the wall, the light radiates brightly and fizzles outward from the point that is directly in front of the camera. Diffuse light is modeled by the following equation:

$$Diffuse_{Color} * Diffuse_{Intensity} * N.L$$

To make the light fade from the center even more dramatic, the light intensity is scaled with a *fallOff* variable. *fallOff* is the inverted exponent of the scaled distance, d, between the light and pixel. *exp(d)* equals e^d where e is approximately 2.718281828.

Because N.L = cos α, as the angle between the surface normal and light vector decreases, cos α approaches 1 and diffuse light increases. Shining a light directly at a surface normal generates a brighter reflection than a light shone at an angle away from the normal vector. `PointLightDiffuse()` calculates the color added by the diffuse light:

```
float4 PointLightDiffuse(VStoPS IN){
    // unit direction of light vector L
    float3 lightDirection
                    = normalize(lightPosition - IN.transformedPosition);
    // brightest angle between L and N = 0
    float diffuseLevel = dot(lightDirection, IN.normal);

    // get distance from light to pixel
    float distance = distance(lightPosition, IN.transformedPosition);
```

```
    // compute a falloff for the lighting
    float scale = 0.2f;
    float fallOff = clamp(1.0f / exp(distance * scale), 0, 1);

    // adjust the light intensity based on the falloff
    lightIntensity *= fallOff;

    // point light diffuse*intensity and color
    return diffuseLevel * lightIntensity * color;
}
```

The point light vertex shader receives the vertex position, texture, and normal data. The position in the window is generated by multiplying the position by the WVP matrix so that each vertex can be seen properly by the camera. *transformedPosition* is calculated by normalizing the product of the position and World matrix, so this unit vector can be used in the specular and diffuse lighting calculations. The normal vector is also transformed with the World matrix and is then normalized for the specular and diffuse calculations. Ambient light is uniform across the entire surface, so this calculation is performed in the vertex shader to save a little processing time:

```
void VertexShader(in VSinput IN, out VStoPS OUT){
    OUT.position          = mul(IN.position, wvpMatrix);
    OUT.transformedPosition
                          = mul(IN.position, worldMatrix);
    OUT.normal            = normalize(mul(IN.normal, (float3x3)worldMatrix));
    OUT.UV                = IN.UV;
    OUT.ambientColor      = AmbientLight();
}
```

The pixel shader combines the different lights together and blends them with the texture for each pixel. The sum of the ambient, specular, and diffuse light component vectors is equivalent to the combination of different lighting components in Phong's reflection model.

```
void PixelShader(in VStoPS IN, out PSoutput OUT){
    float4 diffuseColor  = PointLightDiffuse(IN);
    float4 specularColor = SpecularLight(IN);
    OUT.color            = tex2D(textureSampler,IN.UV)
                         *(IN.ambientColor+specularColor+diffuseColor);
}
```

The technique is identical to others used before this chapter for compiling the vertex and pixel shaders and for calling them:

```
technique PointLightShader{
    pass p0{
        sampler[0]      = (textureSampler);
        vertexshader    = compile vs_2_0 VertexShader();  // set up vs
        pixelshader     = compile ps_2_0 PixelShader();   // set up ps
    }
}
```

It is amazing that such a small amount of shader code can generate such a great lighting effect.

Point Light Example: The XNA Code

All of the shader code just described can be found in the PointLightPS.fx file in the Shaders folder on this book's website. Be sure to add this file to your project in the Shaders folder.

To assist in setting the matrices for the shader, and to provide position data for the lighting calculations, the effect parameters *lightEffectWorld*, *lightEffectWVP*, and *lightEffectPosition* are declared. A texture parameter, *lightEffectTexture*, allows you to set the image applied in the shader from the C# code. The parameter *lightEffectIntensity* lets you set the intensity of the diffuse point light at run time from the application, and *lightEffectColor* allows you to set the color of the light. Add these declarations to the game class module level so you can set these shader variables from your C# code:

```
private Effect          lightEffect;              // point light shader
private EffectParameter lightEffectWorld;         // world matrix
private EffectParameter lightEffectWVP;           // wvp matrix
private EffectParameter lightEffectPosition;      // light position
private EffectParameter lightEffectIntensity;     // point light strength
private EffectParameter lightEffectTexture;       // texture
private EffectParameter lightEffectColor;         // color of point light
```

To be able to use your shader, you must load and compile it when the program starts. Add code to set up the shader in `Initialize()`:

```
lightEffect          = Content.Load<Effect>("Shaders\\PointLightPS");
```

To set the data in the shader variables at run time, you must initialize the effect parameters to reference the correct shader variables when the program begins. To make this possible, assign the effect parameters to their corresponding shader variables from `Initialize()`:

```
lightEffectWVP       = lightEffect.Parameters["wvpMatrix"];
lightEffectWorld     = lightEffect.Parameters["worldMatrix"];
lightEffectPosition  = lightEffect.Parameters["lightPosition"];
lightEffectIntensity = lightEffect.Parameters["lightIntensity"];
lightEffectTexture   = lightEffect.Parameters["textureImage"];
lightEffectColor     = lightEffect.Parameters["color"];
```

The `LightingShader()` method is needed in the game class to apply the PointLightPS.fx shader while drawing with vertices while using an index buffer:

```
private void LightingShader(PrimitiveType primitiveType){
    // avoid drawing back face for large amounts of vertices
    graphics.GraphicsDevice.RenderState.CullMode =
                            CullMode.CullClockwiseFace;
    lightEffect.Begin();
    lightEffect.Techniques[0].Passes[0].Begin();

    // 5: draw object - select vertex type, primitive type, index, & draw
    graphics.GraphicsDevice.VertexDeclaration = positionNormalTexture;
    graphics.GraphicsDevice.Indices           = indexBuffer;
    graphics.GraphicsDevice.Vertices[0].SetSource(vertexBuffer, 0,
                            VertexPositionNormalTexture.SizeInBytes);
    // draw grid one row at a time
    for (int Z = 0; Z < NUM_ROWS - 1; Z++){
        graphics.GraphicsDevice.DrawIndexedPrimitives(
            primitiveType,              // primitive
            Z * NUM_COLS,               // start point in vertex
            0,                          // vertex buffer offset
            NUM_COLS * NUM_ROWS,        // total verts in vertex buffer
            0,                          // start point in index buffer
            2 * (NUM_COLS - 1));        // end point in index buffer
    }
    // end shader
    lightEffect.Techniques[0].Passes[0].End();
    lightEffect.End();
    // disable back face culling
    graphics.GraphicsDevice.RenderState.CullMode = CullMode.None;
}
```

Most of the code used to draw the primitive surface has been explained in previous chapters. This includes transforming the object and drawing the vertices using an index buffer reference. Also, the shader's effect parameters are used here to move the point light with the camera, to set the diffuse light intensity, and to set the texture value. In step 4 of the code, the global variables in the shader are assigned values for the WVP matrix and the World matrix. This combination allows you to generate light in the view space and then to render the objects based on the World matrix. Replace the existing version of `DrawIndexedGrid()` with the following code to draw the surfaces with the point light shader:

```
private void DrawIndexedGrid(string surfaceName){
    // 1: declare matrices
    Matrix world, translate, rotateX, scale, rotateY;

    // 2: initialize matrices
    translate   = Matrix.CreateTranslation(0.0f, -3.6f, 0.0f);
    scale       = Matrix.CreateScale(0.8f, 0.8f, 0.8f);
    rotateY     = Matrix.CreateRotationY(0.0f);
    rotateX     = Matrix.CreateRotationX(0.0f);

    if (surfaceName == "wall"){          // set parameters for wall
        rotateX     = Matrix.CreateRotationX(MathHelper.Pi/2.0f);
        translate   = Matrix.CreateTranslation(0.0f, 9.20f, -12.8f);
        lightEffectTexture.SetValue(wallTexture);
    }
    else if (surfaceName == "ground")    // set parameters for ground
        lightEffectTexture.SetValue(floorTexture);

    // 3: build cumulative world matrix using I.S.R.O.T. sequence
    // identity, scale, rotate, orbit(translate & rotate), translate
    world = scale * rotateX * rotateY * translate;

    // 4: pass parameters to shader
    lightEffectWVP.SetValue(world*cam.viewMatrix*cam.projectionMatrix);
    lightEffectWorld.SetValue(world);
    lightEffectPosition.SetValue(new Vector4(cam.position, 1.0f));
    lightEffectIntensity.SetValue(2.0f);
    lightEffectColor.SetValue(new Vector4(1.0f, 1.0f, 1.0f, 1.0f));

    // 5: draw object - select vertex type, primitive type, index, and draw
    LightingShader(PrimitiveType.TriangleStrip);
}
```

If you compile and run the project, you will see the point light traveling with the camera. Move closer to the wall, and the light reflected back will become brighter because the point light is closer to the wall surface.

Figure 22-4 shows the point light positioned above the center of the ground. The light is brightest directly beneath the light—hopefully this will help you see the point of point light!

Point Light in the Vertex Shader Example

You won't always be able to afford pixel-based lighting, because it is expensive for the processor. Moving specular and diffuse lighting calculations into the vertex shader will drastically reduce the number of times these calculations need to be made each frame. The ambient, diffuse, and specular light can be combined in one color variable in the vertex shader, which can then be sent to the pixel shader so that the pixel shader doesn't have to generate it. When this color data is sent to the pixel shader, it is automatically interpolated between vertices. Using more vertices provides more definition and smoother shading; so for this method to be effective, an index buffer is recommended for primitive surfaces.

This example begins with the solution from the previous example. You could follow the steps here to modify the shader to implement vertex shader–based point

FIGURE 22-4

Point light demo

light, or you could just load and reference the PointLightVS.fx file in place of the PointLightPS.fx file in your project to implement it.

Once you have changed your shader reference, you will need to load the new shader from `Initialize()` when the program begins:

```
lightEffect = Content.Load<Effect>("Shaders\\PointLightVS");
```

With this change, less information needs to be passed to the pixel shader, so a new struct for the vertex shader output is used. This struct is already added to the PointLightVS.fx file for you. However, if you are modifying the effect file from the previous example you will need to add this new struct.

```
struct VStoPS2{
    float4 position    : POSITION0;
    float4 color       : COLOR;
    float2 UV          : TEXCOORD0;
};
```

The revised version of the vertex shader uses the new struct to define the output. Note that the calculations for all lights are now performed in the vertex shader. The color variable that is sent to the pixel shader stores the sum of the ambient, diffuse, and specular lights. Replace the existing vertex shader with this revised version to process the lighting calculations before sending the output to the pixel shader:

```
void VertexShader(in VSinput IN, out VStoPS2 OUT){
    VStoPS vsData; // original output values used for color calculation
    vsData.transformedPosition = mul(IN.position, worldMatrix);
    vsData.normal      = normalize(mul(IN.normal, (float3x3)worldMatrix));
    vsData.position    = mul(IN.position, wvpMatrix);
    vsData.UV          = IN.UV;

    OUT.position           = vsData.position;          // position output
    OUT.UV                 = vsData.UV;                // uv output
    vsData.ambientColor    = AmbientLight();           // color output
    float4 diffuseColor    = PointLightDiffuse(vsData);
    float4 specularColor = SpecularLight(vsData);
    OUT.color = (vsData.ambientColor + specularColor + diffuseColor);
}
```

A slight change is made in the pixel shader to receive the new vertex shader output, which already includes the combined ambient, diffuse, and specular light:

```
void PixelShader(in VStoPS2 IN, out PSoutput OUT){
    OUT.color = tex2D(textureSampler, IN.UV)*(IN.color);
}
```

To view a stationary point light, in your XNA code, set the position of the light to a constant value. (Or you could continue to move the light with your camera if you prefer.) You can make the position of the point light stationary by replacing the instruction that moves the light with the camera in `DrawIndexedGrid()`:

```
lightEffectPosition.SetValue(new Vector4(0.0f, 0.0f, 0.0f, 1.0f));
```

When you run this version of the code, you will still see the point light. It will not be defined as much as the pixel shader point light, but you may notice a performance boost when running it.

A simple lighting system, such as a lone directional light or the sun, can add depth to your game and reveal the details in your environment. Point light can add intriguing details for night-time or indoor settings. As you can see, the effect is quite brilliant.

CHAPTER 22 REVIEW EXERCISES

To get the most from this chapter, try out these chapter review exercises.

1. Complete the step-by-step examples presented in this chapter, if you have not already done so.
2. After completing the directional light demonstration using the `BasicEffect` object, try reducing the number of vertices that are stored in the vertex buffer by lowering the number of rows and columns to two each. Run the demo again (after this change has been made) and notice how the specular detail diminishes. Then, increase the total number of vertices for rows and columns to 50 each. Notice how the specular lighting's effect improves with more vertices.
3. Using the directional light example, change the Y value of the normal in the vertex buffer from +1 to –1. Notice how everything turns black. Explain why this happens.
4. What is a useful intensity level for ambient light during daytime settings in the directional light demo? What is a useful intensity level for ambient light during evening settings in the directional light demo?

CHAPTER 23

Input Devices

EFFECTIVELY handling input is fundamental to every gamer's experience. Nowadays, this means that you need to support the keyboard, mouse, Xbox 360 game controller, Zune controls, and possibly even a wireless racing wheel. The XNA Framework greatly simplifies this task. Specifically, the `Microsoft.Xna.Framework.Input` namespace enables the capture of button press and release events, mouse click events, keyboard presses and game controller button, thumbstick, DPad, and trigger events. You can even use the Input library to send rumbles to users' controllers to let them know when they have exploded.

This chapter focuses primarily on the input handling library for the Xbox 360 and PC. Zune input handling is performed with a subset of this library. A discussion of Zune input handling and an example are included at the end of this chapter.

HANDLING KEYBOARD INPUT

The Input library handles press and release events for all common keyboard keys. To view a full listing of key identifiers, type **Keys.** in the Game Studio code window. This will open a drop-down menu that displays all identifiers available. These are the identifiers for common keyboard keys, as listed in Table 23-1.

TABLE 23-1

A to Z	*Home*	*PageUp*
Add	*Insert*	*PrintScreen*
CapsLock	*Left*	*Right*
D0 to D9	*LeftAlt*	*RightAlt*
Decimal	*LeftControl*	*RightControl*
Delete	*LeftShift*	*RightShift*
Divide	*LeftWindows*	*RightWindows*
Down	*Multiply*	*Scroll*
End	*NumLock*	*Space*
Enter	*NumPad0 to*	*Subtract*
Escape	*NumPad9*	*Tab*
F1 to F12	*PageDown*	*Up*
Help		

Common keyboard keys

D0 to D9 refer to the numbers at the top of the keyboard, whereas keys on the number pad use NumPad0 to NumPad9.

You will capture key events using a `KeyboardState` object. At each frame, this object is updated by polling the keyboard with the `GetState()` method:

```
KeyboardState keyboardState = Keyboard.GetState();
```

Individual key events are distinguished with the `IsKeyDown()` method using a `Keys` identifier as a parameter:

```
bool KeyboardState.IsKeyDown(Keys Keys.Identifier);
```

HANDLING MOUSE INPUT

In many PC versions of major game titles, and even for the 3D graphics engine used in this book, the mouse can be used to control the player's direction. The `Input` namespace enables handling of mouse-based events. Mouse movements and click events are detected with a `MouseState` object. Every frame, the state of the mouse is refreshed with the `GetState()` method, which retrieves information about the cursor's position and the press state of the mouse buttons:

```
MouseState mouseState = Mouse.GetState();
```

With these continuous updates, the `MouseState` object's X and Y properties track the cursor's position in the game window:

```
int MouseState.X
int MouseState.Y
```

Press and release states of each mouse button are retrieved from the `ButtonState` property of each button. Most mice have a `MouseState.LeftButton` and `MouseState.RightButton` property, and some have a `MouseState.MiddleButton` property. The `ButtonState` attribute stores either a `Pressed` value, if the button is pressed, or a `Released` value, if it is not.

HANDLING CONTROLLER INPUT

In addition to the keyboard and mouse, the `Input` namespace also handles events for the game controller. The game controller itself provides several options to obtain user input through presses and shifts of the thumbstick, as well as presses to the DPad, buttons, left and right bumpers, and triggers. Figure 23-1 shows the name of each control.

Game Pad States

The `GamePadState` object for the controller allows you to check the state of each control on each game controller at every frame. Because it is possible to have up to four game controllers connected to your Xbox 360, the `GamePadState` object is often declared as an array with a size of four:

```
private GamePadState[] gamePadState = new GamePadState[4];
```

Although the array has room for up to four controllers, if only one controller is connected, this controller will use the first object in the array; it is referenced with zero as the index.

FIGURE 23-1

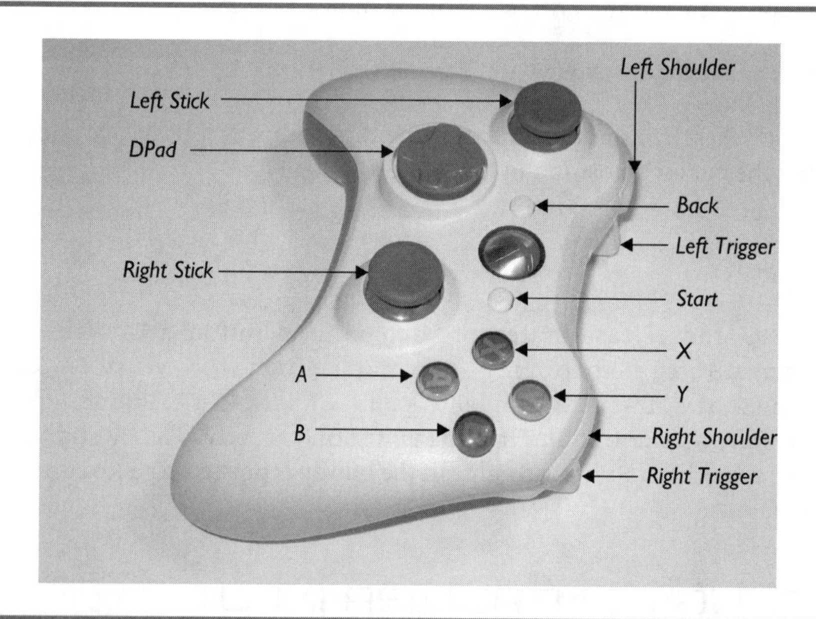

Names of individual controls on the controller

At every frame, the states for each game pad are retrieved with the `GetState()` method and `PlayerIndex` attribute to identify the controller:

```
gamePadState[0] = GamePad.GetState(PlayerIndex.One);
gamePadState[1] = GamePad.GetState(PlayerIndex.Two);
gamePadState[2] = GamePad.GetState(PlayerIndex.Three);
gamePadState[3] = GamePad.GetState(PlayerIndex.Four);
```

Handling Pressed and Released States

Most of the controls on the game controller use a `ButtonState.Pressed` and a `ButtonState.Released` attribute to indicate whether or not the control is pressed. Table 23-2 is a complete listing of controls that store either a `Pressed` or `Released` property.

Thumbsticks

Another way to enable user control is to use thumbsticks. They can be pushed up, down, and sideways to help with tasks such as controlling the player's view or guiding the direction of game characters. Each thumbstick stores a float to measure the deviation from its central resting position. The X and Y values range from -1 to +1, where 0 is the center position. These are the four possible thumbstick properties:

- `float ThumbSticks.Left.X`
- `float ThumbSticks.Left.Y`
- `float ThumbSticks.Right.X`
- `float ThumbSticks.Right.Y`

TABLE 23-2

Buttons.A	*Buttons.Right Shoulder*	*DPad.Down*
Buttons.B	*Buttons.RightStick*	*DPad.Left*
Buttons.Back	*Buttons.Start*	*DPad.Right*
Buttons.LeftShoulder	*Buttons.X*	*DPad.Up*
Buttons.LeftStick	*Buttons.Y*	

Game pad controls

Triggers

You can enable intuitive features such as acceleration or rapid firing with the Xbox 360 controller triggers. On every controller there is one left and one right trigger. Each trigger returns a float that ranges from 0 (for released) to 1 (for fully pressed).

```
float GamePadState.Triggers.Right
float GamePadState.Triggers.Left
```

Adjusting the Input Device Responsiveness

The responsiveness needed for input controls can vary depending on the purpose of the control. The `IsKeyDown()` method and `ButtonState.Pressed` property can be used to check whether a key, mouse button, or controller's DPad, button, or thumbstick is pressed. Similarly, the `Left` and `Right` properties of a trigger and the X and Y properties of a thumbstick will return nonzero values when moved away from their default positions. Most of the time, an immediate response at every frame is useful for events such as rapid fire or speed control. In other situations, press events might be used to toggle through a list of properties to choose a game character, select a map, change weapons, or even enter a name through an input device. When toggling states, tens or even hundreds of true `IsKeyDown()` events or `ButtonState.Pressed` states are registered between the time that the user first presses the control and releases it. For cases like these, it is helpful to compare the current key or button state with the previous one. The following code snippet shows how current and previous states are used to allow a player to alter the display values between "On" and "Off":

```
if (kbstate.IsKeyDown(Keys.T) && kbstatePrevious.IsKeyUp(Keys.T))
    if (keyT == "On")              // alternate On or Off status
        keyT = "Off";              // for keydown events
    else
        keyT = "On";
```

Adding a Rumble

The ability to make a controller rumble is a popular feature among gamers. Whether the player has crashed into a wall or is checked into the boards, sending a rumble through their controller will add to the effect. A rumble can be sent to the left and right sides of the game controller with the method `SetVibration()`. The vibration takes three parameters to identify the control and to set the strength of the rumble. The rumble strength is measured with a float that ranges from 0 to 1.

```
GamePad.SetVibration(int controllerNumber, float LRumble, float RRumble);
```

Input Example

This example demonstrates the handling of input from the keyboard, mouse, and game pad by drawing current information on their press, release, shift, and move states in the window. The cursor and mouse-based input will only appear in Windows, though, because the Xbox 360 is not designed to use mouse input.

To begin with a project that has fonts enabled, this example uses the "Font Example: Displaying Text in the Game Window" solution from Chapter 13. Some adjustments are required to prepare this solution to display the status of all input controls presented during this demonstration. The call to `DrawGround()` from the `Draw()` method should be disabled to clear the screen for drawing text only:

```
// DrawGround();
```

Also, because more data is being presented in this example, to view all of the text output, you need to change the size definition in the MyFont.spritefont file. You can do this by replacing the `<Size>` element with the following:

```
<Size>10</Size>
```

Handling Keyboard Input

Sometimes you will not have your game controller with you, or your intended audience may only have a keyboard and mouse as input devices. For this reason, when running your games on the PC, your code should always consider the keyboard as an alternative for user input.

To handle the input events, a reference to the `Microsoft.Xna.Framework.Input` namespace is required at the top of the Game1.cs file where the game class is located. For this case, the reference is already present, so you don't need to add it.

```
using Microsoft.Xna.Framework.Input;
```

This first portion of the demonstration shows whether or not the 0 on the keyboard, the 0 on the number pad, and the A key are pressed. To store a user-friendly description of each key state, strings are declared for each key to later display the key's current press or release status in the game window:

```
private String numPad0, key0, keyA, keyT;
```

To ensure accurate reporting of the input device status each frame, a function is required to poll the input device. In this routine, a `KeyboardState` object is refreshed each frame. A `KeyboardState` object declaration is needed at the top of the game class for this:

```
KeyboardState kbstate;
```

We will update the `KeyboardState` object with the `GetState()` method. Once the entire keyboard state has been updated, it is possible for you to check whether each key is pressed. If a key is pressed, the string that was defined earlier to display the key state for the key is set to `Pressed`. If the key is not pressed, the string retains a default value of `Released`. This value is set at the beginning of the algorithm. To implement this routine, you will add the `UpdateInputEvents()` method to your game class:

```
void UpdateInputEvents(){
    kbstate      = Keyboard.GetState();
    numPad0      = key0 = keyA = "released"; // refresh each frame

    if (kbstate.IsKeyDown(Keys.A))            // A pressed
        keyA    = "pressed";
    if (kbstate.IsKeyDown(Keys.D0))           // 0 pressed
        key0    = "pressed";
    if (kbstate.IsKeyDown(Keys.NumPad0))      // 0 on numberpad pressed
        numPad0 = "pressed";
}
```

To ensure continuous updates to the `KeyboardState` object, `UpdateInputEvents()` is called from the `Update()` method at every frame:

```
UpdateInputEvents();
```

Now that you have implemented continuous tracking of the A, 0 (keyboard), and 0 (number pad) keys, their status can be reported in the game window. `ShowString()` is a simple method that implements the `SpriteBatch`'s `DrawString()` method. The `ShowString()` method accepts the display string and the X,Y coordinates where that string is to be drawn. It then sets the output color when drawing the string. In this example, `ShowString()` needs to be placed in the game class to display the status of all input devices:

```
private void ShowString(String output, int X, int Y){
    spriteBatch.DrawString(spriteFont, output,
                  new Vector2((float)X, (float)Y), Color.Red);
}
```

This example uses a revision of the DrawFonts() method to trigger the display of the input device states. DrawFonts() first initializes the X and Y values within the title-safe region where new text is to be drawn. (The title-safe area has already been calculated in the code solution used to start this example and is explained in Chapter 13.) Then the ShowString() method is called to show the text in the window. To view the text output, you must replace the existing DrawFonts() method in the game class with this code:

```
private void DrawFonts(){
    Rectangle  drawArea;
    drawArea = TitleSafeRegion("Test string", spriteFont); // start pixel
    int X    = (int)drawArea.X;                            // starting X
    int Y    = (int)drawArea.Y;                            // starting Y

    ShowString("Keyboard            ", X, Y += 20);
    ShowString("               a:   " + keyA, X, Y += 20);
    ShowString("               0:   " + key0, X, Y += 20);
    ShowString("    numberpad 0:   " + numPad0,X, Y += 20);
}
```

The sprite batch will be used later to draw a cursor in addition to the font output. Also, the revised DrawFonts() method has a different signature than the original version. To ensure that you draw with the correct method and to set up the sprite batch so you can draw a cursor without having to reset the render states again, replace the existing DrawFonts() call from Draw() with these instructions:

```
// Start drawing font sprites. See Chapter 12 for a more
// efficient way to manually save and restore render states.
spriteBatch.Begin(SpriteBlendMode.AlphaBlend,  // enable transparency
                  SpriteSortMode.Immediate,    // use manual order
                  SaveStateMode.SaveState);    // store 3D settings

    DrawFonts();
// all 2D drawing above this line
spriteBatch.End();
```

Using Input Devices for Toggle Events

The method you just implemented for displaying the press or release status of the A, 0 (keyboard), and 0 (number pad) keys treats each frame as a separate event. However, sometimes a player may use a button, control, or key to select an option. When the user presses a key, button, or control to select an option, several frames will pass before the user is able to release it. You can easily track whether a brand new press event has occurred by checking for a press event in the current frame just after a release state was registered for the same button or key in the preceding frame for the same key.

To demonstrate the handling of a press and release event that occurs over several frames, you will check for occurrences where the T key's state is pressed and its previous state is released. This condition must be `true` before toggling to allow the user to change between On and Off settings. You will use a string to store the value of On or Off for display purposes. In addition to a string declaration, you should add two other variables for storing the game time and the time of the last keypress to the module level of the game class:

```
KeyboardState kbstatePrevious;
```

Every frame, you need to track the previous `KeyboardState` values to compare current states with these values during the previous frame. Assigning the existing `KeyboardState` value to the `kbstatePrevious` object retains the most recent states. After storing the last states, you can then update `kbstate`. To ensure that these assignments are done in the proper sequence, add this instruction at the very beginning of `UpdateInputEvents()`:

```
kbstatePrevious = kbstate;
```

Once current and previous `KeyboardState` values are tracked, you need to add the following code to the end of the `UpdateInputEvents()` method to alter the output between On and Off whenever the user presses the T key:

```
if (kbstate.IsKeyDown(Keys.T) && kbstatePrevious.IsKeyUp(Keys.T))
    if (keyT == "On")                // alternate On or Off status
        keyT = "Off";                // for keydown events only
    else
        keyT = "On";
```

You have already added the code required to enable a successful toggle, so the status of the toggle state can now be displayed in the window. Code to display the status of the On or Off setting belongs at the bottom of the `DrawFonts()` method just before the `base.Draw()` instruction. Placing the code at the end of the `DrawFonts()` method will ensure that the Y position for the text output updates properly each frame on the PC.

```
ShowString("          toggle t:  " + keyT, X, Y += 20);
```

If you were to run the program now (on the PC), you would be able to press and release the T key to switch back and forth between On and Off display settings in the window.

Handling Mouse Button and Move Events

At some point, you may want to handle mouse button events to enable features such as rapid fire when running your game on a PC. Handling the mouse move and button-click events is even easier than handling keyboard events. To enable mouse event handling, you need a declaration for the MouseState object in the module declaration area of the game class. This has already been added to the base code, so you do not need to add it again for this example. You will notice code that handles all mouse input is enclosed using an #if...#endif condition to ensure that mouse-handling code is only executed on the PC. This check is necessary because the Xbox 360 does not include instructions to handle the mouse, and your code will not compile for the Xbox 360 without this condition. This declaration is already in your code:

```
#if !XBOX
    MouseState                              mouse;
#endif
```

To show the left and right mouse-button press or release states, you will display text output in the game window. A string declaration at the module level of the game class enables storage of mouse-button press states; later, you can use these states to draw text to the window.

```
private String mouseLeft, mouseRight;
```

Every frame, the mouse state must be updated to refresh the button-click values and the X and Y coordinates for the mouse. To ensure regular updates, check that the assignment of the mouse state is maintained in the ChangeView() method. This code is already included in the base code, so you do not need to add it in again.

```
#if !XBOX
    mouse = Mouse.GetState();
#endif
```

Now that the MouseState object is refreshed every frame, it is possible for you to update the string values that store the state of the left and right mouse buttons. This code checks whether either button is pressed and updates the appropriate string accordingly. To perform the check for the left and right mouse buttons and store their states each frame, add this code to the UpdateInputEvents() method:

```
mouseLeft = mouseRight = "released";
#if !XBOX
    if (mouse.LeftButton == ButtonState.Pressed)
        mouseLeft = "pressed";
```

```
    if (mouse.RightButton == ButtonState.Pressed)
        mouseRight = "pressed";
#endif
```

In this book's base code project, code is already in place to allow a player the ability to control direction with the cursor and mouse. In the `ChangeView()` method, there are instructions to set the cursor position back to the middle of the window at each frame. Resetting the cursor position every frame allows the camera to measure the mouse deviation from the center of the window, which can then be used to adjust the view each frame. For this example, the `SetPosition()` instruction must be disabled in the `ChangeView()` method; otherwise, you will not be able to move your mouse. You can do so by deleting the following line of code inside `ChangeView()`:

```
Mouse.SetPosition(widthMiddle, heightMiddle);
```

You should also add code to center the mouse over the window when the program begins. You can do this by adding the next four instructions to `Initialize()`:

```
#if !Xbox
    Mouse.SetPosition(Window.ClientBounds.Width/2,
                      Window.ClientBounds.Height/2);
#endif
```

Add this code block to the end of the `DrawFonts()` method. This will output the mouse button states on the PC window:

```
ShowString("Mouse                 "             , X, Y += 20);
ShowString("    right button:     " + mouseRight, X, Y += 20);
ShowString("     left button:     " + mouseLeft, X, Y += 20);
```

Because the `MouseState` is already being updated each frame, you can add code inside `DrawFonts()` to extract the X and Y coordinates of the cursor and convert them to string values for display in the game window:

```
#if !Xbox
    ShowString("                  x:   " + mouse.X.ToString(), X, Y+= 20);
    ShowString("                  y:   " + mouse.Y.ToString(), X, Y+= 20);
#endif
```

If you were to run the program now, the mouse coordinates would change as you moved the mouse. Pressing the mouse buttons would trigger the display of a `Pressed` listing on the game window.

Adding a Mouse Cursor

To further demonstrate mouse move events, you will add a cursor to visualize the effect of shifting the mouse. By default, the cursor will not appear in the game window mainly because XNA is geared to run video games, where there often is no cursor. To view the cursor on the PC, you can simply add `IsMouseVisible = true` in the main `Game` class to make the Windows cursor visible. However, for this example, you'll create your own.

You will create the cursor using a sprite made from a mouse image. Declarations are required in the module declaration area to load and draw the cursor image as a sprite:

```
private Texture2D   cursorTexture;
```

To load the cursor image with your other images, place the cursor.dds file in the Images folder for your project. You can find this cursor in the Images folder on this book's website. Add the reference to the cursor file in the Solution Explorer so the `ContentManager` object can find it. Then, inside `LoadContent()`, place your code to load the image when the program begins:

```
cursorTexture = Content.Load<Texture2D>("Images\\cursor");
```

Once the cursor image and sprite object have been defined and loaded, drawing the cursor as a sprite is easy. You will extract the X and Y coordinates of the mouse from the `MouseState` object. Adding the `DrawCursor()` method to your game class will display the cursor wherever the mouse is directed over the window:

```
void DrawCursor(){
#if !XBOX
    mouse = Mouse.GetState();
    spriteBatch.Draw(
        cursorTexture,                    // texture

        new Rectangle(mouse.X,mouse.Y, // starting window pixel
        cursorTexture.Width,              // area used on window
        cursorTexture.Height),

        // you can set this third parameter to NULL to repeat the
        // rectangle values from above
        new Rectangle(0, 0,               // starting pixel in sprite
        cursorTexture.Width,              // area used in sprite
        cursorTexture.Height),
```

```
        Color.White);                          // color
#endif
}
```

The cursor display needs to be triggered from the `Draw()` method to show the cursor on the window before `spriteBatch.End()` is called:

```
DrawCursor();
```

To see the states for the keyboard and mouse and to see the cursor move as you move the mouse, compile and run your project.

Handling the Controller

Now that keyboard and mouse handling have been demonstrated, we will shift focus to the game controller. Many people find the game controller better suited to gaming than a keyboard and mouse. Therefore, it's important for Windows games to support both options in case the player has a controller plugged into their PC.

As previously mentioned, it is possible to have up to four controllers attached to the machine, so the controller object is usually declared as a four-element array. Adding this instruction to the top of the game class allows access to the `GamePadState` object for each controller throughout the program.

```
private GamePadState[] gamePadState = new GamePadState[4];
```

Before handling game controller states, you first need to determine whether the game controller is actually connected. String variables, declared in the module declaration area, allow you to store and display the connected status of the controllers within the game window:

```
private String[] gamePadConnected = new String[4];
```

All controller states, including the `IsConnected` property, are retrieved by calling the `GetState()` method for each controller. This code can be implemented from the `Update()` method:

```
gamePadState[0] = GamePad.GetState(PlayerIndex.One);
gamePadState[1] = GamePad.GetState(PlayerIndex.Two);
gamePadState[2] = GamePad.GetState(PlayerIndex.Three);
gamePadState[3] = GamePad.GetState(PlayerIndex.Four);
```

After you check whether a controller is connected, the "connected" or "not connected" status is stored in a string. The default value is "not connected," but if the game pad's `IsConnected` property is true, a "connected" value is stored in this string variable. Adding this code block, after the game controller's states are retrieved in `UpdateInputEvents()`, will ensure that you accurately record the controller's connection state for each frame:

```
for (int i = 0; i < 4; i++)
    if (gamePadState[i].IsConnected == true)
        gamePadConnected[i] = "connected";
    else
        gamePadConnected[i] = "not connected";
```

Now that the controller's connection status is updated every frame, this information can be displayed in the game window. Adding the following lines of code to `DrawFonts()` will display the status that has been stored in the string variables in the game window:

```
ShowString("Controller        "                    , X, Y +=20);
for(int i=0; i<4; i++)
    ShowString("                   " + i.ToString() + ":  "
                                     + gamePadConnected[i], X, Y +=20);
```

If you run the program at this point, the connection states for each of the four controllers in the array will appear. The listing will show a "connected" or "not connected" value in the game window.

Game Pad Buttons

The process of checking whether buttons on the game controller are pressed is similar to checking whether the mouse buttons or keyboard keys are pressed. For this portion of the example, during each update, checks will be made to determine whether the A, Back, and Start buttons on the game controller are selected. Similar to the keyboard and mouse button examples, you will use string variables to store either a `Pressed` or `Released` value. Adding string variable declarations at the module level will enable more than one method in the class to access these values:

```
private String gpA, gpBack, gpStart;
```

After the game controller state has been updated, the status of the game controller buttons is checked inside the `UpdateInputEvents()` method. If a `Pressed` state is found for A, Back, or Start, the value `pressed` is stored in the corresponding string variable:

```
gpA = gpBack = gpStart = "released";
if (gamePadState[0].Buttons.A == ButtonState.Pressed)
    gpA = "pressed";
```

```
if (gamePadState[0].Buttons.Back == ButtonState.Pressed)
    gpBack = "pressed";
if (gamePadState[0].Buttons.Start == ButtonState.Pressed)
    gpStart = "pressed";
```

The results from the button state test can now be drawn to the window using the values stored in the string variables. These instructions for displaying the text must be called at the end of the `DrawFonts()` method:

```
ShowString("Gamepad Button      ", X, Y += 20);
ShowString("               a:   " + gpA,     X, Y += 20);
ShowString("            back:   " + gpBack,  X, Y += 20);
ShowString("           start:   " + gpStart,X, Y += 20);
```

When you run this version of the code, it will show the `Pressed` or `Released` status of the A, Back, and Start buttons on the game controller.

Left Shoulder and Right Shoulder (Bumpers)

Shoulders (or *bumpers)* are another form of button that return a `Pressed` or `Released` state. Declaring these variables in the module declaration area allows you to store the status of the shoulder buttons:

```
private String leftShoulder, rightShoulder;
```

Inside `UpdateInputEvents()`, checks can be made to determine whether a shoulder button is pressed. The status is assigned accordingly.

```
leftShoulder = rightShoulder = "released";
if (gamePadState[0].Buttons.LeftShoulder == ButtonState.Pressed)
    leftShoulder = "pressed";
if (gamePadState[0].Buttons.RightShoulder== ButtonState.Pressed)
    rightShoulder = "pressed";
```

Once the shoulder states have been evaluated and stored in a string, the results can be shown in the game window. But first, you will use some extra code at the end of the `DrawFonts()` method to position the new text listings in a second column that follows:

```
X = Window.ClientBounds.Width/2;
Y = (int)drawArea.Y;
```

You should also add the shoulder state display instructions to the end of the `DrawFonts()` method so that the shoulder states appear in the window:

```
ShowString("Bumpers              ",  X, Y += 20);
ShowString("             left:   " + leftShoulder,  X, Y += 20);
ShowString("            right:   " + rightShoulder, X, Y += 20);
```

When the program is run, you will see the Pressed or Released status of your bumpers.

DPad

The DPad control is unique in that it has Right, Left, Up, and Down attributes. Each attribute has its own Pressed or Released state; it is possible to have two of the DPad's attributes return a Pressed result if the game player presses a corner of the DPad. A module-level string declaration enables the display of the status on the window each frame:

```
private String DPadLeft, DPadRight, DPadUp, DPadDown;
```

To ensure that the DPad press states are checked every frame, the ButtonState.Pressed property for the DPad is checked after the GamePadState is retrieved for the controller in the UpdateInputEvents() method:

```
DPadLeft = DPadRight = DPadUp = DPadDown = "released";
if (gamePadState[0].DPad.Right == ButtonState.Pressed)
    DPadRight = "pressed";
if (gamePadState[0].DPad.Left == ButtonState.Pressed)
    DPadLeft = "pressed";
if (gamePadState[0].DPad.Up == ButtonState.Pressed)
    DPadUp = "pressed";
if (gamePadState[0].DPad.Down == ButtonState.Pressed)
    DPadDown= "pressed";
```

Now the status of the Right, Left, Up, and Down buttons on the DPad can be displayed on the window by adding these instructions to DrawFonts() to output the text:

```
ShowString("Dpad                 ",          X, Y +=20);
ShowString("            right:   " + DPadRight,X, Y +=20);
ShowString("             left:   " + DPadLeft,X, Y +=20);
ShowString("               up:   " + DPadUp,X, Y +=20);
ShowString("             down:   " + DPadDown,X, Y +=20);
```

When you run this program, the output will show the Pressed or Released status for the DPad's Left, Right, Up, and Down attributes.

Left Stick and Right Stick

To track the left and right thumbsticks' `Pressed` and `Released` states, you will follow steps similar to those used for tracking the `DPad` states. However, the thumbsticks don't just track their `Pressed` and `Released` states; each thumbstick also tracks an X and Y value to gauge the distance from its center resting position. Declaring string variables at the module level will enable the storage of press and shift states in string format; this allows you to display the states in the game window:

```
private String leftStick,   rightStick,  leftStickX,
               rightStickX, rightStickY, leftStickY;
```

Inside the `UpdateInputEvents()` method, after the status for each game controller has been updated, the press status of each stick can be checked and stored:

```
leftStick     = rightStick = "released"; // default value
if (gamePadState[0].Buttons.LeftStick == ButtonState.Pressed)
    leftStick = "pressed";
if (gamePadState[0].Buttons.RightStick == ButtonState.Pressed)
    rightStick = "pressed";
```

To track the positions of the left and right thumbsticks, you need to add some more code in the `UpdateInputEvents()` method. This code returns the floating-point attributes for the X and Y values of each stick. The float values in this code are converted to strings using the `ToString()` method so that they can be stored in a string value for display in the window:

```
rightStickX = gamePadState[0].ThumbSticks.Right.X.ToString();
rightStickY = gamePadState[0].ThumbSticks.Right.Y.ToString();
leftStickX  = gamePadState[0].ThumbSticks.Left.X.ToString();
leftStickY  = gamePadState[0].ThumbSticks.Left.Y.ToString();
```

Once the results for the thumbstick press and shift states are stored as string values, they can be displayed as text output in the window. To enable the output, add these statements to the end of the `DrawFonts()` method:

```
ShowString("Right stick          "              , X, Y += 20);
ShowString("           button:   " + rightStick ,  X, Y += 20);
ShowString("                x:   " + rightStickX,  X, Y += 20);
ShowString("                y:   " + rightStickY,  X, Y += 20);
ShowString("Left stick           "              , X, Y += 20);
ShowString("           button:   " + leftStick  , X, Y += 20);
ShowString("                x:   " + leftStickX , X, Y += 20);
ShowString("                y:   " + leftStickY , X, Y += 20);
```

When you run this version of the input example, you will see the press and shift states for the left and right thumbsticks displayed in the game window. Each thumbstick shows one `Pressed` or `Released` state. Also, each thumbstick lists floating-point values for its X and Y positions. These positions are relative to the thumbstick's resting position at the center of the control.

Left Trigger and Right Trigger

Triggers provide yet another unique way of obtaining user input. Each left and right trigger stores a float value that ranges between 0 and 1 to indicate how far the trigger is pulled. When the trigger is released, the value returned is 0. When the trigger is fully squeezed, the trigger returns a value of 1.

To show these floating-point values in the window, you will convert them to string format. These string declarations belong at the module level to ensure that they can be updated and used throughout the game class:

```
private String leftTrigger, rightTrigger;
```

The status of triggers can be updated and stored in the strings just declared—after the game pad status is retrieved in the `UpdateInputEvents()` method:

```
leftTrigger  = gamePadState[0].Triggers.Left.ToString();
rightTrigger = gamePadState[0].Triggers.Right.ToString();
```

Once the trigger states have been gathered and converted to string output, the output can be shown as text in the game window. To do this, add the following code to the end of the `DrawFonts()` method:

```
ShowString("Trigger              ", X, Y += 20);
ShowString("             left:   " + leftTrigger,  X, Y += 20);
ShowString("            right:   " + rightTrigger, X, Y += 20);
```

When you run the program now, it shows changing floating-point values for the triggers as each is pulled and released. The floating-point values shown range between 0 (for fully released) and 1 (for fully pressed).

Setting the Rumble

A rumble can be added to this example with one instruction, `SetVibration()`. The vibration takes three parameters: the controller identifier (which in this case is the zero index), the strength of the rumble on the left side of the controller, and the strength of the rumble on the right side of the controller. The strength of the rumble ranges between 0 and 1. Add this instruction to the end of the

`UpdateInputEvents()` method to send rumbles to the left and right sides of the controller whenever a trigger is squeezed:

```
GamePad.SetVibration(0, gamePadState[0].Triggers.Left,
                        gamePadState[0].Triggers.Right);
```

When you run the program now, you will see the corresponding press, release, and XY values for the keyboard, mouse, and game controller. You can also run this code on the Xbox 360 for similar output; however, the mouse event handling will be disabled.

ZUNE INPUT HANDLING

Input handling on the Zune is a limited subset of the game pad library. Figure 23-2 shows how the DPad, left thumbstick, A button, B button, and Back button map to the Zune.

FIGURE 23-2

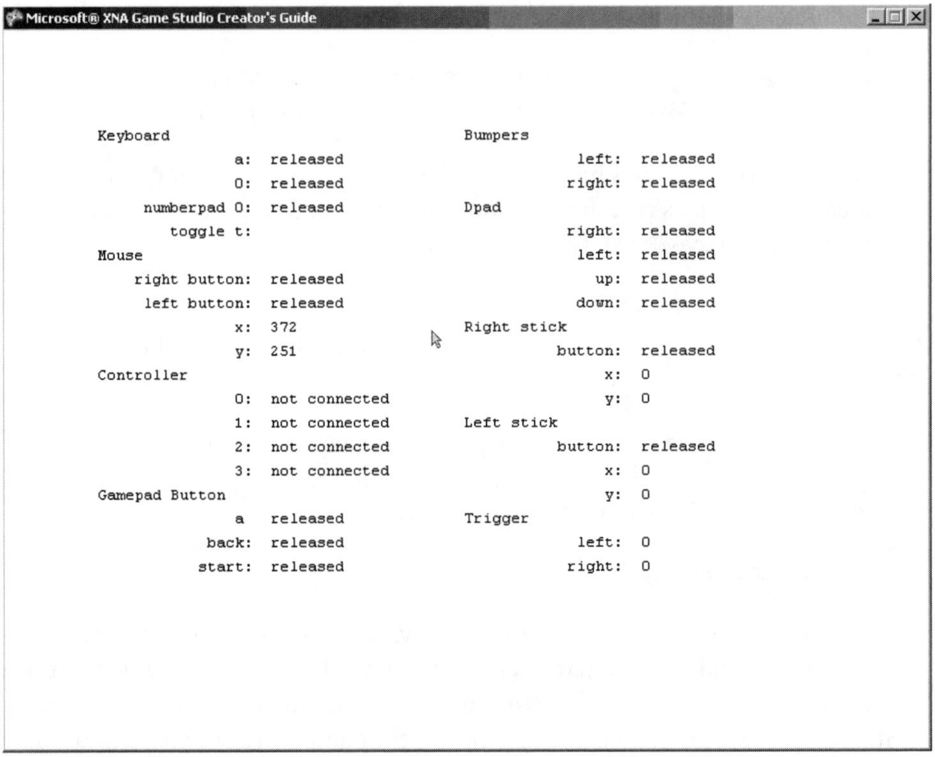

```
Microsoft® XNA Game Studio Creator's Guide

Keyboard                                  Bumpers
                a:  released                      left:  released
                0:  released                     right:  released
     numberpad 0:  released               Dpad
        toggle t:                                right:  released
Mouse                                             left:  released
    right button:  released                         up:  released
     left button:  released                       down:  released
                x:  372                   Right stick
                y:  251                         button:  released
Controller                                           x:  0
                0:  not connected                    y:  0
                1:  not connected         Left stick
                2:  not connected               button:  released
                3:  not connected                    x:  0
Gamepad Button                                       y:  0
                a   released              Trigger
             back:  released                      left:  0
            start:  released                     right:  0
```

Input handling on the Zune

Zune Input Device Example

This example uses text output to demonstrate how the A, B, Back, Up, Down, Right, and thumbstick events are handled on the Zune.

The project begins with a new Zune game template. Once you have created a new Zune game, you will need to add a font file to draw text output. Right-click the Content node in the project and choose Add | New Item | Sprite Font to add it. When prompted to assign this file a name enter **MyFont**. You will reference this name later when you load the font file.

To simplify aligning the text output, replace the FontName element in the MyFont.spritefont file with this change:

```
<FontName>Courier New</FontName>
```

You will need a SpriteFont object to load and reference the font:

```
SpriteFont spriteFont;
```

Now you can load the font from LoadContent():

```
spriteFont = Content.Load<SpriteFont>("MyFont");
```

Input control status is displayed in text on separate lines starting from the top of the Zune window to the bottom. DrawFonts() is needed in the game class to show this output:

```
public void DrawFonts(String output, float top){
    const float LEFT = 10.0f;
    top             *= spriteFont.LineSpacing;

    spriteBatch.Begin();
        spriteBatch.DrawString(spriteFont, output,
                new Vector2(LEFT, top), Color.Yellow);
    spriteBatch.End();
}
```

Add ShowInputDeviceStatus() to the game class to check the states for the A, B, and Back buttons as well as the DPad and leftstick controls. ShowInputDeviceStatus displays the current press state or XY values for each:

```
private void ShowInputDeviceStatus(){
    float line = 0.0f;
    GamePadState zunePad = GamePad.GetState(PlayerIndex.One);
    if (zunePad.DPad.Up == ButtonState.Pressed)      // Up
        DrawFonts("DPad.Up:    pressed",  ++line);
    else
```

```
        DrawFonts("DPad.Up:    released", ++line);
    if (zunePad.DPad.Down == ButtonState.Pressed)    // Down
        DrawFonts("DPad.Down:  pressed",  ++line);
    else
        DrawFonts("DPad.Down:  released", ++line);
    if (zunePad.DPad.Left == ButtonState.Pressed)    // Left
        DrawFonts("DPad.Left:  pressed",  ++line);
    else
        DrawFonts("DPad.Left:  released", ++line);
    if (zunePad.DPad.Right == ButtonState.Pressed)   // Right
        DrawFonts("DPad.Right: pressed",  ++line);
    else
        DrawFonts("DPad.Right: released", ++line);
    // A - press center of Zune pad
    if (zunePad.Buttons.A == ButtonState.Pressed)   // A
        DrawFonts("A:          pressed", ++line);
    else
        DrawFonts("A:          released", ++line);
    // B - press top right button
    if (zunePad.Buttons.B == ButtonState.Pressed)   // B
        DrawFonts("B:          pressed", ++line);
    else
        DrawFonts("B:          released", ++line);
    // running finger on Zune pad
    float X = zunePad.ThumbSticks.Left.X;    // thumbstick X
    float Y = zunePad.ThumbSticks.Left.Y;    // thumbstick Y
    DrawFonts("ThumbSticks.Left.X", ++line);
    DrawFonts("= " + X.ToString(), ++line);
    DrawFonts("ThumbSticks.Left.Y", ++line);
    DrawFonts("= " + Y.ToString(), ++line);

    // show user how to exit game - back button is top left button
    ++line; // Back button is already used to exit in the template
    DrawFonts("Press Back button", ++line);
    DrawFonts("to exit.", ++line);
}
```

With everything in place you can now trigger the code to display the input device status from Draw()

```
ShowInputDeviceStatus();
```

When you run your code, you will see the press and release states of your controls as well as the X and Y position of your finger on the Zune pad. You can see from this tiny example that Zune input handling is simple yet flexible enough to allow players a full range of control over their game play.

After enabling keyboard, mouse, game pad, and Zune input, you literally will have placed control of your game engine in the hands of your players. Your world is now their oyster.

Chapter 23 Review Exercises

To get the most from this chapter, try out these chapter review exercises.

1. Try the step-by-step examples provided in this chapter, if you have not already done so.
2. If you run the solution from Exercise 1, when you left-click the mouse, the word "Pressed" appears in the window. Track the mouse state so you can toggle between displaying pressed and released states in the game window. (A similar check exists that enables you to toggle between On and Off states when pressing the letter T.)
3. In the "Collision Detection Using Lines and Spheres" solution from Chapter 18, make your game pad rumble every time the camera collides with something.

CHAPTER 24

Content Pipeline Processors

UNTIL now, the media you used for the examples in this book has been in formats supported by the XNA content pipeline. Using predefined content types in XNA allows for easy deployment on your PC or Xbox 360. For example, the XNA Framework offers built-in methods for loading and accessing `Texture2D`, `XACT` (audio), `XML`, `Effect` (shaders), Autodesk `FBX` (model), and `X` (model) objects. This chapter shows how to extend the content pipeline to load files not supported out of the box by the XNA Framework.

Aside from allowing you to load any graphics or data file on the PC and Xbox 360, custom content processors can also enable faster game startup times. A custom content pipeline processor will read the bulk data from your media files, process it, and then store it in intermediate form. This compiled binary intermediate data is stored in an .xnb file.

The content processor also tracks changes to your media and to the content-processing code itself. If any changes are detected, when you build your game, the content processor reloads the bulk data from your media files and recompiles it. Otherwise, if no changes are detected, the compiled data is read from the .xnb file that stored it. Being able to read preprocessed data can be a big timesaver when large compressed media files are loaded at game launch.

For the *Quake II* model loader (used in Chapter 26), setting up the model for XNA deployment requires loading the bulk data, organizing the faces in the polygon shapes from the indexed information stored in the file, and generating the normal vectors to enable lighting. This processing time can add unwanted delays to your game launch. However, if you use a custom content processor to decompress and organize your .md2 data in an intermediate format, your game will not read from the *.md2 file again. Instead, the game will read the intermediate data from your compiled .xnb file during any consecutive run. The initial data processing is only performed when either the original media file changes or the processor code is modified. In short, you will notice an improvement to your load times when using the content processor.

CONTENT PROCESSORS

The content processor loads your external media and locates existing processor components. All custom processors must derive from the `ContentProcessor` base class in a manner similar to the following:

```
public class MyContentProcessor : ContentProcessor<Tinput,Toutput>
{}
```

`Tinput` and `Toutput` are the user-defined input and output classes you create to input your bulk data and output your compiled data in the required format.

ContentImporter

The ContentImporter class is defined with an Import method to read unprocessed data from your original media file. The class declaration is preceded by the ContentImporter attribute to list the file extension(s) associated with this loader and the processor used to convert it to a compiled format. Additional extensions, separated by commas, can be added to the string.

```
[ContentImporter(string fileExt, DefaultProcessor = string processorName)]
public class MyContentImporter : ContentImporter<TerrainContent>{
    public override MyCustomContent Import(String filename,
                                    ContentImporterContext context){}
}
```

Inside the Import method, the file is opened and can be read with a System.IO.File method or through the MemoryStream and BinaryReader objects. Using these objects, you can read text and binary formats.

For this example, the System.IO.File ReadAllBytes() method reads in the bytes from the .raw image. However, if you were reading text input, this could be read with the File object's ReadAllText() method. You can also load your data with MemoryStream and BinaryReader objects to read data in specific chunks to handle integers, floats, vectors, and many other data types.

After the data has been read, it is structured according to your own custom data-storage class. You define how you want the data organized and how you want it exported to the .xnb file.

ContentTypeWriter

The ContentTypeWriter class assists in writing your intermediary data as binary output to the .xnb file. Output is written with the Write() method override. The GetRuntimeType() method returns the custom data type of the processed content. The GetRuntimeReader() reader method returns the intermediate format reader's location:

```
[ContentTypeWriter]
public class MyContentWriter : ContentTypeWriter<MyCustomContent>{
    protected override void Write(ContentWriter wr,
                                  MyCustomContent output){}
    public override string GetRuntimeType(TargetPlatform targetPlatform)
    {}
    public override string GetRuntimeReader(TargetPlatform targetPlatform)
    {}
}
```

ContentTypeReader

The ContentTypeReader loads the intermediate binary data you stored in the .xnb file.

The ContentTypeReader must not be placed in your content pipeline project. It can exist in your game library or in a separate project.

Most of the methods available to load the data with the ContentTypeReader object are inherited from the BinaryReader class. You select the read method to fit your data types. Table 24-1 shows some common types but there are many others.

The ContentTypeReader loads your data and returns an initialized instance of your custom data class.

```
public class MyReader : ContentTypeReader<MyCustomContent>{
    protected override MyCustomContent Read(ContentReader input,
                                            MyCustomContent existingInstance){}
}
```

When the Read() method override is finished importing your managed data, it returns this data in the format you defined in your storage class. This data is then made available to your game project.

CUSTOM CONTENT PROCESSOR EXAMPLE

This example demonstrates how to create a custom content processor that loads a height map from a .raw image. This content processor converts the height data to generate position and normal vectors. The vertices created from this newly generated data are used in Chapter 25 to build a rolling landscape. To keep the content processor demonstration in this chapter focused, the terrain is not fully implemented. How-

TABLE 24-1

Method	*Type*
ReadBoolean()	*Boolean*
ReadInt32()	*Integer*
ReadSingle()	*Float*
Vector3()	*Vector3*

Common methods for reading binary data

ever, the height data associated with the current camera position is updated as it moves through the world and this height information is printed in the window.

XNA does not provide a code library for loading .raw images, so you need an alternate way to load them. You can get away with `BinaryReader` methods to load them on Windows. On the Xbox 360, the `BinaryReader` methods will find your .raw files if you place your media resources in the debug folder when deploying your solution. However, to handle these files more gracefully, you should create a custom processor to load them through the content pipeline.

Load performance is another reason to use the content processor to load your terrain data. The .raw image stores an array of bytes. When it is used as a height map, each pixel stores height information between 0 and 255. The pixels from this rectangular .raw image are mapped to the rectangular ground in your world. To superimpose each pixel over the corresponding section of ground, you will need to calculate the position vector associated with each pixel. Also, to enable lighting, you will need to calculate the normal vector associated with each pixel in the .raw file.

This example begins with the "Directional Lighting Example" from Chapter 22. This project can be found in the Solutions folder on this book's website.

Building a Custom Content Processor in Windows

In order to compile the content processor into a DLL that can be used either on Windows or the Xbox 360, you must add a separate Content Pipeline Extension Library project to your solution from the Solution Explorer. To add it, right-click the solution name and choose Add | New Project. When prompted in the Add New Project dialog, select Content Pipeline Extension Library. The Content Pipeline Extension project is used because it already has the proper assembly references and does not contain the Content subproject. For this example, name your content pipeline project as TerrainPipeline.

Once your new library project has been added, you will be able to see it as a separate project in the Solution Explorer. Rename the .cs code file that is generated to TerrainContent.cs. Then replace the code in this file with the following shell to implement your own content processor:

```
using System;
using Microsoft.Xna.Framework;
using Microsoft.Xna.Framework.Content;
using Microsoft.Xna.Framework.Content.Pipeline;
using Microsoft.Xna.Framework.Content.Pipeline.Serialization.Compiler;
using System.IO;

namespace TerrainPipeline{
}
```

Your custom data class is designed by you to store your data in the format you require. For this example, the user-defined class `TerrainContent` stores bulk height data from the .raw file. It then uses this data to generate position and normal vectors along with the terrain dimensions and stores these new values at the class level.

The `TerrainContent` class is referenced throughout your content processor to generate and access your height map data, so it must be made public. Also, to ensure that the height map is mapped properly to the rectangular world, the number of rows and columns, the world dimensions, and the cell height and width are also made public. This terrain-defining code belongs in the `TerrainPipeline` namespace of your TerrainContent.cs file:

```
public class TerrainContent{
    public byte[]         height;
    public Vector3[]      position;
    public Vector3[]      normal;
    public float          cellWidth, cellHeight;

    // hard coded values to match height map pixel and world dimensions
    public int            NUM_ROWS    = 257;
    public int            NUM_COLS    = 257;
    public float          worldWidth  = 16.0f;
    public float          worldHeight = 16.0f;
    public float          heightScale = 0.0104f;

    // constructor for raw data - used during bulk data import
    public TerrainContent(byte[] bytes){
        height     = bytes;
        setCellDimensions();
        generatePositions();
        generateNormals();
    }

    // sets height and width of cells made from pixels in .raw file
    public void setCellDimensions(){
        cellWidth = 2.0f*worldWidth/(NUM_COLS - 1);
        cellHeight = 2.0f*worldHeight/(NUM_ROWS - 1);
    }

    // generate X, Y, and Z position data where Y is the height.
    private void generatePositions(){
        position = new Vector3[NUM_ROWS*NUM_COLS];
```

```
        for (int row = 0; row < NUM_ROWS; row++){
            for (int col = 0; col < NUM_COLS; col++){
                float X = -worldWidth + col*cellWidth;
                float Y =  height[row*NUM_COLS + col]*heightScale;
                float Z = -worldHeight + row*cellHeight;
                position[col + row*NUM_COLS] = new Vector3(X, Y, Z);
            }
        }
    }
    // generate normal vector for each cell in height map
    private void generateNormals(){
        Vector3 tail, right, down, cross;
        normal = new Vector3[NUM_ROWS*NUM_COLS];

        // normal is cross product of two vectors joined at tail
        for (int row=0; row<NUM_ROWS - 1; row++){
            for (int col = 0; col < NUM_COLS - 1; col++){
                tail    = position[col + row*NUM_COLS];
                right   = position[col + 1 + row*NUM_COLS] - tail;
                down    = position[col + (row + 1)*(NUM_COLS)] - tail;
                cross   = Vector3.Cross(down, right);
                cross.Normalize();
                normal[col + row*NUM_COLS] = cross;
            }
        }
    }
}
```

With the TerrainContent class in place to store the terrain data, a derived instance of the ContentProcessor class is needed as a processor interface for the terrain object:

```
// all processors must derive from this class
[ContentProcessor]
public class TerrainProcessor : ContentProcessor<TerrainContent,
                                               TerrainContent>{
    public override TerrainContent Process(TerrainContent input,
                                   ContentProcessorContext context){
        return new TerrainContent(input.height);
    }
}
```

Extending the `ContentImporter` class enables the overridden `Import()` method to read your data from the original media file. The `ContentImporter` attribute precedes the `ContentImporter` class definition to list the file extensions that can use this importer.

For this example, the `ReadAllBytes()` method reads in the bytes from the .raw image. Of course, you can use other methods to read your data:

```
// stores information about importer, file extension, and caching
[ContentImporter(".raw", DefaultProcessor = "TerrainProcessor")]
// ContentImporter reads original data from original media file
public class TerrainPipeline : ContentImporter<TerrainContent>{
    // reads original data from binary or text based files
    public override TerrainContent Import(String filename,
                    ContentImporterContext context){
        byte[]          bytes     = File.ReadAllBytes(filename);
        TerrainContent  terrain   = new TerrainContent(bytes);
        return          terrain;    // returns compiled data object
    }
}
```

Once the data is read, it is passed to your custom data class. This data initializes a custom data object that organizes the data as you need it. The data object is then returned to your processor so it can be written in a compiled binary format to an .xnb file.

Adding the extended `ContentTypeWriter` class to your `TerrainPipeline` namespace allows you to output your compiled binary custom data to an .xnb file. The `Write()` method receives your integer, float, and vector data and then writes it in binary format to the file. When you write your data, you have to write it in the sequence you want to retrieve it. The writer/reader combination uses a "first in first out" sequence for your data storage and access.

A `GetRuntimeType()` method is included in the `ContentTypeWriter` class to return the custom data type of the processed content to be loaded at run time. A `GetRunTimeReader()` method is also added to return the intermediate content reader's location in the solution:

```
// write compiled data to *.xnb file
[ContentTypeWriter]
public class TerrWriter : ContentTypeWriter<TerrainContent>{
    protected override void Write(ContentWriter  cw,
                                  TerrainContent terrain){
        cw.Write(terrain.NUM_ROWS);
```

```
        cw.Write(terrain.NUM_COLS);
        cw.Write(terrain.worldWidth);
        cw.Write(terrain.worldHeight);
        cw.Write(terrain.heightScale);
        cw.Write(terrain.cellWidth);
        cw.Write(terrain.cellHeight);

        for (int row = 0; row < terrain.NUM_ROWS; row++){
            for (int col = 0; col < terrain.NUM_COLS; col++){
                cw.Write(terrain.position[col + row*terrain.NUM_COLS]);
                cw.Write(terrain.normal[col + row*terrain.NUM_COLS]);
            }
        }
    }
    // Sets the CLR data type to be loaded at runtime.
    public override string GetRuntimeType(TargetPlatform targetPlatform){
        return "TerrainRuntime.Terrain, TerrainRuntime,
                Version=1.0.0.0, Culture=neutral";
    }

    // Tells the content pipeline about reader used to load .xnb data
    public override string GetRuntimeReader(TargetPlatform targetPlatform){
        return "TerrainRuntime.TerrainReader, TerrainRuntime,
                Version=1.0.0.0, Culture=neutral";
    }
}
```

At run time, the Content reader reads the compiled data from the .xnb file. A separate project is used for this reader. To create it, right-click the solution, choose Add | New Project, and then choose Content Pipeline Extension Library. In the Add New Project dialog, assign it the name TerrainRuntime to match the value given in the `GetRuntimeReader()` method from inside the content processor. For readability, rename the project code file that is generated to TerrainReader.cs.

The `ContentReader` is derived from the `BinaryReader` class and exposes similar methods for retrieving data in the segments you need. Once the data is read, an object of your custom data class is initialized. This custom data object is then made available to your XNA game project as soon as the data is loaded:

```
using System;
using System.Collections.Generic;
using Microsoft.Xna.Framework;
using Microsoft.Xna.Framework.Content;
```

```
namespace TerrainRuntime{
    public class Terrain{
        // these variables store values that are accessible in game class
        public byte[]       height;
        public Vector3[]    position;
        public Vector3[]    normal;
        public int          NUM_ROWS, NUM_COLS;
        public float        worldWidth, worldHeight, heightScale;
        public float        cellWidth, cellHeight;

        internal Terrain(ContentReader cr){
            NUM_ROWS    = cr.ReadInt32();
            NUM_COLS    = cr.ReadInt32();
            worldWidth  = cr.ReadSingle();
            worldHeight = cr.ReadSingle();
            heightScale = cr.ReadSingle();
            cellWidth   = cr.ReadSingle();
            cellHeight  = cr.ReadSingle();

            // declare position and normal vector arrays
            position    = new Vector3[NUM_ROWS*NUM_COLS];
            normal      = new Vector3[NUM_ROWS*NUM_COLS];

            // read in position and normal data to generate height map
            for (int row = 0; row < NUM_ROWS; row++){
                for (int col = 0; col < NUM_COLS; col++){
                    position[col + row*NUM_COLS] = cr.ReadVector3();
                    normal[col + row*NUM_COLS]   = cr.ReadVector3();
                }
            }
        }
    }
    // loads terrain from an XNB file.
    public class TerrainReader : ContentTypeReader<Terrain>{
        protected override Terrain Read(ContentReader input,
                                        Terrain existingInstance){
            return new Terrain(input);
        }
    }
}
```

The game project must reference the TerrainRuntime project. To reference this assembly, right-click the game project's References folder in the Solution Explorer and choose Add Reference. In the Add Reference dialog, select the TerrainRuntime project from the Projects tab and click OK. You will now see this TerrainRuntime reference listed in your game project (see Figure 24-1). The game project's Content project needs to reference the TerrainPipeline to load the raw content. To add it, right-click the References node under the Content folder and choose Add Reference. Then in the Add Reference dialog, select the TerrainPipeline project from the Projects tab (see Figure 24-1).

Wherever you want to use your custom data type, the new namespace for your runtime content must be included in your original game project:

```
using TerrainRuntime;
```

FIGURE 24-1

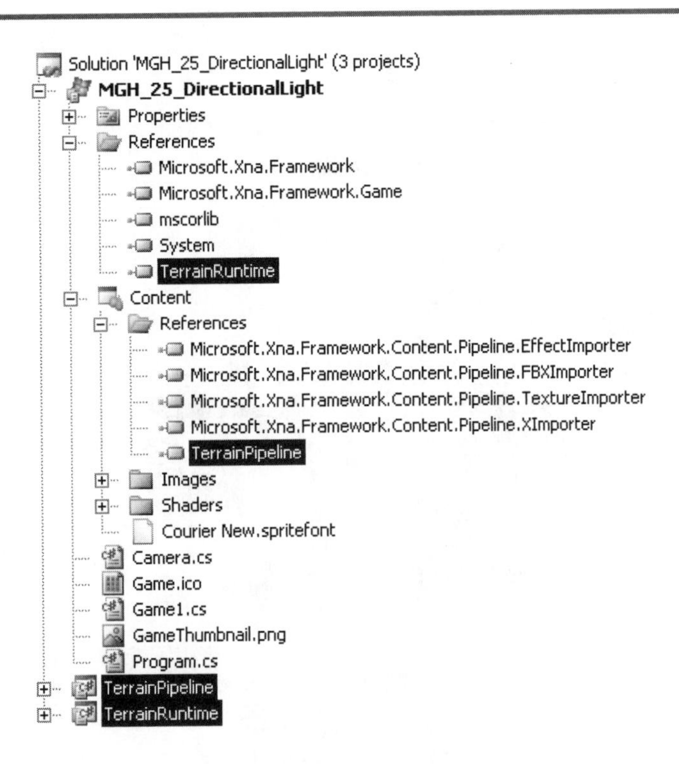

The game project references the runtime project. The content subproject references the pipeline project.

Next, your heightMap.raw file must be referenced in the Images folder for your game project. You can get this file from the Images directory on this book's website.

Once the heightMap.raw file is referenced, you can set its properties to use your custom content processor to load it. First, you need to build your TerrainPipeline and TerrainRuntime projects to see their references when setting up the heightMap.raw file. You can build each project by right-clicking each project name in the Solution Explorer and choosing Build. Then, to assign the custom content processor to read the .raw file, right-click heightMap in the Solution Explorer and select Properties. Under the Build Action property drop-down, select Compile. The Content Importer attribute should be set to `TerrainPipeline`, and the Content Processor attribute should be set to `TerrainProcessor`. Figure 24-2 shows the content pipeline property settings for the heightMap.raw file.

In your game project you need an instance of the terrain object at the class level:

```
Terrain terrain;
```

FIGURE 24-2

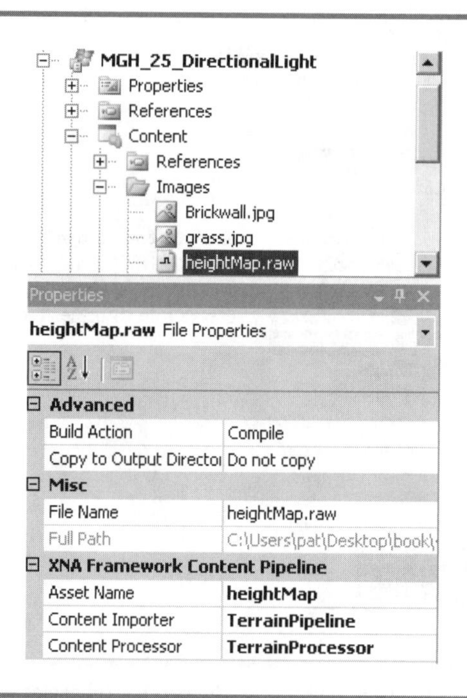

Media file references the custom content importer and processor.

Finally, you can now add the instruction to load your .raw data using the content pipeline. Be sure to load your terrain before you initialize the vertex buffer because the vertex buffer is going to store your terrain vertices. To address this you load the terrain content when the program begins, so it is called from the `Initialize()` method:

```
terrain = Content.Load<Terrain>("Images\\heightMap");
```

Now we can start adding our code to extract height information from your height map. The `HandleOffHeightMap()` method ensures that the rows and columns are on the height map. If not, it chooses the closest row and column on the map:

```
private void HandleOffHeightMap(ref int row, ref int col){
    if (row >= terrain.NUM_ROWS)
        row = terrain.NUM_ROWS - 1;
    else if (row < 0)
        row = 0;
    if (col >= terrain.NUM_COLS)
        col = terrain.NUM_COLS - 1;
    else if (col < 0)
        col = 0;
}
```

`RowColumn()` is added to the game class to determine an object's row and column position relative to the object's world position:

```
Vector3 RowColumn(Vector3 position){
    // calculate X and Z
    int col = (int)((position.X + terrain.worldWidth)/terrain.cellWidth);
    int row = (int)((position.Z + terrain.worldHeight)/terrain.cellHeight);
    HandleOffHeightMap(ref row, ref col);

    return new Vector3(col, 0.0f, row);
}
```

`Height()` is used in the game class to return the height value associated with a row and column on the height map:

```
float Height(int row, int col){
    HandleOffHeightMap(ref row, ref col);
    return terrain.position[col + row*terrain.NUM_COLS].Y;
}
```

When finding an object's height, the object's location relative to a height map cell is first determined. Position vertices at each corner of the cell to store the Y values that contain the height information. These four known height values are then used to interpolate the actual object height inside the cell. The `Lerp()` function performs this linear interpolation with the following calculation:

```
height = height0 + (height1 - height0)*position/(distance from 0 to 1)
```

The height projection is done in three steps. First the height at the top margin at a fixed distance from the left border of the cell is determined. Then the height at the bottom cell margin with the same distance from the left border is determined. These top and bottom height values are then used with the object's distance from the top of the cell to determine the height of the object inside the cell (see Figure 24-3).

`CellHeight()` performs this series of operations to determine the current object height in the game class:

```
public float CellHeight(Vector3 position){
    // get top left row and column indicies
    Vector3 cellPosition = RowColumn(position);
    int     row          = (int)cellPosition.Z;
    int     col          = (int)cellPosition.X;

    // distance from top left of cell
    float distanceFromLeft, distanceFromTop;
    distanceFromLeft     = position.X%terrain.cellWidth;
    distanceFromTop      = position.Z%terrain.cellHeight;

    // lerp projects height relative to known dimensions
    float topHeight      = MathHelper.Lerp(Height(row, col),
                                           Height(row, col + 1),
                                           distanceFromLeft);
    float bottomHeight   = MathHelper.Lerp(Height(row + 1, col),
                                           Height(row + 1, col + 1),
                                           distanceFromLeft);
    return MathHelper.Lerp(topHeight, bottomHeight, distanceFromTop);
}
```

In this example, the height values are not actually used in any practical sense. However, we will print the height that corresponds with the camera's current position in the window, so a font object is needed in the game project. To add the font

FIGURE 24-3

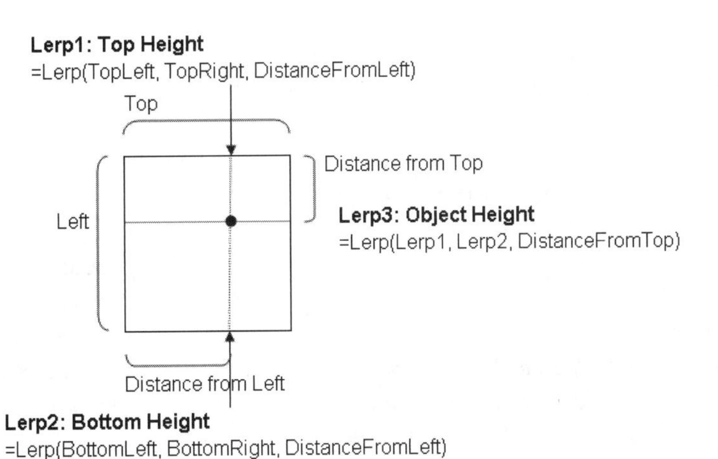

Steps taken to interpolate the object height

XML file, right-click the game project's Content node and choose Add | New Item. Select the Sprite Font icon in the Add New Item dialog and assign it the name "Courier New." You will have to assign a new font value in the FontName element to display this font type:

```
<FontName>Courier New</FontName>
```

Next, an instance of a `SpriteFont` object is required at the top of the game class to access and draw our font:

```
private SpriteFont spriteFont;
```

Here is the code to load and initialize the font sprite. This is needed inside `LoadContent()`:

```
spriteFont      = Content.Load<SpriteFont>("Courier New");
```

To ensure that our font displays in the viewable region on all televisions, add the `TitleSafeRegion()` method to your game class:

```
Rectangle TitleSafeRegion(string outputString, SpriteFont font){
    Vector2 stringDimensions = font.MeasureString(outputString);
```

```
    float   width            = stringDimensions.X; // string pixel width
    float   height           = stringDimensions.Y; // font pixel height

    // some televisions only show 80% of the window
    const float UNSAFEAREA   = 0.2f;
    Vector2     topLeft      = new Vector2();
    topLeft.X = graphics.GraphicsDevice.Viewport.Width  * UNSAFEAREA/2.0f;
    topLeft.Y = graphics.GraphicsDevice.Viewport.Height * UNSAFEAREA/2.0f;

    return new Rectangle(                          // returns margin
    (int)topLeft.X,                                // positions in pixels
    (int)topLeft.Y,                                // around safe area.
    (int)((1.0f - UNSAFEAREA)*(float)Window.ClientBounds.Width  - width),
    (int)((1.0f - UNSAFEAREA)*(float)Window.ClientBounds.Height - height));
}
```

The font-drawing routine, `DisplayCurrentHeight()`, is like any font display method you have used in previous chapters. `DisplayCurrentHeight()` belongs in the game class:

```
private void DisplayCurrentHeight(){
    string    outputString;
    Rectangle safeArea;

    // start drawing font sprites
    spriteBatch.Begin(SpriteBlendMode.AlphaBlend,  // enable transparency
                      SpriteSortMode.Immediate,    // use manual order
                      SaveStateMode.SaveState);    // store 3D settings
    Vector3 position = RowColumn(cam.position);
    int     row      = (int)position.Z;
    int     col      = (int)position.X;
    float   height   = terrain.position[col + terrain.NUM_ROWS*row].Y;

    // show cell height and width
    outputString     = "Cell Height=" + height;
    safeArea         = TitleSafeRegion(outputString, spriteFont);
    spriteBatch.DrawString(spriteFont, outputString, new Vector2(
                           safeArea.Left, safeArea.Top), Color.Yellow);
```

```
    // stop drawing - and 3D settings are restored if SaveState used
    spriteBatch.End();
}
```

`DisplayCurrentHeight()` is called from the `Draw()` method inside the game class. Remember to call it after the 3D objects have drawn so they do not cover your font output:

```
DisplayCurrentHeight();
```

When you run your game project, the Content Pipeline Extension Library is compiled before your XNA game project. The implication from this is that you will have limited ability to use debugging tools such as stepping and tracing in your game library. Outside the `ContentTypeReader` class, breakpoints and tracing are not available for Microsoft Visual C# Express. However, these features are available for full editions of Visual C# or Visual Studio.

Try running your project. When you move through the world, your code will determine the camera's current location over the height map and it will print the current location in the window.

Try the step-by-step example in this chapter to create the custom content processor. Then test it and deploy it on the Xbox 360 to get a better understanding of how it works. You'll have many project references and component dependencies to learn about and digest when studying custom content processors. To avoid the pitfalls of incorrect naming and referencing—until you become more familiar with the content processors—you may find it helpful to start with a working solution like the one from this chapter. Then you can modify it incrementally to turn it into a processor that suits your needs. After doing this a few times, you will be ready to create your own from scratch.

CHAPTER 24 REVIEW EXERCISES

To get the most from this chapter, try out these chapter review exercises.

1. Follow the step-by-step exercise in this chapter to create the custom content processor, and run it on Windows and the Xbox 360.
2. After running the solution on Windows, navigate to the folder where the heightMap.xnb file is located and look at the timestamp. This file is located in the directory MGH_25_DirectionalLight\bin\x86\Debug\Content\Images.

You'll notice that the file is not updated as long as you do not change the media file or alter the content processor code. This shows that the content processor tracks changes made to the media file and processor code and only updates the compiled binary data when changes are detected.

3. Create your own custom content processor to read the string "ABC" from a text file and store it in your user-defined class. You may start with the solution from this chapter, but when you finish, rename all processor components and call your namespace for the processor `ABCimporter`. Make sure it works on both Windows and the Xbox 360.

CHAPTER 25

Terrain with Height Detection

WHEN playing *Halo*, did you ever stop to appreciate the beautiful scenery as you ran toward the Blood Gulch caves while clutching the rocket launcher? It may be tough to take time to enjoy the moment when you have to watch out for players who might suddenly appear from behind a big grassy hill, but this does not mean that gamers will not appreciate the effort you devote to the terrain in your games.

This chapter shows you how to create rolling fields with height detection. This way, you not only see this impressive terrain, but your camera will adjust to rise above the ground as you travel up or down the hilly landscape. The same logic can be used to implement height detection for other objects in your game. The terrain in this chapter is generated using a type of topographical map called a *height map*. Figure 25-1 shows a grassy landscape similar to the one that will be created in this chapter. As you travel over the hills, the camera rises or falls according to the height of the ground.

HEIGHT MAPS

A *height map* is an image that stores information in each pixel about terrain elevation. Using a height map to create terrain is popular because it is easy for designers to generate landscapes with an image-editing tool, and it is easy to convert this information to implement height detection in a 3D environment. The demonstration used in this chapter shows how to create and implement a height map using an 8-bit .raw grayscale image. Each pixel in the .raw image stores information about the elevation—in a range between 0 and 255. This information is read into an array when the program begins; the height data in each pixel can then be accessed with the pixel row and column number. When this technique is applied in a 3D environment, the ground is divided up into the same number of rows and columns as the image. When positioning the camera or other objects, you calculate the elevation by determining the row and column position of the object and then passing this information to the height map array to retrieve the elevation for the corresponding cell on the landscape.

FIGURE 25-1

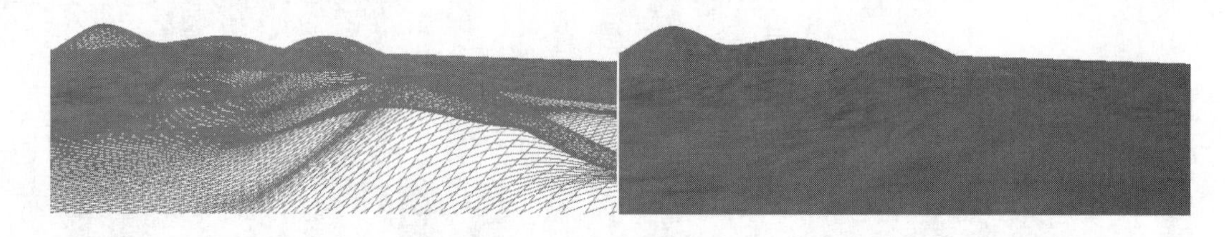

Terrain drawn from elevation data that is contained in a height map

Creating a Height Map Using Terragen

This demonstration shows you how to create a height map using Planetside's Terragen. Terragen does an excellent job in creating realistic terrain. If you configured the landscape before making your skybox (as shown in Chapter 10), you can use it to create terrain that matches your skybox.

Creating the Height Map

Terragen offers many different ways to create a height map. You can select a pattern for creating the terrain randomly or you can sculpt it on your own. This demonstration shows you how to sculpt it so you can have more control over the hills and fields you generate. You can download a trial version of Terragen from www.planetside.co.uk/terragen/. Once you have installed the application, you can launch it by selecting Terragen from the Start menu. This will open the main Terragen window. To create the terrain, select Landscape from the View menu.

Adjusting the Height Map Size

With the noncommercial edition of Terragen, you can choose from several preset sizes for your height map. The size 257×257 will be used for this demonstration because it offers enough pixels to draw smooth hills. Also, the `NUM_COLS` and `NUM_ROWS` values stored in your current terrain loader use these values. However, the size is not so large that it will impact performance on your PC or Xbox 360. To adjust the size, click the Size button in the Landscape dialog. Then select 257 in the Landscape Settings dialog that appears. Note that later in this demonstration you will create a 512×512 texture, which will be applied to the ground surface. Terragen's 257×257 pixel dimensions do not need to match the dimensions of the texture as long as the proportions of the width compared to the height are the same.

Starting with Level Ground

To clear the terrain so you can start with a flat surface, in the Landscape dialog, select the Modify button. Then, in the Terrain Modification dialog that appears, click Clear/Flatten. After returning to the Landscape dialog, you will notice the height map preview area is black; this means the ground is level (that is, no area on it has been elevated).

Adding Hills to Your Terrain

To start adding hills to your terrain, from the Landscape dialog, select View/Sculpt. Select the Basic Sculpting tool in the top-left corner of the View/Sculpt dialog and then left-click the mouse and drag in the dialog to add terrain. Right-clicking the mouse and dragging in the dialog lowers the terrain. Elevated areas will be lighter—bright white indicates high elevation and black indicates ground level. Figure 25-2 shows two clusters of hills that have been created from left-clicking the mouse and dragging in the View/Sculpt dialog.

When you return to the Landscape dialog, the changes you have made to the terrain will appear on the left.

Adjusting the Color

You can also adjust the color of the landscape from the Landscape dialog. This color has no effect on your height map, but it will affect the texture you will generate to cover it. In the Landscape dialog, highlight Surface Map and then click Edit. In the Surface Layer dialog that appears, click Color on the Base Surface tab. The Surface Color dialog will open and you can adjust the red, green, and blue settings to establish a general color for your terrain. To look more realistic, the color will not be uniform across the terrain, but it will use the general value you set. The color will also be affected by shadows from the sun, elevation, and other factors—if you choose these in your project settings. When you are satisfied with the general colors, click OK to exit from the Surface Color dialog, and then close the Surface Layer dialog to return to the Landscape dialog.

Exporting Your Height Map

Your height map is now ready for export. You can export the height map from the Landscape dialog by clicking the Export button. In the Terrain Export dialog, select the Export Method drop-down and choose Raw 8 bits, which is the format needed for this code demonstration. Then click Select a File and Save. When prompted, in the Export Heightfield dialog, after navigating to the folder where you want to save your

FIGURE 25-2

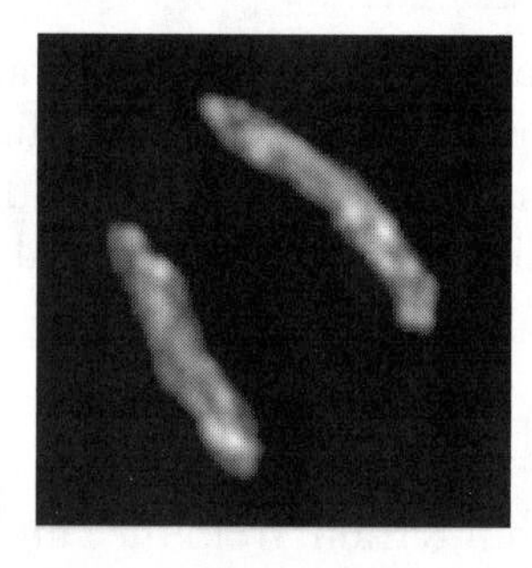

Two clusters of hills created in the View/Sculpt dialog

height map, enter the name **heightMap.raw** and click Save. This action will export your height map. Now you can create the texture to match the height map. Keep the Landscape dialog open to have the height map settings available when you generate the texture.

Creating the Terrain Texture to Match the Height Map

As you may have figured out already, the height map is separate from the texture. You do not have to use Terragen to create your terrain texture. If you want, you can use the tiled grass texture included with the base project for your terrain texture. However, you might consider using Terragen to generate this texture for several reasons. Terragen generates the terrain in a manner that considers many environmental factors, including the following:

- Blending of images
- Shadows based on cloud cover, sunlight, and change in elevation
- Snow, rock, and grass cover quantity, density, and color
- Elevation

When creating the texture for the terrain, you will use the same camera settings as in Chapter 10. This will ensure that the terrain can be viewed from the same perspective as your original skybox. Figure 25-3 shows the Rendering Control dialog settings used to generate the terrain image. Terragen will automatically adjust some of the properties as others are set, so you may not be able to replicate these properties exactly. However, you need to ensure that the Pitch (Y) value for the camera orientation is set to –90 so the camera points at the ground when the texture is rendered.

The camera settings applied for the terrain are summarized in Table 25-1.

Also, as in Chapter 10, the Zoom/Magnification property is set to 1 to ensure that the image is scaled properly when it is rendered by Terragen. This setting can be adjusted in the Camera Settings dialog. You can navigate there by clicking the Camera Settings button in the Rendering Control dialog. Note that the Detail slider is at a maximum setting in the Rendering Control dialog; this ensures the highest quality. Lastly, the texture size is set to 512×512, which matches the size used for the skybox images you created earlier in the book.

At this point, you will make an additional adjustment to reduce the shadows caused by the sun. Shadows look great in many situations, but they will look odd for the current project because they create a large dark area over the ground, which makes it difficult to see. Also, this effect would look odd in the absence of a surround-

FIGURE 25-3

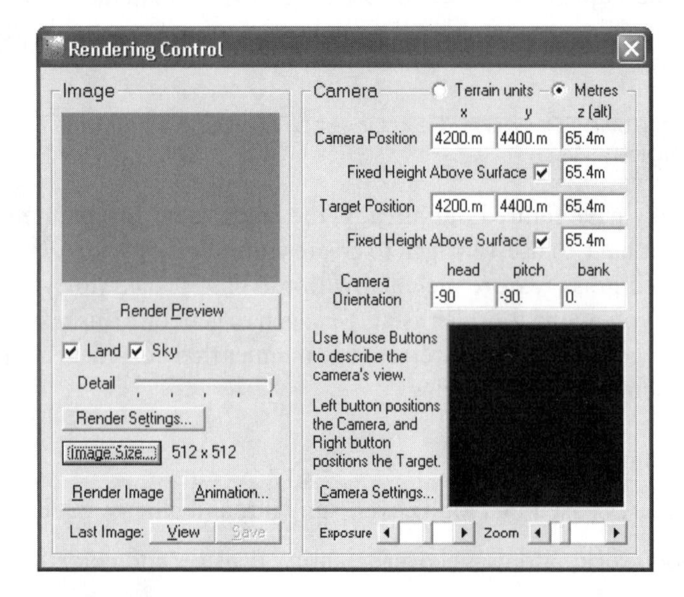

Settings for generating the terrain texture

ing series of mountains. To turn off the shadows, from the View menu select Lighting. In the Lighting Conditions dialog that appears, deselect Terrain Casts Shadows and Clouds Cast Shadows. Then close the Lighting Conditions dialog to return to the main window.

When these settings are in place, click Render Preview to check the color, randomness, and view of the image. If you are seeing sky, it is probably because the camera orientation changed. Before you generate the image, you will have to change the camera orientation's Y value back to –90 to ensure that the camera is looking at the ground when generating the terrain texture. Figure 25-4 shows the Rendering Con-

TABLE 25-1

Setting	**X**	**Y**	**Z**
Camera Position	*4200m*	*4400m*	*65.4m*
Target Position	*4200m*	*4400m*	*65.4m*
Camera Orientation	*-90*	*-90*	*0*

Camera settings for terrain creation

FIGURE 25-4

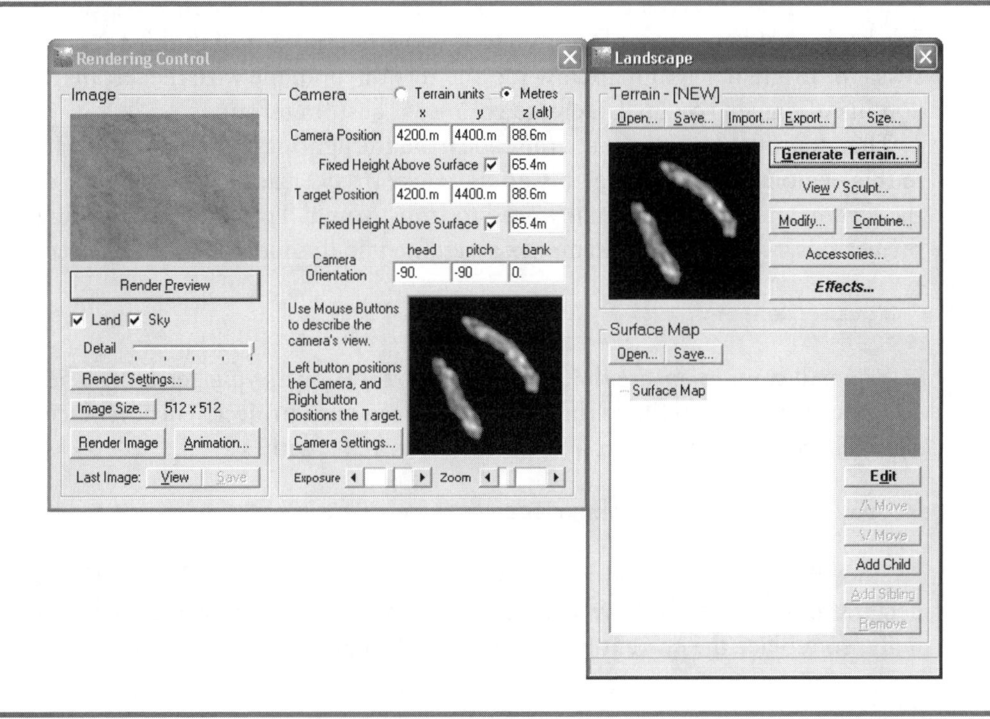

Texture preview on the left and height map preview on the right

trol and Landscape dialogs with settings suitable for exporting the terrain. The height map preview is in the Landscape dialog on the right as well as in the Rendering Control dialog in the lower left. The terrain preview is located in the top-left corner of the Rendering Control dialog.

Once your texture setup looks right, you can export the texture by selecting Render Image. Next, in the Rendering dialog, choose Save. When prompted, you can enter the name of the image and save it as a bitmap.

HEIGHT MAP CODE EXAMPLE

This code example begins with the solution from the first example in Chapter 24. The content processor in this solution already loads and generates the terrain position and normal vector data. This solution also implements code to detect the camera's row and column location on the terrain to determine the corresponding camera height over the terrain vertices.

When you finish adding the code from the demonstration in this chapter, the terrain will appear and your camera will travel above it. In the distance, a spaceship will ride back and forth across the terrain following the contours of the hills. You can also swap the original height map .raw file and terrain .bmp file with the terrain files that you just designed so you can create your own custom terrain.

This example recycles a lot of the code from the lighting demonstration. However, in this demonstration we are only going to use `DrawIndexedGrid()` for drawing the terrain and we don't actually need to transform it. To remove all existing transformations, replace the world matrix assignment in this method with the instruction:

```
world = Matrix.Identity;
```

You will want to ensure that the proper texture covers your terrain, so be sure to add your terrain.bmp file to the Images folder in your project. Then, replace the assignment for `floorTexture` in `LoadContent()` with:

```
floorTexture = Content.Load<Texture2D>("Images\\terrain");
```

Since the original terrain you created is 257 pixels wide by 257 pixels high, the declarations for the total rows and columns in your game class must be set accordingly, so replace the current declarations in the game class with these:

```
const int NUM_COLS = 257;
const int NUM_ROWS = 257;
```

The vertex buffer used for storing the terrain vertices must now use the height information from the height map. To do this, inside `InitializeVertexBuffer()` replace the current nested loop with this revised nested loop:

```
for(int row = 0; row < NUM_ROWS; row++){
    for(int col = 0; col < NUM_COLS; col++){
        vertex[col + row * NUM_COLS].Position              // position
                = terrain.position[col + row*NUM_COLS];

        float U = (float)col/(float)(NUM_COLS - 1);        // UV
        float V = (float)row/(float)(NUM_ROWS - 1);
        vertex[col + row * NUM_COLS].TextureCoordinate = new Vector2(U, V);

        vertex[col + row * NUM_COLS].Normal                // normal
                = terrain.normal[col + row*NUM_COLS];
    }
}
```

The terrain vertices depend on data generated from the terrain loader so be sure to load your terrain inside `Initialize()` prior to calling `InitializeVertexBuffer()`.

With these routines in place, you can now focus on implementing height detection for your game objects. We will first start with the camera.

`UpdateCameraHeight()` determines the camera height at the current location. Then it updates the Y values for the camera position and view:

```
void UpdateCameraHeight(){
    const float      HOVER_AMOUNT = 0.25f;

    float height      = CellHeight(cam.position);
    cam.view.Y       += height - cam.position.Y + HOVER_AMOUNT;
    cam.position.Y   += height - cam.position.Y + HOVER_AMOUNT;
}
```

Updates to the camera height rely on the latest camera position. Also, since the camera view is changing with the height, we need to ensure that the view is also adjusted. To implement move and view changes properly, trigger the camera's height adjustment from the `Update()` method immediately after `SetView()`:

```
UpdateCameraHeight();
```

Lastly, you need to comment out the line:

```
DrawIndexedGrid("wall");
```

If you run your code now, you will see your beautiful terrain, and your camera position and view will rise and fall along with it as you travel through the world.

Now we are going to add a spaceship that travels back and forth on the Z plane. This ship implementation for height detection is similar to the camera's implementation except the ship's `Up` vector will adjust to match the slope of the terrain's face where it is located. Start the spaceship loading and drawing code by declaring variables to store the ship model and to track the ship position:

```
Model    shipModel;
Matrix[] shipMatrix;

Vector3  shipPosition = new Vector3(0.0f, 3.0f, -BOUNDARY/2.0f);
Vector3  shipVelocity = new Vector3(0.0f, 0.0f, 0.318f);
bool     positiveDirection        = true;
```

These next instructions belong inside `LoadContent()` to load the spaceship model:

```
shipModel  = Content.Load<Model>("Models\\alien1");
shipMatrix = new Matrix[shipModel.Bones.Count];
shipModel.CopyAbsoluteBoneTransformsTo(shipMatrix);
```

`UpdateShipPosition()` is used in the game class to not only move the ship on X and Z but also Y to match the height of the terrain below:

```
void UpdateShipPosition(GameTime gameTime){
    const float HOVER_DISTANCE = 0.04f;

    // ship's X, Y, Z position without hover distance above the ground
    shipPosition.Y      = shipPosition.Y - HOVER_DISTANCE;

    // reverse direction if right boundary exceeded
    if (shipPosition.Z < -BOUNDARY && positiveDirection == false){
        shipVelocity *= -1.0f;
        positiveDirection = true;
    }
    // reverse direction if left boundary exceeded
    else if (shipPosition.Z > BOUNDARY && positiveDirection == true){
        shipVelocity *= -1.0f;
        positiveDirection = false;
    }
    // increment position by time scale so speed is same on all systems
    float time     = (float)gameTime.ElapsedGameTime.Milliseconds/200.0f;
    shipPosition.Z+= shipVelocity.Z * time;
    shipPosition.X+= shipVelocity.X * time;
    shipPosition.Y = CellHeight(shipPosition) + HOVER_DISTANCE;
}
```

To update the ship height each frame, trigger the ship update at the end of the `Update()` method:

```
UpdateShipPosition(gameTime);
```

When drawing objects that use the terrain, you need to do more than just update their positions and directions about the Y axis. You also need to update their orientation relative to the slope of the terrain where they are located. This next section of code allows you to do this.

When you're drawing the spaceship, the ship's Up vector is calculated using a weighted average of leading and trailing normal vectors in the ship's path (see Figure 25-5). This weighted average prevents a jerking motion caused as the ship's Up vector changes from one cell to the next. If you want to make it look as if you don't have any shock absorption, you can just use the normal vector for the current cell only.

Whether you are calculating weighted or normal vectors, a method is required to project or interpolate the object's position ahead or behind. When directionScalar equals +1, the position in one cell ahead is determined. When directionScalar equals -1, the position one cell behind is determined. Add ProjectedXZ() to the game class to interpolate the X and Z positions for objects in leading and trailing cells:

```
public Vector3 ProjectedXZ(Vector3 position, Vector3 speed,
                           float   directionScalar){
    // only consider change in X and Z when projecting position
    // in neighboring cell.
    Vector3 velocity = new Vector3(speed.X, 0.0f, speed.Z);
            velocity = Vector3.Normalize(velocity);

    float changeX = directionScalar * terrain.cellWidth * velocity.X;
    float changeZ = directionScalar * terrain.cellHeight * velocity.Z;
    return new Vector3(position.X + changeX, 0.0f, position.Z + changeZ);
}
```

CellWeight() determines the remaining distance within the current cell relative to the total distance projected into the neighboring cell. This fraction is then used to

FIGURE 25-5

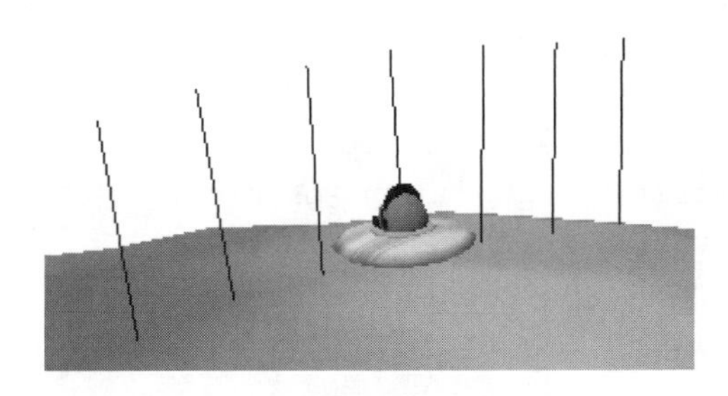

Trailing and loading normal vectors

weight the height values and `Up` vectors in trailing and leading height map cells. `CellWeight()` belongs in the game class:

```
float CellWeight(Vector3 currentPosition, Vector3 nextPosition){
    Vector3 currRowColumn = RowColumn(currentPosition);
    int     currRow       = (int)currRowColumn.Z;
    int     currCol       = (int)currRowColumn.X;
    Vector3 nextRowColumn = RowColumn(nextPosition);
    int     nextRow       = (int)nextRowColumn.Z;
    int     nextCol       = (int)nextRowColumn.X;

    // find row and column between current cell and neighbor cell
    int rowBorder, colBorder;
    if (currRow < nextRow)
        rowBorder = currRow + 1;
    else
        rowBorder = currRow;

    if (currCol < nextCol)          // next cell at right of current cell
        colBorder = currCol + 1;
    else
        colBorder = currCol;        // next cell at left of current cell

    Vector3 intersect = Vector3.Zero;  // margins between current
                                       // and next cell
    intersect.X = -BOUNDARY + colBorder*terrain.cellWidth;
    intersect.Z = -BOUNDARY + rowBorder*terrain.cellHeight;
    currentPosition.Y  = 0.0f; // not concerned about height

    // find distance between current position and cell border
    Vector3 difference     = intersect - currentPosition;
    float   lengthToBorder = difference.Length();

    // find distance to projected location in neighboring cell
    difference = nextPosition - currentPosition;
    float lengthToNewCell = difference.Length();

    if(lengthToNewCell==0)  // prevent divide by zero
        return 0.0f;

    // weighted distance in current cell relative to the entire
```

```
    // distance to projected position
    return lengthToBorder / lengthToNewCell;
}
```

Since the normal vector is projected in the cell ahead or trailing cell behind, an adjustment is required to handle situations where the current and projected cell are both off the height map. Replace the existing `HandleOffHeightMap()` method with this revision to remedy this case. If you don't, you will notice the spaceship disappears when it reaches the end of the world when Z is positive:

```
private void HandleOffHeightMap(ref int row, ref int col){
    if (row >= terrain.NUM_ROWS)
        row = terrain.NUM_ROWS - 2;
    else if (row < 0)
        row = 0;
    if (col >= terrain.NUM_COLS)
        col = terrain.NUM_COLS - 2;
    else if (col < 0)
        col = 0;
}
```

`CellNormal()` receives the height map row and column as parameters and returns the corresponding normal vector. The normal vector serves as a measure of uprightness for the object travelling above this location:

```
Vector3 CellNormal(int row, int col){
    HandleOffHeightMap(ref row, ref col);
    return terrain.normal[col + row * terrain.NUM_COLS];
}
```

`Normal()` projects the normal vector inside the cell according to the position relative to the surrounding height map cell vertices. Chapter 24 explains the `Lerp()` calculation behind this projection:

```
Vector3 Normal(Vector3 position){
    // coordinates for top left of cell
    Vector3 cellPosition    = RowColumn(position);
    int row                 = (int)cellPosition.Z;
    int col                 = (int)cellPosition.X;

    // distance from top left of cell
    float distanceFromLeft  = position.X%terrain.cellWidth;
```

```
    float distanceFromTop   = position.Z%terrain.cellHeight;

    // use lerp to interpolate normal at point within cell
    Vector3 topNormal        = Vector3.Lerp(
        CellNormal(row, col), CellNormal(row,col+1), distanceFromLeft);
    Vector3 bottomNormal     = Vector3.Lerp(
        CellNormal(row+1,col),CellNormal(row+1,col+1),distanceFromLeft);
    Vector3 normal           = Vector3.Lerp(
                               topNormal, bottomNormal, distanceFromTop);
    normal.Normalize();      // convert to unit vector for consistency
    return normal;
}
```

NormalWeight() is needed in the game class to allocate a weighted portion for each normal vector contained in a fixed range along the object's path, as shown in Figure 25-5. These weighted normal vectors are later combined to generate the upright vector for the spaceship. If you only use the current normal vector for your ship's Up direction, you will notice sudden changes in orientation at each cell and the ride will appear to be a rough one:

```
Vector3 NormalWeight(Vector3 position, Vector3 speed,
                     float   numCells, float   directionScalar){
    float   weight            = 0.0f;
    float   startWeight       = 0.0f;
    float   totalSteps        = (float)numCells;
    Vector3 nextPosition;
    Vector3 cumulativeNormal = Vector3.Zero;

    for (int i = 0; i <= numCells; i++)
    {   // get position in next cell
        nextPosition = ProjectedXZ(position, speed, directionScalar);

        if (i == 0){                   // current cell
            startWeight  = CellWeight(position, nextPosition);
            weight       = startWeight/totalSteps;
        }
        else if (i == numCells)      // end cell
            weight       = (1.0f - startWeight)/totalSteps;
        else                           // all cells in between
            weight       = 1.0f/totalSteps;
```

```
        cumulativeNormal+= weight * Normal(position);
        position         = nextPosition;
    }
    cumulativeNormal.Normalize();
    return cumulativeNormal;
}
```

ProjectedUp() drives the normal vector calculation for the ship from the game class. This method ensures that your ship is oriented properly above the terrain face:

```
Vector3 ProjectedUp(Vector3 position, Vector3 speed, int numCells){
    Vector3 frontAverage, backAverage, projectedUp;

    // total steps must be 0 or more. 0 steps means no shock absorption.
    if (numCells <= 0)
        return Normal(position);
    // weighted average of normals ahead and behind enable smoother ride.
    else{
        frontAverage  = NormalWeight(position, speed, numCells, 1.0f);
        backAverage   = NormalWeight(position, speed, numCells,-1.0f);
    }
    projectedUp       = (frontAverage + backAverage)/2.0f;
    projectedUp.Normalize();
    return projectedUp;
}
```

ShipWorldMatrix() assembles the cumulative transformation for the spaceship. It performs the same scaling and translation routine that we have implemented in previous chapters. ShipWorldMatrix() also calculates the ship's orientation according to both the ship's direction and the slope of the terrain underneath. The direction matrix used is described in more detail in Chapter 8. These are the steps used to generate the direction matrix (refer to Figure 26-6):

1. Initialize a direction matrix using a fixed rotation about the Y axis. This is arbitrary but the direction vectors contained within this matrix will be corrected later.
2. Calculate the proper Up vector using a weighted average of leading and trailing normal vectors on the ship's path, as shown in Figure 25-5.
3. Generate the Right vector from the initial Forward and weighted Up vector.
4. Calculate the proper Forward vector using the cross product of the Up and Right vectors.

FIGURE 25-6

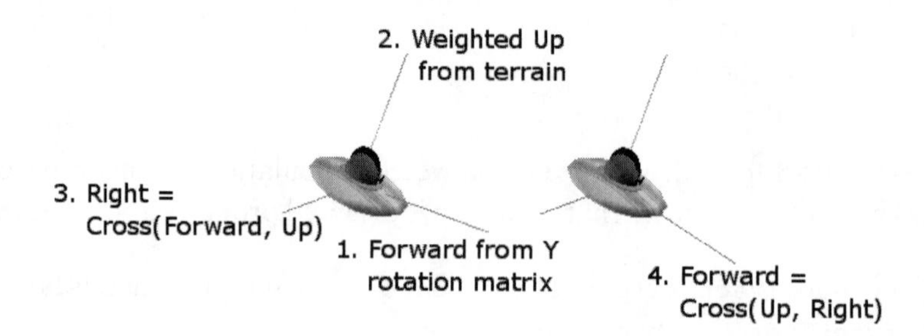

Direction matrix

Add `ShipWorldMatrix()` to the game class to set the ship's direction:

```
Matrix ShipWorldMatrix()
{
    float rotationAngle = (float)Math.Atan2(shipVelocity.Z,
                                shipVelocity.X) + MathHelper.Pi / 2.0f;
    Matrix  rotationY   = Matrix.CreateRotationY(rotationAngle);
    Matrix  scale       = Matrix.CreateScale(0.3f, 0.3f, 0.3f);
    Matrix  translation = Matrix.CreateTranslation(shipPosition);
    // 1.
    // generate direction matrix with fixed rotation about Y axis
    Matrix  dir         = Matrix.CreateRotationY(MathHelper.Pi);
    Vector3 velocity    = Vector3.Normalize(shipVelocity);
    // 2.
    // get UP vector using weighted average of cells in object path
    const int CELL_SPAN = 3; // total trailing and leading cells
    dir.Up = ProjectedUp(shipPosition, velocity, CELL_SPAN);
    // 3.
    // FORWARD stores a fixed direction about Y but it is enough to
    // compute the RIGHT vector which is the normal of FORWARD & UP
    dir.Right = Vector3.Cross(dir.Forward, dir.Up);
    dir.Right = Vector3.Normalize(dir.Right);
    // 4.
    // Re-calculate FORWARD with known UP and RIGHT vectors
    dir.Forward = Vector3.Cross(dir.Up, dir.Right);
```

```
    dir.Forward = Vector3.Normalize(dir.Forward);

    // apply other transformations along with direction matrix
    return scale * rotationY * dir * translation;
}
```

`DrawModel()` is needed in the game class to draw the ship. It draws the ship at the position and with the orientation to fit the terrain location and slope:

```
void DrawModel(Model model){
    // declare matrices
    Matrix world                = ShipWorldMatrix();

    foreach (ModelMesh mesh in model.Meshes){
        foreach (BasicEffect effect in mesh.Effects)
        {   // pass wvp to shader
            effect.World      = shipMatrix[mesh.ParentBone.Index] * world;
            effect.View       = cam.viewMatrix;
            effect.Projection = cam.projectionMatrix;

            // set lighting
            effect.EnableDefaultLighting();
            effect.CommitChanges();
        }
        // draw object
        mesh.Draw();
    }
}
```

`DrawShip()` is called from the `Draw()` method:

```
DrawModel(shipModel);
```

When you run the program, your hills will appear, and as you move over them the camera will rise and fall with their elevation. The spaceship will travel back and forth riding the changes in terrain slope. As you can see, this impressive effect was created with very little effort.

If you like the textures generated by the noncommercial version of Terragen, you should consider purchasing a license so you have the ability to create even larger image sizes and you can access more features.

CHAPTER 25 REVIEW EXERCISES

To get the most from this chapter, try out these chapter review exercises.

1. Implement the step-by-step demonstration discussed in this chapter, if you have not already done so.
2. Reduce the `CELL_SPAN` value to 0 in `ShipWorldMatrix()` and run your game code. Notice the spaceship ride is much rougher because the normal vectors are not weighted.
3. Create your own height map. Load it into your application. To add detail, apply multitexturing to the terrain.
4. Modify the `heightScale` value inside TerrainContent.cs to heighten or flatten your terrain.
5. If you are feeling ambitious, try adjusting the camera's view vector to change with the slope of the terrain just as the spaceship does.

CHAPTER 26

Animated Models

WE are sure you will agree that animated models are among the most exciting features of any game. This chapter presents several options for creating and loading pre-animated 3D models in your code. XNA does not currently ship with a library that automatically animates 3D models, so you have to find a loader that you can integrate into your code or you have to write your own animated model loader. As an alternative, we provide a model loader that loads and displays animated *Quake II* models, which are stored in the .md2 model format.

Of course, you can use MilkShape to create and export your animated models to .md2 format. However, if you are using a different model loader for other 3D model formats, you may still be able to create your model in MilkShape and then export it to your desired format. Alternatively, if you developed your 3D model in another 3D model tool, you may be able to import it into MilkShape, animate it, and then export it to a *Quake II* model format or other format, as needed.

Whatever method you use to develop your models, make sure you test the load and display of your 3D models from your XNA code. It is worth the time to ensure your models load and animate properly in your loader before you invest heavily in creating and animating them.

THE QUAKE II FORMAT

This chapter does not fully explain how the animated *Quake II* model source code works. However, a brief overview of the .md2 format is presented, and if you need to study it more, all of the *Quake II* model loader code is available with this book for you to view and modify. This chapter explains how you can add this MD2 class to play your animations, change animations, play sequences of animations, or pause and resume your animations.

The MD2 format was developed by id Software, and it was first introduced as part of id Software's *Quake II*. id Software has since released the source code for their *Quake II* game engine to the public under the GNU General Public License. Since then, the *Quake II* model format has become popular with game coders because it is reliable for animations, it is easy to implement, and decent low-cost tools are available to create models.

The *Quake II* format implements animation entirely through keyframe animations. The model's vertices are positioned at each keyframe. During the animation, the vertices are projected according to their relative position on the timeline between the closest keyframes.

When creating *Quake II* models in a modeling tool such as MilkShape, you attach the groups of vertices (known as *meshes*) to bones. These bones are connected by a series of joints to create the skeleton. The bones can be moved and rotated at different frames in the timeline to create keyframes. The attached meshes move with the bones when you create the animation. The joints keep the bones together to ensure your meshes move properly within the skeletal system for the model. When you export the

model and keyframes to the .md2 format, the bones are thrown out and you are left with a header file that describes the model's vertex data, the texture or skin information, and the information about the keyframe animations.

Unlike other model formats, *Quake II* models do not use the skeletal hierarchy or skin weights that are assigned during the model-creation process. This absence of information can lead to unrealistic crinkling of skin around model joints. However, you can avoid this crinkling (or minimize it) with careful planning while designing your model. Up close your *Quake II* model skins may appear to be a bit wobbly or watery due to their keyframe animation, but this defect isn't noticeable from most distances.

Quake II models cannot use more than 4,096 triangles. However, this limitation is reasonable because you can still generate decent-looking models with this polygon count.

A Closer Look at the .md2 Data

This section provides a brief overview of how the .md2 file is loaded and how it enables your animated models.

The *Quake II* data is stored in binary format in a manner that permits for some compression of the vertex and frame data. To help you unravel this data, the start of the file contains a header that describes the file type, the texture properties, the vertex properties, the total number of vertices, the total number of frames, and binary offsets in the file (to access details about the vertices and animation frames). Here is the standard .md2 header:

```
struct md2{ int fileFormatVersion; // file type which must equal 844121161
  int version;           // file format version which must be 8
  int skinWidth;         // texture width
  int skinHeight;        // texture height
  int frameSize;         // bytes per frame
  int numSkins;          // total skins used
  int numVertices;       // total vertices per frame
  int numUVs;            // total texture UV's
  int numTris;           // number of triangle coordinates
  int numglCommands;     // number of glCommands
  int numFrames;         // number of keyframes
  int offsetSkins;       // binary offset to skin data
  int offsetUV;          // offset to texture UV data
  int offsetTriangle;    // offset to triangle list data
  int offsetFrames;      // offset to frame data
  int offsetglcmds;      // offset to OpenGL command data
  int offsetEnd;         // offset to end of file
};
```

Each vertex in every frame is indexed. The indexes are ordered in a sequence of triangle lists. When the file is loaded, the indices are used to generate a list of vertex coordinates. The coordinates are then used to build a series of triangle lists. For efficiency, you could use the glCommands data to rewrite your model-loading and animation code to render your models using triangle strips or triangle fans.

As you would expect, it is possible to store more than one animation with the *Quake II* format. For example, your model may have a running, jumping, taunting, saluting, crouching, and idling animation. You will want to be able to switch between these animations on demand. To access this information, use the .md2 header, which contains the offset to the frame descriptions. The frame descriptions can be read in using a binary read at the offset. All frame descriptions are located together sequentially from the starting frame to the very last frame. Each frame description includes an animation name and a frame number.

To determine the starting and ending frames for each individual animation, you must parse each frame description so you can match the animation names. Once you have a series of matching animation names, you can store the starting and ending frame numbers in this series. When you want to play the animation on demand, you can set the frame number to the starting frame in the animation series. When the animation reaches the last frame, you can start the animation over again or you can switch to another animation.

During the animation sequence, the vertices are projected on the timeline between the keyframes used in the animation. The normal vectors must also be interpolated in this manner.

Textures with .md2 Format

For the actual *Quake II* game, *Quake II* models use .pcx files for textures. However, the .pcx format is not supported in XNA's content pipeline. A way to get around this limitation is to use an image-editing program such as the freeware image editor GIMP to load your *.pcx skins and save them to *.tga format, which is supported in the content pipeline. You can then use the *.tga files to texture your *Quake II* models. Although it is possible to have more than one texture for a *Quake II* model, the *Quake II* model loader provided with this chapter only handles one texture or skin.

When you build your Quake II models, be sure to use only one skin. The code used in this chapter can only handle one skin.

Animating Models in MilkShape

To show you how to create an animated model using MilkShape, this example demonstrates how to create an animated lamp that pivots left and right and also performs a bowing animation.

Creating the Quake II Model

Before you can create an animation, you first need to create a model. You can create your own model, use the one that is provided with the book, or search online for one to use.

Creating the Meshes

Your first task is to create two separate meshes for the top and bottom portions of a lamp, similar to the ones shown on the left side of Figure 26-1. For a refresher on how to use MilkShape to create meshes like these, review Chapter 14, "3D Models."

To enable smooth animations, be sure to position your model at the origin.

Once you have created your meshes, you need to position them together so they appear as one lamp. However, to enable the animation, you must ensure that the meshes remain as two separate groups. If your model uses more than two mesh groups, you will need to merge them so you end up with a top mesh group and a bottom mesh group. Merging can be performed on the *Groups* tab using the *Regroup* button. (Merging groups is also explained in Chapter 14.)

Creating the Skeleton

Once you have the top and bottom mesh groups in position, you must add three joints to create pivot points for the animation. The end result is shown in the diagram on the right in Figure 26-1.

Joints can be added in MilkShape from the *Model* tab. While the *Joint* button is selected, click into the viewport to add a joint where the cursor is placed. To enable

FIGURE 26-1

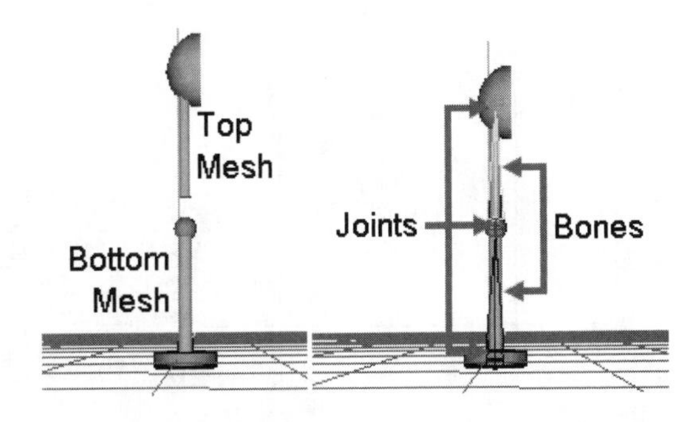

Two model pieces on the left; three joints and two bones for animating on the right

proper mesh positioning with the bones (when animating your lamp model), you must add each of the three joints in sequence from the bottom to the top. The first joint is placed at the base of the lamp. After the first joint is set, whenever a new joint is added, a bone is automatically generated between the new joint and the joint that was previously added.

To enable use of the bones as guides for the mesh animations, you must attach the meshes to the bones. The bottom mesh will be attached to the bottom bone. You can select the bottom bone by clicking the joint listed at the top on the *Joints* tab, then select the bottom mesh. When doing this, choose the *Select* button on the *Groups* tab to ensure the bottom mesh is the only mesh group highlighted in red. When the bottom mesh group is highlighted in red and the bottom joint is also highlighted in red, click the *Assign* button on the *Joints* tab to assign the bottom mesh to the bottom bone. Figure 26-2 shows the viewport and *Joints* tab where the bottom mesh has been assigned to the lower bone.

Next, you must repeat this process to assign the top mesh to the top bone. To select the top bone, click the middle joint, which is *joint2*, to highlight it in red. Then select the top mesh in the viewport on the *Groups* tab and ensure that is the only one highlighted in red. Once both the top joint and top mesh are selected, click the *Assign* button on the *Joints* tab to attach the upper mesh to the upper bone.

NOTE To ensure you have the correct mesh attached to the correct bone, you can select the joint on the Joints tab and click the SelAssigned button to highlight the mesh that is attached.

FIGURE 26-2

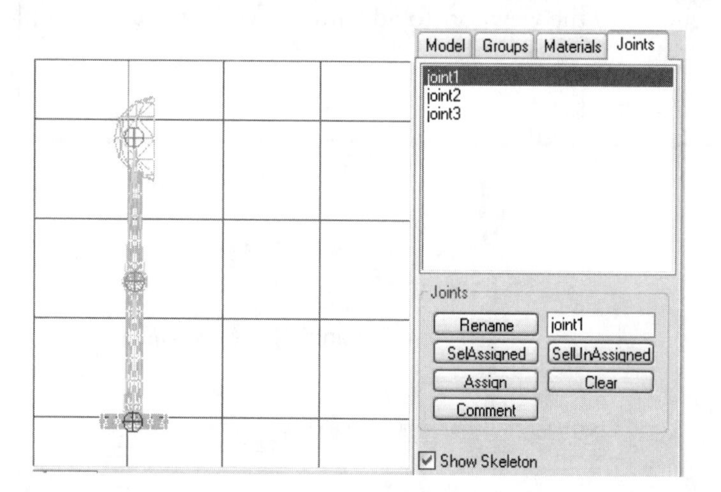

Attaching the bottom mesh to the bottom bone

Creating the Pivoting Animation

Now that you have attached the meshes to the skeleton, you can create your animation. For this example, you will create two separate animations. The first animation is a pivot animation where the lamp turns back and forth from left to right. This animation runs between frames 1 and 29. The second animation is a bowing animation where the lamp bows downward and then returns to the original upright position. This second animation runs from frames 30 to 50. Thankfully, to generate all 50 frames, you don't need to reposition the model each frame. You only need to set keyframes for the animation, and MilkShape will project the model at all frames in between.

To create the animation, you must select the *Anim* button in the lower-right corner of the MilkShape window. Note that if the *Anim* button is not selected, the meshes will not move with the bones. When the *Anim* button is pressed, you must identify the minimum (starting) frame, current frame, maximum (ending) frame, and total frames for the animation in Milkshape on the bottom right of the *Model* tab. Figure 26-3 shows the first keyframe is set 1, the current frame is at 30, and total frame count is 50. The current frame number is entered in the second text box from the left. For our purposes, the last frame number for the entire animation series is always the same value entered for the maximum number of frames in the animation. These maximum and total frame counts appear on the right of Figure 26-3. You also need a viewport projection that shows the model from a perspective that allows you to easily move or rotate the model when creating your keyframe.

A top view like the one in the left of Figure 26-3 offers easy access to permit rotations for the top of the lamp. The middle joint is selected so only the top bone and mesh will move or rotate when you are positioning the model. The middle joint is selected from the *Joints* tab. Once the joint is selected, on the *Models* tab you can rotate the bone and attached mesh when the *Rotate* button is selected. You can also move the bone and attached mesh when the *Move* button is selected. When the lamp is in

FIGURE 26-3

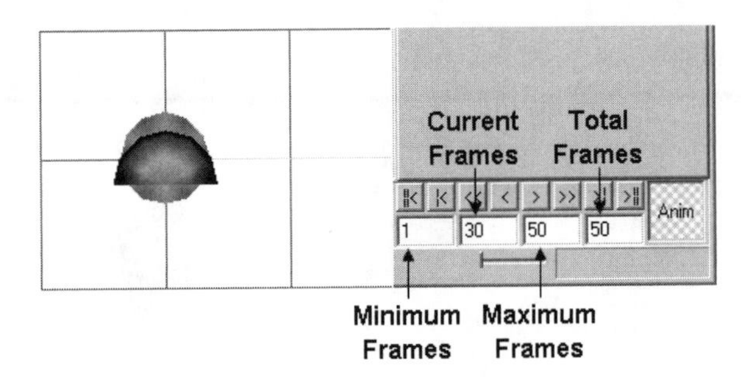

Setup for the animation frames

position to start the animation, you can set the keyframe from the Animate menu by selecting Set Keyframe.

To create the next keyframe, change the frame number in the left text box from 1 to 8. You can do this by clicking in the text box and entering **8** with your keyboard. Then, while the middle joint is still selected, and while the *Rotate* button on the *Models* tab is selected, rotate the lamp 90 degrees in a clockwise direction about the Y axis. When you have done this, you can set a new keyframe by selecting Set Keyframe from the Animate menu.

To create the next keyframe in this animation, change the keyframe number in the text box to **15**. While the middle joint is selected and while the *Rotate* button on the *Models* tab is selected, rotate the upper portion of the lamp so it faces toward the middle again. Once the lamp faces the middle, select Set Keyframe from the Animate menu to set the keyframe. Next, enter **22** as the frame number in the left text box at the lower left of the MilkShape window. Rotate the lamp 90 degrees about the Y axis so it faces toward the right, and set a keyframe there.

To complete the animation, enter **29** in the frame text box and then rotate the upper portion of the lamp 90 degrees so it returns to the starting position where it faces the middle. Set the keyframe at frame 29 to complete the first animation. Figure 26-4 shows how the lamp is positioned for each keyframe at frames 1, 8, 15, 22, and 29.

You can view your animation in MilkShape by setting the starting frame to 1 and the ending frame at 29 in the text boxes at the bottom of the MilkShape window. Then, while the *Anim* button is selected, click the > button (shown back in Figure 26-3). If your animation is set properly, you will see the upper portion of the lamp pivoting back and forth from left to right.

Creating the Bowing Animation

The bowing animation runs from frame number 30 to frame number 50. You will need to use a side view to create the keyframes for this animation. Figure 26-5 shows how to position the lamp for frames 30, 35, 40, 45, and 50 when creating keyframes for this animation.

FIGURE 26-4

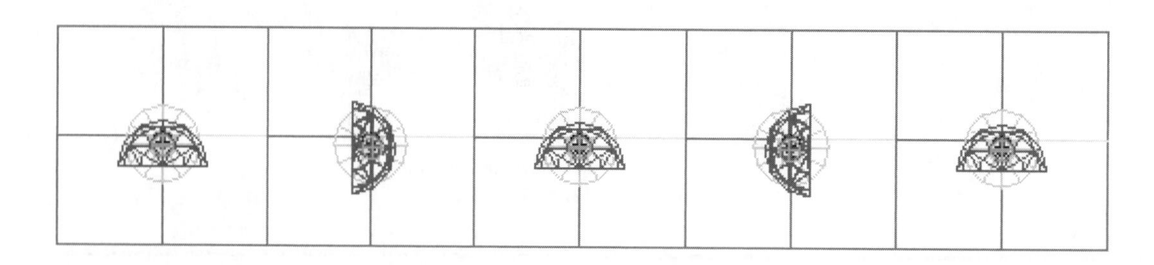

Top view of keyframes set at frames 1, 8, 15, 22, and 29

Previewing Your Animation

When the keyframes have been set, you can preview your animation by clicking the > button in MilkShape while the *Anim* button is pressed. When you are satisfied that the animation looks the way it is intended, you can export your model.

Exporting to QUAKE II .md2 Format

The XNA *Quake II* file loader included with this chapter requires that you export to *Quake II* MD2 format if you want to animate your model with this code. However, you can export to another model format from MilkShape in case you have a different type of loader. When exporting to the *Quake II* MD2 format, you must place an md2.qc file in the same directory where you export your model. The md2.qc file is used to help build the .md2 file. It contains information about the model name, the skin name, and skin pixel dimensions. It also contains the different animation names and their starting and ending frames. The md2.qc file is actually just a text file that you can edit in Notepad. You will have to edit this file or create one to list information about the image you use for your lamp and to document the frames used for the pivoting and bowing animations. If the md2.qc file is not present when you are exporting from MilkShape, you will receive an error. For this example, here are the required contents for the md2.qc file:

```
// Sample MD2 config, copy into export directory
$modelname lamp.md2
$origin 0.0 0.0 0.0
// skins
$skinwidth 128
$skinheight 128
$skin lamp.bmp
// sequences
$sequence pivot 1 29
$sequence bowing 30 50
```

FIGURE 26-5

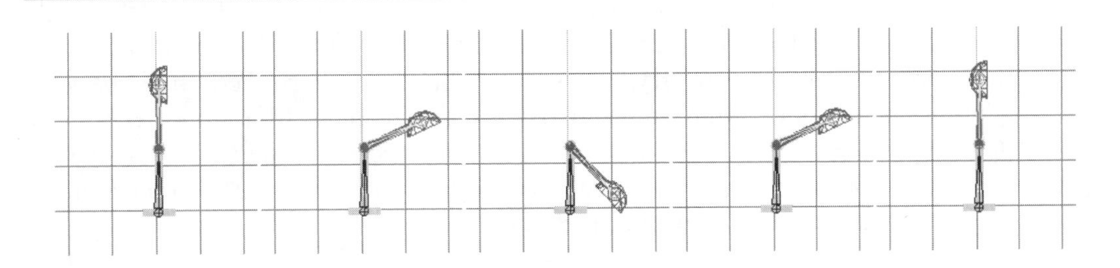

Side view of keyframes set at frames 30, 35, 40, 45, and 50

When your md2.qc file has been created, place it in the same folder where your model's texture is located. You can now export your MD2 model to that directory by selecting File | Export | Quake 2 MD2. Save this file as lamp.md2.

Loading Your Quake II Model in Code

This code demonstration shows you how to load your *Quake II* model in code. It loads the lamp you created and animates it with the pivoting and bowing animations.

The example begins with either the MGHWinBaseCode project or the MGH360BaseCode project, which can be found in the BaseCode folder in the download available from this book's website. You will also need the MD2Pipeline project, the MD2Runtime project, and MD2.cs source file from Source directory. The MD2Pipeline project and the MD2Runtime project must be referenced in your solution. The MD2.cs file must be referenced in your game project from the Solution Explorer.

For either the PC or the Xbox, the custom content processor must be included in your project references. In Chapter 24, "Content Pipeline Processors," you referenced the pipeline and runtime projects in your game project. The steps to reference your *Quake II* loader are similar. The pipeline and runtime projects belong in the same directory as your game project. Then right-click the parent solution node for the base code and select Add | Existing Project. You can then navigate to either the pipeline project or the runtime project to select and add each. Once both projects are added to the solution, you then need to reference them from your game project. To do this, right-click your game project's Content | References node and from the Projects tab of the Add Reference dialog that appears select the Pipeline project. Then, right-click the parent References tab in your game project. From there you choose your runtime project from Projects tab of the Add Reference dialog. Once you have finished your project references will be similar to Figure 26-6.

When your base code is ready, you will have to reference your model and the accompanying texture in your project. In your game project, create a Models folder under the Content node. Then place your .md2 model there. The lamp.bmp texture needs to be placed in the Images folder under the Content node. With your *Quake II* model files in your project, you need to ensure that your lamp.md2 model uses the content pipeline. To be sure, click the .md2 file in the Solution Explorer to view this file's properties in the property browser. The Build Action property must be set to Compile. The Content Importer property needs to be set to MD2Importer, and the Content Processor property must be set to md2Processor. Figure 26-7 shows the properties for the lamp model when it has been referenced properly in the Solution Explorer (i.e., to use the content pipeline).

FIGURE 26-6

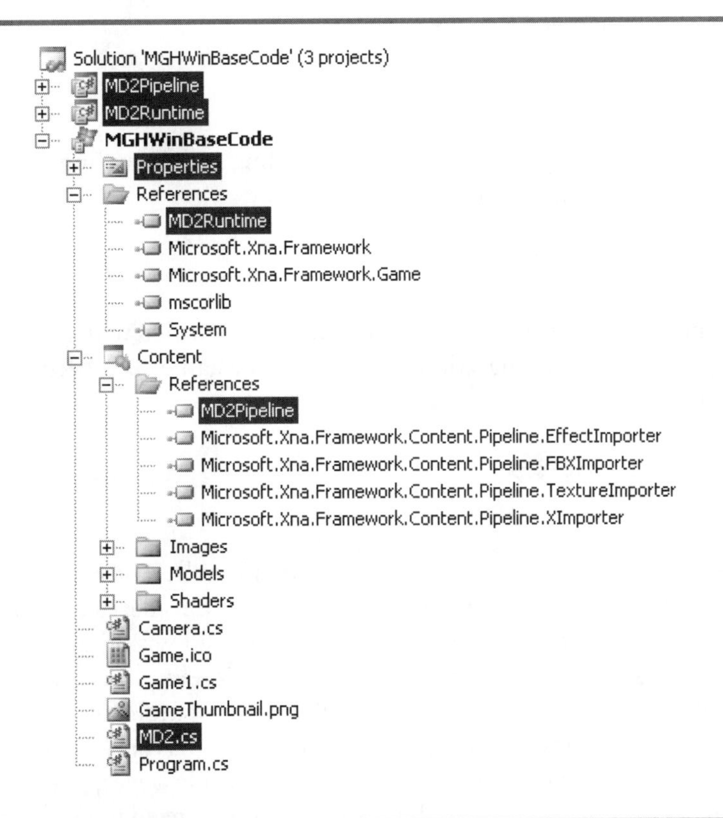

MD2 project references

FIGURE 26-7

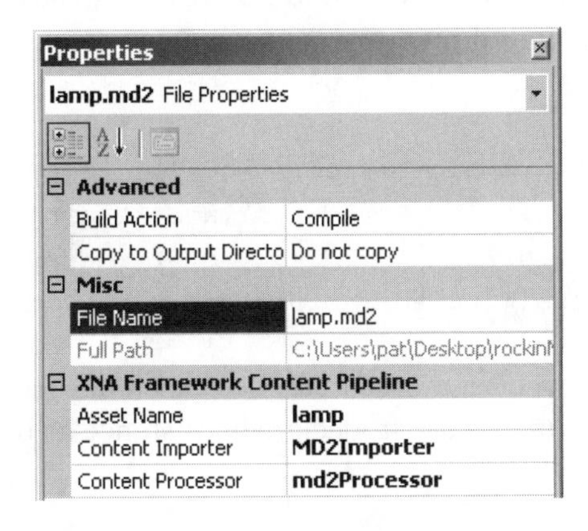

Model properties

Next, your Game1.cs file has to reference the MD2 class to access it, so you must include the namespace for this class:

```
using MD2Animation;
```

To create an object to use this class for loading and animating your *Quake II* models, a class-level object is required:

```
private MD2 md2;
```

The pivoting and bowing animations will be identified with a class-level enumeration. Declaring the enumeration at the top of the game class permits the use of these identifiers throughout the game class:

```
public enum       animations
{     pivot,      bow       }
```

The model setup when the program starts is simple. The MD2 object must be initialized. Then, the model can be loaded from the folder where it is located. The *Quake II* model's texture, lamp.bmp, can be loaded with the ContentManager object as long as the image is referenced in the Solution Explorer. Also, when the model is initialized, the speed is set. The method SetAnimationSpeed(), with a parameter equal to 5.0f, sets the animation rate to a similar playback speed that you experienced when testing your animation in MilkShape. However, you can slow your animation down or speed it up with this method if you need to. To start animating the model when the game begins, the instruction SetAnimationSequence() plays two animations in succession. The first parameter sets the animation to play once only. The second parameter sets the second animation to play in a continuous loop when the first animation ends. Add this code to LoadContent() to set up your model, load it, and play the bowing and pivoting animations:

```
md2 = new MD2();
md2.LoadModel(graphics.GraphicsDevice, "Models\\lamp",
                                       "Images\\lamp", Content);
md2.SetAnimationSpeed(5.0f);                  // default
md2.SetAnimationSequence((int)animations.bow, (int)animations.pivot);
```

XNA's BasicEffect class is used to render the model because it offers an easy implementation of lighting. To use it, declare an instance at the top of the game class:

```
BasicEffect basicEffect;
```

To prepare the BasicEffect shader when the program launches, and to avoid costly cycles used when initializing the BasicEffect object, this object should only be created once when the program begins. With this in mind, the BasicEffect object is set in Initialize():

```
basicEffect = new BasicEffect(graphics.GraphicsDevice, null);
```

Directional lighting only needs to be set once—unless your world has more than one sun. The lighting settings used here are explained in more detail in Chapter 22, "Lighting." To provide a method that can be used by all objects that use BasicEffect's lighting and to enable the texturing when rendering objects with this shader, add the InitializeBasicEffect() method to the game class:

```
public void InitializeBasicEffect(){
    // set up lighting
    basicEffect.LightingEnabled                  = true;
    basicEffect.DirectionalLight0.Enabled        = true;
    basicEffect.AmbientLightColor                = new Vector3(0.8f, 0.8f, 0.8f);
    basicEffect.DirectionalLight0.DiffuseColor   = new Vector3(1.0f, 1.0f, 1.0f);
    basicEffect.DirectionalLight0.Direction      = Vector3.Normalize(
                                            new Vector3(0.0f, -0.3f, 1.0f));
    basicEffect.DirectionalLight0.SpecularColor = new Vector3(0.2f, 0.2f, 0.2f);
    basicEffect.SpecularPower                    = 0.01f;
    basicEffect.TextureEnabled                   = true;
}
```

To initialize the BasicEffect shader's properties when the program begins, call InitializeBasicEffect() from the Initialize() method:

```
InitializeBasicEffect();
```

A suitable VertexDeclaration that permits lighting, with XNA's BasicEffect class, is required. This variable is needed throughout the game class, so a declaration is needed at the top of it:

```
private VertexDeclaration positionNormalTexture;
```

The VertexDeclaration object is initialized when the application starts, so it can be used when drawing the first frame. To enable this setup, add the following code to the Initialize() method:

```
positionNormalTexture = new VertexDeclaration(graphics.GraphicsDevice,
                              VertexPositionNormalTexture.VertexElements);
```

Every frame, the .md2 model vertices must be updated with a time-scaled interpolation between frames. Adding the UpdateModel() instruction to the Update() method allows the MD2 class to take care of this interpolation to enable a smooth animation:

```
md2.UpdateModel(graphics.GraphicsDevice, gameTime);
```

The code used to draw the model is similar to code you have used to draw your .x or .fbx 3D models. A notable difference here is you must reference the model's vertex buffer when setting the data source. Also, this code is designed to use triangle lists when drawing the *Quake II* model, so you must specify this primitive type while rendering it. The total number of triangles drawn is obtained from the model object while it is being rendered. Add the DrawMD2Model() method to your game class to draw your model:

```
void DrawMD2Model(){
    // 1: declare matrices
    Matrix scale, rotationY, translation, world;

    // 2: initialize matrices
    scale       = Matrix.CreateScale(0.2f, 0.2f, 0.2f);
    rotationY   = Matrix.CreateRotationY(0.0f);
    translation = Matrix.CreateTranslation(0.0f, 0.0f, -4.0f);
    // 3: build cumulative world matrix using I.S.R.O.T. sequence
    // identity, scale, rotate, orbit(translate & rotate), translate
    world       = scale * rotationY * translation;

    // 4: set shader matrices, and texture
    // don't draw back face
    graphics.GraphicsDevice.RenderState.CullMode
                = CullMode.CullCounterClockwiseFace;

    basicEffect.Begin();
    basicEffect.World         = world;
    basicEffect.View          = cam.viewMatrix;
    basicEffect.Projection    = cam.projectionMatrix;
    basicEffect.Texture       = md2.GetTexture();

    // 5: draw object - select vertex type, data source, # of primitives
    graphics.GraphicsDevice.VertexDeclaration = positionNormalTexture;
    foreach (EffectPass pass in basicEffect.CurrentTechnique.Passes){
        pass.Begin();
        // get the data and draw it
```

```
            graphics.GraphicsDevice.Vertices[0].SetSource(
               md2.vertexBuffer, 0, VertexPositionNormalTexture.SizeInBytes);
            graphics.GraphicsDevice.DrawPrimitives(
               PrimitiveType.TriangleList, 0, md2.GetNumTriangles());
            pass.End();
        }
        basicEffect.End();
        // turn off culling
        graphics.GraphicsDevice.RenderState.CullMode = CullMode.None;
}
```

As with all objects that are rendered, the instructions to draw the *Quake II* model are triggered from the Draw() method:

```
DrawMD2Model();
```

When you run the code, you will see your lamp performing the bowing animation followed by a continuous pivot back and forth from right to left. You may find that you need to scale your model and rotate it, depending on the scale and orientation used when creating the model.

Loading and Controlling Quake II Models in Code

The last demonstration showed you how to create your own *Quake II* model and animate it in code. This is definitely a useful exercise; however, *Quake II* models have the power to perform far more interesting animations than the one you just created. This next demonstration shows a more interesting animated model to demonstrate how to use the MD2 class to play animations on demand, switch animations, and pause or resume animations. This demonstration loads a model called Zarlag, which is stored in the tris.md2 file. The Zarlag.tga image is used for the skin. You can download this model and skin from the Models folder in the book's download.

The Zarlag model was created by Phillip T. Wheeler. Thank you very much, Phillip, for a great model.

Zarlag has many interesting animations, and this example shows you how to use the MD2 class to switch between them. Figure 26-8 shows Zarlag in the heat of battle.

This example begins with the solution code from the previous example. To be able to handle all of Zarlag's animations, replace the existing enumeration with the following revision, which provides friendly identifiers for all of Zarlag's animations. These enumerated values will be referenced later so you can play Zarlag's animations on demand:

```
public enum animations{
stand,   run,    attack,   pain1,
pain2,   pain3,  jump,     flip,
```

```
salute,  taunt,  wave,     point,
crstand, crwalk, crattack, crpain,
crdeath, death1, death2,   death3
}
```

To load Zarlag instead of the lamp model, replace the LoadModel() instruction inside LoadContent() with this version. Also, make sure you place the tris.md2 file in the Model's folder and reference the Zarlag.tga image from the Image's folder in Solution Explorer.

```
md2.LoadModel(graphics.GraphicsDevice, "Models\\tris",
                                       "Images\\Zarlag", Content);
```

To begin with a standing animation, inside LoadContent() replace the SetAnimationSequence() call to start the bowing and pivoting animations with the following instruction, which sets a standing animation:

```
md2.SetAnimation((int)animations.stand);
```

When drawing the animation, you need to position, rotate, and scale Zarlag differently from the lamp. Replace the scaling, translation, and rotation calculations in DrawMD2Model() with these revisions so Zarlag faces the viewer and appears to be standing on the ground when the program begins:

```
scale       = Matrix.CreateScale(0.02f, 0.02f, 0.02f);
translation = Matrix.CreateTranslation(0.0f, 0.5f, -3.0f);
rotationY   = Matrix.CreateRotationY(-MathHelper.Pi/2.0f);
```

FIGURE 26-8

Zarlag on the move

The MD2 class has a few different methods to allow you to play an animation on demand, play an animation sequence for two animations, and to pause and resume an animation. These commands will be triggered by press events. To ensure that multiple animations are triggered in one press event, which can last over several frames, current KeyboardState and GamePadState objects are compared with previous ones to check for new press events that indicate a change is needed. Add these declarations to track the input device states for switching animations:

```
KeyboardState currentKB, previousKB;
GamePadState  currentGP, previousGP;
```

The first animation handler allows you to advance through the list of the *Quake II* model's animations by pressing either the SPACEBAR or the left thumbstick on the game pad. The MD2 class's AdvanceAnimation() scrolls through the list of animations. Add this code block to the Update() method to allow your users to view all animations for the *Quake II* file:

```
// refresh new input states
previousKB = currentKB; // store keyboard state from last frame
previousGP = currentGP; // store previous gamepad state
currentKB  = Keyboard.GetState();
currentGP  = GamePad.GetState(PlayerIndex.One);

// if new space bar or left stick press advance the animation
if(currentKB.IsKeyDown(Keys.Space) && previousKB.IsKeyUp(Keys.Space)
|| currentGP.IsButtonDown(Buttons.LeftStick) // new left stick press
&& previousGP.IsButtonUp(Buttons.LeftStick)){
    md2.AdvanceAnimation();                     // move to next animation
}
```

This next animation handler triggers the running animation if either the A key is pressed or the right trigger on the game pad is pulled. This code is added to the Update() method to catch these press events and start Zarlag running:

```
// show running animation when A key pressed or right trigger pulled
if(currentKB.IsKeyDown(Keys.A) && previousKB.IsKeyUp(Keys.A)
|| currentGP.Triggers.Right> 0 && previousGP.Triggers.Right==0
&& !md2.IsPlaying((int)animations.run)){
    md2.SetAnimation((int)animations.run);  // switch to run animation
}
```

This next code block triggers a one-time jump followed by a running loop when either the J key or right thumbstick is pressed. Add this code to the Update() method to enable this feature:

```
// if J key or right stick pressed jump then run
if(currentKB.IsKeyDown(Keys.J) && previousKB.IsKeyUp(Keys.J)
|| currentGP.IsButtonDown(Buttons.RightStick)
&& previousGP.IsButtonUp(Buttons.RightStick)){
    md2.SetAnimationSequence((int)animations.jump, (int)animations.run);
}
```

You may also pause or resume your animation when the R key or B button is pressed. Add the following code block to Update() to handle these pause and resume events:

```
if(currentKB.IsKeyDown(Keys.R) && previousKB.IsKeyUp(Keys.R)
|| currentGP.IsButtonDown(Buttons.B) && previousGP.IsButtonUp(Buttons.B))
{
    if(md2.paused){                                    // resume
        md2.Resume();
    }
    else{                                              // pause
        md2.Pause();
    }
}
```

Try running your program now. The model should first appear standing idle. You can make it run by pulling the right trigger or by pressing the SPACEBAR. You can advance it through all animations by pressing the left thumbstick or the SPACEBAR. Press the A key or pull the right trigger to start the running animation. A one-time jump followed by a running animation can be called when either the J key or right thumbstick is pressed. You can pause and resume animations with either the P and R keys or the B and A buttons on the game pad.

Loading the Quake II Weapon

Quake II weapons are usually separate from the actual character model. Separate weapons enable you to switch between holding a rifle, plasma gun, rocket launcher, or other artillery to fit the occasion. These weapons are animated to match the character's animation. As the model runs, jumps, crouches, or falls in pain, the weapon moves with the model's arms and hands. In the unfortunate event of death, the weapon may fall from the character's hands.

To add the weapon, the weapon.md2 file must be referenced from the Models folder and the weaponSkin.tga file must be referenced from the Images folder. These files can be found in the Models folder from the book's download.

To enable use of the MD2 class for a weapon object in addition to the *Quake II* character, some changes are needed. Identifiers at the top of the game class distinguish between the two separate models:

```
const int CHARACTER = 0;
const int WEAPON    = 1;
```

Also in the game class, a new instance of the MD2 class is needed, so this object must be declared at the module level:

```
private MD2 md2Weapon;
```

The weapon and texture are loaded when the game begins, place the code to load them inside LoadContent():

```
md2Weapon = new MD2();
md2Weapon.LoadModel(graphics.GraphicsDevice,
                    "Models\\weapon", "Images\\weaponSkin", Content);
md2Weapon.SetAnimationSpeed(5.0f);
md2Weapon.SetAnimation((int)animations.stand);
```

Note the animation speed, 5.0f, and the starting animation are set to match the starting speed and starting animation for Zarlag. This ensures that the weapon will animate properly with the character.

Each frame, the weapon animation must be updated. This can be done from the Update() method with the following instruction:

```
md2Weapon.UpdateModel(graphics.GraphicsDevice, gameTime);
```

Inside the Update() method, five conditions were implemented above to handle user input for changing the character's animation to the next animation, setting a specific animation, setting an animation sequence, and pausing and resuming animations. To ensure the weapon also moves properly with these animation changes, the following five instructions must be included with their respective conditions in the Update() method:

```
md2Weapon.AdvanceAnimation();
md2Weapon.SetAnimation((int)animations.run);
md2Weapon.SetAnimationSequence((int)animations.jump,(int)animations.run);
```

```
md2Weapon.Resume();
md2Weapon.Pause();
```

Some minor changes are also needed in the DrawMD2Model() method. It needs to be able to handle an identifier for the model so it knows which one to draw. Replace the header with this revision that includes a parameter to identify the model:

```
void DrawMD2Model(int modelNum)
```

Next, inside the DrawMD2Model() method, some additional changes are required to ensure Zarlag and the weapon are textured with the correct skin. A check is needed to determine which model is being drawn before skinning it. Replace the code that textures Zarlag with this code block:

```
if(modelNum == WEAPON)
    basicEffect.Texture = md2Weapon.GetTexture();
else
    basicEffect.Texture = md2.GetTexture();
```

Then, inside the DrawMD2Model() method, when setting the data source and drawing primitive surfaces from it, a check is needed to make sure the correct set of vertices and the correct number of triangles are used. Replace the existing code that selects the vertices and draws the primitive surface with this version:

```
if (modelNum == WEAPON){
    graphics.GraphicsDevice.Vertices[0].SetSource(
    md2Weapon.vertexBuffer, 0, VertexPositionNormalTexture.SizeInBytes);
    graphics.GraphicsDevice.DrawPrimitives(
        PrimitiveType.TriangleList, 0, md2Weapon.GetNumTriangles());
}
else{
    graphics.GraphicsDevice.Vertices[0].SetSource(
    md2.vertexBuffer, 0, VertexPositionNormalTexture.SizeInBytes);
    graphics.GraphicsDevice.DrawPrimitives(
        PrimitiveType.TriangleList, 0, md2.GetNumTriangles());
}
```

Lastly, to draw your character model and weapon with the identifier parameter, replace the existing instruction inside draw with this change:

```
DrawMD2Model(CHARACTER);
DrawMD2Model(WEAPON);
```

When you run the code now and change the animations, Zarlag and the weapon will animate together.

This chapter has shown how easy it is to create your own animated models. You may build your models in other modeling tools and then load them in MilkShape to animate them and/or convert them to .md2 format. If you have a loader for a different model format, you can still use MilkShape to create 3D models for it. Whatever method you use to create and load your 3D models, just make sure they load and animate properly in code before investing a lot of time building them.

The demonstration for Zarlag shows how powerful and diverse the *Quake II* format is for enabling animations. Combining pre-animated models with the techniques discussed in Chapter 8, "Character Movement," and Chapter 21, "Keyframe Animations," opens up all kinds of possibilities to unleash lifelike creatures in your 3D game play.

CHAPTER 26 REVIEW EXERCISES

1. Follow the step-by-step exercises in this chapter to create your own animated model and load it in code.
2. Create a model that animates with four bones or more and has three or more animations. Load this model and at least one other model in your game project. Code it so you have the ability to view all animations for each model loaded. Use the SetAnimationSequence() sequence at least once to trigger an animation and follow it with another looping animation.

CHAPTER 27

Adding Audio to Your Game

AUDIO effects not only raise the appeal of a game, but you can also use them to challenge players to make judgments based on sound. This chapter shows you how to add audio to your game and create audio depth.

With 3D audio enabled, you can actually tell where things are just by their sounds. For example, if you heard distant footsteps in your right ear, but could not see anybody walking, you would know that somebody is walking behind you off to the right. If you were to turn 180 degrees, you would see the person walking and the sound would be louder in your left ear. Your game will offer far more appeal and vibrancy with sounds throughout the environment—and with music to match.

ABOUT XACT

In addition to enabling 3D audio, the XACT audio studio is intended to simplify the process of managing your audio files and sound cues. You can use it to organize wave files and to set their playback properties. XACT is installed as part of XNA Game Studio.

Currently, WAV (wave), AIF, and AIFF (audio interchange file format) files are the only audio formats supported in XACT. If you want to play back other formats—such as MP3—you can use the *Song* class in conjunction with the *MediaPlayer* class to load and play these types of files.

THE SONG AND SOUNDEFFECT ALTERNATIVE

3D Audio from XACT will not work on the Zune. However, a separate audio Application Programming Interface (API) is available to enable playback for your 2D games on the Zune. You can use this API in your PC and Xbox 360 projects as well.

This audio library includes a *Song* class for playing MP3 audio files in conjunction with the *MediaPlayer* class.

A *SoundEffect* class allows you to play wave files. Basically, all you have to do is load your wave file and play it. This process is so much simpler than implementing audio with XACT, the XNA community refers to it as "play and forget." If you want to pause, resume, or set the volume of your SoundEffect objects, you can access these routines by storing your *SoundEffect* object in a *SoundEffectInstance*.

PROGRAMMING XACT AUDIO

To implement XACT audio, you must (at least) use these five main objects:

- XACT audio project file
- Audio engine
- Global settings
- Wave banks
- Sound banks

XACT Audio Project File

The XACT audio project file is the file created from XACT—also known as the *XACT authoring tool*. The XACT project file has an .xap extension. This file stores the audio file references, sound cue instances, and their playback settings. The .xap file extension is useful for deploying on both Windows and on the Xbox 360.

You don't need to reference this project file in the code you write. However, when the .xap file is referenced in your XNA game project (from the Solution Explorer), your game project will automatically generate a global settings file, a wave bank file, and a sound bank file for you to regulate audio playback according to your audio project settings.

You could export the global settings, wave bank, and sound bank files separately from the audio authoring tool and then reference them manually in your project. However, to simplify referencing and loading your audio files in both your Windows and Xbox 360 game projects, referencing the .xap file in your project is recommended. When you reference the .xap file in your game project, it also provides a relative file path reference to the wave files used in your project.

Audio Engine

The `AudioEngine` object instantiates and manipulates core sound objects for playing game audio. This object is initialized with a set of properties loaded from a global settings file generated from the XACT authoring tool. As mentioned earlier, if you reference the .xap project file in the Solution Explorer, the global settings file will automatically be generated in your project at run time. Even though you cannot physically see the global settings file in the same folder as your .xap file, you can load it in code as long as the directory path is the same as your project file, as shown here:

```
AudioEngine audioEngine = new
AudioEngine("AudioProjectFileFolder\\GlobalSettings.xgs");
```

Once you have initialized the sound engine in your code, it is then used to initialize the `WaveBank` and the `SoundBank`. As with the global settings file, these files will not be physically present in the audio folder when you use the .xap project file to generate them. However, virtual references to them are required from the same directory in your project as your *.xap project file:

```
WaveBank waveBank      = new
WaveBank( audioEngine, "Content\\AudioProjectFileFolder\\Wave Bank.xwb");
SoundBank soundBank    = new
SoundBank(audioEngine, "Content\\AudioProjectFileFolder\\Sound Bank.xsb");
```

When you are loading your audio project, engine, wave bank, and sound bank files in this manner, your *.wav, *.aif, and *.aiff files will need to be in the same directory path (relative to the location where your .xap project file is saved).

Global Settings

Global settings are the definitions for the audio controls created by the sound designer. You use this file to initialize the sound engine.

Wave Banks

A *wave bank* is a collection of wave files loaded and packaged in an .xwb file.

Sound Banks

A *sound bank* is a collection of instructions and cues for the wave files to regulate how the sounds are played in your program.

Cues

You can use *cues* to trigger audio playback from the sound bank. Cues may contain a list of sounds to play in a specific sequence when an event is triggered, or they may provide a list of sounds that can be selected randomly for playback.

Categories

Categories are used to group sound banks with similar properties. You might consider categorizing sounds by how they are played back. For example, sounds with volumes that need to be adjusted together or sounds that need to be paused and resumed at the same time can be grouped in the same category.

Cue Instance Variables

Cue instance variables set limits for sound cue properties, such as pitch and volume, in the XACT tool. You can alter values within your cue instance variable ranges to control playback.

Runtime Parameter Control Preset (RPC Preset)

An RPC preset allows you to define how your sound properties change within their designated ranges. You can then attach these RPC presets to specific instances of sound.

Playback Methods

You have the option of using two methods for audio playback. The first involves using the SoundBank's GetCue() method to retrieve the sound instance and then the Play() method to play it:

```
cue = soundBank.GetCue(String cueName);
cue.Play();
```

This method is useful if you need to set the volume, or pause or resume the sound. However, if you are constantly using the GetCue() method, playing your sound, and disposing of the cue, you will hear the sound cutting out during playback. If you know you will be using these cues later, you can avoid this problem by placing your idle cues on a stack.

Another method that can be used to play your audio is the SoundBank's PlayCue() method. This method is useful for playing sounds in quick succession, such as the sound of a rapid-fire machine gun:

```
PlayCue(String cueName);
```

With this method, there is no disposal of the cue. This helps to avoid disruptions to the audio that can be caused by the garbage collection that happens when cues are disposed.

Programming 3D Audio

3D audio scales the volume of your sound sources and positions them in each speaker. The volume and position properties for each sound are derived from the listener's relative distance and orientation to the sound source. The listener object is defined by the AudioListener class. This object governs what you hear and how you hear it.

Normally, there is only one listener in a game, and it moves and changes direction with the camera. Moving this listener object with the camera allows you to update the position and orientation of each sound as the viewer travels through the world.

The AudioEmitter class stores the sound source's position, speed, and orientation. An AudioEmitter object is required for each sound source.

Both the listener and emitter objects store the following four vectors:

```
Vector3 Forward; // direction
Vector3 Speed;   // direction and magnitude
```

```
Vector3 Position;
Vector3 Up;       // uprightness
```

The vectors are updated for the listener and all emitters every frame. Then the calculations to position the sound and scale the volume for each are applied with the method `Apply3D()`:

```
void Cue.Apply3D(AudioListner listener, AudioEmitter emitter);
```

Because the cue is used to apply 3D audio, `GetCue()` must be used to retrieve the cue for playback.

XACT Authoring Tool

The XACT audio authoring tool provides a sound designer studio that allows you to create wave banks, add sound banks, and edit the properties for controlling how they are played from within your code.

The authoring tool is feature-rich, and you may be pleased to discover how much you can customize your audio beyond the standard settings. You can use the audio authoring tool to randomize how sounds are played back, add reverb, randomize the sound volume, and implement great audio effects such as a Doppler effect.

SPACE AUDIO EXAMPLE: PART A

This demonstration shows how to use the audio authoring tool to generate an .xap project file that stores references for your wave files and their playback properties. Later on, you will reference this project file in your XNA project to regulate the playback of the wave files within your game. Whether you are building a 2D or a 3D game, the steps taken here to build your XACT audio project are the same. If you are building a 2D game for Windows or the Xbox 360, then parts B and C of this example are relevant for you. If you are building a 3D game, then all sections are relevant.

The audio portion of this example begins with an introduction. When the introduction finishes, two spacecraft engines start playing in a loop. For no particular reason other than to create an interesting soundscape and to demonstrate XNA audio features, each spacecraft also emits a telemetric beep. These telemetric beeps start after the introduction. Ship0 travels with the camera and ship1 moves back and forth along the Z plane in the distance. You can left-click the mouse or pull the right trigger to play a laser firing sound. When you move or strafe, the pitch and volume of your craft (ship0) changes according to your acceleration level.

This project uses six WAV files: an introduction, two engines, two beeps, and a laser fire noise. The audio files for this project can be found in the Audio folder on this book's website. The audio files for this demonstration are from the XNA Spacewar project that ships with Game Studio.

Launching the XACT Authoring Tool

The XACT authoring tool can be found in the Start menu folder with Game Studio. There you will see Tools | Microsoft Cross-Platform Audio Creation Tool (XACT). Selecting Microsoft Cross-Platform Audio Creation Tool (XACT) launches this authoring tool. The authoring tool will appear as shown in Figure 27-1.

Creating a Wave Bank

To load a wave file, click the Wave Banks menu and then choose New Wave Bank. You can now add wave files to your wave bank. Start by adding the intro.wav file. To do this, click the Wave Banks menu and choose Insert Wave File(s). When the Open dialog launches, select the intro.wav file. Your wave file now appears in the Wave Bank panel.

Adding a Sound Bank

Next, you need a sound bank so you can customize properties that determine how the wave file will be played. The sound bank consists of two parts—a sound bank name and a cue name. To add a sound bank, select the Sound Banks menu and then click New Sound Bank.

You then need to create a cue that your code will use to trigger playback. This can be done by left-clicking the wave file in the Wave Bank panel and dragging it down, with the left mouse button pressed, into the lower panel of the Sound Bank panel. Your wave file instance should now appear in both the upper and lower sections of the Sound Bank panel (see Figure 27-2).

FIGURE 27-1

XACT authoring tool

FIGURE 27-2

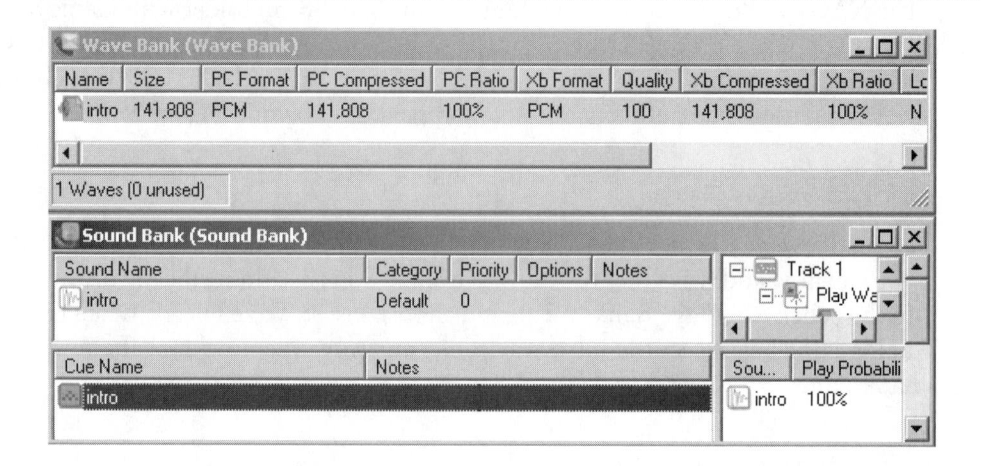

XACT authoring tool with a wave file referenced on the wave bank panel at the top and the sound bank panel on the bottom

Referencing the Spaceship Engines, Firing Sound, and Beeping Sounds

For this part of the example, you repeat the steps you just completed for the intro.wav file for the beep0.wav, beep1.wav, engine0.wav, engine1.wav, and fire.wav files. When you are finished, these files will appear in wave bank, sound bank, and sound bank cue panels, as shown in Figure 27-3.

Setting the Category Property for Beep0

Sometimes you will want to group your sound banks by category. Having sounds that fulfill a similar role under the same category simplifies your ability to control how the sounds are played back in your code. Some code instructions can be applied once to an entire category rather than individually for each sound in the category.

For this example, you need a different category for beep0. This will enable the beeping noise to be paused and resumed separately in your code. The intro, engine0, engine1, beep1, and fire sound banks have been assigned by default to the Default category. If you were to set the volume to the Default category, the intro, beep1, engine0, engine1, and fire sounds would all be affected. The beep0 sound bank will be assigned to the Beep0 category so we can pause and resume it midstream. To create a Beep0 category, right-click the Category node in the XAP project and select New Category. When prompted, name the category as **Beep0**. Then, click on the `beep0` instance in the Sound Bank panel under the Category column. In the left panel, select the Beep0 category setting in the lower-left property panel (see Figure 27-4).

FIGURE 27-3

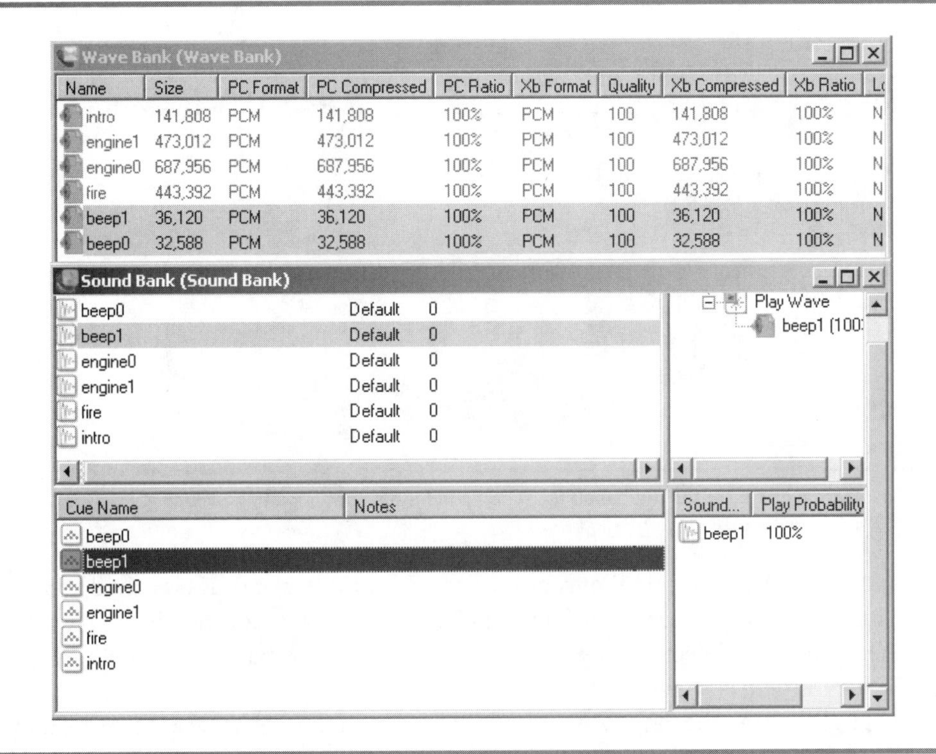

Wave bank, sound bank, and cues after the wave files have been added

Creating an Infinite Loop

The beep0 file is meant to play in an infinite loop, so the playback repeats every time the track finishes. To enable the loop, select the beep0 sound bank and highlight Play Wave in the tree view in the top-right panel of the XACT authoring tool.

Once you have highlighted Play Wave for beep0's sound bank, you can set the `loop property` at the bottom of the left panel in the XACT authoring tool. Checking Infinite under looping enables the infinite loop for the beep0 sound (see Figure 27-4).

Both engine0 and engine1 sound banks also have to play in an infinite loop so they can be heard continuously throughout the game. You will need to set the `Infinite` property for these objects just as you did for beep0. However, when you do this, just use the Default category.

Adding a Finite Loop

For the second telemetric beep sound, beep1, the corresponding wave file only stores one beep. This example requires the beep1 sound to play twice so the sound is heard

FIGURE 27-4

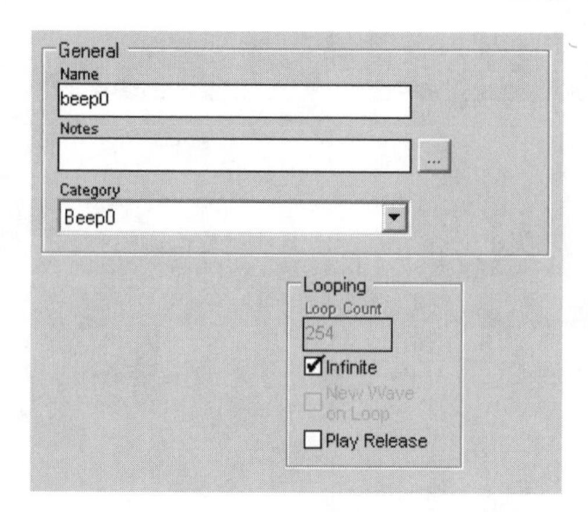

The Beep0 category is set for the beep0 file. The sound is also set for infinite looping.

as "beep, beep." A loop that repeats a specific number of times is called a *finite loop*. You can add the "beep, beep" sound by creating a finite loop with one repeat. To set the finite loop, select the beep1 wave file in the sound bank and then highlight Play Wave in the tree view.

Highlighting the Play Wave property button in the tree view at the top-right of the XNA authoring tool will display the Play Wave Properties panel at the bottom left. In the Play Wave Properties panel, expand the LoopEvent attribute. Select Finite in the LoopEvent drop-down. You can then expand the LoopEvent drop-down where you can enter **1** for the `LoopCount` property.

Testing Your Audio

Now that you have created the sound banks and you have assigned properties, you can test their playback with the XACT Auditioning Utility. This tool allows you to hear how they will sound when played in your game. Launch the XACT Auditioning Utility by navigating from the Start menu to Programs | Microsoft XNA Game Studio Express | Tools. A command-prompt window will appear with the message "Waiting for the XACT authoring tool to connect...." When you want to test a sound bank, select it, right-click Play Wave in the right panel, and choose Play Sound.

Cue Instance Variables

Say you want to increase the ship's engine volume and pitch whenever the player increases speed. You are going to need some way to tie pitch and volume values in your XNA code to the player's move and strafe events. The authoring tool allows you to create cue instance variables for this purpose. You then define ranges of values for the variable and corresponding properties with an RPC preset object in the XACT tool. You can then attach your sound files to these RPC preset objects. In your code you can reference your cue instance variables to set their values at run time.

To create a cue instance variable, right-click the Cue Instance node in the left panel and choose New Cue Instance. Your cursor will be placed at the bottom of the variable settings dialog in the Name column. Here you can assign your cue instance variable a name. For this example, assign your new cue instance variable the name *`Engine0Variable`*. Next, set the variable `Min` and `Max` properties to 0 and 1 respectively. These values will map nicely to values obtained from the move and strafe keys and the left thumbstick whose absolute values range between 0 and 1 (refer to Figure 27-5).

In your code, you can use the `Cue` object's `SetVariable()` method to set these values:

```
Cue cue.SetVariable("Engine0Variable", float value);
```

Creating a New RPC Preset

For our example, a Ship0RPC preset is created to specify how different sound properties are affected over the range of values of a cue instance variable. You can start by right-clicking the RPC Presets node, and in the dialog that appears, select your cue instance variable. From there, you can choose your new cue instance variable, *`Engine0Variable`*. Choose the Sound value for the Object and use the Volume selection as the Parameter. You are then presented with a curve, which you can shape to specify how your volume changes between 0 and 1. Two control points define the graph initially.

FIGURE 27-5

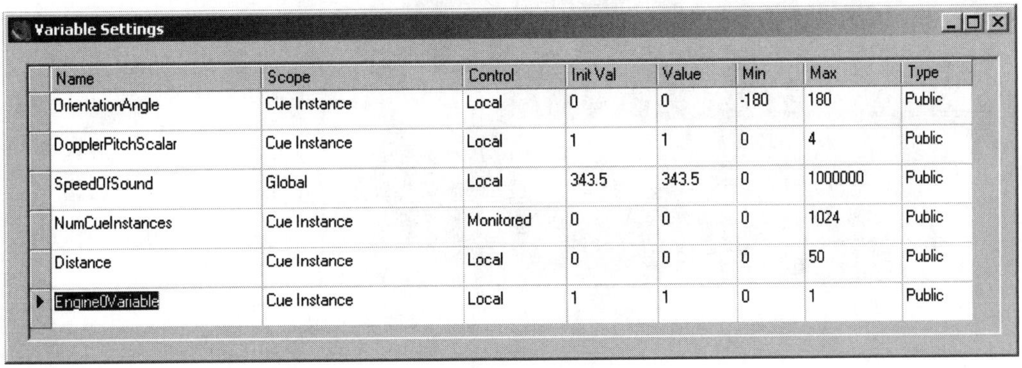

Variable Settings

Name	Scope	Control	Init Val	Value	Min	Max	Type
OrientationAngle	Cue Instance	Local	0	0	-180	180	Public
DopplerPitchScalar	Cue Instance	Local	1	1	0	4	Public
SpeedOfSound	Global	Local	343.5	343.5	0	1000000	Public
NumCueInstances	Cue Instance	Monitored	0	0	0	1024	Public
Distance	Cue Instance	Local	0	0	0	50	Public
Engine0Variable	Cue Instance	Local	1	1	0	1	Public

Cue instance variable

To add a control point to shape your graph, right-click the rows of data under the Points heading and choose Insert Point in the drop-down that appears. You can then left-click these control points and drag them into position while your left mouse button is pressed. This finished curve defines volume for different values of your cue instance variable. Changes in volume are shown by the top curve in Figure 27-6.

The process used to define the range of values for Pitch is similar to the steps taken to define the volume. First, you have to add another instance of the `Engine0Variable` value under the Variable heading. Then, you must pick Sound as an Object and Pitch as a Parameter. The bottom curve in Figure 27-6 shows the pitch values over the range where `Engine0Variable` ranges between 0 and 1.

For this example, name your RPC preset to **Ship0RPC**. Then right-click it to choose Add/Detach Sounds where you can select engine0. After you do this, you will see the reference to the sound (refer to Figure 27-7).

FIGURE 27-6

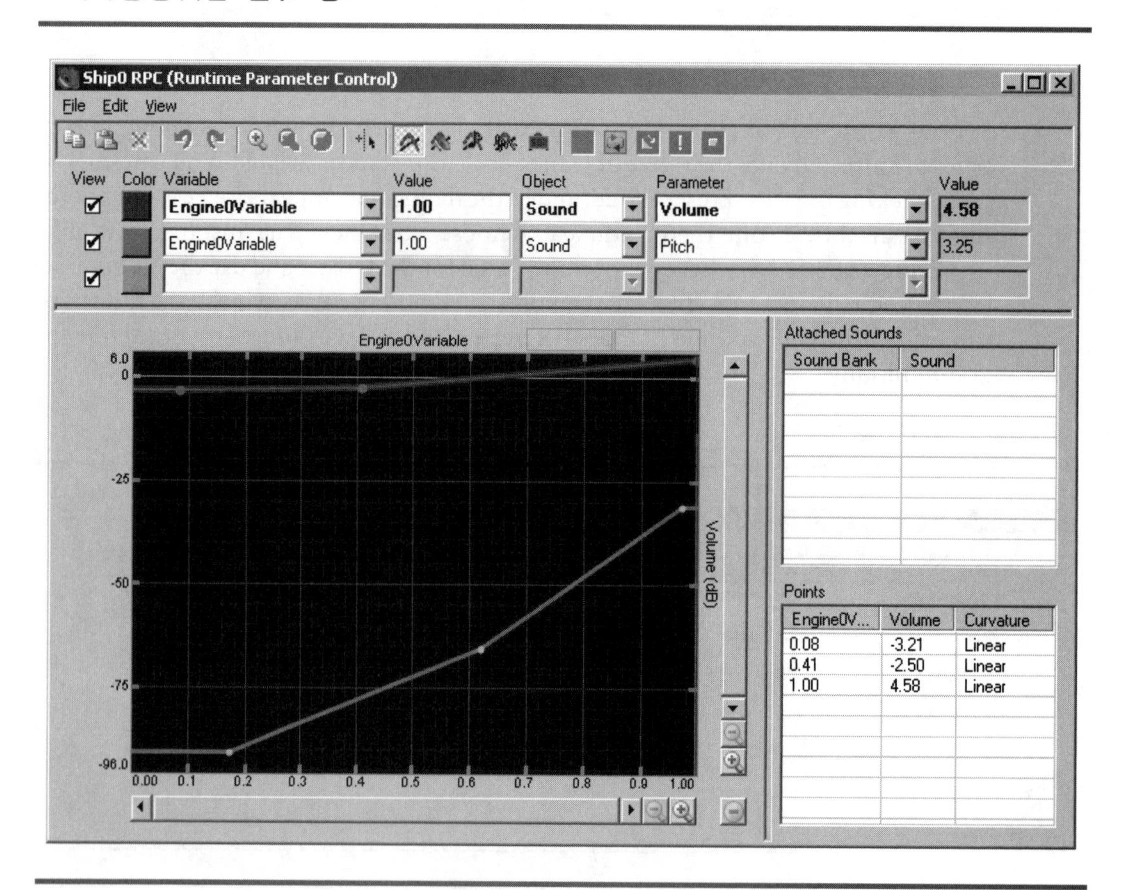

RPC preset for controlling engine0's volume and pitch between values of 0 and 1

FIGURE 27-7

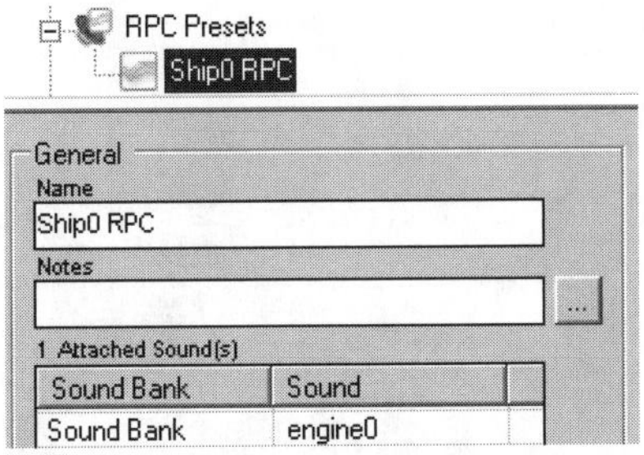

RPC preset for references engine0

Later, you will be able to control the pitch and volume of your engine0 with this instruction:

```
Cue cue.SetVariable("Engine0Variable", float value);
```

Enabling Volume Attenuation

Audio attenuation refers to how the volume changes as the sound source travels toward and away from the listener. First, you must adjust the maximum distance value for the cue. To do this, in the left panel of the XACT project, expand Cue Instance and click Distance to select it. While Distance is selected, in the Properties panel that appears, change the MaximumValue property to **50** (see the earlier Figure 27-5).

Next, to enable volume attenuation, you have to attach the sound to a Runtime Parameter Control (RPC) preset. To create an RPC preset, right-click RPC Presets in the left panel and choose New RPC Preset. Under the Parameter column choose Sound: Volume. Under the Variable column, choose Distance. The line that appears shows how the sound fades as it travels away from the listener. When you are finished, the distance curve should be similar to the one in Figure 27-8. This volume level simulates how sound volume fades over distance.

To associate this attenuation with engine1, right-click your new RPC preset that appears in the left panel and choose Attach/Detach Sounds. When prompted, choose Sound Bank engine1 and click Attach. Click OK when you are finished.

The engine1 will now be listed as one of the attached sounds in the properties display for the `AttachedSounds` property under the RPC preset. Engine1's sound volume will now adjust according to the increase or decrease in distance between it and the listener. Figure 27-9 shows the new RPC preset, named Ship1 RPC, with the engine1 sound attached.

FIGURE 27-8

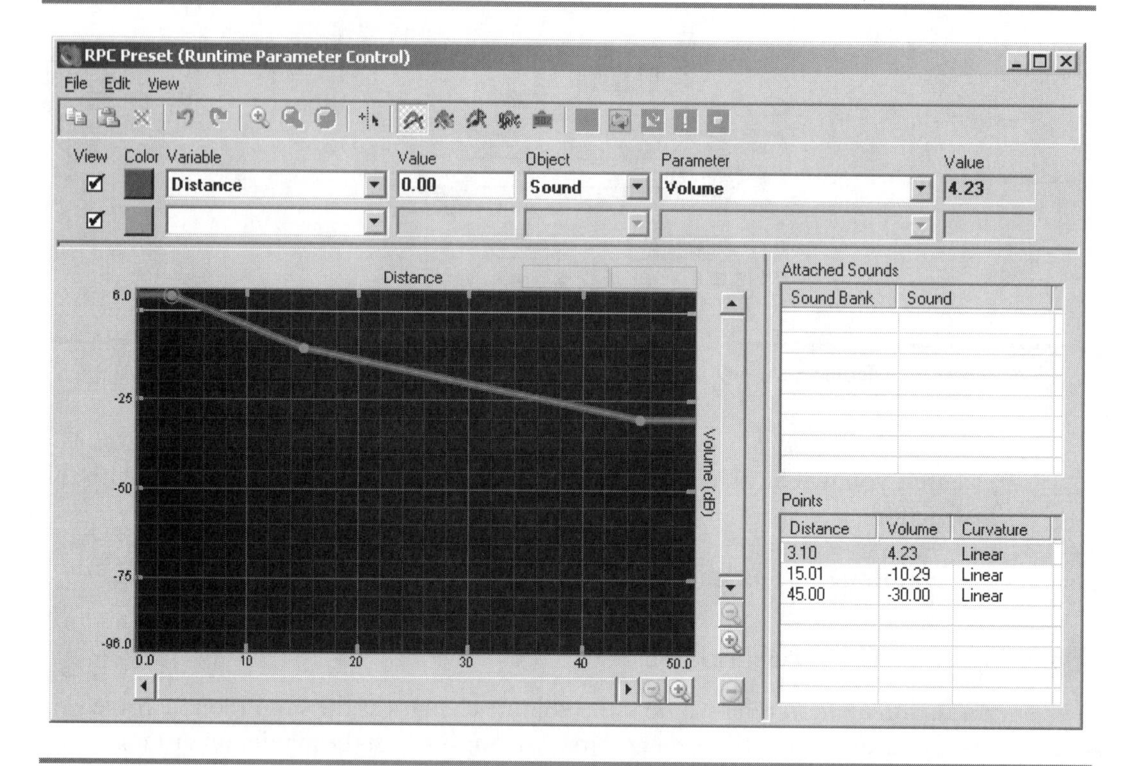

Runtime Parameter Control settings to adjust volume with distance

FIGURE 27-9

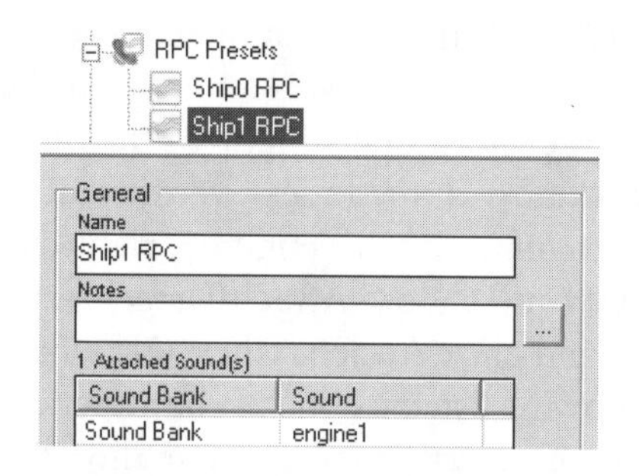

RPC preset with engine1 sound attached

Saving Your Audio Project

Now your wave banks and sound banks are prepared to play sounds as required for this example. The next step requires that you save your XACT project. The .xap project file that is generated is used by your XNA game project to set the playback properties for your wave files. To generate the .xap project file, on the XACT authoring tool's File menu, select Save Project As. In the Save Project As dialog, browse to the directory where you want to export your project.

For the code portion of the example that follows, the .xap project file needs to be saved to the folder where the wave files are located; this ensures that the project file's directory has the same relative path as the wave files. Enter the name **audioProject** in the File Name text box and click the Save button. This action generates an audioProject.xap file that stores your project and includes your wave bank, sound bank, and sound bank cue settings. Also, be sure to keep this .xap file in case you want to edit your XACT authoring tool project later.

SPACE AUDIO EXAMPLE: PART B

Part B of this example adds some 3D models and animates them to make the example a little more dramatic.

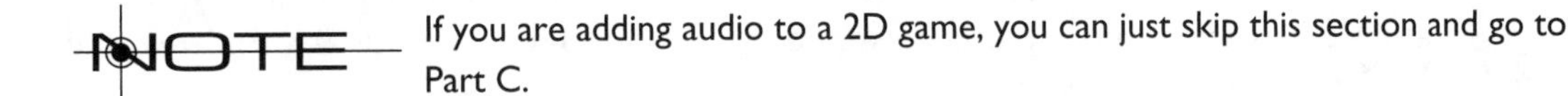

NOTE If you are adding audio to a 2D game, you can just skip this section and go to Part C.

If you are adding audio to a 3D game, you can start the code portion of this example with either the MGHWinBaseCode project or the MGH360BaseCode project, found in the BaseCode folder on this book's website.

Loading, Drawing, and Animating the Spacecraft

For this first portion of code, you will load and draw two spaceship models. Ship0 travels with the camera and ship1 moves continuously from side to side off in the distance. All together, the model files consist of the alien0.fbx, alien1.fbx, and spaceA.bmp files. The two .fbx files must be referenced from a Models folder under the Content node in your game project. You can find these files in the Models folder on this book's website.

Two model objects and matrices for storing their meshes are needed in the game class to store, transform, and draw the model:

```
Model    ship0Model,  ship1Model;
Matrix[] ship1Matrix, ship0Matrix;
```

You must initialize the spacecraft models and their bone transformation matrices when the game begins. You can add this code to the game class to load and initialize them:

```
void InitializeModels(){
    ship0Model  = Content.Load<Model>("Models\\alien0");
    ship0Matrix = new Matrix[ship0Model.Bones.Count];
    ship0Model.CopyAbsoluteBoneTransformsTo(ship0Matrix);

    ship1Model  = Content.Load<Model>("Models\\alien1");
    ship1Matrix = new Matrix[ship1Model.Bones.Count];
    ship1Model.CopyAbsoluteBoneTransformsTo(ship1Matrix);
}
```

To ensure that the spacecraft models are set up properly when the program begins, add the call statement for `InitializeModels()` to the `Initialize()` method in your game class:

```
InitializeModels();
```

Ship1 is going to be animated, so it translates back and forth on the X axis. To perform this animation, you use variables to store ship1's current position and velocity, and ship1's direction. These corresponding class-level declarations are needed at the top of your game class:

```
bool        rightDirection     = false; // track ship 1
Vector3     ship1Position      = new Vector3(0.0f, 0.2f, -BOUNDARY);
Vector3     ship1Velocity      = new Vector3(-1.3f, 0.0f, 0.0f);
```

This next method, `UpdateShip1Position()`, allows you to update ship1 each frame so it translates side to side in your world along the X axis.

A check is made to determine if ship1 has reached the left or right edge of the world on the X axis. If it reaches the edge of the world, ship1's direction is reversed and its position is then incremented.

Adding the `UpdateShip1Position()` method ensures that the position and direction of ship1 are updated each frame for a smooth animation:

```
void UpdateShip1Position(GameTime gameTime){
    // reverse direction if pass right boundary
    if (ship1Position.X > BOUNDARY && rightDirection == true){
        ship1Velocity.X  *= -1.0f;
        rightDirection    =  false;
    }
```

```
    // reverse direction if pass left boundary
    else if (ship1Position.X < -BOUNDARY && rightDirection == false){
        ship1Velocity.X  *= -1.0f;
        rightDirection    =  true;
    }
    // increment position by time scale so speed is same rate all systems
    float time            = (float)
                            gameTime.ElapsedGameTime.Milliseconds/200.0f;
    ship1Position.X      += ship1Velocity.X * time;
}
```

The code for updating ship1's angle and position is triggered from the `Update()` method with a call to the `UpdateShip1Position()` method:

```
UpdateShip1Position(gameTime);
```

Next, a method called `WorldMatrix()` is needed in the game class to generate transformations for both spaceships:

```
Matrix WorldMatrix(string modelName){
    Matrix rotationY, rotationYOrbit, translation, translationOrbit;
    Matrix world            = new Matrix();

    switch (modelName){
        case "ship0":
            translation   = Matrix.CreateTranslation(
                            cam.position.X, 0.0f, cam.position.Z);
            translationOrbit
                          = Matrix.CreateTranslation(0.0f, 0.0f, 1.9f);
            Vector3 look  = cam.view - cam.position;
            rotationYOrbit= Matrix.CreateRotationY((float)
                           (Math.Atan2(look.X, look.Z)));
            world = translationOrbit * rotationYOrbit * translation;
            break;
        case "ship1":
            translation   = Matrix.CreateTranslation(ship1Position);
            if (rightDirection)
                rotationY = Matrix.CreateRotationY( MathHelper.Pi/2.0f);
            else
                rotationY = Matrix.CreateRotationY(-MathHelper.Pi/2.0f);
            world         = rotationY * translation;
            break;
    }
```

```
    return world;
}
```

The code you add to the game class to draw the spaceships is similar to code you have already seen in this book for drawing models. This time, though, the routine calls the `WorldMatrix()` method to generate the cumulative transformation:

```
void DrawModel(Model model, string modelName){
    // declare matrices
    Matrix world              = WorldMatrix(modelName);

    foreach (ModelMesh mesh in model.Meshes){
        foreach (BasicEffect effect in mesh.Effects)
        {   // pass wvp to shader
            switch(modelName)
            {   case "ship0":
                effect.World   = ship0Matrix[mesh.ParentBone.Index]*world;
                    break;
                case "ship1":
                effect.World   = ship1Matrix[mesh.ParentBone.Index]*world;
                    break;
            }
            effect.View        = cam.viewMatrix;
            effect.Projection = cam.projectionMatrix;

            // set lighting
            effect.EnableDefaultLighting();
        }
        // draw object
        mesh.Draw();
    }
}
```

To draw each spacecraft, you call `DrawModel()` separately with the correct model and identifier as parameters from the `Draw()` method:

```
DrawModel(ship0Model, "ship0");
DrawModel(ship1Model, "ship1");
```

Since ship0 travels with your camera, you will want to set your view direction so the camera does not bounce up and down. To do this, replace the return statement inside `ChangeView()` with this revision:

```
return new Vector2(change.X, 0.0f);
```

When you compile and run the program, you will see ship1 flying from side to side in your 3D world and ship0 will travel with your camera.

SPACE AUDIO EXAMPLE: PART C

Part C of this demonstration takes the .xap project file you have created, and the accompanying wave files, and loads them for playback in your game project. You can add the code from this section to either your 2D game or your 3D game project. For this section though, we are only going to focus on adding audio for ship0. Ship0's engine, beep, and laser audio are appropriate for both 2D and 3D games because the audio is always positioned in front of the viewer.

After you add the code from section C, you will be able to hear the introduction when the game begins. When the introduction ends, the engine0 and telemetric beep0 of ship0 will play in an infinite loop. Whenever you accelerate, the engine volume and pitch increase. A laser will fire whenever you pull the right game-controller trigger or left-click the mouse.

Adding Audio

You can use the intro.wav, engine0.wav, engine1.wav, beep0.wav, beep1.wav, and fire.wav files in the Audio folder in the book's download. You may use the audioProject.xap file you created, or you can find a copy in the Audio folder that is included in the book's download. To reference these files in your project, add an Audio folder to your solution, add each of the .xap and wave files to it, and then reference each file within the Audio folder from the Solution Explorer. At this point, the wave files are referenced in your project and are located in the Audio folder with your .xap project file. To enable audio in the code project, a reference is required at the top of your Game1.cs file to include the XACT audio library. This reference has already been added to your project by the XNA template wizard when the initial project shell was generated:

```
using Microsoft.Xna.Framework.Audio;
```

Since the focus of this section is to add audio for the intro and for ship0, you will need to declare sound cue objects to control each sound:

```
Cue ship0Cue, beep0Cue, introCue;
```

Some additional preparation in code is needed to store the different components of your audio system. As mentioned earlier, the project file will be referenced in the project and will generate the global settings file, the wave bank, and the sound bank. Module-level declarations for loading and storing the sound engine, wave bank, and

sound bank files will make these objects available for loading and playing your audio files throughout your game class:

```
private static AudioEngine  soundEngine;
private static WaveBank     waveBank;
private static SoundBank    soundBank;
```

Your global settings, wave bank, and sound bank can now be loaded from the `Initialize()` method when the program begins. The file path specified leads to the same directory where your audioProject.xap project file is located. Even though these files are not physically present when your project is not running, the directory references are needed:

```
soundEngine =new AudioEngine("Content\\Audio\\audioProject.xgs");
waveBank    =new WaveBank(soundEngine,"Content\\Audio\\Wave Bank.xwb");
soundBank   =new SoundBank(soundEngine,"Content\\Audio\\Sound Bank.xsb");
```

At every frame, you must update the sound engine. If you omit this update, it may seem for many frames that your audio is working. However, Microsoft warns that without continuous updates, the sound engine will inevitably crash.

Before you actually update the sound engine, an additional check is made to ensure that the sound engine exists. You use the sound engine's `IsDisposed` property for this check. Trying to update the sound engine when it has been disposed will cause a program crash. To implement the sound engine update, add the following code to the `Update()` method:

```
if (!soundEngine.IsDisposed){
    soundEngine.Update();
}
```

To ensure that your audio files unload when the program ends, add some code to dispose of them when the user exits from the program. `DeleteAudio()` will remove your sound bank, wave bank, and engine from memory when the application is shut down:

```
void DeleteAudio(){
    soundBank.Dispose();
    waveBank.Dispose();
    soundEngine.Dispose();
}
```

To ensure that `DeleteAudio()` is called when the game ends, inside `Update()` (just before `this.Exit()`) add a call statement to dispose of the audio:

```
DeleteAudio();
```

The introduction sound plays once at the start of the program so the code that follows is needed in the game class after the sound engine, wave bank, and sound bank are initialized inside `Initialize()` to retrieve the cue and to play it:

```
if (!soundEngine.IsDisposed){
    introCue = soundBank.GetCue("intro");
    introCue.Play();
}
```

When the introduction finishes, the ship0's engine and beep start and repeat for the rest of the game. Before this happens though, the introduction Cue object's `IsPlaying` attribute is used to determine if the introduction is still playing. When the introduction ends, a Boolean flag, `gameStarted`, is set to `true`. To ensure that no other audio is played until after the introduction has finished, this variable declaration is added to the top of the game class:

```
private static bool gameStarted = false;
```

To enable proper timing for pausing and resuming audio and for playing the laser fire with the game pad, add class-level declarations for variables to compare press and release states for the game pad and mouse:

```
GamePadState  gpCurrent, gpPrevious;
#if !XBOX
     MouseState mouseCurrent, mousePrevious;
#endif
```

The gamer controls the firing noise by left-clicking the mouse or by pulling the right trigger. A new firing sound is only triggered whenever a new press event is registered. In other words, a firing event is cleared to play when a press event in the current frame follows a release event from the previous frame. The `PlayCue()` method is used to play the laser audio because it is a rapid-fire sound. The `PlayCue()` method is not prone to disruptions to the audio, which can be caused by garbage collection that occurs with the `GetCue()` and `Dispose()` methods. The `PlayCue()` method requires that the cue be stored in memory for as long as the audio is needed during the game.

```
void Fire(){
    if(gpCurrent.Triggers.Right!=0.0f && gpPrevious.Triggers.Right==0.0f
        #if !Xbox
            || mouseCurrent.LeftButton  == ButtonState.Pressed &&
               mousePrevious.LeftButton != ButtonState.Pressed
        #endif
```

```
        )
        soundBank.PlayCue("fire");
}
```

As with the Fire() method, when you're coding the routine for toggling between the beep0's paused and resumed states, a check is made for any new B-button press or new right-mouse-button press events. For each new press event, the beep's pause and resume states are changed. PauseAndResumeBeep() is needed in the game class to enable this routine:

```
void PauseAndResumeBeep(){
    if(
        #if !Xbox
            mouseCurrent.RightButton  == ButtonState.Pressed
        &&  mousePrevious.RightButton == ButtonState.Released  ||
        #endif
            gpCurrent.Buttons.B  == ButtonState.Pressed
        &&  gpPrevious.Buttons.B == ButtonState.Released){
            if (!beep0Cue.IsPaused)
                soundEngine.GetCategory("Beep0").Pause();  // pause beep
            else if (beep0Cue.IsPaused)
                soundEngine.GetCategory("Beep0").Resume(); // play beep
    }
}
```

In part A of this example, you created a cue instance variable to control ship0's engine volume and pitch from code. You must add the GetAccelerationVolume() method to the game class to implement the first part of this routine to generate the level of acceleration that drives these values:

```
float GetAccelerationVolume(){
    float accelerate, accelerateX, accelerateY;
          accelerate = 0.0f;

    // left stick forward, back, or side shift sets acceleration volume
    if (GamePad.GetState(PlayerIndex.One).IsConnected){
        accelerateX =
        Math.Abs(GamePad.GetState(PlayerIndex.One).ThumbSticks.Left.X);
        accelerateY =
        Math.Abs(GamePad.GetState(PlayerIndex.One).ThumbSticks.Left.Y);
        accelerate = Math.Max(accelerateX, accelerateY);
    }
```

```
    // no controller so use arrow keys to set acceleration volume
    else{
        KeyboardState kbState = Keyboard.GetState();

        if (kbState.IsKeyDown(Keys.Right)|| kbState.IsKeyDown(Keys.D)
        ||  kbState.IsKeyDown(Keys.Left) || kbState.IsKeyDown(Keys.A)
        ||  kbState.IsKeyDown(Keys.Up)   || kbState.IsKeyDown(Keys.W)
        ||  kbState.IsKeyDown(Keys.Down) || kbState.IsKeyDown(Keys.S)){
            accelerate = 1.0f;
        }
    }
    return accelerate;
}
```

After the introduction begins inside the `Initialize()` method, the code for driving the sound events in each frame is called from the `Update()` method. Before anything is done in this routine, a check is made to ensure that the audio engine actually exists. Failing to check whether this object exists will cause the program to crash if the sound banks or cues are used after the audio engine has been disposed.

The engine0 and telemetric beep0 are started only after the introduction finishes. When the program begins, a check is made each frame to determine whether the introduction is playing. When the introduction's `IsPlaying` attribute is `false`, the engine0 audio and beep0 audio are started and a Boolean flag is set so that this condition is never entered again during the game.

Once the audio has started, checks are made each frame to update the acceleration, handle any trigger firing, and to pause and resume beeping:

```
if (!gameStarted){
    if (!soundEngine.IsDisposed){
        if (!introCue.IsPlaying){                          // intro over
            gameStarted = true;
            beep0Cue    = soundBank.GetCue("beep0");       // play beep0
            soundBank.PlayCue("beep0");                    // lower volume
            soundEngine.GetCategory("Beep0").SetVolume(0.1f);
            ship0Cue    = soundBank.GetCue("engine0");     // start engine 0
            ship0Cue.Play();
        }
    }
}
else{
    if (!soundEngine.IsDisposed){
        #if !XBOX                              // update mouse state
```

```
            mousePrevious = mouseCurrent;
            mouseCurrent  = Mouse.GetState();
        #endif
        gpPrevious        = gpCurrent; // update gamepad states
        gpCurrent         = GamePad.GetState(PlayerIndex.One);

        Fire();                         // check input for fire
                                        // change volume with acceleration
        ship0Cue.SetVariable("Engine0Variable", GetAccelerationVolume());
        PauseAndResumeBeep();           // for beep 0 with ship 0
    }
}
```

If you run your code now, you will hear the introduction play first, and then you will hear ship0's engine and telemetric beep. You will also hear the firing sound every time you pull the right trigger or left-click the mouse. Ship0's engine audio will rise in volume and pitch every time you accelerate.

SPACE AUDIO EXAMPLE: PART D

The audio implemented until now plays at the same volume in the left and right speakers. However, you can create even more depth with 3D audio to reflect the relative position and direction of sound sources within our world.

Adding 3D Audio

The last sounds that are played in this demonstration are emitted by ship1. 3D audio is used here to give ship1's sounds some depth. The 3D audio positions the sound in your speakers according to the distance and orientation between the camera and sound source.

Two game class–level objects are required for 3D audio to calculate the proper volume for each speaker. The `AudioListener` stores the position, speed, and orientation of the viewer, which is usually defined at the camera. The `AudioEmitter` stores the position and orientation of the object that makes the noise (which is engine1 and beep1 in this case).

```
AudioListener listener          = new AudioListener();
AudioEmitter  ship1Emitter      = new AudioEmitter();
AudioEmitter  beep1Emitter      = new AudioEmitter();
```

As mentioned previously, `GetCue()` must be used to retrieve the cue before playback when you're using 3D audio. However, after every queue is played, it is automatically disposed and removed later through garbage collection. When cues are frequently disposed and regenerated, this causes unwanted static in your audio during playback. To avoid this problem, you will place a helper class just inside the game class to store the cue for reuse and to track the sound emitter attached to it:

```
private class  Audio3DCue{
    public     Cue          cue;
    public     AudioEmitter emitter;
}
```

With this helper class in place, a class-level list and stack are declared to track the active sound cues and to store inactive cues:

```
List<Audio3DCue>  activeCueList = new List<Audio3DCue>();
Stack<Audio3DCue> cueStack      = new Stack<Audio3DCue>();
```

The previous ship0 and ship1 positions can be assigned at the start of the `Update()` method before the current positions are reassigned. Later you can use these values to calculate the speed of the camera and ship1:

```
Vector3 previousCamPosition, previousShip1Position;
```

`UpdateAudioListener()` is added to the game class to update the listener position and orientation vectors. You will use these listener vectors to later position the audio in the speaker:

```
void UpdateAudioListener(){
    // update direction with position, uprightness, and direction
    listener.Position    = cam.position;
    listener.Up          = cam.up;
    listener.Forward     = Vector3.Normalize(cam.view - cam.position);
    // calculate speed
    Vector3 speed        = cam.position - previousCamPosition;
    listener.Velocity    = speed;
}
```

For this demonstration, you will update the emitter vectors just before the calculation that positions the sound in the speaker. In the game class, the `Apply3DAudio` method first updates ship1's position, speed, and direction vectors. Since beep1 travels with ship1, the beep1 vectors are also updated with the ship vectors. In either case, the ship1 and beep1 `Cue` object's `Apply3D()` method uses the listener and emitter data to set the volume and position for each sound:

```
private void Apply3DAudio(Audio3DCue cue3D){
    if (!cue3D.cue.IsDisposed && !soundBank.IsDisposed
```

```
    &&  !soundEngine.IsDisposed){
        switch (cue3D.cue.Name){
            case "engine1":
                // calculate speed based on change in position
                Vector3 speed0 = ship1Position - previousShip1Position;
                ship1Emitter.Velocity = speed0;
                previousShip1Position = ship1Position; // track position
                // calculate orientation via speed and direction vectors
                ship1Emitter.Position = ship1Position;
                ship1Emitter.Up       = new Vector3(0.0f, 1.0f, 0.0f);
                ship1Emitter.Forward  = Vector3.Normalize(speed0);
                cue3D.cue.Apply3D(listener, ship1Emitter);
                break;
            case "beep1":
                Vector3 speed1        = ship1Emitter.Velocity;
                beep1Emitter.Velocity = speed1;
                beep1Emitter.Position = ship1Emitter.Position;
                beep1Emitter.Up       = ship1Emitter.Up;
                beep1Emitter.Forward  = Vector3.Normalize(speed1);
                cue3D.cue.Apply3D(listener, beep1Emitter);
                break;
        }
    }
}
```

The `UpdateAudioEmitters()` method calls the `Apply3DAudio` method after managing the existing cues. If a cue has stopped playing, `UpdateAudioEmitter()` disposes of it and pushes the cue instance on the stack for reuse later to prevent unwanted garbage collection. The cue is no longer active, so it is removed from the active cue list. Otherwise, if the cue is playing, it is retrieved from the active cue list and `Apply3DAudio()` is called to perform the 3D audio calculations:

```
void UpdateAudioEmitters(){
    for (int i = 0; i < activeCueList.Count; i++){
        Audio3DCue audio3Dcue = activeCueList[i];
        if (!audio3Dcue.cue.IsDisposed && audio3Dcue.cue.IsStopped){
            audio3Dcue.cue.Dispose();    // dispose when stops playing
            cueStack.Push(audio3Dcue);   // store Audio3DCue for reuse
            activeCueList.RemoveAt(i);   // remove inactive cue from list
        }
        else
```

```
            Apply3DAudio(audio3Dcue);    // cue playing so update 3D
    }
}
```

The emitter and listener objects must be updated each frame so they are called from the `Update()` method. The emitter and listener updates must be called immediately after the call to `SoundEngineUpdate()` where a check has been made to ensure that the sound engine has not been disposed:

```
UpdateAudioListener();
UpdateAudioEmitters();
```

`Play3DAudio()` is placed in the game class either to retrieve an available cue from the stack (if it exists) or to create one if it does not exist. Once the cue is ready, `Apply3DAudio()` is called to calculate the volume and sound position in each speaker. After these calculations have been performed, the cue is played and the active cue is added to the active cue list. Add `Play3DAudio` to your game class to implement this routine:

```
public Cue Play3DAudio(string strCueName){
    Audio3DCue audio3Dcue;

    if (cueStack.Count > 0)                 // re-use cue if any exist on stack
        audio3Dcue = cueStack.Pop();
    else                                    // otherwise create new one
        audio3Dcue = new Audio3DCue();

    // store current cue and emitter
    audio3Dcue.cue      = soundBank.GetCue(strCueName);
    audio3Dcue.emitter  = ship1Emitter;
    Apply3DAudio(audio3Dcue);               // set position and orientation
    audio3Dcue.cue.Play();                  // play it
    activeCueList.Add(audio3Dcue);          // store in active audio list

    return audio3Dcue.cue;
}
```

The beep1's sound was set in the XACT authoring tool to repeat once every time it is played. The result is that you hear the sound twice in succession—"beep, beep." You will use a timer to play ship1's beep every 1 second. In the module declarations section of your game class, a declaration for the time of the previous frame will assist in tracking the time lapse between beeps:

```
public double   intervalTime, previousIntervalTime;
```

A timer like the one that was first used in Chapter 12 enables playback of the beep audio every second:

```
bool Timer(GameTime gameTime){
    bool    resetInterval = false;

    // add time lapse between frames and keep value between 0 & 1 second
    intervalTime += (double)gameTime.ElapsedGameTime.Milliseconds;
    intervalTime  = intervalTime % 1000;

    // intervalTime has been reset so a new interval has started
    if (intervalTime < previousIntervalTime)
        resetInterval = true;

    previousIntervalTime = intervalTime;
    return resetInterval;
}
```

As long as the sound engine has not been disposed, the timer triggers the beep1's audio playback event every 2 seconds at the end of the `Update()` method. Add the following code to verify the sound engine and to check for the timer event before playing the audio:

```
if(!soundEngine.IsDisposed && Timer(gameTime)){
    Play3DAudio("beep1");
}
```

As with engine0, the start event for playing engine1 occurs only once and it does not begin until the introduction audio is over. Start playing engine1 after starting engine0 audio inside `Update()`.

```
Play3DAudio("engine1");
```

When you run the program, the game will begin with the introduction sound. When the introduction is finished, the engines and telemetric beeps start. You have the option to pause or resume ship0's beep by pressing B on the keyboard or the B button on the game pad. A laser fire sound can be triggered by left-clicking the mouse or pulling the right trigger of the game controller. The ship1 engine and telemetric beep can still be heard in each speaker—according to the listener's position and angle relative to ship1.

This demonstration has shown how to create several different types of sound. You can employ the same logic used in the demonstration to create most other types of audio you would need in a game. Scenarios covered include audio that is suitable for 2D and 3D games. Parts A and C of the demonstration are essential for 2D game developers who want to implement great sound effects in their games. Part D is essential for 3D game developers who want to implement 3D audio to match their visual environment.

ZUNE AUDIO EXAMPLE

The following example demonstrates implementing audio on the Zune. The steps shown here explain how to play a looping telemetric beep noise with an mp3 file, a looping engine sound effect from a wave file, and a firing audio effect from a wave file. You can pause and resume the looping audio by pressing the center of the Zune pad button. You can trigger the firing audio by pressing the B button.

This demonstration begins with a new project that is created using the Zune Game template. Also, you will need to add the telemetricBeep.mp3, engine0.wav, and fire.wav files to an Audio folder that is referenced under the content node to load them at runtime. You can find these files in the Audio folder from this book's website.

To load the three different sound objects, their declarations are required at the top of the game class:

```
SoundEffect         fireSound, engineSound;
SoundEffectInstance engineInstance;
Song                backgroundAudio;
```

Next, to track the game pad state from the previous frame and to pause and resume playback, add this declaration to the game class to track your game pad state:

```
GamePadState gpPrevious;
```

The parameters used when calling Play() for both SoundEffect objects are almost identical so they are declared as constants at the top of the game class. The parameter value ranges are explained in comments:

```
const float VOLUME  = 1.0f;    // range between 0 and 1
const float PITCH   = 0.0f;    // -1 down an octave. +1 up an octave
const float PAN     = 0.0f;    // -1 full left. +1 full right
const bool  LOOP    = true;    // true for continuous. false for 1 time.
```

The Audio needs to be loaded from the LoadContent() method. The telemetricBeep.mp3 file is loaded into the Song object and is played back in a loop using the MediaPlayer class. The ship engine audio also plays in a loop but it is loaded in a SoundEffect object. A SoundEffectInstance is created from this SoundEffect object which gives you the ability to loop, pause, and resume your individual sound effects. The firing audio is loaded into a SoundEffect object which is used later for playback whenever the B button is pressed.

```
// load and play background audio
backgroundAudio          = Content.Load<Song>("Audio\\telemetricBeep");
MediaPlayer.Play(backgroundAudio);
MediaPlayer.IsRepeating = true;

// load and play engine as SoundEffectInstance for playback control
engineSound      = Content.Load<SoundEffect>("Audio\\engine0");
engineInstance   = engineSound.Play(VOLUME, PITCH, PAN, LOOP);
// load fire sound effect for playback later
fireSound        = Content.Load<SoundEffect>("Audio\\fire");
```

Lastly, inside Update(), you can add this code to trigger the firing audio whenever the B button is pressed. This code will also allow your players to pause and resume the ship engine and telemetric beep whenever they press the center of the Zune pad.

```
// get new game pad states
GamePadState gpCurrent = GamePad.GetState(PlayerIndex.One);

// play fire sound at each new B button press event
if (gpCurrent.IsButtonDown(Buttons.B)&& gpPrevious.IsButtonUp(Buttons.B))
    fireSound.Play(VOLUME, PITCH, PAN, !LOOP);
// toggle engine audio pause and resume states for DPad.Down events
if (gpCurrent.Buttons.A  == ButtonState.Pressed &&
    gpPrevious.Buttons.A == ButtonState.Released)
    if (engineInstance.State == SoundState.Playing){
        engineInstance.Pause();
        MediaPlayer.Pause();
    }
    else{
        engineInstance.Resume();
        MediaPlayer.Resume();
    }
// store game pad state for next frame
gpPrevious = gpCurrent;
```

You are now ready to deploy this to the Zune for an audio-enabled experience. You may have found the process so simple that you might also decide to use this library in your 2D and 3D game projects on the PC and Xbox 360 as well.

We are sure you will notice how much more enjoyable your games are when you add audio using any of the alternatives provided in XNA.

CHAPTER 27 REVIEW EXERCISES

To get the most from this chapter, try out these chapter review exercises.

1. Implement the step-by-step example in this chapter to create your own XACT audio project file. Then load your audio and play it from code.
2. Using the solution for the arcing projectiles example from Chapter 19, add in audio to handle a launch sound and a 3D audio-enabled explosion sound when the rocket hits the ground.
3. Using the solution for "Adding a Car as a Third-Person Object" from Chapter 14, add a looping noise that repeats to create a continuous engine sound whenever the car moves forward or backward.

CHAPTER 28

Multiplayer Gaming

WE'RE sure you can appreciate the difference between playing video games against the computer and against your friends. Whether you're knocking baseballs over their heads, swerving in front of them to maintain a lead, or volleying rockets at them, it's all good. Most people have a lot more fun playing against an unpredictable human opponent who puts up a tough fight and trash-talks while doing it.

Until now, the examples in this book have been geared for single-player games. You can easily change this by converting your base code to enable a multiplayer environment—where up to four people at a time can take the controls in a split-screen game. This type of environment is exactly what you would expect in a 3D first-person shooter game or a racing game.

You could actually split the screen into more than four sections, but the controller limit is four. You might want additional dimensions, though, if you were to show different views of the world. For example, maybe you want to create a radar screen with an aerial view of your entire world in addition to the main viewer for navigation. The split-screen technique offers many useful possibilities for dividing up the graphics that are rendered in your window.

The code changes required to enable a split-screen game are surprisingly simple. The `Viewport` class makes it easy to split your screen. And if your camera is carefully designed, as it is in the examples this book, you can easily create separate instances to give each additional player control over her own viewport.

VIEWPORT

A *viewport* is a section of the window that you use to draw a scene from a specific view. As you'll see, using the `Viewport` class to split the screen is actually very simple. The `Viewport` class is used to create a viewport object:

```
Viewport viewport = new Viewport();
```

Each viewport object has several properties to set the position and area covered in the game window. Each section of the window is assigned values for the starting top-left pixel, the width and height in pixels, and the depth for clipping, so your physical game objects draw properly:

```
int      viewport.X          // top left pixel X coordinate
int      viewport.Y          // top left pixel Y coordinate
int      viewport.Width      // width in pixels
int      viewport.Height     // height in pixels
float    viewport.MinDepth   // minimum depth of clip volume (usually 0)
float    viewport.MaxDepth   // maximum depth of clip volume (usually 1)
```

The bulk of the code changes needed to convert to a multiplayer game are in handling a separate instance of the camera for each player. However, even this task is relatively simple.

When your multiplayer games are rendered on the Xbox 360, your viewports may be truncated on the televisions where they are played. In fact, it is possible that up to 20 percent of the screen will be hidden. This issue can be addressed by implementing a routine to create margins that equal 10 percent of the window height at the top and bottom and 10 percent of the window width for the left and right. An example of how to do this is presented in the demonstration later in this chapter.

CREATING SEPARATE CAMERAS FOR EACH PLAYER

To give each user the ability to navigate through the world, a separate camera instance is required for each player. The camera instance gives the players the ability to change their position and view within the 3D world.

Adjusting the View

For the graphics engine used in this book, whenever a player moves the mouse or shifts the right thumbstick, he changes his view. In other words, his position in the world stays the same, but his `Look` direction changes as his view target changes. A separate view is needed for each player in the game. For example, in a racing game you might need to focus your camera to watch the contours of a hairpin turn so you don't crash. Your friend might need to watch out for an oil slick to maintain control of the car, and yet another player might be focused on the finish line.

When you assign a separate viewport for each player, every object that is drawn in the viewport must be rendered according to that player's view. Even the base code, which draws nothing but ground, must draw the ground once for each viewport according to the viewport owner's `Look` direction. To handle this need for separate views, the camera's view matrix is updated separately for each player.

Adjusting the Projection

The Projection matrix transforms vector coordinates into clip space (a cone that the viewer sees through). In a split-screen window, you must also adjust the projection to match the area in each viewport. If you do not resize the perspective's aspect ratio properly, you could end up with a viewport(s) that displays everything in a bloated manner—as if the scene were either viewed through a fish-eye lens or in a house of mirrors. The aspect ratio considers the viewport width relative to the viewport height. Until now we have used the window width over height to calculate this ratio. Now though, the current viewport's width over height is needed.

To implement this modification for a split-screen environment, for each different viewport size on display, a Projection matrix is defined when the application begins with the following syntax:

```
// parameters are field of view, viewport w/h, near clip, far clip
Matrix projection = Matrix.CreatePerspectiveFieldOfView(
                    float fieldOfView, float aspectRatio,
                    float nearClip,    float farClip)
```

If you divide the window into top and bottom viewports, the aspect ratio becomes this:

```
Window.ClientBounds.Width/(Window.ClientBounds.Height/2)
```

HANDLING THE USER INPUT

It is possible to have up to four game controllers on one Xbox 360 or PC, so you could write code to handle up to four different players and split the screen accordingly at run time. For the PC, you can even use the mouse and keyboard as one of these inputs. Handling the different controllers is easy with the `GamePadState` class because each controller is referenced by a separate instance of the class. The states for each control on the game pad can be obtained using the `GetState()` method with a `PlayerIndex` attribute as a parameter to specify each player.

SPLIT-SCREEN CODE EXAMPLE

This example demonstrates multiplayer 3D gaming in a split-screen environment. Two aliens will be rendered and controlled in two separate viewports. Each player has her own viewport and is given control of one alien's spaceship, which moves with her camera as she travels. Figure 28-1 shows a split screen for two players. Each player can control her view and position inside the viewport and ultimately travel within the world independently of the other player.

A multiplayer racing game or first-person shooter game uses the same code foundation, so converting the logic to suit a different type of 3D multiplayer game is a simple task. Converting this logic to handle more than two players is also straightforward.

When you run this code on the Xbox 360, you will be able to handle two players, each with her own controller. When the code is run on the PC, you can handle either two controllers, or one controller and a mouse/keyboard combination. If you run this code on the PC with only a mouse and keyboard, you will be able to control one of the viewports, but the other viewport will be disabled until a controller is connected.

This example begins with either the MGHWinBaseCode or MGH360BaseCode project, which can be found in the BaseCode folder in the download available from this book's website.

To enable a two-player game, and to identify each player, you declare the NUMPLAYERS, ALIEN0, and ALIEN1 definitions at the top of the game class:

```
const int NUMPLAYERS        = 2;
const int ALIEN0            = 0;      const int ALIEN1 = 1;
```

To give each player control to move through the 3D environment, and to allow them to view it independently, you declare an array with two separate instances for the camera. Use this revision to replace the existing camera object declaration:

```
private Camera[] cam = new Camera[NUMPLAYERS];
```

FIGURE 28-1

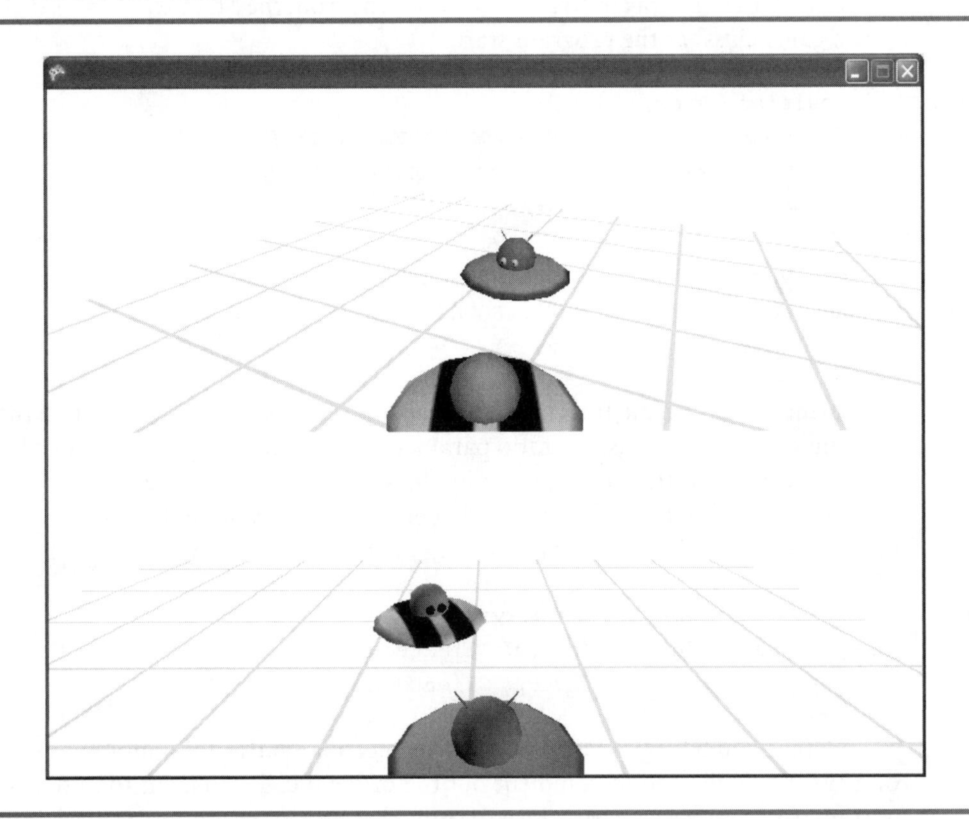

Two viewports for a two-player game. Each player controls her view of the world and can travel independently.

When you're initializing each camera, the starting position and view position for each person needs to be different. Otherwise, with just a default position and view, when the game begins, the players would all be positioned in the same place, one on top of the other. To set the players up at opposite ends of the world, and to have them looking at their opponent, each instance of the camera is initialized with parameters to set the position and view.

An override to the camera constructor allows you to set the position and view of the camera when it is initialized for each player:

```
public Camera(Vector3 startPosition, Vector3 startView){
    position    =  startPosition;
    view        =  startView;
    up          =  new Vector3(0.0f, 1.0f, 0.0f);
}
```

To initialize the camera for the players, you pass their individual starting positions and views to the camera constructor. This is done from the `Initialize()` method (in the game class) at the program start:

```
Vector3     position, view;
position = new Vector3( 0.5f, 0.9f, BOUNDARY - 0.5f);
view     = new Vector3( 0.5f, 0.7f, BOUNDARY - 1.0f);
cam[0]   = new Camera(position, view);

position = new Vector3(-0.5f, 0.9f,-BOUNDARY + 0.5f);
view     = new Vector3(-0.5f, 0.7f,-BOUNDARY + 1.0f);
cam[1]   = new Camera(position, view);
```

As mentioned earlier in this chapter, because both viewport heights are half the actual window height, the aspect-ratio parameter in the Projection matrix must be adjusted. The aspect ratio for the projection becomes (width/(height/2)). To apply this to the Projection matrix, after initializing each camera, replace the call to initialize the Projection matrix in the `Initialize()` method:

```
for (int player = 0; player < 2; player++)
    cam[player].SetProjection(Window.ClientBounds.Width,
                              Window.ClientBounds.Height/2);
```

Now that you have properly set up the projection matrix for a multiplayer environment, you will need to comment out the original call statement to initialize the projection matrix. You can find this call statement inside the `InitializeBaseCode()` method of the game class:

```
// cam.setProjection(Window.ClientBounds.Width,
//                   Window.ClientBounds.Height);
```

A routine is needed in the game class to determine how many game controllers are connected so it can assign control to both players accordingly. The `TotalControllersUsed()` method needed for this example only considers a situation where up to two controllers are used:

```
int TotalControllersUsed(){
    GamePadState gp0 = GamePad.GetState(PlayerIndex.One);
    GamePadState gp1 = GamePad.GetState(PlayerIndex.Two);
    if (gp0.IsConnected && gp1.IsConnected)
        return 2;
    else if (gp0.IsConnected)
        return 1;
    return 0;
}
```

The `ChangeView()`, `Move()`, `Strafe()`, and `DrawGround()` methods inside the game class need to be modified so they can be used for each player. Since each player is a viewport owner, these method headers must be adjusted to accept the player number, as follows:

```
Vector2  ChangeView(GameTime gameTime, int player)
float    Move(int player)
float    Strafe(int player)
void     DrawGround(int player)
```

The `ChangeView()`, `Move()`, and `Strafe()` methods are called once for each viewport owner. These methods must then select the correct input device to allow each player to control their view and position.

For this example, by default, a `GamePadState` object is set for the first player using the `PlayerIndex.One` parameter value regardless of whether a controller is connected or not. If zero or one controllers are connected on a PC, the mouse is designated for the first player to control their viewport. If two game controllers are connected on the PC, the `GamePadState` object is set for the second player using the `PlayerIndex.Two` parameter.

The following code must be added in the `ChangeView()`, `Move()`, and `Strafe()` methods after the `GamePadState` object, gp, is declared:

```
bool useMouse          = false;
int totalControllers = TotalControllersUsed();
```

```
// when fewer than two controllers connected use mouse for 1st player
if (totalControllers <2 && player == 0)
    useMouse = true;
// when 2 controllers connected use 2nd controller for 2nd player
else if (totalControllers == 2 && player == 1)
    gp = GamePad.GetState(PlayerIndex.Two);
```

Also, to ensure that code for the game pad is executed on the PC when either one or two controllers are connected, inside the `ChangeView()`, `Move()`, and `Strafe()` methods, replace:

```
if(gp.IsConnected == true)
```

with

```
if(!useMouse)
```

The code that sets the WorldViewProjection matrix inside `DrawGround()` must also be adjusted according to the player's view. This adjustment sets the WorldViewProjection matrix so it is drawn according to each viewport owner's view:

```
textureEffectWVP.SetValue(world * cam[player].viewMatrix
                          * cam[player].projectionMatrix);
```

Because each player has a separate instance of the camera, each camera must be updated separately; this gives the players the ability to travel independently in the game world. To enable this, inside `Update()`, replace the code that handles the camera's time tracking, forward movement, backward movement, and strafing with this revision to update these values for each player:

```
for (int player = 0; player < NUMPLAYERS; player++){
    // update timer in camera to regulate camera speed
    cam[player].SetFrameInterval(gameTime);

    // adjust camera position and view
    cam[player].Move(Move(player));
    cam[player].Strafe(Strafe(player));
    cam[player].SetView(ChangeView(gameTime, player));
}
```

When the viewports are being drawn (while your code is run on the Xbox 360), it is possible that the full window may not be visible—it may fall outside the title-safe region. As discussed previously in examples where 2D graphics are used, on some televisions, this nonvisible range may be as high as 20 percent. To adjust for this possibility, the starting top-left pixel that is used as the viewport should allow for this potential difference. When viewports are used, you are going to want to account for this possibility so that your 3D graphics do not appear to be off center if truncation occurs. To fix this, add this version of the `TitleSafeRegion()` method to obtain the bounding margins for the top viewport. These margins in turn will be used to determine the starting top-left pixel for each viewport in this demonstration:

```
Rectangle TitleSafeRegion(){
    int windowWidth  = Window.ClientBounds.Width;
    int windowHeight = Window.ClientBounds.Height;
#if Xbox
    // some televisions only show 80% of the window
    Vector2     start          = new Vector2();    // starting pixel X & Y
    const float UNSAFEAREA     = 0.2f;             // 80% not visible on
                                                   // Xbox 360
    start.X =  windowWidth  * UNSAFEAREA/2.0f;
    start.Y =  windowHeight * UNSAFEAREA/2.0f;

    // ensure viewport drawn in safe region on all sides
    return new Rectangle(
           (int)start.X,
           (int)start.Y,
           (int)((1.0f-UNSAFEAREA)* windowWidth),
           (int)((1.0f-UNSAFEAREA)* windowHeight/2));
#endif
    // PC show the entire region
    return new Rectangle(0, 0, windowWidth, windowHeight/2);
}
```

The next method needed in your game class is the CurrentViewport() method to set your viewport. In a multiplayer game, the `Draw()` method must trigger rendering of the entire scene for each viewport. Before drawing each viewport, you must set the top-left pixel where the viewport begins, the height and width properties for each viewport, and the clip minimum and maximum. If the clip minimum and maximum values are not set between 0 and 1, your 3D models will not render properly:

```
Viewport CurrentViewport(int player){
    Viewport  viewport        = new Viewport();
    Rectangle safeRegion      = TitleSafeRegion();
    Vector2   startPixel      = new Vector2((float)safeRegion.Left,
                                            (float)safeRegion.Top);
```

```
    // get starting top left pixel for viewport
    if (player == 1)                              // 2nd player - bottom
        startPixel.Y += (float)safeRegion.Height;

    // assign viewport properties
    viewport.X          = (int)startPixel.X;          // top left pixel X
    viewport.Y          = (int)startPixel.Y;          // top left pixel Y
    viewport.Width      = safeRegion.Width;           // pixel width
    viewport.Height     = safeRegion.Height;          // pixel height

    viewport.MinDepth = 0.0f;                         // depth is between
    viewport.MaxDepth = 1.0f;                         // 0 & 1 so models
                                                      // appear properly
    return viewport;
}
```

When multiple viewports are used, each one is rendered separately. In effect, the same scene is drawn more than once. With careful planning, the same methods can be used for drawing your primitive objects and models. Note also that when drawing with multiple viewports, the viewport is set first before the viewport is cleared. The drawing is performed afterward.

Replace the existing `Draw()` method with this revision to draw all objects in each viewport according to the view and perspective of each player:

```
protected override void Draw(GameTime gameTime){
    for (int player = 0; player < NUMPLAYERS; player++) {
        // set the viewport before clearing screen
        graphics.GraphicsDevice.Viewport = CurrentViewport(player);
        graphics.GraphicsDevice.Clear(Color.CornflowerBlue);
        // draw objects
        DrawGround(player);
    }
    base.Draw(gameTime);
}
```

If you ran the project now, you would see two viewports. Remember that this code can serve as a base for any multiplayer game.

To make this demonstration more interesting, two aliens will be added. Each player will be given control of an alien, which will be used as a third-person character. The alien will move with the camera. This not only allows each player to control her own spaceship, but also enables her to view the movements of her opponent in her own viewport.

For this example, you can use the alien models in the Models folder in the book's download. To do this, obtain the alien0.fbx, alien1.fbx, and spaceA.bmp files from the Models folder. Create a Models folder in your project and reference the .fbx files from the Solution Explorer.

To load these models and to control their transformations, declarations for the model objects and their bone-transformation matrices are required at the top of the game class:

```
Model    alien0Model;  Model    alien1Model;
Matrix[] alien0Matrix; Matrix[] alien1Matrix;
```

The code used to load these two models and their accompanying transformation matrices is contained in the InitializeAliens() method. To initialize the models, add this method to your game class:

```
void InitializeAliens(){
    alien0Model         = Content.Load<Model>("Models\\alien0");
    alien0Matrix        = new Matrix[alien0Model.Bones.Count];
    alien0Model.CopyAbsoluteBoneTransformsTo(alien0Matrix);

    alien1Model         = Content.Load<Model>("Models\\alien1");
    alien1Matrix        = new Matrix[alien1Model.Bones.Count];
    alien1Model.CopyAbsoluteBoneTransformsTo(alien1Matrix);
}
```

To load the aliens when the program begins, add the call statement InitializeAliens() to the `Initialize()` method:

```
InitializeAliens();
```

For this two-player game, one alien and its spaceship are controlled by each player. Each alien's spaceship moves with the player's camera. To rotate the alien about the Y axis—so it always points in the direction it is traveling—use the following method to calculate the angle of direction based on the camera's `Look` direction:

```
float RotationAngle(Vector3 view, Vector3 position){
    Vector3 look = view - position;
    return        (float)Math.Atan2((double)look.X, (double)look.Z);
}
```

To save on code, the same method is used to draw both aliens. When these items are rendered in a viewport, this method is called once for each model. This process is repeated for each player. For this example, `alien0`'s position and angle of orientation is based on the first player's camera. `Alien1`'s position and orientation is based on the second player's camera. The view is adjusted for each player. The rest of the routine is identical to the routines you have already used in this book for drawing models.

```
void DrawAliens(int player, Model model, int modelNum){
    foreach (ModelMesh mesh in model.Meshes){
        // 1: declare matrices
        Matrix world, scale, rotationY, translation, translationOrbit;

        // 2: initialize matrices
        scale            = Matrix.CreateScale(0.5f, 0.5f, 0.5f);
        translation      = Matrix.CreateTranslation(Vector3.Zero);
        rotationY        = Matrix.CreateRotationY(MathHelper.Pi);
        translationOrbit = Matrix.CreateTranslation(0.0f, 0.0f, 1.0f);
        translation      = Matrix.CreateTranslation(         // one alien
                           cam[modelNum].position.X,         // is located
                           cam[modelNum].position.Y - 0.6f,  // at each
                           cam[modelNum].position.Z);        // camera
        float angleY     = RotationAngle(cam[modelNum].view,
                           cam[modelNum].position);
        rotationY        = Matrix.CreateRotationY(angleY);

        // 3: build cumulative world matrix using I.S.R.O.T. sequence
        // identity, scale, rotate, orbit(translate & rotate), translate
        world =  scale * translationOrbit * rotationY * translation;
        foreach (BasicEffect effect in mesh.Effects){
            // 4: pass wvp to shader
            effect.View           = cam[player].viewMatrix;
            switch (modelNum){
                case ALIEN0:
                    effect.World =
                    alien0Matrix[mesh.ParentBone.Index] * world;  break;
                case ALIEN1:
                    effect.World =
                    alien1Matrix[mesh.ParentBone.Index] * world;  break;
            }
            effect.Projection     = cam[player].projectionMatrix;
            // 4b: set lighting
            effect.EnableDefaultLighting();
```

```
            }
            // 5: draw object
            mesh.Draw();
        }
    }
```

To draw each model, add these call statements to the end of the `Draw()` method inside the for-loop that triggers drawing for each player's viewport:

```
DrawAliens(player, alien0Model, ALIEN0);
DrawAliens(player, alien1Model, ALIEN1);
```

When you run this version of the code, each of the two players can control the movement of her alien separately. In addition, she can view her world and travel independently of the other player.

Being able to shift the view up and down might be useful for a first-person shooter game, but it doesn't look right for this setup. Inside `ChangeView()`, you can prevent the camera from bobbing up and down by modifying the return statement to set the Y view to zero:

```
return new Vector2(change.X, 0.0f);
```

When you run the code now, each player will be able to control her view of the world. This example was kept simple, but you can apply this logic for different types of games, such as first-person shooter, racing, role-playing, or adventure games.

CHAPTER 28 REVIEW EXERCISES

To get the most from this chapter, try out these chapter review exercises.

1. If you have not already done so, implement the step-by-step demonstration presented in this chapter.
2. Create a three-person viewport window. The first two viewports should split the top half of the window, and the third viewport should be located in the bottom half of the window. The user input should be handled in such a way as to permit up to three controllers. If the code is run on the PC, and fewer than three controllers are detected, the mouse and keyboard should be enabled for the third player. You will need to create a separate Projection matrix method to permit proper viewing from each viewport if one of the viewports is sized differently than the others.

CHAPTER 29

Networking

THANKS to Microsoft XNA's developer-friendly framework, building network games is simple and powerful. The examples presented in this chapter use 3D graphics, so they will only work on the PC and Xbox 360. However, the network-specific code is identical for the Xbox 360, PC, and Zune. If needed, you could easily adapt these solutions for game play in a 2D environment to run on the Xbox 360, PC, or Zune.

This chapter offers two different ways to implement the XNA networking framework through: peer-to-peer network and a client/server network.

PEER-TO-PEER NETWORKS

The simpler option for developing XNA network games is to use a peer-to-peer network. The peer-to-peer network is generated by the first machine to create a game session. Once the session is started, the other peer machines may join. Each peer system reads data sent from all other peers, so the traffic load is equivalent for all of the machines using the network. When all peer machines have similar processing capabilities, the peer-to-peer network may be ideal for enabling efficient and balanced game performance. However, a peer-to-peer framework creates more network traffic than a client/server structure. As more gamers join the peer-to-peer network session, performance will generally degrade more quickly than on a client/server-based network.

CLIENT/SERVER NETWORKS

On a client/server network all remote machines, referred to as *clients*, send their game data to the server, and the server distributes the entire data collection to all clients. The machine that creates the session is designated as the server.

A client/server network offers better scalability for games because it cuts down on data packet traffic and it lets gamers decide where the server-side processing should be performed. Having the data managed in one location also enables better security enforcement.

EFFICIENT BANDWIDTH USE

Exchanging data over a network presents challenges since there are delays between the time data packets are sent and when they are received. More data and more gamers will slow the network traffic. Because of this, ensuring efficient data delivery speed is crucial not only for game performance but also for game play. If two cars are in a dead heat and each car is controlled from a remote machine, you need to be sure to reward the true winner. In a networked environment this can be difficult. Data delivery may fall behind the game action when two cars are jockeying for position. In close calls like these, it is hard to know who really won. You could just assign a tie if

you are unsure who won, but your players will eventually catch on and get upset if tied results occur too frequently. Also, if the network is too slow, your animations will lag and could appear fragmented.

To ensure efficient use of your network, you should aim to minimize the amount of data exchanged. For this reason, your game design should arrange your data packets such that only critical data has to be sent. During a grenade explosion, random smoke, flames, shrapnel, and collateral damage result. Given all of the events and assets affected by an explosion, you cannot afford to transfer all of this descriptive data over the network to create an identical explosion on each client. To reduce traffic, much of the randomization should be done on the client—this is how commercial games do it. If you actually compare the aftermath of an explosion on two different machines in a networked game, you will see differences in how the windows, buildings, and vehicles are damaged and dispersed. Still, when an explosion takes place, players on different machines are seeing this action from different directions. Game play in games like these is usually so fast that minor differences aren't noticeable and they certainly do not detract from the experience.

XNA'S CODE FRAMEWORK

XNA offers a very simple interface to build your network while it also allows you room to customize how it operates.

GamerServicesComponent

A networked XNA game is enabled with the `GamerServicesComponent`. The `GamerServices` namespace must be referenced from the game class to use it:

```
using Microsoft.Xna.Framework.GamerServices;
```

The `GamerServicesComponent` is added when the game begins:

```
Components.Add(new GamerServicesComponent(this));
```

NetworkSession

A multiplayer network game is conducted through one network session. Each system that joins the networked game contains the same instance of this session.

```
NetworkSession      session;
```

Creating the Network

The first machine must initialize the `NetworkSession` object using the `NetworkSession` class `Create()` method. `Create()` receives three parameters.

The first parameter is the NetworkSessionType, which offers four different types of network connectivity:

1. Local Does not generate network traffic but does enable networking on the Xbox 360 for split-screen gaming.
2. PlayerMatch Enables a connection over the Internet using Xbox LIVE servers. Use on Windows requires a LIVE Silver membership and use on the Xbox 360 requires a LIVE Gold membership.
3. Ranked All session matches are ranked. This feature is only available for commercial games that have passed Xbox LIVE certification.
4. SystemLink Connects computers and Xbox 360s via a local subnet. This option does not require a connection to an Xbox or an Xbox LIVE account.

The example for this chapter uses NetworkSessionType.SystemLink because it allows you to test your PC network games without having to purchase an XNA Creators Club membership. Any development on an Xbox 360 requires the Creators Club subscription, but you only need one subscription. However, if you are testing over LIVE you will require two subscriptions—one for each machine. Here is the syntax for NetworkSession.Create() when the SystemLink option is specified:

```
session = NetworkSession.Create(NetworkSessionType.SystemLink,
                                int MAX_LOCAL_GAMERS, int MAX_GAMERS);
```

Joining a NetworkSession

When joining a network, the NetworkSession's Find() method searches for and returns a listing of the best possible sessions. AvailableNetworkSessionCollection stores the sessions that are accessible to your game:

```
AvailableNetworkSessionCollection availableSessions =
    NetworkSession.Find(NetworkSessionType.SystemLink, MAX_LOCAL_GAMERS,
                        null)
```

Here the default is set to join the first available session that is found:

```
NetworkSession session   = NetworkSession.Join(availableSessions[0]);
```

Session Events

The NetworkSession class allows you to create several events to capture changes that affect your session. These events include GameStarted, GamerJoined, GamerLeft, GamerEnded, and SessionEnded.

GamerJoined Event

As the name suggests, the GamerJoined event lets you track new gamers that join your session. This event handler is added on every machine that joins the current network session:

```
NetworkSession networkSession.GamerJoined  += GamerJoinEvent;
```

The GamerJoinEvent handler used in our example later is shown below:

```
void GamerJoinEvent(object sender, GamerJoinedEventArgs e){
    int gamerIndex = session.AllGamers.IndexOf(e.Gamer);
}
```

SessionEnded Event

The SessionEnded event informs all gamers of session termination and the reasons why. For example, one reason would be that the network host has left. This event is added on each machine when the NetworkSession is initialized:

```
session.SessionEnded += SessionEndEvent;
```

Your SessionEnd handler may look similar to the following:

```
void SessionEndEvent(object sender, NetworkSessionEndedEventArgs e){
    errorMessage    = e.EndReason.ToString();
    session.Dispose();
    session         = null;
}
```

LOCAL NETWORK GAMER

The LocalNetworkGamer class provides attributes and methods for identifying and handling players in your session. LocalNetworkGamer properties like IsHost and IsLocal allow you to determine whether the current gamer is located on the network host or on another client machine.

UPDATING THE SESSION

In between draws, when updating the game, the network session is also updated. During the update, current data packets are written to the network and new ones are read.

PacketWriter

Data is sent to the network using a packet writer. The `PacketWriter` object is initialized on every machine on the network.

```
PacketWriter packetWriter  = new PacketWriter();
```

The `PacketWriter` object allows you to send Boolean values, color, string, common numeric types, vector, and matrix data from your client. Most of the built-in data types you'd use with XNA can be sent across the network. You don't need to specify the type of data either, because the `Write()` method overloads do this for you. This `Write()` method, which is used in a later example, implements the `SendDataOptions.InOrder` type so that the data packet write and read routines must send the data using a first-in, first-out basis:

```
void Write(LocalNetworkGamer gamer,
           Vector3 cameraPosition, Vector3 cameraView){
    packetWriter.Write(cameraPosition);
    packetWriter.Write(cameraView);
    gamer.SendData(packetWriter, SendDataOptions.InOrder);
}
```

PacketReader

Data is read from the network using the packet reader. A `PacketReader` object is initialized on each machine located in the session.

```
PacketReader packetReader  = new PacketReader();
```

When you use the `PacketReader` object, you have to specify the read method that matches the data format being read from the network. For example, in the following code, `Vector3` data is being read:

```
Vector3 vector3 = packetReader.ReadVector3();
```

Table 1 shows all of the data types that the `PacketReader` reads.

TABLE 29-1

ReadBoolean	*ReadDecimal*	*ReadQuaternion*	*ReadUInt64*
ReadByte	*ReadDouble*	*ReadSbyte*	*ReadVector2*
ReadBytes	*ReadInt16*	*ReadSingle*	*ReadVector3*
ReadChar	*ReadInt32*	*ReadString*	*ReadVector4*
ReadChars	*ReadInt64*	*ReadUInt16*	
ReadColor	*ReadMatrix*	*ReadUInt32*	

PacketReader methods for reading different data types

Updating the Network

The code used to update the session must write local data to the network, check to ensure the session still exists, and then read the incoming data from the network. Also, during the update, you must update the `NetworkSession` parent's `Update()` method:

```
networkSession.Update();
```

NETWORK EXAMPLE: PEER TO PEER

This example shows how to create a network that allows two players to control their own alien ship remotely in the same game. A peer-to-peer network will first be created and later this project will be converted into a client/server networked game. The example begins with either the MGHWinBaseCode or MGH360BaseCode project found in the BaseCode folder on this book's website.

Setting Up the Network Class

A new code file called Network.cs will be used to contain our networking code. Add a Network.cs code file to the project and place the following code shell in it to get the `XNANetwork` class started. This code includes the `Session`, `PacketWriter`, and `PacketReader` objects to create the network and to transfer data within it. Since the data transfer requirements for this game demonstration are actually very light, you only need to transfer the player `position` and `view` data from each controller. The rest of the processing can be handled on the client. Some constants are declared at the top of this class shell to set maximum totals for local and remote players in addition to identifying the data source for each gamer. Here is the code to start the XNANetwork class:

```
using System;
using Microsoft.Xna.Framework;
using Microsoft.Xna.Framework.Net;
using System.Collections.Generic;
namespace MGHGame{
    public class XNANetwork{
        public  String                errorMessage;
        public  NetworkSession        session;
        PacketWriter packetWriter     = new PacketWriter();
        PacketReader packetReader     = new PacketReader();
        public Vector3 remotePosition, remoteView;
        const int MAX_GAMERS = 16;    const int MAX_LOCAL_GAMERS = 4;
        public int MaxLocalGamers{ get { return MAX_LOCAL_GAMERS; } }
```

```
        const int CAMERA_DATA = 0;     const int NETWORK_DATA     = 1;
    }
}
```

Next, to track when gamers join your game and when the session ends, add the following handlers to your XNANetwork class:

```
void GamerJoinEvent(object sender, GamerJoinedEventArgs e){
    int gamerIndex = session.AllGamers.IndexOf(e.Gamer);
}
void SessionEndEvent(object sender, NetworkSessionEndedEventArgs e){
    errorMessage   = e.EndReason.ToString();
    session.Dispose();
    session        = null;
}
void AddSessionEvents(){
    session.GamerJoined  += GamerJoinEvent;
    session.SessionEnded += SessionEndEvent;
}
```

A `CreateSession()` method is also needed in the `XNANetwork` class. This routine creates a session using the `SystemLink` type, so that you can test your networked PC and Xbox 360 games on a local subnet. This method also sets a limit of four players—to comply with XNA's four-player limit per Xbox 360—as well as a `MAX_GAMERS` limit of 16 to keep the game session from becoming too big to handle. This code uses the non-asynchronous networking methods, so there will be some lockup during the session creation, finding, and joining process:

```
public void CreateSession(){
    try{session = NetworkSession.Create(NetworkSessionType.SystemLink,
                                        MAX_LOCAL_GAMERS, MAX_GAMERS);
        AddSessionEvents();
    }
    catch (Exception e){
        errorMessage   = e.Message;
    }
}
```

Now that the `XNANetwork` class has enough code in place to create a session, you can add this `JoinSession()` to let new machines also join the session. The `Find()` method searches for a list of sessions within the `SessionType` scope. This example assumes you will take the first available session:

```
public void JoinSession(){
    try{
```

```
        // search for sessions.
        using (AvailableNetworkSessionCollection availableSessions =
                NetworkSession.Find(NetworkSessionType.SystemLink,
                            MAX_LOCAL_GAMERS, null)){
            if (availableSessions.Count == 0){
                errorMessage = "Network session not found.";
                return;
            }
            // join first session we found.
            session   = NetworkSession.Join(availableSessions[0]);
            AddSessionEvents();
        }
    }
    catch (Exception e){
        errorMessage = e.Message;
    }
}
```

The `XNANetwork.Write()` method packages our local data and sends it across the network in a packet. The `SendDataOptions.InOrder` type specified in the `SendData` parameter enforces a first-in, first-out delivery:

```
void Write(LocalNetworkGamer gamer,
           Vector3 cameraPosition, Vector3 cameraView){
    packetWriter.Write(cameraPosition);
    packetWriter.Write(cameraView);
    gamer.SendData(packetWriter, SendDataOptions.InOrder);
}
```

The `XNANetwork.Read()` method inputs all position and view data from remote players. It then stores the remote data in the `remotePosition` and `remoteView` `Vector3` objects so that the receiving client can use this data to properly position and angle the remotely controlled alien ship:

```
void Read(LocalNetworkGamer gamer){
    // read all available incoming packets
    while (gamer.IsDataAvailable){
        NetworkGamer sender;
        // read single packet from network.
        gamer.ReceiveData(packetReader, out sender);
        // don't read local packets
        if (sender.IsLocal)
            continue;
        remotePosition = packetReader.ReadVector3();
```

```
        remoteView      = packetReader.ReadVector3();
    }
}
```

The XNANetwork class code that updates our network is called in between draws. First this routine writes local data and if the session has not ended, it also reads remote data. Also, the parent Session object's parent routine is updated:

```
public void UpdateNetwork(Vector3 cameraPosition, Vector3 cameraView){
    // write locally generated data
    foreach (LocalNetworkGamer gamer in session.LocalGamers)
        if (gamer.IsLocal)
            Write(gamer, cameraPosition, cameraView);
    // update session object
    session.Update();
    // ensure that session has not ended
    if (session == null)
        return;
    // read packets for remotely controlled aliens
    foreach (LocalNetworkGamer gamer in session.LocalGamers)
        Read(gamer);
}
```

Adding Network Capability to the Game Class

To enable networking objects in your game, you must reference the GamerServices framework in your game class:

```
using Microsoft.Xna.Framework.GamerServices;
```

You can then add in an instance of the GamerServicesComponent for the game from the game class constructor:

```
Components.Add(new GamerServicesComponent(this));
```

At the top of the game class, an instance of the network is needed:

```
XNANetwork network      = new XNANetwork();
```

Also at the top of the game class, a Boolean variable is used to track whether or not the current machine is the network host:

```
bool host = false;
```

When running games over a network, you need a menu screen to allow users to sign in and join the game. To enable this, you also need a font object in the game class. You can add the font by inserting this declaration:

```
SpriteFont font;
```

Of course, you also need to add a spritefont file to your class under the Content node. You need to name it `Font.spritefont` so that it can be loaded using code presented later in this demonstration. Assign the `<FontName>` Arial in the Font.spritefont file:

```
<FontName>Arial</FontName>
```

To load your font, add this instruction to the `LoadContent()` method:

```
font = Content.Load<SpriteFont>("Font");
```

Add the `DrawString()` routine to display the text on the game menu in addition to the error messages that may be written during a game session. `SaveStateMode.SaveState` is used here to restore the graphics device:

```
void DrawString(String msg){
    spriteBatch.Begin(SpriteBlendMode.AlphaBlend, // see chapter 12
                                                   // for more performance
                                                   // friendly alternative
                                                   // to SaveState
              SpriteSortMode.Immediate, SaveStateMode.SaveState);
    spriteBatch.DrawString(font, msg, new Vector2(152, 152), Color.White);
    spriteBatch.End();
}
```

`DrawMenu()` and `DrawMessage()` are needed in the game class to display user options for starting or joining a game and for informing the user of errors that may occur during the course of a game session:

```
void DrawMenu(){
    string msg = string.Empty;

    if (!string.IsNullOrEmpty(network.errorMessage))
        msg += "Error:\n"
               + network.errorMessage.Replace(". ", ".\n") + "\n\n";

    msg     += "A = Start game\n" +
               "B = Join game";
    DrawString(msg);
}
void DrawMessage(string message){
    if (!BeginDraw())   // starts drawing of frame
```

```
        return;
    GraphicsDevice.Clear(Color.CornflowerBlue);
    DrawString(message);
    EndDraw();              // ends drawing of frame
}
```

When initializing the game, code is needed to assign starting positions for the camera depending on whether the alien ship is controlled locally or remotely. When setting the starting positions for each alien, an offset is used to differentiate the camera view from the camera position on the Z access.

```
const float VIEWOFFSET_Z = 0.5f;
```

Another constant is needed at the top of the game class to describe whether the alien being drawn or updated is controlled locally. The constant is used to make our code easier to read:

```
const bool LOCAL_CONTROL = true;
```

The `CameraStartPositions()` method is needed in the game class to set up the cameras based on the local and remote controller orientation when the game begins:

```
void CameraStartPositions(){
    const float YOFFSET          = 0.9f;

    // handles only two gamers - each at opposite ends of the world
    if (host){  // host gamer
        cam.position             = new Vector3(0.0f, YOFFSET, -BOUNDARY);
        cam.view                 = new Vector3(0.0f, YOFFSET, -BOUNDARY
                                                       + VIEWOFFSET_Z);
              // assign remote positions (but don't draw yet)
        network.remotePosition   = new Vector3(0.0f, YOFFSET, +BOUNDARY);
        network.remoteView       = new Vector3(0.0f, YOFFSET, +BOUNDARY
                                                       - VIEWOFFSET_Z);
    }
    else{       // other gamer
        cam.position             = new Vector3(0.0f, YOFFSET, +BOUNDARY);
        cam.view                 = new Vector3(0.0f, YOFFSET, +BOUNDARY
                                                       - VIEWOFFSET_Z);
    }
}
```

The introductory screen and menu selections are displayed from `UpdateGameStart()`. When no gamers are signed in locally, `Guide.ShowSignIn()` displays Microsoft's SignIn window where your gamers select or create their profile. Once a profile is selected, the gamer can then either create or join a network session. You can, of course, customize this chain of events if you want more players to play locally, but you will have to add a split-screen environment:

```
void UpdateGameStart(){
    KeyboardState kbState = Keyboard.GetState();
    GamePadState  gpState = GamePad.GetState(PlayerIndex.One);

    if (this.IsActive){
        if (Gamer.SignedInGamers.Count == 0)
            Guide.ShowSignIn(network.MaxLocalGamers, false);
        // create new session
        else if (kbState.IsKeyDown(Keys.A)
        || gpState.IsButtonDown(Buttons.A)){
            host = true;
            network.CreateSession();
            CameraStartPositions();
        }
        else if (kbState.IsKeyDown(Keys.B)
        || gpState.IsButtonDown(Buttons.B)){
            // join existing session
            DrawMessage("Joining session...");
            network.JoinSession();
            CameraStartPositions();
        }
    }
}
```

You are just about ready to start drawing. To prepare for this, these model objects and identifier declarations are needed in the game class to control the model content:

```
Model     alien0Model;      Model     alien1Model;
Matrix[]  alien0Matrix;     Matrix[]  alien1Matrix;
const int ALIEN0 = 0;       const int ALIEN1 = 1;
```

Before you begin loading or drawing the models, the alien0.fbx, alien1.fbx, and fbx\spaceA.bmp files must be referenced from a Models folder under your Content node. Once you have done this, you can load your model files from the LoadContent() methods:

```
alien0Model      = Content.Load<Model>("Models\\alien0");
alien0Matrix     = new Matrix[alien0Model.Bones.Count];
alien0Model.CopyAbsoluteBoneTransformsTo(alien0Matrix);
alien1Model      = Content.Load<Model>("Models\\alien1");
alien1Matrix     = new Matrix[alien1Model.Bones.Count];
alien1Model.CopyAbsoluteBoneTransformsTo(alien1Matrix);
```

To orient the aliens according to their direction on the Y axis, the YDirection() method is required in the game class:

```
float YDirection(Vector3 view, Vector3 position){
    Vector3 forward = view - position;
    return (float)Math.Atan2((double)forward.X, (double)forward.Z);
}
```

To transform the alien models when drawing and updating them, add these methods to the game class:

```
Matrix Scale(){
    const float SCALAR = 0.5f;
    return Matrix.CreateScale(SCALAR, SCALAR, SCALAR);
}
Matrix TransformAliens(bool host, bool controlledLocally,
                       Vector3 position, Vector3 view){
    // 1: declare matrices
    Matrix yRotation, translateOffset, rotateOffset, translation;

    // 2: initialize matrices
    yRotation           = Matrix.CreateRotationY(0.0f);
    float offsetAngle   = YDirection(view, position);
    rotateOffset        = Matrix.CreateRotationY(offsetAngle);
    const float YOFFSET  = 0.3f;
    const float Z_OFFSET = 2.0f;
    translateOffset = Matrix.CreateTranslation(0.0f, YOFFSET, Z_OFFSET);
    translation     = Matrix.CreateTranslation(
                      new Vector3(position.X, 0.0f, position.Z));
    // 3: build cumulative world matrix using I.S.R.O.T. sequence
    // identity, scale, rotate, orbit(translate & rotate), translate
    return yRotation * translateOffset * rotateOffset * translation;
}
```

To update the local position and view data each frame, add `UpdateGameNetwork()` to your game class. `Vector3.Transform()` updates the view and position coordinates according to the changes of the locally controlled aliens. Once the local view and position data is calculated, these values are passed to the network class for distribution across the network:

```
public void UpdateGameNetwork(){
    if (network.session == null){ // update menu if no game yet
        UpdateGameStart();
    }
    else{                         // otherwise update network
                                  // with latest position and view data
        Matrix world     = Scale() * TransformAliens(host, LOCAL_CONTROL,
                           cam.position, cam.view);
        Vector3 position = Vector3.Zero;
        Vector3 view     = Vector3.Zero;
                view.Z   =-VIEWOFFSET_Z;
        Vector3.Transform(ref position, ref world, out position);
        Vector3.Transform(ref view, ref world, out view);
        network.UpdateNetwork(cam.position, cam.view);
    }
}
```

To update your game, call `UpdateGameNetwork()` at the end of the `Update()` method in the game class:

```
UpdateGameNetwork();
```

This generic `DrawModels()` routine will draw your models:

```
void DrawModels(Model model, Matrix[] matrix, Matrix world){
    foreach (ModelMesh mesh in model.Meshes){
        foreach (BasicEffect effect in mesh.Effects){
            // 4: set shader variables
            effect.World      = matrix[mesh.ParentBone.Index] * world;
            effect.View       = cam.viewMatrix;
            effect.Projection = cam.projectionMatrix;
            effect.EnableDefaultLighting();
            effect.CommitChanges();
        }
        // 5: draw object
        mesh.Draw();
    }
}
```

Add DrawAliens() to your game class to render your alien models. This method is called when the game is active, and it switches views depending on whether the game is being run on the network host or from a network client:

```
public void DrawAliens(){
    Matrix world;

    if (network.session.RemoteGamers.Count > 0){
        if (host){        // host
            world = Scale() * TransformAliens(host, LOCAL_CONTROL,
                    cam.position, cam.view);
            DrawModels(alien0Model, alien0Matrix, world);
            world = Scale() * TransformAliens(host, !LOCAL_CONTROL,
                    network.remotePosition, network.remoteView);
            DrawModels(alien1Model, alien1Matrix, world);
        }
        else{             // client
            world = Scale() * TransformAliens(host, !LOCAL_CONTROL,
                    network.remotePosition, network.remoteView);
            DrawModels(alien0Model, alien0Matrix, world);
            world = Scale() * TransformAliens(host, LOCAL_CONTROL,
                    cam.position, cam.view);
            DrawModels(alien1Model, alien1Matrix, world);
        }
    }
    // 1 player only
    else{
        world = Scale() * TransformAliens(host, LOCAL_CONTROL,
                cam.position, cam.view);
        DrawModels(alien0Model, alien0Matrix, world);
    }
}
```

The code for drawing your aliens is triggered from the Draw() method. Since menus are displayed before 3D graphics (when the game begins), a conditional structure is used to select the appropriate output based on the user's choice. To implement this drawing code, replace the existing DrawGround() statement in Draw() with this revision:

```
if (network.session == null){
    DrawMenu();
}
```

```
else{
    DrawGround();
    DrawAliens();
}
```

When you have finished adding this code, you will then be able to run your game on two machines. Each player will be able to control one of the aliens in the game.

NETWORK EXAMPLE: CLIENT/SERVER

This next example starts with the code from the peer-to-peer solution and converts it to a client/server-based network. The main difference with this example is that the clients send their data directly to the server rather than to all of the other clients. The server then distributes the entire collection of data to the clients.

To start, an extra class is needed in Network.cs to store the alien position, view, and identification:

```
public class Alien{
    public Vector3  position;
    public Vector3  view;
    public int      alienID;

    public Alien() { }
    public Alien(int alienNum){
        alienID = alienNum;
    }
}
```

The server collects all of the remote client and local data and stores it in a list, so a list declaration is needed in the XNANetwork class:

```
public List<Alien> alienData = new List<Alien>();
```

A new version of GamerJoinEvent() stores the instance of each new gamer locally as each new player joins the game. The structure, e.Gamer.Tag, stores each new gamer's identity. e.Gamer.Tag will be referenced later during reads and writes to identify the gamer data. Each new gamer is added to the XNANetwork list. To add this code, replace GamerJoinEvent() with this new version:

```
void GamerJoinEvent(object sender, GamerJoinedEventArgs e){
    int gamerIndex      = session.AllGamers.IndexOf(e.Gamer);
```

```
    e.Gamer.Tag          = new Alien(gamerIndex);

    Alien tempAlien      = new Alien();
    tempAlien.alienID    = gamerIndex;
    alienData.Add(tempAlien);
}
```

ClientWrite() belongs in the XNANetwork class to write local data from the client to the network:

```
void ClientWrite(LocalNetworkGamer gamer,
                 Vector3 localPosition, Vector3 localView){
    Alien localAlien = gamer.Tag as Alien;

    // find local players in list and write their data to the network
    for (int i = 0; i < alienData.Count; i++){
        if (alienData[i].alienID == localAlien.alienID && gamer.IsLocal){
            Alien tempAlien      = new Alien();
            tempAlien.alienID    = localAlien.alienID;
            tempAlien.position   = localPosition;
            tempAlien.view       = localView;
            alienData[i]         = tempAlien;

            // Write our latest input state into a network packet.
            packetWriter.Write(alienData[i].alienID);
            packetWriter.Write(localPosition);
            packetWriter.Write(localView);
        }
    }
    // Send our input data to the server.
    gamer.SendData(packetWriter,
                   SendDataOptions.InOrder, session.Host);
}
```

The routine that writes data packets from the server, ServerWrite(), is different than ClientWrite(). ServerWrite() sends local data to the network and also distributes all data generated on other clients as one collection. ServerWrite() must be placed inside the XNANetwork class to perform this data transfer:

```
void ServerWrite(Vector3 localPosition, Vector3 localView){
    // iterate through all local and remote players
```

```
    foreach (NetworkGamer gamer in session.AllGamers){
        Alien alien = gamer.Tag as Alien;

        for (int i = 0; i < alienData.Count; i++){
            // update local data only
            if (gamer.IsLocal && alienData[i].alienID == alien.alienID){
                Alien tempAlien      = new Alien();
                tempAlien.alienID    = alien.alienID;
                tempAlien.position   = localPosition;
                tempAlien.view       = localView;
                alienData[i]         = tempAlien;
            }
            // write data for all players
            packetWriter.Write(alienData[i].alienID);
            packetWriter.Write(alienData[i].position);
            packetWriter.Write(alienData[i].view);
        }
    }

    // send all data to everyone on session
    LocalNetworkGamer server = (LocalNetworkGamer)session.Host;
    server.SendData(packetWriter, SendDataOptions.InOrder);
}
```

Next, add `ServerRead()` to the `XNANetwork` class to read all remote data and store it locally in the list:

```
void ServerRead(LocalNetworkGamer gamer){
    // read all incoming packets
    while (gamer.IsDataAvailable){
        NetworkGamer sender;

        // read single packet
        gamer.ReceiveData(packetReader, out sender);

        // store remote data only
        if (!sender.IsLocal){
            int tag        = packetReader.ReadInt32();
            remotePosition = packetReader.ReadVector3();
            remoteView     = packetReader.ReadVector3();
            for (int i = 0; i < alienData.Count; i++){
```

```
                if (alienData[i].alienID == tag){
                    Alien tempAlien        = new Alien();
                    tempAlien.alienID      = tag;
                    tempAlien.position     = remotePosition;
                    tempAlien.view         = remoteView;
                    alienData[i]           = tempAlien;
                }
            }
        }
    }
}
```

Then, add `ClientRead()` to read all data from the network and to store the remote data in the alien data list:

```
void ClientRead(LocalNetworkGamer gamer){
    while (gamer.IsDataAvailable){
        NetworkGamer sender;
        // read single packet
        gamer.ReceiveData(packetReader, out sender);

        int gamerId  = packetReader.ReadInt32();
        Vector3 pos  = packetReader.ReadVector3();
        Vector3 view = packetReader.ReadVector3();

        // get current gamer id
        NetworkGamer remoteGamer = session.FindGamerById(gamer.Id);

        // don't update if gamer left game
        if (remoteGamer == null)
            return;

        Alien alien = remoteGamer.Tag as Alien;

        // search all aliens and find match with remote ones
        for (int i = 0; i < alienData.Count; i++){
            if (alienData[i].alienID == gamerId) {
                Alien tempAlien        = new Alien();
                tempAlien.alienID      = gamerId;
                tempAlien.position     = pos;
```

```
                tempAlien.view        = view;

                alienData[i]          = tempAlien;
                remotePosition        = alienData[i].position;
                remoteView            = alienData[i].view;
            }
        }
    }
}
```

A revised `UpdateNetwork()` method must replace the existing one to handle the client/server processing. If the session is in progress, this method triggers read and write routines on the client and the server:

```
public void UpdateNetwork(Vector3 localPosition, Vector3 localView){
    // ensure session has not ended
    if (session == null)
        return;

    // read incoming network packets.
    foreach (LocalNetworkGamer gamer in session.LocalGamers)
        if (gamer.IsHost)
            ServerRead(gamer);
        else
            ClientRead(gamer);
    // write from clients
    if (!session.IsHost)
        foreach (LocalNetworkGamer gamer in session.LocalGamers)
            ClientWrite(gamer, localPosition, localView);
    // write from server
    else
        ServerWrite(localPosition, localView);
    // update session object
    session.Update();
}
```

When you run your code now, your client/server network will allow you to control two different aliens, each on its own machine. With either the peer-to-peer framework or the client/server framework, you have a performance-friendly way to exchange data between machines in your game as long as you design the game for efficient data transfer.

CHAPTER 29 REVIEW EXERCISES

To get the most from this chapter, try out these chapter review exercises.

1. If you have not already done so, follow the step-by-step examples shown in this chapter to implement the peer-to-peer network sample and the client/server network sample.
2. Modify the code to allow more than one player locally. You will need to use a split-screen environment to do this.

Index

A

abs function, 76
Acceleration of projectiles, 308
Accept New Key option, 14
Accuracy settings for skyboxes, 147
Add/Detach Sounds option, 470–471
Add Existing Item dialog
 images, 34
 shaders, 77
 source files, 12
Add New Item dialog
 fonts, 193, 415
 projectiles, 309
 shaders, 76
Add Reference dialog, 446
Add Watch option, 18
Add Xbox 360 Name and Connection Key dialog, 14
Addition of vectors, 234–236
AddSessionEvents method, 512
AddSphere method, 292–293
AdjustBlueLevel method, 83
AdvanceAnimation method, 453
AIF files, 460
AIFF files, 460
Airplane, 109–110
 direction angle, 115–118
 flying with spinning propeller, 114–115
 stationary with spinning propeller, 110–114
Alias FBX File format, 213
Alien class, 521
alien0.fbx file, 473, 501, 517
alien1.fbx file, 473, 501, 517
Aliens
 creating, 500–503
 peer-to-peer networks, 517–521
Alpha channels, 127
AlphaBlendEnable method, 138
Ambient light, 355
AmbientLight method, 367
Angles
 airplane direction, 115–118
 dot products, 244
Animated textures, 174–178
Animation, 92
 asteroids, 43–45
 characters. *See* Character movement
 keyframe, 344–351
 matrices, 93–95
 Quake II. *See* Quake II model
 Right Hand Rule, 92–93
 spaceships, 473–477
 sprites. *See* Sprites
 windmill, 217–219
animations enum, 446, 451–452
Application flow, 22
Apply3D method, 464, 483
Apply3DAudio method, 483–484
Arcing Projectile algorithm, 306
Arcing projectiles
 example, 319–320
 overview, 306–309
Arctangent function, 104–107
Assemblies, 23
Assembly language, 73
Asteroid example, 42
 asteroid animation, 43–45
 collision detection, 48–52
 completing, 52–53
 images for, 42–43
 rocket ship control, 45–48
Atan function, 105–106, 115–116
Atan2 function, 107, 116, 140
Atmosphere setting, 147
AttachedSounds property, 471
Attenuation of audio, 471–472
Audio, 460
 adding, 477–482
 attenuation, 471–472
 XACT. *See* XACT (Cross Platform Audio Creation Tool)
 Zune, 487–489
Audio3DCue class, 483
AudioEmitter class, 463, 482
AudioEngine class, 461–462
AudioListener class, 463, 482
audioProject.xap file, 473, 477–478
Auditioning Utility, 468
Authoring tool, 461, 464–468
AutoComplete format, 12
AvailableNetworkSessionCollection class, 508

B

backwall.jpg file, 135
Ballistics
 arcing projectiles, 306–309
 arcing projectiles example, 319–320
 linear projectiles, 306–307
 linear projectiles example, 309–319
Bandwidth for networks, 506–507
Bank setting for images, 148
base.fbx file, 216
Base for windmill
 creating, 205–206
 exporting, 213
Base Surface tab, 422
Basic Sculpting tool, 421
BasicEffect class, 70
 car object, 226
 default lighting, 356–357
 directional lighting, 357–362
 Quake II model, 448–449
 shaders, 86–89
 windmill, 215–216

BasicShader technique, 71
Beep0 file, 466–468
beep0.wav file, 466, 477
beep1.wav file, 466, 477
Beeping sound, 466–468, 481
Begin method, 35
Bezier curves, 344–348
bigCarSpheres.fbx file, 296
Billboarding effect, 139–140
BinaryReader class, 403–405, 409
Blades for windmill
  duplicating, 209
  materials, 207–209
  rotating, 209–210, 217
Bold font style, 194
Bold Italic font style, 194
Bone animation, 214–215, 438–443
Bounding boxes
  BoundingBox type, 286–289
  collision detection implementation, 302–304
Bounding spheres
  BoundingSphere type, 286–288
  collision detection implementation, 299–302
  initialization and drawing, 290–299
Bowing animation, 440, 443–446
Boxes
  bounding, 286–289, 302–304
  windmill, 205, 209
Breakpoints, 17–18
Brickwall.jpg file, 360
Buffers, index, 156
  grids using, 159–163
  vertices, 156–159
BufferUsage settings, 157
Bui Tuong Phong, 362
Build Action property, 446
Bumpers, 41, 392–393
Button events, 387–388
ButtonState property, 379

C

C#, 2–4, 8, 120–122
Camera class, 271–272, 496
Camera.cs file, 271, 274–275
Camera Settings dialog
  skyboxes, 147
  terrain, 423
CameraCopy method, 300
Cameras
  base code, 284
  car object, 224–227, 299–301
  changing views, 282–284
  class initialization, 272–273
  class structures, 271–272
  matrices, 268–270
  moving and strafing, 274–277
  multiplayer gaming, 493–496
  rotating views, 277–282
  skyboxes, 144–145, 147
  terrain, 423, 427
  vectors, 268
CameraStartPositions method, 516
CameraViewer namespace, 271
Car object, 219–231
car.tga file, 221
Cartesian coordinates
  3D graphics, 56
  Right Hand Rule, 92–93
CarYDirection method, 224
Categories of sound banks, 462
Cell method, 249–250
CellHeight method, 414
CellNormal method, 431
CellWeight method, 429–430
CF-18 Hornet fighter jet example, 345–351
cf18.x file, 349
cf18Color.jpg file, 349
ChangePosition method, 83, 85
ChangeView method
  cameras, 281–283
  car object, 222–224
  mouse, 387–388
  spaceships, 476
  split-screen environment, 497–498
Character movement, 104, 109–110
  airplane direction angle, 115–118
  direction, 104–109
  flying airplane with spinning propeller, 114–115
  stationary airplane with spinning propeller, 110–114
CheckCollisions method, 51–52
clamp function, 76
Class-level variables, 84
Clear method, 341
Client/server networks
  example, 521–525
  overview, 506
ClientRead method, 524–525
ClientWrite method, 522
Clip planes, 270
Closing games, 26
Cloud Shading setting, 147
Clouds Cast Shadows option, 424
Code files
  adding and removing, 12
  managing, 8–9
Collision detection, 37, 286
  asteroid example, 48–52
  bounding box implementation, 302–304
  bounding spheres implementation, 299–302
  bounding spheres initialization and drawing, 290–299
  BoundingBox, 288–289
  BoundingSphere, 288
  containment types, 287
  early warning systems, 287
  per pixel, 39–40
  rectangle, 37
  transformation matrices, 37–39
Collision method, 299
Color
  landscape, 422
  shaders, 71–72, 75, 81–86
  textures, 48–49, 128, 140–141
Combining images
  multitexturing, 178–189
  sprites. *See* Sprites
CommitChanges method, 78, 87, 126, 133
Compatibility of shaders, 73
Compiling Xbox 360 Game projects, 12–13
Conjugate quaternions, 279
Connect to Computer screen, 14–15
Connection Key dialog, 14
Connections to PC and Xbox 360, 3–4
ContainmentType type, 287
Contains containment type, 287
Contains method
  BoundingBox, 289
  BoundingSphere, 288
Content Importer property, 446
Content node, 34
Content pipeline and processors, 402
  ContentImporter, 403
  ContentTypeReader, 404
  example, 404–417
  images, 34
  overview, 33
Content Pipeline Extension projects, 405
ContentImporter class, 403, 408
ContentManager class
  description, 24
  models, 312
  particles, 334
  textures, 121
ContentProcessor class, 402, 407
ContentReader class, 409
ContentTypeReader class, 404
ContentTypeWriter class, 403–404, 408
Continue option, 18
Control points for curves, 344
Controllers, 379–380, 390–391
  bumpers, 392–393
  DPad, 393
  game pad buttons, 391–392
  game pad states, 380–381
  pressed and released states, 381

rumble, 395–396
thumbsticks, 381, 394–395
triggers, 382, 395
Coordinates
3D graphics, 56
mouse, 389
multitexturing, 182
point sprites, 325–328
Right Hand Rule, 92–93
skyboxes, 150
texture, 120–121
two-dimensional, 32
UV. *See* UV coordinates
vectors, 234
CopyAbsoluteBoneTransformsTo method, 215, 217, 221
cos function, 76
Courier New font, 249
Create method, 507–508
CreateLookAt method, 272
CreatePerspectiveFieldOfView method, 270
CreateRotationX method, 260, 314
CreateRotationY method, 112, 116, 140, 262
CreateRotationZ method, 38, 263
CreateScale method, 100, 258
CreateSession method, 512
CreateTranslation method, 38, 115, 256
Creators Club, 3, 49
Cross method, 239–240
Cross Platform Audio Creation Tool. *See* XACT (Cross Platform Audio Creation Tool)
Cross products of vectors, 239–240
Cues, audio, 462
instance variables, 462, 468–469
sound banks, 465
Culling, 70
problems in, 273
sprites, 168
Cumulative transformation matrices, 38
CurrentViewport method, 499–500
Cursors, mouse, 389–390
Curves in keyframe animations, 344–348
CustomVertex struct, 332
Cylinders for windmill, 206–208

D

dangersign.png file, 174–175
Data types for shaders, 74–75
Debugging
breakpoints, 17–18
Error Lists, 15–16
errors, 15–16
pausing, 16–18
stepping through code, 18
warnings, 16–17
watch lists, 18–19
Declaring matrices, 96
Delays, network, 506
DeleteAudio method, 478
Delta Halo level, 139
Deploying games
Xbox 360 projects, 14–15
to Zune, 4–5
Depth of animated sprites layers, 36
Detail setting for skyboxes, 147
Developer basics, 8
code project management, 8–9
debugging, 15–19
deploying, 14–15
editing, 12–13
Windows Game projects, 9–10
Xbox 360 Game projects, 10–11
Zune game projects, 11
Development environment setup, 2–5
DeviceReset events, 25
Diffuse light, 355
DiffuseColor property, 357
Direction, 104
airplane angle, 115–118
cameras, 269
scaling in, 108–109
speed for, 105–107
trigonometry for, 104–105
vectors for, 107–108
Direction property, 357
Directional lights, 354, 356–362, 449
DirectionMatrix method, 117
DirectX, 212
Disjoint containment type, 287
Display
bumpers, 392–393
fonts, 193–198
frames-per-second count, 198–199
game pad button state, 392
heads-up, 169–173
input device states, 385–386
mouse states, 388
thumbsticks, 394–395
triggers, 395
DisplayCurrentHeight, 416–417
Dispose method, 479
Dot method, 76, 244
Dot products of vectors, 243–245
Down attribute in DPad, 393
Downloading examples, 5–6
DPad control, 41, 380–382, 393
Draw method
animated sprites, 35–36
animated texture, 178
fire, 339–341
fonts, 197–198
images, 43
meshes, 216, 218–219
overriding, 28
purpose, 26
shaders, 82
split-screen environment, 499–500
sprites, 167–168, 172–173
textures, 137–138
triggering, 25
DrawAirplaneBody method, 112, 114–117
DrawAliens method, 502–503, 520–521
DrawAnimatedHud method, 172–173
DrawAnimatedTexture method, 177
DrawCar method, 226
DrawCF18 method, 350
DrawCursor method, 389–390
DrawEarth method, 99–101
DrawFonts method, 197–198
bumpers, 392–393
controllers, 391
game pad button state, 392
input device states, 385–386
matrix display, 251
mouse states, 388
thumbsticks, 394–395
triggers, 395
vector calculations in, 235
Zune, 397
DrawGround method
grass, 134
ground, 88–89
skyboxes, 149
split-screen environment, 497–498
DrawIndexedGrid method, 162–163
multitexturing, 184–186
point lights, 372, 375
terrain, 426
DrawIndexedPrimitives method, 159, 162–163
Drawing
bounding spheres, 290–299
fonts, 197–198
games, 25–26
with shaders, 78, 80–81
spaceships, 473–477
windmill, 215–219
DrawLauncher method, 314–315
DrawMatrix method, 250–251
DrawMD2Model method, 450–452, 456
DrawMenu method, 515
DrawMessage method, 515–516
DrawModel method
car object, 226
spaceships, 435, 476
DrawModels method, 519

DrawMoon method, 100–101
DrawObjects method
 Martian eyes, 64, 67–68
 Martian mouth, 63
 Martian nose, 66
DrawParticles method, 338–339
DrawPrimitives method, 330
DrawPropeller method, 112–115, 117
DrawRectangle method, 82
DrawRockets method, 318–319
DrawShip method, 435
DrawSkybox method, 151–152
DrawSpheres method, 298
DrawString method
 fonts, 197
 peer-to-peer networks, 515
 vector calculations in, 235
DrawSurfaces method, 136–138, 140
DrawTorch method, 339–340
DrawUserPrimitives method, 59, 62, 133
DrawWater method, 185–186
DrawWindmill method, 217–219
Duplicating windmill blades, 209
DynamicVertexBuffer class, 158, 182

E

Early warning collision detection systems, 287
Earth example, 97–101
Editing code, 12–13
Effect class
 fire, 331
 shaders, 75, 77, 79–80
 textures, 130
Effect1.fx file, 76
EffectParameter class
 global shaders, 75, 77–78
 textures, 126, 130–131, 134
 WVP matrix, 79–80
Enabled property, 357
EnableDefaultLighting method, 216, 218, 356
Enabling Volume Attenuation option, 471
End method, 35
End points for curves, 344
engine0.wav file, 466, 477, 487
engine1.wav file, 466, 477
Engines sound, 466
Error Lists, 10–11, 15–16
Errors, debugging, 15–16
Events
 input devices, 385–388
 network sessions, 508–509
Examples, downloading, 5–6
Existing Game Studio projects, 8–9
Export Heightfield dialog, 422
Exporting
 height maps, 422–423
 to .md2 format, 445–446
 windmill, 213
ExtractBoundingSphere method, 296–297
Eyebrows, Martian, 60, 66–67
Eyes, Martian, 59–60, 63–65, 67–68

F

Face, Martian, 59–60
 eyebrows, 66–67
 eyes, 59–60, 63–65, 67–68
 mouth, 60–63
 nose, 60, 65–66
Fade with point sprites, 327
Fan, windmill, 206–213
fan.fbx file, 213, 216
Far clip planes, 270
.fbx format, 202–203, 207, 212–213
Field of view, 270
Fighter jet example, 345–351
Filters for textures, 123, 128
Find method, 508
Finite audio loops, 467–468
Fire example, 331–341
Fire method, 479–480
fire.wav file, 466, 477, 487
Firing sound, 466
float data type for shaders, 75
Flow control for shaders, 75
Flowing river effect, 179–187
Fonts
 bumpers, 392–393
 drawing, 197–198
 frames-per-second count example, 198–199
 game pad button state, 392
 height, 416–417
 input device states, 385–386
 loading, 193–196
 monospace, 249
 mouse states, 388
 peer-to-peer networks, 515
 thumbsticks, 394–395
 triggers, 395
 in visible window portion, 196
 Zune, 397
Force with projectiles, 308
Forward vector
 direction calculations, 107–108
 spaceship, 433–434
 textures, 139
Fractions, scaling vectors by, 237
Frame swapping, 166
Frames-per-second count display, 198–199
FramesPerSecond method, 199
Friction with projectiles, 308
Frustum, 270
.fx extension, 76

G

Game controllers. *See* Controllers
Game pad buttons, 391–392
Game stats
 fonts for, 193–198
 frames-per-second count, 198–199
Game Studio projects, 8
Game windows, 22
 closing, 26
 drawing and updating, 25–26
 example, 26–28
 game foundation, 22–25
Game1 class, 27–28
Game1.cs file
 audio, 477
 cameras, 272
 color shaders, 83
 fire example, 336
 input events, 383
 MD2 class, 448
 namespaces, 23
 new projects, 12, 27
 particles, 336
 projectiles, 312
 vertices, 97
GamePadState class
 input, 494, 497
 Quake II animation, 453
 states, 41, 380–381, 390
GamerEnded event, 508
GamerJoined event, 508–509
GamerJoinEvent method, 509, 512, 521–522
GamerLeft event, 508
GamerServices class, 507, 514
GamerServicesComponent class, 507, 514
GameStarted event, 508
Generate Connection Key option, 14
generateNormals method, 407
generatePositions method, 406–407
GetAccelerationVolume method, 480–481
GetCue method, 463–464, 479, 482
GetPositionOnCurve method, 348
GetPositionOnLine method, 348
GetRuntimeReader method, 403, 408–409
GetRuntimeType method, 403, 408
GetState method
 controllers, 381, 390
 GamePad, 41
 KeyboardState, 40, 379, 384

MouseState, 379, 387
multiplayer gaming, 494
GetViewerAngle method, 140
Global settings in XACT, 462
Graphics engine cameras. *See* Cameras
Graphics pipeline, 70. *See also* Shaders
GraphicsDevice class
index buffers, 162
particles, 337
shaders, 80
sprites, 173
textures, 131
GraphicsDeviceManager class, 24–25
grass.jpg image, 132
Grass texture, 130–134
Gravity with projectiles, 308–309
Grids, 159–163
Group enum, 294
Groups, merging
Quake II model, 441–442
windmill, 210–211

H

Halo 2, 139
HandleOffHeightMap method, 413, 431
Hargreaves, Shawn, 328
Head setting for images, 148
Heads-up display, 169–173
Height
camera view, 273
images, 146
windows, 32
Height maps, 412–413, 420
example, 425–435
Terragen for, 420–425
Height method, 413
heightMap.raw file, 412, 423
Hierarchies, skeletal, 214–215
High Level Shader Language (HLSL)
data types, 74–75
functions, 75–76
overview, 72–73
textures, 123–124
Hills, 421–422
Horizons
overview, 144–145
Terragen software for, 145–153
hotrod.fbx file, 221, 296
hotrodSpheres.fbx file, 296

I

Identity matrices, 94–95, 263–265
Identity transformations, 92, 94
Image frame animations, 169
animated textures, 174–178
heads-up display, 169–173
Images
2D games, 33
adding, 42–43
frame swapping, 166
loading and storing, 33–34
skyboxes, 146–153
sprites. *See* Sprites
Import method, 403, 408
Index buffers, 156
grids using, 159–163
vertices, 156–159
IndexBuffer class, 157
Indexes for Quake II vertices, 440
Indices class, 159, 162
Infinite audio loops, 467
Infinite property, 467
Initialize method
aliens, 501
audio, 478–479, 481
BoundingBox, 302
cameras, 273, 496
example, 27
fire example, 332–333
linear projectiles, 312
overriding, 25
particles, 337
terrain, 413
InitializeAirplaneBody method, 111
InitializeAliens method, 501
InitializeAnimatedSurface method, 175
InitializeBaseCode method
cameras, 273
directional lighting, 358
shaders, 80, 83, 85
textures, 131
InitializeBasicEffect method, 449
InitializeGround method, 127, 132–133, 149
InitializeIndices method, 160
InitializeLineList method, 66
InitializeLineStrip method, 65
InitializeModels method, 312–313, 474
InitializeModelSpheres method, 297
InitializeParticleVertex method, 333
InitializePointList method, 67
InitializePropeller method, 111
InitializeRoutes method, 346–347
InitializeSkybox method, 150–151
InitializeSpeed method, 114
InitializeSphere method, 291–292
InitializeSurface method, 135–136, 141
InitializeTimeLine method, 347
InitializeTorch method, 339
InitializeTriangle method, 97–98
InitializeTriangleList method, 64
InitializeTriangleStrip method, 61
InitializeVertexBuffer method
directional lighting, 358–359
grids, 161–162
multitexturing, 182–183
terrain, 426–427
InitializeVertices method, 81–82
InitializeWallSpheres method, 294–296
Initializing
bounding spheres, 288, 290–299
game applications, 23
matrices, 96
Input devices, 378
controllers, 379–382, 390–396
handling, 40–41
keyboard, 378–379, 383–385
mouse, 379, 387–390
multiplayer gaming, 494
responsiveness, 382
rumbles, 382
shaders, 73–74
toggle events, 385–386
Zune, 396–399
Installing required software, 3
int data type for shaders, 75
Interpolation
keyframe animations, 344
linear, 123
Intersect containment type, 287
Intersects method, 38
BoundingBox, 289
BoundingSphere, 288
Intrinsic functions, 75–76
intro.wav file, 465–466, 477
Irregular shapes in collision detection, 286
IsConnected property
controllers, 390
GamePad, 41
IsDisposed property, 478
IsHost property, 509
IsKeyDown method, 40, 379, 382
IsKeyUp method, 40
IsLocal property, 509
IsPlaying attribute, 479, 481
I.S.R.O.T sequence, 94
Italic font style, 194

J

Jet example, 345–351
Join method, 508
JoinSession method, 512–513
Joints
Quake II model, 441–443
windmill, 211–212
Joints tab, 442

K

kbstatePrevious class, 386
Key identifiers, 378

Keyboard, 40, 378–379, 383–385
KeyboardState class, 40, 379, 383–384, 386, 453
Keyframe animations, 344
 curves, 344–348
 example, 345–351
 interpolation, 344
KeyFrameNumber function, 347
Keys class, 40

L

lamp.bmp file, 446, 448
lamp.md2 file, 446
Land option, 148
Landscape dialog, 421–423
Landscape settings, 421
Launch method, 310
Launch speed of projectiles, 306
launcher.bmp file, 312
launcher.fbx file, 312
LaunchRocket method, 315–318
Layer depth, 36
Left property
 DPad, 393
 triggers, 382
Left shoulders, 392–393
Left thumbsticks, 394–395
Left triggers, 395
LeftButton property, 379
Length method, 242
Length of vectors, 241–242
Lerp function, 414
Life of particles, 336
lightEffectPosition setting, 370
lightEffectWorld setting, 370
lightEffectWVP setting, 370
Lighting, 354
 BasicEffect, 215–216
 directional, 356–362
 point, 362–375
 reflective, 355–356
 source, 354
 terrain, 424
Lighting Conditions dialog, 424
LightingEnabled property, 356, 359
LightingShader method, 371–372
Line lists
 Martian eyebrows, 66–67
 primitive objects, 56–58
Line strips
 Martian nose, 65–66
 primitive objects, 56–58
Linear interpolation, 123
Linear Projectile algorithm, 306
Linear projectiles
 example, 309–319
 overview, 306–307
LineList type, 58
LineStrip type, 58
Lists
 Martian eyebrows, 66–67
 Martian eyes, 63–65, 67–68
 primitive objects, 56–58
LIVE Arcade, 32
LIVE Community Games, 5
Load method
 shaders, 77
 textures, 121, 132
 windmill, 217
LoadContent method
 audio, 487
 car object, 221
 cursor, 389
 danger sign, 175
 directional lighting, 360
 font sprites, 415
 fonts, 195, 397
 images, 43, 149
 keyframe animations, 349
 linear projectiles, 313
 multitexturing, 181–182
 overriding, 25, 28
 particles, 334
 peer-to-peer networks, 515, 518
 Quake II weapon, 455
 spaceship, 428
 sprites, 34
 terrain, 426
 textures, 34, 132, 135, 138
 warning light, 171
 windmill, 217
 Zarlag, 452
Loading
 fonts, 193–196
 images, 33–34
 Quake II model, 446–451
 Quake II weapon, 454–457
 spaceships, 473–477
 textures, 120–121
 wave files, 465
 windmill, 214–217
Local network connectivity type, 508
Local rotation quaternions, 278
LocalNetworkGamer class, 509
Logic, viewing, 16–18
Look direction
 cameras, 274
 linear projectiles, 314, 316
Look vector
 cameras, 268, 275
 direction angle, 117
 direction calculations, 107–108
 linear projectiles, 306
 quaternions, 278–279
 textures, 139
LoopCount property, 468
LoopEvent attribute, 468
Loops
 audio, 467–468
 shaders, 75

M

magfilters, 123
Magnification of skyboxes, 147
Maps, height, 412–413, 420
 example, 425–435
 Terragen for, 420–425
Martian face, 59–60
 eyebrows, 66–67
 eyes, 59–60, 63–65, 67–68
 mouth, 60–63
 nose, 60, 65–66
Masks, pixels, 127
Materials
 reflective lighting, 355–356
 windmill blade, 207–209
 windmill box and sphere, 209
Matrices, 93, 248
 camera, 268–270
 declaring and initializing, 96
 identity, 94–95, 263–265
 matrix arrays, 214–215
 multiplication, 248–253
 rotation, 95
 scaling, 95, 256–258
 transformation. *See* Transformation matrices
 translation, 95–96
 types, 248–249
Matrix data type, 75, 94
Max property, 469
MaximumValue property, 471
MD2 class, 438, 453, 455
MD2.cs file, 446
.md2 format, 438–440, 445–446
md2.qc file, 445–446
md2 struct, 439
MD2Pipeline project, 446
MD2Runtime project, 446
MeasureString method, 196
MediaPlayer class, 460
MemoryStream class, 403
Merging groups
 Quake II model, 441
 windmill, 210–211
Meshes
 drawing, 216, 218–219
 Quake II model, 438, 441–442
MGH360BaseCode projects, 60, 79
MGHGame namespace, 291–292
MGHWinBaseCode projects, 60, 79
Microsoft.Xna.Framework library, 234
Microsoft XNA Game Studio, 8
MiddleButton property, 379

MilkShape application, 202–203
- animated models, 440–457
- windmill example. *See* Windmill

Milliseconds attribute, 113
Min property, 469
minfilters, 123
mipfilters, 123
Model class, 214–215
Model tab, 441, 443–444
ModelMesh class, 215
Momentum with projectiles, 308–309
Monospace fonts, 249
Moon example, 97–101
Mouse, 379
- button and move events, 387–388
- cursors, 389–390

Mouse class, 282
MouseState class, 282, 379, 387, 389
Mouth, Martian, 60–63
Move method
- cameras, 274–277
- split-screen environment, 497–498

Movement
- cameras, 274–277
- character. *See* Character movement
- mouse events, 387–388

MoveShip method, 47–48
mul function, 76
Multipass shader rendering, 178–179
Multiplayer gaming, 492
- cameras, 493–494
- input, 494
- split-screen environment, 494–503
- viewports, 492–493

Multiplying
- matrices, 94, 248–253
- quaternions, 279

MultiplyMatrix method, 251–253, 256–257, 260
MultiTexture technique, 179, 181
Multitexturing, 178
- multipass shader rendering, 178–179
- water example, 179–189

MyContentWriter class, 403
MyFont.spritefont file, 193, 397

N

Namespaces, 23
Near clip planes, 270
Network.cs file, 511, 521
Networks, 506
- bandwidth, 506–507
- capability, 514–521
- client/server, 506
- client/server example, 521–525
- LocalNetworkGamer, 509
- peer-to-peer, 506
- peer-to-peer example, 511–521
- session updating, 509–510

NetworkSession class, 507–508
NetworkSessionType class, 508
New Cue Instance option, 469
New Item dialog, 12
New Project dialog
- asteroid game, 42
- source files, 26
- sprites, 166
- terrain, 409
- windmill project, 204
- Windows Game projects, 9
- Xbox 360 Game projects, 11

New RPC Preset option, 471
Nonproportional fonts, 249
Normal method, 431–432
Normal vectors
- cross products, 238–240
- reflective, 355

Normalization of vectors, 108, 240–243
Normalize method, 76, 243
NormalWeight method, 432–433
Nose, Martian, 60, 65–66
NUM_COLS setting, 421
NUM_ROWS setting, 421

O

.OBJ files, 203
OffsetFromCamera method, 224
Opaque textures, 134–137
Open dialog
- materials, 207
- wave files, 465

Opening
- Game Studio projects, 8–9
- Microsoft XNA Game Studio, 8

Orbits, 92, 94
Origins
- animated sprites, 36
- windmill, 211

Outputs, shaders, 73–74
Overlapping objects. *See* Collision detection

P

PacketReader class, 510
PacketWriter class, 510
Particle.cs file, 334
Particle effects, 324
- fire example, 331–341
- point sprites, 324–329
- VertexDeclarations, 330–331

ParticleShader method, 337–388
Passes, shaders, 72, 179
PauseAndResumeBeep method, 480
Pausing programs, 16–18
PC video cards, 6
.pcx files, 440
Peer-to-peer networks
- example, 511–521
- overview, 506

Per pixel collision checking, 39–40
Performance of collision detection, 287
Phong reflection model, 362–363
Pins for windmill, 206
Pipeline. *See* Content pipeline and processors
Pitch setting for images, 148
Pivoting animation, 443–444
PivotWheel method, 228–229
Pixel shaders, 70–72
- point lights, 365–375
- point sprites, 326–328
- texture coloring, 128

PixelCollision method, 49–50
PixelColor method, 48–49
Pixels
- columns and rows, 32
- masks, 127

PixelShader method, 71, 128
- point lights, 369, 374–375
- point sprites, 328

Planetside website, 145
Play method, 463, 487
Play Sound option, 468
Play Wave property, 468
Play3DAudio method, 485–486
Playback methods, 463
PlayCue method, 463, 479–480
PlayerIndex attribute, 381, 494
PlayerMatch network connectivity type, 508
Point lights, 354
- calculating, 364
- Phong reflection model, 362–364
- pixel shader example, 365–375

Point lists
- Martian eyes, 67–68
- primitive objects, 56–58

Point sprites
- fire example, 331–341
- overview, 324–329

PointLightDiffuse method, 368–369
PointLightPS.fx file, 365, 370–371
PointLightShader technique, 370
PointLightVS.fx file, 374
PointList type, 58
Points option for index buffers, 157
PointSprite.fx file, 331

PointSpriteTechnique technique, 328–329
Porting 2D games to Zune, 41
Position color shaders, 81–86
Position vector
  cameras, 268, 274–275
  linear projectiles, 306
PositionColor.fx file, 61, 71, 79–83
PositionColorEffect method, 80–81
PositionColorShader method, 62, 64–67, 80–81
PositionColorTexture type, 358
Positioning
  animated sprites, 35–36
  car object, 222
  windmill, 211
pow function, 76
Pressed state
  controllers, 381–382
  DPad, 393
  game pad, 391–392
  keyboard, 384
  thumbsticks, 394–395
Previewing Quake II animation, 445
Primitive objects, 56–57
  drawing example, 59–68
  drawing steps, 96–101
  drawing syntax, 57–59
Program1.cs file, 12, 26
Project files in XACT, 460–461
ProjectedUp method, 433
ProjectedXZ method, 429
Projectile class, 309–312
Projectile.cs file, 309
Projectiles
  arcing, 306–309, 319–320
  linear, 306–307, 309–319
Projection matrix, 269–270
Projection property, 87–88
Projections in multiplayer gaming, 493–494
Projects tab, 446
PSinput struct, 326–327
PSIZE semantic, 326
PSoutput struct, 125, 367
Pythagorean Theorem, 241–242

Q

Quake II model, 438–440
  bowing animation, 444
  controlling, 451–454
  exporting to .md2 format, 445–446
  loading, 446–451
  meshes, 441–442
  pivoting animation, 443–444
  previewing animation, 445
  skeletons, 441–442
  weapons, 454–457
Quality setting for skybox images, 147
Quaternion theory, 277–280

R

Random class, 336
RankedAll network connectivity type, 508
Raw image files, 33
Read method
  ContentTypeReader, 404
  XNANetwork, 513–514
ReadAllBytes method, 403, 408
ReadAllText method, 403
ReadBoolean method, 404
ReadInt32 method, 404
ReadSingle method, 404
ReadVector3 method, 510
Rectangle class, 37, 44
Rectangle collision checking, 37
Red dots for breakpoints, 17
References tab, 446
Referencing shaders, 75–80
Reflective lighting, 355–356
Reflective normals, 355
Regular font style, 194
Released state
  controllers, 381–382
  DPad, 393
  game pad, 391–392
  keyboard, 384
  thumbsticks, 394–395
Removing code files from projects, 12
Render Settings dialog, 146–147
Render states, saving, 197
Rendering, 26
  images, 148
  skybox settings, 146–147
  sprites, 168–169
Rendering Control dialog
  skyboxes, 147
  terrains, 423–425
ResetParticle method, 335
Resizing animated sprites, 36
Resolution in Zune, 41
Responsiveness of input devices, 382
Resuming programs, 18
Revolutions, 92, 94
Right Hand Rule, 92–93
  distance calculations, 104
  linear projectiles, 313
  transformation matrices, 254
  vector cross products, 238
Right property
  DPad, 393
  triggers, 382
Right shoulders, 392–393
Right thumbsticks, 394–395
Right triggers, 395
Right vector
  cameras, 268, 275
  direction angle, 117
  direction calculations, 107–108
  spaceship, 433–434
RightButton property, 379
rocket.bmp file, 312
rocket.fbx file, 312
Rockets. *See* Spaceships and rockets
RootDirectory attribute, 34, 131
RotateShip method, 45–46
Rotation, 92, 94
  animated sprites, 36
  camera views, 277–282
  linear projectiles, 314
  Quake II model, 443–444
  rocket ship, 45–46
  windmill blades, 209–210, 217
Rotation matrices, 95
  X axis, 258–260
  Y axis, 260–262
  Z axis, 262–263
RotationAngle method, 115–117, 501
RotationQuaternion method, 279–280
RowColumn method, 413
RPC Preset (Runtime Parameter Control Preset), 463, 469–471
Rumble, 382, 395–396
Running Xbox 360 Game projects, 12–13
Runtime logic and variable values, 16–18
Runtime Parameter Control Preset (RPC Preset), 463, 469–471

S

Sampler class, 123–124
saturate function, 76
Save Project As dialog, 473
SaveState property
  peer-to-peer networks, 515
  render states, 168, 197
Saving
  audio projects, 473
  images, 148
  render states, 197
  sprite settings, 168
  windmill, 212–213
  Xbox 360 Game projects, 13
Scale method
  aliens, 518
  scaling matrices, 95
ScaleModel method, 224
ScaleSpheres method, 297–298
Scaling, 92, 94
  aliens, 518

boxes, 205
point sprites, 327–328
time lapse between frames, 108–109
vectors, 236–237, 240–243
Scaling matrices, 95, 256–258
Score tracking and game stats
fonts for, 193–198
frames-per-second count, 198–199
Screen resolution in Zune, 41
Selling games, 5
ServerRead method, 523–524
ServerWrite method, 522–523
SessionEnded event, 508–509
SessionEndEvent method, 509, 512
Set Keyframe option, 444
SetAnimation method, 452
SetAnimationSequence method, 448, 452
SetAnimationSpeed method, 448
setCellDimensions method, 406
SetData method, 158, 161–162
SetDirectionMatrix method, 310–311, 320
SetFrameInterval method, 272–273
SetPosition method, 282, 388
SetProjection method, 272
SetSource method, 158, 162
SetValue method, 77–78, 126, 136
SetVariable method, 469, 471
SetVibration method, 382, 395–396
SetView method
cameras, 272, 282–283
car object, 224
terrain, 427
SetWaterHeight method, 188
Shaders
BasicEffect objects, 86–89
changes, 78
data types, 74
description, 60
drawing with, 78, 80–81
Effect objects, 77
EffectParameter objects, 77–78, 87
flow control, 75
graphics pipeline, 70
HLSL, 72–73
inputs and outputs, 73–74
intrinsic functions, 75–76
passes, 72, 178–179
pixel, 71–72
point lights, 365–375
point sprites, 325–329
position color, 81–86
referencing, 75–80
semantics, 73–74
structure, 71
textures, 122–123, 126
UV coordinates with, 123–124
values setting, 96
vertex, 71–72
Shadows for terrain, 423
ShipWorldMatrix method, 433–435
Shoulders, 392–393
Show Viewport Caption option, 205
ShowInputDeviceStatus method, 397–398
ShowSignIn method, 517
ShowString method, 384–385
sidewall.jpg file, 135
sin function, 76
Sine wave equations, 187–188
SineCycle method, 188
Size
aliens, 517
animated sprites, 36
height maps, 421
point sprites, 327–328
skybox images, 146
Skeletal hierarchies, 214–215
Skeletons in Quake II model, 441–442
Skin
Martian, 60
Quake II model, 439–440, 445
Sky option, 148
Skyboxes
overview, 144–145
Terragen software for, 145–153
Snapshots of images, 148
Solution Explorer, 10–12
Song class, 460
Sound, 460
adding, 477–482
attenuation, 471–472
XACT. *See* XACT (Cross Platform Audio Creation Tool)
Zune, 487–489
Sound Bank panel, 465
Sound banks, 462–465
SoundBank class, 461
SoundEffect class, 460, 487–488
SoundEffectInstance class, 460
SoundEngineUpdate method, 485
Source files, 26
Source lights, 354
SourceBlend property, 138
spaceA.bmp file, 473, 501, 517
Spaceships and rockets
arcing projectiles, 308, 319–320
audio examples, 464–487
collision detection, 48–52
linear projectiles, 309–319
loading, drawing, and animating, 473–477
in terrain, 427–435
Specular light, 355
SpecularColor property, 357
SpecularLight method, 367–368
Speed
direction calculations, 105–107
projectiles, 306
Sphere class, 292–293
Sphere.cs file, 292
SphereData struct, 293
Spheres
bounding, 286–288, 290–302
for windmill, 206, 209
SphereScalar method, 297–298
SphereVertices method, 291
Spin method, 227
Spinning propeller
flying airplane with, 114–115
stationary airplane with, 110–114
Split-screen environment, 494–503
SpriteBatch class, 24, 33–34, 166–167, 169
SpriteBlendMode option, 172
SpriteFont class, 195, 397
Sprites, 24, 34
drawing and animating, 35
fire example, 331–341
heads-up display, 169–173
image frame swapping, 166
layer depth, 36
origins, 36
overview, 324–329
point, 324–329, 331–341
resizing, 36
restoring settings, 167–168
rotating, 36
SpriteBatch class, 166–167
title safe regions, 37, 168–169
transparency, 35
SPRITETEXCOORD semantic, 326
Start Debugging option, 15
Start points for curves, 344
Stationary airplane with spinning propeller, 110–114
Status information
fonts for, 193–198
frames-per-second count, 198–199
SteamWriter class, 19
Step Into feature, 18
Step Over feature, 18
Stepping through code, 18
Stonefloor.jpg file, 360
Storing images, 33–34
Strafe method, 275, 277, 497–498
Strafing
cameras, 274–277
keys for, 60
split-screen environment, 497–498
Strips
Martian mouth, 61–63
Martian nose, 65–66
primitive objects, 56–58

struct data type, 75
Subtraction of vectors, 236
Surface Color dialog, 422
Surface Layer dialog, 422
SystemLinkConnects network connectivity type, 508

t

tan function, 76
Tangent function, 104
Target positions for skybox images, 147
Techniques, 72
telemetricBeep.mp3 file, 487
Templates, 23
Terragen software
  for height maps, 420–425
  for skyboxes, 145–153
terrain.bmp file, 426
Terrain Casts Shadows option, 424
Terrain class, 410
Terrain Export dialog, 422
Terrain height detection, 420
  example, 425–435
  Terragen for, 420–425
Terrain Modification dialog, 421
TerrainContent class, 406–407
TerrainContent.cs file, 405–406
TerrainPipeline class, 405–406, 408
TerrainReader class, 410
TerrainReader.cs file, 409
TerrainRuntime namespace, 410–411
Testing audio, 468
tex2D function, 76, 124, 128
Text display. *See* Display
Texture Coordinate Editor dialog, 207–208
Texture.fx file, 124, 128–130, 181
Texture2D class
  directional lighting, 360
  images, 33–34
  multitexturing, 181
  shaders, 75
  sprites, 35, 167, 169–170
  storing textures, 134, 137
  texture loading, 120–121, 131
textureEffectWVP value, 136
TextureEnabled property, 359
Textures, 120, 123
  adding, 134–137
  animated, 174–178
  animated sprites, 35
  applying, 124–125
  billboarding, 140
  C# syntax, 120–122
  classes, 33–34
  color, 48–49, 128, 140–141
  EffectParameter, 126, 130–131, 134
  grass, 130–134
  height maps, 423–425
  HLSL, 123–124
  multitexturing, 178–189
  point sprites, 327–328
  Quake II model, 440
  shaders for, 122–123
  tiling, 127
  transparent, 127, 137–139
  tree example, 129
  UV coordinates. *See* UV coordinates
  vertices, 122
  windmill, 206–207
textureSampler filter, 128
TextureShader technique, 126, 133–134
.tga files, 440
3D audio, 463–464, 482–487
3D graphics programming, 56
  primitive objects, 56–68
  shaders. *See* Shaders
3D models, 202–203
  car example, 219–231
  drawing steps, 96
  windmill example. *See* Windmill
3D view ports, 208–209
3D views, 204
Thumbstick events, 41
Thumbsticks, 381, 394–395, 397
Tiling textures, 127
Time lapse in scaling, 108–109
Timer method
  audio, 486
  frame counts, 198–199
  image frame animation, 170–171
  textures, 176
Tinput class, 402
Title safe regions
  animated sprites, 37, 44
  fonts, 196, 385
  frames-per-second count, 199
  rendering sprites, 168–169
  split-screen environment, 498–499
TitleSafeRegion method
  animated sprites, 44
  fonts, 196, 415–416
  image frame animation, 169, 171–172
  split-screen environment, 499
Toggle events, 385–386
ToolTips, 12, 17
torch.bmp file, 339
Torch example, 331–341
torch.fbx file, 339
ToString method, 394
TotalControllersUsed method, 497
Toutput class, 402
Transform method, 50, 519
TransformAliens method, 518
Transformation matrices, 253–254
  collision detection, 37–39
  identity, 263–265
  rotation X axis, 258–260
  rotation Y axis, 260–262
  rotation Z axis, 262–263
  scaling, 256–258
  translation, 254–258
Transformations
  applying, 97–101
  car wheel, 229–231
  order, 94
  types, 92
TransformCar method, 224
transformedPosition setting, 366, 369
Transforming rectangles, 37
TransformRectangle method, 49–51
TransformWheel method, 230–231
Translation matrices, 38, 95–96, 254
  CreateTranslation, 256
  example, 254–256
  W component, 254
Translations, 92, 94
Transparency
  sprites, 35
  textures, 127, 137–139, 178
tree.png file, 137
Trees
  texture, 129
  transparent, 137–139
Triangle lists
  Martian eyes, 63–65
  primitive objects, 56–58
Triangle strips
  Martian mouth, 61–63
  primitive objects, 56–58
Triangle vertices, 256–258
TriangleList type, 58
Triangles
  Quake II model, 439
  rotating, 98
TriangleStrip type, 58
Trigger events, 41
Triggers, 382, 395
Trigonometry
  direction calculations, 104–105
  primer, 46–47
tris.md2 file, 452
TrueType fonts, 194
Two-dimensional coordinate systems, 32
2D games, 32
  animated sprites, 34–37
  collision detection, 37–40
  coordinate systems, 32
  example. *See* Asteroid example

image files for, 33–34
input devices, 40–41
porting, 41

U

Unit vectors, 49, 240–243
UnloadContent method, 26, 28
Up attribute for DPad, 393
Up vector
cameras, 268, 275
direction angle, 117
direction calculations, 107–108
spaceship, 429, 433–434
Update method and updating
animated sprites, 35
cameras, 273, 275–276, 283
car object, 222, 227
controllers, 390
frames-per-second count display, 199
games, 25–26
keyframe animations, 346
linear projectiles, 317
network sessions, 509–511
networks, 511
overriding, 28
primitive rotation, 98
purpose, 26
Quake II animation, 453–454
Quake II weapon, 455
spaceship, 428
split-screen environment, 498
sprite rotation, 36
terrain, 427
triggering, 25
UpdateAirplanePosition method, 114–115
UpdateAsteroid method, 44–45
UpdateAudioEmitters method, 484–485
UpdateAudioListener method, 483
UpdateBlueLevel method, 84
UpdateCamera method, 300–304
UpdateCameraHeight method, 427
UpdateGameNetwork method, 519
UpdateGameStart method, 517
UpdateInputEvents method
controllers, 391–392
DPad, 393
keyboard, 384, 386
mouse, 387
rumble, 396
thumbsticks, 394
triggers, 395
UpdateKeyframeAnimation method, 348–349
UpdateModel method
Quake II model, 450
Quake II weapon, 455
UpdateMovingSurface method, 183–184, 189
UpdateNetwork method, 514, 525
UpdateParticle method, 336
UpdatePosition method, 85–86
UpdatePositionAndView method, 274
UpdateProjectile method, 311–312, 319–320
UpdateShip1Position method, 474–475
UpdateShipPosition method, 428
UpdateTextureUV method, 176–177
UpdateView method, 280–282, 315
Updating. *See* Update method and updating
User input devices. *See* Input devices
UV coordinates
animated texture, 176
description, 120–121
grass texture, 132
multitexturing, 182
opaque textures, 135
point sprites, 325–328
with shaders, 123–124
skyboxes, 150
sprites, 166
texture color, 128
texture tiling, 127

V

Variables
asteroid example, 42
class-level, 84
viewing, 16–18
watch lists, 18–19
Vector2 data type, 75, 234
Vector3 data type, 75, 234, 404
Vector3 method, 404
Vector4 data type, 75, 234
VectorCalculation method
addition, 235
cross products, 240
dot products, 245
length, 241–242
scaling, 237
subtraction, 236
unit vectors, 242–243
Vectors, 234
addition, 234–236
cameras, 268
direction angle, 117–118
direction calculations, 107–108
dot products, 243–245
normal, 49, 238–240, 355
normalization, 240–243
scaling, 236–237
subtraction, 236
types, 234
unit normal, 49
Velocity of arcing projectiles, 308
Vertex shaders, 70–72
point lights, 373–375
point sprites, 325–328
VertexBuffer class, 161, 330
fire example, 333
multitexturing, 182
VertexDeclaration class, 59, 62, 80, 325
custom declarations, 330–331
fire example, 333
Quake II model, 449
textures, 131
VertexDeclaration property, 360
VertexElement class, 330, 332
VertexPositionColor format, 58, 62–63, 65, 158
VertexPositionColorTexture format, 58, 122, 131, 135, 158, 359
VertexPositionNormalTexture format, 58, 122, 158, 358
VertexPositionTexture format, 58, 122, 158
VertexShader method, 71
point lights, 369, 374
point sprites, 327–328
texture color, 125, 128
Vertices
bounding spheres, 291
format storage, 59
graphics pipeline, 70
index buffers, 156–159
lighting, 356
Martian face, 59–68
multitexturing, 182
primitive objects, 56–57
Quake II model, 438–440
rendering, 56
rotating, 38
scaling matrices, 256–258
shaders. *See* Shaders
skyboxes, 150
stationary airplane, 110–111
textures, 122
types, 58
Vertices.cs file, 291
Video cards, 6
View matrix, 269
View property, 87–88
View/Sculpt dialog, 421–422
View vector
cameras, 268, 274
linear projectiles, 306
Viewing logic and variable values, 16–18
Viewport class, 492–493
Views
cameras, 277–284
multiplayer gaming, 492–493
windmill project, 204

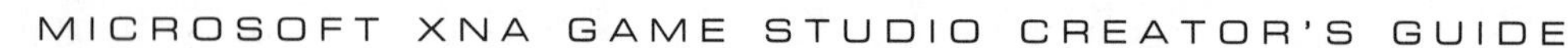

Viscosity with projectiles, 308
Visibility of cameras, 269–270
Visible display area, 196
Visual Studio, 2–4, 8, 42, 417
Volume attenuation, 471–472
VSinput struct, 71
  point lights, 366
  point sprites, 326
  textures, 124–125
VSoutput struct, 326–327
VStoPS struct, 71
  point lights, 366
  textures, 124–125
VStoPS2 struct, 374

W

W component
  translation matrices, 254
  vectors, 234
WallCollision method, 299, 302–303
WallSphere method, 294
warninglight.png file, 171
Warnings, debugging, 16–17
Watch lists, 18–19
Water effects, 179–189
WAV files, 460, 464
Wave banks, 462, 465
WaveBank class, 461
Waves effect, 187–189
weapon.md2 file, 455
Weapons in Quake II models, 454–457
weaponSkin.tga file, 455
Weighted averages, 429
wheel.fbx file, 221, 296
Wheeler, Phillip T., 451
WheelOffset method, 230
Wheels for car object, 227–231
wheelSpheres.fbx file, 296
Width
  camera view, 273
  images, 146
  windows, 32
Windmill, 203
  animating, 217–219
  blade duplication, 209
  blade material, 207–209
  blade rotation, 209–210, 217
  boxes for, 205, 209
  conclusion, 213–214
  cylinders for, 206
  drawing, 215–219
  exporting, 213
  group merging, 210–211
  joints, 211–212
  loading, 214–217
  positioning, 211
  project for, 204–205
  saving, 212–213
  spheres for, 206, 209
  textures, 206–207
windmill.bmp file, 207, 213, 216
Windows Game projects, 8
  creating, 9–10
  custom content processors, 405–417
WindowsGame1 namespace, 23, 26–27
World matrix, 93
  building, 96, 99
  description, 269
  identity matrices, 264
  point lights, 372
  windmill, 216
World property for shaders, 87–88
World-view-projection (WVP) matrices
  point lights, 366, 369, 372
  setting, 79
WorldMatrix method, 475–476
WorldViewProjection matrix
  split-screen environment, 498
  textures, 136
Write method
  ContentTypeWriter, 403, 408
  PacketWriter, 510
  XNANetwork, 513
WriteOnly option, 157
WVP (World-view-projection) matrices
  point lights, 366, 369, 372
  setting, 79

X

X axes in Right Hand Rule, 92–93
X coordinates
  mouse, 389
  pixels, 32
  vectors, 234
X planes
  3D graphics, 56
  linear projectiles, 306
X property for mouse, 379
X rotation matrix, 258–260
XACT (Cross Platform Audio Creation Tool), 5, 460
  AudioEngine, 461–462
  global settings, 462
  programming, 460–461
  project files, 460–461
  Song and SoundEffect, 460
  sound banks, 462–464
  space examples, 464–487
  wave banks, 462
.xap project files, 461–462, 464, 473
Xbox 360 Game projects, 8
  compiling and running, 12–13
  creating, 10–11
  deploying, 14–15
  saving, 13
Xbox LIVE Arcade, 32
Xbox360Game1 namespace, 23
XNA Creators Club, 3
XNA Game Studio Connect application, 3–4, 14
XNA game template wizard, 34
XNANetwork class, 511–514, 521–523

Y

Y axes in Right Hand Rule, 92–93
Y coordinates
  mouse, 389
  pixels, 32
  vectors, 234
Y planes
  3D graphics, 56
  linear projectiles, 306
Y property for mouse, 379
Y rotation matrix, 260–262
YDirection method, 518

Z

Z axes in Right Hand Rule, 92–93
Z coordinates for vectors, 234
Z planes
  3D graphics, 56
  linear projectiles, 306
Z rotation matrix, 38, 262–263
Zarlag model, 451–452, 456–457
Zarlag.tga file, 451–452
Zoom magnification for skyboxes, 147
Zune Game projects, 8
  audio, 460, 487–489
  creating, 11
  deploying games to, 4–5
  input handling, 396–399
  porting 2D games to, 41
ZWriteEnable setting, 329, 340–341